Heaven
on
Earth

The Rise, Fall, and
Afterlife of Socialism

JOSHUA
MURAVCHIK

Encounter
BOOKS

New York • London

First American edition published in 2002 by Encounter Books,
an activity of Encounter for Culture and Education, Inc.,
a nonprofit, tax exempt corporation.
Encounter Books website address: www.encounterbooks.com

Manufactured in the United States and printed on
acid-free paper. The paper used in this publication meets
the minimum requirements of ANSI/NISO Z39.48-1992
(R 1997) (*Permanence of Paper*).

First paperback edition published in 2003.
Second paperback edition published in 2019.
Paperback edition ISBN: 978-1-59403-963-8

THE LIBRARY OF CONGRESS HAS CATALOGUED
THE HARDCOVER EDITION AS FOLLOWS:
Muravchik, Joshua.
Heaven on earth : the rise and fall of socialism /
Joshua Muravchik. p. cm.
Includes bibliographical references and index.
ISBN 1-893554-45-7 (alk. paper)
Socialism—History. I. Title.

HX36.M87 2002
335'.009—dc21
2001055681

To Sally

The Christian . . . imagines the better future of the human species . . . in the image of heavenly joy. . . . We, on the other hand, will have this heaven on earth.

—Moses Hess, *A Communist Confession of Faith*, 1846

CONTENTS

PREFACE TO THE
SECOND EDITION

In 2002, when *Heaven on Earth* first appeared, an unusual event was held in Washington, D.C. It was a reunion of members of the Young People's Socialist League from the 1960s and 1970s. I had been one, even for a time its leader. Indeed it had been the center of my life for a stretch of years, as it had been for others, so a reunion was a natural thing. And we all recalled that back then we hosted, as fundraisers, reunions of YPSL members from the 1930s—to great success. This reunion of YPSL members of my generation was no fundraiser, just for nostalgic pleasure, but it doubled as a launchpad for my book.

The most remarkable thing about the event was that my 85-year-old father, now of blessed memory, came to protest. He distributed a flyer containing a statement he had written in rebuttal to the book. It described his own circumstance at that time, explaining how he and my mother relied on Social Security and Medicare, suggesting this proved the value of socialism.

His decision to leaflet the event was a little gauche, but I understood that he saw this book as an act of apostasy, a betrayal of the faith he had bequeathed to me. I had hurt him, and I was deeply sorry I had.

I was, nonetheless, not much impressed by his argument. Social Security and Medicare are fine things, but they do not add up to socialism, the dream that had captivated my father and millions of others, including me. Norman Thomas, the six-time Socialist Party nominee for president (whose original party membership card was mounted and presented to my father late in life in token of his decades of service to the party), was asked once whether President Franklin D. Roosevelt had not carried out his program. To this, Thomas replied that FDR had "carried it out on a stretcher."

Socialism meant so much more than the welfare state, which was at best a kind of consolation prize to socialists and at worst a way of buying off the masses so that they would not pursue deeper change. Indeed, the welfare state had been pioneered by Prussian Chancellor Otto von Bismarck for precisely that purpose. It was not for goals as modest as the welfare state that my father and others like him had devoted their lives to the pursuit of socialism. Rather, they envisioned, as I too had in my socialist years, an end to exploitation; a new dawn of brotherhood; a different, kinder and more wholesome way of living. The power of this image had made socialism a monumental force driving the history of the twentieth century. And this, I believed, was over.

I still believe it. What I had not predicted, although looking back it seems to have been inevitable, was that any force as powerful as socialism would have an afterlife, and not merely in the form of the welfare state. Now, nearly two decades into a new century, that afterlife is evident in two forms that I find particularly worthy of note.

On the one hand, here and there around the world, as a new generation has grown up without any direct memory of the Cold War or the countless failures and abuses of socialism, that old dream has shown that it retains the capacity to enchant even in the most unlikely places. In the United States, that least socialist of countries, presidential candidate Bernie Sanders, a proclaimed "democratic socialist" and a veteran of the YPSL, nearly won the Democratic nomination in 2016 and inspired other proclaimed socialists to win seats in Congress and statehouses in 2018. Meanwhile, in Great Britain, the Labour Party, once the exemplar of a socialist party that had gone conservative, was taken over by Jeremy Corbyn, who is not merely a radical socialist but a warm supporter of various Communist regimes and movements. I cannot imagine that either the United States or the United Kingdom will be remade as socialist, but the rise of Sanders and Corbyn shows anew the power of this idea.

On the other hand, Russia and even more so China, the two Communist giants of the twentieth century, seem poised to shape and perhaps to dominate international life in the decades ahead. Russia is no longer Communist. And China, though still ruled by the Communist Party, is no longer socialist. Yet these influential countries, one with the world's largest population, the other with its largest land mass, were largely shaped—or misshaped—by their Communist experience and retain its earmarks in their current guises.

In this new edition, I have not emended any of the chapters of the original book, which cover the history of the previous centuries, other than to correct a few small (though embarrassing) errors and to update my account of the evolution of Israel's kibbutzim. But I have added a long Epilogue, telling the story of this afterlife as it has unfolded thus far in the first decades of the new century.

PROLOGUE:
CHANGING FAITHS

SOCIALISM WAS THE FAITH IN WHICH I WAS RAISED. It was my father's faith and his father's before him.

My grandfather, Avraham Chaim Muravchik, grew up in a small *shtetl* outside Kiev in what was then the Russian Empire. Born in 1878, he received the orthodox religious training of every boy of his time and place. But like many others of that generation he turned away from formal Judaism by the time he entered high school, or *gymnasium,* as it was called.

It was in the radical student circle at *gymnasium* that he met my grandmother, Rachel. She was several years his junior since he had not been able to afford the school until he had worked for a time as a lumberman, while her family, which manufactured paper bags and lived in Kiev proper, was better off. Together they joined the most radical of the newly formed Russian leftist parties, the Socialist Revolutionaries. It was distinguished from the more Marxist-oriented Social Democrats by its endorsement of terror tactics and by its theory that the leading role in the revolution would be played by Russia's peasantry rather than its proletariat.

Avraham Chaim and Rachel left for America in 1905, part of a wave of Jewish emigration touched off by an orgy of anti-Semitic violence that followed Russia's defeat by Japan and the abortive attempt to overthrow the tsar. The peasants, it turned out, were more easily mobilized for pogroms than for revolution.

In America, the couple found work with the Yiddish-language *Jewish Daily Forward,* whose masthead was emblazoned with the famous injunction of the *Communist Manifesto*: "Workers of the world unite!" They settled in a Harlem tenement, in which my father, Emanuel, was born in 1916.

Emanuel's boyhood was filled with the comings and goings of the exile branches of the Russian Students Organization and the Left Socialist Revolutionaries. (The party had split in 1917, and my grandparents stuck with the more radical half.) In 1929, Norman Thomas ran for mayor of New York on the Socialist Party ticket, and the campaign crystallized my father's budding interest in socialism. He chose it as the topic of an eighth-grade paper, and after four intense days in the library, pronounced himself a convert. A few months later, just after his thirteenth birthday, he joined the Socialist Party. It was a coming of age that substituted for a bar mitzvah.

My mother, Miriam, whom he met in college, shared my father's views albeit with softer ideological definition. Being of liberal spirit, however, they decided to refrain from systematically indoctrinating me and my brother as they raised us. Systematic indoctrination was scarcely necessary, at any rate, for the political cause was the center of their lives. It was discussed at the family dinner table and with their friends, who were mostly "comrades." On car excursions, we whiled away the time by singing "We Shall Not Be Moved" and other old labor songs. I first visited our nation's capital in 1958 at the age of eleven when my parents took us on the Youth March for Integrated Schools, one of the earliest civil rights demonstrations. By my teens, I was a seasoned protestor.

By then I, too, had joined the Socialist Party, eventually becoming the leader of its youth wing, the Young People's Socialist League. It was a small organization because socialism never caught on in this country, despite my father's efforts and my own. (His persisted for more than seventy years, while I became an apostate in my thirties and began to grope my way back to Judaism.)

If we were out of step with America, we took heart from knowing that America was out of step with the world. My comrade Michael Harrington—the famous writer who became chairman of the Socialist Party in 1968, at the same moment that I became chairman of the YPSL—boasted: "Most of the people in the world today call the name of their dream 'socialism.'"[1] I could not vouch for his math, but socialism undoubtedly was the most popular political idea ever invented.

Arguably, it was the most popular idea of any kind, surpassing even the great religions. Like them, socialism spread both by evangelization and by the sword, but no religion ever spread so far or so fast. Islam conquered an empire that at its height embraced 20 percent of mankind. It took 300 years before Christianity could speak for 10 percent of the world's people, and after two millennia it can claim the adherence of about one-third of the human race. By comparison, within 150 years after the term "socialism" was coined by the followers of Robert Owen in the late 1820s, roughly 60 percent of the earth's population found itself living under socialist rule of one kind or another.† Of

† The word "communism" came into use in French and English in the 1840s. The words "socialism" and "communism" have often been used interchangeably, as have the terms "socialism" and "social

course, not all who lived under socialism believed in it, but not all who were counted as Christians or Muslims were believers either.

Once empowered, socialism refused to yield its promised rewards. The more dogged the effort to achieve it, the more the outcome mocked the humane ideals it proclaimed. Yet for a century and a half, no amount of failure dampened socialism's appeal. Then suddenly, like a rocket crashing back to earth, it all collapsed. Within a couple of decades, socialism was officially repealed in half the places where it had triumphed. In the other half, it continued in name only. Today, in but a few flyspecks on the map is there still an earnest effort to practice socialism, defended in the manner of those marooned Japanese soldiers who held out for decades after 1945, never having learned that their emperor had surrendered.

In this book I trace socialism's phenomenal trajectory. It is the story of man's most ambitious attempt to supplant religion with a doctrine about how life ought to be lived that claimed grounding in science rather than revelation. Although its provenance was European, it was taken up with ardor in China and Africa, India and Latin America and even in that most tradition-bound of regions, the Middle East. No other faith ever appealed as widely. It was not confined to salons and libraries but exerted itself as well in statehouses and on picket lines, barricades and battlefields. It did more than anything else to shape the history of the twentieth century.

Ironically, the power of this faith was to some degree obscured by the popularity of Marxist theory, which held that ideas were merely the surface froth thrown up by underlying currents of technological progress and material interests. This, too, was a seductive notion because it answered that most puzzling question: why do people think what they do? But this "materialist" interpretation of ideology has not stood the test of time, least of all in explaining socialism's own history. What material interests or technology caused the triumph of socialism, or its defeat, in Russia? Its transmission to China, Cuba and North Korea? Its appearance in other forms in Sweden, Israel, Tanzania, Syria?

democracy." At other times, these have been treated as differentiable doctrines and various definitions have been formulated, but none of these have won general acceptance, and they have sometimes been mutually contradictory. Since my purpose is history not theory, I stipulate no definitions. In general I will describe movements by the terms they themselves favored. After the Bolshevik seizure of power in Russia in 1917, those who followed Lenin's trail assumed a near monopoly on the word "Communist," although they also still often called themselves socialists, too. Those who rejected Lenin's approach generally used the label "socialist" or "social democrat." Except where I am referring to a specific party or movement, I use the term "socialism" broadly to encompass all the various branches that grew out of the socialist acorn.

The idea of socialism did not march through history of its own accord. It was invented, developed, popularized, revised, exploited and in some cases abandoned by a chain of thinkers and activists. It was modified again and again, sometimes for ulterior motives but also because, for all its unmatched allure, it proved maddeningly difficult to implement. I have chosen to tell the story of socialism through sketches of key individuals, each of whom exemplifies a critical stage or form in its evolution. Some of these were seminal figures, responsible more or less single-handedly for a major turning point. Who can imagine communism without Lenin, fascism without Mussolini, or the peaceful self-nullification of the Soviet Union without Gorbachev? Other important episodes, such as the rise of utopianism or social democracy or the embrace of socialism by "Third World" states, cannot be traced to a single individual, so I have selected for portraiture the one whom I believe best represents each of these chapters in the drama.

The manger in which socialism was born was the French Revolution, with its emphasis on equality, its profound anticlericalism and its promise that all things could be made new. Amidst the chiliastic confusion of serial upheavals, one impassioned visionary, "Gracchus" Babeuf, proposed that the way to give substance to the slogan "liberty, equality, fraternity" was to collectivize all property. Thus did his Conspiracy of Equals, as it called itself, serve as midwife to the new idea, which grew and developed over the next 120 years. In the early 1800s, with most of Europe still recoiling from the Napoleonic bloodbath, socialism turned away from revolution to experimentation, in the form of small communities in which people could practice the life of collective ownership. The most important of these—in America and England—were led or inspired by Robert Owen.

These experiments in socialism did not turn out well, and the idea itself might have wasted away in infancy had it not been taken up by a symbiotic team of unique prophetic power: Karl Marx and Friedrich Engels. They shifted the basis of socialist hopes from individual experiments to broader historic trends, which shielded the idea against empirical failure. Although Owen's movement had adopted the physical trappings of religion, erecting church-like "halls of science" where sermons were delivered at Sunday services, Marx and Engels achieved the far more profound breakthrough of imbuing socialism with something of the intellectual and spiritual force of the great religious texts. Their doctrine provided an account of man's history, an explanation of current sorrows and a vision of a redemptive future.

But half a century after the publication of *The Communist Manifesto,* the social-ist idea hit another crisis as Marx and Engels' leading heir, Eduard Bernstein, observed that economic development was confounding the prophecy. The theory was rescued by Lenin, who kept it alive by performing heart transplant surgery, replacing the proletariat by the vanguard. Still, although socialism had stirred millions by the early twentieth century, it remained a dream.

Then, World War I gave Lenin the opportunity to put his idea into prac-tice, and in 1917 socialism achieved its first momentous triumph. Even those socialists who decried Lenin's methods, or who viewed his state as little more than a caricature of their goals, nonetheless felt strengthened in the conviction that history was flowing from capitalism to socialism. Yet the debate over the Russian model, along with the war's demonstration of the power of nationalism, shattered the movement. Of the fragments, the most outré was fascism, which seemed to turn socialism on its head. Still, the leap from Lenin to Mussolini was no bigger than that from Marx to Lenin; each man distilled theory from the exigencies of revolutionary action.

The fascist chapter was explosive and brief, and socialism emerged strength-ened from the defeat of this heresy in World War II. Not only did many more communist regimes emerge, but social democracy found a new lease on life, spearheaded by Clement Attlee's stunning electoral triumph over Churchill in Britain at the end of the war. The aftermath also saw the appearance of dozens of new postcolonial states and with them the birth of "Third World socialism." This was a hybrid of communism and social democracy, exemplified by Julius Nyerere's Tanzania, modeled partly after Chinese Maoism, partly after British Fabianism.

At some point in the late 1970s, socialism reached its apogee, with com-munist, social-democratic or Third World socialist regimes governing most of the world. There were, however, two chinks in the socialist armor. One was its dismal economic performance: much of socialism's appeal sprang from the wish to ameliorate want and deprivation, yet in practice it often made things worse. The other was its utter inability to gain a foothold in America, the world's most influential nation, where—to add insult to injury—the leading antisocialist force seemed to be none other than the working class, personified by labor leaders like Samuel Gompers and George Meany. As America's contin-ued economic success mocked socialism's failures, various Third World nations began to rethink their economic direction. Astoundingly, so did the two com-munist giants, China and the U.S.S.R., which, under the stewardship of restless reformers Deng Xiaoping and Mikhail Gorbachev, embarked on uncharted courses away from socialism. It remained only for the social-democratic branch of the socialist family to beat a retreat in order for the reversal to be complete. And in 1997, Tony Blair resuscitated Attlee's moribund party by campaigning with the slogan "Labour is the party of business." Thus, 201 years from the date of Babeuf's failed coup, the story was brought full circle.

I complete my telling with a digression from history to laboratory science, as it were, by training a microscope on an Israeli kibbutz. Like most such settlements, kibbutz Ginosar was secular, built by Jews who, like my father and grandfather, preferred the teachings of Marx to those of Moses. And like most, they succeeded where people in other lands had failed, creating a pure socialism, faithful to the blueprint—only to see their progeny turn its back on this way of life.

After so much hope and struggle, and so many lives sacrificed around the world, socialism's epitaph turned out to be: If you build it, they will leave.

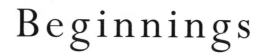

Beginnings

1
—

CONSPIRACY OF EQUALS:
BABEUF PLOTS A REVOLUTION

EASTER SUNDAY, 1911, WAS A GLORIOUS SPRING DAY in the region of Picardy, with a "superb azure sky" beckoning locals to their gardens and fishing holes, so the newspaper reported. But four to five thousand residents of Saint Quentin had more serious things in mind. Led by marching bands and illustrious delegates from all across France, they paraded past city hall and gathered around a flag-draped red platform erected in front of the central labor headquarters. There, they commemorated an anniversary—not of Christ's resurrection, but of the birth in that town, 151 years earlier, of "the first fighter and martyr for the socialist idea," according to the keynote speaker, Jean Jaurès, the leader of the main party of French socialists.

Although images of socialism had been sketched by philosophers as far back as Plato, these had never been more than intellectual exercises. Like Oz or Lilliput, Plato's Republic and Thomas More's Utopia (which means "Nowhere") were conjured up in order to make a point about life and existing society. The French Revolution, however, made things that had once been taken as fanciful suddenly seem possible. "Nowhere . . . first became somewhere in the Palais-Royale," remarks James Billington.[1]

The most consequential of these new possibilities was socialism, although this was not in view when the Revolution began. The stormers of the Bastille had not aimed at a socialist objective, nor did the actors in any of the other increasingly radical moments—*journées,* they were called—of the next five years. On the contrary, from Mirabeau to Robespierre, the revolutionists, it has often been noted, were mostly of the bourgeoisie, and their key *pronunciamentos* affirmed the right of property.

The 1789 Declaration of the Rights of Man and Citizen tracked the U.S. Declaration of Independence in proclaiming that the reason for government was to secure men's rights. And its designation of those rights—"liberty, property, security"—resembled the American triad of "life, liberty, and the pursuit of happiness." (The French included a right of "resistance to oppression," but this was little more than a rhetorical flourish.) However, as the Revolution unfolded and new constitutions were written, the French added a fourth substantive right: equality. To be sure, the Americans had proclaimed that men were "created equal," but this was not a statement of policy; it was a postulate about the nature of man and his relation to God. The French innovation was to include "equality" among the essential purposes of government.

The impetus behind this was not hard to understand. Whereas the core issue for the Americans in 1776 was political legitimacy, for the French in 1789 it was social status. The rebellion in France was aimed against an onerous and pervasive structure of invidious distinction. Its first act was to demand that representatives meet in one body as a "national assembly" rather than as separate "estates." The promise of equality, thus, expressed the very soul of the Revolution, but there was no explanation of how this might be achieved or even what, exactly, it meant.

As the break with the old regime accelerated into an avalanche, the right of property remained sacrosanct. The constitution of 1793, the formal expression of the most extreme phase of the Revolution, reaffirmed it in the strongest terms: "No one may be deprived of the least portion of his property without his consent, unless a legally established public necessity requires it, and upon condition of a just and previous indemnity."

It was only in the dying days of the Revolution that someone came forward to argue that there was a contradiction within the revolutionary agenda—that fulfilling the promise of equality would require not merely the abolition of feudal titles and privileges, but the institution of a new way of economic life in which individual ownership would be abolished and each citizen would be furnished with an identical portion of nature's bounty.

The man who put this forth was named François-Noël Babeuf, and he called himself Gracchus. He was the native son whom the diverging factions of French socialists united to honor that day in Saint Quentin, as he had been lauded in the writings of Marx and Engels, and as he would be extolled again at the founding of the "Comintern."

At the trial following the abortive insurrection he was to lead in 1796, Babeuf claimed that his socialist beliefs were not original. In his defense he quoted at length from Rousseau and Mably, and from writings that were ascribed to Diderot (although subsequent scholarship showed them to have been written by the less-known Abbé Morelly). His ideas were borrowed from them, said Babeuf: "In condemning me, gentlemen of the jury ... you place these great thinkers ... in the dock," for "the man who wills an end also wills the means to gain that end."[2] But this is no more persuasive historically than it was found to be juridically. However closely Babeuf's goals may have resembled those of the *philosophes* or earlier utopians, none of them had ever organized to seize power as Babeuf had done through an underground organization calling itself the "Conspiracy of Equals." Babeuf may have taken his philosophy from others, but before he came along, socialism had been only a speculative fancy. He transformed it into a fighting creed.

• • •

Unlike most subsequent socialist leaders and most of the key French revolutionaries, Babeuf came from humble origins. How humble is hard to know, since a great deal of what was written about him was ideological, and because he and his family provided embroidered accounts that either elevated or depressed his class status as the occasion might require. It is unlikely that Babeuf, as he told it, was asked by Emperor Joseph II of Austria to tutor his children. On the other hand, the tale that the Babeuf clan was so poor that the priests would not baptize François-Noël is given the lie by the baptismal certificate that a researcher uncovered in an archive.[3] As for Babeuf's claim that a breadbox had to serve him as an infant's cradle, stunting his growth, his adult height of five foot six was average for a Frenchman of his day.

What education Babeuf received came from his father, a professional soldier. He made enough of it to escape the rigors of canal-digging, his first occupation, for "white collar" work. He became a "feudist," performing archival research for nobles aimed at assuring that they were receiving all the fees and concessions to which they might conceivably be entitled. As was the norm for feudists, Babeuf's contracts afforded him one-third of the arrears collected as a result of his discoveries, which were likely to come out of the hide of the peasantry. Later he was to explain, perhaps in apologia: "I was a *feudiste* under the old regime, and that is the reason I was perhaps the most formidable scourge of feudalism in the new. In the dust of the seigneurial archives I uncovered the horrifying mysteries of the usurpations of the noble caste."[4]

For a time, Babeuf's business prospered so well that he was able to employ a handful of clerks. But some of his noble clients failed to pay him—whether out of haughty disdain of obligations to a commoner or because of some inadequacy in his work is disputed. Ultimately, however, it was the Revolution that put him out of business by bringing an end to feudal entitlements.

Babeuf next tried exercising his talents as a writer. His masterpiece, *Le Cadastre Perpetuel* ("The Permanent Land-Register"), combined his expertise as a feudist with his burgeoning passions as a reformer. It set forth a method that he believed would both modernize land records and provide succor to the poor. Babeuf invested great hopes in it, declaring, "It will serve for ages."[5] But months after its publication, his friend Jean-Pierre Audiffret, who had fronted the costs, complained that it had sold only four copies.

In the absence of earnings, Babeuf survived on loans from friends. When Audiffret had lent his limit, Babeuf cadged one last advance from him by showing him a letter from a wealthy client offering Babeuf a fat contract. It was a forgery that Babeuf had directed his wife to send him.

The outbreak of the Revolution found Babeuf in Paris. His explanation of its origins was surprisingly irreverent:

> The causes of the revolution are not, perhaps, such as many writers have
> wished to represent them. . . . Undoubtedly the kingdom of France was ill-
> governed but not worse than many others; the people were very miserable,
> but not more so than in other parts of Europe. There was light in the country,
> but the greater number of those persons who possessed it, did not possess
> virtue in due proportion, and the love of their fellow kind. That which, in my
> opinion, contributed most to the first popular commotion is this—we had
> just seen the revolution in North America, and movements in Holland and
> Brabant: the spirit of novelty and of imitation, so natural among the French,
> made them wish to do in their turn what, as it appeared to them, had given
> celebrity to people whom they did not think better than themselves.[6]

At first Babeuf was more a spectator than a participant. Watching the mob parade the head of a Bastille defender on a pike, he was repelled, although he exonerated the masses from their own coarseness. "Punishments of all kinds...have demoralised us," he wrote to his wife about these displays. "Our masters, instead of policing us, have made us barbarians....[A]ll this...will have...terrible consequences! We are as yet only at the beginning!"[7] Over time his misgivings about violence were overcome by the logic of revolutionary necessity—much as Robespierre began his political career as an opponent of capital punishment, but ended as its leading practitioner.

Babeuf's own part in the Revolution began as he returned from Paris to his native Picardy, which by 1790 had become one of the most active centers of agitation against the old regime's taxes on salt (the *gabelle*) and beverages (the *aides*). Long resented, these taxes became a prime target once the populace began to voice its grievances. Resistance to the *aides* was buttressed by the financial backing of brewers and saloonkeepers. In Picardy, Babeuf quickly established himself as a leader of this movement, resulting in the first of his many arrests.

Carried back to Paris for incarceration, Babeuf began to contribute from behind bars to radical journals, especially Jean-Paul Marat's famous *Ami du Peuple,* for which he wrote polemics on prison conditions among other matters. After a couple of months, Marat's agitation succeeded in winning a kind of parole for Babeuf, who soon returned to Picardy and widened the ambit of his militancy. After the official abolition of feudalism left unsettled a welter of claims between lords and peasants, Babeuf made himself a spokesman for the latter, both as an advocate in legal proceedings and also before the court of public opinion through a newssheet and various petitions. He called himself "the Marat of the Somme."

For more than two years, this mini-Marat built his reputation within the region as a revolutionary personage. He won election to various local offices, and formal designation as a "notable." In this period, writes the biographer R. B. Rose, Babeuf "appears to have adopted a revolutionary presence appropriate to the majesty of a people's representative. He was wearing his hair long and cut low on the brow in the Jacobin style, and had a long grey cloak and a huge sabre."[8] He also took to calling himself "Camille" after the Roman hero Camillus, known as the second founder of Rome and a reconciler of classes.

Babeuf's gifts, however, were not those of a reconciler. On the contrary, he was better suited to fulfill the order that came down to his municipality, following the abolition of the monarchy, to conduct a ritual purging of "the signs of ancient servitude." As Rose describes it:

Anything burnable was to be handed over for a public bonfire at the foot of the Tree of Liberty, in the market square, after proper provision had been made for "fuel for the poor." . . . Babeuf—acting alone, and amidst the jeers and menaces of a hostile crowd . . . carr[ied] out his *auto-da-fé*. To the fleur-de-lis tapestries from the tribunal and the town hall he added "twelve superb portraits of kings," garnered from the same places and from the district offices. The demonstration had been staged with the intention of celebrating the execution of Louis XVI on 21 January. But all it seemed to show was that the majority of the inhabitants of at least one Picard town were still royalists at heart.[9]

Thus Babeuf made enemies, and when he let himself get caught indulging his weakness for forgery, they pounced. He fled to Paris to escape arrest. There he threw himself into the arena of national revolutionary activity. Now calling himself Gracchus to signify his identity with the Roman tribune Tiberius Gracchus, author of an agrarian reform that confiscated surplus land for distribution to the needy, he wrote home to his wife: "This is exciting me to the point of madness. The sans-culottes want to be happy, and I don't think it is impossible that within a year, if we carry out our measures aright and act with all necessary prudence, we shall succeed in ensuring general happiness on earth."[10]

Robespierre's protégé Saint-Just once explained that "happiness is a new idea in Europe."[11] It came from the American Declaration of Independence. But while the Americans aimed to protect the pursuit of it, the French revolutionists wanted to guarantee the thing itself.

Babeuf rallied behind first one and then another of the leading lights of the Revolution, finally settling on Robespierre on the grounds of his solicitousness for the lower classes and his advocacy of limitations on property rights. Attuned for the moment to the prevailing political tide, Babeuf found employment within the revolutionary administration. However, the charge of forgery remained against him, and the law caught up with him in November 1793. Spending the next eight months in prison, he was isolated from the most frenzied phase of the Terror and the ensuing downfall of Robespierre and the Jacobins. They had accelerated the use of the guillotine to an unimagined tempo, but then it was their turn for the scaffold. Being under lock and key at this time may have been a stroke of luck for Babeuf since he had antagonized many people, and by falling afoul of one faction or another he might have paid with his head before he had the chance to make his mark on history.

Released on bond (supplied by anonymous friends or supporters), Babeuf found his way back to Paris in July 1794 and threw his lot in with the newly ascendant crowd of "Thermidorians," the moderates who had overthrown Robespierre. Although he had once supported Robespierre, Babeuf now lambasted him for his repressions. He went so far as to charge that Robespierre's hidden aim had been to create so much death and flight that the population would be reduced, thereby alleviating the food shortage. Within three months, however, Babeuf turned against the Thermidorians on the grounds of *their* repressiveness.

Soon the police were after him again, forcing him to publish his new journal, *Le Tribun du Peuple,* from hiding. In February 1795 they caught up with him, and he spent another eight months behind bars. During this incarceration he drew around him a few other political prisoners to form the Conspiracy of Equals. Throughout that year, the ruling Thermidorians alternately put down risings by the sans-culottes on their Left and by royalists on their Right. In October, to strengthen itself for a showdown with the Right, the regime released a number of radicals from custody, among them Babeuf.

Days later, the Convention was dissolved and the Directory took power, a further step in moderating the Revolution. The Directory proclaimed that its mission was "to consolidate the republic . . . to regenerate morals, to revive commerce and industry . . . to restore social order." Part of its strategy was to propitiate or co-opt the Left. Some publishers of radical sheets quietly accepted subventions from agents of the Directory, but Babeuf, who resumed publishing *Le Tribun du Peuple* immediately after regaining his freedom, was irreconcilable. Within two months his vitriolic diatribes against the Directory and exhortations to class war had the police at his door again.

Foolishly, the government sent but a single officer to arrest Babeuf, who resisted and fled his lodging. With the inspector in pursuit, the champion of the plebeians took refuge inside a food warehouse, with which he was probably familiar from his tenure in the food administration under the Jacobins. Inside, Rose recounts, "the grain porters . . . intervened and took Babeuf under their protection. While they were busy giving the inspector a rough time, beating him and covering him with mud and ordure, Babeuf was guided to a hiding place."[12]

Babeuf continued to publish, and two months later, in February 1796, the frustrated police took his wife, the devoted Marie-Anne, into custody. The pretense for the arrest was her part in distributing *Le Tribun,* but it was widely assumed that the real motive was to bring pressure on Babeuf himself. That, and reports that Marie-Anne was held without food for the first days, aroused indignation not only within Babeuf's circle but throughout the Left. The various factions that made up the Left—Babeuf's circle; veterans of the Jacobin regime; followers of the more radical sans-culotte leaders, Jacques-René Hébert and Anaxagoras Chaumette, who had been guillotined by the Jacobins—all participated in something called the Pantheon Club. This was a discussion and agitation society, said to number some two or three thousand, which took its name from its meeting place in a convent near the Pantheon. Reaction to the treatment of Marie-Anne swung support behind Babeuf's radical position, thereby exhausting the authorities' patience with "the den of brigands," as the club was called by its detractors. A military contingent commanded by General Napoleon Bonaparte was dispatched to close it down, and the general himself is said to have padlocked the doors. Thereafter, the Conspiracy of Equals emerged as the chief source of radical agitation.

• • •

At the center of the Conspiracy was the self-proclaimed Insurrectionary Committee of Public Safety, made up of seven members. The name was a reprise of the body through which Robespierre and his collaborators had ruled the nation and visited upon it their Reign of Terror. By this time, Babeuf had radically revised his assessment of Robespierre. Conveying his new view with characteristic asperity in the pages of *Le Tribun,* Babeuf waxed indignant at a recent attack on the memory of the fallen ruler: "Urn of Robespierre! Beloved ashes! Spring once more to life, and deign to confound your grovelling slanderers. . . . The whole French people . . . for which your genius alone did more than anyone else . . . is arising to avenge you."[13]

In correspondence with another leftist, Babeuf acknowledged his change of opinion and addressed the awkward fact of Robespierre's having sent the leaders of the sans-culotte radicals to the guillotine:

> I freely confess today that I am vexed with myself for having formerly taken
> an unfavorable view of the Revolutionary Government. . . . [T]heir dictatorial
> government was a devilish good idea. . . . I will not enter into an inquiry as to
> whether Hébert and Chaumette were innocent. Even if that were the case, I
> should still justify Robespierre, for it was he who might justly pride himself
> upon being the only man capable of guiding the chariot of the Revolution
> to its true goal. . . . The salvation of 25,000,000 men cannot be weighed in

the balance against consideration for a few shady individuals. A regenera-
tor . . . must mow down all that impedes him . . . all that might hinder his safe
arrival at the goal he has set before him. . . . Robespierre knew all this. . . . This
is what makes me see in him the genius in whom resided truly regenerative
ideas![14]

In addition to Babeuf, the Insurrectionary Committee included some
veterans of Robespierre's regime. One was Augustin-Alexandre-Joseph
Darthé, a law student who had taken part in storming the Bastille and then
made his mark as the public accuser for the regions of Arras and Cambrai
during the Reign of Terror. He boasted that "a stern decree led to the confinement of those aristocratic wives whose husbands were incarcerated and
those husbands whose wives were. From that moment, the guillotine never
ceased working; dukes, marquis, counts and barons, males and females, fell
like hail."[15] According to an 1831 article in the Tory journal *Quarterly Review,*
"Two thousand persons perished at Arras and Cambrai under the tyranny of
this monster; and . . . when Robespierre's overthrow put a stop to their career,
a trench had just been dug under the scaffold large enough to receive sixty-
four heads at a time."[16]

Another Jacobin veteran on the committee was Filippo Michele Buonarroti,
an expatriate Italian of noble birth, descended of the family of Michelangelo.
While the other Conspirators went to their deaths or dropped from sight,
Buonarroti lived another forty years, mostly in exile in Geneva, achieving iconic
status in the eyes of later revolutionaries. He sustained the memory of the group
through his celebrated book *La Conspiration des Égaux,* which was translated into
several languages and remains the authoritative account of its activities.

The other most important member of the inner circle of Conspirators
was Sylvain Maréchal, who composed the "Manifesto of the Equals," one of the
principal codifications of the goals and philosophy of the Conspiracy. Maréchal
was known above all as a militant atheist. He liked to call himself *l'HSD,* which
stood for *l'Homme sans Dieu* ("The Man without God" or "The Godless Man").[17]
He had previously published *The Atheist's Dictionary,* a famous work at the time,
as well as an atheist opera[18] and atheist poems which Babeuf sometimes read
to his son.[19]

The Equals aimed to redeem the promise of the Revolution. They wanted
"to add to the revolution in power and rank that incomparably more just and
necessary one of property and intelligence, whose final result should be an

impartial distribution of riches and knowledge amongst all the citizens."[20] The overriding goal was "Equality! the first wish of nature, the first need of man."[21] The motive for egalitarianism was both spiritual and material. The Equals wanted a "truly fraternal union of all Frenchmen" in which each member viewed his own well-being as inextricably entwined with that of every other.[22] "If there is a single man on earth who is richer and more powerful than his fellows," said Maréchal's "Manifesto of the Equals," "...then the equilibrium is broken: crime and misfortune are on earth."[23] Therefore, it was imperative to "remove from every individual the hope of ever becoming richer, or more powerful, or more distinguished by his intelligence."[24] This would lead to "the disappearance of boundary-marks, hedges, walls, door-locks, disputes, trials, thefts, murders, all crimes . . . courts, prisons, gallows, penalties . . . envy, jealousy, insatiability, pride, deception, duplicity, in short all vices."

In addition to these estimable spiritual benefits, an egalitarian society would also, the Equals believed, serve to eliminate want. In the image of the economic world projected in the writings of Babeuf and his fellows, nature provided a relatively fixed bounty. Therefore, a person could "only succeed in having too much by arranging for others to have not enough."[25] That alone would justify equal distribution, but in addition, Babeuf speculated that an egalitarian society would turn scarcity into abundance. "A few hours' occupation per day would secure to every individual the means of living agreeably," he wrote.[26] Indeed it was just this image that drew Babeuf to the philosophy of Morelly (a little-known thinker whose book *Code de la Nature* had been mistakenly attributed to Diderot). Babeuf explained his preference for Morelly in a letter:

> [F]ar from sending us back into the woods, as M. Rousseau does, in order to live thus, to sate ourselves under an oak, refresh ourselves at the nearest stream, and then repose serenely under the same oak where we first found our food, instead of all this, [Morelly] has us eat four good meals a day, dresses us most elegantly, and also provides those of us who are fathers of families with charming houses worth a thousand louis each.[27]

The way to create a system of equality would be to "organize a communal regime which will suppress private property, set each to work at the skill or job he understands, require each to deposit the fruits of his labor in kind at the common store, and establish an agency for the distribution of basic necessities. This agency will maintain a complete list of people and of supplies, will distribute the latter with scrupulous fairness, and will deliver them to the home of each worker."[28] Money would be abolished, the circulation of gold or silver forbidden. Thus provisioned, "no member of the community may possess anything other than what the law makes available through the agency of the governors."[29] Each would be supplied alike with furniture and clothing. Buonarroti explained, "It is essential . . . that the citizen should habitually find in all his fellow countrymen equals, brothers; and that he should nowhere meet with the least sign of even apparent superiority."[30]

Citizens would be divided into occupational groups and would be attached to their location of residency. They could "receive the common ration only in the district where they live, except in the case of movements authorized by the administration." The authorities not only would have to approve any moves, but could command them: "the movement of workers from one [locale] to another may be ordered by the supreme administration in the light of the resources and needs of the community."[31] Babeuf foresaw "the extinction of those receptacles of every vice, large cities; and covering France with villages."[32]

The goal was not just to change the system but to change people. Said Babeuf: "Society must be made to operate in such a way that it eradicates once and for all the desire of a man to become richer, or wiser, or more powerful than others."[33] In designing their new society, the Equals devoted a great deal of attention to planning the upbringing of the young and also to the ongoing instruction of the adult population. As Buonarroti recalled:

> In the social order conceived by the Committee, the country takes possession of every individual at birth, and never quits him till death. It watches over his first moments, secures him the nourishment and cares of his mother, keeps out of his reach every thing that might impair his health or enervate his constitution, guarantees him against the dangers of a false tenderness, and conducts him, by the hand of his parent, to the national seminary, where he is to acquire the virtues and intelligence necessary to make him a good citizen.[34]

The "national seminary" alluded to here would comprise same-sex boarding schools where all children would be raised. The goal of their education would be "to make [the citizens] love equality, liberty, and their country, and place them in a condition to serve and defend it,"[35] said Buonarroti. To accomplish this fully, the educators would strive "to render all affections of family and kindred subordinate to" the "love of country."[36] After a number of years in the

boarding schools, "so soon as the children would have acquired strength, they
would have been habituated to military works.... [It is necessary] to preclude
the introduction of young people into social life until inured to discipline,
and to the privations of the camp, inflamed with love of country, and burning
to serve it."[37] Thus would the young people pass several years encamped on
France's frontiers, securing the national boundaries while being hardened in
final preparation for "the rights of citizenship."

Yet education would not conclude at that point. Buonarroti reported that:
"In the Committee's opinion, it was of sovereign importance to the cause of
equality to keep the citizens incessantly exercised—to attach them to their
country, by making them love its ceremonies, its games, its amusements."[38] The
majesty of government would be augmented by intermixing it with religion.
Buonarroti foresaw "the establishment of that sublime worship, which, by blending the laws of the country with the precepts of the divinity, doubled, as it were,
the force of the legislator, and armed him with the means of extinguishing all
superstitions in a short time, and of realizing all the miracles of equality."[39] In
speaking of "superstitions," Buonarroti of course meant traditional religion,
toward which the Equals, led by Maréchal, were strongly antagonistic. (The
historian Patrice Higonnet notes "the curious view of Jews that Babeuf had at
that time: their *stupide crédulité* was indeed *pitoyable* but it was to their credit
that they had seen through Christ."[40])

In their hostility to established religion and their plan to bend it to political ends, the Equals were carrying forward a spirit that had suffused the
Revolution from its early months, when the National Assembly adopted the
Civil Constitution of the Clergy, aiming to subject the church to government
control. Anticlericalism intensified during the reign of the Jacobins, when hunts
were organized for "nonjuring" priests, those who refused to swear ultimate
allegiance to civil authorities. Hundreds or thousands of them were killed. It
was, by Simon Schama's account, one such episode—the guillotining of the
priest who had given last rites to her mother—that launched the extraordinary
young woman Charlotte Corday on the path that culminated in stabbing to death
Jean-Paul Marat in his bath.[41] In November 1793, the Paris Commune ordered
all the churches in the city shut down. Throughout the country, churches were
forcibly closed to worship and ransacked for war materiel or booty. Mockeries
of Christian rituals were performed, including the so-called "republican mar-
riages" in which a priest and nun were tied together naked and tossed into a
body of water to drown.

The Gregorian calendar, measuring history from the birth of Christ, was replaced by one designating the founding of the French Republic as Year I. The biblically rooted seven-day week was replaced by a ten-day cycle, and the Sabbath by a so-called *decadi*. In place of the saints associated with the various days of the year, each day was given a fruit or flower or fish or garden implement, and new names were invented for the months to reinforce the cult of nature: Vendémiare for harvest, Thermidor for hot, and so on.

Given the temper of the times, Babeuf must have thought he had a strong argument when at trial he appealed to the sympathy of the jurors on the grounds that the defendants "have only been dreaming of the happiness of their fellow-creatures. The revolution . . . became to them a new religion."[42] The universalization of this sensibility was the goal of the Equals. They longed for the day, said Babeuf, when "the great principle of equality, or universal fraternity would become the sole religion of the peoples."[43]

• • •

As much as they wrestled with the contours of the egalitarian order they were out to build, Babeuf and his fellow Conspirators also spent long hours formulating a vision of the path that would bring them there. They aimed to direct one final *journée,* those brief outbursts of insurrectionary frenzy by the mass of Parisian sans-culottes that had impelled the Revolution through its increasingly radical stages. They formalized their plans by adopting an "Insurrectionary Act" which they intended to distribute throughout the city at the moment chosen to ignite the rebellion.

It called upon citizens to take up their arms, or to seize arms wherever they could be found, and to rally "at this very hour" to the sound of the tocsin and trumpet. They were to follow the leadership of "patriots to whom the Insurrectionary Committee shall have entrusted banners bearing the inscription 'The Constitution of 1793: Equality, Liberty, and Common Happiness.'" Under the command of "generals of the people distinguished by tricolor ribbons floating conspicuously around their hats," they were instructed to seize the national treasury, the post, the homes of ministers and "every public or private building containing provisions or ammunition." The rivers were to be carefully guarded. "No one may leave Paris without a formal and special order of the Insurrectionary Committee; no one shall enter but couriers, conductors, porters, and carriers of foodstuff, to whom protection and security will be given."

With the city thus secured, "all opposition shall be suppressed immediately by force. Those opposing shall be exterminated." The ruling Directory and both houses of the legislative body, the Council of 500 and the Council of Elders, were to be dissolved at once and all their members "immediately judged by the people." Buonarroti explained that what was needed was "a great example of justice, capable of terrifying . . . traitors . . . a day of just and salutary terror, which would have left behind it only the remembrance of a legitimate and too tardy retribution."[44]

The Equals did not imagine, however, that suppression could be limited to those at the pinnacle of the old regime. The Insurrectionary Act specified that "any public functionary whatsoever" attempting to perform any official act "shall be immediately put to death." The same fate was prescribed for anyone trying to sound an alarm and for "foreigners of whatever nation, found in the street." The insurgents were instructed "not [to] take rest until after the destruction of the tyrannical government." To keep them going, "provisions of all kinds shall be brought to the people in the public places." In particular, all bakers were ordered "to continue to make bread, which shall be distributed free to the people." Any who refused were to be strung up from the nearest lamppost, wrote Darthé, who, on the strength of his experience as a public accuser under the Terror, took on the task of drawing up a list of those marked for execution.[45] In addition to recalcitrant bakers, any citizens caught hiding foodstuffs or refusing to surrender their flour were to face the ultimate punishment.

To bind the people to the Revolution, all the possessions of emigrants, of leaders of the previous regime and of "all enemies of the people" would be seized and distributed to the masses. In addition, wrote Buonarroti, "For the purpose of giving the people a sensible idea of the new Revolution, and of strengthening its zeal, the Insurrectionary Committee proposed to publish, during the insurrection, two decrees, by virtue of which the poor should be immediately clothed at the expense of the Republic, and on the same day lodged in the houses of the rich."[46]

Power in hand, the entire people of Paris was then to gather in the Place de la Revolution to elect a new National Assembly and a provisional government, the members of both to be nominated by the Insurrectionary Committee.[47] Even after this was accomplished, the Insurrectionary Committee would "remain in permanence until the complete accomplishment of the insurrection," said the plan. Buonarroti explained that the committee itself was unsure how long this might take. On the one hand they recognized that to retain in their own hands "a permanent, and necessarily very extended power, would expose the members of the Insurrectiona[ry] Committee to the suspicion of having ambitious and interested views."[48] But "on the other hand, the . . . Committee saw but few men in whom purity of principle was to be found united with courage, with firmness, and the intelligence necessary to reduce them to practice; it felt how dangerous it would be not to leave the completion of so hazardous a work to those who had had the boldness to commence it."

The Equals knew they would have to hold onto power "until this new revolution shall be consolidated" because so many of the people had been led astray by "the horrible cunning of the Patriciate," as Babeuf put it,[49] This was the obstacle that later socialist thinkers would call "false consciousness." According to his biographer, R. B. Rose, Babeuf's personal papers show that he believed that the phase of dictatorial rule by the Insurrectionary Committee would be completed within three months, by which time "the level of opinion will be raised."[50] But Buonarroti's account suggests that the Insurrectionary Committee knew this might require more time. "The sovereign power was to be rendered to the people only gradually and according to the progress of the new manners," he said.[51] "It will be easily felt that the Insurrectiona[ry] Committee itself could neither foresee all the measures which circumstances might have rendered necessary, nor determine beforehand the epoch when the mission of the reformer would have been completed."

In the meanwhile an ongoing war would be waged against the defenders of the old order. Babeuf explained in an article in *Le Tribun* that "in order to govern judiciously it is necessary to terrorize the evilly disposed, the royalists, papists and starvers of the public. . . . [O]ne cannot govern democratically without this terrorism."[52] Even in the long term, the Equals apparently believed that liberty as it was spelled out in the 1789 Declaration of the Rights of Man and Citizen was not readily reconciled with the preservation of equality. Thus, Buonarroti argued that free expression ought not to be extended to the point of "risking . . . again calling in question the justice of equality, and the rights of the people, or delivering the Republic to interminable and disastrous discussions."[53] For this reason, he reported, the Insurrectionary Committee was considering a decree ordering that "no one may promulgate opinions directly contrary to the sacred principles of equality, and of the sovereignty of the people" and that "no writing about any pretended revelation whatever can be published." Writings on other subjects might be published "if the conservators of the National Will shall judge that their publication may be useful to the Republic" or upon petition of "a prescribed number of citizens, above the age of thirty."

Armed with these plans and visions, the Equals set about building a clandestine network capable of carrying out the great rising. They selected a chief agent in each of Paris' twelve *arrondissements*. Those so honored had not necessarily been inducted previously into membership in the Equals, nor did they know they were under consideration for the mission for which they were chosen. Simply, they were men of stout revolutionary reputation. Each was notified of his appointment by a written message delivered by courier. The message did not reveal the names of the members of the Insurrectionary Committee, but in proof of authenticity it was stamped with the seal of the Conspiracy of Equals.

Though this seems a strange way to commission agents, the Insurrectionary Committee chose well, since most of those who received this surprise summons apparently accepted it. Thereafter they continued to receive instructions and supplies by secret courier, authenticated by the Equals' seal. The tasks of the agents consisted mainly of intelligence and propaganda. They canvassed the play of opinion within the workshops and barracks of their districts, and reported to the leaders. They also passed along the names of likely sympathizers and the locations of provisions and weapons. They organized cells and with their help pasted up flyers and posters such as the "Analysis of Babeuf's Doctrine."

France continued to be enmeshed in a triangular political battle. The ruling Directory was opposed on one side by the remnants of sans-culotte radicalism now led by the Equals, and on the other by those wishing to restore the old regime. The three groups waged a daily contest of posters, affixing their own polemics and ripping down those of the others.

The agents of the Equals were also charged with assuring that Babeuf's *Le Tribun* and another paper on which Babeuf and other Equals collaborated, *L'Éclaireur du Peuple* ("The People's Enlightener"), were read aloud. This was done sometimes at open-air meetings in the Tuileries or on street corners, but most often in cafés. The favorite café was the Bains Chinois, a well-known center of radical agitation where the readings were relieved by song. The beautiful seamstress Sophie Lapierre, a member of the Equals, crooned tunes with revolutionary messages composed by the Conspiracy. In their agitation, notes historian Ian Birchall, the Equals "stressed the importance of women because of the influence exercised by 'this interesting sex.'"[54] They were thought especially important in attracting soldiers to the revolutionary cause.

As reflected in the banners they designed for their planned uprising, restoration of the Constitution of 1793 was a main slogan of the Equals. This was the most democratic of the constitutions promulgated during the course of the Revolution. Drawn up by the Jacobins, it was no sooner ratified than it was superseded by a decree proclaiming "the provisional government of France revolutionary until the peace." William Doyle has described the document's fate:

> The promulgation ceremony [was held] on 10 August . . . with a huge procession wending its way through Paris to where eighty-three pikes, one brought from each department by a patriot ripe in years, were bound into a huge fasces symbolizing republican unity. The constitution itself was deposited in a cedar box and suspended from the roof of the Convention hall.
>
> Theoretically, the Convention's work was now done. Like the Constituent Assembly before it, it could dissolve itself and make way for regular, constitutional government. Delacroix proposed just this. . . . That same night, however, Robespierre denounced [this] proposal which could only bring to power "the envoys of Pitt and Coburg." The current emergency, when the very survival of the Republic was at stake, was not the time to increase political uncertainties. The constitution could not safely be brought into force in time of war. So long as the emergency lasted it would remain suspended, in every sense.[55] After the fall of the Jacobins, the stillborn Constitution of 1793 was supplanted by the Constitution of 1795, which sharply limited suffrage on the basis of property qualifications. The Equals viewed the 1793 constitution as no more than a step in the right direction, objecting in particular to its recognition of the right to property, but they saw the call for its restoration as an effective organizing device. They believed, said Buonarroti, "that to this Constitution would rally not only the Equals, but also the Democrats, who did not go so far, and a large portion of the people; that all further changes would become easier as soon as the spirit of equality had resumed its energy." The goal, he said, was "to unite all the popular forces."[56]

Indeed, the Equals entered into a tense negotiation with the Jacobins who, despite executions and defections, continued to function as an organized group. The key issue was not philosophical. It was how to divide power on the morrow of the insurrection. Should it revert to the Jacobin deputies in office at the time of Thermidor, or should it be entrusted to new representatives nominated by the Equals' Insurrectionary Committee? The Jacobins finally gave way, and a pact was reached during the first days of May 1796.

The Insurrectionary Committee planned its uprising for later that month. Deliberations among its military commanders intensified. But the day was never to arrive. The Conspiracy had been penetrated, and the police swooped in to arrest the leading participants before they could give the call to sound the tocsin of revolt. (Just to make sure, the Directory had taken the precaution of removing from their respective structures throughout Paris the various bells suitable for this function.)

• • •

The arrest of the Conspirators was not yet the final chapter of the Conspiracy of Equals, for Babeuf proved to be as ingenious and colorful a prisoner as he had been in his other roles. Two days after his arrest he addressed a long letter to the five-member Directory. From his cell he proposed to open negotiations with them "as between power and power." He warned that if they proceeded to try him, he would turn the court into a stage on which to propagate his views. "I should demonstrate with all the force of character, with all the energy of which you have known me to be possessed, the righteousness of the conspiracy, of which I never denied having been the ringleader," he said. If he were executed he would become a martyr with "altars raised to me beside those where today Robespierre and Goujon are revered." In that case, the Directors would have aroused against themselves "the whole democracy of the French Republic," and he bluffed that the lists of sympathizers that the police had seized from the Conspirators constituted "only . . . a fragment."

In case that did not suffice to intimidate the Directors, Babeuf next reminded them of their opponents on the Right. "You have need of a party to support you, and if you removed that of the patriots [i.e., Babeuf and his comrades] you are left alone in the face of royalism." Babeuf realized that this appeal to the Directors to look upon the Equals as a bastion of support was compromised by the fact that the police had captured documents in which the Conspiracy spelled out its intent to visit a summary and exemplary justice upon them. This had apparently been leaked to the press. Babeuf denied it indignantly: "you will not find that [we] desire your death, and it is a calumny to have allowed the statement to be published."

The Conspiracy did not seek the death of the Directors, he said, merely the confession "that you have made an oppressive use of power." With such a confession, the breach between the two factions could be healed. For his part, Babeuf allowed: "I have seen, on reflection, that in the last resort you have not always been the enemies of this republic." As far as Babeuf was concerned, their acknowledgment of error (plus the release of himself and his colleagues) would square everything. "Why will you not believe that you . . . are men who have been temporarily led astray?" Above all, he appealed to their sense of civic duty: "Declare that there has never been any serious conspiracy. Five men, in thus showing themselves great and generous, can today save the country."

It is hardly surprising that the Directors were unmoved by this appeal. Not only did various of the Equals' documents speak somewhat euphemistically of their plans for the Directors, but one that was seized stated quite plainly, *"Tuer les Cinq"* ("Kill the Five"). When, in the course of the investigation, the officers of the court asked Babeuf to initial the documents seized in connection with his arrest, he managed to run his pen through these three words, partially obscuring them. This resulted in hours of wrangling in court over their legibility, but the Directors could have had no doubts about what had been written.

The months before the trial were busy ones for the prisoners. They debated the approach to take in the courtroom; worked at tunneling their way out of prison; endeavored to arouse a popular uprising to liberate them; and protested their conditions. Babeuf was unhappy with the food he was given and took to breaking his plates as a form of resistance. One such occasion, described by the biographer Rose, gives a feeling of his combative spirit:

> The routine was for the cook to set off each evening for the prisoners' quarters . . . accompanied by a boy carrying a great pot. On this occasion Babeuf announced that he had broken his plates. The cook impatiently refused to supply any more, and in a fury Babeuf tendered his chamber-pot, which the cook promptly filled with everything (soup, stew and entrée), then received the lot thrown at his head in return. . . . Babeuf was awarded another five days' solitary, deprived of wine for the duration, and restricted to wooden plates henceforth.[57]

Outside the prison, the Equals retained enough of an organized following to launch one last desperate insurrectionary thrust. They had addressed a great deal of their propaganda to soldiers, and there were persistent reports that the ten thousand troops encamped at Grenelle were throbbing with discontent. In September 1796 several hundred radicals marched on the camp, hoping to win the defection of major units. But their approach was anticipated, and they were met with steel. Those who were able fled, leaving scores of fallen comrades behind. It was, writes Ernest Bax, "the last dying flicker of the spirit of popular insurrection . . . the closing episode of the French Revolution."[58]

The prisoners' efforts at escape (except for one of their group) proved no more effective than the efforts of their comrades to liberate them by force. Their last hope was the judicial system which afforded them a meticulous due process, in contrast with the summary justice that they had planned for their captors should their rebellion have succeeded.

In their legal strategy, the defendants were torn between the wish to deny as much as possible in the hope of acquittal and Babeuf's desire to use the trial as a stage on which to propound his philosophy. In the end they did both, papering over the apparent contradiction by acknowledging that they constituted some kind of "club or reunion of democrats" but insisting that they were being tried for their ideas alone. Thus at one point Babeuf proclaimed that "there was not such an organisation, directory, body of empowered agents, institution, execution, intention, and aim, as pretended by the prosecution."[59] This denial, however, aroused an indignant riposte from the president of the court, reminding Babeuf of his letter to the Directory boasting that he was the leader of the Conspiracy. Babeuf responded lamely that he had only pretended as much in order to frighten the Directors.

Babeuf was much more in his natural voice when it came to turning the trial into a political debate. This was what the relatively moderate Jacobin leader Georges Jacques Danton had attempted at his trial during the Terror, but he was stymied at once by Robespierre, who decreed that the defendant could speak no further. The court under the Directory was more scrupulous. Despite evidencing its impatience, it allowed Babeuf to orate for days at a time. The prisoners insisted on punctuating the sessions by rendering choruses of the *Marseillaise,* and the galleries were filled with their partisans, who volubly made their views known.

Babeuf argued that his was not "a trial of individuals, [but] of the Republic itself."[60] Not only was there no conspiracy, but there could have been none, he said, because there is no such thing as a conspiracy against illegitimate authority. No one, he pointed out, called those who stormed the Bastille conspirators. Likewise, the current government was illegitimate because it was not "established in accordance with the true principles of popular sovereignty."[61] Not only did he associate his aims with the luminous names of Rousseau, Diderot and other figures of the Enlightenment, but he added (setting aside for the moment his contempt for Christianity) that "when Jesus spread His message of human equality, he too was treated as the ringleader of a conspiracy."[62]

These tactics proved surprisingly effective. Some government witnesses, influenced by the gallery, ended up supporting the defense. But the prosecution had an ace in the hole: the military officer, Jacques-Charles-Georges Grisel, who had been in the inner circle of the Conspiracy and whose betrayal of the insurrectionists' plans had triggered their arrest. He now appeared as the government's star witness, and his detailed account of the Conspirators' intent was unshakeable. Nonetheless, after a three-month trial, the jury returned a mixed verdict: 56 out of the 65 defendants were acquitted, 7 were ordered deported, and 2—Babeuf and Darthé, who had steadfastly refused to take part in the proceedings—were sentenced to death. On the announcement of the verdict, each of the two immediately pulled a handmade dagger from his clothes and stabbed himself. Neither died of his self-inflicted wounds, however, and both were delivered to the guillotine the next day.

•   •   •

During his final imprisonment, Babeuf wrote to his comrade Félix LePeletier, a wealthy nobleman who had been a member of the Conspiracy of Equals' Insurrectionary Committee, beseeching him to look after his family. LePeletier was one of the many co-defendants who were acquitted, and he fulfilled Babeuf's plea, adopting the eldest son (christened Robert but called Émile by his father in homage to Rousseau) and placing the others with a friend. Through Émile, Babeuf enjoyed a certain revenge. Some years after his father's death, Émile is reported to have made for Spain and there encountered none other than the traitor Grisel, challenged him to a duel and killed him. (Subsequently, after serving in Napoleon's army, Émile emigrated to America, where he spent the remainder of his life.)[63]

As much as Babeuf was concerned for the fate of his family, he was no less concerned about his intellectual legacy. In his final letter, he gave his wife, Marie-Anne, detailed instructions for the preservation of his defense, in which, over the course of days of oratory, he had recapitulated, sometimes almost verbatim, the main points of the various polemics he had written for *Le Tribun*.[64] He told her that "this defense is precious . . . will be always dear to virtuous hearts and to the friends of their country. The only legacy which will remain to you from me will be my reputation. And I am sure that the enjoyment of it will console greatly both you and your children." One of his comrades had announced the intention to print the various defenses, and he asked Marie-Anne to urge him to give "as much publicity as possible to mine." He also enjoined her not to give copies of it to his comrades "without keeping another correct copy" in order to make sure that it "will never be lost."

As it turned out, Babeuf's *Defense* was published and saved, and its fame and endurance proved to be all that he might have wished. "There is consolation in dying for the sake of truth, justice, honor," it said. "Such a death ... confers immortality."[65] It was published not just in French but several other languages. Some 170 years later, during the radical *journées* of the 1960s, it was published afresh in English, complete with an essay by the popular leftist scholar Herbert Marcuse.

Even with this success, the *Defense* turned out to be but a small part of Babeuf's enduring legacy. For it was his revolutionary example, far more than his thought, that made a mark on history. His comrade Buonarroti, one of those convicted at the trial and sentenced to exile, promised to vindicate them all by one day telling the true story of the Conspiracy of Equals. Devoting the rest of his life to radical agitation, Buonarroti brought out his history in 1828 in Brussels. Those of his former fellow Conspirators who were still alive and whose roles were not already in the public record he attempted to shield from what he took to be a still present danger of government retribution by yielding their names only in the form of anagrams. Although it could not then be published in France, his work circulated there illicitly (so much that it was reviewed in an influential journal), adding its measure to the ferment that was soon to spark a second revolution.[66]

When the Revolution of 1830 ushered in the liberal monarchy of Louis Philippe, the first of many French editions of Buonarroti's *La Conspiration des Égaux* was published, and he was able to return to France. Until his death in 1837 he served as a kind of living oracle of the ideas of the Equals, consulted by Auguste Blanqui, Louis Blanc and others of the generation of revolutionaries then coming of age. He was, wrote French historian Armand Marrast, "the inheritor of the ideas of the great revolutionary epoch ... the high-priest of a proscribed religion who guarded, almost alone and in mysterious refuge, the sacred fire of equality."[67]

Buonarroti's tale "came to rank almost as a 'Revolutionists' Handbook'" for the agitators of 1830 and 1848, as socialist historian G. D. H. Cole put it.[68] In 1838 in Britain, Bronterre O'Brien, the "schoolmaster" of the Chartist movement, published an English translation. Marx is reported to have read the book in 1844 and to have sought to arrange its translation into German (a task ultimately carried out by his colleague Moses Hess).[69] The next year, in their first collaborative work, *The Holy Family,* the young Marx and Engels paid this bow to the Equals: "The revolutionary movement which began in 1789 . . . and which with Babeuf's conspiracy was temporarily defeated, gave rise to the communist idea which Babeuf's friend Buonarroti reintroduced in France after the Revolution of 1830."

Marx and Engels made a second passing reference to Babeuf in the *Communist Manifesto,* distinguishing him from the derided "utopians," as an early voice of proletarian struggle. Indeed, they might have been more generous in their acknowledgment since fifty years before the *Manifesto,* Babeuf's *Defense* had anticipated its main theme. "Class war," it said, arises when "the masses can no longer find a way to go on living; they see that they possess nothing and that they suffer under the harsh and flinty oppression of a greedy ruling class. The hour strikes for great and memorable revolutionary events . . . when a general overthrow of the system of private property is inevitable, when the revolt of the poor against the rich becomes a necessity that can no longer be postponed."[70]

At the turn of the nineteenth century, when the modern French socialist movement gelled, both major wings embraced the heritage of Babeuf: the militants led by Jules Guesde, who called the Conspiracy of Equals the movement's "cradle," and the moderates led by Jean Jaurès, who presided at the 1911 memorial meeting at Saint Quentin. The legacy of the self-made feudist from Picardy did not stop at the borders of France. In 1919, the founding manifesto of the Comintern declared: "We Communists, united in the Third International, consider ourselves the direct continuators of the heroic endeavors and martyrdom of a long line of revolutionary generations [starting] from Babeuf."

2

NEW HARMONY:
OWEN CONDUCTS AN
EXPERIMENT

MARCH 5, 1825, WAS JOHN QUINCY ADAMS' first full day as President. Nonetheless, he found time to walk over to the Hall of Representatives after dinner to take in a discourse by Robert Owen, the renowned British industrialist and visionary who had come to America to launch an experiment in replacing the existing "individual selfish system" with a "united social" one.

Owen's fame, flowing from the innovative and humane manner in which he governed the employees of his cotton mill in Scotland, had preceded him across the Atlantic. He was received by the panoply of the New World's leading citizens, culminating in an address to Congress on February 25. His audience included not only senators and representatives, but also members of the cabinet, justices of the Supreme Court, and outgoing President Monroe. President-elect Adams had attended part of it. Owen had informed this luminous gathering of "changes at hand greater than all the changes which have hitherto occurred in the affairs of mankind."[1] It was hard to do justice to so momentous a topic even in the several hours that Owen lectured that day, so it was agreed to reconvene on March 5 in order that he might complete the picture.

Something compelled a postponement, but no one bothered to inform the new President, so Adams' walk down to Congress was for naught. Nonetheless, he returned when the postponement date arrived to hear the final three-hour installment of Owen's disquisition, parts of which, the President noted dryly in his diary, Owen seemed to read from a book.

Owen announced that he had purchased a large, developed tract on the banks of the Wabash in Indiana on which he would organize a model community to prove to the world the benefits of the "social system" and thereby usher in the millennium:

> [H]ere it is, in the heart of the United States . . . that that power which directs and governs the universe and every action of man, has arranged circum-stances . . . to permit me to commence a new empire of peace and good will to man, founded on other principles, and leading to other practices than those of the past or present, and which principles, in due season, and in the allotted time, will lead to that state of virtue, intelligence, enjoyment, and happiness, in practice, which has been foretold by the sages of past times, would, at some distant period become the lot of the human race![2]

Hearing of these plans from his exile in Brussels, Babeuf's surviving co-conspirator, Buonarroti, noted with satisfaction that "what the Democrats of the Year IV were unable to execute in France, a generous man has recently essayed, by other means, to put in practice in . . . America . . . communities founded on the principles of equal distribution of enjoyments and of labours."[3]

Whereas "Babeuf's doctrine" had no name, Owen and his followers coined the term "socialism." Buonarroti was right that the two had the same end in mind, but the difference in approach was of the utmost consequence. Babeuf had conceived of no way to collectivize property except through the power of the state. Owen recognized that there was no need to seize power. Endowed with some land and capital, socialists could form their own communities. They need not wait for the government to be overthrown before enjoying a life of brotherhood and sharing. And the demonstration they would offer of the happiness and efficacy of collective living would hasten the spread of their philosophy.

This approach was later dismissed by Marx and Engels as "utopian," a label under which they grouped Owen with such other radical thinkers of the late eighteenth and early nineteenth centuries as Count Saint Simon and Charles Fourier. Nonetheless, Engels acknowledged Owen's unparalleled influence: "Every social movement, every real advance in England on behalf of the workers links itself on to the name of Robert Owen."[4]

Of the "utopians," Owen was by far the most respected, as was evidenced by the eagerness of the American government's leaders to give him a thorough hearing. He was also the clearest in his socialism. Saint Simon and Fourier both accepted private property and neither was much interested in democracy, but Owen was a firm advocate of democracy and collective ownership. In addition he was more determined to put his ideas into practice. Within a few months of Owen's announcement before Congress of his planned settlement, some eight to nine hundred Americans rushed to join him on the Wabash.

• • •

For Robert Owen, pioneering was second nature. After just two years of education, from age five to seven, followed by two years spent assisting with the instruction of younger students, he declared himself ready to strike out on his own. But his parents made him wait until he turned ten, when they took him to Shrewsbury, the stop nearest their home of Newtown in Wales, and put him on board a coach for London with the goodly sum of forty shillings in his pocket.

Owen's family had not left him entirely to his own devices. A grown brother gave him temporary lodging in London, and his father corresponded with acquaintances to help Robert find his first job, as an assistant to a clothing retailer in Stamford. Compensated at first only by room and board, he proved a bright and diligent employee and climbed rapidly in his position while accumulating knowledge of textiles. Still in his teens he joined with a partner on his first business venture, manufacturing "mules," a recently invented machine for spinning cotton. After a few months he traded his share in the partnership for a few of the machines and launched his own shop.

Soon his little business was netting six pounds a week, but he gave it up when Peter Drinkwater, the owner of a spinning mill with five hundred employees, agreed to pay him an equivalent amount to become its manager. With a salary of three hundred pounds the first year and substantial increments to follow, Owen boasted that he was "now placed in an independent position for one not yet twenty years of age."[5] The accomplishment was all the more remarkable for the fact that, as he later recalled: "I was yet but an ill-educated awkward youth, strongly sensitive to my defects of education, speaking ungrammatically, a kind of Welsh English, in consequence of the imperfect language spoken in Newtown."

Unschooled he may have been, but the young Owen had a flair for business. He secured his employer's permission to stamp his own name on the spools of yarn, and within a few years Owen's reputation in the field was established. Leaving Drinkwater, he readily found partners to provide the capital for a major new firm under his management, the Chorlton Twist Company.

This business took him to Scotland, where he met Anne Caroline Dale, daughter of the mill owner David Dale. Owen was so shy with women that Anne had to send a friend to let it slip that she would welcome his courtship. He took up the invitation with alacrity, but her father stood as an obstacle. As a stratagem in this courtship, Owen offered to purchase Dale's mills on the Clyde in New Lanark. Owen bought the mills, softened the father, won the girl. His chivalry was doubly rewarded, for the mills at New Lanark brought him fame and fortune.

It was while still managing Drinkwater's establishment that Owen first "noticed the great attention given to the dead machinery, and the neglect and disregard of the living machinery," that is, the employees. Gradually the plan formed in his mind to run New Lanark in a very different way. It was to be, he said, "the most important experiment for the happiness of the human race that had yet been instituted."[6]

When Owen took possession of New Lanark, the mills employed some 1,700 to 1,800 employees. Of these, 400 to 500 were pauper children indentured as wards to industrialists who provided food, clothing and shelter in exchange for the right to work them however they wished. The ages of these charges were recorded as between seven and twelve, but Owen said he discovered that they were in fact between five and ten. Of the workforce as a whole, said Owen, "the great majority were idle, intemperate, dishonest" and "theft was very general, and was carried on to an enormous and ruinous extent."[7]

Owen probably exaggerated the ills to dramatize his own subsequent accomplishment, but there is little dispute that he rendered the place far happier than he found it.[8] He did not raise wages, but he did marginally reduce the hours of work, and he brought order and cleanliness to the mill.[9]

Since New Lanark was a company village, Owen oversaw not only the workplace but all aspects of his employees' surroundings. He provided a better store at which they could make their purchases, and added a second room to each of their dwellings. Before Owen's arrival many of the villagers allowed dunghills to accumulate in front of their doors. Owen had these carried off to a nearby farm and forbade their renewal. Thereafter, as son Robert Dale Owen recollects, "the streets, daily swept at the expense of the company, were kept scrupulously clean; and its tidy appearance in every respect was the admiration of strangers."[10]

Owen endeavored to uplift his employees without resorting to the two most familiar methods of his time, religious instruction and harsh punishments. For improving their performance in the workplace, Owen invented a device he called the "silent monitor," which, he explained,

> consisted for a four-sided piece of wood, about two inches long and one broad, each side coloured—one side black, another blue, the third yellow, and the fourth white. . . . One of these was suspended in a conspicuous place near to each of the persons employed, and the colour at the front told the conduct of the individual during the preceding day, to four degrees of comparison. Bad, denoted by black . . . indifferent by blue . . . good by yellow . . . and excellent by white. . . . I could thus see at a glance, as I passed through each room of every factory or mill, how each one had behaved during the preceding day.[11]

To reinforce the evaluations, Owen had his managers maintain "books of character" in which was entered each employee's daily score, on a scale of 1 to 4. Owen said he found it "gratifying to observe the new spirit created" by this system. As time passed, the predominant color he observed as he wended his way among the work stations shifted from darkest to lightest. "Never perhaps in the history of the human race," he ventured, "has so simple a device created in so short a period so much order, virtue, goodness, and happiness."[12] How his employees felt about this method of daily judgment we do not know.

He also looked to their behavior outside the mill. Although he felt compelled to tolerate the consumption of alcohol, he refused to abide drunkenness. As Robert Dale tells us, "He had village watchmen, who patrolled the streets at night, and who were instructed to take down the name of every man found drunk. The inebriate was fined so much for the first offence, a larger sum for the second, the fines being deducted from his wages, and the third offence resulted in dismissal, sometimes postponed if he showed sincere repentance."[13]

Nor did Owen's effort to reform his employees stop at their doors; he undertook as well to police the cleanliness of their abodes. He devised a method for this that might be seen as an early antecedent of the "block committees" that Fidel Castro created to police daily life in Cuba. An anonymous pamphlet written by one of the villagers relates that Owen advised that they should appoint a committee from amongst themselves, every week, to inspect the houses in the village and to insert in a book . . . a faithful report of the state of each house as they might happen to find it. This recommendation was upon the whole pretty cordially acceded to by the male part of the population, but the rage and opposition it met with from the women, I well remember, was unbounded. They almost unanimously resolved to meet the visitants with locked doors. They bestowed upon them the appellation of "Bug Hunters," and Mr. Owen escaped not without his share of the general odium.[14]

In addition to the good order and cleanliness and the general spirit of benevolence that Owen brought to New Lanark, what made the place famous was its educational system. Owen devoted great sums to his schools, often quarreling with his partners over the expenditure. He provided education up to the age of twelve, although book-learning began only in the last of these years since Owen believed that the natural environment was a great source of instruction. The principal subjects were singing, dancing and military drill, for both sexes, which he said were the disciplines most conducive to good character.

Education until age twelve was a lot longer than was commonly available, particularly to a mill worker's child, but the most remarkable aspect of Owen's system was the age at which the schooling began—at one year old or as soon as the children were able to walk.

The cardinal rule of this early childhood education was kindness, although not praise. Owen hit on the theory, still in vogue in some schools of child-rearing, that it was best to avoid all praise or blame. (How he reconciled this with his cherished "silent monitors" which passed judgment on his employees every moment of their working lives was never explained.) The students were not to be struck nor spoken to harshly, and they were constantly exhorted to show kindness to their fellows.

The fame of Owen's schools spread far and wide, and many illustrious guests came to observe them. Grand Duke Nicholas of Russia, who later became tsar, was so impressed that he offered to provide land for two million Englishmen to emigrate to Russia under Owen's governance, in order to alleviate the overpopulation of Britain about which Doctor Malthus was warning. Among the others who made the pilgrimage to New Lanark were Princes John and Maximilian of Austria; Peter, Regent of Oldenburg; and, by Owen's estimate, most of the nobility of England, as well as "Foreign Ambassadors,—many bishops—and clergy innumerable . . . learned men of all professions from all countries,—and wealthy travellers . . . of every description."[15] In all, the guest book at New Lanark showed some twenty thousand entries over the ten years before Owen first left for America. Numerous other dignitaries received Owen and embraced his work, including the Duke of Kent, father of queen-to-be Victoria.

For the boy who had left Wales atop a coach with forty shillings in his pocket, the attention he was receiving from the high and mighty was quite heady. He estimated that he had become "the most popular individual in the civilised world," and his already robust confidence in his ideas grew all the stronger.[16]

Owen never departed from graciousness in an argument; but neither did he ever pay the least attention to what anyone who disagreed with him said. Robert Dale Owen recollected that his father "usually glanced over books, without mastering them; often dismissing them with some such curt remark as that 'the radical errors shared by all men made books of comparatively little value.'"[17] His friend, the writer Harriet Martineau, put it best: "Robert Owen is not the man to think differently of a book for having read it."[18]

• • •

Owen's socialist philosophy was derived from two fundamental pillars of his thought. The first was that no human "is responsible for his will and his own actions." This is because "his whole character—physical, mental, and moral—is formed independently of himself."[19] Each person is entirely the product of his "constitution or organization at birth, and of the effects of external circumstances upon it from birth to death."[20] Therefore, it is futile to call individuals to account for their behavior. Instead, society should recognize its power to shape each of its members into a person of high character.

The second pillar, a natural complement to the first, was a fierce opposition to religion. "There is no sacrifice . . . which I . . . would not have . . . willingly and joyously made to terminate the existence of religion on earth," he declared.[21] After reflecting in childhood upon the great diversity of faiths, Owen concluded that all were "based on the same absurd imagination, that each [person] . . . determined his own thoughts, will, and action,—and was responsible for them to God and his fellowmen."[22] This faulty notion, he said, turned man into "a weak, imbecile animal; a furious bigot and fanatic; or a miserable hypocrite."[23]

Owen's socialist economics crystallized in the course of a national inquiry into the issue of poverty. The revolution in the technology of the textile industry had displaced many workers, giving rise, from 1811 to 1816, to "Luddite" riots in numerous cities in which labor-saving machinery was smashed. The contraction of demand at the end of the Napoleonic wars drove a growing number of indigents into the public workhouses and prompted a parliamentary inquiry into the Poor Laws. This inspired Owen to develop a plan for "villages of unity and cooperation."

Owen designed the villages down to the last detail, and even had a scale model built. Each village was to accommodate twelve hundred people. The buildings were to be arranged in the shape of a parallelogram, three sides of which would consist of flats, with one room allocated to each married couple and their very young children. The fourth side would comprise dormitories for all children over the age of three, and an infirmary and a guest house. In the middle would be schools and dining halls and kitchens, since all meals would be taken communally. Gardens and playgrounds would surround these central buildings. Owen even prescribed the dress of the villagers, favoring loose garments like Roman togas or Scottish kilts.

These villages would take "men, women, and children, of all ages, capacities, and dispositions; most of them very ignorant; many with bad and vicious habits,"[24] and transform them into superior beings. They would live together in the closest harmony—"intimately acquainted with each other's inmost thoughts"—and would produce enough to provide for themselves abundantly.[25]

The committee of inquiry was unresponsive to Owen's proposal. As G. D. H. Cole put it, they "had asked for a mouse; they received a mountain."[26] But while Parliament failed to embrace the idea, Owen became ever more convinced that villages of unity and cooperation held the key not merely to alleviating the plight of the poor, but to the reconstitution of the entire society.

As Owen developed the idea, he envisioned a life of virtually effortless abundance. Villagers would proceed from birth through three five-year stages of education, preparing them to become at age fifteen "men and women of a new race, physically, intellectually and morally; beings far superior to any yet known to have lived upon the earth."[27] At this point they would embark upon "a most interesting period of human life," namely the finding of mates. The stress would have been removed from this portentous choice by communal upbringing in which none would have any secrets and all would "naturally make known . . . their undisguised thoughts and feelings."[28] Thus it would easily be "ascertained who by nature . . . have the strongest attachment for each other; and these will naturally unite."

Courtship thus dispensed with, the fifteen- to twenty-year-old group would have ample time for their large responsibilities. They would perform virtually all of society's productive work and also would see to the education of those just younger than themselves. Owen estimated that, with the assistance of the younger children, this age cohort would be able to "produce a surplus of all the wealth which a rational and superior race of beings can require."[29] However, to guarantee against any possible shortfall, those from age twenty to twenty-five would work as directors and supervisors. Beyond this age, "none need be required to produce or instruct, except for their own pleasure and gratification."[30] This would still leave the work of storage and distribution, which would be the task of those from the age of twenty-five to thirty, although it would require no more than two hours a day of their time.

When people were raised in these villages, the human race would change—and not only it. "There will be no cruelty in man's nature," not even toward other creatures, and as a result, "the animal creation will also become different in character." More species would be domesticated, and those that could not be tamed would be "destroyed," so that "a terrestrial paradise be formed, in which harmony will pervade all that will exist upon earth."[31]

These musings about transforming wildlife were fanciful, not to mention ecologically unsound, but they were not unique to Owen. In fact, Charles Fourier went further, predicting the domestication of lions and whales whose strength would free humans from most work. Such fantasies about new beasts did not outlive the utopians, but the idea of a new man, dimly foreseen by Babeuf but sketched sharply by Owen, became the enduring centerpiece of the socialist vision. Socialism promised a surfeit of material goods and brotherly harmony among people, but its ultimate reward would be the transformation of humans, if not into gods, then into supermen able to transcend the pains and limits of life as it had been known.

Owen was confident that the great transition to the "terrestrial paradise" could be achieved by the force of example. Once one or several villages of unity and cooperation would have the chance to demonstrate their success, other people would be eager to emulate them. Even the most privileged of the existing society would come to see that their present enjoyments were nothing in comparison with what this new way of living offered. "Your titles, your rank, shall not be meddled with," he wrote. "You may shut yourselves up in your parks as usual; but when you peep over the walls, you will find us all so happy in our villages of co-operation, that you will of your own accord throw away privileges that only interfere with your own happiness."[32] Owen stressed that he sought no violent confrontation, and that he was not out to destroy the existing system, merely to render it obsolete. He likened the process to that by which rail travel had supplanted old gravel roads. More and more villages would be "made ready to receive willing passengers from the old road . . . until the new shall gradually . . . become sufficient to accommodate . . . the population of the world."[33]

•   •   •

The prompt for launching such a village—as opposed to mere theorizing about it—came to Owen quite fortuitously. In the United States, a sect of German Lutheran schismatics, led by the charismatic preacher George Rapp, lived communally since emigrating from Württemburg in 1804. The Harmony Society, as they fashioned themselves, had built a flourishing community in Butler County, Pennsylvania. In 1814, something inspired Rapp to move his flock to Indiana and found a new community, which was christened "Harmonie."[34] Here, in addition to bringing forth verdant fields, orchards and vineyards on the four thousand acres of rich soil they cleared, they built highly remunerative industries which produced an array of textiles, clothing, shoes, lumber, bricks, cooking oil, candles, glue, beer and even whiskey. The latter they did not touch themselves, but marketed, along with about twenty other products, as far away as New Orleans. Then, after ten years, prompted by some new revelation, Rapp determined to move his band once again. He commissioned Richard Flower, a leader of an English settlement across the Wabash in Albion, Illinois, to find a buyer for Harmonie.

Flower traveled to New Lanark and approached Owen, who had already heard of Harmonie and had even corresponded with Rapp about communal living. "The success of the Rappites . . . wonderfully encouraged my father," wrote Robert Dale Owen. "He felt sure that he could be far more successful than they."[35] Owen could see at once that the site of Harmonie would be an excellent setting for launching a model village of unity and cooperation. And doing it on American soil offered social and political benefits, as well. Robert Dale recalled: "Here was a village ready built, a territory capable of supporting tens of thousands in a country where the expression of thought was free, and where the people were unsophisticated."[36] The time had come for the great experiment.

Thus Owen and his son William, then twenty-two, set sail for the new world. After landing in New York, they traveled upstate to visit a Shaker colony.

William recorded in his diary a conversation the Owens had with some of the Shakers: "When my father talked of establishing communities, they asked: of Quakers? or Jews? or what? and shook their heads when they found it was for all sects."[37] But Owen was confident in his plans. William continued: "one asked if we would like to remain with them. We said we would make some communities still better than theirs and that they would come to us."

Owen then lectured his way down the East Coast to Washington, where in addition to the two discourses delivered before Presidents Monroe and Adams and the other assembled leaders of the United States government, he met with a delegation of Choctaw and Chickasaw chiefs whom he found sympathetic to his vision. William recorded in his diary that "At the end of almost every sentence, my Father said they cried out 'say, sa' or 'na, na say sa,' which implied that they agreed and were pleased."[38] All in all, Owen's reception in America left him exultant. He wrote home to a friend:

> The proceedings exceed the most sanguine anticipations that I had formed. The United States . . . have been prepared in the most remarkable manner for the new system. The principle of union & cooperation . . . is now universally admitted to be far superior to the individual selfish system. . . . In fact the whole of this country is ready to commence a new empire upon the principle of public property & to discard private property. . . . For years past every thing seems to have been preparing in an unaccountable & most remarkable manner for my arrival. This new colony will be filled up to its full number before the end of this [month or year?[†]] by useful & valuable families & individuals accustomed to the climate & habits of the country without one coming out from Europe. . . . Our operations will soon extend to the blacks, & the Indians who by singular circumstances have been prepared in a peculiar manner for the change which I propose.[39]

The property transfer was completed. Rapp and his followers boarded a riverboat for their new settlement in Pennsylvania, which they called "Economy." Harmonie was rechristened "New Harmony," and it filled with Americans answering Owen's call. On April 27, 1825, he assembled the new arrivals for a welcoming speech. "I am come to this country, to introduce an entire new state of society;" he said. "To change it from the ignorant, selfish system, to an

---

† Owen omitted a word here.

enlightened social system which shall gradually unite all interests into one, and remove all cause for contest between individuals."[40] And he concluded solemnly: "I now live but to see this system fairly established in the world."

Owen drafted a constitution for the Preliminary Society of New Harmony. He envisioned this as a three-year transitional phase to a fully cooperative and egalitarian community. For the short term, some elements of inequality would be allowed to endure. Despite his hopes for the blacks and Indians, the charter of the Preliminary Society said membership was open to all, "exclusive of persons of color."

Within two months of greeting his new followers, Owen departed, entrusting command to his son William and a British disciple, Donald MacDonald. He had some business affairs to attend to in Scotland, but mostly he spent his time making speeches in America and England. Owen's decision to leave his fledgling community at this time defies understanding. Not only were all of his hopes and visions invested in it, but also the preponderance of his fortune. The only conceivable explanation is that he was so certain of the validity of his theories that he had not entertained the possibility that the project might fail.

But if doubt never entered Owen's mind, the same was by no means true for the son whom he left at the helm. William confided to his diary:

> The enjoyment of a reformer, I should say, is much more in contemplation, than in reality. . . . Did I not expect that those who were brought up in a community . . . will enjoy more happiness than I anticipated for myself, and more than they can experience [who have been] brought up and liv[e] under the old mode of society, I should not be disposed to promote the formation of a society, as I at present am inclined to doubt whether the happiness of the present generation will be increased.[41]

William was tormented by the knowledge that his own feelings did not correspond with those appropriate for the social system, and he recorded his surprise at how difficult it was to "get over one's old habits." He wrote to his father in England about "how delighted I shall be, when we all meet here & again form a family circle. A Society Circle is, as yet a little too large for me."[42]

The village purchased from Rapp contained some 160 buildings, ranging from log cabins, which had been erected when the Rappites first settled Harmonie and which they were in the process of phasing out, to large frame and brick structures including dwellings, barns, granaries, factories, workshops, a tavern and an immense church. However, since the Owenites outnumbered the Rappites by several hundred, William was at his wit's end finding sufficient sleeping quarters for all. Moreover, despite the surfeit of population, there was nonetheless a shortage of labor. This was felt most markedly in the colony's various industries, every one of which experienced a falloff in output and several of which ceased operation altogether.

Historian Arthur Bestor traces this collapse to a dearth of skilled workmen and supervisors, few of whom were attracted to New Harmony where their compensation would have been much less than in the surrounding economy.[43] In a letter home to one of his brothers, William bemoaned the lack of any "potter, ager, saddler, or good tinner" among the New Harmonians.[44] Owen did think to provide some differential material rewards, but only for the more highly educated professionals. Ironically, this was probably superfluous; for unlike the skilled workmen, many intellectuals were drawn to New Harmony by their interest in its philosophy.

Bestor's analysis may account for the atrophy of the colony's workshops, but it does not explain why the Owenites did not manage to plant sufficient crops that spring or summer on the vast fertile lands they had purchased or to adequately protect those they did plant. Of the several surviving accounts from within New Harmony, the letters of William Pelham, an elderly retiree, to his son constitute the only one that retained its hopefulness. He blamed the Rappites for the community's woes. "Vegetables of every kind are very scarce," he wrote, "for the old Harmonites left the garden fences in a wretched condition, and before they could be repaired by the newcomers the hogs and cows had materially injured the gardens." But it is hard to believe that the notoriously punctilious Rappites had in fact left the fences in disrepair, and it is impossible to understand why, if they had, the Owenites could not have made timely repairs.

Other accounts describe similar difficulties but do not join Pelham in pointing fingers outside the group. Paul Brown, who wrote a book about his disillusion with Owen, reports that "the gardens and fields were almost entirely neglected."[45] And Thomas Pears, another whose correspondence survives, wrote during the late summer: "The hogs have been our Lords and Masters this year in field and garden. We are now, as we have been, without vegetables except what we buy; and I believe that we shall go without potatoes, turnips, or cabbages this winter."[46]

The corollary to the shortage of skilled hands was a surplus of unskilled or unbusy ones. Owen complained, "we have also been much puzzled to know what to do with those who profess to do any thing or every thing, they are perfect drones."[47] The same observation was put more bluntly by an outsider, R. L. Baker, a Rappite who returned to New Harmony on business: "the streets are filled with idlers who all have something to do or to say, which one could do for ten."[48] Even the imperishably hopeful Pelham acknowledged in one letter that "there has been much irregularity of effort." This "irregularity" in turn led to bickering. Pears remarked that "instead of striving who should do most, the most industry was manifested in accusing others of doing little."[49] He added that this had given rise to what he called "the Reign of Reports."[50]

In September, Pears wrote that "until lately our Committee gave up all idea of farming till Mr. Owen's return, except the sowing of fifty or sixty acres of winter barley, which they wisely concluded would be wanted for our beer the ensuing year."[51] In apparent desperation, he and several other "agriculturalists" met and drafted a resolution calling on the committee "immediately to ascertain the situation of the land which is to receive the crops of winter grain," including "its location" and "whether it be subject at any time to inundation" and also to determine "what number of horses and oxen are in the possession of the Society" and "what number of wagons, tools, ploughs, harrows, axes, spades, etc. [are] now possessed by us." This is information any ordinary farmer would gather on day one, but in New Harmony, all the farmers could do was form a caucus. Pears reported that the resolution languished.[52]

The prevailing inefficiency at New Harmony extended to its distribution system. Each member of the community had a passbook in which his hours of labor were credited and the supplies taken from the village store were debited. Apparently all consumables were supposed to be disbursed this way. "Even salads were deposited in the store, to be handed out—making ten thousand unnecessary steps, and causing them to come to the tables in a wilted deadened state," complained Brown.[53] The scene was vividly described by William Shephard, a neighbor who visited often while serving as an intermediary in some of the continuing financial transactions between Old and New Harmony:

> The store is literally constantly thronged by . . . consumers with their little books. The storekeepers and clerks seem abundantly busy in attending them—and altho there is so many persons officiating behind the counters, it is frequently very difficult for country people to obtain attention—It has been remarked by many persons in my hearing that three *Dutch* storekeepers would do more business than them all and with far less confusion—It seems

to me an *expensive system!* plenty of storekeepers, clerks, committee men and rangers—few smiths, artizans [*sic*] & farmers![54]

Laggard in production, bureaucratic in distribution, New Harmony survived only because Owen subsidized it, pouring in some thirty thousand dollars those first months, in addition to the cost of his purchases from Rapp. Even this subsidy was not enough to raise the living standards above a spartan level. Brown complained that "a great part of the time the people were very much stinted in their allowances of coffee and tea, butter, milk, &c."[55] And even the resolutely upbeat Pelham confessed that "our privations are sometimes such as to test the strength of our principles."[56] In a letter to friends planning to join him at New Harmony, he urged them to bring items that were in short supply, including ham, despite complaints that the pigs had the run of the place.

Perhaps in consequence of this general feeling of want, or perhaps because of the character of some of the people drawn to New Harmony, "a pilfering disposition very much prevailed," reported Brown. "Scarce a week passed but shirts, handkerchiefs, or stockings, were filched from . . . out of the laundries or yards of the boarding houses."[57]

The only things that seemed to be pursued with energy at New Harmony were meetings and entertainment.[58] One of the few instructions that Owen had given before his departure was that the community should convene three nights a week: once for general discussion, once for a musical recital, once for a ball. These occurred unfailingly, it seems, on Wednesday, Friday and Tuesday nights, and to them were added, according to Pears, parade and drill on Monday nights and "fire engine" and debates on Saturdays.

Despite these diversions, New Harmony was an uneasy place throughout 1825. Pelham remained confident that "the present inconveniences will gradually be supplanted," but he also had to report that his two friends who had reached New Harmony after a journey of two weeks had decided one week later to return at once to Zanesville.[59] And Thomas Pears' wife, Sarah, lamented: "If ever I should be fortunate enough to get into civilized society once more, I think I should never wish to leave it again."[60]

The young community pined for its founder. After two months in Scotland and England, Owen headed back to America accompanied by his oldest son, Robert Dale, who described himself as having exulted over the journey "as an Israelite may have exulted when Moses spoke to him of the Land of Promise."[61] Owen's party also included an architect named Stedman Whitwell. Owen had retained Whitwell to explain the six-by-six-foot scale model of the ideal cooperative village that he was bringing back with him. It is not easy to understand why Owen attached so much importance to this model when he had nearly a thousand followers living in a flesh-and-blood community patterned according to his social, if not his architectural, ideas. Soon after disembarking, he arranged for Whitwell to convey the thing to Washington, where President Adams allowed them to display it for some weeks in a White House anteroom.

Before returning to New Harmony, Owen traveled to Philadelphia to link up with William Maclure. A Scotsman who had settled in Philadelphia, Maclure was himself a wealthy reformer who had visited Owen's mills at New Lanark and had been powerfully impressed. He had agreed to join Owen in the New Harmony venture and to help finance it. Although Maclure supported Owen's socialist ideas, the goal dearest to his heart was educational reform. It was agreed that he would take charge of education at New Harmony, utilizing it to experiment with new methods. He gathered to himself several educators from Europe and also several scientists of distinction, which he himself was in the field of geology. The coterie included Thomas Say, sometimes called the father of American entomology, and two well-known Europeans, the Dutch geologist Gerard Troost and the French naturalist and illustrator Charles Alexandre Lesueur. So impressive were the group's scholarly credentials that the vessel which carried them to New Harmony was nicknamed the "boatload of knowledge."

Owen's arrival at New Harmony in January 1826 brought great rejoicing. The schoolchildren gathered to greet him and accompanied him to his quarters at the tavern.[62] In contrast to the widespread sense of distress among the denizens, Owen declared himself mightily pleased with the progress of New Harmony in his absence. Within a week he announced his intention to dissolve the "Preliminary Society," then in only the ninth month of its intended three-year duration, and to replace it at once with a permanent society in which all lingering inequality of rewards would be done away with. It was to be "liberty, equality, and fraternity in downright earnest," wrote Robert Dale Owen.[63]

For two weeks, New Harmony was alive with meetings and drafting sessions culminating on February 5 with the adoption of the constitution of the New Harmony Community of Equality. Its preamble echoed the Declaration of Independence: "When a number of the human family associate in principles which do not yet influence the rest of the world, a due regard to the opinions of others requires a public declaration of the object of their association, of their principles, and of their intentions."[64]

Apparently, however, the constitution was not pleasing to everyone. Within days, one group, discontent with Owen's antireligious views, broke away and formed an independent community on land that Owen agreed to lease or sell to them. They called their community "Macluria," although Maclure himself was not among them, and he was no less a nonbeliever than Owen. In the main community, after two weeks the populace despaired that the new constitution sufficed to set them on a sound course, so the governing committee unanimously voted to give Owen dictatorial powers for a year. A month later, another split ensued and a third community was formed, taking the name "Feiba Peveli."[65]

This peculiar name derived from an invention of the architect Stedman Whitwell. He found it confusing that so many places in America were named Washington, and troubling that the name of a place told nothing of its whereabouts. To remedy this, he devised a new system of geographic notation in which each degree of longitude or latitude received an alphabetic designation. Whitwell ingeniously assigned consonants and vowels in such a way as to assure that each place would be pronounceable. By his system London became "Lafa Vovutu," Pittsburgh "Otfu Veitoup," and the site of community number three at New Harmony came out as "Feiba Peveli." When challenged about the lack of euphony of his system, Whitwell responded that his place names were a breeze compared with the name of a nearby Indian chief, known as "Occoneocoglecococachecachecodungo."

In the main community, Owen undertook a reorganization designed to elicit more work and responsibility from the members. The new constitution contained a provision reminiscent of Owen's "silent monitors" at New Lanark. A record was to be kept of "the Intendants opinion of the daily character of each person attached to their Occupation." Then, at public meetings each Sunday, Owen would read aloud the character ratings and the amount of work performed by each member of the society. By March the community's newspaper, the *Gazette,* was boasting that "by the indefatigable attention of Mr. Owen, a degree of order, of regularity, of system, has been introduced.... Our streets no longer present groups of idle talkers."[66] Spirits were brightened to the point that the weekly balls in April saw the introduction of an original cotillion, called the "New Social System."

Not all of Owen's initiatives succeeded. He banned liquor, but never succeeded in making the ban stick. Decades later one of the community members, using the pseudonym Squire B., recalled to an interviewer his own role in subverting this rule:

[Squire B.] informed us that he came from Illinois to New Harmony, and that a man in Illinois was "owing him," and asked him to take a barrel of whisky for the debt. He could not well get the money; so took the whisky. . . . Not long after, Mr. Owen found that the people still got whisky from some quarter, he could not tell where, though he did his best to find out. At last he suspected Squire B., and . . . accused him of it; on which Squire B. had to own that it was he who retailed the whisky. "It was taken for a debt," said he, "and what was I to do to get rid of it?" Mr. Owen turned round and in his simple manner said, "Ah, I see you do not understand the principles."[67]

The schools, which functioned under Maclure's aegis, were also a source of mixed satisfaction. Some of the parents were unhappy with the forced separation from their children, and undoubtedly many of the children shared this feeling. I am aware of only one surviving memoir recounting childhood experience in the schools of New Harmony, that of Mrs. Sarah Cox Thrall, who recalled many decades later:

> We had bread but once a week—on Saturdays. I thought if I ever got out, I would kill myself eating sugar and cake. We marched in military order. . . . We went to bed at sundown in little bunks suspended in rows by cords from the ceiling. Sometimes one of the children at the end of the row would swing back her cradle, and, when it collided on the return bound with the next bunk, it set the whole row bumping together. This was a favorite diversion, and caused the teachers much distress. . . . Children regularly in the boarding-school were not allowed to see their parents, except at rare intervals. I saw my father and mother twice in two years. We had a little song we used to sing:
>
> > Number 2 pigs locked up in a pen,
> > When they get out, it's now and then;
> > When they get out, they sneak about,
> > for fear old Neef[†] will find them out.[68]

By May, things were felt to be faltering to the extent that Owen attempted another reorganization of the community, this time, following a suggestion of Maclure's, subdividing it into occupation groups. Each unit—farmers, mechanics, educators—could then see to the productivity of its own and would trade goods and services with the others.

---

† Joseph Neef, an associate of Maclure's, was one of the chief schoolteachers.

In addition to his administrative efforts, Owen aimed to give his follow-ers renewed inspiration. That summer marked the fiftieth anniversary of the Declaration of Independence, and on July 4 Owen delivered an oration that he believed would be at least as important to posterity. He called it the Declaration of Mental Independence, and in it he declared that:

> man, up to this hour, has been, in all parts of the earth, a slave to a TRINITY of the most monstrous evils that could be combined to inflict mental and physical evil upon his whole race. . . . PRIVATE, OR INDIVIDUAL PROPERTY—ABSURD AND IRRATIONAL SYSTEMS OF RELIGION AND MARRIAGE, FOUNDED ON INDIVIDUAL PROPERTY COMBINED WITH SOME ONE OF THESE IRRATIONAL SYSTEMS OF RELIGION.[69]

Thereafter, the masthead of the *Gazette* took to counting time from the moment of the address, as in "First Year of Mental Independence," and so forth. The effect of the speech, however, was less to energize Owen's followers than to bring down the obloquy of those scandalized by his attitudes toward religion and marriage.

His critics charged him with advocating free love, and he gave them basis for the charge. Owen argued that the institution of marriage was "unnatural" and "rendered prostitution unavoidable."[70] Because "men and women have not been formed with power to create their own feelings . . . it is blasphemy . . . against the laws of their nature, for man or woman to make any promises or engage-ments relative to their future feelings."[71] Owen's design for "villages of unity and cooperation" had been criticized for their proposal that boys and girls share common dormitories in their teen years. These criticisms were dismissed as scandal-mongering by Owen's defenders, but later Owen asserted that in the new moral world "celibacy, beyond the period plainly indicated for its termination by nature . . . will be known . . . to be a great crime." In his view "real chastity" consisted not in abstinence from sex but in abstinence from sex without affection.[72]

No hint of personal scandal can be found in any of Owen's biographies, but there is an arresting passage in a letter from Maclure to his protégé Madame Fretageot during the days of New Harmony. "I did not conjecture that Mr. O. was quite so amourous as the stories make him," said Maclure. "The wives of the greatest part of those that have left . . . lately have declared to their husbands that it was in consequence of the freedom that Mr. O. took with them that they could not think of remaining under such dreadful risk of their virtue."[73]

By fall, Owen attempted still another reorganization plan, this one designed to root out some of the indolent or otherwise undesirable members of the community. Around the same time, community number two, Macluria, split and a few weeks later dissolved entirely. In the winter, Owen attempted a fifth and last reorganization, breaking the community down into numerous smaller communities. This was accompanied by the expulsion of twenty more undesirable families, an event memorialized by Paul Brown as "Doomsday." A few days later, wrote Brown wryly, came "Dogs' Doomsday." It consisted of a "general dog killing; when all citizens of the canine brood were to be shot. Many were those that fell on that day."[74]

In connection with the final reorganization, Owen agreed to sell parcels of land to small groups wishing to establish their own communities. One of the residents, William Taylor, quickly agreed to this plan. He and Owen signed a contract conveying a certain plot "with all thereon." The night before the effective date, the unscrupulous Taylor moved quantities of the community's valuable assets onto this land, thereby gaining legal title to them. Thus capitalized, Taylor added insult to injury by setting up a distillery on his new property.

The final blow to New Harmony was an angry falling out between Owen and Maclure. One of its chief causes was Owen's sudden plan to institute a program of mass education at New Harmony for adults and children alike, consisting of thrice-weekly lectures. Maclure took this as a direct challenge to his authority over educational matters. In addition, Owen proposed to take back a choice piece of land from Maclure's educational society. The various other subgroups at New Harmony were all Owen's beneficiaries, so their property claims may have been somewhat notional. Maclure, on the other hand, was a full partner in the investment, so his rights were concrete. In the end, the two men sued each other and the courts resolved the dispute, largely in Maclure's favor.

In the winter of 1826-27, with the handwriting on the wall, "a funeral of the social system was projected by some of the New Harmonites," recounts the turn-of-the-century historian George Lockwood. "A coffin was procured and properly labeled, and arrangements were made for an imposing procession; but the night before the day set for the funeral the building in which the coffin was concealed was broken into and all the paraphernalia destroyed, so that the project was abandoned, and the system was allowed to die in its own way."[75]

In May 1827, before departing once again for England, Owen delivered a farewell address to New Harmony, claiming triumph for the project. "The social system is now firmly established. . . . I could not but feel an almost inexpressible delight . . . from reflecting upon the obstacles which have been overcome," he said.[76] But with Owen gone, the bickering among his followers intensified, a few drifted away and others turned to private pursuits. By the time the leader returned ten months later, what he found could no longer be sugarcoated. Instead, Owen pointed the finger of blame both at Maclure, for failing to make the schools a force binding the community together, and at the members themselves. "This proves that families trained in the individual system have not acquired those moral characteristics of forbearance and charity necessary for confidence and harmony," he said.[77] Unsurprisingly, this did not go down well with the assembled listeners, and the old schoolmaster Neef spoke for many when he replied that "People that had sense enough to perceive that a community of co-operation [and] common property would be the best . . . were . . . the very best materials to form such a community."[78]

Despite Neef's telling rejoinder, Owen's attribution of New Harmony's failure to the character of its residents was often repeated, and it has echoed down throughout the historiography of the experiment. As Taylor exemplified, some unsavory types were indeed drawn to New Harmony, but so were a great many unusually accomplished individuals, those for whom the "boatload of knowledge" got its moniker. Moreover, placing the blame on the quality of people attracted to New Harmony ran counter to Owen's own repeated claims that he had formed his ideas in the process of successfully reforming the "idle, intemperate, dishonest" workforce he had inherited at New Lanark. The point was made best by Abram Combe, whom Owen described as one of "the most faithful and honest of my disciples."[79] In 1826, while Owen's attentions were focused on New Harmony, Combe led a group of Owenites in Scotland in launching a model village at an estate called Orbiston, near Glasgow. Orbiston, too, was short-lived, but Combe rejected the argument that the participants were at fault. "We set out to overcome Ignorance, Poverty and Vice," he said. "It would be a poor excuse for failure to [argue] that the subjects of our experiment were ignorant, poor and vicious."[80]

In short, Owen's argument was circular. Socialism, he said, would produce a "new man." Until then, all people were necessarily products of the old system. If it required people reared under socialism to create socialism, then how could you get there from here?

Robert Dale Owen made a more honest attempt to diagnose New Harmony's collapse. The "most potent factor," he concluded, was that "All cooperative schemes which provide equal remuneration to the skilled and industrious and the ignorant and idle, must work their own downfall, for by this unjust plan of remuneration they must of necessity eliminate the valuable members—who find their services reaped by the indigent—and retain only the improvident, unskilled, and vicious members."[81]

While the son's explanation was quite different from the father's, they both pointed to the same underlying question: was socialism suited to men as they were? Tailoring institutions to human nature was the guiding motif of America's founders. In the *Federalist Papers,* Madison observed famously that government was necessary because men were not angels and that controls on government were necessary because those who governed were not angels. Had Madison commented on socialism, he might have come up with an analogous paradox: if men were angels then an economy might succeed without selfish incentives, but if men were angels it would not matter whether the economy succeeded since they would have no material needs.

Men, alas, are not angels, and it was socialism's unique departure to attempt their uplift through an economic rather than a spiritual system. This point was in fact made at the outset of Owen's experiment by George Rapp in a letter to his son: "It goes with these people as with the Jews at the time of Jesus, they are seeking and want a sensuous kingdom of God, and not a spiritual one."[82]

The distinction was evident in the fates of the numerous cooperative villages established in the New World. According to several different scholarly efforts to count them, by the dawn of the twentieth century there had been somewhere between 250 and 300.[83] The majority had a religious basis, and many of these endured for long periods. Indeed, the Rappite community survived its founder, lasting one hundred years, and this was despite the fact that from around the time he sold Harmonie to Owen, Rapp required his followers to be celibate. Without procreating, they kept their society alive by recruiting new members.

In contrast, the secular communities, whose primary purpose was to create socialism, all went the way of New Harmony. There were somewhere from ten to twenty inspired by Owen and about another thirty that followed the ideas of Fourier. None of them rivaled New Harmony in scale or promise, and none improved significantly upon its outcome. Their median life span was two years.

· · ·

The failure of New Harmony cost Robert Owen much of his fortune, but it did not shake his faith in his ideas. He paid it little more attention than he paid to the arguments of his adversaries. In his autobiography he devoted a total of three sentences to the entire New Harmony venture, commenting that he "found the population of the States far too undeveloped at that period for the practice of a full true and social life."[84]

So little was Owen fazed by the denouement of the New Harmony experiment that within months of returning to Britain, he took it in mind to persuade the government of Mexico to grant him Texas as a site to renew his experiment on a grander scale. On his way to Mexico, Owen stopped in Jamaica, which afforded his first opportunity to observe slavery first hand. Perhaps still smarting from the effort to govern an unruly multitude at New Harmony, he came away from the island with a surprisingly positive impression. He wrote:

> I request with all the earnestness such a subject demands, that our good religious people in England will not attempt to disturb these slaves in the happiness and independence which they enjoy in their present condition. For while they are under humane masters—and almost all slave proprietors are now humane, for they know it to be to their interest to be so—the West Indian "slave" as he is called, is greatly more comfortable and happy than the British or Irish operative manufacturer or day-labourer.[85]

When Owen reached Mexico, the government turned down his request to rule Texas on the grounds that the territory elected its own governor. But it did discuss the possibility of granting him a swath of land along the border with the United States, some 150 miles in width and stretching from the Gulf of Mexico to the Pacific. Owen insisted, however, that he could govern the territory only if Mexico would amend its laws so as to allow religious tolerance rather than recognize Roman Catholicism as the established religion. And this proved an insuperable stumbling block.

With his adventures in the New World behind him and his share of New Lanark sold, Owen returned to England, but not to his wife and remaining family in Scotland. Instead, he settled in London. G. D. H. Cole observes that:

> Owen had apparently no need of his wife's companionship. He writes to her reporting his public doings. . . . Her letters . . . dwelling especially on the poor health of their daughter Anne, can only be described as plaintive. Again and again she speaks of her need for him, and urges him to come to her. "Oh, my dear husband, how much I feel the want of you . . . in a time of so much anxiety."[86]

But he did not come, and Anne died at twenty-two years old. Months later, her mother, perhaps brokenhearted, followed her into the grave. Cole's assessment is that "Owen, from the time when he became a public man, ceased to have any 'private life.'. . . He became a humanitarian, and lost his humanity."[87]

For the next thirty years he continued his activism, serving as the pioneer or inspiration of numerous progressive causes, even some toward which he was ambivalent. For example, the founders of the consumer cooperatives, which began in the 1830s, declared that they had been inspired by Owen, even though he was uninvolved in their efforts and not supportive. Spearheaded by the famous Rochdale movement, the cooperatives grew over generations into a mighty economic force.

No less awkward was Owen's role as leader of the early labor movement. With his ceaseless entreaties to Kent, Nicholas, Castlereagh, Metternich, Santa Anna and the like, Owen was the consummate believer in change from the top. Nonetheless, he was chosen president of the first countrywide labor organization, the Grand National Consolidated Trades Union. Formed in 1834, it brought together a large array of local groups that had emerged over the previous years. Some comprised employees striving for higher wages, others were artisans endeavoring to form producer cooperatives, and still others were organized in pursuit of political reform, or as Mason-like secret fraternal orders. The Grand National pulled off one mass demonstration in behalf of six Dorset workers who had been harshly sentenced for their labor activities, but within a year it disintegrated.

Dearer to Owen's heart than either the consumer cooperatives or the Grand National was the effort to create "labor exchanges." This was Owen's own brainchild. Foreshadowing Marx's more subtle theory, Owen adapted from the early-nineteenth-century economist David Ricardo the idea that the source of value of any item was the labor that went into it. From this, Owen concluded that middlemen were an unnecessary drain on wealth and that money was superfluous. Hence, he went about organizing a center where artisans could exchange goods free from these impediments but with greater flexibility than barter would allow. Members of the exchange could bring their wares and receive credits for the number of man-hours required to produce them. They could spend these credits to purchase other goods from the exchange, priced in man-hours.

Owen opened his exchange in London, and initially it attracted enough participants and apparent success to inspire emulators in other cities.

Gradually, however, Owen and his confreres discovered that it was not so easy to transcend the old methods of commerce. The credits that they issued in exchange for goods took the form of "labor notes," which differed little from currency, except they were not backed by metal. Moreover, the administrators quickly realized that they could not value the goods they accepted according to the number of hours the producer claimed to have invested, since the time varied. Instead, they took to inferring the worth in labor-hours from prices on the general retail market. Finally, they discovered that even though the exchange distinguished itself from traditional merchants by eschewing profits, it could not avoid taking a markup in order to meet overhead and maintain inventory. When the Owen-sympathizer who had initially donated the building that housed the exchange began to charge rent, the managers moved the enterprise to less convenient facilities, and the ensuing decline in business soon led to the project's collapse.

In the middle 1830s, after the failure of the labor exchanges and the Grand National Consolidated Trades Union, Owen and his followers—the "socialists," as they by now were coming generally to be known—turned their efforts more toward spiritual and proselytizing activities. In 1835 they founded the Association of All Classes of All Nations. Owen was given the title of Preliminary Father. This was later changed to Rational Social Father, and the group itself became the Universal Community Society of Rational Religionists. Later it changed its name again, to the Rational Society, and then again to the Home Colonization Society.

The group's dual goals were social change along collectivist lines, and moral reform based on Owen's pet theory that the individual was in no sense responsible for his own character. Its chapters erected buildings in which they held Sunday services. They did not call these buildings "churches," but rather "halls of science." The services included readings from Owen's masterwork, the *Book of the New Moral World*; sermons, generally given by Owen himself when he was present; and the singing of hymns. An example of the latter, drawn from the society's own hymnal, *Social Hymns,*[88] gives a flavor of its gospel:

> Outcasts on your native soil,
> Doom'd to poverty and toil,
> Strangers in your native land;
> Come, and join the social band.

Leave, oh leave, your wretched state,
Scene of discord, scene of hate,
Take the brother's hand we give,
Come and in communion live.

Leave your selfish cares behind,
Turn your loves from self to kind.
Let the claims of *mine* and *thine*
In all-blessing *ours* combine.

On each other cast our care,
All each others' comforts share;
Hand in hand and heart in heart,
Bliss enjoy and bliss impart.[89]

In addition to erecting its church-like "halls of science," the society commanded enough resources to appoint six paid missionaries, known as the "socialist bishops."

After a few years, many of the members grew eager for a demonstration of the efficacy of their social theories. In 1839 a large estate called Queenwood was leased and a socialist community was launched. Owen, perhaps inwardly chastened by the collapse of New Harmony a decade before, was uneasy with the venture and declined to be its governor. Nonetheless, the society threw its resources into the experiment, eventually laying off the "socialist bishops." In addition, members made cash subscriptions, and innumerable in-kind contributions were recorded in the society's weekly newspaper, the *New Moral World*: "seventeen pairs of razors, a handbook of mathematics, a complete set of harness, a French grammar, *Horace, a Poem,* pocket-knives, a patent corkscrew, and implements innumerable for the stables, the farm, the shambles, the kitchen, and the dining-room."[90]

The few score initial settlers brimmed with enthusiasm. Like the French revolutionists and the New Harmonists, they inaugurated a new calendar, marking off time from the date they took possession of the estate, which was designated "Day 1 of the New Moral World." Before long, however, enthusiasm gave way to discontent over material privations, lack of privacy, and a system of management in which the residents had little voice. In 1841, hoping to rescue the experiment, Owen announced his readiness to assume governorship, bringing with him an infusion of additional capital raised from a few wealthy backers. He sank it all into the construction of a magnificent three-story building, comprising sleeping, dining and meeting quarters. The structure was christened "Harmony Hall," and Owen had the initials C.M. carved on the front, standing for "Commencement of the Millennium."

Owen's reputation as a businessman of the first order endured, but decades of visionary activism separated him from his days as a prosperous cotton magnate. He spent the colony, and with it the Rational Society, into a deepening hole. Only gradually did it register with some of the disciples that, as one remarked, "Mr. Owen was no financier, and had no idea of money."[91] In the face of discontent with his leadership, Owen resigned as governor of Queenwood in 1842, and then resumed the position a year later, but none of these comings and goings arrested the project's steady decline. In 1844, real dissension against Owen's leadership burst forth, and Owen insisted that he could hold no position with Queenwood or the society unless given absolute authority, which by this time his disciples were no longer willing to grant.

The story of Queenwood and Owen's society-of-ever-changing-names for moral and political regeneration ended in tragic-comic wrangles. The last governor of Queenwood, John Buxton, remained on the property with his family after the other residents departed, until the trustees had him evicted. The Buxtons then camped in a tent on the outskirts, and there convened still one more congress of the society. In the end, after Owen's death, the surviving officers of the society fell to suing one another over what was left of the assets and liabilities.

Even as Owen was getting up in years, he remained energetic. The thrilling revolutionary upheavals of 1848 ignited in him a burst of activity, and he left at once for France, where he saw to the distribution of translations of his various works, supplementing them with two new pamphlets. "Paris was deluged with Owenite literature," says biographer Frank Podmore, and Owen was invited to address the National Assembly.[92]

Around the time he turned eighty, the still vigorous founder of the Rational Society embraced "spiritualism," that is, the practice of communicating with the dead through the assistance of mediums. This was all the rage in the middle of the nineteenth century, starting in America and carried back from there to England. Owen was initiated into the practice by an American medium named Mrs. Hayden, but when she was exposed as a fraud, he simply found a new medium. Owen knew full well that others doubted the legitimacy of the

process, but he insisted that he had carefully tested it and that the spirits with
whom he communicated told him things that only they could know. "To com-
municate in a material manner with our past and now . . . invisible relatives and
friends, is an idea as monstrous to receive by the so-called enlightened of this
day, as the monstrous statement of Galileo in his day . . . that the earth was not
flat," he said.[93]

In his séances, Owen communed with many of the famous people he had
known, including Benjamin Franklin, Thomas Jefferson, whom he dubbed "my
friend and warm disciple" (although in life Jefferson had written sharp criticisms
of Owen's ideas), and his old supporter the duke of Kent. Owen had frequent
sessions with the late duke, and he extolled his noble courtesy: "never in one
instance . . . has this Spirit not been punctual to the minute he had named."[94]

Despite the turn to spiritualism, Owen never wavered in his opposition to
the "superstition" of religion. In 1858, at age eighty-seven, his powers clearly
failing, Owen traveled back to his birthplace, Newtown, to die. "I will lay my
bones whence I derived them," he told his manservant.[95] He had been away from
Wales for more than seventy years, and he let out a cheer as his coach crossed
back into it. He remained himself until the end, writing ahead to one of the
town elders with the offer to deliver an important message if a public meeting
of the leading citizens would be organized. On his deathbed he staunchly refused
the offer of a pastoral visit from the town's rector, and when, a few hours before
his death, the rector visited nonetheless, Owen engaged him in a discussion of
a plan he was hatching for the regeneration of Newtown.

Owen passed from the world under the loving attention of his son, Robert
Dale Owen, who had traveled from Naples, where he was serving as the
American chargé d'affaires. "My dear father passed away this morning . . . as
gently and as quietly as if he had been falling asleep," he wrote.[96] Cole, the
celebrated socialist historian, pronounced this epitaph:

> No man has been forerunner and patron-saint of so many movements as he.
> New Lanark at once suggests the pioneer of popular education and factory
> reform; the events of 1830-1834 recall the leading figure in the first broad
> concerted movement of the working class. Socialism and Cooperation alike
> found in him their first systematic exponent in Great Britain. Secularism and
> Rationalism, too, took shape under his guidance.[97]

•   •   •

Robert Owen had created a movement, or at least a large milieu, that called itself "socialist." There is no record whether it was he, himself, or one of his followers who first used the term, but by the time of his death they had brought it into wide currency. Through the halls of science with their hymns and Sunday meetings, the movement had been shaped into the simulacrum of a religion. The failures of New Harmony and the other Owenite colonies had not proved fatally discouraging; instead, they had pointed socialists back in the direction of political action. The hope that a model socialism could be constructed in isolation from the surrounding community had been dashed. Socialism would have to be achieved by transforming society as a whole.

Across the Atlantic, Owen left a legacy of a different kind, which would help to undermine all that he had worked for. His four sons and one of his daughters remained in America and contributed more than their share to shaping and strengthening the country that would prove to be the insuperable obstacle to socialism. They were among the several hundred survivors of Owen's experiment who took possession of individual holdings at New Harmony. Relieved of his blueprints, the community thrived. Robert Dale Owen wrote five years later that "the progress back to the state of order and prosperity in which Rapp's people left it, is, I think, very apparent."[98] And in another article around the same time, he explained:

> If I expect (as I do expect) to see New Harmony flourish and maintain its rank among the Western Colonies that surround it, it is because we are pursuing there (now that the experiment of United Labor, is, for the present, no longer carried on) a policy the very reverse of this; giving to each respectable citizen every facility and encouragement to become (what every adult ought to be) a landed proprietor.[99]

On this new basis, the Owen progeny and what was left of the "boatload of knowledge"—among them Fretageot, Say, Lesueur and Neef—turned the town into a great intellectual center. It was famed throughout the remainder of the century for its contributions to the natural sciences, education and even the dramatic arts, thanks to a thespian society that William had founded. What did not endure at New Harmony was any remnant of socialism, as the researcher A. J. MacDonald discovered. An admirer of Owen's who set out in the 1850s to interview veterans of New Harmony, he reported: "I was cautioned not to speak of Socialism, as the subject was unpopular. The advice was good; Socialism was unpopular, and with good reason. The people had been wearied and disappointed by it; had been filled full with theories, until they were nauseated."[100]

The Owen children made notable contributions to their adopted country. David Dale Owen became the state geologist of Indiana and Arkansas and then head of the U.S. Geological Survey. He and Robert Dale were instrumental in the creation of the Smithsonian Institution. Richard Owen succeeded David as Indiana's geologist, later taking up an academic career that culminated in his selection as the first president of Purdue University. He wrote of the link he perceived between the country's natural endowment and its social message: "Here amid nature's wild, human hope expanded, a new regime was founded, and America took up her appointed mission of exemplifying to the world the inalienable rights of man."[101] In contrast to his father, Richard became deeply religious and authored some works on the compatibility of natural science with scriptural revelation. William Owen, the son so overburdened with New Harmony's early management, became a bank director.

The greatest distinction was achieved by Robert Dale Owen, who served in the Indiana legislature, then for two terms in the U.S. House of Representatives, and later as secretary of the Freedman's Bureau. In between, he represented the United States as a diplomat, which occasioned his presence in Europe at the time of his father's death. He wrote of the difference between the Old World and the New:

> In Europe, where men are trained to bear any and every thing, even steady, respectable heads of families are content to be life-renters or mere tenants at will.... But here, fortunately, the state of things is very different.... [A]ny man who has the smallest share of honest ambition, and who can wield an axe or plough a corn-row, chooses to have his own homesteading [from which no] haughty landlord [can] dispossess him. So ought it to be every where; so is it, in these United States.[102]

Thus, the son who had written of his rapturous expectations as he first crossed the Atlantic to join his father's colony found the "Land of Promise" not in New Harmony, but in America itself.

3

SCIENTIFIC SOCIALISM:
ENGELS INTERPRETS
THE ORACLE

THE HALL OF SCIENCE IN MANCHESTER was an imposing structure, all stone and block, dwarfing the surrounding buildings. It was only two stories, but its first story alone reached almost as high as the roofs of the neighboring three-story buildings. The architecture was a testament to man's mastery of geometry, not to his imagination. It had no steeples or spires, but was built all in right angles, rectangular walls and doors and windows, topped with a flat roof. High along the full length of the longer exterior wall was the inscription in large block letters: "Sacred to the Investigation of Truth." It held three thousand people, and it was filled each Sunday by adherents of Robert Owen's New Moral World.

Throughout 1843, the congregation included a twenty-two-year-old German journalist named Friedrich Engels. In an account he wrote for a newspaper back home, Engels described the gatherings:

[T]hese meetings partly resemble church gatherings; in the gallery a choir accompanied by an orchestra sings social hymns; these consist of semi-religious or wholly religious melodies with communist words, during which the audience stands. Then, quite nonchalantly, without removing his hat, a lecturer comes on to the platform, on which there is a table and chairs; after raising his hat by way of greeting those present, he takes off his overcoat and then sits down and delivers his address, which usually gives much occasion for laughter, for in these speeches the English intellect expresses itself in superabundant humour. In one corner of the hall is a stall where books and pamphlets are sold and in another a booth with oranges and refreshments. . . . From time to time tea-parties are arranged on Sunday evenings at which people of both sexes, of all ages and classes, sit together and partake of the usual supper of tea and sandwiches; on working days dances and concerts are often held in the hall.[1]

The butt of much of the joviality that Engels so admired was conventional religion. Engels reported that "frequently . . . Christianity is directly attacked and Christians are called 'our enemies.'" He particularly liked the lectures of the atheist pamphleteer John Watts, who taught Sunday school at the hall. Watts and his colleagues

always start out from . . . verifiable or obvious facts. . . . If anyone tries to carry the argument into a different sphere they laugh in his face. If, for example, I say: For man the existence of God does not depend on facts for its proof, they retort: "What a ridiculous proposition you put forward: if God does not manifest Himself through facts, why should we want to trouble ourselves about Him? . . . [W]e keep to the basis of 'real facts,' where there can be no question of such fantastic things as God. . . ." So the rest of their communist propositions are supported by proof based on facts.[2]

All of this held great appeal for the young German, who was in the throes of full-bore rebellion against the devout faith of his parents and had recently been converted to communism. Indeed, he had landed in Manchester as a result of his newfound radicalism and of his father's efforts to tame it.

Engels had grown up in Barmen (now Wuppertal, near Düsseldorf), a center of Pietism, a German evangelical movement. The Engels family owned a textile business that had been passed down through three generations to Engels' father, and he hoped that his children, especially the talented eldest son, Friedrich, would take it on in turn. But although Friedrich was good-natured as well as gifted, he was also something of a free spirit, and this was a source of worry to his parents. When he was fourteen, his father wrote to his mother, who was away visiting her family:

As you know, his manners have improved; but in spite of severe punishment in the past, he does not seem to be learning implicit obedience even from the fear of chastisement. Today I was once more vexed by finding in his desk a dirty book from a lending library, a romance of the thirteenth century. May God guard the boy's heart, for I am often troubled over this son of ours, who is otherwise so full of promise.[3]

Indulging his adolescent prurient curiosity in medieval romance novels was only the beginning of Friedrich's rebellion, and the tug-of-war between father and son continued throughout the remaining decades of the older man's life. Friedrich left *gymnasium* at seventeen, a year short of completing his diploma, but there is no record of paternal alarm over this. Instead, the father arranged a kind of unpaid internship for him in the offices of a business friend in the town of Bremen, another stronghold of Pietism. He also procured suitable lodging, in the home of a clergyman. But the demands of the job were light, leaving Friedrich ample time to gratify his appetites, both intellectual and sensuous, much as he might have done at university. He read avidly, learned languages, for which he had a remarkable facility, sketched cartoons, composed music, swam, rode and fenced. He also boasted, in letters home to his younger siblings, about the beer he drank and the cigars he smoked while on the job.

Writing for a Hamburg newspaper under the pseudonym Friedrich Oswald, young Engels produced a series of "Letters from Wuppertal" that described the life of his native region with merciless sarcasm. Focusing sharply on the exploitation of industrial workers and the hypocrisies of Pietism, Engels wrote:

But the wealthy manufacturers have a flexible conscience, and causing the death of one child more or one less does not doom a Pietist's soul to hell, especially if he goes to church twice every Sunday. For it is a fact that the Pietists among the factory owners treat their workers worst of all; they use every possible means to reduce the workers' wages on the pretext of depriving them of the opportunity to get drunk, yet at the election of preachers they are always the first to bribe their people.[4]

There was much more in this vein, which created an uproar among the Wuppertalians and even attracted considerable notice beyond the region. Had Oswald's identity been revealed, it is unlikely his father would have welcomed him home; but only a few knew the secret, and Engels returned to Barmen in 1841. A few months later, a bit shy of his twenty-first birthday, he left for a year's military service in the Guards Foot Artillery in Berlin. The duty was light and did not require residence in the barracks. Engels rented a room and took full advantage of the metropolis to explore his cultural and political interests. Berlin, he wrote, "has excellent wine, cheap living, a very good theatre, and many newspapers in the cafes."[5]

The young soldier pursued his journalism, attended classes at the University of Berlin, and gravitated toward a milieu of anti-establishment intellectuals of his generation who were called the "Young Hegelians." The group's first interest was philosophy, especially the critique of religion. As one of their number, Karl Marx, put it: "Criticism of religion is the prelude of all criticism."[6]

Two books in particular contributed to the rise of this movement. One, *The Life of Jesus* by David Friedrich Strauss, published in 1835, subjected the New Testament to historical scrutiny and concluded that the Gospels constituted essentially a body of mythology. Engels counted himself "a wholehearted disciple of Strauss," whom he credited with putting him on "the road that leads straight to Hegelianism."[7] The second influential book, published in 1841, was *The Essence of Christianity* by Ludwig Feuerbach. It carried the assault on revealed religion further, arguing that God was an invention onto which man projected his own hopes and imaginings. "Enthusiasm was universal and we all immediately became disciples of Feuerbach," recalled Engels.[8]

To counteract this subversive tendency among the students, a conservative philosopher, Friedrich von Schelling, was transferred, on order of King Friedrich Wilhelm himself, to the University of Berlin, where Engels was auditing courses. After hearing Schelling, the young artillery-man proceeded to produce an anonymous pamphlet, *Schelling and Revelation: Critique of the Latest Attempt of Reaction against the Free Philosophy*. It attracted an international audience, perhaps more for its audacious atheism than for its logical rigor.[9]

That year, 1842, Engels and Marx each began contributing to a liberal paper, *Rheinische Zeitung,* which had been inspired by Moses Hess, one of the older of the Young Hegelians. Having broken with his strict Jewish upbringing, Hess became the first in this circle to embrace the idea of communism, which he had picked up from reading French and British radicals. On the way home from his completed military duty, Engels stopped in Cologne for what proved a momentous meeting with Hess. "We talked of questions of the day," said Hess. "Engels, who was revolutionary to the core when he met me, left a passionate Communist."[10]

Engels did not remain long back in Barmen. Hess had forecast that England, roiled by the agitation of the Chartists, would be the first country to experience the coming revolution, and Engels wanted to observe the scene himself. He surely could not have explained this to his parents, but his father believed that a visit to England would separate Friedrich from his unsavory radical associates and allow him to advance his knowledge of the textile business. Hence, it was agreed that the young man would go to Manchester where the family firm, Engels & Ermen, maintained a second production center.

On his way, Engels again stopped in Cologne, this time to meet Marx, who by then had become editor of the *Rheinische Zeitung*. But Marx, who had begun to weary of the Young Hegelians, received Engels coolly, and the encounter gave no clue of the singular partnership that was to develop between the two.

Within days of his arrival in England, his bags only partly unpacked, Engels dispatched two articles to the paper, reporting that he had found England to be headed for revolution.[11] The English whom he had met denied this, he said, but they were mistaken. Although Engels did not find revolutionists among the English, he did find socialists to whom he was drawn, chiefly Robert Owen and his followers, and he began to attend their Sunday gatherings. Soon, in addition to his reports for the German press, Engels began to contribute to Owen's periodical, the *New Moral World*.

He also drank in the accounts he found in its pages of the success of communist settlements. These inspired him to compose a synoptic piece for a German publication, which was later translated for the *New Moral World* as well. Titled "Description of Recently Founded Communist Colonies Still in Existence," it began:

> When one talks to people about socialism or communism, one very frequently finds that they entirely agree with one regarding the substance of the matter and declare communism to be a very fine thing; "but", they then say, "it is impossible ever to put such things into practice in real life." One encounters this objection so frequently that it seems to the writer both useful and necessary to reply to it with a few facts which are still very little known in Germany and which completely and utterly dispose of this objection. For communism, social existence and activity based on community of goods, is not only possible but has actually already been realised in many communities in America and in one place in England, with the greatest success.[12]

Engels went on to describe the colonies of the Shakers, the Rappites and other such sects, the example of which "have caused many other people in America to undertake similar experiments" with the result that the "community of goods will soon be introduced over a significant part of their country." He then furnished a glowing account of the Owenites' Harmony Hall in Queenwood, England. Summing up, he said: "We see then that community of goods is by no means an impossibility but that on the contrary all these experiments have been entirely successful."[13] Curiously, although Engels described the successful development of the town of Harmonie by the Rappites and its sale to Robert Owen, he wrote not a word about what became of it after Owen's purchase.

In addition to contributing to the *Rheinische Zeitung,* Engels agreed to contribute to a new publishing venture undertaken by Marx in 1843, the *Deutsch-Französische Jahrbücher.* Its aim was to promote cooperation between German and French radicals, but no French contributions could be secured for the single edition that appeared in early 1844. Engels contributed two pieces, one of which, "Outlines of a Critique on Political Economy," seized Marx's imagination and pointed him on the road to communism.

In this polemic against market economics, Engels sketched the rudiments of the doctrine that the world would come to know as "Marxism." Private property is theft. Capital has dissolved old boundaries, subjecting the entire world to its domain. It has also destroyed human bonds, especially the family. Man himself has been turned into a commodity, compelled to renounce "every truly human purpose" and sell himself in a morbid act of "self-alienation." Every ostensible morality serves only as a cloak for naked interest. Bitterest of ironies, although man is now a slave to capital, capital itself is nothing but stored-up labor.

However, Engels continued, deliverance is on the way. Inevitably, due to the dynamics of competition, large capital swallows up or drives out small, leading to a concentration of wealth. "The middle classes must increasingly disappear until the world is divided into millionaires and paupers." The paupers, moreover, are increasingly impoverished: "only the very barest necessities, the mere means of subsistence, fall to the lot of labor." Hence the contradiction between an ever-expanding productive capacity, due to the modernization of industry, and the inability of the vast majority to purchase the goods. Ergo a cycle of overproduction and slump: "the people starve from sheer abundance." In the end, the inflammation of this contradiction will lead to social revolution. Thus the early collectivist ideas of Babeuf, preserved by Buonarroti, and those of

Owen, Saint Simon and the like, brought home to Engels by Hess, were recast into a historical narrative.

Years later, Marx was to recall that he found the "Outlines of a Critique" to be a work of "genius."[14] He studied it carefully. Terrell Carver, biographer of both men, reports that "Marx's manuscript notes on Engels's essay prefigured the course of his lifework."[15]

• • •

Until that time, Marx's writing had focused more on issues of abstract philosophy. Of the two articles he contributed to the *Jahrbücher*, one was a critique of Hegel. The other, entitled "On the Jewish Question," purported to be nothing more than an objective analysis of the quest by Jews in Germany for civic emancipation. But since this issue had had considerable impact on Marx's own upbringing, it is hard not to see the essay as a struggle to come to terms with his own heritage, much as Engels was wrestling with Christianity.

Karl Marx was the scion of two distinguished lines of rabbis. His mother's father had been rabbi of Nijmegen, Holland. On his father's side, his great-great-grandfather had been the well-known Joshua Heschel Lvov. And in turn, Joshua's great-great-grandfather had been Meier Ben Isaac Katzenellenbogen, a renowned rabbi of the sixteenth century.

Although European Jewish communities of the eighteenth century still lived in great isolation, Karl's paternal grandfather, Rabbi Mordechai Levy, had taken a first tiny step toward assimilation when he stopped using the given name Mordechai and began to call himself Marx Levy, Marx being the German equivalent of Mark. While one of his sons continued the rabbinical line, another son, Heschel, became a lawyer. At some point, Heschel stopped calling himself Levy, substituting his father's adopted first name of Marx, and then he changed Heschel to Heinrich. Thus, Heschel Levy became Heinrich Marx. When the wave of post-Napoleonic reaction swept Prussia and Jews were barred from the law, Heinrich, rather than sacrifice his career, had himself baptized a Lutheran. He had his children baptized around the time Karl entered primary school.

Since Heinrich had abandoned Judaism, Karl cannot be said to have rebelled against the faith of his father as Engels had done. In a sense he took his father's act of renunciation as a model for the solution of the "Jewish question." Marx's essay began with the premise that the Jews were in some sense victims, but he suggested that it was their own fault. "We discern in Judaism . . . a universal antisocial element of the present time," he wrote. Marx explained it with this catechism: "What is the worldly cult of the Jew? Huckstering. What is his world-ly god? Money? . . . Money is the jealous god of Israel, beside which no other god may exist." So what is the solution? Marx reached his answer in the essay's peroration: "As soon as society succeeds in abolishing the empirical essence of Judaism—huckstering and its conditions—the Jew becomes impossible, because his consciousness no longer has an object. . . .The social emancipation of the Jew is the emancipation of society from Judaism."

Not only Marxists but many non-Marxist scholars too have attempted to explain away these jarring words. In an otherwise fine biography, David McLellan exemplifies this incredulity: "Whether Marx himself possessed anti-semitic tendencies is a matter of much controversy: certainly a superficial reading of his pamphlet On the Jewish Question would indicate as much; and his letters contain innumerable derogatory epithets concerning Jews; but this does not justify a charge of sustained anti-semitism."[16]

To be sure, Marx was only twenty-five when he wrote "On the Jewish Question," but its vicious sentiments were reiterated not only in his private correspondence, but in many of his public writings as well. A year later, in his 1845 Theses on Feuerbach, he distinguished "theoretical" activity from "dirty-Judaic" practical activity. And a dozen years after that, in the New York Tribune, Marx wrote: "Christ drove the Jewish money-changers out of the temple, and that the money-changers of our age enlisted on the side of tyranny happen again to be Jews is perhaps no more than a historic coincidence."[†]

Still later, in his 1860 book, Herr Vogt, Marx mocked the "Jewish nose" of Joseph Moses Levy, the publisher of the Daily Telegraph: "Levy wants to be an Anglo-Saxon. Hence at least once a month he attacks the un-British policies of Disraeli. . . . But of what use is it for Levy to attack Mr. Disraeli . . . so long as Mother Nature has inscribed, with the wildest black letters, his family tree in the middle of his face." And in his final book, Das Kapital, he wrote: "The capi-talist knows that all commodities, however scurvy they may look, or however badly they smell, are in faith and in truth money, inwardly circumcised Jews." In addition, as McLellan suggests, the abuse of Jews was even more frequent and virulent in Marx's private letters.[‡]

---

† According to Lewis Feuer, one of the reasons that Charles A. Dana, Marx's editor, was fired from the Tribune by Horace Greeley, the paper's chief, was that Greeley disliked the anti-Semitic articles that Dana sometimes ran, three of which had been by Marx. Feuer, Marx and the Intellectuals (Garden City, New York: Anchor Books, 1969), p. 38.

‡ Marx was particularly derogatory about the German socialist leader Ferdinand Lassalle, whom he saw as a rival. In his correspondence with Engels, he usually alluded to Lassalle as "Itzig,"

But if hostility to Jews and Judaism was one of the earliest features of Marx's spirit and thought, and one that endured throughout his life, in other areas he was still forming his ideas at age twenty-five, and Engels' "Outlines" pointed him toward unexplored paths. Naturally this obliged him to view Engels in a newly respectful light, and the two began to correspond. That summer Engels decided to conclude his sojourn in England and return home to Barmen. On the way he stopped in Paris, where he and Marx had their second face-to-face. This meeting was as fertile as their first had been barren. "We found ourselves in complete agreement on questions of theory," said Engels, and they decided to join forces in propagating their ideas.[17]

As a first collaboration, Marx suggested a polemic against their erstwhile Young Hegelian colleagues, the Bauer brothers. Engels completed his short section at once, but Marx scribbled on for months and hundreds of pages. This verbosity took Engels somewhat by surprise, and he commented that it tended to undercut their argument that the works of the Bauers were unworthy of serious consideration.

Bruno Bauer had been something of a mentor to Marx, helping him with school and jobs, while Edgar Bauer had been one of Engels' best friends. None of this inhibited the two co-authors from dousing their subjects in vitriol. The book's very title, *The Holy Family,* was intended as ridicule of the Bauers, whose philosophy, Marx wrote, "still dares to reproduce all the old trash in a new form."

Marx and Engels' next joint endeavor was *The German Ideology.* It continued the tirade against Bruno Bauer and also took into its sights Feuerbach and the so-called "true socialists" Max Stirner and Karl Gruen. It was not published for nearly a hundred years, but the authors circulated their vituperation by other means. Marx wrote to the French radical leader Proudhon that "Gruen . . . is nothing but . . . a type of charlatan who . . . attempts to conceal his ignorance in pompous and arrogant phrases, but he is only a parvenu who has made himself ridiculous."[18] Proudhon apparently was appalled by this attack, which must have

intended as a derision of his Jewishness (like Jesse Jackson's "Hymie") and sometimes as "our nigger," because Lassalle was swarthy, or as the "Jewish nigger." In one letter, he waxed poetic in his animus: "Lazarus the leper . . . is . . . the prototype of the Jews and of Lazarus-Lassalle. But in our Lazarus, the leprosy lies in the brain. His illness was originally a badly cured case of syphilis." Saul K. Padover, ed. and trans., *The Letters of Karl Marx* (Englewood Cliffs: Prentice-Hall, 1979), p. 459. Engels held his own in this obloquy, responding that Lassalle was "a real Jew. . . . [I]t is disgusting to see how he is always trying to push his way into the world of the upper classes. He is a greasy Jew disguised under brilliantine and flashy jewels." W. O, Henderson, *The Life of Friedrich Engels* (Abingdon: Routledge, 1976), vol 1, p. 471.

seemed all the more vicious because he knew that Gruen had been a friend of Marx's. In his reply he defended Gruen, and he appealed to Marx: "Let us have decent and sincere polemics; let us give the world an example of learned and farsighted tolerance.... [S]imply because we are at the head of a movement, do not let us ourselves become the leaders of a new intolerance."[19] Marx's response was to break with Proudhon and to make him the next target—in a book titled *The Poverty of Philosophy* (a play on Proudhon's *Philosophy of Poverty*).

More than Marx, Engels had already made a name for himself, and his stature was soon to grow. At about the same time in 1845 that *The Holy Family* appeared, so did the main fruit of Engels' two-year sojourn in Manchester, *The Condition of the Working Class in England in 1844,* a book which deservedly drew much more attention. In the dedication "to the working classes of Great Britain," Engels explained that he had

> wanted more than a mere *abstract* knowledge of my subject, I wanted to see you in your own homes, to observe you in your every-day life, to chat with you on your condition and grievances, to witness your struggles against the social and political power of your oppressors. I have done so: I forsook the company and the dinner-parties, the port-wine and champaign [sic] of the middle-classes, and devoted my leisure-hours almost exclusively to the intercourse with plain Working-Men.

It may be doubted that Engels, who was a great oenophile, forsook wine altogether, but there is little doubt that he did actively rub elbows with the lower classes. During this time he took up with Mary Burns, his intimate companion over the next twenty years. She was an Irish working girl who lived with her family in Manchester, and it seems that she showed Engels the byways of working-class life.

Most of the book consisted of an unflinching portrayal of the squalor, dirt and disease in the city's teeming slums. This was interwoven with a continuation of the theoretical indictment of capitalism that he had launched in the "Outlines of a Critique." It was published at a propitious time in Germany. Demonstrations by weavers in Silesia in 1844 had drawn public attention to the new social ills caused by industrialization. *The Condition of the Working Class*, says W. O. Henderson, "was the most important socialist work to be published in Germany between the weavers' rising and the appearance of the Communist

Manifesto. It was widely reviewed, widely read, and widely quoted. The first edition of 1845 was reprinted three years later."[20]

Not only was the young Engels more accomplished than Marx, but he originated as many or more of the key ideas that came to be called "Marxism." The British scholar Gareth Stedman Jones observed that "theoretical ability, even when possessed in as exceptional degree as Marx, is a necessary but not sufficient condition of a theoretical revolution." What is also required are "the raw components of a new theoretical structure. It was Engels in his writings of 1844 and 1845 who provided these." Why then do we have Marxism, rather than Engelsism or Marx-Engelsism? Why was an implicit hierarchy established early in their relationship in which Marx was dominant?

Part of the answer is that both men believed Marx to be a genius. Yet genius alone cannot explain Marx's dominance. Nor can the fact that Marx was two years older; nor that Engels was a high school dropout, while Marx, as he let no one forget, was a "doctor." (He had received a Ph.D. by submitting a dissertation to the University of Jena without ever having attended it.) The balance in the relationship was largely a consequence of the differing temperaments of the two men: whereas Marx was hard, forbidding, self-important, Engels was soft, gregarious and self-effacing.

But Marx's more aggressive personality is not the whole explanation of his dominance, either. The principal reason why we know their doctrine as "Marxism" is that Engels promoted the term! It was first coined in derision by socialist rivals of Marx and Engels. While Marx responded by saying, "All I know is that I am not a Marxist," Engels made authentication of the term his mission.

Although audacious and opinionated, Engels exhibited normal human modesty and self-doubt. When he heard his own ideas reflected back with the fierce authoritativeness with which Marx invariably expressed himself, they sounded so much more compelling. As Jones writes, "For Engels . . . the relationship fulfilled a deep-felt need for intellectual certainty. . . . Engels did not possess the certainty of self to be a great original theorist; he therefore sought this quality in others."[21]

No one could have been better suited to play this demigod role than Marx, who was preternaturally self-possessed and aloof. Indeed, he seemed strangely devoid of any shred of self-doubt, as well as other softer sentiments. This vacuum was evident in his relations with his parental family even before he reached adulthood.

His father, with whom Karl had a loving relationship, had an eerily penetrating insight into the character of his most gifted child. He articulated it in a letter of great pathos sent to the eighteen-year-old during his first year at college:

> From time to time, my heart revels in the thoughts of you and your future. And yet, from time to time, I cannot escape the sad, suspicious, fearful thoughts that strike like lightning: does your heart match your head and your talents? Does it have room for the earthly but gentler feelings that are such an essential consolation to the sensitive human being in this vale of sorrows? . . .[22]

When Karl was at university, his father and then his remaining brother died, leaving his mother with four daughters, three of them grown but all unmarried. Karl, then twenty-four, had received his doctorate a year before and launched his career in radical journalism. He never thought to offer the five women any help, but rather, he expected his mother to continue to support him. She was hurt and eventually cut him off almost entirely, an offense for which he never forgave her. She did allow him to claim some of his inheritance in advance, and he waited impatiently for the rest. When Engels wrote reporting the death of his mistress, Mary Burns, Marx consoled him with the wish that it had been "my own mother, who is now full of physical infirmities and has already lived her life, instead of Mary."[23]

Other than cutting Karl off financially, had his mother done anything to invite the stony heart he turned toward her? The paradigms of modern psychology demand that we search for such evidence. In the notes she wrote him at college we find, however, only a very loving mother. "Scrub my beloved Carl weekly with sponge and soap," she exhorts, adding, with admiration for him and embarrassment about her own incomplete literacy, "your amiable Muse will not feel offended by the Prose of your Mother, tell Her that through the inferior the superior and the better are attained." And she closes with: "if you have a wish for Christmas that I can satisfy I am prepared for it with pleasure so keep well my beloved Carl be worthy and good and always keep God and your Parents before your eyes, adieu, your loving Mother."[24] No doubt, like every mother who ever lived, she hurt or failed her son on occasion, but the picture that emerges from her writings and his is one of love repaid in hatred.

Early in 1845, only months after Engels and Marx had begun their partnership, the French government, yielding to the behest of Prussia, shut down the radical exile newspaper, *Vorwärts,* and expelled its main contributors. Marx found refuge in Brussels, with Engels soon following, and the two lived as neighbors for the next three years. In addition to their literary efforts, they began their collaboration as activists. They traveled together to England, where Engels showed Marx around Manchester. In London, Engels introduced him to various British socialists as well as some exiled German communists who bore the distinction of actually being from a lower class.

Until he had come to England, all of the other communists Engels had known were fellow intellectuals. As he had written in the *New Moral World*, "It will appear very singular to Englishmen that a party which aims at the destruction of private property is chiefly made up by those who have property: and yet this is the case in Germany. We can recruit our ranks from those classes only which have enjoyed a pretty good education."[25] But the band of communist exiles he had befriended in London, and to whom he introduced Marx, were different. Chief among them were a shoemaker named Bauer (no relation to the philosopher brothers against whom *The Holy Family* was aimed), a compositor named Schapper and a watchmaker named Moll. "They were the first proletarian revolutionists I had ever met," recalled Engels.[26] (They might have been better described as artisans, but they did work with their hands.) "I can never forget the profound impression these three men made upon me, a youngster at the time, just entering upon manhood." They were, he said, "three real men," and their example imbued the young journalist with "the will to become a man."

Bauer, Schapper and Moll were members of something called the "League of the Just," a secretive revolutionary band that had been founded in the late 1830s by Wilhelm Weitling, an apprentice tailor and bastard son of a working-class woman. Marx and Engels initially had no interest in joining the league, which they adjudged deficient in theory and reckless in revolutionary zeal. Instead, after returning home they founded a Brussels Correspondence Committee, which aimed to foster a network of communists in several countries. Weitling visited them, and a meeting of the Correspondence Committee was convened in Marx's home at which Marx tore into Weitling's shaky doctrine. Stunned by the ferocity of the assault and unable to hold his own against Marx in theoretics, Weitling replied by pointing out that he enjoyed a substantial following, which Marx did not. Paul Annenkov, a Russian friend of Marx's who was present, recalled the scene that ensued:

> On hearing these last words Marx finally lost control of himself and thumped so hard with his fist on the table that the lamp on it rung and shook. He

jumped up saying: "Ignorance never yet helped anybody!" We followed his
example and left the table. The sitting ended, and as Marx paced up and down
the room, extraordinarily irritated and angry, I hurriedly took leave of him
and his interlocutors and went home, amazed at all I had seen and heard.[27]

The gentle Moses Hess, to whom Weitling turned for solace, wrote to
Marx in protest, saying that the episode "makes me want to vomit."[28] But Marx
and Engels were unrepentant, and Weitling, under the fury of their continuing
scourge, took flight for America. This paved the way for a rapprochement of
Marx and Engels with the League of the Just. Their entry was sealed at a conference in the summer of 1847, attended by Engels, at which the group was
renamed the "Communist League."

The new organization also began debating various drafts of a platform or
"confession of faith," as it was called, which was to be considered at a second
London conference scheduled for that November. Marx got himself elected as
a delegate from Brussels, and Engels, who was then staying in Paris, was chosen
from there. He also managed to hijack authority for drafting the confession, as
he wrote smirkingly to Marx:

> *Strictly* between ourselves, I've played an infernal trick on Mosi [Hess]. He had
> actually put through a delightfully amended confession of faith. Last Friday at
> the district [committee of the Communist League] I dealt with this, point by
> point. . . . I got them to entrust me with the task of drafting a new one which
> will be discussed next Friday by the district and will be sent to London *behind*
> *the backs of the* [communist] *communities.* Naturally not a soul must know about
> this, otherwise we shall all be unseated and there'll be the deuce of a row.[29]

Engels had prepared a draft "confession" for the summer meeting, but he
now wrote out a much lengthier version, which he called the "Principles of
Communism." He was not satisfied with his handiwork, however, and en route
to the conference he wrote to Marx:

> Give a little thought to the Confession of Faith. I think we would do best to
> abandon the catechetical form and call the thing Communist *Manifesto.* Since a
> certain amount of history has to be narrated in it, the form hitherto adopted
> is quite unsuitable. I shall be bringing with me the one from here, which I did;
> it is in simple narrative form, but wretchedly worded, in a tearing hurry.[30]

At the November conference, he and Marx won recognition as the group's leading theoreticians and were authorized to prepare a final version of the statement by early the next year. They began working on it at once and continued as both traveled to Brussels in December. At the end of the year, Engels returned to Paris, while Marx used January to complete the *Manifesto,* which was published the following month.

Twenty years later, Engels wrote that the *Manifesto,* which bore both of their names, was "substantially [Marx's] work."[31] But he asserted this in the course of his efforts to publicize the newly published *Das Kapital,* and he may have inflated Marx's share of the credit in deference to the public relations task at hand or out of his customary self-effacement vis-à-vis Marx. The major ideas and themes echo earlier works of Engels—such as "The Outlines of a Critique," *Condition of the Working Class* and "Speeches at Elberfeld"—more than those of Marx.[†] It is true that the form and style of the *Manifesto* are quite different from the "Principles of Communism" that Engels brought to the London conference. But Terrell Carver, who has published the most systematic comparison of the two documents (at least in English), has detailed their substantial similarities. Carver argues that the *Manifesto*

> was in a sense very largely Engels's work and was almost the last one to demonstrate unambiguously his authorial virtues. . . .The level of the Communist Manifesto was very much that of [Engels' 1845] "Speeches in Elberfeld" [rather than] Marx's more abstruse analyses of idealist and realist ontology, the ultimate contradictions of the liberal state, and the peculiar nature of ideological consciousness.[32]

The *Manifesto* was eventually to become one of the most influential pamphlets ever written, and its aura was heightened in hindsight by the fact that it appeared in 1848, just as revolutions were erupting all over Europe. But it was published in London in German, an obscure emigré pamphlet that by common account went entirely unnoticed at the time.

When the revolutionary wildfire of 1848 was ignited in January in Palermo,

---

† A caveat to this is that much of this material may also be found in the *German Ideology*, written in 1845-46 but still unpublished when the *Manifesto* appeared. It was signed by the two jointly, and we do not know who contributed what. It was written in Engels' hand, but this does not prove anything about authorship, since his penmanship was superior and the decision that he should do the scribbling probably rested on this.

the leaders of the Communist League were still sending Marx and Engels ulti-
matums demanding a final draft of the *Manifesto*. In February, the outbreak of
revolt in Paris, cockpit of European politics, fanned the sparks into a blaze of
nearly fifty uprisings engulfing the area between Russia and the English Channel.
Marx had recently received an inheritance from his father, and he soon spent
most of it buying guns and daggers for German rebels in Belgium, leading to
his arrest and expulsion from that country. Fortunately for him, the new regime
in France opened its arms to him, and it also welcomed back Engels, who had
been expelled when the upheaval began.

In March, rebellion in Berlin elicited concessions from the king and drew
a stream of radical exiles back to Germany, among them Engels and Marx. In
Cologne they launched a new newspaper, *Neue Rheinische Zeitung,* with Marx
as editor. Engels said that "Marx's dictatorship was self-evident, acknowledged
and unquestioned." But Engels wrote most of the editorials and probably as
much of the copy as Marx.

In September, agitation in Cologne reached fever pitch, and, borrowing a
name from the Jacobins, a "Committee of Public Safety" was proclaimed which
included most of the editors of the *Neue Rheinische Zeitung.* After a declaration
of martial law, the paper was ordered to suspend publication. Amidst a wave of
arrests, charges were brought against Engels, who fled. After hiding out briefly
in his native Barmen, he escaped to Belgium and from there made his way to
France.

There ensued one of the odder episodes of Engels' revolutionary career.
Within a few weeks, tensions eased in Prussia, and the *Neue Rheinische Zeitung*
was allowed to resume publication, albeit under continuing legal pressure.
Engels, however, rather than returning at once to the struggle in Cologne,
decided to go on to Switzerland. Since he was short of funds and it was early fall,
the loveliest season to oenophiles, he determined to go there by foot, devoting
the next two months of that revolutionary year to a solitary walking tour. The
notes he kept of his journey suggest that he did not much miss the barricades:

> The French certainly have a beautiful country and they are right to be proud of
> it. . . . And what wine! What a diversity, from Bordeaux to Burgundy . . . from
> Petit Mâcon or Chablis to Chambertin . . . and from that to sparkling cham-
> pagne! . . . If only one could have had one's pockets full of money in that red
> republic! The 1848 harvest was so infinitely rich . . . better than '46, perhaps
> even better than '34! . . . It will therefore readily be believed that I spent more

time lying in the grass with the vintners and their girls, eating grapes, drinking wine, chatting and laughing.[33]

By the time he returned to Germany in January 1849, the tide of revolution had ebbed and the forces of reaction had gained the upper hand across the continent. In May, Marx was ordered expelled from Prussia and he returned to Paris as the *Neue Rheinische Zeitung* published its last issue—in defiant red ink. Engels went on to Baden-Palatinate in Bavaria, where a provisional government was maintaining one of the last outposts of insurrection in Germany.

The following month, when Prussia dispatched forces to aid the Bavarian regime in breaking the resistance of the Baden insurgents, Engels put himself at the disposal of the revolutionary armed forces. With his year of military training, he was chosen as aide de camp to August von Willich, a Prussian artillery officer who threw in with the rebels and who commanded a motley force of some seven to eight hundred fighters. They held out for a few weeks against heavy odds, and made their last stand along the river Murg where Moll the watchmaker fell. Together with Willich, Engels escaped into Switzerland. He traveled from there to Genoa, whence he sailed to England to reunite with Marx.

In London, Marx and Engels revived the Communist League. But as 1849 gave way to 1850 they grew pessimistic about prospects for a rapid renewal of revolutionary energy and focused more on their literary endeavors. Marx published *The Class Struggles in France* and Engels *The Peasant War in Germany*. Other members of the Communist League, however, did not share their discouragement. A split ensued until Marx and Engels pushed through a motion to move the league's headquarters to Cologne, which had the intended result of burying the organization, since all of its experienced members were living in London.

Marx and Engels seemed to rejoice in the league's demise. Marx wrote to Engels: "The system of mutual concessions, half-measures tolerated for decency's sake, and the obligation to bear one's share of public ridicule in the party along with all these jackasses, all this is now over."[34] And Engels replied: "Truly, it is no loss if we are no longer held to be the 'right and adequate expression' of the ignorant curs with whom we have been thrown together over the past few years."

The Communist League may have died unlamented, but it constituted an important milestone in socialist history. When Marx and Engels joined forces with the League of the Just, they changed not only its name but its motto: from "All men are brothers" to "Workers of the world, unite." The impact of this change was not confined to the life of one organization. Robert Owen and the other "utopians" of the first half of the nineteenth century had separated the socialist cause from the bloody-mindedness of the French Revolution and infused it instead with a spirit akin to Christian love—albeit an atheist and materialist version. Marx and Engels heaped scorn on their do-good approach and reconnected socialism to the thrill of violence, now dressed up in the high theory of "class struggle."

There was, however, something curious about their notion of class. Marx and Engels were journalists, the former the son of a high-ranking lawyer, the latter of an entrepreneur. Both received financial support from their well-heeled families throughout their early adulthood. They maintained an unembarrassed—one might even say supercilious—awareness of their class status, glaringly apparent in their derision of their working-class comrades as "jackasses" and "ignorant curs." Stephen Born, a member of the Communist League who, like Schapper, worked as a compositor, complained in his memoirs that Engels was unable to get along with men of a lower class, and Engels' admiring biographer, Gustav Mayer, confirmed as much while offering this lame excuse:

> His honesty and the natural pride of one who was the son of an old family, unaccustomed to dissembling, prevented him from fawning on men of inferior education and character. He was irritated by the backwardness of the artisans, and he may have let them feel his superiority more clearly than was prudent. Yet that was not bourgeois arrogance, but the inexperience of youth.[35]

As for Marx, he supported himself his entire life by begging, as we shall see, but he still was unwilling to settle for a meager existence. The Marx household, even through the most penurious times, always kept one servant and for some years, two. Marx's wife, Jenny, once complained that "we live in a veritable palace which, in my view, is far too big and far too expensive." But Marx justified this in a letter to Engels:

> I do, indeed, live too expensively for my conditions. . . . But it is the only means whereby the children . . . can maintain contacts and relationships to assure their future. I believe that you yourself will agree that, even from a mere business point of view, a purely proletarian household establishment, while quite acceptable to me and my wife or even the girls when they were young, would be unbecoming now.[36]

A year later, appealing to Engels for the gift of a shipment of claret and Rhine wine for a dance which his daughters were hosting, he had explained the urgency: "they have been unable to invite anyone for the whole of this year . . . and are therefore about to lose caste."[37]

Despite the fact that Engels and Marx neither came from the working class nor had any interest in joining it, they viewed themselves not primarily as theorists but as leaders of the proletariat. On the other hand, they did not hesitate to confer the anathema "bourgeois" upon socialist or communist workers with whom they differed, such as Schapper, the mammoth-sized compositor who had filled the young Engels with a yearning for manliness. Thus these terms proletarian and bourgeois—did not signify anything about the class status of those to whom they were applied, but rather about their ideas.

In the program of "class struggle" that Marx and Engels imprinted upon the socialist movement, therefore, the idea of struggle was a lot clearer than the idea of class. The socialist ideal which Owen had bathed in tones of kindliness took on instead the coloration of justice, retribution and hatred. And this, as we have seen, was the hard spirit of Marx's and Engels' cutting remarks about the other members of the Communist League, as well as their polemics against the Bauers, Feuerbach, Weitling, Proudhon and later Lassalle, Bakunin, Duhring and countless others.

Marx and Engels extolled violence, regarding it as not merely a means to power but also an exercise for heightening the sensibilities of the proletarians. Marx explained this in his 1850 address to the Central Committee of the Communist League just before its demise. The coming revolution, he said, like those of 1789 and 1848, would involve a multiplicity of forces fighting for varying goals. "Bourgeois democrats" would fight for political rights while the "proletarians" would fight for socialism. But there was a danger that the latter forces might be lulled into stopping short of their own goals. Therefore, he argued,

> the workers must counteract . . . the bourgeois endeavors to allay the storm, and must compel the democrats to carry out their present terrorist phrases. Their actions must be so aimed as to prevent the direct revolutionary excitement from being suppressed again immediately after the victory. On the contrary, they must keep it alive as long as possible. Far from opposing so-called excesses, instances of popular revenge against hated individuals or public buildings that are associated only with hateful recollections, such instances must not only be tolerated but the leadership of them taken in hand.[38]

In the short term, violence could help to keep the workers in a state of revolutionary excitement, while in the long term it could toughen them and prepare them to rule. The communists, Marx wrote, must say: "You will have to go through fifteen or twenty or fifty years of civil wars and international wars not only in order to change extant conditions, but also in order to change yourselves and to render yourselves fit for political dominion."[39]

As this made clear, in addition to revolutionary violence, Engels and Marx welcomed strife between states, although they decried loyalty to any, because they believed that war would serve as a spur to progress and revolution. Writing in the *New York Tribune* in 1851 under Marx's name, Engels explained that during the upheavals of 1848-49, "the advanced party in Germany [the Communists and the Left-Wing Democrats] deemed a war with Russia necessary to keep up the Continental [democratic] movement," and that such a war "would have called more active and energetic men to the helm."[40]

In applauding the progressive consequences of war, Engels and Marx did not shirk from facing its destructive effects. They welcomed those, too—if the objects of destruction were regressive or outmoded. In this way, entire nations might be consigned to the ash heap of history. Slavs, in particular, needed to be done away with so that more progressive races might reach their fulfillment. Engels declared in the *Neue Rheinische Zeitung*: "The universal war which [is coming] will crush the Slav alliance and will wipe out completely those obstinate peoples so that their very names will be forgotten. . . . [It] will wipe out not only reactionary classes and dynasties but it will also destroy these utterly reactionary races . . . and that will be a real step forward."[41] Marx said much the same, looking forward to the "annihilation" of "reactionary races" such as "Croats, Pandurs, Czechs and similar scum."[42]

• • •

In 1850, with the Communist League defunct and the prospects for an early resumption of European revolution bleak, Engels began to consider the need for a livelihood. A like thought seems never to have entered Marx's head, although of the two it was only he who had a family. Engels accepted this, and indeed hoped to contribute to Marx's support. Both men agreed on the paramount importance of Marx's completion of a book presenting an overarching interpretation of economics from their joint perspective.

While Engels might have earned a living in journalism, a better prospect for making a surplus that would enable him to assist Marx lay with the family firm. He had bowed to his father's wishes and gone to work in the business in 1845 shortly after returning from his youthful sojourn in England. But he had quit after only a short while, complaining that "the waste of time is too horrible. Above all it is too horrible to belong to the middle classes and actually to be associated with factory owners. It is too horrible to play the part of a member of the bourgeoisie and to be actively engaged in opposing the interests of the workers."[43] Now, he saw little choice but to swallow his pride and revulsion in order to help his idol write the bible of class warfare.

The stern senior Engels was of no mind to give the wayward son a cushy position. He did, however, have some real use for him. The Manchester branch of the firm of Engels & Ermen was run by two of the Ermen brothers, while Engels senior was based in Barmen. He feared that they were misusing assets of the joint business to benefit some other enterprises of their own in Manchester. Despite his tensions with his son, he trusted him to protect the family's interests, and so he arranged a minor office job for him, the essence of which was to keep an eye on the Ermen partners.

The job allowed Engels to support himself and to give some financial assistance to Marx during the short interval, as he expected it would be, until revolution broke out anew. He often thought he could glimpse the coming upheaval on the horizon, but he was repeatedly disappointed, and so he spent twenty years—from the time he was thirty until fifty—working for Engels & Ermen in Manchester. Though apparently he continued to dislike the work, he was good enough at it to win raises and promotions that could not have resulted from mere paternal indulgence. When his father died in 1860, a small quarrel ensued between Friedrich and his brothers who worked in the firm's headquarters in Barmen. In the end, Friedrich received the family's share of the Manchester branch of the business, and for the next ten years he worked to amass enough of a fortune to retire on.

In Manchester, Engels maintained two homes. One he used for business entertaining and similar public purposes, while in the other he lived in common-law partnership with Mary Burns. He had brought her to Brussels in 1845 and she had lived with him most of the time since, although she did not join in his many peregrinations during the late forties. Judging from his open and avid pursuit of other women in that period, it is not clear how bound he had felt. Now, however, they settled into a stable relationship, which lasted until Mary's death in 1863. Engels was deeply grieved then, but soon took up with Mary's sister, Lizzy, with whom he maintained a similar relationship until her death

some thirteen or fourteen years after that. Touchingly, he married Lizzy on her
deathbed, his only experience of matrimony.

Housekeeping with Mary Burns was not the only thing about which Engels
exercised discretion. Because the Ermens had the upper hand in the firm, he
avoided offending them by flaunting radical involvements. He attended con-
scientiously to his business responsibilities, restricting political activities to his
spare time. Moreover, he maintained memberships in the appropriate clubs
for a man of his station, such as the Cheshire Hunt Club. He frequently spent
weekends riding to the hounds with other gentlemen, an activity in which he
took great pleasure, but which he justified as a way of keeping himself in shape
for the revolution.[44] Nor did he neglect charitable activities more conventional
than his support of Marx, serving on the board of the Society for the Relief of
Really Deserving Distressed Foreigners.

Soon upon his arrival in Manchester, perhaps out of his first paycheck,
Engels sent Marx two pounds. The method that became their custom, in those
days of limited banking services, was for Engels to tear a bill in half and mail
each in a separate envelope. As his income grew, so did these remittances. Years
later, as he tried to calculate how much income he would require to leave the
business, he said in a letter to Marx: "and this has always been on my mind—
what are we to do with you then? But if things turn out now as they promise,
that will soon settle itself, even if the revolution does not come meanwhile and
do away with all this financial planning."[45]

For his part, Marx never did any financial planning. Nor was there a moment
in his life when he was self-supporting. Edmund Wilson noted the irony that "the
man who had done more than any other to call attention to economic motivation
should have been incapable of doing anything for gain."[46] Marx himself once
repeated his mother's quip that she wished he had been making capital instead
of writing about it. Most of the time, however, he expressed great anguish over
his economic dependency but did nothing to alleviate it.

Throughout his life he appealed over and again for handouts from every
friend or relative he could think of, even eventually from one of his grown
children. While he scorned his mother and siblings, the only relative with
whom he maintained active relations was his aunt Sophie, who had married a
banker. Leaving his wife, Jenny, at home, he visited them several times in the
effort to borrow money—and also, perhaps, to be near their beautiful daughter,
Nannette, twenty years his junior. (When she was in her young twenties, reports
Saul Padover, "he paid unrestrained court to her, and she frankly reciprocated
by falling in love with him.")[47]

The only other substantial source of income in the Marx household was a series of bequests from his relatives and some of Jenny's. He got his mother to give him some of his inheritance in advance, and Jenny's mother, though she herself had fallen on hard times in widowhood, scratched out contributions.

The Marxes got a windfall when one devoted comrade, Wilhelm Wolff, died and it was discovered that he had squirreled away considerable savings and bequeathed most of it—about nine hundred pounds—to Marx. This ought to have been enough to support him for two or three years, but Marx managed to go through it in little more than one year.

All of these other beggings, borrowings and inheritances paled in comparison with the lifelong subsidy provided by Engels, both literal and literary. The only significant earned income that Marx ever received consisted of fees for articles published over several years in the 1850s in the *New York Tribune*. He was hired as a European correspondent by Charles Dana, the newspaper's second in command, who had befriended the founder and chief editor, Horace Greeley, when both were members of the Fourierist commune, Brook Farm. Marx did not hesitate to accept the assignment, even though the articles had to be in English, which he did not then speak. Bearing in mind Engels' great facility with languages, Marx simply asked him to ghostwrite the articles. Engels dutifully accepted the burden, coming home from his day job at the firm, where he earned money to help support Marx, to spend his evenings doing Marx's job.

In a couple of years, Marx learned enough English to write the articles himself, but not before more than a hundred had been ghostwritten for him by Engels. A year after Engels' death, Marx's daughter Eleanor published a book in Marx's name titled *Revolution and Counter-Revolution in Germany in 1848*, a compilation of articles from the *Tribune* signed by Marx. Twenty years after the book appeared it was discovered that these had all come from the pen of Engels.

As Engels' fortune grew, so did his generosity, but Marx always adjusted his standard of living to a level above what he received. Thus he was never out of debt, and he never stopped asking Engels for more. Even when he was living well, he had little trouble finding room to expand the ambit of his mendicancy. When his oldest daughter married and moved to France, Marx asked Engels to pay her rent, pointing out, as if it explained all, that nonpayment of rent was taken seriously in France.

At one stage Engels moved into cheaper lodgings so as to spare more for Marx. He did all of this out of something more than friendship: he was convinced that Marx was producing a great work that would be the touchstone of the communist movement. In his twenties he had taken confidence in the

validity of socialist ideas from their alleged demonstration in the Owenite and
similar communities, but now he had come to write dismissively about "utopian
socialism" and to confess that Owen's New Harmony had been a flop. In the
face of socialism's failure to prove itself experimentally, he hoped that Marx's
genius could bring forth a masterwork furnishing the validation that could not
be found in naked experience.

Marx had been talking about this book for years already when Engels moved
to Manchester in 1850. Early in 1851 Marx wrote to Engels that he hoped "to
finish the whole economic shit"[48] in another five weeks. Engels wrote back that
he was "delighted that you have at last finished your book on economics. The
whole business has taken too long." But five weeks grew into five years, and then
another five and another five.

Engels did grow a touch cynical in this later period, as he wrote to another
friend:

> Alas we are so used to these excuses for the non-completion of the work!
> Whenever the state of his health made it impossible for him to go on with it,
> this impossibility preyed heavily upon his mind, and he was only too glad if
> he could only find some theoretical excuse why the work should not then be
> completed. All these arguments he had at the time made use of *vis-à-vis moi;*
> they seemed to ease his conscience.[49]

The cynicism never mushroomed into resentment, however, and his support—financial and otherwise—remained steadfast to the end.

No one knows how much money passed between the two friends. Between
1850 and 1869, Marx's requests and Engels' invariably compliant responses
flowed back and forth in a constant stream of letters. Biographers have tried
to add the sums involved, but a good deal of the correspondence does not survive, so they are working from fragments. Even these incomplete records show
transfers of £33 in 1851, £41 in 1852, £57 in 1853, £12 in 1854, £10 in 1856,
£70 in 1857, £61 in 1858, £52 in 1859, and £159 in 1860.[50] Throughout this
era, the average individual in Britain lived on £27 per year.[51]

When Engels calculated that he had accumulated enough to live off the
proceeds and walk away from his tedious job at Engels & Ermen, he literally
jumped for joy. His calculations included support for Marx, whom he asked
to work up a complete sum of his outstanding debts, and when Marx supplied
the number, Engels sent a check to cover them. Then he allotted an annuity of

£350—more than twelve times the per capita GNP—to be paid to Marx in quarterly installments for the rest of his life.

Marx's financial worries should have been over. They were not. To begin with, after a few months he wrote to Engels to explain that the final tally of debt he had sent had been short by £75. He attributed the error entirely to Jenny, commenting that this showed why "women need guardians."[52] The ever-indulgent Engels sent the difference but asked Marx not to let this happen again, as he had calculated his budget carefully. Soon, however, Marx found himself with more bills than the £350 per annum could cover, so the pattern of repeated appeals to his friend—now for £15, now for £30, now for £50 resumed. As Marx's health weakened in his sixties, he began to go for weeks or months at a time to various fashionable spas in search of cures. Usually he took along one of his daughters, and usually he asked Engels to foot the bills above and beyond his regular remittances.

Engels' generosity was matched by patience. Occasionally he inquired after the progress of Marx's masterpiece, but even as year melted into year he did not grow plaintive. In 1857 and 1858 Marx gave forth a great burst of productive activity, and he reported to Engels that he was finally synthesizing his economic studies. Engels hoped that the great work might be at hand. But the notebooks Marx produced were unpublishable and remained unpublished until the middle of the twentieth century, when they were released under the title *Grundrisse* by Moscow's Marx-Engels-Lenin Institute. Marx did succeed in boiling his thoughts down into a small book published the next year, 1859, with the title *Contribution to a Critique of Political Philosophy*. The book achieved little notice and few sales. Marx attributed this response to a "conspiracy of silence" on the part of his adversaries. But even friends found little good to say about the *Contribution*. Marx's loyal disciple Wilhelm Liebknecht called it the most disappointing book he had ever read.[53]

Finally, in 1867, Marx completed the first of what were to have been six volumes of *Das Kapital*. After those sixteen years, Engels waited another sixteen—until Marx's death—for the subsequent volumes, but they never arrived. *Das Kapital* began where Engels' own youthful work in Manchester left off. It borrowed numerous sources and arguments and referred to the earlier work ten times.[54] But evoking the miseries of working-class life was only the beginning of Marx's project, which was six or eight times longer than Engels' book, and far more ambitious. The renowned literary critic Edmund Wilson described it this way:

> The book is a welding-together of several quite diverse points of view, of several quite distinct techniques of thought. It contains a treatise on economics, a history of industrial development and an inspired tract for the times; and the morality, which is part of the time suspended in the interests of scientific objectivity, is no more self-consistent than the economics is consistently scientific or the history undistracted by the exaltation of apocalyptic vision. And outside the whole immense structure, dark and strong like the old Trier basilica, built by the Romans with brick walls and granite columns, swim the mists and the septentrional lights of German metaphysics and mysticism always ready to leak in through the crevices.[55]

How many ordinary readers were prepared to tackle eight to nine hundred pages of stuff such as this? Peter Fox, a British radical colleague to whom Marx sent a copy, is reported to have remarked that "he felt like a man who had been given an elephant and did not know what to do with it."[56]

Length was only the beginning of the problem. Whereas *The Condition of the Working Class* had made compelling reading, *Capital*—though some great scholars have found it profound—was on the whole inaccessible. If Fox had begun to read the book, as he may have done, he would have encountered at once a series of ponderous banalities. It begins: "The wealth of those societies in which the capitalist mode of production prevails presents itself as 'an immense accumulation of commodities,' its unit being a single commodity." The text continues: "A commodity is, in the first place, an object outside us, a thing that by its properties satisfies human wants of some sort or another. Every useful thing, as iron, paper, etc., may be looked at from the two points of view of quality and quantity. It is an assemblage of many properties, and may therefore be of use in various ways."

After three paragraphs of such blather, Fox at last would have arrived at something he did not already know—and, if he had a normal mind, would not comprehend when he read it:

> The utility of a thing makes it a use-value. But this utility is not a thing of air. Being limited by the physical properties of the commodity, it has no existence apart from that commodity. A commodity, such as iron, corn, or a diamond, is therefore, so far as it is a material thing, a use-value, something useful. This property of a commodity is independent of the amount of labour required to appropriate its useful qualities. When treating of use-value, we always assume

to be dealing with definite quantities, such as dozens of watches, yards of linen, or tons of iron.

Fox was not the only recipient of the book who was left scratching his head. Editors and potential reviewers were confounded, too, and at first scarcely a review appeared. Marx blamed this on the perfidy of the ruling classes. The "learned and unlearned spokesmen of the German bourgeoisie tried at first to kill *Das Kapital* by silence, as they had managed to do with my earlier writings," he alleged.[57]

Unlike Marx, Engels was not one to wallow in rage or anguish. Instead, he threw himself into the task of remedying the book's neglect. He composed as many as ten different reviews and, using friends as intermediaries, he managed to place them, generally anonymously as was common then, in a variety of dailies and weeklies all across Germany. He cleverly adjusted not only the content but also the writing style for the differing outlets. These efforts accounted for most of whatever attention the book received.[58]

• • •

The production of volume one of *Capital* marked the culmination of Marx's literary work. He did devote a good part of his remaining years to research for the subsequent volumes, but he never composed them. His only significant piece of writing was the 1871 pamphlet *The Civil War in France,* an account of the Paris Commune. This was written as a statement on behalf of the International Workingman's Association, or, as it is often called, the First International.

Founded more than a decade after the disbanding of the Communist League, the International occasioned a return to activism by Marx and Engels. It was not, however, their brainchild. After the defeat of the revolutions of 1848, the remnants of the Left had sunk into quiescence, but voices of protest began to regain some vigor in the 1860s. In 1863 a group of British and French trade unionists cooperated in a show of support for the Polish uprising against Russian rule, and the experience prompted them to reconvene the following year to set up a permanent organization. Labor and Leftist groups from across Europe were invited, and Marx attended as a representative of German exiles in England. A variety of progressive causes were in the air—work conditions, Polish and Italian independence, the defeat of slavery in the United States—and the conference displayed more spirit than focus.

Marx managed to get named to the committee charged with drafting a constitution for the International Workingman's Association, and he soon emerged as its leader. He wrote the constitution, yielding to the inclusion of some verbiage about "right and duty, truth, justice and freedom" on the grounds that "they could do no possible harm," even though he viewed such moralism as sentimental cant. He found it tolerable because he was able to win approval of an "Inaugural Address" of the association, which was in essence a clarion to class struggle.

Marx then secured a position on the group's governing body, the General Council, which was based in London, and he quickly came to dominate that as well. As Saul Padover tells it:

> From the very first, other members of the General Council, less literate and less sure in their purpose than Marx, were glad to have him to take over responsibility. This was particularly true when it came to the all-important function of formulating positions. "I am in fact the head of the thing," Marx told Engels in 1865.[59]

Throughout the remainder of the 1860s, the International continued to attract new affiliates from among all of the major European countries and the United States. These ranged from middle-class associations of socialists or anarchists to ordinary labor unions. Marx was exhilarated by the feeling of being at the helm of the international revolutionary movement.

But strains developed within the organization, and the General Council, with Marx in control, attempted to compel reluctant affiliates to accept the policy pronouncements it set forth. The strains reached a breaking point when rebellion broke out in the streets of Paris in 1871.

Generations after the Great Revolution, the breach between progressive Paris and the conservative countryside revealed itself to be unhealed, and France's defeat by Prussia tore open the wound. In the ensuing turmoil, Paris declared its own government, the Commune. It lasted ten weeks, ending in the destruction of much of the city and tens of thousands of deaths.

The lion's share of carnage came at the hands of the military authorities who suppressed the rebellion with pitiless brutality; but the rebels contributed, too. They executed prisoners and hostages—including the archbishop of Paris—and torched the Tuileries Palace and other national monuments as symbols of the old regime. And although the Parisian rebels suffered more bloodshed than they perpetrated, it was they who had initiated the conflagration.

While the image of the Commune sent shivers down most European spines, Marx was thrilled by it. He had not advocated rebellion by the Parisians, and few of the rebels were followers of his, yet many of them were workers, so Marx thought he saw in these events the beginnings of the proletarian revolution. His *Civil War in France* warmly embraced the Commune. This was seized upon in fanciful rightist exposés identifying Marx, a Prussian—in some versions even a hireling of Bismarck's—as the dark hand behind the Commune. Marx reveled in his newfound notoriety, calling himself "the most abused and threatened man in London," and adding that it "really does me good after the tedious twenty-year idyll in my den!"[60] But the British trade union leaders in the International refused to give their endorsement to the pamphlet, and two of the more prominent ones, including George Odger, the original president of the General Council, resigned from the International in protest.

The last blow to the organization was the climax of the bitter rivalry between Marx and Michael Bakunin. An immense, swashbuckling, charismatic Russian aristocrat who made a career of revolution, Bakunin had received death sentences in more than one country. These he survived, as well as years of imprisonment and Siberian exile, from which he escaped. He admired Marx, and had even translated some of his works into Russian, but diverged from him in philosophy. Bakunin distrusted all political authority and advocated anarchism. With remarkable prescience, he argued that only tyranny would result from the political revolution that Marx advocated: "The so-called people's state will be nothing other than the quite despotic administration of the masses of the people by a new and very non-numerous aristocracy of real and supposed learned ones."[61]

The final showdown came at the 1872 annual conference of the IWA at The Hague. Because of the group's apocryphal role in fomenting the Paris Commune, armed soldiers patrolled the streets. Engels had been entrusted by the General Council with preparing the conference and, from a factional standpoint, he had done his work well. He and Marx held a decisive majority among the delegates. They began by expelling Bakunin and his leading supporter, the Swiss James Guillaume.

Although their majority at the 1872 conference was secure, Marx and Engels must have feared that this might not reflect the true balance of opinion among the International's constituents. Before the meeting concluded, Engels stunned the delegates by proposing to move the headquarters from London to New York. Communications across the Atlantic were difficult; the organization had already had trouble keeping its American affiliates in line. To move the head-quarters to the New World meant to consign the International to oblivion. The French delegate, physician Edouard Vaillant, commented that they might as well be moved to the moon.[62] Yet Marx and Engels knew exactly what they were doing. They had made a cold-blooded calculation that burying the organization was preferable to risking that it might yet fall under the spell of Bakunin or the popular French revolutionary Auguste Blanqui. And they were employing the same stratagem by which they had finished off the Communist League, except that New York was a lot more remote than Cologne. Despite their commanding majority, they managed to push Engels' motion through only by a hair.

The International did not last long in America. The headquarters were moved from New York to Philadelphia, where in 1876 a final conference, num-bering only fourteen delegates in all, voted its official dissolution.

Although Marx lived until 1883, much of his final eleven years was spent in the search for cures for his numerous ailments. Just as *The Civil War in France* marked the conclusion of his literary career, so the conference at The Hague was the final episode of his activism. In all, his political work met with scant success. When he was interred at London's High Gate cemetery, fewer than twenty mourners attended.

The loneliness of his death and the failure of his life both owed much to a central paradox about Marx. He thought of himself as a man who had devoted his life to "working for humanity," as he liked to phrase it, comparing himself invidiously with "so-called practical men," who busied themselves with career and family.[63] But whatever his devotion to humanity in general, to the concrete individuals with whom he came in contact, from childhood until old age, he was never kind and often cruel.

Of all his interactions with other people, he was best toward his wife and children. Yet though he undoubtedly loved them, he disdained the ordinary responsibilities of husband and father. He never tried to get a job,[†] but was content to let his family share the sufferings of living on whatever they could help him beg or borrow. In a letter to a future son-in-law, Marx wrote: "I have sacrificed my whole fortune to the revolutionary struggle. I do not regret it. Quite the contrary. If I had to start my life over again, I would do the same. But I would not marry."[64]

---

† He once claimed that he had applied for a position as a railway clerk but was turned down on the grounds of poor handwriting. There is no reason to believe that the story is true, but even if it is, he never tried to improve his handwriting or seek a different position.

Although his brilliance and self-confidence constituted natural attributes of leadership, Marx's political work suffered from his great difficulty in getting along with people. Not only was he vicious toward his rivals, he was often contemptuous of his own supporters. When Wilhelm Liebknecht, his most devoted follower within Germany, had a child, Marx quipped, "Liebknecht has finally achieved something."[65] Marx described Karl Kautsky, who was to become the leader of German Marxism, as "a small-minded mediocrity" who "busies himself with statistics but does not derive anything intelligent from them, belonging by nature to the tribe of Philistines."[66]

Engels was capable of similar coarseness, but he was far more of a regular guy. The Russian Marxist Georgi Plekhanov called him "a great man and also an amiable man at the same time."[67] This amiability was displayed in an elaborate Christmas tradition he developed, despite his atheism, following his return to London in 1870 upon retiring from the firm. Two weeks in advance he would invite a group of friends to help him prepare a vat of rum pudding during a night of champagne and revelry. Then, as his disciple Eduard Bernstein recalled, Christmas Day itself

> was kept by Engels after the English fashion, as Charles Dickens has so delightfully described it in *The Pickwick Papers*. The room is decorated with green boughs of every kind, between which, in suitable places, the perfidious mistletoe peeps forth, which gives every man the right to kiss any person of the opposite sex who is standing beneath it or whom he can catch in passing. At table ... the dish of honour [is] the plum-pudding, which is served up, the room having been darkened, with burning rum....An enormous quantity was made, for there was not a single friend of the house who did not receive a Christmas pudding from 122 Regent's Park Road.[68]

Engels' sociality made him an effective mentor to a generation of acolytes, and it reflected itself in a literary style that reached many more readers than Marx's forbidding prose. As Marx's career was winding down with the publication of volume one of *Capital* and the disintegration of the IWA, Engels' career was just recommencing. During the quarter-century between his retirement and his death in 1895, he devoted all his extraordinary energy to advancing "Marxism" and building a movement.

The first task was the production of *Capital,* which Engels called the "Bible of the Working Class."[69] He had underwritten Marx's labors on the first volume, which drew heavily on his own earlier research in Manchester. That, however, was only the beginning of Engels' contribution. He was shocked to discover the unfinished state of the notes that Marx had left for the remaining parts. Engels took these in hand, and from them produced volume two in 1885 and volume three in 1894. Not only did the notes need to be turned into finished prose, but the statistics were all wrong. For all his work in economics, Marx, it turns out, was as inept with math in general as with his household finances. Engels wrote to one of Marx's daughters about her father's "tables being almost without exception miscalculated . . . and having to be recast." He added sardonically, "you know what a genius he was for figures!"[70]

Padover calls *Capital* "the masterpiece on which Marx's worldwide reputation rests."[71] This may be true in some sense, but large parts of it are difficult to read and in fact have rarely been read. As Gustav Mayer said about the German Socialist Workers' Party, the mid-nineteenth-century party most directly shaped by Marx and Engels:

> hardly any influential person in the party (far less the mass of ordinary members) understood the basis of Marx's and Engels' theory or the political deductions which they drew from it. The leaders had no time to plunge into a book like *Capital*. At most they knew the *Communist Manifesto* and realized that it developed the doctrine of the class-conflict more thoroughly than Lassalle's *Workers' Program,* which was the usual introduction to socialist education in Germany at that time.[72]

Marx's masterpiece was of such little immediate consequence that when Bismarck's antisocialist law led to the banning of hundreds of the party's books and periodicals, the authorities did not bother to include *Capital* among the proscribed works.

If few read or understood *Capital,* what was its importance? Despite Engels' characterization, it was less a bible than a talisman. Unlike the Torah, the New Testament or the Holy Koran, all of which are studied assiduously by believers, *Capital* fulfilled its purpose just by existing. Believers could assure themselves that it contained profound evidence that their worldview was more correct than any other. Eric Hobsbawm, a historian sympathetic to Marxism, explained: "*Capital* vol. I was indeed frequently reprinted . . . but it may be doubted whether it lent itself to wide popular reading. Many of those who bought it were probably content to have it on their shelf as a living proof that Marx had proved the inevitability of socialism scientifically."[73]

How, then, did most socialists learn their doctrine? Some through the *Communist Manifesto* or the work of Lassalle, as Mayer says, but even more learned it through the later works of Engels, including *Anti-Dühring,* published in 1878. Eugen Dühring, a popular blind lecturer in philosophy and economics at the University of Berlin, was perceived by Marx and Engels as an emerging rival, and a good part of Engels' book was reminiscent of their bitter diatribes against earlier rivals. But in three chapters Engels presented the basic ideas of "scientific socialism": historical materialism, class struggle, surplus value, the contradictions of capitalism, the dynamic of the business cycle, the economic impoverishment and concomitant political rise of the proletariat, the inevitable revolution, the subsequent dying out of the state, and the ultimate fulfillment of mankind as it ascends from "the kingdom of necessity to the kingdom of freedom." There was even a brief exegesis on "dialectic," allegedly a more profound method of reasoning. This was hopelessly turbid (and absurd to that one reader in a hundred who could comprehend it), but it served to give the whole piece an aura of deep philosophy.

The three chapters were translated into French by Marx's son-in-law Paul Lafargue and issued as a pamphlet titled *Socialism: Utopian and Scientific,* which allowed the thought of Marx and Engels to penetrate the French radical movement for the first time. The booklet was then published in German and translated into English by Edward Aveling. At forty-five pages it was a perfect length for wide consumption. For an hour or two of his time, the reader was rewarded with a comprehensive explanation of political history, the problems of the day and the key to their solution. For decades it was the most widely translated and widely sold work in the library of Marxism. Engels himself said that "most people are too idle to read thick books like *Capital,* and so a little pamphlet does the job much more quickly."[74]

This was true not only for workers, but intellectuals, too. Among those who were won to Marxism by reading *Anti-Dühring* were the lawyer Karl Kautsky and the bank clerk Eduard Bernstein, young socialists destined to play important roles in the movement. Engels' pamphlet, which they studied together, distilled their cloudy, eclectic radicalism into crystalline Marxist doctrine.[75] The virtue of *Anti-Dühring* lay not only in its brevity, as Kautsky explained:

> while complaints are made about the unintelligibleness of Marx, and most
> people have read more about *Capital* than they have of *Capital* itself, Engels
> stands as a master of popular exposition; his writings are read by all thinking
> proletarians, and the majority of those who have accepted socialism have

obtained their knowledge and understanding of the Marx-Engels theory from these writings.[76]

After Marx's death, Engels published two other books, *The Origin of the Family* and *Private Property and the State,* in 1884 and *Ludwig Feuerbach and the End of Classical German Philosophy* in 1888. These did not endure as well but achieved celebrity in their time. As George Lichtheim recounts, they, together with *Anti-Dühring* and *Socialism: Utopian and Scientific,* "achieved canonical status in the labour movement at the very peak of Social-Democratic influence ... from 1890 to 1914. It was from them, rather than from *Capital* ... that most Socialists drew their mental picture of the world."[77]

Also during these twelve years, the works of Marx, as well as their collaborative effort, the *Manifesto,* all of which had had tiny initial print runs, were being reissued or translated, and Engels glossed no fewer than twenty-two of these with introductory essays to help readers understand them. It is to Engels the popularizer that we can trace many of the catch-phrases of Marxism: "historical materialism," "withering away of the state," "dialectical materialism," "scientific socialism" and, above all, "Marxism."

In addition to this prodigious literary output, Engels resumed his political activity. He had kept up an active correspondence with key disciples August Bebel and Wilhelm Liebknecht, guiding them in their leadership of one of the two German socialist parties, which had merged at an 1875 congress in Gotha to form the German Socialist Workers' Party.

The other branch of the movement had been founded by Marx's rival, Ferdinand Lassalle. Although there were some ideological differences between the two men (Lassalle was more meliorist, more open to class compromise, more favorable toward the Prussian state), the competition between them was mostly personal. Marx, seven years older, was the superior theoretician, as Lassalle acknowledged, but Lassalle was the more charismatic. He was successful in his practice of law, cut a figure in elite society, and commanded an ardent following of workers, who had in fact appealed to him to form his party. Marx bitterly envied Lassalle's popularity. If he had not gotten himself killed at age thirty-nine in a duel over the honor of a lovely countess, Lassalle might have remained the dominant figure of German socialism. As it was, it took decades after Lassalle's death in 1864 until the Marxists gained the upper hand over his disciples.

That triumph was engineered by Engels with the help of not only Bebel and Liebknecht, but also the younger Bernstein and Kautsky, whom he mentored closely. Bernstein was chosen editor of the party newspaper, *Der Sozialdemokrat,* and Kautsky founded another, more theoretical party periodical, *Die Neue Zeit.* Both publications were influential in swaying the party from the heritage of Lassalle toward Marxism, a process that culminated in 1891 with the adoption of a new program, drafted by Kautsky with Engels' help, to replace the compromises of 1875.

The electoral success of the German Socialist Workers' Party after the repeal of the antisocialist laws in 1890 lent it immense prestige in the eyes of socialists abroad. This buttressed Engels' efforts to win them, too, to Marxism, and he became mentor to Viktor Adler in Austria and Jules Guesde and Paul Lafargue in France. He also corresponded busily with the Italian Antonio Labriola and the Russians Pavel Axelrod and Georgi Plekhanov, who also traced their views to the formative influence of *Anti-Dühring.*[78]

In 1889, the Guesde-Lafargue faction of French socialists invited their sister parties to Paris for a conference that founded the Second International, a far more powerful and enduring institution than its predecessor. Engels was given the title "Honorary President," and a leader of the Belgian party penned this description of his appearance at the International's 1893 congress in Zurich:

> We wanted to close the meeting; the last votes were taken in feverish haste.
> One name was on every lip. Friedrich Engels entered the hall; among storms
> of cheering he came to the platform. And after he had spoken (in the three
> official languages of the congress) of the battles of the past, the successes of
> the present, and the unlimited hopes of the future—it was as if the sunshine
> had suddenly dispersed the mists. The spiritual unity of socialism shone out
> bright as day from among the peculiarities of individual nations; and the whole
> assembly re-echoed the words with which Engels closed the congress, as he
> had once ended the *Communist Manifesto*: "Workers of the world, unite!"[79]

Engels was seventy-five when he died of cancer of the esophagus, under the care of his Austrian disciple, the physician Viktor Adler. In his last days, no longer able to talk, he used chalk and slate to erase a stain from his memory. In 1851, the Marxes' longtime maid, Helene Demuth, had given birth to a son, although she had neither husband nor boyfriend. To shield Marx from rumors he said his enemies were spreading, Engels agreed to claim paternity, and the child was named Henry Frederick. Neither Marx nor Engels took any responsibility for his support, and he was given to a family to raise, although he would come to visit his natural mother, always using the servants' entrance. Engels had taken in

Helene upon Marx's death, and when she died seven years later, he had written that he would "sadly miss her tactful advice on party affairs."[80] (She was, after all, the one member of the working class nearest to hand.) Now on his deathbed, wanting to make clear why he did not mention "Freddy" Demuth in his will, Engels confessed to his devoted disciple and caregiver, Louise Freyberger, that Marx, not he, was the father of Helene's son.

After earmarking a thousand pounds for the German party's electoral campaign, Engels divided the bulk of his substantial estate among Freyberger; Lizzy Burns' niece, Pumps; the children of Marx's deceased daughter, Jenny; and Marx's two surviving daughters, Laura and Eleanor.

Laura had married Paul Lafargue, a leader of the French socialists. Lafargue emulated Marx not only in politics but in his means of livelihood: rather than work, he begged from Engels. His relentless stream of importunate letters came much to resemble those of his father-in-law, except without Marx's frequent notes of embarrassment. After Engels' death, since Paul could apparently figure out no other way to support them, he and Laura agreed that when the bequest ran out, they would commit suicide. It did (when they were in their late sixties), and they carried out their plan.

Marx's youngest, Eleanor, called "Tussy," also died by suicide. At nineteen she had fallen in love with a veteran of the Paris Commune, but Marx would not allow the match. She and her lover, Prosper Olivier Lissagaray, remained mutually devoted for many years, but eventually Marx's efforts to break the bond succeeded. Subsequently, she fell for Edward Aveling, a British radical who had made his mark as the author of atheist tracts such as *A Godless Life the Happiest and Most Useful* and *The Wickedness of God*. Aveling became a Marxist and was a major translator into English of works by Marx and Engels, including *Das Kapital* and *Socialism: Utopian and Scientific*.

Aveling told Eleanor that a wife from whom he was separated would not consent to divorce, so Eleanor agreed to live with him unwed. Whereas Marx had begged from his friends, Aveling stole from his and embezzled from the causes in which he took part. It seems he managed to spend most of Eleanor's inheritance from Engels as well, all while repeatedly abandoning her to pursue other women. Finally, just after she had nursed him through a long illness, Eleanor was informed that Aveling had gotten free to marry again, and had secretly wed a young actress. A confrontation ensued in which Aveling must have feigned remorse, and he and Eleanor, who had not long before executed a codicil leaving her entire estate to him, agreed on a suicide pact. Aveling supplied the poison, and Eleanor, after writing a note declaring her eternal love for him, took a lethal dose. Whereupon Aveling immediately left the house and proceeded to party headquarters to establish an alibi.

While Engels' material bequests did little good for Marx's posterity, his political legacy was far more fruitful. With typical self-effacement he said: "For all that I contributed—at any rate with the exception of my work in a few special fields—Marx could very well have done without me. What Marx accomplished I would not have achieved."[81] But it was Engels who formulated and popularized Marxism and who launched the Marxist movement. He was Moses to Marx's God, Mohammed to Marx's Allah. He was the High Priest and Marx the Oracle. "Marx stood higher, saw farther," said Engels. Perhaps he did. But it was Engels who told the world what Marx saw, spreading the message that shaped the history of the dawning century.

4

WHAT IS TO BE DONE?: BERNSTEIN DEVELOPS DOUBTS

IN HIS WILL, ENGELS HAD ASKED TO BE CREMATED and to have his ashes scattered at sea. And so, on a blustery autumn day in 1895, four stalwart socialists pushed out into rough seas from the harbor of Beachy Head in Eastbourne, England, with an urn containing his earthly remains. Despite the swells, the dutiful quartet sailed some five or six miles from shore to reach what they deemed a suitable distance to discharge their solemn mission.

The group included Friedrich Lessner, a last surviving comrade from the original Communist League of 1847, and Tussy (Eleanor) Marx, Karl's adored youngest daughter. In addition, there were two prominent disciples. One was Tussy's faithless common-law husband, Edward Aveling. The other was Eduard Bernstein, the forty-five-year-old German exile who had become Engels' closest protégé. Despite the devotion displayed that day (all the more impressive on Bernstein's part in view of his chronic sea-sickness), these two were soon to wreak havoc upon the Marx-Engels legacy. The unscrupulous Aveling was to bring about Tussy's tragic early death. The upright Bernstein was to inflict damage of a different kind, destroying forever the movement's doctrinal unity.

How was it that Bernstein could have such a devastating effect? Because he was the leading apostle of the new science of Marxism—of such high standing that Engels had asked him to produce volume four of *Capital* from Marx's difficult notes, just as Engels himself had produced volumes two and three. He had also designated Bernstein executor of his literary estate. So when Bernstein challenged the accuracy of Marxian prophecy it was as if the pope declared there would be no Second Coming. His pronouncement touched off an internecine imbroglio that would reverberate for a century as competing heirs vied to possess the Marxist legacy.

Engels' esteem for Bernstein had blossomed despite initial misgivings. In his early twenties, Bernstein had been an admirer of Eugen Dühring's and had distributed his books to other socialists. It was precisely to counteract such activities that Engels had penned his epochal *Anti-Dühring*. Bernstein avowed that this book won him to Marxism, but nonetheless he helped his employer, Karl Hochberg, publish a socialist *Jahrbuch* which contained an article urging closer cooperation with the liberal bourgeoisie. Marx raged against this effort to "give socialism a 'higher, idealistic' orientation, that is to say, to replace its materialistic basis . . . by modern mythology with its goddesses of Justice, Liberty, Equality, and Fraternity."[1]

Because of these dalliances, Bernstein was far from the good graces of Marx and Engels when, in 1880, socialist leader August Bebel proposed that the thirty-year-old author be elevated to the editorship of *Der Sozialdemokrat*. This paper, clandestinely circulated to thousands of loyal subscribers, was the lifeline of the German Socialist Workers' Party during the years of Chancellor Bismarck's antisocialist laws, under which scores of socialist publications had been silenced. Before such a critical post could be conferred, Bebel felt he needed the blessings of the movement's twin patron saints, of whose skepticism he was aware. So he decided "to take Bernstein with me to the lions' den. . . . I wanted to show them that he was not the terrible fellow that the two old ones believed him to be."[2]

After a voyage across the channel wracked by nausea, Bernstein and Bebel reached London and set out, *Baedeker* in hand, to find Engels' home. Since Bernstein had studied English he served as guide, but, as he noted with his usual levity, he soon "discover[ed] that the English did not pronounce their own language correctly. . . . I could not understand any of the policemen to whom I addressed my inquiries."[3] Eventually they found their destination, where "the general" held the younger man in thrall. Bernstein recalled:

> Engels' stormy temperament, which concealed such a truly noble character, and many good qualities, revealed itself to us as unreservedly as the joyous conception of life peculiar to the native of the Rhineland. "Drink, young man!"

And with these words, in the midst of a violent dispute, he kept on refilling my glass with Bordeaux, which he always had in the house.[4]

No doubt there was much wine, a standard feature of Engels' hospitality, but if there was a "violent dispute" it must have been one-sided. To be sure, Bernstein was opinionated, but he was diffident by nature and clearly awed by Engels. He had not even supposed that Bebel intended to include him in the meeting with the great man until Engels bade him enter. Whatever clash of views there was could not have been too sharp, since the audience satisfied Engels enough for him eventually to ask his guests to come along to see "the Moor," as he called Marx.

In the course of the next days, Bernstein and Bebel spent considerable time with Marx and Engels. The social highlight of their sojourn was a performance being given by Tussy, then twenty-four and an aspiring actress. It was a dramatic reading of *The Pied Piper of Hamelin,* presented as a benefit for the widow of a hero of the Paris Commune. What most impressed Bernstein, whose English was not strong enough to follow the recitation (although he loyally extolled Tussy's vivacity), was that first among the listed patrons of this event was Queen Victoria, who pledged ten pounds for the red martyr. One could scarcely imagine the kaiser choosing a similar object for his philanthropy. By the end of the visit, the "old ones" had warmed to Bernstein, and his appointment to the critical post was approved.

•   •   •

Unlike most other major figures in the history of socialism, Bernstein was actually raised in poverty. Born in 1850, he was the seventh of fifteen children, ten of whom survived. His father, Jacob, a nonpracticing Jew, supported this brood first as a plumber, then as a railway engineer. The family could afford little meat, and what there was went mostly to the breadwinner. Eduard was small and weak; yet in light of the Bernsteins' circumstances and the child's meager prospects, the doctors did not think it worth the investment to provide the boy with medicine.[5] Given the medical knowledge of the time, this may well have been what saved him.

In any event, Eduard thrived, and as he demonstrated his intellectual gifts, his parents sacrificed to provide him with a better education than they could offer other of their offspring. They sent him to *gymnasium,* or high school, until the age of sixteen. At that point they could do no more, and Ede, as he was

called, took an apprenticeship as a bank clerk. Thereafter he both supported
and educated himself.

As he began to develop ideas about the political world, young Bernstein and
some friends formed a drinking and discussion club which they called "Utopia,"
a name inspired more by the beer than by the subject matter. Together they
explored the various liberal, democratic and nationalist ideas that were in the
wind. Then, in 1872, a highly publicized political trial crystallized Bernstein's
diffuse liberal sentiments into socialist ideology. Bebel and Wilhelm Liebknecht,
the leaders of one of the two branches of German socialism, were put in the
dock for opposing the annexation of Alsace-Lorraine during the Franco-Prussian
War. Like Babeuf a few generations earlier, they used their witness box as a pul-
pit. The principled eloquence of these defendants impelled Bernstein to delve
into the writings of socialist thinkers, and soon he was a convert. He was so
gripped by Marx's account of the Paris Commune, *The Civil War in France,* that
he wrote and performed a drama based on it.[6]

By the time he was twenty-five, Bernstein was well enough known in the
socialist movement to be chosen a delegate to the historic 1875 Gotha conference, at which the two socialist groups—one more influenced by Lassalle, the
other by Marx and Engels—merged to form the Socialist Workers' Party, which
later became the Social Democratic Party of Germany (SPD). In the course of
his activities he met Karl Hochberg, a wealthy party benefactor and publisher
of socialist literature.

In 1878 the fragile Hochberg was ordered by his doctors to repair to
Switzerland for the beneficial quality of its climate. He asked Bernstein to come
along as his secretary and help him continue to publish the influential magazine
Die Zukunft from there. The straitened circumstances of Bernstein's upbringing
had allowed almost no opportunity for travel, so he leapt at the offer, scarcely
imagining that it would be nearly a quarter-century before he would be able
to return.

No sooner had Bernstein and Hochberg settled in Switzerland than
Chancellor Bismarck succeeded in pushing the "antisocialist laws" through the
Reichstag. Two recent attempts had been made on the life of the kaiser, one
of which succeeded in wounding him. Even though the socialists had been
responsible for neither attack, there ensued a conservative backlash, which
Bismarck was able to exploit. Socialist books, periodicals and clubs of all kinds
were banned, and various individual socialists were indicted for *lèse majesté* and
other crimes. One of those indicted was Bernstein, and a warrant was issued
for his arrest.

Hochberg agreed to finance a new publication to serve as the party's voice from exile. *Der Sozialdemokrat* was launched from Zurich, where he and Bernstein had resettled, in 1879. The tasks of writing and editing it and then smuggling it to thousands of subscribers in Germany made it the center of the party's activity in exile.

The Zurich exile circle working on Hochberg's various publications was enlivened the next year by the arrival of Karl Kautsky, a precocious twenty-five-year-old who had just completed his first book, on the theories of Malthus. Kautsky was the eldest child of a comfortable Prague family immersed in the theater business. He had, it seems, acquired some dramatic flair from his parents. His comrades nicknamed him "Baron" because of his penchant for elegant clothes. Bernstein recounts: "Kautsky, a nimble and extremely inventive person, delighted us, when our mood was more than usually extravagant, by irresistibly amusing imitations of acrobats, or as a fantastic dancer."[7]

Bernstein and Kautsky soon became the closest pair in a tight-knit group. As Kautsky described it, they "became so much of one heart and one soul that we were considered as a sort of red Orestes and Pylades."[8] During their frequent beer hall evenings, Bebel recalled, "Eduard Bernstein and Karl Kautsky—who were then the two inseparables—would sing a duet, in a manner which would break one's heart, or soften a stone."[9] But their collaboration was not all frivolity. Together they studied the works of Marx and Engels, often working at it from morning to night and stopping only for lunch and a walk.[10] Together they would compose correspondence to the masters, requesting clarification on this point or that. Together they translated into German *The Poverty of Philosophy*, which Marx had written in French since it was a diatribe against Proudhon aimed at undermining his influence with his countrymen. Together they blossomed as the party's outstanding Marxist thinkers.

Although they were a pair, they were not at first esteemed equally in the eyes of their heroes. After Bernstein's 1880 visit to London, he was well approved, as was evidenced by an incident a few months after he commenced his work as editor. Beset by feelings of inadequacy, which were an abiding feature of his psyche, Bernstein proposed to relinquish the post, but Marx and Engels would not hear of it. Engels wrote him: "We can see absolutely no reason for [you to leave *Der Sozialdemokrat*], and it would be *very agreeable* [emphasis in original] to us if you would reconsider. You have edited the paper skillfully from the very beginning, you have given it the right tone and developed the necessary wit."[11] This was an assessment from which Engels never deviated. Ten years later, when the end of the antisocialist laws meant that the mission of *Der*

Sozialdemokrat had been completed, he wrote for the final issue that Bernstein had made the publication into "unquestionably the best newspaper this party has ever had."[12]

Kautsky, in contrast, had a long struggle for acceptance, perhaps because he shared little of Bernstein's natural modesty. In a letter to one of his daughters, Marx wrote witheringly of his first meeting with Kautsky, whose mother had published some romantic novels with a socialist twist: "When this charmer first appeared at my place ... the first [words] which escaped me [were]: are you like your mother? Not in the very least, he assured me, and I silently congratulated his mother."[13]

For his part, Engels in 1881 allowed that although Kautsky was "an extremely good fellow," he was also "a born pedant and hair-splitter in whose hands the complicated questions do not become simple, but the simple complicated."[14] While these comments were not made to his face, Kautsky must have smarted at the attitude Engels adopted toward *Die Neue Zeit*. Founded as a monthly in 1883, just before Marx's death, it was the world's first journal of Marxist theory, and Kautsky was its editor. He sought contributions from Engels, who demurred, preferring to publish in *Der Sozialdemokrat,* even though as a topical newspaper it might have seemed less suited for his reflections. Eventually, in the hope of winning Engels' favor, Kautsky moved to London so that he might receive "private lessons" at the foot of the sage, who in time declared himself fully satisfied with the pupil's "progress."[15]

Thus by 1890, when the Reichstag refused to renew the antisocialist laws, Engels looked confidently to these two disciples to lead the SPD on the right course. Bismarck's effort to eradicate the party had backfired. The "Iron Chancellor" was himself brought down, in part by his differences with the new kaiser, Wilhelm II, over how to handle the socialists. They, on the other hand, were flourishing in the face of repression. The rigors of clandestine operation—distributing *Der Sozialdemokrat* and convening national congresses in secret locations abroad—had served to anneal and bond the party cadre. Moreover, socialist candidates had continued to stand for the Reichstag even while the party was banned from functioning as an organization. In 1881, the first election after the laws were enacted, their vote fell, but not catastrophically: twelve of them won seats. In 1890, after twelve years of repression, the party won thirty-five seats, and more important, it ran first in the popular vote, with 20 percent.

While the antisocialist laws lapsed in 1890, the indictment against Bernstein did not. Thus, as newspapers and periodicals began to roll off the party presses within Germany once again, Bernstein was stranded in London, where he had lived since 1888 when pressure from the German government had induced the Swiss authorities to evict him. The day of *Der Sozialdemokrat,* designed as an exile publication, was done. Bernstein supported himself by contributing from afar to the revived socialist press back home and writing some books on historical subjects. It was at this time that Engels asked him to take over the preparation of volume four of *Capital.* However, Bernstein was aware that his selection for this prestigious task was wounding to Kautsky. Of the two, Bernstein's reputation was for journalism, while Kautsky's was for theory. So, exhibiting his characteristic largeness of spirit, Bernstein deferred to his friend.[16]

Kautsky's pride suffered still another blow when Engels left his literary estate in Bernstein's hands. Within a few years of Engels' death, however, Tussy Marx expressed the fear that Bernstein had begun to deviate from Marxist doctrine, a development for which she blamed the Fabian Society.

This was a club of eminent intellectuals who were socialists but not Marxists, and it was unrivaled in its influence in the world of British letters. Bernstein had indeed grown friendly with such Fabians as George Bernard Shaw and Sidney and Beatrice Webb, and he was in fact entertaining heterodox thoughts. But what was changing him was not so much the Fabians as England itself, beginning with the queen's patronage of Tussy's long-ago benefit performance. How, exactly, could orthodox Marxism, in which all behavior is said to flow from economic self-interest, account for Her Majesty's solicitude for the veterans of the Paris Commune?

The problem did not end with a single performance of *The Pied Piper.* The longer he lived in England, the harder Bernstein found it to align his observations of its open political process and cooperative relations between classes with the Marxist map. Similar questions were beginning to present themselves even in illiberal Germany. The kaiser was proposing enhancements of the social insurance initiated by Bismarck. To be sure, this embryonic German welfare state had been created in order to steal the thunder of the socialists, but by now it was unmistakably clear that this ulterior motive had been disappointed, as the socialists continued to gain at the polls. Nonetheless, Wilhelm concerned himself with the well-being of his subjects, sometimes supporting workers in disputes with employers.

For a time Bernstein managed to wrestle his empirical observations into the ill-defined contours of Marxian theory. But then he tired of the labor. In a letter to Bebel in 1898, he explained:

Up to two years ago I tried, by stretching Marxist teachings, to bring them
into accord with practical realities. Characteristically, or if you wish under-
standably, I fully realized the impossibility of such tactics when I gave a lecture at the Fabian Society on the subject, "What Marx really taught," about a
year and a half ago. I still have the manuscript of that talk; it is a frightening
example of a well-meaning rescue attempt. I wanted to save Marx; I wanted to
show that he had predicted everything that had and had not happened. When
I got through with my "artistic performance," when I read my lecture over,
the thought flashed through my head: You are doing Marx an injustice, what
you are spouting about is not Marx. . . . I said to myself—this cannot go on.
It is idle to try to reconcile the irreconcilable. What is necessary is to become
clear just where Marx is right and where he is wrong.[17]

Toward this end, Bernstein began in 1896 to publish a series of articles in
Die Neue Zeit titled "Problems of Socialism" which scrutinized aspects of the
Marxist canon that he had come to doubt. He pointed out that the growth
of trade unions and democracy had vitiated the raw power of capitalists and
had ameliorated capitalism. It no longer made sense, he said, to draw "a heavy
line . . . between capitalist society on the one side and socialist society on the
other," nor to assume "an abrupt leap" from one to the other. Moreover, to
believe that socialism would somehow accord a solution to all problems was
to "assume . . . miracles."[18] In place of the stirring black and white images
which had been the movement's inspiration, Bernstein painted social issues in
tones of gray. His approach was epitomized in this challenging formulation:
"I have extraordinarily little interest or taste for what is generally called the
'final goal of Socialism.' This aim, whatever it be, is nothing to me, *the movement everything*."[19]

Some critics hastened to point out the obvious contradiction: how can
movement be meaningful without an endpoint toward which it is aiming? This
rejoinder, however, was arid. What Bernstein was suggesting was that it was
possible to fight for the well-being of workers—more political and social legislation, better pay and working conditions—without envisioning a new society.
The real fault with his argument was that by rejecting teleology, Bernstein's
approach would rob socialism of the religious mystique in which Marxism
had clothed it. No longer would it offer the promise of a "new age . . . which
establishes the 'kingdom of God' on earth and which will make all people into
humans!" as a young, enthusiastic Kautsky had put it.[20]

A departure this fundamental by so key a disciple tore at the heart-strings of the Marxist inner circle. Tussy Marx's last letter to Kautsky, two weeks before taking her own life, begged him to bring Bernstein back into the fold. "Ede's present unhappy sceptical pessimism . . . hurts me more than I can say," she wrote. "Ede is so dear a friend that it is horrible to see things as they are just now." Only Kautsky's intervention could "make Ede our own Ede again."[21]

In truth, there was nothing Kautsky could do to dissuade Bernstein of opinions that had incubated in his thoughts over several years. He had argued with him by letter, but to no avail. The question, he knew, was not how to resurrect the old Ede but how to cope with the new one. As the party's top theoretician, he was being pressed to attack Bernstein, yet the grassroots leaders of the party's growing electoral base and affiliated trade unions were sympathetic to Bernstein's incremental approach. Kautsky wanted to combat Bernstein's apostasy without antagonizing them.

However, the party's young militants shared no such scruples. Two in particular sprang to the attack: Israel Lazarevich Helphand (or Gelfand), who called himself "Parvus," and Rosa Luxemburg. Both had immigrated to Germany from the east only a few years before. Both came from economically privileged Jewish families. Both had Ph.D.s and were eager to make their mark in the German socialist party. And both saw at once that Bernstein's deviation presented the opportunity to do so.

It was Parvus who struck first. Raised in the cosmopolitan port city of Odessa, he was a man of flamboyant gestures and opinions and of out-sized appetites and physical stature. (Kautsky's children nicknamed him "Dr. Elephant.") Having moved to Germany in 1891, he already had made a reputation as a radical journalist. He aspired to be a theoretician, and later he did lay the basis for the "theory of permanent revolution" that Trotsky, with whom he was to collaborate in 1905, made famous. But it was as a Machiavellian servant of the German general staff, rather than as a theoretician, that he was to make his main contribution to socialist history, as we will see in the next chapter.

In the span of two months in early 1898, Parvus penned no fewer than seventeen articles castigating Bernstein. He accused Bernstein of rejecting "*all the scientific foundations of current party tactics*," namely "its intention to seize *political power* by as swift a process as possible in order to use this power—the 'dictatorship of the proletariat'—to expropriate the capitalists and [create] a socialist society."[22]

By summer, Parvus' jeremiads against Bernstein were overshadowed by those of Luxemburg. She was the inverse of Parvus: a truly talented theoretician and a disastrous operator, who ironically became known as the theorist of direct action. Her works became an enduring part of the socialist library, but she got herself martyred in a short-lived rebellion before she turned fifty.

Though of Jewish background, Luxemburg's parents "thought and spoke Polish," says her biographer.[23] Rosa, a brilliant, unsocial, homely girl who acquired a limp at age thirteen from a hip ailment, was at ease neither with her Polishness nor with her Jewishness. The leading issue of Polish politics was national independence, and for most Polish socialists of the late 1800s the socialist cause was entwined with the national. But not for Rosa Luxemburg. She became the leader of a small faction that rejected nationalism on the orthodox Marxist grounds that the working man has no country.

This conviction led her to Germany to be on the front line of the international socialist revolution. The antisocialist laws had been lifted, but German officials were not opening their arms to itinerant Jewish radicals. In order to secure residency, Luxemburg contrived a marriage to the son of a German female comrade with whom she was close. Its only consummation was her residency permit. This in hand, she searched for lodgings in Berlin, where she intended to live with her boyfriend and chief political collaborator, Leo Jogiches. He, too, was a Polish Jewish socialist who found meaning only in the last of these three identities. He was from a family even wealthier than hers, and they lived largely off remittances from the two sets of parents.

Luxemburg set out to capture the limelight in her newly adopted party by leaping into the fray against Bernstein. She composed a series of five articles which later were expanded into a Marxist classic, *Reform or Revolution?* Taking aim at Bernstein's claim that unions and democracy would ameliorate capitalism, she said that, on the contrary, the only reason why socialists should participate in elections or collective bargaining is that "through political and trade union activity ... the proletariat is brought to realise that such activity cannot possibly bring about a fundamental improvement in their situation and that it is therefore imperative that they should, once and for all, take over the means of political power ... by means of a social revolution."[24]

Bernstein's position, she wrote, amounted to "rejection of the class standpoint."[25] This was brassy, not to say ridiculous, coming from a twenty-seven-year-old child of privilege who had never supported herself, perhaps never held a job. But while her worldly experience was limited, she had a mind for abstraction. Better than any of the other disputants, including Bernstein himself, she recognized how fundamentally his emendations undermined the entire scaffolding of Marxism. If capitalism was susceptible to amelioration, then it could not be expected to suffer the catastrophic breakdown that would produce a socialist revolution. In that case, "socialism ceases to be a historical necessity and becomes anything you please.... [It] becomes utopian."[26] In others words, socialism would revert to Owen's whimsy rather than Marx's law.

As she hoped, Luxemburg's incisive polemic propelled her into the center of the debate. And she won election as a delegate to the party congress held 1898 in Stuttgart, where a spirited exchange was anticipated on the "Bernstein question."

Bernstein, however, could not be there; he was stuck in exile in London. All he could do was defend himself in a brief letter, which was duly read aloud by Bebel so that it might be attacked. Luxemburg demanded Bernstein's expulsion from the party, but the party leadership opposed this. They knew that Bernstein's position found receptive ears among the electoral and labor officials, that is, among those closest to the party's mass base. In private correspondence Kautsky asked Bernstein to resign from the party, but he did not want the repercussions of an expulsion.[27] Nor did he want to leave the argument against Bernstein to the radicals. Thus Kautsky took the floor at Stuttgart, "with great reluctance," for his first major public attack on his old companion.

Kautsky argued that while Bernstein's notion of a piecemeal, democratic path to socialism might be possible for England, German conditions allowed no alternative to a violent revolution. "A hard battle lies before us," he said, "and what we chiefly need for this battle is faith in ourselves, confidence of victory... confidence... which says... the victory must be ours in the end." If Bernstein was right that "it is capitalism, not socialism which is establishing itself... we shall never reach our goal." But Bernstein was wrong, he concluded, "and we shall win." The minutes show that this peroration was greeted with "tumultuous applause and ovation."[28] In closing the gathering, Liebknecht, the party's senior leader, declared that "the entire... conference gave [Kautsky] their jubilant support.... [W]e have in essence reached agreement."[29]

This was wishful thinking. Kautsky's oratory was more stirring than persuasive, and all sides girded for a renewal of the debate at the next congress, scheduled for Hanover a year later. In anticipation, Kautsky prevailed upon Bernstein to organize his ideas into a book so that party members could more readily confront them. Thus in 1899 was published the short volume which in English translation was titled *Evolutionary Socialism*.

The starting point of Bernstein's presentation of what came to be called "revisionism" was empirical. More than fifty years had passed since Marx and Engels formulated their sociological forecast that the rich would become fewer, the poor poorer and the middle classes negligible. Bernstein observed that something nearly opposite had occurred: the rich were more numerous, as were the middle classes, and the poor were better off. He focused on the prediction that capital would become ever more concentrated, apparently because data on this was easy to come by. He was able to show that the number of small businesses was growing and so was the number of well-off people. Indeed, as a result of research in economic history, it is now estimated that per capita income in Germany and England, adjusted for inflation, had roughly doubled between the publication of *Communist Manifesto* in 1848 and of *Evolutionary Socialism* in 1899.[30] Such statistics were not available to Bernstein, but the practical evidence of changes in standard of living were observable all around. As Peter Gay has summarized it:

> All departments of life showed improvements. People ate and dressed better. . . . Many items, once considered luxuries, now were being mass produced. Furniture, books, pictures, carpets, cigarets, pianos, watches, neckties, and roller skates entered general circulation. Similarly, entertainment became more universally accessible. . . . Annual consumption of goods increased markedly: Consumption of sugar rose from 12 pounds per person in 1870 to 34 pounds in 1907; that of beer from 78 liters in 1872 to 123 liters in 1900. In 1873, average annual consumption of meat was about 59 pounds per person. That had gone up to 105 pounds in 1912.[31]

The implications for Marxian theory were profound. The progressive reduction of society to just two classes, one small and immensely rich and the other vast and utterly impoverished, was to form the crucible of social transformation. Without that process, as Luxemburg had pointed out, there was no reason to expect a socialist revolution. Socialism was still possible, but it would have to be brought about by human will, not by impersonal historical forces, and therefore it would have to be justified because it was desirable, not because it was inevitable. Recognizing this, Bernstein proposed to detach the socialist project from its link with Hegel, the apostle of historical determinism, and reattach it to Kant, the theoretician of ethics. As he punned in English, he was advancing "Kant against cant."

By repeatedly citing Marx or Engels, Bernstein demonstrated that he was far from wishing to reject their teachings wholesale. But he wanted to treat their works like those of any other writer, rather than as scripture. He challenged many specific points, but the essence of his argument was that socialism must rest on empiricism and on an extrinsic moral standard. He did not shrink from pronouncing this ambivalent judgment on Marx: "[his] work aims at being a scientific inquiry and also at proving a theory laid down long before. . . . [T]his great scientific spirit was, in the end, a slave to a doctrine."[32]

At the Hanover conference in 1899, the main agenda item was "the Bernstein question." August Bebel opened the conference with a polemical discourse on the subject that lasted more than six hours, which did not stop him later from excoriating Bernstein, still marooned in London, for being "long-winded." Bebel also charged him with indulging in "Talmudic sophistries," which was taken as a dig at Bernstein's Jewishness. After three days of debate—for Bernstein had his defenders among the labor and electoral leaders—Bernstein's views were officially repudiated by a vote of 216 to 21.[33]

The attacks impelled Bernstein to new efforts to persuade German authorities to lift his indictment so he could return to the country and participate in his own political defense. In 1901, some eleven years after the expiration of the antisocialist laws, the state relented. That it took this long was a tribute to the unusual tenacity with which Bernstein had defied those laws, establishing himself in the eyes of the monarchy as one of its most dangerous opponents. Hard upon his return, his admirers among the party's electoral leaders asked him to stand for the Reichstag. Although there is no evidence that he had ever contemplated such a career, he agreed, and proved to be a popular politician. He won his first race with a vote that exceeded the combined total of all his competitors and then was reelected continually from 1902 until 1928, when at age seventy-eight he retired to "make room for youth."

· · ·

The debate over Bernstein's revisionism spilled over frontiers. Socialists saw themselves as part of a worldwide movement, in which Germany, home to the largest, most powerful party in the International, was the cockpit. Some foreign socialists, like Parvus and Luxemburg, migrated to Germany to be in the forefront of the class struggle. Others followed developments in the SPD from afar as if they were part of it. Thus, among the first socialists to challenge Bernstein were the British Marxist Ernest Belfort Bax and the Russian Georgi Plekhanov.

Soon, H. M. Hyndman in England, Jean Jaurès in France, Anton Pannekoek in Holland and Max Adler in Austria jumped into the fray.

The most fateful contribution to the debate was slower in coming. Thousands of miles away, in the small Siberian town of Shushenskoye, just north of Mongolia, a twenty-nine-year-old exile awaited the arrival of Bernstein's newly published *Evolutionary Socialism* in a state of agitation. Lenin, as he called himself, had followed Bernstein's articles and the debates at the Stuttgart conference as best he could across a span of six time zones.

He was particularly incensed over the inspiration that the revisionists' arguments had given to Ekaterina Kuskova, a young Russian socialist who published a pamphlet espousing a turn away from revolution toward aiding Russian workers in the fight for better wages and conditions. This obscure, untitled pamphlet had been sent to Lenin by his sister, Anna, whose frequent packages helped keep him *au courant* of radical debate. Lenin not only composed a scathing rebuttal, he convened a meeting of seventeen other exiles from nearby towns, including one carried in on his deathbed, so that he might read it aloud for their concurrence.[34]

The day after *Evolutionary Socialism* arrived, Lenin wrote to his mother that "Nadya [his wife] and I started reading Bernstein's book immediately. . . . [I]t is . . . unbounded opportunism . . . and cowardly opportunism at that."[35] When, next, they received Kautsky's refutation, a pamphlet titled *Bernstein and the Social Democratic Program: An Anti-Critique,* the couple dropped everything and spent two tireless weeks translating it into Russian. This, however, did not begin to exhaust Lenin's spleen. Months later, upon completion of his years of exile, he was greeted at the Moscow train station by his younger brother, Dmitri, who recalled that almost the first words out of Lenin's mouth were that "a decisive and relentless struggle [against Bernstein] had now become imperative."[36]

He was to wage this struggle with a ferocity that never wavered. "There is only one answer to revisionism: smash its face in!"[37] he told a follower several years later. While face-smashing expressed the spirit of Lenin's reaction, it was not the sum of it. In the year or so after reading Bernstein's book, Lenin formulated an answer that was more cogent than those of Kautsky, Luxemburg and the rest, one that was to change forever the face of socialism. Most workers might not be growing poorer or more ready to overthrow the system, but the "proletarian revolution" did not need to be carried out by proletarians; it could be done for them!

As the package from his sister, the letter to his mother and the reception by his brother suggest, "Lenin" came from a close family, the Ulyanovs. Vladimir, as he was christened, was born in 1870, the third of seven children, six of whom survived infancy. There is debate among biographers about the family's ethnicity. Some say, and others deny, that Lenin's mother, Maria, was half Jewish. Others argue about whether his father, Ilya, was Great Russian or Asiatic.

Information about their occupational backgrounds is much clearer. Maria's father had been an eccentric but successful physician who managed to retire young to an estate he had purchased to live the life of the gentry. Ilya, the son of a serf who had bought his freedom and become a tailor, had, with the help of scholarships, reached the level of candidate in mathematics, comparable to a master's degree. He entered the field of education and rose rapidly until he was appointed director of schools for the province of Simbirsk. This position carried the rank that is usually translated into the indigestible English phrase "actual state councilor." Whatever that may mean, on the table of ranks it was equivalent to a major general, and it conferred a heritable title of nobility.

Ilya and Maria settled in the province's capital, also called Simbirsk (later renamed Ulyanovsk), a sleepy town of thirty thousand on the banks of the Volga, where European and Asian Russia meet. After living for a while in more modest quarters, the Ulyanovs moved into a large, comfortable house with a grand piano in the living room and a garden, orchard and field for playing cro-quet out back. Each of the three oldest children had his or her own bedroom. There appear to have been three or four servants.[38] Summers were spent far-ther up the Volga at Kokushkino, Maria's father's thousand-acre estate. He had bequeathed it in shares to his five daughters, who came there often with their families. It offered many entertainments, including a billiard room, some boats and much natural beauty. Lenin became a strong swimmer, an expert hunter of mushrooms and, according to his one-time companion Valentinov, a skilled hand with a pool cue.

Lenin was bright, a top student, but at times unpleasant and usually friend-less. Most biographers offer the same paltry harvest of anecdotes: upon receiv-ing a toy horse, young Vladimir twisted off each of its legs; he tormented his younger siblings with frightening verses; he ordered his cereal served however Sasha, his admired older brother, took his. In all, he seems to have been a boring child who led a boring, pampered life.

Change came in 1886 when Vladimir was fifteen. His father died suddenly of a cerebral hemorrhage. From her own resources and the generous widow's pension to which Ilya's position entitled her, Maria was able to sustain the fam-ily financially. But a year later it was to suffer a still more grievous blow. Maria received word that Anna and Alexander (Sasha), the two oldest children, were being held in St. Petersburg, where they attended university, on charges of plotting to assassinate the tsar.

Maria rushed to St. Petersburg, incredulous at the charges. The ethos of the household that she and Ilya had made was culturally enlightened but reverent toward God and the tsar. Accordingly, it turned out that the police had nothing on Anna, who had been arrested merely because she was found in Sasha's room when they raided it, and Maria was able to win her release. As for Sasha, however, he had indeed been lured, like so many Russian students, by the mystique of revolution.

A decade earlier, in the 1870s, young radicals, fired with populist ideology, had "gone to the people," taking to the countryside to rouse the peasantry. But often the peasants would listen while drinking vodka bought by their student enlighteners, then tie them up and deliver them to the cops. The revolutionary generation of the 1880s turned to a top-down strategy: regicide. In 1881, after numerous failed attempts, a youthful cabal styling itself the "Executive Committee" of *Norodnaya Volya,* or "People's Will," succeeded in blowing up Alexander II as he rode through the capital. This tsar, who had liberated the serfs, abolished corporal punishment and initiated some other reforms, was succeeded by his son, Alexander III, who decided at once that a firmer hand was called for. Although the Executive Committee was entirely eradicated, soon there were others ready to follow in its footsteps, finding all the more justification in the harsh policies of the new ruler.

The radical faction that recruited Sasha Ulyanov believed that it had made a valuable catch. As a biology major he knew his way around laboratories, so they made him their bomb-maker. But this band of aspiring assassins could not shoot straight. Their plot was exposed when three of their number were picked up after having been observed loitering on the streets near the palace several days in succession. One of them, Osipanov, brandished his revolver but could not get it to fire. In the police station, not yet having been frisked, he pulled a bomb from beneath his coat and tossed it at his warders, but it clattered to the ground, failing to detonate.

Interrogation soon led to the arrest of Sasha and other accomplices and co-conspirators who had not been present at the opéra bouffe attempt at revolutionary violence. Sasha exhibited the strength of character that his mother knew, but in a way that brought her little joy. In an effort to shield his comrades, he insisted on taking as much responsibility on his own shoulders as he could—indeed more, as the prosecutor sardonically noted, than the facts warranted. Had he asked for mercy, the tsar, who followed the case in detail and read and annotated an appeal Maria addressed to him, would have granted it. But Sasha likened himself to a party to a duel who had fired first and missed. What kind of man would he be if he now begged his adversary not to shoot back? Poor Maria understood only that her son was determined to die. And so he did, on the gallows, along with four others, on May 20, 1887.

The effect on Vladimir, who had just turned seventeen, was searing. Thirty years later, on the eve of taking power, he began a self-description with these lines: "My name is Vladimir Ilyich Ulyanov. I was born in Simbirsk April 10, 1870. In the spring of 1887, my older brother Alexander was sentenced to death by Alexander III for an attempt... on his life."[39]

Being the younger brother of a would-be regicide clouded Vladimir's prospects for admission to university, but the way was smoothed by Fyodor Kerensky, the director of Vladimir's *gymnasium* and also the family guardian named in Ilya's will. Kerensky awarded him the school's gold medal for being the best in his class in "ability, development and conduct," a medal that Sasha had also won and later pawned in St. Petersburg to purchase explosives. As if out of the script of some Greek drama, Fyodor's son, Alexander Kerensky, was to become the democratic prime minister driven from power by Lenin in 1917. For now, Fyodor's warm recommendation helped persuade Kazan University to take in young Vladimir.

He had not been there long before he participated in a demonstration. By most accounts his was a minor role, but in view of his late brother's record, he was immediately expelled. Maria persuaded the authorities to limit his punishment to banishment to the family estate in Kukoshkino, where elder sister, Anna, was already in enforced residence in consequence of her arrest at the time of the failed attempt on Alexander III. In the ensuing period of enforced idleness, Vladimir began to study the books Sasha had left behind, including various revolutionary classics. His favorite was a novel by Nikolai Chernyshevsky, titled *What Is to Be Done?* Widely acknowledged to be devoid of literary merit ("by any reckoning, one of the most appallingly bad novels ever published... implausible, melodramatic and mawkishly sentimental," as the historian Tibor Szamuely put it),[40] it nonetheless electrified a generation of Russian intellectuals.

Its appeal was not as a work of art, but as a tract. Chernyshevsky, born in 1828, had been influenced by the ideas of Owen, Fourier, Saint Simon and other utopian socialists. His novel depicted, as their writings often had done, a blissful future of effortless abundance and egalitarian harmony. What it added that was new was a description of how this utopia would be reached—or, more precisely, who would bring it to realization. The heroes of *What Is to Be Done?* were a class of "New Men." This was an unmistakable euphemism for "revolutionaries," coined, as were many code words of the time, to dodge the censor. The New Men are "courageous, unwavering, unyielding" and utterly devoted to the "common cause." Their destiny is to rescue society: "In a few years, in a very few years they will be implored: 'Save us!'—and whatever they say will be obeyed by all."

Young Vladimir Ulyanov, nursing the hurt of his brother's execution and his own expulsion, read this book again and again. He said of Chernyshevsky, "My brother . . . was captivated by him, and so was I. *He completely transformed my outlook.*"[41]

Since the authorities were deaf to appeals to readmit Vladimir to university or to allow him to study abroad, the indefatigable Maria created other opportunities for him. When he was released from enforced residence in Kokushkino, she purchased an estate in Alakayeva in the hope that Vladimir would settle down to the life of a gentleman farmer, much as her father had done. But he had neither taste nor aptitude for it. (He later told his wife that relations with the peasants who worked his land had quickly grown "abnormal.") So Maria set out again on the thousand-mile journey to St. Petersburg. This time her destination was the ministry of education, where she succeeded in winning permission for Vladimir to take his law exams. Even though he had not done the coursework, he scored first in his cohort.

•   •   •

After getting his degree, Vladimir practiced almost no law and continued to depend on Maria for financial support. He held down a junior position in a firm mostly as a cover for the political activities that had by now, at age twenty-three, become the sole focus of his life.

Before long he was recognized as "first among equals" of the growing coterie of St. Petersburg socialists. The failure of "going to the people" in the 1870s and of the tactic of regicide in the 1880s gave rise to a growing interest in Marxism among Russia's radical intellectuals, despite the country's lack of industrialization. The interest was requited because Marx and Engels were flattered by the avid attention to their writings. Marx noted in 1880 that *"Das Kapital* is more read and appreciated [in Russia] than anywhere else."[42] Marx and Engels both

corresponded respectfully with Vera Zasulich, a notorious young revolutionary who had turned to Marxism. She had achieved celebrity by shooting the
governor of St. Petersburg at point-blank range, then winning acquittal from a
jury although she did not deny the deed. In this correspondence, the two sages
encouraged the Russians in their hope that the socialist revolution might reach
them via some kind of shortcut through the Marxian "stages of history."

The Russian Marxists formed a group called the "St. Petersburg Union of
Struggle for the Liberation of the Working Class." Lenin, like several others,
found a worker to whom he could read *Capital*. Although the tutee grumbled
that he could read himself, he was grateful for the explications—as anyone
might be. Then, Lenin's closest friend and comrade, Julius Tsederbaum, hit
upon a better tactic: "agitation." Tsederbaum, the son of wealthy Russified Jews,
called himself Martov. His simple idea was that the Marxists should support the
workers in efforts to unionize and to ameliorate their conditions. For Lenin,
this entailed a reversal of attitude. Two years earlier, he had opposed efforts at
famine relief by other progressives on the grounds that this would only rescue
the regime from popular wrath. But Lenin now accepted Martov's point that by
siding with the workers in small battles, they could win them to a larger cause.

Soon, powerful strikes shook St. Petersburg. Although it is not clear how
much the highborn agitators contributed to this development, the police undertook a sweep of the Marxists, and in 1895 Lenin and Martov were arrested.
Lenin was held in prison for more than a year until being sentenced to three
years of internal exile. In legend, the phrase "sent to Siberia" has an ominous
ring; but the conditions were humane in "those sentimental tsarist times" (as the
widow of an early Bolshevik would say to a fellow camp inmate decades later)[43]
in comparison with what they became once Lenin himself came to power.

In deference to appeals from the indefatigable Maria, Lenin was assigned to
the relatively mild, southern region of Minusinsk. He was released from prison
without guard and ordered to make his own way to Krasnoyarsk, the nearest
stop on the Trans-Siberian Railway. First, he was given three days free in St.
Petersburg to put his affairs in order, and when he asked for a few extra days
plus a stop for a family visit in Moscow, the request was granted. He passed
a restful month or two in Krasnoyarsk, enjoying the famous private library
of a local merchant before being directed to settle in Shushenskoye. There he
rented quarters and was free to come and go as he wished, although the local
constable was supposed to keep an eye on him. He traveled about for holidays
and meetings with other radicals in nearby towns, and he often went hunting

after his mother reluctantly complied with his request to send him a gun. He also received and dispatched quantities of socialist literature, including an 1897 essay, "The Tasks of the Russian Social Democrats," the first of his works to be signed "Lenin."

The government provided him with a monthly stipend of eight rubles, sufficient to cover his rent and buy food. Naturally, his mother supplemented this, so when he was joined by his partner, Nadezhda (Nadya) Krupskaya, who was also of the nobility and unused to doing her own housework, they were able to employ a peasant girl as a servant.

Krupskaya and Lenin had met in St. Petersburg socialist circles, and they had become companions, although they had no plans to marry formally. After Lenin's banishment, she, too, was arrested and sentenced to a similar term of exile in the city of Ufa in the Urals. She appealed to be allowed to spend her exile together with him in Shushenskoye and to have her term shortened so that it might end at the same time as his. The authorities refused the latter request, but granted the former—on the condition that the two wed. This they agreed to do, even though the service had to be performed in church, a fact that scholar Adam Ulam says Soviet historians treated as the worst skeleton in Lenin's closet. Krupskaya was accompanied to Shushenskoye by her mother, who came along to look after the young couple. It was not uncommon for the mothers of young exiles to join their sons in Siberia to see to the cooking and cleaning. One can well imagine Maria Ulyanova doing as much were she not held down by the requirements of fending for her younger offspring, who by this time were following their older brothers' footsteps and beginning to have run-ins with the law.

The arrest of the St. Petersburg Marxists did not discredit the tactic of agitation; on the contrary, it was a badge of success. But agitation proved to be a two-edged sword. While it afforded the socialists, who were almost all from the middle class or higher, greater contact with the workers and thus greater opportunity to persuade them that their plight required a revolutionary solution, the influence flowed both ways. As the workers won advances, the path of piecemeal reform grew more attractive to them, and this inference rubbed off on some of the socialists. Thus there arose within the socialist movement a trend called "economism," which attached an intrinsic value to workplace struggles and relegated revolution to the back burner. This evoked Lenin's disdain. "The struggle for reforms is but a means of marshalling the forces of the proletariat for the struggle for a final revolutionary overthrow," he inveighed.[44]

Kuskova, author of the pamphlet Lenin received in Shushenskoye, was a minor figure among the economists, but they were not a minor force within Russian socialism. One of their spokesmen, for example, was Peter Struve, author of the program adopted at the first attempt to form a nationwide socialist party. In Lenin's view, Bernstein's writing undergirded them with all the authority of his status as Engels' disciple and as a leader of the most advanced socialist party. Until he read Kuskova's pamphlet, Lenin's term of exile had been a period of calm and contentment, but now, according to Krupskaya, he lost his appetite and developed insomnia. Apparently he was upset about the rise of economism and revisionism, seeing in them a direct threat to what he regarded as "the decisive aspect of Marxism, namely, its revolutionary dialectic."[45]

This understanding of Marxism separated Lenin not only from Bernstein but also from many other followers of Marx who found the materialist interpretation of history or the centrality of class struggle or the destiny of the proletariat to be more important aspects of his teaching. But Lenin believed, as he wrote in his private notes, that "not a single Marxist has understood Marx!"[46] He, Lenin, was the first to do so, with his single-minded emphasis on revolution. Had not the young Marx and Engels declared: "Communists everywhere support every revolutionary movement against the existing social and political order of things"? Had not the mature Marx waxed rapturous over the Paris Commune ("history has no example of similar greatness") even though the rebels were neither Marxists nor mostly workers? In this attitude, despite discrepancies in doctrine, "Lenin was the spiritual reincarnation of Marx," as Jacques Barzun trenchantly observed. For neither Lenin nor Marx was the revolution the answer to the question: what can be done for the proletariat? Rather the proletariat was the answer to the question: what can be done for the revolution?[47]

Thus it is easy to understand why the nonrevolutionary policies of the revisionists and economists infuriated Lenin, but it is harder to explain why he seemed to grow so worried. After all, a great many things infuriated him, and he often seemed to revel in his rages. Perhaps what robbed him of his sleep was not anger at Bernstein's errors, but fear that Bernstein might be right. The criticism of Bernstein in Germany and from abroad had been impassioned and voluminous but hardly dispositive. Plekhanov, an aristocrat with a Ph.D., sniffed that Bernstein lacked formal training in philosophy. Bebel, who had gone to considerable lengths to endear Bernstein to Marx and Engels, now allowed that he had never regarded him as a first-rate intellect. Other attacks, like those of

Parvus, Luxemburg and Kautsky, boiled down to the circular argument that
Bernstein could not be right because if he was, then the movement had been
mistaken in some of its cherished beliefs.

None of these adversaries had come up with a compelling rejoinder to
Bernstein's essential empirical point that the proletariat was not evolving in the
direction that Marx and Engels predicted. His case was implicitly strengthened
by the fact that his strongest defenders were in fact labor leaders and others
closest to the SPD's working-class constituency. Kautsky himself had observed
that the natural tendency of the workers was nonrevolutionary, although he did
not acknowledge how much this contradicted the doctrine of Marx and Engels.
"The class condition of the proletariat produces socialist *inclinations,* but not
socialist knowledge," he wrote.[48] That deficit had to be compensated through
the tutelage of educated, middle-class socialists. Absent such intervention, the
workers tend to "come to an English conception of things which only concerns
itself with the tangible, the obvious, the practical." Such a mentality had already
grown up in the German trade unions. "We must do everything we can to root
it out," he said, "because it is the grave of revolutionary thinking."

Lenin built on Kautsky's sense of crisis in formulating his own solution
to the issues raised by revisionism. In the months after his release from exile,
he composed an article titled "The Urgent Tasks of Our Movement." In it he
averred that "isolated from Social-Democracy, the working class movement
becomes petty and inevitably becomes bourgeois." This problem could not
be solved by socialists' lending support to the workers' economic struggles.
Instead, a revolutionary party had to be built. Until recently, socialist circles in
Russia had been mostly local. The first effort to convene a national party had
taken place in 1898 when a congress was convened in Minsk (where Struve's
program was adopted). According to different sources, the total number of
attendees was either nine or ten, and these were all arrested soon after, apparently because at least one was a police spy. A stronger, more centralized, more
secretive party was required, wrote Lenin, consisting of "people who will
devote the whole of their lives, not only their spare evenings, to the revolution." These would be the "political leaders," the "prominent representatives"
of the proletariat.

The vehicle for building this party would be a newspaper. According to
Adam Ulam, Lenin's model was the *Bell,* the revolutionary periodical published
from exile by Alexander Herzen, which became the most influential publication in Russia during the late 1850s and 1860s.[49] Lenin may have had Herzen

in mind, but he undoubtedly also had absorbed some lessons from the German party, which managed to grow stronger in the face of repressive antisocialist laws. One source of its success was Bernstein's newspaper, *Der Sozialdemokrat,* which the comrades worked hard to distribute inside Germany. This very activity was beneficial to the party, quite apart from the impact of the paper's content, because it served to develop cadre. Smuggling each issue into the country and then circulating it clandestinely; dodging the authorities to arrange subscriptions or dispatches or discussions about articles—these were satisfying, even thrilling tasks. Party militants thrived on them.

In order to launch his paper, Lenin left Russia in 1900 for Geneva, where many other Russian exiles had settled. He named the paper *Iskra* or Spark, from the verse of one of the Decembrists, the Russian revolutionaries of the 1820s: "Out of the spark will come a conflagration." Lenin aimed to establish *Iskra* as a central organ which would unite scattered revolutionaries into a tight party. To do this he needed cooperation from others, above all Plekhanov, the granddaddy of Russian Marxism. After bitter haggling, the two agreed to an editorial board of six: Lenin and two of his close comrades, Martov and Alexander Potresov; and Plekhanov and his two chief collaborators, Vera Zasulich and Pavel Axelrod. The factional divide here was defined not by ideology but by generation. In reality, it boiled down to a personal tug-of-war between Lenin and Plekhanov for dominance. For the moment Plekhanov was given the decisive vote on the board, but the all-important task of organizing the distribution of the paper was left in Lenin's hands. His wife, Krupskaya, became the secretary of *Iskra* as soon as she finished her term of exile and joined him in Munich, where it was initially published. (Later it moved to London, then Geneva.)

It was in the first issue of *Iskra,* appearing in December 1900, that Lenin printed his essay "Urgent Tasks." Then he set to work on elaborating these ideas into a book, perhaps his most famous. Its title deliberately echoed Chernyshevsky: *What Is to Be Done?* Again invoking Kautsky, Lenin asserted more forcefully than before the uselessness of the proletariat left to its own devices. "The history of all countries shows that the working class, exclusively by its own effort, is able to develop only trade union consciousness." Thus "class political consciousness can be brought to the workers only from without." After all, he pointed out, instancing Marx and Engels, "The theory of socialism . . . grew out of the philosophic, historical, and economic theories elaborated by educated representatives of the propertied classes, by intellectuals." Rather than trying to make themselves one with the people, the socialists should make themselves their champions: "the Social-Democrat's ideal should not be the trade union secretary, but the tribune of the people."

To achieve this on a large scale, what was needed was "a military organization of agents" made up of people "who make revolutionary activity their profession." This organization "must perforce not be very extensive and must be as secret as possible." Although its members would be drawn "without distinctions as between workers and intellectuals," they would constitute "the genuine vanguard of the most revolutionary class." In turn, the Russian proletariat could become "the vanguard of the international revolutionary proletariat."

Apparently, this party—the vanguard of the vanguard—would have a vanguard of its own. Years later, Lenin would say plainly that "the dictatorship of individuals was very often the expression, the vehicle, the channel of the dictatorship of the revolutionary classes."[50] For now he was less explicit, and limited himself to tackling the objection that the party he was envisioning would not be democratic. He argued that the repressive circumstances of Russia made party democracy unfeasible. He did not, however, say that the party ought to be as democratic as possible within the constraints under which it operated. Rather, he poured scorn upon those who advocated such an approach, accusing them of "infantile playing at 'democratic' forms" which were nothing but "a useless and harmful toy." Then he added, somewhat chillingly, that the members of his party would "have not the time to think about toy forms of democratism [but instead they will] have a lively sense of their *responsibility,* knowing as they do from experience that an organization of real revolutionaries will stop at nothing to rid itself of an unworthy member."

• • •

The publication of Bernstein's *Evolutionary Socialism* in 1899 followed by Lenin's *What Is to Be Done?* in 1902 distilled the crisis of Marxism. The elegant answer that Marx and Engels had hit upon to the question of how a socialist revolution might be achieved had collapsed. Their answer was the proletariat, but their expectation that it would grow increasingly universal, impoverished and revolutionary had been confounded. The progress of the capitalist economy was raising living standards throughout society and providing more channels of entry into the middle class and beyond. In addition, the growth of trade unions and the democratization of political processes provided the workers with safer methods of fighting for their interests than taking up arms.

Until this point, there had been something to Marxism's claim to be "scientific," namely that its forecasts rested on empirical observations of mid-century capitalism. (Never mind that some later scholars faulted the data.) The failure of its central forecast, however, showed the essential theory to be false and thus confronted socialists with a dilemma that was to haunt them throughout the remaining life of their movement. They could retain their identity with the workers by pursuing further incremental gains and giving up any serious notion of revolution; or they could keep their devotion to the revolutionary transformation of society but focus their hopes on forces other than the proletariat.

Most socialists closed their eyes to the evidence that made this choice necessary, but Bernstein and Lenin, in opposite ways, found the courage to confront it. The divergent paths they chose each led to the dire consequences that the other predicted. Lenin's revolution for the workers but not by them resulted in greater repression and exploitation than they had ever suffered under capitalism. Bernstein's insistence that the final goal meant nothing led to a rejection of socialism altogether, not on his part but by those who were his spiritual heirs—American labor leaders like Samuel Gompers and George Meany and a generation of social-democratic politicians who came to the fore in Europe late in the twentieth century.

Meanwhile, mainstream social democracy, exemplified by Kautsky and other leaders of the Socialist International, managed to reject both these choices but only at the price of an ever widening chasm between theory and practice as, in one country after another, notional revolutionaries became members of the "establishment." They would heave themselves out of their chairs at the climax of rich party banquets, thrust their fists into the air and intone the socialist anthem: "Arise ye prisoners of starvation."

While these orthodox Marxists resisted Bernstein's appeal to revise dogma just as traditionalists had once spurned Copernicus, Lenin was like Ptolemy, adding ever more farfetched emendations in order to keep the central doctrine intact. "From the philosophy of Marxism, cast of one piece of steel, it is impossible to expunge a single basic premise, a single essential part, without deviating from objective truth, without falling into the arms of bourgeois-reactionary falsehood," he wrote.[51] But his pessimism about the workers' revolutionary consciousness did not square with Marx's assertion in *The Holy Family* that "it is not a matter of what this or that proletarian or even the proletariat as a whole pictures at present as its goal. It is a matter of what the proletariat ... will historically be compelled to do." And his claim that the party must bring political consciousness to the workers was a far cry from the *Manifesto*'s insistence that "Communists ... do not set up any sectarian principles of their own, by which to shape and mold the proletarian movement."

Why, then, could he not acknowledge that he, too, was proposing revisions? He recognized how the sense of possessing an unshakeable dogma can serve as a source of motivation, especially in the kind of tightly disciplined, top-down organization that he aimed to build. "Marxist doctrine is omnipotent because it is true," he said. "It is comprehensive and harmonious, and provides men with an integral world outlook."[52] He understood, as Luxemburg underscored in her polemic against Bernstein, that much of the power of Marxism lay in its discovery that socialism was "a historical necessity." Therefore, instead of admitting that he was amending the doctrine, Lenin redefined empirical realities. Even while Russia remained more than 90 percent pastoral, he announced that private ownership of land made it a "capitalist" country, hence ready to move on to socialism. And he insisted that his party, admittedly composed mostly of intellectuals, would nonetheless in some sense be "the proletariat."

Lenin was not interested in theory for its own sake. He was above all a practitioner, and his writing was almost always in the service of practice. When *What Is to Be Done?* was published in 1902, he was already at work on a draft program for the Russian Social Democratic Workers' Party. The diffuse elements of Russian socialism agreed that year to hold a congress the following summer in order to work out a platform and a structure for a national party. The gathering was dubbed the "second congress" of the RSDWP, counting the tiny 1898 Minsk gathering as the first, even though it had eventuated only in prison terms for the participants, not in any organization. The second congress, in contrast, brought together nearly sixty delegates, although, as Trotsky recalled, "there were only three workmen . . . and that was only accomplished with trouble."[53]

The deliberations opened in Brussels on July 30, 1903, but after a week, police harassment impelled the body to pick up and transfer to the more tolerant environs of London, where deliberations continued throughout most of August. A few delegates each represented the "economists," the Jewish Labor Bund and a miscellany of other tendencies. The largest bloc, a majority, was identified with *Iskra*. This was not because *Iskra* represented the greatest number of grassroots members; on the contrary, the Jewish Bund probably had more followers. But Lenin, and apparently he alone, had been preparing for the congress with an eye to control. He had directed his network of *Iskra* agents within Russia to get themselves designated as delegates and had closely guided their efforts. As Axelrod said afterward with a mixture of admiration and regret: "There is no other man who is absorbed by the revolution twenty-four hours a day, who has no other thoughts but the thought of revolution, and who, even when he sleeps, dreams of nothing but the revolution."[54]

In bitter disputes in the early sessions, the *Iskra* majority visited such uncompromising defeats on the economists and the Jewish Bund that their representatives eventually left the congress. Then the *Iskra* adherents fell out among themselves. The line was first drawn over a clause in the party program that defined the conditions of membership. The difference in wording between the version offered by Lenin and that of Martov was so abstruse that it is impossible for a reader today to tease from the text the point at issue. But what it boiled down to was Lenin's conception of a compact, disciplined party of professional revolutionaries versus a broader, looser organization that would have room for "amateurs." When it was put to a vote, Martov's position prevailed by a small majority, though that was including the votes of the Bundists and the economists who were licking their wounds but had not yet decided to depart. Once they left, the balance shifted to Lenin, and he had his way on the remaining organizational questions.

The most important of these made the editorial board of *Iskra,* based outside of Russia, the supreme authority within the party, while a "central committee" inside Russia would be subordinate to it.

"Doesn't that mean complete dictatorship" by the editorial board? protested Trotsky, who had come to the congress a Lenin disciple but had grown increasingly alienated from him.

"What is bad about that?" Lenin replied.

Lenin's crowning maneuver was to reduce the editorial board from six members to three: himself, Martov and Plekhanov. He had wooed Plekhanov during the months leading up to the congress and the dean of Russian Marxism had responded by throwing his backing to Lenin throughout the meeting. It was an impressive measure of Lenin's control at the culmination of the congress that he won his way on the issue of the editorial board. But he had overreached. Almost immediately after adjournment a backlash began to gather against his rough tactics. Within three months, his honeymoon with Plekhanov had ended, the older man likening the younger to Robespierre. "Lenin desires unity as a man desires unity with a piece of bread," he said later.[55]

Lenin's scheme for dominating the party had for the moment collapsed. But from the latter part of the "second congress," when the walk-out of the Bund and the economists left him with a two-vote margin over his remaining opponents, he clung to the label "majority group," or "Bolsheviks." This was a useful moniker for a faction that had no regard for formal democracy, whether in the state or in the party. Lenin and his followers continued to refer to themselves by it until they were the rulers of Russia.

Triumphs

5

REAL EXISTING SOCIALISM:
LENIN SEIZES POWER

I T WAS NOT ONLY YOUNG RUSSIANS, like Lenin and his brother, who fell under the spell of Chernyshevsky's *What Is to Be Done?* but other Slavs as well. Three such were the Serbs Gavrilo Princip, Nadjelko Cabrinovic and Trifko Grabez, members of a group called Young Bosnia. Abjuring alcohol and sex as an exercise in self-discipline, they yearned to be among the "new men" ready to sacrifice all for the "common cause." How they defined that cause, given that they were all of nineteen, was a bit vague. They knew, though, that they were revolutionaries, socialists, above all patriots. And they were ready to strike a blow for the fatherland and a better world.

They spotted their opportunity when Archduke Franz Ferdinand of Austria, heir to the Hapsburg throne, accepted an invitation from General Potiorek, military governor of Bosnia-Herzegovina, to visit Sarajevo and review military exercises. The sojourn was to climax on June 28, 1914, a special date to Ferdinand since it was the anniversary of his marriage to Sophie, for whose love he had defied the emperor, his uncle Franz Josef. It was an anniversary, as well, but a bitter one, for the Serbs who made up a majority of the population of Bosnia-Herzegovina. Exactly 525 years earlier, on the battlefields of Kosovo, they had been vanquished by the Turks, and the wound in the Serb psyche still festered. After centuries, Serbia had regained its independence, but the Serbs of Bosnia-Herzegovina remained subjugated, having been delivered by the great powers from the hands of the Ottomans to those of the Hapsburgs.

The three young militants had recruited a few collaborators, and with arms furnished by Serbian intelligence, they lay in wait at intervals along the Appel Quay, Ferdinand's announced route. When he saw the royal motorcade, Cabrinovic hurled his hand grenade. It landed on the folded-back top of the archduke's carriage, but he alertly pushed it off onto the road, where it exploded beneath the following car. As the injured were evacuated, the rest of the procession went on to Town Hall. There, as scheduled, the mayor welcomed the archduke with assurances that "all the citizens of Sarajevo, overwhelmed with happiness, greet your Highness' most illustrious visit with the utmost enthusiasm."[1] Ferdinand is reported to have made some show of skepticism. Then he insisted that before proceeding as planned to view the new museum, they stop at the hospital to show their concern for Potiorek's adjutant, who had been among the wounded.

Ferdinand, Sophie and Potiorek piled back into their motor carriage, but with the military efficiency later immortalized by Jaroslav Hasek's satirical good soldier Schweik, no one informed their driver of the change in destination. Instead of continuing along the Appel Quay, which would have led to the hospital, the car turned right onto the road to the museum. Realizing the error at once, Potiorek told the driver to stop and back up. By chance, one of the conspirators, Princip, was standing just at this intersection. The car had passed before he could do anything, but as it stopped and shifted into reverse, he must have thought that fortune was smiling on his mission. Rushing forward and drawing his Browning, he fired two shots into the car at close range, all the while averting his head, as he had almost no experience with handguns. Nonetheless, he managed to hit Ferdinand and Sophie. Within the hour the royal couple were both dead. And the fuse to war had been lit.

Thus began the crisis that socialists all over Europe had dreaded. The Second International, by now twenty-five years old, had flourished in the years since the passing of its honorary president, Friedrich Engels. This was the "golden age" of classical Marxism, as Leszek Kolakowski has dubbed it.[2] Across the continent, democratization had broadened the franchise and created new electoral offices. Industrialization had given rise to enlarged working-class constituencies to which the socialist (or "social-democratic" or "labor") parties directed their appeals. Although the party leaders and theoreticians were mostly of middle-class background, theirs were the only parties to champion the workers' interests above all; and their job was often made easier by discriminatory laws which were all but designed to breed "class consciousness" among those at the lower rungs. By the time Princip fired his fateful shots, socialists had achieved electoral prominence in many countries. The German SPD had garnered as much as 35 percent of the popular vote; the Swedish socialists had topped that, with 36 percent. The Belgian and Danish parties had won 30 percent, the Austrians 25, the Italians 21 and the French 17.[3]

Despite their rising electoral strength, the socialists feared they would be powerless to prevent a war. Since the turn of the century, turmoil in the Balkans, squabbles over colonial possessions and the unsettling of the balance of power caused by Germany's rapid rise had strained the capacity of the Concert of Europe to preserve peace. Although Marx and Engels had welcomed war as a midwife of progress, most socialists were sobered by knowing that the casualties would be drawn overwhelmingly from among the poor. Meetings of the Socialist International repeatedly debated proposals to resist war by means of general strikes. But most of the leaders believed that this tactic was more likely to lead to repression of the labor unions than to a crippling of the war machine. Instead, the International settled on a proclamation that the parties would endeavor to exploit any war to "hasten the overthrow of capitalist rule."[4] The fiery rhetoric was in part a bow to militants like Lenin and Luxemburg, but it was also a way of masking the sense of helplessness.

However, in the first weeks after the Sarajevo outrage, few people foresaw the catastrophic result to which it was leading. Royals had been shot before without war ensuing. In mid-July the Socialist International proceeded with its plans to host a convocation in Brussels of the various Russian socialist groups in the hopes of persuading them to unify. Over the previous decade, the International had often tried to adjudicate among these squabbling factions. The bad blood of the Russians' 1903 Second Congress, at which the "Bolshevik" and "Menshevik" division appeared, had never been washed away. Still, for nearly another decade they had all remained part of the same social-democratic party. The fractiousness of the leaders, who were usually in exile, was constrained by their followers inside Russia, where the struggle to survive in a repressive environment put a premium on cooperation.

For their part, the Mensheviks, although often bitter toward Lenin, never abandoned the goal of maintaining a unified party. Their leader, Martov, was, in Lenin's scornful description, a "conciliator."[5]

Lenin's own approach was quite the opposite. He would convene his followers and declare it to be a meeting of the whole party. At moments of outward reconciliation, he created new secret bodies to strengthen his factional apparatus. Once,

he engineered a division, then ordered his subalterns in the party headquarters
to make off with the funds and the records. As Plekhanov, who straddled the two
factions, once put it: "The bolsheviks behave as if the split were already achieved,
while the mensheviks behave as if it will never take place."[6]

When, in 1907, the Mensheviks invoked a party tribunal because of a particularly vicious calumniation Lenin had aimed at them, he coolly acknowledged
that his words were

> calculated to evoke in the reader hatred, aversion and contempt . . . calculated
> not to convince but to break up the ranks of the opponent, not to correct the
> mistake of the opponent but to destroy him, to wipe his organization off the
> face of the earth. . . . Against *such* political enemies I then conducted—and
> in the event of repetition or development of a split *shall always conduct*—a
> struggle of *extermination.*[7]

Lenin defended this ferocity on the grounds that actions that would be
impermissible against party comrades were permissible, even obligatory, against
those who had "split"; but in truth, he and his targets were still members of the
same party. Moreover, the splits of the past, and those still to come, were invariably fomented by him. As he spelled out in *What Is to Be Done?* Lenin aimed to
create a party that was "not . . . very extensive and . . . as secret as possible" and
that would function like a "military organization." Splits and purges served to
keep the organization compact and disciplined. He engineered breaks with the
Mensheviks several times, only to have them papered over under pressure from
inside Russia and from the International. He also often expelled groups from
his own faction, sometimes for being too conciliatory toward the Mensheviks.
In 1912, he convened a "party conference" to which the Mensheviks were not
invited and made his divorce from them final.

Although by any fair measure the Mensheviks could adduce a longer list
of grievances, and many found Lenin repugnant, they could never match the
obsessive depths of his animus toward them. A female comrade and close friend
recounted this story of climbing a peak near Montreux with Lenin, who was
known as a nature lover.

> To reach the top more quickly we left the road and pushed recklessly upward.
> With every step the climb grew more difficult. Vladimir Ilyich strode strong
> and secure, laughing at my effort not to fall behind. . . .

Finally we got there. A limitless landscape, an indescribable play of colors. In front of us, as on one's palm, were all the zones, all the climates. Brightly the snow shines; somewhat lower, the plants of the north, and further down the succulent alpine meadow and the turbulent vegetation of the south. I attune myself to a high pitch and am ready to recite Shakespeare, Byron. I glance at Vladimir Ilyich: he sits, deep in thought, and suddenly exclaims: "The Mensheviks really mess things up."[8]

Lenin held a practical advantage in the power struggle: he had more money at his disposal. He used it to finance a variety of Bolshevik publications, to cover the travel expenses of loyal delegates to party congresses, and to pay salaries to his party men, his "professional revolutionaries." Where did the funds come from? At least once, in 1911, he filched the party treasury.[9] But there were fatter pickings to be had. Over a period of years beginning around 1906, Lenin's minions carried out armed robberies of banks and armored cars, sometimes killing the guards. They made off with large hauls of cash in these "expropriations," as the Bolsheviks liked to call them. It was through his skill at such work that Stalin first won Lenin's admiration.

• • •

In July 1914 the Socialist International invited the Bolsheviks and Mensheviks, as well as the smaller Russian groups associated with Plekhanov and Trotsky and the parties representing the empire's Poles, Letts and Jews, to a mediating session in Brussels. Lenin refused "on principle" to attend in person, as he wrote to Inessa Armand, the vivacious comrade who is widely believed to have been his mistress.[†][10] He sent her in his stead. He knew she could be relied upon to adhere to his instructions to make no compromise. And he knew, too, that the others would not accept his demand that they "unconditionally submit" to the command of the Bolsheviks.[11] The other ten groups (except the Letts) did reach a meeting of minds, and the foreign mediators gave the Bolsheviks only until the pending congress of the International, scheduled in August, to join the consensus. That gathering, however, was forestalled by larger events.

---

† Bertram Wolfe, David Shub, Richard Pipes and Robert Payne credit this interpretation. Louis Fischer describes the closeness of the two without characterizing the relationship. Adam Ulam expresses agnosticism on the subject. Lenin's former friend Nikolay Valentinov comments: "indeed, he was in love with . . . Inessa Armand . . . in his own way—no doubt stealing a few kisses between a discussion on the perfidy of the Mensheviks and drafting a resolution stigmatizing imperialism and the capitalist sharks." *Encounters with Lenin* (London: Oxford University Press, 1968), p. 59.

On July 23, the Austrian government sent Serbia a devastating ultimatum. All at once it was apparent that the diplomatic temperature was near the combustion point. The Bureau of the Socialist International convened in emergency session in Brussels on July 27. Most of the movement's leading lights attended: Karl Kautsky and Rosa Luxemburg from Germany, Max Adler from Austria, Pavel Axelrod from Russia, Jean Jaurès from France and many others. The meeting closed the next day with a great rally in the Cirque Royale with thousands chanting "war against war." But that very day, July 28, Austria declared war on Serbia. On July 31, after the Bureau members had returned to their respective countries, a pro-war French extremist shot the much beloved Jaurès dead in a Paris café, bitterly symbolizing the socialists' impotence to soothe Europe's martial fever.

On August 1, Germany declared war on Russia. Two days later the conflagration spread west, as Germany and France declared war on one another. The following day, the socialist members of Parliament in both countries voted to approve war credits. The socialists of Belgium, Austria and England also took a patriotic tack. Together, "these acts struck a mortal blow to the International," wrote its chronicler, Julius Braunthal. "The Socialist parties did not withhold their support for a contest they lacked the power to prevent. . . . [T]hey gave their enthusiastic support, both morally and politically, to the war effort."[12] In most countries, they even agreed to join in governments of national unity, breaking a long taboo on coalitions with "bourgeois parties."[13]

Socialist leaders were taken aback by the alacrity with which the working classes harkened to the call of country. They must have been even more surprised to discover how the spirit of patriotism welled within their own breasts. The German SPD declared: "A victory of Russian despotism, stained with the blood of the best of its own people, would gravely jeopardize the future of our people. . . . [I]n the hour of danger we are not prepared to let our Fatherland down."[14] The French party asserted that France was "struggling that the world [be] freed from the stifling oppression of imperialism."[15] And from exile, Plekhanov, the dean of Russian Marxism, said that were he "not old and sick I would join the army. To bayonet your German comrades would give me great pleasure."[16]

This failure of "the spirit of international solidarity," as Braunthal put it, drove a stake through the heart of Marxist theory, already enfeebled by the upward economic trends Bernstein had cited in his "revisionist" writings. The single most fundamental idea of Marxism was that class is the most important political variable, yet the response to the war proved that nationality was a more powerful bond, and few socialists were able to resist its pull.

There were, of course, exceptions. In Germany, an antiwar minority split away from the SPD and formed an independent social-democratic party. Naturally, it included Luxemburg, a diehard supranationalist. (She and her husband, Jogiches, had continued to play active roles in the Polish and Russian parties as well as the German.) More surprisingly, it was joined by the centrist Kautsky, who sacrificed his standing as the SPD's leading theoretician, and the conservative Bernstein, who risked his seat in the Reichstag. Concluding that Germany was to blame for the war, Bernstein and Kautsky took a stand of principle that few other mainstream socialists dared. It reunited these two old friends after years of estrangement. But the vitriolic attacks upon them by other old comrades now gushing with patriotism—attacks which were often laced with anti-Semitism when directed at Bernstein, and even sometimes at Kautsky, who was not a Jew—were a grim augury of things to come in Germany.

In America, the socialists were stalwart against militarism, a stance that was painless as long as their country remained neutral but costly once it entered the fighting in 1917. Socialist leader Eugene V. Debs, who had garnered 6 percent of the popular vote for president in the 1912 election, was thrown in jail, and the party never recovered its popularity. The Italian socialists also remained steadfast as their country, too, initially refused to join the fray, but a prominent leader, Benito Mussolini, editor of the party newspaper, *Avanti!,* bolted to form a new group of leftists clamoring for war against the country's erstwhile allies, Germany and Austria.

With the notable exception of Plekhanov, most Russian socialist leaders were unmoved by the national call to arms. Unlike their French and German counterparts, they did not serve in Parliament but lived in exile, completely isolated from their government, which hounded and spied on them. This is not to say that the fighting dismayed them all. On the contrary, as a faithful disciple of Marx and Engels, Lenin welcomed it. Only the year before, he had speculated that "a war between Austria and Russia would be a very useful thing for the revolution—in all of Eastern Europe—but it is not likely that Franz Josef and Nikolasha [the tsar] will give us that pleasure."[17] He believed that in the event of war "the workers will pay a dreadfully heavy price . . . but in the end they will gain. It is the will of history."[18]

When the war began, Lenin was living in Cracow,[†] which was then within the Hapsburg Empire, and he was promptly arrested as an enemy alien. Although he raged against the socialist patriots for their betrayal of principles, that did not prevent his asking, and receiving, their help. Through local comrades he appealed to Viktor Adler to intervene on his behalf. Since the Austrian socialists were supporting the war, Adler was able to see the foreign minister. The resultant government order freeing Lenin explained: "It is the opinion of Dr. Adler that under the present circumstances Ulyanov could be of great service" in undermining Russia, Austria's main enemy.[19] It was an insight which the Central Powers would exploit further as the war progressed.

For its first two and a half years, however, the war proved a great disappointment to Lenin. Around the world, those socialists who had not turned patriot mostly cried out for an end to the bloodshed, but Lenin had no patience for this position. He chastised those antiwar socialists who sought merely to stop the carnage. "Objectively, who profits by the slogan of peace?" he asked. "Certainly not the revolutionary proletariat. Not the idea of *using* the war to *speed* up the collapse of capitalism."[20] However, this unflinching revolutionary approach won few adherents, and his party's fortunes reached low ebb. In January 1917, he conjectured that his generation might not live to see "the decisive battles of the coming revolution." But even as he spoke, the ground had already begun to crumble beneath the tsarist regime. Across Europe, hereditary autocracy proved to be an anachronism that could not withstand the strains of twentieth-century "total war."

Many factors contributed to Russia's February Revolution, but it was planned by no one. In addition to military debacle, the war had brought inflation, which had discouraged peasants from selling grain, and cities were experiencing shortages of food. They were low on fuel as well, due to military demands, and this slowed the economy. Strikes broke out in some factories, followed by open air rallies protesting the food shortage. Soldiers were ordered to disperse the crowds, and a few fired directly into them, killing dozens.

As often with conscript armies, most soldiers were uneasy being sent against their civilian countrymen. During the next twenty-four hours, as word of the massacre passed from barrack to barrack in Petrograd,[‡] one unit after

---

[†] He had spent two years there after four in Paris, several in Geneva and a spell in Finland during the course of his long exile.

[‡] The name of the capital city was changed from St. Petersburg to the more Russian Petrograd in 1914 as an expression of the nationalist spirit evoked by the war.

another mutinied and joined the demonstrators. The tsar calculated that the rabble could be dealt with if isolated from the Duma, the body of elected representatives that, although constitutionally toothless, could offer it leadership and legitimacy. He therefore ordered the Duma to adjourn, but the legislators defied him and instead appointed a provisional government. Russia's military commanders began to fear that the mutiny of the Petrograd soldiers would spread to the front. Bowing to their counsel, the tsar abdicated.

Given that the Russian state was virtually synonymous with the person of the tsar, the abdication left an immense vacuum. Nicholas ceded the crown to his younger brother, Michael, but the latter, intuiting that it might be worth his life, renounced it.[†] The throne remained empty. The provisional government looked ahead to the election of a Constituent Assembly. In the meantime, having defied the sovereign and lacking any constitutional basis for its authority, it anxiously invoked an ephemeral popular mandate. But as an expression of the voice of the people, it had a competitor.

During the upheavals of 1905, Pavel Axelrod, a Menshevik and one of the few socialist leaders to come from a background of true poverty, was concerned that the workers should develop more of a voice of their own. He came up with the idea of a council, or *soviet*, of representatives chosen by factory. These were formed in St. Petersburg and other locales, and they briefly proved to be effective centers of agitation until the uprising was smothered. Now in 1917, the Mensheviks and Socialist Revolutionaries, a leftist party of populist bent, took the initiative of renewing the soviets.

With large numbers of men in uniform, military units as well as factories were invited to send deputies. Given the circumstances, there were no consistent rules of selection or apportionment. The Petrograd soviet grew willy-nilly to a few thousand delegates. This unwieldy size, and the lack of established procedures, rendered it useless as a deliberative body. Most of its decisions were made by an executive committee, which was not chosen by the body as a whole but made up of representatives from each of the socialist parties. These representatives were almost all intellectuals of middle-class background, in effect vitiating Axelrod's goal.

Nonetheless, the soviets had an aura of being the authentic voice of the people. Even the provisional government was awed by this mystique as the two bodies jockeyed for position. The members of the provisional government were painfully aware that they had not been elected to the responsibilities they were

---

† Michael's intuition was accurate but renunciation did not save him. He was murdered by the Cheka, the Bolshevik secret police, in June 1918, a month ahead of the rest of the royal family.

now executing, so to bolster their legitimacy they appealed to the soviets to endorse their rule.

For their part, the leaders of the soviets saw the world through the prism of Marxism. To them, the fall of the tsar and the rise of the provisional government constituted the overthrow of "feudalism" by the "bourgeoisie." Next, their theory told them, it was the turn of the bourgeoisie to be overthrown by the "proletariat." In other words, they wanted the provisional government in place so they could get busy destroying it.

This was awkward for the Mensheviks and Socialist Revolutionaries who were prominent both in the soviets and in the provisional government. In fact, one of them became prime minister: Alexander Kerensky, son of Fyodor, the schoolmaster who had shielded young Vladimir Ulyanov. This personal debt did not stay Lenin's hand, and the Bolsheviks, initially a minor force, gathered support by attacking the hapless new leaders relentlessly.

Despite these attacks, the moderate leftists in the provisional government stuck reflexively to the idea that their enemies were on the Right. They could not recognize that the specter of a tsarist "restoration" posed a far smaller threat to their lives and liberty than did their own one-time comrades. Marx, as Isaiah Berlin observed, had "divi[ded] mankind into good sheep and evil and dangerous goats," and Lenin, however obnoxious, was still a sheep.[21] Even when French intelligence furnished proof of Lenin's ties to the German government, they declined to publicize the documents.[†]

Lenin's path to power was cleared when Kerensky fell out with his military commander, the charismatic, lowborn General Kornilov. Kerensky summoned all the forces of the Left to repulse the "counterrevolution." Kornilov's coup was defeated, but this left Kerensky and the moderate leftists naked before the Bolsheviks, who alone among the parties had organized their own military forces.

Under Leon Trotsky's command, the "revolution" was launched on October 21 by the Gregorian calendar. It was carried out not by workers but by soldiers—and not that many of them. Altogether there may have been a few tens of thousands of troops at Bolshevik command, but far fewer were prepared to fight to defend Kerensky's provisional government. Some tsarist officers remained so bitter toward Kerensky that they threw in with the Bolsheviks.

---

† The link had been forged by Bernstein's old scourge, "Doctor Elephant" Parvus, who had left behind radical journalism, made a fortune in unidentified business dealings in Turkey, and returned to Germany as a well-connected wheeler-dealer.

They probably believed that this gang of madmen could not hang onto power for long, anyway. Key buildings and transit points were seized, and a new government was proclaimed. From beginning to end it took five days. It had all been "as easy as picking up a feather," Lenin commented later. He had, said Bertram Wolfe, "seize[d] power not in a land 'ripe for socialism' but in a land ripe for seizing power."[22]

Wolfe's quip aptly characterizes the situation in Russia, but it begs a question: when is a country ripe for socialism? According to this Marxian concept, a new society will be born when its time is due, as measured by its economic development. Ever since 1917, many critics and supporters of Lenin's have agreed that the basic problem facing the infant Bolshevik regime was that Russia was not advanced enough for socialism, its economy being more agricultural than industrial.

Though Russia was poor, it was, however, no poorer than Germany had been seventy years earlier when Marx and Engels had bent every effort to foment a socialist revolution there.[23] The problem, then, was not so much Russia's backwardness as the black hole at the center of the theory to which Lenin looked for guidance. Marx and Engels offered only a few hazy images of life under socialism, where each individual would be provisioned "according to his needs" while having to work only in pursuit of self-fulfillment. On the mechanics of transition they were mute. What was a Marxist to do once he got his hands on power?

• • •

Lenin knew well that the new regime's most burning economic challenge was to put bread on city tables, since he had played upon the bread shortage in his drive to power. And he believed, as did all socialists, that profit was theft; so he ordered the peasants to sell grain to the state at fixed, low prices. Naturally, they were reluctant, and their reluctance grew with inflation as the government printed unbacked currency to cover the disappearance of revenue caused by the upheavals and property seizures. Growers preferred to route their produce to the black market, mostly peasants who traveled by train to the cities and sold grain out of sacks on their backs.

Lenin ordered these "bagmen" shot when caught, and he ordered growers to turn over to the state all of their crop beyond what was required for their own table. If they would not yield it, armed teams of workers and soldiers would be sent to take it by force. He exhorted his followers "not to spare dictatorial methods . . . not to refrain from barbarous means in the struggle against barbarism."[24]

Russia's autocracy had long been notorious in Europe for its cruelty, but no tsar had ever shed blood so freely. Then again, no tsar ever had such lofty aims. "How could they . . . act otherwise," asked former Yugoslav Communist leader Milovan Djilas of the Bolsheviks, "when they ha[d] been named by . . . history to establish the Kingdom of Heaven in this sinful world?"[25] The opponents of his noble goal, Lenin knew, must be capitalists—even if they appeared to be mere peasants. Thus was invented the *kulak,* a Bolshevik term for the more success-ful peasants. The thin margin of their prosperity and the absurdity of calling them exploiters was revealed in Soviet census data examined by Richard Pipes, showing that only 2 percent of peasant households had any hired help, and these averaged one employee each.[26]

Lenin's policy backfired politically as well as economically. Peasant rage fueled the civil wars waged by "Whites" against "Reds" during the first years of Bolshevik power. Even when the various imperial officers were all defeated, the peasants fought on in a wave of uprisings in 1920 and 1921. Through it all, little grain was successfully requisitioned. Lenin complained that he felt as if he were trying to steer a bicycle whose wheels were unconnected to its handlebar. Finally he concluded, as he reported to the tenth party congress, that "only agreement with the peasantry can save the socialist revolution in Russia." They would be allowed to sell their produce on the market. Moreover, some freedom to manufacture and sell finished goods would also be restored so there would be something for the countryside to buy with the rubles it earned from its grain.

This New Economic Policy, Lenin confessed, amounted to "turning back towards capitalism." But he was confident that as long as "the proletariat"—that is, the party—was in power, the eventual emergence of socialism was assured. Thus he could loosen the economic screw as long as it entailed no political relaxation. On the contrary, explained *Pravda* editor Nikolai Bukharin, "We are making economic concessions to avoid political concessions."[†27]

The legitimacy of Bolshevik power was impugned at the outset by elec-tions to a Constituent Assembly which had been scheduled by the provisional

---

† Nor was the truce with the peasantry permanent. The Bolsheviks licked their wounds, and in the 1930s under Stalin they renewed with a vengeance the campaign to "liquidate the kulaks" and collectivize agriculture. To crush resistance they took about fifteen million lives, and Russia was never able to feed itself again. See Robert Conquest, *Harvest of Sorrow* (New York: Oxford University Press, 1986), p. 301.

government for November. Ever since the tsar's abdication, the Bolsheviks had been demanding such elections in order to create a new constitution and government for Russia. The ulterior motive of this demand was to undermine the provisional government. Had they been democrats, the Bolsheviks would not have taken power by force with the elections just weeks away. Now that power was theirs, they would have preferred to cancel the pending vote, but they opted not to risk the obloquy that this would have evoked. They hoped that the levers of coercion they now held, as well as the prestige of their new position, would bring a tolerable result. But they were bitterly disappointed, winning less than 24 percent.

Still, they believed that history conferred a more valid mandate than the voters did. When the Constituent Assembly convened in January 1918, the halls were lined with armed soldiers and sailors loyal to the Bolsheviks. Some of them playfully aimed their rifles at representatives of the other parties, who were repeatedly hooted down when they took the floor. Although not a representative, Lenin attended. He did not speak, but made a show of his disdain. In David Shub's account: "He sat on the stairs leading to the platform, smiled derisively, jested, wrote something on a slip of paper, then stretched himself out on a bench and pretended to fall asleep."[28] After the first day, seeing that the crowds that had been summoned by the opposition in support of the assembly were not large enough to overcome the Bolsheviks' armed guard, he ordered the hall locked and the delegates dispersed when they tried to return the next day. "The breaking up of the Constituent Assembly by the Soviet power is the complete and public liquidation of formal democracy in the name of the revolutionary dictatorship. It will be a good lesson," he told Trotsky.[29]

The chief resource of the "revolutionary dictatorship" was Lenin's iron will. "The greatest inward mobilization of all his forces...made him the greatest revolutionary of history," said Trotsky.[30] He was abstemious, sitting at his desk on a plain wooden chair, dining with his wife and sisters on soup and black bread which Krupskaya carried from the Kremlin restaurant. "He worked from morn till night, and out of great anxiety he could not sleep," recalled Krupskaya. "He would awake in the middle of the night, get out of bed, and begin to check by telephone: had this or the other of his orders been carried out? think up some kind of additional telegram to send."[31]

The old machinery of government had been smashed. Existing law in Russia was abolished. Lenin built a new apparatus from the ground up, or rather, from

himself down. All authority flowed from him—or from the committees that he
dominated, which amounted to the same thing. He fined cabinet members for
coming late to meetings. His orders, even on small administrative matters, were
sent in a blizzard of telegrams all over the vast expanse of Russia. Yet the British
philosopher Bertrand Russell found him "entirely without a trace of *hauteur*. If
one met him without knowing who he was, one would not guess that he is possessed of great power or even that he is in any way very eminent."[32] Angelica
Balabanoff, who served as secretary to the Comintern in its early days, wrote
that even though Lenin was "intoleran[t] of any deviation from his way of thinking," he "avoided everything that might . . . lead toward the establishment of a
personality cult."[33] Anatole Lunacharsky, the commissar of education, explained
the apparent contradiction: "He does his work imperiously, not because power
is sweet to him but because he is sure that he is right and cannot endure to have
anybody spoil his work."[34]

Alas, he had so little to work with. His regard for his followers was
always laced with contempt. His so-called "testament," a deathbed mis-
sive to the Central Committee, read like a painstaking catalogue of each of
their faults. During the years of exile he had repeatedly had to fortify them
against the temptation of compromise with other factions, and then during
October he had had to goad them on to the seizure of power. No sooner was
it theirs, than many were wavering once again. Fearing that their party could
not succeed on its own, several Bolshevik leaders endorsed the proposal of
the Mensheviks and Socialist Revolutionaries for a governing coalition of all
socialist parties.

Lenin would not hear of it. To him, the others were "petty bourgeois" and
had to be treated as a part of the "class enemy." He called for "ruthless war on
the kulaks! Death to them!" and "Hatred and contempt for the parties which
defend them—the Right Socialist-Revolutionaries, the Mensheviks, and today's
Left Socialist-Revolutionaries!"[35]

He received decisive backing from Trotsky, who himself had once been
aligned with the Mensheviks. For that reason, and because he ended as a martyr
to Stalin, Trotsky has often been imagined as embodying a more humane or
democratic strain of communism. But from 1917 on, he was joined at the hip
to Lenin in implacable, merciless antipathy to all non-Bolsheviks.

Some of Lenin's other comrades felt so strongly about the need to compromise that a group of commissars resigned in protest after the first weeks. They
warned that if they kept all power in their own hands, the Bolsheviks would have

to rule "by the means of political terror."[36] This warning did not faze Lenin. "Do you think we can be victors without the most severe revolutionary terror?" he admonished a cabinet member who objected to a decree prescribing summary executions.[37] Trotsky recalled that this "was the period when Lenin, at every passing opportunity, emphasized the absolute necessity of the terror."[38]

True, a civil war was raging. Therefore, in provinces experiencing rebellion against the Bolsheviks he ordered "merciless mass terror against kulaks, priests, and White Guards; persons of doubtful standing should be locked up in concentration camps."[39] But he also demanded similar measures as a preventative in locales where revolt had not broken out:

> In Nizhni Novgorod there are clearly preparations for a White Guard uprising. We must gather our strength, set up a dictatorial *troika* and institute mass terror "immediately"; shoot and ferret out hundreds of prostitutes who get the soldiers drunk, former officers, etc. . . . It is necessary to act all-out. . . . Mass seizures of Mensheviks and other unreliables.[40]

Lamenting his followers' lack of resolve, he pleaded, "Is it impossible to find among us a Fouquier-Tinville [chief prosecutor of the Jacobin Terror] to tame our wild counter-revolutionists?"[41] As biographer David Shub puts it, Lenin found his in Feliks Dzerzhinsky. The scion of Polish aristocrats, Dzerzhinsky had been one of the non-Jewish minority in Rosa Luxemburg's antinationalist Polish socialist party before ending up a Bolshevik. Lenin appointed him the first chief of the Cheka, or Bolshevik secret police.

Russia had had a secret police force under the tsars, the dreaded Okhrana. But its work—which consisted mostly of internal espionage—was child's play compared with that of the Cheka. If Fouquier-Tinville was once Europe's exemplar of terror, his exploits paled alongside Dzerzhinsky's. Whereas the former sent his victims to the guillotine after a parody of judicial procedure in which perhaps one-fourth were acquitted, Dzerzhinsky's were mostly shot without any formalities. And while Fouquier-Tinville's toll numbered at most a couple of thousand souls, Dzerzhinsky dispatched tens of thousands. The Okhrana had rarely killed anyone.

The writer Maxim Gorky, a friend of Lenin's and a public relations asset to the regime, used his unusual access to appeal for the commutation of the sentences of various intellectuals. "Don't you think you are wasting your energies on a lot of rubbish?" the ruler asked, even while sometimes acquiescing.[42] Gorky owed his sway to his ability to understand Lenin or at least to picture him as he wished to be understood. "In this accursed world," Gorky wrote, Lenin shone forth as "a splendid human being, who had to sacrifice himself to hostility and hatred, so that love might be at last realized."[43]

Terrorizing resistors, kulaks and other recalcitrants was only part of the process of consolidating Bolshevik power. After the fall of the tsar in February 1917, Russia had become, Lenin said, the freest country in the world. Now it was time to reverse that process. Within two weeks after its formation, the Bolshevik government issued a decree restricting the press and began shutting down newspapers. Liberal papers were special targets because they were "bourgeois," but papers reflecting non-Bolshevik shades of socialist opinion were also closed because they "objectively" served capitalist interests. At first these measures were described as temporary, but in short order a decree was issued in the name of the Central Executive Committee, declaring: "re-establishment of the so-called freedom of the press . . . would be an unpardonable surrender to the will of capital, that is to say, a counter-revolutionary measure."[44]

A similar fate awaited the political parties. The Constitutional Democrats, pillars of the provisional government, felt the harshest repression the earliest. Soon the Mensheviks and Socialist Revolutionaries and other socialist splinters were harassed and in effect outlawed. But Lenin was not satisfied. He wrote to his justice minister: "In my opinion it is necessary to extend the application of execution by shooting to all phases covering activities of Mensheviks, Socialist Revolutionaries and the like; a formula must be found that would place these activities in connexion with the international bourgeoisie and its struggle against us."[45]

Only the Left Socialist Revolutionaries for a time escaped persecution because they had supported the Bolshevik takeover. In contrast to the Bolsheviks, who always had a steely glint beneath their revolutionary rhetoric, the Left SRs (my grandparents' party), led by a young woman, Maria Spiridonova, were genuine wild-eyed radicals. When they broke with the Bolsheviks over the humiliating peace with Germany, they took up arms and managed to take Dzerzhinsky hostage. They were in a position to seize the Kremlin, says Pipes, but "they emphatically did not want the responsibility of governing. Their rebellion was not so much a coup d'état as a coup de théâtre."[46] Soon, the Bolsheviks brought up military reinforcements and regained the upper hand.

A month later, a disciple of Spiridonova's, the veteran terrorist Fanya Kaplan, managed to pump two bullets into Lenin as he emerged from a meeting.

He was a "traitor [to] socialism," she said before being shot.[47] The Left SRs had aided the Bolshevik coup because the policies of the provisional government, in which moderate socialists were prominent, so little resembled the socialist dream. But once in power, Lenin had not fulfilled their dream, either.

The suppression of opposition parties did not suffice to safeguard socialism. Lenin recognized that if his own party remained an open forum, enemies would find a voice inside. What brought this danger home to him was the emergence in 1920-21 of a group of Bolsheviks calling themselves the "Workers' Opposition." Led by Alexander Schliapnikov, the highest-ranking Bolshevik of proletarian background, and based mainly in the trade unions, they advocated that control of the factories be entrusted to the workers themselves instead of the party.

Lenin quite rightly saw this proposal as a threat to the party's monopoly of power. To allow workers to control the workplaces would undermine the "dictatorship of the proletariat." The logic was odd, but it was the logic of the system. Therefore Lenin had a resolution on "party unity" put through, banning any activity that smacked of factionalism. It was to enforce this ban on factions, says Pipes, that the post of general secretary was created.[48] The man Lenin chose for this job was Joseph Stalin.

In addition to muzzling "counterrevolutionaries," it was essential to indoctrinate the public in Bolshevik ideas and begin to mold a new socialist man. Louis Fischer describes how the effort was launched under Lenin's characteristic whip:

> Lenin was anxious to have monarchist monuments removed and appropriate inscriptions (like "Religion is the opiate of the people") displayed on walls and buildings in Moscow and Petrograd. "I am astonished and outraged," he wrote Lunacharsky [the commissar of education], that this had not yet been done. . . . In September, 1918, Lenin reprimanded Lunacharsky . . . for failing to display busts of Marx and propaganda texts in city streets: "I demand that the names of those responsible be sent to me so that they can be put on trial."[49]

• • •

The immense challenge of consolidating the "dictatorship of the proletariat" in Russia would have constituted the life's work of a less driven leader, but Lenin never expected that this alone would complete his mission. He believed devoutly in the dictum of Marx and Engels that the working man has no country, and he had proved his fidelity to this principle with his counter-patriotic stand during the war. Moreover, the justification that Russian Marxists developed for pursuing a socialist revolution in Russia despite its backwardness was that it would trigger revolution in the more advanced countries. They, in turn, would help Russia to build socialism. Although this was a non sequitur—no one ever explained what the workers of Germany or France could do to develop Russia—still it was an article of faith among Bolsheviks and many other Marxists. Lenin knew, therefore, that the success of his revolution depended not only on maintaining the Bolsheviks' grip on Russia, but also on spreading the revolution abroad.

He began in the non-Russian parts of the tsarist empire. Within weeks of the Bolsheviks' seizure of power, Lenin and Stalin (who was in charge of nationalities) had issued a declaration recognizing "the equality and sovereignty of all the peoples of Russia" and "the right of . . . self-determination including secession." This fulfilled a tenet of the program by which the Bolsheviks had appealed for support among the empire's restive non-Russians. Lettish riflemen, for example, were among the most loyal and effective military units at Lenin's deploy. In the chaotic aftermath of the October Revolution, one by one the various national groups, acting from their own aspirations or prodded by Russia's neighbors looking to extend their own influence, declared their independence.

Quickly, Lenin reversed course. Many of the new republics were more backward than Russia; they could not help her build socialism. Still, what sense did it make to allow the capitalists to regain power in the near abroad? Through coups by local Communists or direct invasion by the Red Army, the Ukraine and the central Asian and trans-Caucasian parts of the empire were reunited with Russia to form the Union of Soviet Socialist Republics. The last major piece to be restored—until the Stalin-Hitler Pact a generation later—was Georgia, where Menshevism held sway. The Menshevik government had begun to create a noncoercive social democracy, which made it, in the words of Adam Ulam, "the toast of the Western socialists, whose delegations visited Georgia and rendered glowing accounts of its democratic virtues."[50] This gave Lenin pause about the tactics to be used in subduing it. His scruples were overcome by Stalin, himself a Georgian, and after an invasion by a hundred thousand Red Army troops, the Menshevik government fled and Georgia joined the "free union of free nations."

As the Bolsheviks saw it, the most important battleground of the world socialist revolution was destined to be Germany, the industrial heartland of Europe. Encouragingly, events there seemed to reprise those in Russia. In late 1918, military defeat forced the kaiser to abdicate, just as it had the tsar. He was replaced by a provisional government of moderate socialists pledged to convene a Constituent Assembly. Meanwhile, inspired by the example of the soviets, councils of workers and soldiers sprang up in German cities. More radical elements denounced the provisional government as handmaidens of capitalism. The most vociferous of these were the so-called Spartacists, led by Rosa Luxemburg and Karl Liebknecht, son of SPD founder Wilhelm Liebknecht, a descendant of Martin Luther's.

The Spartacists were the Left of the Left: a faction among the Independent Social Democrats that had split from the SPD over the war issue. At the beginning of January 1919, working with Karl Radek, leader of a high level delegation of Bolshevik emissaries sent by Lenin, the Spartacists broke away and formed the Communist Party of Germany. Within a week, their followers were in the streets of Berlin trying to imitate the Bolshevik coup. But their effort was ill-planned. (Luxemburg, whose mantra was "the spontaneity of the masses," was opposed on principle to planning.) Worse, their adversaries had learned well from Russian events, especially the fatal split between the moderate left provisional government of Kerensky and the military establishment led by General Kornilov. Mindful of that example, the moderate socialists and the military stuck fast to one another and the rising was promptly quelled, as were several in other German cities in the next months. Liebknecht and Luxemburg were arrested by paramilitaries, then taken out separately and shot. Her body was dumped in a canal, where it was found months later.

Even as the last Communist uprisings were being put down in Germany, Bolshevik military veteran Béla Kun managed to gain power in Hungary by co-opting the more popular Social Democrats. Lenin counseled: "Be firm. If there are waverings among the Socialists who came over to you yesterday, or among the petty bourgeois, in regard to the dictatorship of the proletariat, suppress the waverings mercilessly. Shooting is the proper fate of a coward in war."[51] Lenin's willingness to practice mercilessness far beyond a level contemplated by his adversaries was one of the keys to his triumph in Russia, but in Hungary it backfired. Domestic resistance undermined the newly christened Red Army of Hungary as it tried to fend off Romanian and Czech forces, and Soviet Hungary collapsed after four months.

Lenin's boldest stroke in spreading the revolution abroad came in Poland in 1920. Newly liberated after a century of Russian rule, Poland was led by Josef Pilsudski, who as a student had been prosecuted as a co-conspirator of Sasha Ulyanov's. As he watched the Bolsheviks reconquer the various parts of the tsarist empire, Pilsudski concluded that Poland, too, was on Lenin's menu. He decided to strike first while Russia was still weak, hoping to win generous boundaries for Poland and to reestablish an independent Ukraine as a long-term counterpoise to Russia.

After some Polish victories, the Red Army gained the initiative and drove the Poles all the way back across the River Bug. This was roughly the boundary that had been proposed by British diplomats at the Versailles conference (the so-called Curzon Line), although it was well to the west of what the Poles had hoped. Western diplomats now called on the Russians to halt their advance, since Poland was not a historic part of the Russian Empire proper and Lenin himself acknowledged that the Curzon Line "was very advantageous for us."[52] Instead, the Red Army pushed on toward Warsaw. In a secret speech, revealed only in the 1990s after the disappearance of the Soviet Union, Lenin explained his reasoning to a party conference: "From the projected borders [of a conquered Poland] we would have won a solid, comfortable, firm base for operations against central Europe."[53] Indeed, he said elsewhere in the speech, it would have provided "a base against all the contemporary states." But as Russian forces encircled Warsaw to the north, Pilsudski, with a smaller force, swung to the south and struck a devastating blow to the exposed Russian flank, neutralizing hundreds of thousands of Red Army troops and forcing Lenin to agree to the terms proposed by the Western powers.

As a result of this debacle, Lenin told his party, "we must limit ourselves to a defensive posture with regard to the Entente, but despite the complete failure in the first instance, our first defeat, we will keep shifting from a defensive to an offensive policy over and over again until we finish all of them off for good."[54] In other words, the goals were boundless and implacable but the tactics would have to be flexible and patient.

To prepare for a long-term struggle, Lenin created the Third International or Comintern. Superficially it resembled the Second International, in that it consisted of individual parties from numerous states, but it functioned more like a worldwide extension of the Bolshevik party. By its statutes, the decisions of the executive, which were unfailingly determined by the Russians, were "binding on all affiliated parties." In turn, each party was required to work by means of top-down "iron discipline," with "final authority and . . . broad powers" concentrated in its Central Committee. Each was required, moreover, to create a secret underground apparatus, even in countries where Communist parties were entirely legal. In short, just as Lenin had once commanded Bolshevik activities in Russia from the perch of exile, so now from Moscow he could command revolutionary activities in every corner of the globe.

It was not given to Lenin, however, to enjoy this control room. In May 1922, less than two years after the adoption of the statutes of the Comintern, he suffered a stroke. After some months, he was able to return to work, but in December a second stroke followed. In March 1923 came the third, which left him largely incapacitated until his death ten months later.

He had forged the instruments of the greatest system of absolutism history had ever known. And he had placed them within the reach of a favorite disciple, Stalin, although it is safe to assume that he never envisioned anyone but himself wielding them. Too late, he seems to have sensed what Stalin was up to, and to have glimpsed the Georgian's sinister side. He struggled to thwart him, but no longer had the strength to attend the necessary meetings, and Stalin had secured the authorization of the Politburo to isolate Lenin for the sake of his health. The failing leader was reduced to fighting by means of notes he dictated, and these had little sting. He complained that Stalin was "rude," but what was the force of this criticism among people whose métier was terror?

Lenin proposed that the Central Committee be expanded to include large numbers of rank-and-file workers, whose presence he felt would somehow purify it of the factional intrigues percolating in his absence. But it was late in the game for the Bolsheviks to add workers to positions of power. There had been few if any present when the party was founded, and few in authority at any time. The last worker to rise high had been Schliapnikov, the disgraced leader of the Workers' Opposition. The whole meaning of Bolshevism, beginning with Lenin's seminal *What Is to Be Done?,* was that socialism should be created for the workers, not by them. Now that the old man was unable to wield power himself, his proposal that his deputies yield it to a bunch of workers rather than take it in their own hands must have made them laugh.

6

FASCISM: MUSSOLINI
BECOMES A HERETIC

LENIN'S EFFORTS TO EXTEND HIS RULE beyond the bounds of imperial Russia failed, but his influence reached far and wide. It was felt not only in the network of Communist parties he established around the world, but in other important political movements as well. In China, the nationalist Guomindang allowed itself to be reorganized under the tutelage of Mikhail Borodin, an envoy from the Comintern. When Lenin died, Sun Yatsen, the father of Chinese nationalism, called him a "great man" and delivered this eulogy: "I wish to proceed along the path pointed out by you."[1] A closer disciple, albeit an eccentric one, was Italy's Mussolini, whose star was rising in 1922 just as Lenin's began to decline. Mussolini had by now abandoned socialism and was forging a new ideology that he called "fascism," yet he still felt a bond with Lenin. The journalist Margherita Sarfatti, one of Mussolini's deputies and mistresses, recalled:

> No one followed the developments of Bolshevism more closely than Mussolini. When the great magnates and high officials did not consider the movement worth studying and dismissed it with a shrug of their shoulders, he declared, "It will last! It will last! It has lasted some time already!"... [W]hat seemed like a tyranny did not horrify him sufficiently to prevent him from seeing the other side, realizing as he did that a temporary suspension of liberty may in the end be productive of much good to a great nation.[2]

Mussolini may in fact have been the original "red diaper baby." His father, Alessandro, a blacksmith, had been a member of the First International, along with Marx and Engels. As was common among Italian leftists, he leaned toward anarchism and was, according to Mussolini's one-time companion Angelica Balabanoff, a follower of Bakunin's.[3] His anarchism did not run so deep, however, as to deter him from assuming elective office as a Socialist member of the council of Predappio, the district in which his famous son was born on July 29, 1883. The boy, Benito Andrea Amilcare Mussolini, was named after three separate heroes of the revolutionary Left: a Mexican, Benito Juárez; and two Italians, Andrea Costa and Amilcare Cipriani. The son later recalled that his father's "heart and mind were always filled and pulsing with socialistic theories. . . . He discussed them in the evening with his friends and his eyes filled with light."[4] At home, he read sections of *Das Kapital* aloud to his family.[5]

The boy admired his father and embraced his ideals, but by all accounts, he was not an easy child. Perhaps he was troubled by the conflicts in the values that his two parents tried to instill in him. He dearly loved his mother, Rosa, the village schoolmistress, but she was a devout Catholic, while Alessandro, the revolutionary, was staunchly anticlerical. At age nine Benito was sent to a strict boarding school run by Silesian priests, but he was unhappy there and eventually got expelled for taking a knife to a fellow student. His parents sent him next to a secular boarding school at Forlimpopoli, where he completed his primary and secondary education. The rules were considerably more lax at this school, but nonetheless Benito got into trouble, at fourteen, for once again stabbing a classmate. (Apparently the problem of boys bringing weapons to school is not unique to twenty-first-century America.)

Despite Benito's checkered career as a student, his first job, at eighteen, was as a schoolteacher in the village of Gualtieri, which had a socialist administration. There he became politically active as the secretary of a socialist group. Soon, however, with a military call-up approaching, he left Italy for Switzerland, home to many expatriates, where he lived off friends and odd jobs, and, like so many other revolutionaries, received the occasional subvention from his parents. There are conflicting accounts about whether he encountered Lenin, who was also in exile in Switzerland at the time. Undoubtedly, however, he encountered Angelica Balabanoff, the rebellious daughter of Ukrainian aristocrats and close disciple of Lenin's, who had moved to Italy and was then carrying out socialist agitation among Italians in Switzerland. Together they translated a pamphlet of Karl Kautsky's into Italian, inaugurating a relationship of close collaboration that turned to hatred some twenty years later when she became secretary of the Comintern and he turned away from the Left.

In Switzerland, Mussolini began to publish articles and poems in socialist publications, including a sonnet about Babeuf. Despite Thermidor's triumph, it says, "Babeuf still smiles, the future in which his Idea will be realized flashed before his dying eyes."[6] And he developed his skills as a soapbox orator, specializing in anticlerical themes. Exhibiting in these stemwinders a penchant for theatrics, he would defy God to prove His existence by striking him down on the spot. He called religion a form of mental illness deserving psychiatric treatment (begging the question of what a psychiatrist might make of such pronouncements from the son of a devout mother). Around this time, Mussolini published his first small book, an atheist tract titled *Man and Divinity* in which he proclaimed grandly: "Faithful, the Anti-christ is born."[7]

In 1905, at age twenty-two, he took advantage of a general amnesty for draft dodgers and returned to Italy to do his service. While he was at it, his mother died and his father moved to Forlì, where Benito joined him after his discharge late in 1906. Like many a bachelor in his twenties, he found time both for some serious reading—Marx, Nietzsche, Sorel, classics of philosophy—and for a good deal of carousing, boasting of his "gigantic" drinking bouts.[8] He also engaged in an unending string of love affairs, mostly with married women.

He claimed to have written a history of philosophy in this period, which, according to the account given by Sarfatti, was lost forever when one of his jealous mistresses threw the manuscript into the fire in a fit of pique. But few other biographers believe this work ever existed. Still, his writing shows that he did develop his socialist ideas, mirroring Lenin in the hope that a "revolutionary vanguard" would lead the masses.[9] Like many of his compatriots, Mussolini was influenced by syndicalism, an ill-defined variant of socialism that stressed violent direct action and was simultaneously elitist and anti-statist. However, Mussolini did not leave the Socialist Party when its syndicalist faction was expelled in 1910.

In 1909 he accepted an offer from the Socialists in Trentino, a region populated by Italians under Austrian rule, to work there as editor of a weekly paper and party organizer. His no-holds-barred polemics with clerical adversaries got him several libel convictions. He made something of a specialty of accusing various priests of moral turpitude. Although he often lacked evidence, the subject was dear to him. Finally he hit upon a way to labor the issue without fear of legal reprisal: he published a pulp novel titled *Claudia Particella, the Cardinal's Mistress.*

When the Austrian authorities expelled him, he left behind two mistresses, one with his child (who died in infancy) and another with whom he would later have a child. But for now, back in Forlì at age twenty-seven, he set his heart on marrying eighteen-year-old Rachele, who had been his girlfriend before he went to Trentino. Her widowed mother worked in his father's home as his housekeeper. Both parents took a jaundiced view of the union, and they are unlikely to have been won over when Benito drunkenly pulled a revolver and threatened to kill himself if denied Rachele's hand. Nonetheless, the parents eventually acquiesced, and the couple, spurning bourgeois ceremony, moved in together. Seven months later their daughter Edda was born, the first of five children of a tumultuous, but not loveless, marriage that lasted thirty-five years.

Mussolini became secretary of the Socialist Federation of Forlì and editor of its paper, *La Lotta di Classe* ("The Class Struggle"), from which platform he established himself as a leading voice of the party's radical left wing. And a strident voice it was. Propounding proletarian internationalism, he declared: "The national flag is for us a rag to be planted on a dunghill." When, in 1911, Italy invaded Tripoli and Cyrenaica to wrest Libya from the Ottomans, the leaders of the party's large conservative faction supported the government while Mussolini emerged as the most intransigent opponent of the war. He was arrested for urging his followers to blow up railway lines to thwart military activity, and he served five and a half months in prison, long enough for the twenty-eight-year-old to compose his first autobiography.

The gap between revolutionaries and reformists among the Italian Socialists became unbridgeable when two of the more conservative Socialist deputies did something the left wing found unconscionable, offering the king congratulations on having survived an anarchist's assassination attempt. At the party's 1912 congress, with Balabanoff urging him on, Mussolini, a year shy of thirty, led a purge of the moderates. Lenin, writing in *Pravda,* registered his approval: "the party of the Italian socialist proletariat has taken the right path by removing the syndicalists and Right reformists from its ranks," he said.[10] He quoted approvingly "our compatriot" Balabanoff's injunction to the delegates not to be deterred from the purge by "sentimentality."

Mussolini and Balabanoff were both elected to the new executive, and four months later he was named editor of the party's national paper, *Avanti!* Thus he became the symbol of revolutionary militancy. Over the next two years, a growing number of Socialist Party adherents began to call themselves "Mussoliniani," including Antonio Gramsci and Amedeo Bordiga, who were to be founders of the Communist Party.[11] By the time of the Socialists' next party congress, in April 1914, Mussolini emerged as the party's dominant leader. The Mussoliniani participated in electoral politics, but unlike their less radical comrades they placed no ultimate hope in the ability of parliamentary institutions to bring the redemptive transformation of society they envisioned.

In addition to *Avanti!* Mussolini launched a monthly theoretical journal that he christened *Utopia*. He used it to try to resolve the problems that he, like Bernstein, Lenin and some of the French and Italian syndicalists, saw in classical Marxism, namely the invariable tendency of the average worker to become absorbed with the prosaic issues of improving his own life and to show little interest in the prospect of a new world. Political scientist A. James Gregor enumerated the many similarities between Mussolini's approach and Lenin's:

> Both insisted on intransigent opposition to bourgeois parliamentarianism, reformist policies, and compromissary political strategies. Both considered the Party a hierarchically organized agency for the effective furtherance of socialist objectives. Both envisioned a leadership composed of a minority of professional revolutionaries, who would serve as a catalyst in mobilizing mass revolutionary sentiment. Neither had any faith in the spontaneous organization of the working classes. Both argued that the preoccupation with immediate economic interests condemned exclusively economic organizations to a bourgeois mentality of calculation for personal profit and well-being. Both argued that only organized violence could be the final arbiter in a contest between classes. And both agreed that revolutionary consciousness could only be brought to the masses from without, through a tutelary, revolutionary, and self-selected elite.[12]

When war broke out, Lenin and Mussolini were each quoted as having uttered the identical response when informed of the French and German socialists' support for their governments: "The Socialist International is dead."[13] Both saw at once that some traditional socialist hopes had just died, and both sensed that some new opportunities were aborning. Briefly, as if on autopilot, Mussolini reprised his antiwar past, denouncing the conflict as an "unpardonable crime," but within two months he began to gravitate toward those who advocated entering the war on the side of the Entente. This led to a showdown within the editorial board of *Avanti!* and when Mussolini lost, he resigned. Within weeks, he launched his own paper, *Il Popolo d'Italia,* which espoused belligerency on the grounds that this would kindle revolution. His critics charged that *Il Popolo* was subsidized by the French government, which was eager to draw Italy into the war.

A month after his resignation from *Avanti!*, at a raucous meeting in Milan, Mussolini was expelled from the Socialist Party for "political and moral unwor-thiness." He shouted at his accusers: "You think you can turn me out, but you will find I shall come back again. I am and shall remain a socialist and my convic-tions will never change. They are bred in my very bones."[14] But Mussolini did not return to the party. Instead he joined a band called the Fascio Autonomo d'Azione Rivoluzionaria, which had been founded earlier by pro-war leftists, mostly revolutionary syndicalists. What a triumph it was for them when such a prominent leader of Italian socialism joined their ranks! Naturally, he became their leader almost at once.

The adoption of a pro-war stance did not signify a shift to the political Right. On the contrary, *fascio,* meaning "bundle" and suggesting people tightly bonded, was a symbol adopted by the French Revolution. The original Italian Fascists were pro-war leftists, and the reasons they advanced for Italy's entry into the war were couched in the terms of the Left. Like the French socialists, they described Germany as the main bastion of reaction on the Continent. Defeating the Hohenzollern and Hapsburg empires would liberate many captive people, including Italians such as those in Trentino. This would complete the process of national unification, creating the necessary framework for Italy's transition to socialism. Like Lenin, Mussolini said that the war would be a beneficial catalyst.

Although unshaken in his socialist convictions, Mussolini began to weigh the implications of the collapse of the Second International under the impact of nationalist sentiment. "I saw that internationalism was crumbling," he later recalled, and he concluded that it was "utterly foolish" to suppose that even a socialist state could transcend "the old barriers of race and historical conten-tions."[15] "The sentiment of nationality exists and cannot be denied," he wrote, and he pondered the ideological implications: "I have asked myself if interna-tionalism is an absolutely necessary constituent of the notion of socialism. A future socialism might well concern itself with finding an equilibrium between nation and class."[16]

In his new paper, *Il Popolo d'Italia,* Mussolini argued that the support for maintaining Italy's neutrality was coming only from the forces of reaction, except for the traditional socialists who had sold out to Germany. "It is necessary to assassinate the Party in order to save Socialism," he wrote. In the spring of 1915, he exhorted readers to take part in mass demonstrations for entry into the war: "Proletarians, come into the streets and piazzas with us and cry: 'Down with the corrupt mercantile policy of the Italian bourgeoisie' and demand war against the Empires responsible for the European conflagration. Long live the war of liberation of the peoples!"[17]

In May 1915 Italy went to war, and within a few months, Mussolini was called to service. Eager to see action, he turned down a desk job, and by all accounts served competently, even earning a few promotions. In February 1917 he suffered severe shrapnel wounds, and after a few months in the hospital he was discharged from the service. The experience of battle affected him deeply. In 1914 he had begun to recognize the power of nationalism; after two years of war he began to feel it within his own breast. He discovered that he was, as he put it, "desperately Italian."[18]

From the time he left the army until the armistice, he agitated, in the pages of *Il Popolo* and through the bands of men that he influenced, for maximal prosecution of the war. He lashed out against the Socialists and the pope for advocating peace short of victory, and against the Bolsheviks for taking Russia out of the war. He began to propound substantial territorial claims for Italy. And he spoke of the need for a *trincerocrazia,* meaning rule by those who had been in the trenches. If sharing a workplace was an experience that could bind people into a political class, as Marxist theory asserted, how much more powerful was the experience of sharing combat? The *trincerocrazia* was less a proposal than a slogan designed to encourage veterans to see themselves as a political constituency. Mussolini recognized that just as the Socialist parties had prospered by directing their appeal to industrial workers, something similar could be done by championing the cause of veterans. Numerous *arditi,* rough-and-tumble bands of former servicemen who distinguished themselves by wearing black shirts as shock troops had done in the army, rallied to the fascist banner, and this item of dress became the movement's symbol.

Early in 1919, shortly after the war's end, Mussolini determined to unite the various local fascist groups into a national organization. On March 23, fifty-odd delegates met in Milan and founded the *Fasci di Combattimento.* The participants were an ideological potpourri, of which the largest contingents were revolutionary syndicalists and "futurists." Futurism was an early-twentieth-century art movement that aimed to overthrow classical sensibilities by exalting machinery and motion as paradigms of beauty. It was, says political scientist

Zeev Sternhell, "the first intellectual current to give a political formulation to an aesthetic conception."[19] But it might be more accurate to say that futurism gave aesthetic formulation to a political sentiment: it was a reaction against Italy's weakness and backwardness, against the image of the country as a placid repository of antiquities. Thus, it shared the nationalist and revolutionary passions that were fascism's essential ingredients.

Although nationalism was beginning to overshadow socialism in Mussolini's political thought, and although he begrudged the Socialists their pacifism, nonetheless the program advanced by the fascist movement in its early months was still cut from socialist cloth. As Denis Mack Smith summarizes:

> It called for "land to the peasants" and workers' representation in management, as well as a progressive tax on capital, expropriation of land and factories, greater inheritance taxes and confiscation of excessive war profits. In addition, it demanded nationalization of the armaments industry, a legally fixed minimum wage, abolition of the senate, votes for women and a large-scale decentralization of government.[20]

In reconciling socialism and nationalism, fascism embraced an interpretation advanced by Enrico Corradini, a prominent nationalist intellectual. Because Italy was poorer and weaker than the leading European powers and was exploited by them, it was a "proletarian nation." Its struggle against the "rich nations" therefore took on the same urgency and righteousness as the struggle of workers against capitalists.[†]

Parliamentary elections in November 1919 gave the Fascists their first popular test. Most of their candidates, including Mussolini, presented the party as a part of the Left not only in the tenets of its platform but also in its readiness to ally with other leftist parties in the proportional representation system then in effect. The results were painful. The Fascists did not win a single seat, while the Socialists came out best, winning a third of the total vote and over 150 seats. From this, Mussolini apparently deduced, as historian Robert O. Paxton put it, that "there was no space in Italian politics for a party that was both nationalist and Left."[21] And so, step by step, he repositioned the party.

[†] The identical argument was formulated independently in 1920 with regard to China by Li Dazhou, the intellectual father of the Communist Party of China, and became a hallmark of Maoism. See Jonathan D. Spence, *The Search for Modern China* (New York: W. W. Norton, 1990), p. 308.

Il Popolo ceased calling itself "socialist," but rather a "journal of the combatants and producers."[22] While dropping the term "socialism," Mussolini "was quick to remind his readers that he was prepared to assimilate everything that remained vital in its tradition," says Gregor.[23] Moreover, there were sound Marxian grounds for abandoning (or at least postponing) the quest for socialism, as had been argued by various of the revolutionary syndicalists who had helped to found fascism. Since Italy was not yet an industrialized country, it needed first to experience full capitalist development before it would be ready for socialist transformation. The Bolsheviks had believed they could transcend this progression and leap directly to socialism; but Lenin had acknowledged that his New Economic Policy of 1920 constituted a retreat to capitalism, and Mussolini took careful note of this. Here was proof that the capitalist phase could not be skipped over.[24]

Further spurring Mussolini away from the Left was his hostility toward the Socialist and Communist parties. He could not forgive the former for the way it had cast him out, while the latter had been founded by one-time Mussoliniani who had abandoned him. Moreover, he cursed the Socialists for their opposition to the war and was even more antagonistic toward the Communists because Lenin had allowed himself to be used by Italy's great enemy, Germany. He railed against the "tyranny" of the Bolsheviks, professing himself a pure libertarian (much as Lenin had done in *State and Revolution,* the pamphlet he wrote less than a year before coming to power). More important, however, than Mussolini's visceral hostility toward the two main leftist parties was his sense that these were his rivals in the struggle for power. "Two religions are today contending . . . for sway over the world—the black and the red," he wrote. "We declare ourselves the heretics."[25]

Mussolini's ideas were also growing more antidemocratic. The weakness of Italy's democracy was underscored in September 1919 when another Socialist military veteran turned nationalist, the poet and playwright Gabriele D'Annunzio, led a band of irregulars in occupying the city of Fiume, which had been awarded to Yugoslavia by the Treaty of Versailles. The Italian government, overawed by the popularity of D'Annunzio's action, stood by inert, signaling a breakdown in the rule of law. This suited Mussolini, for whom the attraction of extraparliamentary methods was intensified by the Fascists' humiliating defeat in that year's election. He was envious of D'Annunzio and reinforced in his conviction of the power of nationalism. He hit upon a strategy signified by his description of himself as a heretic: he would work in tandem with the

Left to bring down the constitutional system, while building his base among those frightened by the Left and those for whom country was the most potent political symbol.

Over the next two years, Socialists and Communists sponsored an unprecedented wave of strikes. These were often accompanied by the seizure or destruction of property and violence against strikebreakers. In parallel, in the countryside, property was taken from landowners and turned into collective farms, whether or not the peasants wished it. To the radicals who organized these actions, they constituted the cutting edge of the movement to overthrow the bourgeois democratic order. In localities where the Left gained control of the government, including Rome, the Italian flag was removed from government buildings and replaced by the red flag. In some places, Sunday was replaced by Monday as the official day of rest, in riddance to clerical "superstitions." In Bologna, a "soviet" was proclaimed. In Viareggio, Bolshevik stamps and currency were issued. In Milan, anarchists detonated a bomb in the Diana Theater during a performance, killing eighteen. As a whole, this period came to be called the "Red Biennium."

Many parties contributed to the violence in the streets and workplaces, but the Fascists usually took it further than their adversaries. Given Mussolini's own taste for violence and his constituency of footloose veterans, it was a realm of competition for which they were best equipped.

For a time, even while his strong-arm squads burned Socialist properties or mixed it up with Communists and anarchists, Mussolini remained vaguely on the Left. He was anticlerical and antimonarchical. He supported some of the factory seizures in 1920, and he tried to induce the workers to embrace him as their leader. But he found his niche as a strikebreaker, and when the deterioration of civil order impelled the government to call new elections in 1921 he blocked with the Right. His party, now rechristened the National Fascist Party, entered Parliament for the first time, with thirty-five representatives. With his characteristic theatricality, Mussolini, fresh from the Left, now announced that he represented the extreme of the Right, and Fascist deputies ostentatiously took up seats in the far right side of the chamber. But this did not prevent him a few months later from proposing an alliance with the Socialists and Left Catholics when the mainstream conservatives faltered.

Like Lenin, who had disingenuously advocated power to the soviets and the election of a Constituent Assembly, all in order to undermine the provisional government, Mussolini played a double game in the quest of taking power into his own hands. He was both a parliamentarian and the author of street violence.

He lacerated the government for its failure to maintain order, while his own minions contributed more than their share to the mayhem. He posed at struggling to restrain his followers; and in fact there was an element of genuineness to this, as some of his lieutenants were more reckless than he, yet he bestowed his blessings on whatever escapades they got away with.

The parliamentary coalition with the Left that Mussolini proposed in mid-1921 did not come to fruition, and the Fascist Party Congress late that year embraced a program that Mussolini described as "decidedly antisocialist." By 1922 the confrontation in the streets between the Fascists and the parties of the Left reached its apogee. The Socialists and Communists called a general strike on July 31 to protest the government's failure to suppress Fascist violence. During the preceding months, squads of Blackshirts had rampaged through Mussolini's native region of Romagna, a traditional bastion of the Left, systematically burning Socialist and Communist offices.

These *squadristi* had been formally organized, on Mussolini's orders, by the twenty-five-year-old tough Italo Balbo. They were assigned uniforms and officers and organized into "legions," each commanded by a "consul," with the top officers directly appointed by *Il Duce,* which means "the commander." The legions were subdivided into "cohorts," "*centurie*" and "squads." Their members were taught a stiff-armed "Roman salute," popularized by D'Annunzio in Fiume. It was, in short, all military histrionics and evocations of ancient Rome.

When the parties of the Left announced their general strike, the Fascists delivered an ultimatum to the government: stop the strike or we will stop it ourselves. Without waiting for the authorities to act (although there was little likelihood that they would), the *squadristi* were dispatched to maintain public services abandoned by strikers. They proved themselves capable of operating streetcars and the like—and even more capable of suppressing violently any who tried to impede them. Within a day the strike was broken. The battle for the streets had been decided. Not only had Fascists demoralized the Left, but they had won the appreciation of many Italians who were fed up with constant strikes and the disorder they symbolized. By their efficient, albeit ruthless, strikebreaking, the Fascists created the image that they could provide more effective governance than the feckless parliaments of recent years.

• • •

This triumph generated a momentum that within three months carried fascism to power. Mussolini's "March on Rome" is as mythical as Lenin's "October Revolution." Lenin took power in a coup, not a popular uprising, and Mussolini's marchers did not arrive in Rome until after King Vittorio Emanuele had asked him to form a government. During the weeks before, he and his deputies had planned to send their "legions" to Rome to seize the government, much as D'Annunzio took Fiume. They did not conceal their intent, and in late October thousands of Blackshirts began to assemble north of the capital, while in other cities they seized administrative offices. Few observers doubt that the army could have routed the Fascist squads easily, as garrisons in fact did in several locales. At the last minute, the cabinet asked Vittorio Emanuele to declare martial law. Until then, few mainstream political leaders had recognized the threat to the constitutional order posed by the Fascists. Just as the moderate socialists in Russia abetted Lenin's triumph because they were mesmerized by the illusory fear of a tsarist restoration, so the center in Italy had been alert to a revolutionary danger only from the Left. Now it was too late. The king spurned their belated pleas to stand against the Fascists, as he feared for the loyalty of the troops. Instead he reshuffled the government, offering Mussolini a portfolio. But this was like blood to a shark. Recognizing that he held the advantage, Mussolini held out for the top position, and the king acquiesced. On October 30, Mussolini was appointed prime minister. His wife, Rachele, is reported to have exclaimed when she heard the news: "What a character!"[26]

Riding an initial wave of popularity, Mussolini asked Parliament for a grant of emergency powers, and this was authorized by an overwhelming vote, only the Communists and most Socialists opposing. Then, a combination of legal formalities and raw force was employed to bring opposition parties and newspapers to heel. None were banned, but politicians who dared to be outspokenly critical were liable to be assaulted, as were editors, who also might see their offices or presses vandalized.

To complete the consolidation of power, a new electoral law was pushed through by the same intimidation tactics that Lenin had used against the Constituent Assembly: armed militiamen filled the galleries and threatened the deputies. Elections under the new rules were held in the spring of 1924, and thousands of politicians, not all of them Fascists, sought to be listed on the Fascist slate. Amidst many irregularities, including Blackshirt violence and fraud, the Fascist list won an overwhelming majority of popular votes and seats.

When the new Parliament convened, the most pointed denunciations of the election procedures came from the prominent Socialist deputy Giacomo Matteotti. Several times already, Matteotti had been accosted by Blackshirts, but he was a large and fearless man, and these attacks did nothing to cow him.

Now, however, he turned up missing. His building attendant at once reported the license plate number of the car in which he had been carried away, and it was traced to a prominent Fascist. Amidst an international outcry as well as personal dogging by Matteotti's wife, Mussolini pledged a thorough investigation. The bloodstained car was found, and a couple of months later so was Matteotti's body. The men who had dragged him away were identified—all of them members of a particularly rough group of *squadristi* known as the Cheka, after Lenin's secret police. (However fierce they grew in their antipathy to communism, the Fascists never ceased mimicking it, implicitly underscoring their claim to be the true or superior heirs to the same legacy.) The trail of command led right to Mussolini's inner circle. One of its number, Cesare Rossi, admitted under questioning that he had arranged the killing—on Mussolini's veiled orders. He claimed that Mussolini had ranted: "What is the Cheka doing?...That man [Matteotti], after that speech, should no longer be in circulation."[27]

Mussolini denied Rossi's account—denied that there was any "Cheka," except as a term of slander used by his opponents. But public opinion and much of the usually quiescent political elite were roiled. Mussolini complained that it was difficult to act "with a corpse under my feet." As rumors of his downfall spread, Blackshirt leaders from around the country converged on Rome to buck him up. Finally, he rallied to make a remarkable speech in Parliament in January 1925. While denying that he had ordered the murder, he said:

> I declare here before this assembly, before all the Italian people, that I assume, I alone, the political, moral, historical responsibility for everything that has happened. If sentences, more or less maimed, are enough to hang a man, out with the noose! If Fascism has only been castor oil or a club, and not a proud passion of the best Italian youth, the blame is on me! If Fascism has been a criminal association, if all the violence has been the result of a determined historical, political, moral delinquency, the responsibility for this is on me.[28]

At one stroke this speech disarmed his critics for its apparent contrition, while making more plausible his denial of direct guilt. There was a further cunning ploy in it. His acknowledgment that power implies responsibility pointed to a corollary, namely that those who bear the burden of responsibility must have power. With this as the implicit rationale, he hinted it was time for more iron-fisted rule. "Italy, Gentlemen, wants peace, wants quiet, wants work, wants calm: we will give it with love, if that be possible, or with strength, if that be

necessary," he warned. He invoked the constitutional provision on impeachment, inviting the deputies to make use of it. Otherwise, he suggested, the
Matteotti affair should no longer be dwelt upon.

The next month, Roberto Farinacci was named to the post of secretary of
the Fascist Party. An ex-Socialist like Mussolini, Farinacci was identified with
the more brutal and reckless elements among the *squadristi*. Indeed, he served
as defense counsel for the men accused of carrying out Matteotti's murder. On
the heels of Farinacci's elevation, a new wave of violence ensued against opposition politicians and critical journalists. The ratcheting up of Fascist power was
executed not only in the streets, but also through formal actions. The cabinet
was narrowed, with the remaining liberals replaced, and a new restrictive press
law was decreed requiring police permission for the opening of a publication.
It authorized local prefects to confiscate any issue that "complicated" the work
of the government or "incited" readers to any one of a long list of misdemean-
ors. In April 1926 a new labor law was promulgated banning strikes by public
employees or for political goals. More important, it required all officers of
labor, business or professional associations to "give proof of their competence,
good moral behavior, and positive faith in the nation." Fascist labor unions were
decreed to be the sole legal representatives of employees.

This increased repression, which foreclosed peaceful means of opposing the
regime, was followed by a series of assassination attempts against the emerging
dictator. In November 1925, the Socialist deputy Tito Zaniboni was arrested
in a hotel room, aiming his rifle through the window at the balcony across the
street where Mussolini was due to appear. Within the next year there were three
additional attempts on the leader's life. These provocations led in turn to further
repressive measures. The death penalty was introduced for attempting to kill top
officials, and "revolutionary tribunals," reminiscent of those created by Lenin,
were established to try political "crimes." Also probably inspired by Lenin, a
formal secret police force was created, called the Organizzazione Vigilanza
Repressione Antifascismo, or Ovra. (The so-called "Cheka" was nothing more
than a particularly violent coterie of Blackshirts.)

Socialist, Communist and other Left deputies were expelled from
Parliament, and those parties were effectively banned. Gramsci and Bordiga,
old Mussoliniani and now leaders of the Communists, were imprisoned. A further electoral reform enacted in 1928 provided that all four hundred deputies
would be elected as a block from a single slate, which the electorate could either
approve or disapprove. The four hundred candidates were nominated by the

Grand Council of Fascism, a kind of mock cabinet appointed by Mussolini that wielded no effective power. But creating a one-party system was not enough. Like Lenin, Mussolini discovered that effective suppression of opposition parties could be vitiated by pluralism within the ruling party. Hence he abolished elections of party officials, making them all appointed from the top, and he drastically curtailed debate within the party.

Finally, Mussolini undertook to "fascistize" society, speaking often of his aim to create a "new Italian"—socialism's "new man" with a nationalist twist. Toward this end, he created a Fascist children's organization, the Opera Nazionale Balilla, along the lines of the Soviet Komsomol. Participation was mandatory up to the age of fifteen; and the Boy Scouts and the Catholic youth organization, seen as potential competitors, were banned. He put forth the motto: "Everything inside the state; nothing outside the state." And he coined the term "totalitarian state" to express his ideal. This term was later taken up by scholars examining Nazi and Communist regimes, in comparison to which, ironically, Fascist Italy, though quite repressive, did not seem very totalitarian. Mussolini's rule rested far more on popular support than Lenin's and far less on killing. Altogether the number of Italians executed by Fascist courts or murdered by Fascist thugs numbered in the dozens, whereas Lenin ordered tens of thousands of deaths. Still, the similarities were deep.

While some socialists saw themselves as libertarians, others grasped that a goal as lofty as a new world and a new man implied a great exercise of power, and they were thrilled by it. This was a sensation shared by Lenin and Mussolini and by their followers. Thus, not only did the Fascists freely imitate the Communists, but often, too, the two movements proceeded on parallel tracks because they had common origins and similar impulses.

The Fascist regime, like the Soviet, carried popular indoctrination to unheard-of lengths. In Italy, as in the U.S.S.R. under Stalin, this included promoting a cult of the leader. Crowds at public events were encouraged to chant *"Du-ce, Du-ce, Du-ce."* The party ordered that pronouns referring to him in print be capitalized, as they are for God. Among the officially sanctioned graffiti splashed across walls around Italy was the slogan "Mussolini is always right."

Not only did underlings and other ambitious Italians fall over each other in flattering the Duce, but many foreign visitors joined the comedy. Much as famous Western intellectuals believed they had seen a "future [that] works" in Soviet Russia, so such eminent figures as Winston Churchill and Mahatma Gandhi waxed lyrical on what they encountered in Fascist Italy. And just as one U.S. ambassador to Moscow babbled inanely about the "Soviet Robin Hood (Stalin),"[29] so the American ambassador to Italy, Richard Washburn Child, heaped praise on its dictator: "In our time it may be shrewdly forecast that no man will exhibit dimensions of permanent greatness equal to those of Mussolini."[30]

In keeping with Mussolini's personality, a great deal of Fascist governance consisted of showmanship. The handshake was officially replaced with the "Roman salute," said to be more manly and more hygienic. In fulfillment of the Fascist promise to restore order to Italy, one-way pedestrian traffic was ordered on some streets. A wide "Avenue of Empire" was constructed, down which Mussolini rode on horseback upon its opening. Marble maps of the Roman Empire were installed near the Forum, and *Il Duce* posed before them. Boxing was encouraged as an "exquisitely fascist" sport, in Mussolini's words, and when an Italian, Primo Carnera, won the world heavyweight championship, the Fascists were ecstatic. The Duce himself vetted plays and movies before public release, sometimes improving the endings. And in the effort to develop a distinctly Fascist art, much like Soviet "socialist realism," an annual award was given for the finest painting on a prescribed theme, such as "listening to a speech by the Duce on the radio."[31]

In the cause of national grandeur, Mussolini tried to foster population growth. Toward that end he forbade emigration and urged large families, banned birth control and levied a tax on "unjustified celibacy." For Italian women he extolled a lifestyle focused on homemaking and childrearing. Ironically, given the Duce's own compulsive philandering, new penalties on adultery were enacted. None of this caused the birthrate to rise. In 1928, eerily foreshadowing Pol Pot, the regime unfurled the slogan "Empty the cities," hoping to encourage the preservation of rural life with its higher birthrates. Yet despite the idealization, life on the farms was not prospering, and the Fascist government resorted to campaigns of exhortation ("the battle for grain"), with Mussolini posing on tractors, in the hope of boosting the harvests.

The Fascist regime also inaugurated a major extension of the welfare state and public works projects. The Charter of Labor announced in 1927 by the Grand Council of Fascism, and later implemented through a variety of legislation, entailed insurance against accidents, illness, old age and occupational diseases; assistance for disabled workers; measures against malaria and tuberculosis; and scholarships for children.[32] Contracts promulgated under its aegis by the state labor associations provided for minimum pay scales, paid vacations and other fringe benefits. Businesses were required to hire disabled war veterans. A national system of summer camps was set up. Children were assigned for a month either to the seashore or to the mountains, according to a health official's judgment of what would most benefit each child. In addition, an agency for adult leisure-time activities sponsored vacations, athletic programs and cultural activities. Summarizing all of this, Mussolini boasted: "Italy is advanced beyond all the European nations....There is little which social welfare research has adjudged practical to national economy or wise for social happiness which has not already been advanced by me."[33]

This elaborate welfare state was introduced within the context of an economic policy that officially lauded the benefits of private enterprise. But this changed in the face of the Depression when Mussolini introduced the concept of "corporatism." Although ill-defined, its essence was to make the state the dominant force in the economy. Capitalism, he explained, betraying the earmarks of his early Marxist training, evolves through three historic stages, "the dynamic, the static, the declining." With the advent of corporatism in Italy, "the method of capitalistic production is superseded and with it the theory of economic liberalism which illustrated and provided the apology for it." This did not mean that corporatism was synonymous with socialism; rather, corporatism "overcomes Socialism as well as it does Liberalism [and] creates a new synthesis."[34] Thus was the "dialectic"—the creative clash of opposites—carried a step beyond where Marx and Engels thought it would end.

· · ·

Whatever the twists or achievements of Fascist economic and social policies, the regime's preeminent goal was national greatness. And the realm in which this might be achieved was not domestic, but international. Less than a year after Mussolini took power, an Italian delegation mediating the border between Greece and Albania was ambushed on Greek soil. Mussolini took this as an opportunity to assert Italian honor. He demanded monetary reparations and other acts of obeisance from the Greek government. To enforce this demand, he sent a fleet to bombard and occupy the Greek island of Corfu, at a cost of several deaths, primarily of orphans in a bombed hospital. Eventually, Greece ceded most of the Italian demands and Italy withdrew.

One voice notably missing from the international criticism of Italy over Corfu was the Kremlin's. While he had invoked the domestic Bolshevik menace as a foil in his rise to power, warning that Italy's Communists were "directed from Moscow" like an "invad[ing]" force,[35] Mussolini had in fact always gotten along well with the U.S.S.R. In 1924 he had raced with Britain's new Labour prime minister, Ramsay MacDonald, to be the first to recognize the Soviet Union. A few months later, when indignation over Matteotti's murder led other foreign missions to shun Mussolini, the Soviet ambassador had him in for a well-publicized lunch.

The Russian and Italian dictators seemed to catch a glimpse of themselves when they looked at one another. The British journalist George Slocombe, who interviewed Mussolini at the 1922 Cannes conference, reported that "Lenin was the only contemporary for whom he would express respect."[36] Meanwhile, Comintern chief Nikolai Bukharin commented that in their methods of combat, the Fascists "more than any other party, have adopted and applied . . . the experiences of the Russian Revolution."[37] Later, Mussolini perceived that the Soviet system under Stalin had become a kind of "Slav fascism" or "crypto-fascism."[38] And a leading Italian Fascist theoretician, Ugo Spirito, speculated on the likely "synthesis" of the two systems.[39]

While Mussolini borrowed much from the Bolsheviks, he in turn became a model for revolutionaries and power-seekers in other nations. During the 1920s and 1930s fascist movements arose to play important parts in the political lives of more than a dozen European countries. Although Mussolini was often quoted as having declared that "fascism is not for export," in fact he offered aid and encouragement to a number of these parties, often through secret channels. For example, Italy set up training bases for the gunmen of the Croatian Ustase movement and gave its leader, Ante Pavelic, sanctuary when he fled a murder charge in Yugoslavia and evaded another one in France.[40] The Ustase aimed for independence from Yugoslavia, a goal which dovetailed with Mussolini's territorial aspirations in Dalmatia. Thus, ideological affinity was reinforced by practical reasons of state.

While succoring the fascist movements, Mussolini did not try to control them the way Moscow controlled the parties of the Comintern. Thus there was little uniformity among them ideologically. Like Mussolini, other fascist leaders patched their programs together opportunistically, often indulging in self-contradictions and vagueness. They were usually antidemocratic, but their common denominator was extreme nationalism and anti-Bolshevism. Most were also anti-Semitic, some for traditionalist reasons, such as clericalism, others because of the prominence of Jews among the Bolsheviks in Russia, Germany and Hungary. As with Italian fascism, the fact that they were anti-Bolshevik did not mean they were pro-capitalist; more often they were quite the opposite. And many of the parties and leaders had leftist strains in their backgrounds.

The British Union of Fascists, for example, was led by Sir Oswald Mosley, a former Labour MP. He had been the youngest member of the Labour cabinet in 1930 when he broke from the party to protest its failure to intervene more vigorously in the economy. With some other leftists he had founded the more radical New Party, but after a visit to Italy to study Mussolini's accomplishments, he merged his group with the small Imperial Fascist League to form the Union, which changed its name in 1936 to the British Union of Fascists and National Socialists. When the war began, its leaders were arrested and locked away.

France was home to the greatest multiplicity of fascist groups, of which the original, Charles Maurras' Action Française, antedated Italian fascism by more than a decade. Maurras was a monarchist and clericalist. His demons were Jews, Protestants, foreigners, Freemasons—and especially democracy. But not social-ism! On the contrary, he once said: "*A socialism liberated from the democratic and cosmopolitan element* fits nationalism as a well-made glove fits a beautiful hand."[41] When a bitter confrontation with the Vatican sent Action Française into decline, some half-dozen groups attempted to fill the void. Among them were the Parti Populaire Français, led by Parliament member Jacques Doriot, who came over from the Communists, and another group led by the breakaway Socialist Marcel Déat, coiner of the famous antiwar slogan "Die for Danzig?" Déat declared: "Let us unite the revolutionary tradition and the socialist aspiration . . . and . . . by a specifically French path we will find ourselves on ground extremely close to that of German National Socialism."[42]

In Belgium, a smattering of fascist groups were all pro-worker and anticapi-talist, and the ones that were Flemish were also anti-French. More interesting than any of these parties, however, was the role played by a leader of the Socialist Party, Henry De Man. A socialist theoretician of global reputation, De Man in 1930 exchanged warm letters with Mussolini.[43] In 1940, he hailed Belgium's surrender to Nazi forces as "a deliverance" from "capitalist plutocracy."[44] He announced that the "political role" of the Socialist Party, of which he was then president, was "terminated"; and he called on his comrades to "prepare . . . to enter the cadres of a movement of national resurrection" under the Nazis that would "realize the Sovereignty of Labor."

In Spain, where syndicalism was as strong within the Left as in Italy, the Groups of National Syndicalist Offensive merged into José Antonio Prima de Rivera's Falange movement, which declared itself neither Left nor Right, while putting forward a program of land reform based on the creation of cooperative farms. It became the political constituency for General Franco's antidemocratic rebellion.

In Hungary, the military officer Gyula Gombos, one of the leaders of the campaign to oust Béla Kun's brief Bolshevist regime (and of the "white terror" that ensued), went on to become defense minister and later prime minister. He called himself a "national socialist" before Hitler's party began using that term. Another military officer, Ferenc Szalasi, founded the Arrow Cross movement. It expounded a vaguely socialist philosophy of "Hungarism," which aimed to do away with the "obsolete system of private capital."[45] Szalasi became head of the government under the German occupation, assisting eagerly in the Holocaust.

The man whose collaboration with Nazi occupiers was so notorious that his name has entered the English language as a synonym for "traitor," Norway's Vidkun Quisling, was no mere puppet but a devout adherent of National Socialism, and he liked to insist that the Nazis were doing his work, rather than vice versa. His ideological evolution had also wound through the Left: in 1924 and 1925 he had served as an organizer for the Red Guards, a Norwegian Communist group.

Other fascist groups and leaders did not have roots in the Left, but the common attributes of fascism stamped it as an offshoot of revolutionary socialism. Unlike any previous movements of the Right, fascism aimed to mobilize the common man through the promise of a secular millennium. It sought to achieve this by means of a popular revolution to sweep away the stodginess, loneliness and mediocrity of bourgeois existence. In its place would arise a kingdom of fraternal solidarity and heroic achievement, all of which would be expressed and fostered through the organs of the state.

Fascism also borrowed much of the paraphernalia of socialism. Where the socialists decked out their legions in red shirts, the fascists countered with black or brown or silver. Where the socialists sang the *Internationale,* so the fascists had their anthems, such as the Italian *Giovinezza* or the German *Horst Wessel Lied.* Where the socialists hailed each other with a clenched-fist salute, the fascists, and not just in Italy, adopted the stiff-armed "Roman salute." Like variations on a musical theme, these small changes were reminiscent of the way the Christian church devised its own versions of the Sabbath and the sacramental bread and wine of Judaism. They were reminders of Mussolini's point that fascism was a heresy of socialism—bearing much the same relationship as Christianity to Judaism or other heretical schisms.

The linkage was made explicit in the name of the most consequential of the fascist movements, the National Socialist German Workers' Party. It was founded in 1919 by the Munich locksmith and toolmaker Anton Drexler.[46] During the war, Drexler had abandoned the Social Democratic Party, which he found insufficiently nationalistic, for the Fatherland Party. Then he left this, too, because of its lack of concern for workers, and launched the German Workers' Party. When Hitler joined the party some months later, he was instrumental in changing its name by adding the words "National Socialist" to emphasize the blending of nationalism with socialism. The point was reinforced in the design of the party flag: red with a white disk encompassing a black swastika. As Hitler explained in *Mein Kampf*, "In *red* we see the social idea of the movement, in *white* the nationalistic idea, in the *swastika* the mission of the struggle for the victory of the Aryan man."[47] Red was used, as well, for the background of party placards, and members addressed and spoke of one another as "comrades" (*Genossen*), the same term used by the parties of the Left.

Not only the party's symbols, but also its "eternal" program, drawn up by Drexler and Hitler in 1920, was socialistic. In addition to chauvinism and violent antipathy to Jews, it contained the following points: "abolition of incomes unearned by work"; "ruthless confiscation of all war gains"; "nationalization of all . . . trusts"; "profits from wholesale trade shall be shared out"; "extensive . . . provision for old age"; "immediate communalization of department stores"; "confiscation without compensation of land for common purposes; abolition of interest on land loans, and prevention of all speculation in land"; "usurers, profiteers, etc., must be punished with death, whatever their creed or race"; "opening to every capable and industrious German the possibility of higher education . . . [and] development of the gifted children of poor parents, whatever their class or occupation, at the expense of the State"; and "The state must see to raising the standard of health in the nation by protecting mothers and infants, prohibiting child labor . . . by obligatory gymnastics and sports . . . and by extensive support of clubs engaged in the bodily development of the young."

What distinguished Nazism from traditional forms of socialism was its febrile nationalism, although not its virulence against despised peoples. Marx, as we have seen, looked forward to the "annihilation" of "reactionary races." The examples he gave were "Croats, Pandurs, Czechs and similar scum."[48] He did not in this passage mention Jews, but his desire for their disappearance was amply expressed elsewhere. His aspiration for "the emancipation of society from

Judaism" because "the practical Jewish spirit" of "huckstering" had taken over the Christian nations[49] is not that far from the Nazi program's twenty-fourth point: "combat[ting] the Jewish-materialist spirit within us and without us" in order "that our nation can . . . achieve permanent health."

What also distinguished National Socialism from the mainstream Left was Hitler's insistence that he aimed to "destroy Marxism," and he railed in *Mein Kampf* against "scatterbrains" who "have not understood the difference between socialism and Marxism."[50] Yet on other occasions he confessed himself an heir to the Marxian legacy. "National Socialism derives from each of the two camps the pure idea that characterizes it, national resolution from the bourgeois tradition, [and] vital, creative socialism from the teachings of Marxism," he told an interviewer in 1934.[51] And his one-time disciple Hermann Rauschning wrote that Hitler once said to him:

> I have learned a great deal from Marxism as I do not hesitate to admit. . . . The difference between them and myself is that I have really put into practice what these peddlers and pen-pushers have timidly begun. The whole of National Socialism is based on it. . . . National Socialism is what Marxism might have been if it could have broken its absurd and artificial ties with a democratic order.[52]

What was repugnant to Hitler about Marx was not his philosophy but his Jewishness. Of course, he detested the internationalism, but this only strengthened his conviction that Marxism was a Judaic doctrine. When he spoke of destroying it, he really meant destroying Judaism. In a 1920 speech titled "Why Are We Anti-Semites?" Hitler summarized Marx's writings on "the Jewish question," saying:

> Others explained to us [that] our further political organization is entirely unnecessary; it is sufficient that the scientific perception of the danger of Jewry gradually be deepened and each individual, in light of this perception, begin to eliminate the Jew from himself. . . . Then it was further explained to us: political organization is also unnecessary. It is sufficient to strip the Jew of his economic power.[53]

But Hitler rejected these solutions as inadequate, since Jewishness in his view was an indelible trait, and the Jews had to be attacked politically. So he added this note of ridicule: "I very much fear that this entire beautiful chain of thought was developed by none other than a Jew himself."

Some other leading Nazis were more friendly to the traditional Left than Hitler. Goebbels, who was identified with the party's left wing, wrote in 1926, "We look towards Russia, because Russia is that country most likely to take the road to socialism with us: because Russia is an ally nature has given us against the devilish contamination and corruption of the West."[54]

When the Nazis took power, they did not carry out all of the provisions of their 1920 program. Most of the economy was left in private hands, although state control was imposed through official "four-year plans," a transparent imitation of Soviet "five-year plans." They did implement the promised social welfare measures, and they promoted a national ethos that was socialistic and egalitarian—with the exception of those whose non-"Aryan" blood excluded them from the *Volksgemeinschaft* (national community). Soon after taking power, Hitler declared May Day, the traditional socialist holiday, a national holiday, and the regime propounded the slogan "Equality of all racial Germans." The legal distinction between white-collar and blue-collar status was abolished. The Third Reich, writes historian David Schoenbaum, espoused "an undifferentiated glorification of 'the worker,' in the form of an almost unlimited appeal to social mobility and in an aggressive emphasis on social egalitarianism."[55] Public statuary mimicked the grotesque "socialist realism" of the Soviet Union, featuring immense, prodigiously muscled workmen performing arduous physical feats. Foreshadowing the practice of Mao Zedong's Cultural Revolution, the Nazi labor law of 1935 compelled every young man to spend six months working in farm or factory in order "to inculcate in the German youth a community spirit and a true concept of the dignity of work, and above all, a proper respect for manual labor."

After Mussolini's March on Rome, the Nazis increasingly looked to the Fascists as a model, for their amalgamation of nationalism and socialism as well as for their successful seizure of power. Hitler wrote in *Mein Kampf*: "What will rank Mussolini among the great men of this earth is his determination not to share Italy with the Marxists, but to destroy internationalism and save the fatherland from it."[56] A bust of Mussolini was displayed in Nazi party headquarters. The Nazi daily, *Völkischer Beobachter*, replied to charges by the socialist-led German labor unions that the Fascist regime repressed workers and that the Nazis would do likewise:

Your leaders tell you lies! We are not an enemy of the workers. We call on the
working classes to fight against all the profiteers and fat cats.

    We are compared, in a manner to frighten, with fascism. And even if
national socialism were identical with fascism, workers, have you not given
any thought to the fact that when the all-powerful Marxist organization in Italy
was shattered over night, thousands and thousands, rejoicing, with banners
waving, went over to the camp of Mussolini (a worker and former Socialist
leader!!)? Have you not considered that in Bavaria thousands and thousands of
former Communists and Social Democrats stand today in the camp of Hitler
and Drexler (a worker)?[57]

However, the Duce did not at first requite Hitler's admiration. In 1926
Hitler had asked at the Italian embassy in Berlin for an autographed photograph of Mussolini, and the Italian foreign minister cabled back this response:
"Please thank the above-named gentleman for his sentiments and tell him in
whatever form you think best that the Duce does not think fit to accede to his
request." When Hitler and Mussolini met for the first time, in Venice, a year
and a half after Hitler came to power, Mussolini is said to have told colleagues:
"Instead of talking about concrete problems, Hitler only recited *Mein Kampf*
from memory—that dreary book which I have never been able to read."[58] The
Führer, he said, struck him as "a clown." A month later, however, Nazis assas-
sinated Austria's right-wing chancellor, Dollfuss, a close ally of Mussolini's, in a
country that formed the strategic buffer between Italy and Germany. Mussolini
was aggrieved, but he began to take Hitler more seriously. Soon he commenced
a long slide down the path of ever greater dependency on his steelier German
disciple.

    During the first dozen years of his rule, Mussolini had been content with
a foreign policy of bluster. In addition to the bombardment of the flyspeck,
Corfu, there were demands that the other powers acknowledge "the new prestige of Italy." Mussolini successfully pressured Yugoslavia to cede Fiume (which
D'Annunzio had been compelled to evacuate) and Greece, the Dodecanese.
After 1926 the Duce had insisted that other statesmen who wished to see him
come to Italy. There was also much boasting about Italy's growing military
capability, with Mussolini taking the key military portfolios into his own hands.
Already by 1926 he had claimed that Italy's armed forces were mightier than
those "of any other country,"[59] but military expenditures did not match the
vaunting assertions.

Now, however, Hitler brought fancy down to earth by demolishing the structures of peace created at Versailles. After withdrawing Germany from the League of Nations in 1933, he launched a military buildup culminating in a new naval agreement with London which implicitly legitimated German rearmament. This sequence had a profound impact on Mussolini. He had made much of the claim that Versailles had cheated Italy. It was time for him to put up or shut up.

Since World War I Mussolini had dreamed of an African empire. In December 1934 a confrontation at the border between Ethiopia and Italian Somaliland led to bloody Italian reprisals. Ethiopia appealed to the League of Nations, but London and Paris, following the deadly logic of appeasement, placed highest priority on maintaining friendly ties with Mussolini as a counterpoise to Hitler. Exploiting this leverage, Mussolini ordered an all-out attack on October 3, 1935. He appeared on the balcony of his headquarters of Palazzo Venezia to announce it to the throng below and, by broadcast, to millions of others who had been assembled by the party in piazzas all over Italy. "Proletarian and Fascist Italy . . . arise!" he exhorted. "Let Heaven hear your shouts of encouragement to our soldiers who are waiting in Africa, so that they are heard by our friends and enemies in every part of the world, the cry for justice, the cry of victory!"[60] After a seven-month campaign, General Badoglio captured the capital, Addis Ababa. King Vittorio Emanuele was proclaimed "Emperor of Ethiopia," but the real magistrate of the empire was suggested in the subsequent announcement that Mussolini was studying Amharic so as to be able to converse with his new subjects.

While Italian poison gas was falling on Ethiopian defenders, Hitler observed the dithering "great powers" and gave his troops the order to reoccupy the Rhineland, from which the peace treaty had barred them. Far from securing Mussolini's gratitude, British and French pusillanimity had had the opposite effect. Before the year was out, Italy and Germany were collaborating in assisting General Franco's rebellion against the Spanish Republic. In October 1936, Mussolini sent his new foreign minister, his son-in-law Count Ciano, to Germany to work out details of what the Duce began to call in public the "Rome-Berlin axis." A year later, Italy announced its adhesion to the "anti-Comintern pact" that had been formed by Germany and Japan.

Already the balance within the new alliance had begun to shift toward Hitler, with Mussolini increasingly in the role of a follower. After visiting Germany he decreed that Italian troops would adopt the goose step, and he

demonstrated it himself before the press. More darkly, although the Italian
Fascist movement had once included numerous Jews and had been distinct
from the fascists of other countries by its absence of anti-Semitism, now anti-
Jewish laws were promulgated. (The path to such racism within Italy had been
paved by apartheid-like laws that Mussolini had imposed on his new "empire" in
Africa.) Also in keeping with Nazi policy, Mussolini abandoned the posture of
piety toward the Vatican that he had adopted after taking power, and resumed
a spirit of anticlericalism.

His demonstrations of fealty to his new senior partner extended to important matters of geopolitics as well. Whereas a few years earlier he had sworn to
use force to defend Austria's independence and had reinforced the Brenner Pass
as a warning to Germany, in March 1938 when German troops annexed Austria,
Mussolini acquiesced blithely. The *Anschluss* of Austria put the world on a fast
track to war, and Mussolini's blood stirred as he sped along in Hitler's sidecar.

As Hitler's demands against Czechoslovakia grew more shrill, British prime
minister Neville Chamberlain begged Mussolini to mediate so as to avert a
European war. The result was the Munich summit of September 1938, which
made that city's name ever since a synonym for appeasement. Chamberlain
and French prime minister Edouard Daladier agreed to Mussolini's proposal
(dictated to him by the Germans) that the western powers compel the Czech
government to yield the so-called Sudetenland to Germany. The British press
saluted Mussolini as a champion of peace, while the Italian press, more accurate
for once, crowed that Chamberlain "had licked his boots."

Six months later, Hitler destroyed what was left of Czechoslovakia.
Mussolini is said to have been annoyed that he had not been told in advance,
but as Germany was giving every demonstration that destiny was on its
side, Mussolini certainly wanted to be there too. So rather than complain,
he endorsed German actions and then undertook a surprise offensive of his
own, sending Italian troops to conquer puny Albania, which was in any event
substantially under Italian influence. To glorify this easy victory he arranged
to have Vittorio Emanuele proclaimed "King of Italy and Albania, Emperor
of Ethiopia." A month later, in May 1939, he and Hitler signed the "pact of
steel," a formal military alliance that supplemented the more limited anti-
Comintern pact.

The final trigger of world war was the Stalin-Hitler pact, initiated when
Soviet ambassador Alexei Merekalov suggested to German state secretary Ernst
von Weiszacker that Moscow's friendly relations with Italy could be a model

for Soviet-German relations. A week after the pact was signed, German armies invaded Poland, and the war in Europe was on.

Mussolini wanted to enter the war against France after Germany had brought it to its knees, though in time to claim a share of the spoils; but the speed with which German armies swept around the Maginot Line nearly left him flatfooted. On June 10, after a night during which he kept Rome blacked out for dramatic effect, he proclaimed war from the balcony of the Palazzo Venezia. The Duce had often bragged about the size and modernity of Italian forces, but quite a different picture was painted by his top commander, Marshall Badoglio: "we have no arms, we have no tanks, we have no aeroplanes, not even shirts for our soldiers."[61] Wherever they went, it seemed, Italian forces either battened on German victories or looked to the Germans to bail them out.

In June 1943, Allied warplanes bombed Rome for the first time. Mussolini proposed to Hitler that they seek a separate peace with Moscow, but Hitler was not interested, and it is inconceivable that Stalin would have relented now that he was winning.

• • •

With the scent of defeat in the air, the Grand Council of Fascism convened on July 25, 1943. Quietly, and in concert with the royal household, the majority of Fascist leaders had decided it was time to extricate Italy from the war and to extricate their regime, if they could, from the man who had created it. They had determined to put through a motion calling upon the king to replace Mussolini. Knowing they had the votes, but uncertain of the outcome nonetheless—since the legal authority of the council was uncertain and fascism, in any case, did not always operate according to Robert's Rules of Order—several of the conspirators came to the meeting with pistols concealed on their persons and hand grenades in their briefcases.

The debate lasted from five in the afternoon until two in the morning. Mussolini acknowledged that he had become the "most . . . hated man in Italy," but he warned that they were all in the same boat because "reactionary and antifascist circles" would use any move against him to "liquidate" the entire regime.[62] He claimed that he had in mind a political stratagem—which he could not reveal at the moment—that would rescue their situation. Max Ascoli, in his preface to some of Mussolini's memoirs, says that the plan was to "wave, again, as in the days of his youth, the red flag of socialism. He would appear once more as the blacksmith's son and talk confiscation of large estates, workers' councils . . . and soak the rich. By going radical he could out-flank the anti-fascists on the left and perhaps re-establish his bargaining position in front of the Allies."[63]

But having mustered the courage to come this far in defying the man before whom they had always cowered, the Fascist hierarchs could not turn back now. The motion passed by a vote of 19 to 7. Still, no one knew for sure what its effect would be. The next day, the king summoned Mussolini and relieved him of the responsibilities that he had conferred upon him more than twenty years before. More than once over the past years, Mussolini had mused aloud about abolishing the monarchy, so Vittorio Emanuele took no chance that his action might be disregarded. As Mussolini got set to depart, the guards insisted—allegedly for Mussolini's own protection—on providing a military ambulance to take him home, rather than the car he had arrived in. The erstwhile Duce was driven instead to a barrack and placed under arrest.

Still one act remained in the Mussolini drama. In September, the new Italian government, which the king had appointed Badoglio to head, accepted the British and American demands for unconditional surrender. But before Allied troops could occupy the country, Hitler's forces swooped down and took most of the north, reaching just beyond Rome. In a dashing operation, German paratroopers plucked Mussolini off the nine-thousand-foot peak of one of the Gran Sasso mountains in the Apennines, where he was being held at a resort, and brought him to Munich. From there he returned to Italy as a German puppet to establish a republic, with its headquarters at Salo on Lake Garda. Several members of the Grand Council of Fascism who had voted for his ouster now calculated that they would be better off in *this* Italy, even if they were in disgrace with Mussolini, than in the Italy of Badoglio, based at Brindisi, which was allied with the Anglo-Americans and increasingly antifascist. They misjudged. Mussolini had them arrested and executed, including his son-in-law Ciano, thereby widowing Edda, his favorite child.

The Italian Social Republic, as it was fashioned, adopted a constitution written by Nicola Bombacci, a longtime Communist and friend of Lenin's, who had come over to the Fascists as late as the war in Ethiopia in the mid-1930s. Mussolini took to railing against the bourgeoisie, reprising the socialism of his youth.[64] He decreed the nationalization of firms with more than one hundred employees. And he pronounced this legacy to the socialist journalist whom he selected to record his thoughts and doings of this last period: "I bequeath the republic to the republicans and not to the monarchists, and the work of social reform to the socialists and not to the middle classes."[65] The republic also undertook roundups of Jews for delivery to Nazi death camps. Until this time, despite Mussolini's adoption of anti-Semitic rhetoric and laws, few Jews had been delivered to the Germans thanks to the passive resistance of the Italians. In addition to the bourgeoisie, Mussolini alternately blamed the Jews, the Freemasons, President Roosevelt and the Germans for his plight; but mostly he blamed the Italians, who turned out, so he said, to be unworthy of him.[66]

Meanwhile, Allied forces fought their way north, launching their last offensive in April 1945. As the vestiges of the Italian Social Republic melted away, Mussolini headed north toward the Swiss border. He dashed off a final letter to Rachele, asking her "forgiveness for all the harm which I have involuntarily done you, but you know that you are the only woman that I have really loved. I swear it before God and our son Bruno."[67] He met up with a group of German soldiers also in flight, and they agreed to try to take him across the border disguised as one of their own, in a Wehrmacht helmet and greatcoat. He was followed by Claretta Petacci, thirty years his junior, who had been his paramour throughout the last decade. Hitler had had her installed in a house near Salo during the time of the Social Republic so as to keep Mussolini content, although when Rachele discovered it, the Duce paid a price. Over the years, Claretta's family had exploited the connection shamelessly, often accompanying her to her assignations with Mussolini. But her own devotion to him was undoubtedly genuine.

A band of Communist partisans stopped the column before it reached the border, and one of them recognized Mussolini, whom they took gleefully into custody. He and Claretta, who insisted on staying with him, were held overnight until the unit got orders from Communist headquarters to shoot him. She was shot, too—by some accounts throwing her body in front of his—and so were a dozen or so of his aides including Bombacci, who shouted: "Long live Mussolini! Long live Socialism!"[68]

7

SOCIAL DEMOCRACY: ATTLEE TAKES THE SLOW ROAD

TWO DAYS AFTER MUSSOLINI'S EXECUTION, Hitler shot himself. The ideology of fascism died with the men who invented it—buried, as it were, beneath the rubble of their fallen regimes.[†] The death of this twisted offshoot of the tree of socialism made room for other branches to grow. Although Mussolini and Hitler had risen to power as the nemeses of Bolshevism, their war enabled communism to spread as never before. The Baltic states as well as parts of Poland and Romania had been swallowed into the Soviet Union under the Stalin-Hitler pact. The Red Army now occupied Poland, Hungary, Czechoslovakia, Romania, Bulgaria, the eastern part of Germany and the northern half of Korea. Local communist movements backed by Moscow stood poised to capture power in Yugoslavia, Albania, Vietnam and China, where the old orders had been demolished in the war.

Meanwhile, in Western Europe, Australia, New Zealand and a few other places, a different kind of rebirth was taking place—that of the democratic socialist heirs to Bernstein and Kautsky. They had seen their dream metastasize into the nightmares of communism and Nazism, but the democratic socialists or social democrats (the terms were now interchangeable) remained

---

† The rule of Franco endured in Spain for decades, as did a cognate regime under Antonio Salazar in Portugal, but these bore more resemblance to commonplace military dictatorships than to the ideologized regimes of Italy and Germany.

convinced that the true, humane and democratic essence of socialism could still be reclaimed from impostors "who falsely claim . . . a share in the Socialist tradition."[1] The calamitous breakdown of European civilization was attributable, they said, to the crisis of capitalism. Was it not the worldwide depression of the 1930s that had led to the triumphs of fascism?

If the barbarous episode that mankind had just endured had defied social-ists' expectations, it also illustrated how badly the world needed the soothing balm of a "cooperative commonwealth." And the practical viability of socialism had been proven, it seemed, by the unprecedented government intervention in the economy that the war required. "In us, and in us alone, lies . . . economic salvation," said Aneurin Bevan of the British Labour Party, which was ready to play the leading role in the global revival of social democracy.

Democratic politics in the other major European countries had been suspended by the war, but even before that, neither the French nor the Italian socialists nor even the Germans had enjoyed as much electoral success as their British comrades. Twice the Labour Party had captured the office of prime min-ister, albeit without controlling a parliamentary majority. The party had now emerged from the war strengthened by its crucial role in the coalition that led the nation through its hour of peril. With the thoughts of Britain turning to the pursuits of peacetime, Labour stood poised for its greatest triumph.

The party's leader, Clement Attlee, was unprepossessing but effective. During the war, he was the only one besides Churchill to remain a member of the inner "war cabinet" from the time Churchill took over, becoming almost an alter ego to the prime minister. They made an odd couple. In contrast to the flamboyant, charismatic Churchill, Attlee was once described by the *Economist* as "smaller than life."[2]

Within two weeks after Germany's collapse, the Labour Party decided to end the coalition government, forcing new elections. The close partnership between the voluble Tory and the taciturn socialist gave way to intense electoral rivalry. Most of the world assumed that Churchill would be reelected since his leadership was credited with having saved England, and his oratorical prowess far exceeded Attlee's. But the voters delivered a stunning surprise. Not only did the poll go to Labour, but by a larger margin than any socialist party had ever achieved outside of Scandinavia. For the first time, Labour would command an absolute majority in the House of Commons, indeed an overwhelming one.

The election had come during a recess in the Potsdam conference. Although Attlee had been a member of Churchill's delegation from the opening of the meeting, he had made himself so inconspicuous that Stalin asked one of the lesser British officials to point him out.[3] When he returned to Potsdam as prime minister, he remained just as reticent as before. He left the talking to his new foreign minister, the earthy former union leader Ernest Bevin. The new prime minister "recedes into the background by his very insignificance," sniffed Sir Alexander Cadogan, the permanent under-secretary of state for foreign affairs who staffed the British delegation throughout the summit.[4]

Cadogan was scarcely the first to form a low estimate of Attlee. When Attlee was chosen as the party's parliamentary leader, a prominent Labour figure, Hugh Dalton, jibed in his diary, "and a little mouse shall lead them." If any of this got back to Attlee, he never revealed a sense of injury, but in retirement he composed a gloating limerick:

> Few thought he was even a starter
> There were many who thought themselves smarter
> But he ended PM
> CH and OM
> An earl and a knight of the garter.[†]

Attlee's father, Henry, was a prominent solicitor, and his mother, Ellen, had come from a wealthy family. Though commoners, the Attlees lived in great comfort. Their spacious home included a billiard room and the grounds featured a tennis court. They also acquired a vacation home on a two-hundred-acre estate near the Essex coast. They employed five full-time servants: two maids, a cook, a gardener and a governess. Each morning, Henry led the family and servants in prayers at 7:30, before breakfast commenced at 8:00.

Clement, the seventh of eight children, was born in 1883, the same year as Mussolini. He was small and frail, soon surpassed in size by his younger brother, Laurence, and so painfully shy that he was not enrolled in boarding school at age six like the other Attlee sons, but taught at home by his mother and a governess until he was nine. Then he was sent to join his older brother Tom at Northaw, a small, mediocre prep school run by family friends, where the emphasis was on cricket and religion.

The diminutive Clement was not much of a cricket player, but he developed a lifelong passion for the game. (Fifty years later, an aide was able to persuade

---

† CH stands for Companion of Honour, OM for Order of Merit, titles of distinction conferred on a select few by the British monarch, as is Knight of the Garter. PM means Prime Minister.

the tradition-bound Prime Minister Attlee of the utility of installing a news wire by pointing out that it would enable him to check the midday cricket scores.) The biblical instruction, however, was lost on him. As he recalled in his autobiography: "The history of the Jews was taken straight through from Joshua and Judges to Ezra and Nehemiah. It is incredible the amount of time wasted in acquiring this useless knowledge."[5] Within a few years, he was to turn decisively against the Christian piety of his parents.

After "public school" (private residential high school), he went to Oxford and spent three "exceedingly happy years" reading history (focusing on the Renaissance) and "taking life easily and as it came." His father had provided each of the children with an annual allowance of two hundred pounds, which was more than enough to live on. Thus, Clement was impelled neither by financial urgency nor by any clearly formed ambition, for the want of which he gravitated toward the law. "It seemed a fairly obvious course to take. My father was a solicitor and, therefore, I might look to some help at the start."[6] He was apprenticed and soon passed his bar exam. But he handled very few cases, instead continuing a rather languid existence, living with his parents, taking up horseback riding and spending "a good deal of time practicing billiards," as he later recalled.

This idyll was interrupted when Clement decided that "in accordance with family practice" he ought to include good works in his leisurely routine. So in October 1905 he acceded to his brother Laurence's suggestion that they visit a boys' club, "Haileybury House," which provided a couple of hours of daily recreation, some military drill and other constructive activity for poor working lads. It was located in impoverished East London, where a decade earlier the tragic Tussy Marx had spent her happiest moments agitating among low-paid Jewish immigrants and found herself unexpectedly drawn to the racial heritage that her father so despised. Alighting from a train, as biographer Francis Beckett describes it, "Clem, still in his [lawyer's garb of] silk hat and tail-coat, walked gingerly through the disgusting, uncleaned streets" to reach the club.[7] His shyness marred this first visit, but he soon became a regular day-a-week volunteer, and a year and a half later he took over as the club's resident manager.

In East London's slums, Attlee came of age. He had found something to do with himself that seemed important, and working with younger people of inferior social status also apparently helped him rise above his shyness. He had never taken strong interest in political issues before, but the poverty to which he was now daily exposed filled him with outrage. Conventional Tory opinion, with which he had until then vaguely identified, portrayed poverty as the fault of the poor, but Attlee found "abundant instances of kindness and much quiet heroism in these mean streets," he said. "These people were not poor through their lack of fine qualities."[8] Far from being culpable, they were victims.

Though famously laconic in speech, Attlee secretly yearned to be a poet. He gave voice to his new convictions in a poem titled "Limehouse," the name of the district where the club was located:

> In Limehouse, in Limehouse, before the break of day,
> I hear the feet of many men who go upon their way.
> Who wander through the city,
> The grey and cruel city,
> Through streets that have no pity,
> The streets where men decay.
> In Limehouse, in Limehouse, by night as well as day
> I hear the feet of children that go to work or play,
> Of children born to sorrow,
> The workers of tomorrow,
> How shall they work tomorrow
> Who get no bread today?
> In Limehouse, in Limehouse, today and every day
> I see the weary mothers who sweat their souls away:
> Poor, tired mothers trying
> To hush the feeble crying
> Of little babies dying
> For want of bread today.
> In Limehouse, in Limehouse, I'm dreaming of the day
> When evil times shall perish and be driven clean away.
> When father, child and mother
> Shall live and love each other
> And brother help his brother
> In happy work and play.

Clem and his brother Tom examined the issue together. Tom encouraged Clem to read the reformist writers John Ruskin and William Morris. The two Attlee brothers saw most things alike, apart from a striking divergence over religion, with Tom holding true to their parents' devotion. Together they decided to embrace socialism, although for Tom it was an expression of his Christian faith, whereas for Clem it was a substitute. "Henceforward," he wrote, "everything in life was bound up with the progress of Socialism."[9]

First they set about to join the Fabian Society, the country's leading platform for socialism. It had been founded in 1883 as the Fellowship of the New Life by a small band of earnest, middle-class do-gooders out to cultivate their own moral perfection. The members soon concluded that it would be more productive to work for the transformation of political institutions than for the transformation of themselves. They espoused a socialist philosophy rooted in Bentham and Mill and Owen rather than Marx and Engels, rejecting the ideas of class struggle, revolution and historical inevitability. They believed that they could attain their goal by education and persuasion and the gradual accretion of piecemeal reforms. Their new name, the Fabian Society, came from the Roman general Quintus Fabius, a practitioner of drawn-out guerrilla warfare. To signify their slow but steady approach the Fabians adopted the tortoise as their symbol.

They were bohemian, nerdy and remarkably effective despite their small numbers. The British writer Ann Fremantle describes them as "a cranky lot, full of the dietetic and sartorial fads of their age, 'cycling along country lanes, the ladies in bloomers, their consorts sandalled' . . . innocuous enough, if not a little absurd' . . . . Nevertheless, among these nut-cutlet-eating cultists were at least half a dozen of the most brilliant minds of the twentieth century."[10] She was referring to the likes of George Bernard Shaw, Graham Wallas, Annie Besant, H. G. Wells, Havelock Ellis, R. H. Tawney and Bertrand Russell.

Of all the intellectual stars, the most important to the society were the remarkable couple Sidney and Beatrice Webb. He, a short, slight man with a large head and a big nose, was an accountant's son, born in 1859, who entered the civil service at age sixteen and thereafter educated himself, making all the more remarkable the encyclopedic knowledge that dazzled his acquaintances. She was a year older, beautiful, intellectually accomplished, well-to-do and unhappy until she found a fulfilling partnership with him when both were past thirty. It lasted more than fifty years and was more fruitful politically than perhaps any other marriage in modern times.

Her inheritance enabled him to retire from the civil service, and they published prolifically, singly and together. Sidney wrote two-thirds of the Fabian Society's early tracts. Among their earliest collaborations was *The History of Trade Unionism,* which Lenin and Krupskaya translated feverishly in Siberia. The Webbs were not just writers; they were activists, too. They founded the London

School of Economics as a "center for collectivist-tempered research." Beatrice launched the magazine *New Statesman*. Sidney served in Parliament and in the cabinet and as chairman of the Labour Party's National Executive Committee. They were responsible for the reorganization of the British educational system to provide more opportunities for the less well off and for poverty proposals that formed the germ of the welfare state.

When young Tom and Clem Attlee came knocking at the Fabians' door they found the atmosphere forbidding. All of the males among these luminaries sported beards as if it were the uniform of the elect, and they seemed far more interested in discoursing with one another than in welcoming proselytes. Attlee said that he and Tom were observed "as if we were two beetles." He soon found a warmer reception in the Independent Labour Party.

The ILP had been founded in 1893 by sundry union members, but it grew increasingly middle-class and ideological, devoted to socialism. Its branches ordinarily met in churches, while the unions preferred to conduct their business in pubs. Then, in 1900, the Labour Party was created by the Trades Union Congress, the coordinating body of the various British unions, in order to get more labor representatives into Parliament. It was not socialist, and at first it was not even a party. Initially called the Labour Representation Committee, it aimed to work within the other parties. Once the Labour Party was formed, the ILP affiliated with it and worked at converting it to socialism. Eventually it succeeded, but only after great effort. Clem Attlee himself, writes biographer Kenneth Harris, "never had any illusions about the difficulty of making working men into socialists. In this respect he had learned a lesson from the club. In spite of their poverty the boys who came to Haileybury House had no inclination to join the ILP. With rare exceptions they were Conservatives."[11]

The year Attlee joined the Independent Labour Party, 1908, was also the year of his father's death. The estate brought an increase in his allowance to four hundred pounds a year. Although still filing the occasional legal brief, Attlee subsisted mostly off this inheritance, and since his work at the club absorbed only a few hours each day, he enjoyed greater freedom for party work than most of his ILP comrades. Thus, within a few weeks of joining he was asked to serve as secretary of the local branch. There is no reason to believe that Attlee, still focused on his poetry, nourished any political ambitions, and yet circumstance had begun to give him a leg up on a political career. His superior education equipped him to be a spokesman for the grievances of his neighbors, while his free time enabled him to concentrate on political activity. And as an affluent, benevolent social worker among the poor, he began to build for himself a grass-roots constituency that was to prove loyal and enduring.

Attlee's dalliance with the Fabians had been initially disappointing, but it, too, was to yield some benefits. In 1909 the Webbs hired him to work for the National Committee for the Prevention of Destitution, a group they had founded to agitate for reform of the poor laws. A few years later, they were instrumental in creating a social service department at the London School of Economics, which they had founded. Sidney, the chairman of the selection committee, hired Attlee as a tutor on the strength of his experience in the slums and with the poor law campaign. This was Attlee's first regular job. Still, the hours of a college teacher left time for activism. As Francis Beckett describes it:

> In these years Clem became a figure in the ILP without consciously trying to do so. He took on all the humble, time-consuming jobs which have to be done, and which ambitious politicians generally consider are for lesser mortals. He cut up loaves to feed dockers' children during the 1911 dock strike, and stood at the bottom of Petticoat Lane with his brother Tom holding collecting boxes during the Irish Transport and General Workers' Union strike in 1913. He carried the Stepney ILP branch banner on demonstrations through Central London. He went to court to plead mitigation when a half-starving boy was caught thieving. In 1909 he spoke at fifty-three indoor and outdoor public meetings; in 1910, eighty-eight; in 1911, sixty-three; and in 1912, seventy.[12]

Through passionate socialist commitment, the boy who in high school and college was "afflicted with a most painful shyness, so that to do anything in public was a torture to me," had at last found his tongue.[13] Perhaps no lesser motive would have enabled him to overcome his natural reticence. But the fears that afflict humans are capricious things. The same man who had been terrified of speaking in front of others proved entirely unfazed by the prospect of being shot at, as he showed when war broke out in 1914.

The onset of hostilities provoked a wrenching debate among British socialists, just as it had among their German, French and Italian comrades in the Socialist International. Within the ranks of the ILP—the more middle-class and ideological part of the Labour Party—antiwar sentiment ran strong. Typical was Clement's brother Tom, who as a Christian socialist held the conviction that violence was never justifiable.

But Clement, the atheist, was too pragmatic to accept absolute pacifism. And Germany's invasion of innocent Belgium for no reason except to outflank France—enhanced in the telling by exaggerated atrocity stories—convinced him that guilt for the war was not equally shared among the belligerent "capitalist powers." In this, his reaction was like that of many of his countrymen, indeed of Britain's Liberal government. Germany's transgression of Belgium sealed Britain's entry into the war.

Within two days, Clement set out to join the fighting. He was thirty-one years old and under no obligation to serve; indeed, he had difficulty enlisting due to his age. His own public explanation of his action was opaque even by Attlee's tight-lipped standards. "It appeared wrong to me to let others make a sacrifice while I stood by, especially as I was unmarried and had no obligations," he said.[14] But the plainer reason for his enlistment was the same one that made war hawks out of French and German and other European socialists despite the supranational theories they had once espoused. He discovered that his socialist philosophy had not nullified his capacity for patriotism, which he called "the natural emotion of every true Briton."[15] Attlee acknowledged the sense of revelation: "It was not until the Great War that I fully grasped the strength of the ties that bind men to the land of their birth."[16]

Clem had to use connections to get posted to a unit that would bring him into the action, the South Lancashire regiment, and in June of 1915 it sailed for Gallipoli. There followed weeks in the trenches in the heat and mud and flies, without reliable food or water, and Attlee was one of many who succumbed to dysentery. "Our diet of [preserved] beef, biscuit and tea without milk was not very suitable" for curing it, he observed.[17] Attlee's response to the illness, as recounted by biographer Kenneth Harris, makes a tale of gallantry:

> Attlee . . . collapsed, was sent down to the beach on a stretcher, rested for three days, started to walk back up to the line, collapsed again, and, unconscious, was put on [a] hospital ship . . . bound for England. When he woke up next day, he protested at having been evacuated without his consent, and demanded to be put off the ship at Malta.[18]

His request was granted, and after a period of recuperation, he made his way back to the front. In his absence, his unit's turn had come to undertake one of those mindless direct assaults that characterized the carnage of World War I, and most of the men had been lost. "It was a great relief to be back again although so many of the old lot had gone," commented Attlee.[19] But the high command was souring on the Gallipoli campaign and ordered a withdrawal. Attlee's unit was assigned to hold the beachhead as the forces were pulled out, and he was among the last men to leave.

His group was withdrawn to Egypt, then sent to the front in Mesopotamia. There, while planting a marker to guide the British artillery, he took a bullet in a thigh and shrapnel in a buttock, and for a time lost the use of both legs. From his hospital bed he wrote jokingly to Tom that "it may interest the comrades to know I was hit while carrying the red flag to victory."[20] These wounds, suffered in April 1916, required a long recovery, but by 1918 he was fit again and determined to get back into the action. He managed to get sent to the French front, but there an injury from some falling timber and additional illnesses landed him back in the hospital, where he lay at war's end.

•   •   •

Upon his discharge, Attlee made his way back to London's East End and rented a large, dilapidated house which he renovated. He turned the ground floor into a clubhouse for the local Labour Party and fashioned residential units above it, living in one and renting two others to Labour comrades. He resumed teaching and threw himself into local political activity.

The Labour Party was poised for new advances. The participation of Labour ministers in cabinets during the war had given the party a new respectability, while the vast expansion of government activity necessitated by the war was cited by socialists as demonstrating the feasibility of government control over the economy in peacetime. Moreover, the Bolshevik triumph in Russia, although repellent to most Britons, seemed to vindicate the Marxian prophecy that socialism was mankind's future.

In 1918 the party strengthened itself by revising its constitution. The leader, Arthur Henderson, said his goal was to "weld the Socialist and trade union elements firmly together."[21] The strategy was to give each side what it prized most. To the trade unions, the most important thing was power, so a system of block voting was devised to assure their dominance. To the socialists, the most important thing was the clarity of the party's ideology, so "Clause IV" was written into the party constitution. Drafted by Sidney Webb, it declared that the party's goal was "to secure for the producers by hand and brain the full fruits of their industry, and the most equitable distribution thereof that may be possible, upon the basis of the common ownership of the means of production and the best obtainable system of popular administration and control of each industry or service." Though the Fabians chose gradual methods, their goal, said George Bernard Shaw, was "complete socialism."[22]

In 1919 Attlee made his first run for office, as a candidate for county council. He "was presented as a middle-class philanthropist who had sacrificed the prospect of a remunerative but unspecified career in the great world outside in order to devote himself to the East End poor," writes Harris.[23] Attlee lost, but the margin was narrow enough that his prospect for future nomination was not dimmed, and the local Labour Party leader, Oscar Tobin, eyed him as a candidate in the next parliamentary election. Beckett explained part of Attlee's attraction:

> However much socialists might have wanted workers to trust men of their own class, Tobin knew the workers would feel more comfortable voting for a man who spoke in the accent of the ruling class. For many years . . . Clem was always referred to in [the borough of] Stepney as "the Major" which was a subtle way of telling his future constituents, not just that he was a gallant soldier, but also that he came from the class which was born to rule, because working-class soldiers did not become commissioned officers.[24]

In the meantime, Attlee managed the party's campaign for the borough council, formulating a platform calling for more open spaces and public baths, subsidized milk for mothers and infants, cheaper housing and better street cleaning. Labour won in a sweep, and Stepney as well as several other London boroughs had their first Labour majority. Although he was not one of the members, the new council appointed Attlee mayor of the borough. His hard work, party loyalty, soft edges and ample free time led to his appointment to a variety of boards and commissions. He was, however, "somewhat handicapped in my work as a Mayor by being unmarried."[25] This was soon remedied.

In 1921, Attlee, by now thirty-eight, arranged to join a college chum of his brother Tom's for a holiday in Italy. This companion brought along his mother and his twenty-five-year-old sister, Violet. As the tour proceeded, Clem spent less time with his friend and more with "Vi," ostensibly on the grounds that she was eager to absorb his knowledge of Italian history. "She listened to everything he had to say with a naive respect he found relaxing," says Harris, adding this climacteric which occurred during the course of an overnight train ride: "In the small hours Vi woke up, and through lidded eyes looked across at Attlee. Thinking she was still asleep, he was gazing at her. 'That was when I thought he might be in love with me,' she told her daughter, Felicity, thirty years later. 'Of course, *I* was in love with *him* already.'"[26]

Her intuition was accurate, and although Attlee chose to introduce Vi in his autobiography by reference to his need for a mayoress, his attraction to her was more than utilitarian. "I am mad as a march hare with joy," he reported in correspondence—probably the most exuberant turn of phrase he ever used.[27] Vi was from a similar social background as Clem, and the two were married in 1922 in a service conducted jointly by his brother Bernard and her brother Basil, both of whom were vicars.

It was out of the question for Vi to move into the slums of Stepney. Instead the newlyweds acquired a comfortable place in the suburbs, but the move did not mean the sacrifice of Clem's political base in the East End. When his term as mayor was expiring, he got himself appointed alderman, which kept him in the thick of local politics.

The same year that he married, Attlee made his first run for Parliament. He campaigned with "meetings in every street," he recalled, using the slogan "Life against wealth." The peroration of his stump speech was socialist boiler-plate: "Instead of the exploitation of the mass of the people in the interests of a small rich class, I demand the organisation of the country in the interests of all as a co-operative commonwealth in which land and capital will be owned by the nation and used for the benefit of the community."[28] One of his handouts contained a cartoon of a war-profiteer clutching a money bag, accompanied by an unattributed poem probably written by Attlee:

> My name is Mr Profiteer
> And talk of taxes makes me queer.
> I made my millions in the war,
> That's why your living costs you more.
> Let homeless heroes starve in ditches,
> But don't make levies on my riches.
> And if the Empire needs a tax
> Well—shove it on the workers' backs.
> The Tory-Libs, they love me so,
> They'll never make me pay, I know.
> But oh! when Labour wins, I fear,
> It's goodbye Mr Profiteer.[29]

Labour won 142 seats, more than double its previous high, surpassing the Liberals for the first time to become Britain's second-largest party. Attlee reaped the fruits of the political soil that he had been cultivating for years, ousting a sixteen-year incumbent who ran with the support of both the Liberals and the Conservatives. Labour's vastly enlarged parliamentary contingent was dominated by the ILP. The charismatic journalist Ramsay MacDonald was chosen party leader, and he in turn chose Attlee as one of his two parliamentary private secretaries. In his maiden speech in Parliament, Attlee set out "the socialist approach to the economic problem":

> Why was it that in the war we were able to find employment for everyone? It was simply that the Government controlled the purchasing power of the nation. They said what things should be produced....That is what we are demanding shall be done in time of peace....[E]xactly as they told manufacturers and workers that they must turn out shells and munitions of all sorts to support the fighting men, so they must turn out houses and necessities for those who are making the country a country of peace.[30]

Throughout the 1920s, Labour's vote continued to rise (as did Attlee's) until the election of 1929 gave the party its first plurality in Parliament, albeit not a majority. MacDonald formed a minority government, ruling by the forbearance of the other parties. This dictated cautious policies just as the world economic downturn seemed to demand bold responses, and this alienated the party's left wing. Before long, eighteen ILP MPs split from Labour, and more splits followed. Sir Oswald Mosley, a dashing young aristocrat who seemed destined for leadership, had been included in the cabinet as chancellor of the Duchy of Lancaster. But when his demands for vast public works programs to alleviate unemployment were unmet, he and some followers bolted to form the more radical New Party, which soon evolved into the British Union of Fascists. Attlee was named to replace him in the government.

Buffeted by economic crisis, MacDonald found it impossible to steer between Labour's own constituency, especially the trade unions, and the opposition parties whose acquiescence he needed. Secretly, in August 1931 he cut a deal with the Liberals and the Conservatives to form a "national government," that is, a coalition of the three major parties. Its policy was one of austerity, which few Labour members were willing to support. The maneuver, wrote Attlee, was "the greatest betrayal in [English] political history." The next month, the party's annual conference voted to expel MacDonald and the other Labour MPs who joined his team. Seeking a clear mandate,

MacDonald decided to call elections in which his new coalition would present itself as a bloc.[31]

The strategy paid off handsomely. Of 612 seats, MacDonald's government won 556. Of the remainder, the Labour Party was able to hang on to 46, down from 287 two years before. Many of these were from the solidly Labour coal-mining districts. Attlee eked out a winning margin of 2 percent in his well-tended Stepney constituency, which previously had returned him by a vote of 2 to 1. Although Attlee rued his party's debacle, it turned out to be his big break. Of the top Labour leaders who had refused to join the "national government," all but George Lansbury were defeated. He was named party leader, and Attlee, who had ranked in the second tier of the party's hierarchy, moved up to the post of deputy leader.

Never in modern history had the parliamentary opposition consisted of so few. The forty-six Labour members developed a rare esprit de corps, once marching into the voting lobby singing the revolutionary dirge "The Red Flag." ("The people's flag is deepest red; It shrouded oft our martyred dead. . . .Though cowards flinch and traitors sneer; We'll keep the red flag flying here.") Later, the Labour benches would fill up again and some of Attlee's seniors would regain their seats, but the bonds formed among the lonely forty-six during this time of the party's duress assured Attlee of retaining his elevated role. In fact, he was soon to ascend further.

The rise of Hitler pushed international issues toward the foreground, and in 1935 Italy's invasion of Ethiopia brought the issue to a head. Attlee's denunciations of Italy's action were so pointed that the editor of the Italian Fascist newspaper *Secolo Fascista* challenged Attlee to a duel for having "rous[ed] . . . feelings of resentment" in "the heart of every Italian."[32] In contrast, Lansbury, though no fan of Mussolini's, was, like many from Labour's Left, a pacifist, and when the party repudiated this position, he resigned as leader, opening the way for Attlee.

• • •

Over the next five years, as the world hurtled toward a new conflagration, Attlee's role as party leader entailed a balancing act. On the one hand, the gathering war clouds created pressure to put aside domestic differences in the interest of national unity. On the other hand, the thrust of socialist rhetoric, even on the lips of an avowed non-Marxist like Attlee, invoked implacable class struggle. What made it possible to manage this contradiction was the deep duality in Attlee's nature. Decades later, Vi chirped to biographer Kenneth Harris:

"Clem was never really a socialist, were you, darling?"[33] What Vi, who took pride in her husband's career but no interest in his political ideas, did not understand was, as Beckett remarked, "Clem [was] conservative about everything except socialism."[34] As early as 1927 a newspaper had noted the tension. Attlee and one other Labour MP, it said, were "such good Englishmen that we often wonder how they contrive to remain in the Labour Party."[35]

Attlee was, in fact, a devoted monarchist. In 1936, when Prime Minister Baldwin learned of King Edward's wish to marry the twice-divorced American Wallis Simpson, he conferred privately with Attlee. Baldwin was opposed to the match; divorce was not condoned by the Anglican Church, and this woman was not suitable for the throne. He feared, however, that the monarch might strike a bargain, asking Labour to form a new government in exchange for a promise to grant approval to his matrimonial wishes. Attlee assured Baldwin that he shared his view of His Majesty's unseemly love. Although not a religious believer, Attlee was certain that the somehow unsavory Mrs. Simpson could not make a proper queen. Edward was true to his heart and yielded the throne to George VI, who continued to occupy it during Attlee's administration. George's death in 1952 was the only event over which Attlee was reported to have cried in public.

At the same time, Attlee's socialist conviction burned with an inextinguishable flame. In 1937, two years after becoming party leader, he penned *The Labour Party in Perspective* for the publisher Victor Gollancz and the Left Book Club, a largely pro-Soviet operation. Attlee was already forty-four, so the work cannot be written off to boyish enthusiasm. Its theme was that "the controversy between Socialism and Capitalism is the dominant public question of the day."[36] In that conflict, moreover, Attlee saw little room for compromise:

> There are those who will say that this is a playing with words; that "We are all Socialists now"; that there is no absolute Socialism or Capitalism; that it is all a matter of degree and so forth. I cannot accept this. Socialism to me is not just a piece of machinery or an economic system, but a living faith translated into action. I desire the classless society.[37]

In other words, the goal was not merely to eliminate poverty. "Without reducing the standards of life of the wealthy, a great advance in the material well-being of the masses is possible, but this is not enough."[38] Attlee argued that "all the major industries" as well as land and investment should be "owned and controlled by the community."[39] He would allow "smaller enterprises" to be "carried on individually," but only "for a time."[40] And he warned against "watering down Labour's Socialist creed in order to attract new adherents who cannot accept the full Socialist faith."[41]

Attlee was never a Communist, but he wrote that the difference between socialists like himself and the Communists was one of "method," not "end," referring to the conflict between the Socialist International and the Comintern as "internecine strife."[42] He lauded "the great experiment in Socialist Russia . . . a community actually putting into operation the Socialist economic system which [socialists] twenty years ago could only contemplate as a distant dream."[43]

Eclectically, Attlee also praised Sweden as "perhaps the most remarkable example of the successful development of Socialism through constitutional means."[44] Swedish Socialists had come to power together with their Agrarian Party allies in 1933 on a reformist, not revolutionary, platform. It did not promise to socialize ownership but rather to fix prices, manage relations between employers and labor, and weave a sturdy social safety net.

Though small in population and geographically isolated, Sweden caught the world's attention during the Great Depression. While most industrial economies languished, unemployment in Sweden was largely eliminated between 1932 and 1937. Whether this was the result of the Socialist government's Keynesian-style programs or of Sweden's strong trade balance is debated to this day. Thanks largely to Hitler and Mussolini, the demand for Sweden's export products—lumber and ores—suffered no slack, for the production of armaments in many countries remained robust even as the global economy weakened. Nonetheless, a blizzard of articles in British and American magazines[45] and the highly popular 1936 book by Marquis Childs, *Sweden: The Middle Way,* extolled a way of life superior to both capitalism and communism. The "Swedish model" of cradle-to-grave government benefits in a context of prosperity and social harmony was to remain a powerful attraction for generations to come. To Attlee, its inspiration was not as a Hegelian synthesis but rather as a way station on the road to a more complete socialism.

With the peace crumbling, the Labour Party found itself at a loss for a persuasive response to the increasingly aggressive behavior of the fascist powers. Labour criticized the Baldwin and Chamberlain governments for being too soft, claiming that some Conservatives secretly welcomed the fascists as a counterpoise to the Communists. At the same time, as antimilitarists, the Labourites were hard put to offer alternative policies. Attlee argued pathetically that "the way to meet Fascism is not by force of arms, but by showing that with co-operation in the economic sphere far better conditions are obtainable than by pursuing a policy of aggression."[46]

The socialists, who measured the world around them against the standard of an imaginary utopia, were ill-prepared to face squarely the grim choices that global politics now presented. And, judging their own society harshly, they had difficulty supporting dangerous and costly measures to defend it. In Parliament, the Labour Party routinely voted against military expenditures, claiming that the Conservative government could not be trusted to use weapons for the right reason. Labour's position was that it would be right to resort to arms on behalf of the League of Nations but not on behalf of narrow national interest. As Attlee put it:

> The Labour Party is opposed to the policy of the National Government in seeking security by piling up huge competitive armaments. It can only toler-ate armaments as a necessary support for a policy of collective security. It is fully alive to the dangers which exist in Europe to-day owing to the aggressive policy of the Fascist Powers, but it has no confidence in the will of a Capitalist Government to oppose them. There is every indication that the policy pursued is an attempt to play the old game of alliances based on the maintenance of the balance of power.[47]

As Hitler's depredations multiplied, Attlee became an increasingly strong critic of appeasement. When Chamberlain returned from Munich with his infamous "peace in our time" agreement, Attlee denounced it as "one of the greatest diplomatic defeats that this country and France have ever sustained." Nonetheless, when Hitler's forces captured Prague half a year later, vindicating Attlee's initial assessment and impelling Chamberlain to ask for a renewal of conscription, Attlee led his party in opposing it. The motive was a justifiable distrust of Chamberlain, but the effect was to weaken the nation's demonstra-tion of resolve.

However, once Germany invaded Poland and England declared war, Attlee's patriotism came to the fore. "The Labour Party . . . has taken its stand with the rest of the country to stop this evil thing spreading," he declared in a BBC broadcast; yet he felt constrained to add: "although we have our own quarrel with the present system of society."[48]

The collapse of Norway's resistance to Germany in the early spring of 1940 brought to a head the disillusionment in Parliament with Chamberlain's leadership. The Labour Party offered a motion of no-confidence. The debate that ensued is among the most famous in British parliamentary history. Leopold Amery, one of the dozens of Conservatives who defected, turned toward his leader and reprised Cromwell's admonition: "You have sat too long here for any good you have been doing. . . . In the name of God, go!" And the elderly David Lloyd George, who had led the nation through World War I and still occupied one of the few Liberal seats, said: "the prime minister . . . has appealed for sacrifice. . . . I say solemnly that the prime minister should give an example of sacrifice, because there is nothing that can contribute more to victory in this war than that he should sacrifice the seals of office."

Although Chamberlain survived the vote, he was broken. The next day he summoned Attlee to a meeting with the Conservative leadership and asked him whether Labour would join a "national government." Attlee replied that he was sure the party would not serve under Chamberlain but that it might under another Tory prime minister. In short order the reins of power were handed to Churchill.

A war cabinet of five was formed, comprising Churchill, Chamberlain and Halifax for the Conservatives, and Attlee and Arthur Greenwood for Labour. "In Clement Attlee I had a colleague of war experience long versed in the House of Commons," Churchill wrote later on. "Our only differences in outlook were about Socialism, but these were swamped by [the] war. . . . We worked together with perfect ease and confidence during the whole period of the Government."[49] They did so despite—or perhaps because of—their contrasting styles. An anonymous minister gave an interviewer this description of the difference: "when Attlee takes the chair, Cabinet meetings are business-like and efficient; we keep to the agenda, make decisions and get away in reasonable time. When Mr. Churchill presides, nothing is decided; we listen enthralled and go home, many hours late, feeling that we have been present at an historic occasion."[50] Nor did their collaboration amount to personal friendship. In private, Churchill once described Attlee as "an admirable character, but not a man with whom it is agreeable to dine."[51]

At first Attlee proposed to link the war to the advancement of social-ism. He argued that a statement of "revolutionary" war aims would stimulate public support. The government should "admit . . . that the old order has col-lapsed and ask . . . people to fight for the new order."[52] But Churchill would have none of it. Apart from his own antipathy to socialism, he argued quite convincingly that war aims should be broad, not divisive. Attlee relented, and as the war continued he found himself coming in for sometimes bitter criticism within his party for failing to advance a distinctly Labour position. The attacks grew especially sharp after the government agreed to shelve the so-called "Beveridge Report" of December 1942, which proposed large advances in social insurance.

In 1943, as the war news turned favorable, Attlee persuaded Churchill to set up a Reconstruction Committee to begin planning for the aftermath. The success of the Normandy landing and the Allied advances that followed made the war's ultimate outcome all but certain. This generated pressure for the dissolution of the unity government and a return to normal political competition. Just days after Germany surrendered, Labour convened a national conference. Attlee proposed preserving the government until the defeat of Japan, as he and Churchill had concurred was best, but with Labour showing strength in the polls and in recent by-elections, his party had no such patience.

No sooner were elections announced than the Labour Party chairman, Harold Laski, wrote to Attlee asking him to step aside so that the party might find a champion with greater "power to ... lead ... to reach out to the masses."[53] Herbert Morrison, who had run against Attlee for party leader in 1935; Stafford Cripps of the party's Left; and Ernest Bevin, the leader of the trade unions, had played prominent roles in the war government and stood higher than Attlee in some popularity polls. Attlee replied with a fifteen-word letter (counting salutation and signature) affording a glimpse of the steely core that was among his underestimated strengths: "Dear Laski, Thank you for your letter, contents of which have been noted. C. R. Attlee."

Attlee was also canny about exploiting his own unprepossessing image. In those days when most campaigning was still done in person, Attlee crisscrossed the country in his own car, with Vi as his driver, while Churchill traveled in a proper motorcade. The contrast, much noted in the press, gave Attlee a homey, down-to-earth flavor that worked to his benefit. Although Churchill was much revered, he was the hero of the war, and the country ached for the pursuits of peace, which Labour seemed to have more clearly in focus. Attlee's persona was also proof against scare stories about socialism. Churchill had launched the campaign with a tirade that socialism would inevitably entail "some kind of Gestapo," but the tactic backfired. The historian Trevor Burridge remarked: "Applied to Bevin, Cripps or Morrison in a mudslinging contest, the charge might perhaps have passed muster; applied to Clement Attlee (whom Churchill had just invited to Potsdam), it was ludicrous."[54]

Labour, in effect, promised the people a well-deserved reward for their painful sacrifices, a peace dividend. Paid for from where? The war itself had shown what prodigious accomplishments could be achieved when government mobilized the resources of the nation. Now, said Labour, it could perform similar feats in the aim of giving every Briton a better life.

The result was a landslide. Never before, anywhere, had socialism won so strong a mandate. Communists and fascists had taken power as violent minorities. Various democratic socialists had formed governments, but never with such a decisive majority without coalition partners. Labour's share of the vote, 48.3, had only once been exceeded by a socialist party—in 1940, when the Swedish Social Democrats polled 53.8 percent. But that party had removed explicit calls for socialism from its program eight years before, and with war raging around their country, the Social Democrats formed a multiparty government.

The Labour Party, in contrast, had not changed Clause IV of its 1918 charter, calling for common ownership, except to expand it by including commerce as well as production. And at its 1944 conference, it had concretized this idea by proposing at once to nationalize land, heavy industry, banking, transport, fuel and power. Nor was this mere rhetoric. The Labour government, said Attlee,

> came to power with a well-defined policy worked out over many years. It had been set out very clearly in our Election Manifesto and we were determined to carry it out.... Our policy was not a reformed capitalism but progress toward a democratic socialism....I...determined that we would go ahead as fast as possible.[55]

• • •

Attlee composed his government of men (and a woman) who had devoted their lives to socialism. He, himself, was sixty-three years old, and many of his ministers were of like age or older; the youngest was forty-eight. Socialism for them was no passing romance. They believed they were remaking the world. One of them, Aneurin Bevan (not to be confused with the homonymic Ernest Bevin) declared that "the eyes of the world are turning to Great Britain. We now have the moral leadership of the world, and before many years we shall have people coming here as to a modern Mecca."[56] Despite personal rivalries, the government was united in its goals. "To an extent unprecedented in British political history the legislation of a government was dictated by a party programme," observes Burridge.[57]

The program had two main pillars, one being nationalization. "Social justice," said Attlee, "could only be attained by bringing under public ownership and control the main factors in the economic system."[58] To symbolize this grand transformation, the Bank of England was chosen as the first business to be nationalized. Next came the coal mines, which produced the lifeblood of the economy. Coal mining is murderous work, and labor/management relations in the British mines were legendarily bitter. "No single measure in the earlier phase of the Attlee government aroused more genuine or spontaneous enthusiasm than did the nationalization of the coal-mines," writes historian Kenneth Morgan. "There were mass demonstrations of rejoicing in mining communities from South Wales to Nottingham, Yorkshire, Durham and Fife."[59]

Civil aviation, cable and wireless communications, railroads and trucking were taken over next, then electricity and gas. But events in the mines in early 1947 slowed the momentum of nationalization. They had barely begun to operate under public ownership when a bitter winter frost hit. The minister of fuel and power, Emmanuel Shinwell, had suggested that nationalization would assure adequate supplies. "Our mining difficulties are over," he had exulted, confident that the miners would produce more now that they were no longer being exploited by greedy owners.[60] The harsh weather shook the government's complacency, leading it to launch an emergency allocation plan, but this just seemed to make things worse. Households faced inadequate heating and interruptions of electricity due to shortages of fuel for power stations. A wave of factory closings ensued, driving the unemployment rate above 15 percent. By the time the weather abated, the government's economic program had lost some of its luster.

Within the Labour Party leadership itself, doubts about the advantages of government ownership began to be voiced. As 1947 gave way to 1948, the party debated its next steps. The left wing urged that the state proceed to take over more banks, as well as insurance, food importation, and the manufacture of ships, aircraft, automobile parts and machine tools. But these proposals met resistance. In particular the labor unions, despite the initial excitement of the miners, were lukewarm toward the whole project of nationalization. To the workers, it was far from certain that life would be better under a government board than under a private corporation, and it might be harder to fight for their interests. Already the mines had begun to witness a renewal of disputes and strikes. The debate within the party crystallized around the issue of iron and steel, the cornerstones of the industrial economy. Within the party executive, the leader of the iron and steel workers' union voted against a government takeover of the industries. Attlee tipped the balance in favor. The House of Lords was able to delay the proposal, but it was finally enacted in 1951.

The second main pillar of Labour's socialist project was social welfare. The National Insurance Act of 1946 supplied universal coverage for illness, unemployment, retirement, widowhood, maternity and death. The Industrial Injuries Act provided for occupational disability. The Family Allowances and National Assistance Acts mandated direct subsidies to the poor, liquidating the last memory of the odious poor-house. In addition, universal education was extended by raising the school-leaving age to fifteen. The government conducted a campaign of public housing construction and took steps to discourage private home-building. The centerpiece of the new welfare state was the National Health Service, providing free medical care paid for by the government. Within short order, Health Minister Aneurin Bevan announced that more than 93 percent of the population had enrolled in the program.[61] Attlee boasted that these measures constituted the most complete network of social protection in the history of the world.

However, the costs of operating the medical service soon exceeded estimates, and there ensued a running battle within the cabinet about whether to keep it completely free to users. Those with responsibility for the national budget repeatedly proposed modest charges for prescriptions, eyeglasses or dentures, but each of these was resisted strenuously by Bevan, who was the official in charge of health and also the champion of the party's Left. He argued that fees would be a hardship for poorer citizens and that the principle of free health care was a bedrock of socialism. Any derogation from it would constitute "a shock to [Labour's] supporters and a grave disappointment to Socialist opinion throughout the world."[62] Attlee's heart was with Bevan, but he decided that some fees were unavoidable. Bevan resigned his ministry in protest.

Labour's problem was to find sufficient resources for all the benefits it wished to provide. Britain had exhausted a large part of its national wealth in the life-and-death struggle with Hitler. According to socialist theory, public ownership of industry would be not only more just but also more productive, since it would eliminate the waste and irrationality of the market as well as the alienation felt by workers. But Labour's nationalizations yielded no such immediate benefit. On the contrary, compensation had to be paid to the former owners, and several of the newly acquired industries—coal, rail, aviation—soon required operating subsidies. The country faced many shortages, and Attlee felt compelled to take the unpopular step of adding bread as well as some other items to the list of rationed commodities still in effect from the war.

What kept the economy afloat was American aid, a loan of $3.75 billion in 1945 and then the Marshall Plan beginning in 1948. These subsidies enabled Labour to pursue its social welfare goals, but the economy soon encountered other hard realities. The government had at first encouraged inflation on the theory that loose money would spur growth and benefit the less well off, but this fed a disastrous run on the pound when it yielded to American pressure to free exchange rates. To save the currency, Attlee shifted to a policy of tight money and more cautious budgets. And to rein in inflation, he imposed wage controls, making raises dependent on increases in productivity. It all amounted to a drastic retreat from socialist economics.

Although there was gratitude for American aid, it was hard for socialists to look across the Atlantic without seeing the caricature of greedy capitalism. Nonetheless, the international situation was driving the Labourites toward a warmer view of America. The motor behind this change was an increasingly sober appreciation of the menace posed by Moscow.

The Labour Party was turning away from its tradition of optimism about Soviet Russia. In 1936, Sidney and Beatrice Webb, the party's leading literary couple, had written a two-volume paean to the U.S.S.R., where, they said, "the interests and desires of all the different sections of the population will be fulfilled . . . to a degree never yet attained in any other community."[63] In 1937, Attlee had sung similar praises in *The Labour Party in Perspective*.[†] But Stalin's pact with Hitler turned him against the Soviet Union, and not even the wartime alliance could soften his newfound distrust. Indeed, by the time of Potsdam, Attlee worried about stiffening the Americans who, romanticizing their ally, had developed their own cult of "Uncle Joe" Stalin. "The combination of Russian old-time and Communist modern Imperialism . . . threatened the freedom of Europe," he said. "The Americans had an insufficient appreciation of this."[64]

Ernest Bevin, his surprising choice for foreign minister, was perhaps the most anti-Soviet of the first-tier Labour leadership. Born poor, orphaned before the age of ten, self-supporting from eleven with barely an elementary school education, Bevin had helped to build the unions and had risen through

---

† He reissued the book in 1949, demonstrating that neither the passage of time nor the burdens of office had diluted his strong socialist conviction. The one revision of opinion he acknowledged was a "sharpened . . . distinction . . . between the socialism of the British Labour Party and the totalitarianism of the Communists." See Clement R. Attlee, *The Labour Party in Perspective—and Twelve Years Later* (London: Victor Gollancz Ltd., 1949), Foreword (not paginated).

their ranks to become the most powerful labor leader in Britain. His antipathy toward communism was nurtured over years of internecine battle for control of the unions, in the course of which he had once won a libel suit against the Communist Party newspaper, *Daily Worker,* for calling him a traitor to the workers.[†] Although Bevin had never served in Parliament, Churchill brought him into the war government as labor minister. In that post he became one of the architects of British victory.

Broad-shouldered, portly, thick-featured, speaking cockney English with few rules of grammar, famously mispronouncing foreign names, Bevin looked and sounded the part of union boss. But he was arguably the most brilliant British foreign minister in the twentieth century and a real hero of the Cold War, the contours of which he recognized sooner than any other leading Western statesman except perhaps Churchill. When Secretary of State George Marshall delivered the 1947 Harvard commencement address that proffered U.S. financing for European recovery, it was Bevin who seized the initially inchoate offer and took the lead in developing what became the Marshall Plan. It was also he who, recognizing the urgency of entwining America in Europe's security, conceived the embryo that grew into NATO.

At Potsdam and in other meetings with Soviet officials, Attlee was content to let Bevin do the talking. When challenged on this he replied: "If you have a good dog, don't bark yourself, and in Mr. Bevin I had an exceptionally good dog."[65] So strong did Attlee, backed by Bevin, become in his anti-Sovietism that, with the knowledge of only a few officials, he took the bold decision to develop Britain's independent nuclear deterrent when Washington failed to fulfill what British officials believed was a commitment to share nuclear weaponry. And despite his allegiance to the workers, Attlee did not balk at using government forces to break politically motivated strikes staged by Communist-run dock unions.

• • •

Attlee's attempt to transform Britain into a socialist society seems all the more remarkable in light of the momentous foreign policy issues he had to face. Not only were the early acts of the Cold War being performed, but so was the drama

---

† The article had described Bevin as "maneuvering here, retreating a little there, but all the time consciously working to secure the acceptance of worsened conditions by the men." The court awarded him the goodly sum of £7,000. "King's Bench Division: Alleged Libel in the Daily Worker: Mr. Ernest Bevin's Action," *Times (London)*, 19 November 1933, p. 4.

of decolonization. Drained by war, England no longer had the wealth or forces to hold its great empire, nor the political strength to resist American support for the cause of independence. In any event, Labour rejected colonialism in principle. On the issue of empire, Attlee exhibited none of the monarchist traditionalism that he displayed on other questions. His goal for the colonies consisted of two points, he said: independence and socialism.

Drawing on the expertise he had gained while serving in the late 1920s on the India commission, he cut the Gordian knot of this most daunting colonial issue, leading to early statehood for India and Pakistan and the inclusion of both in the British Commonwealth. Several historians and biographers consider this his most important achievement, notwithstanding the Hindu-Muslim bloodletting that accompanied the transfer of power. Less widely admired was his handling of Britain's Palestine mandate. Neither he nor Bevin showed any sympathy for Zionism. Historian Kenneth Morgan explains, mystifyingly, that "Bevin was not . . . anti-semitic. But, without doubt, he was emotionally prejudiced against the Jews." Something similar could be said about Attlee, who entertained his children with derogatory "Moses and Ikey" jokes and sometimes included the like in his letters to Tom. Attlee and Bevin resisted Jewish immigration to Palestine and the creation of a Jewish state as long as they could, finally returning the mandate to the United Nations, which partitioned the territory.

Independence proved to be a lot easier to achieve for the colonies than socialism. The government spent millions of scarce pounds on public corporations in a futile effort to stimulate socialist development of the lands being decolonized. This was capped off with the East Africa Groundnut Scheme, which turned a three-million-acre swath of Tanganyikan outback into a vast state-run peanut farm that collapsed in fiasco.

This demonstration of the fallibility of government economic planning reinforced the lessons of the fuel and currency crises of 1947 and the uneven performance of the nationalized industries. Together they served to weaken Labour's confidence in its socialist program. Not that it followed Bernstein in foreswearing the "final goal"; Attlee, for one, strongly reaffirmed his commitment to it. But in practice the party engaged in a form of "revisionism" more radical than Bernstein's. He had written off the utopian image of a socialist future in favor of constant pressure for piecemeal reform. The Labour government now proceeded more fitfully than this, fearing the economic consequences of further measures to enlarge the public sector or expand the welfare state. Even the party's "Keep Left" faction, which demanded fidelity to truly socialist policies, chose to concentrate its fire on foreign policy, criticizing Attlee and Bevin for being too anti-Soviet and pro-American. By 1949, fiscal pressures forced the government to present a budget that reduced spending on social programs and housing, raised the prices of subsidized food, and imposed a charge of a shilling for medical prescriptions.

As the party prepared for new national elections in 1950, its focus was more on consolidating the advances it had made than on marching forward. The welfare state had been launched and, with the addition of iron and steel anticipated later that year, some 20 percent of the British economy would then have been nationalized. The party's electoral program called for taking over next the meat and sugar industries, as well as cement, water and insurance, but many observers felt that this potpourri only served to emphasize the absence of a convincing blueprint for socialist progress.

For the campaign, Attlee again toured the country in the family car, Vi still at the wheel, although news accounts of her erratic driving had become, if not a scandal, a source of national mirth. In deference to his status as prime minister, the car carried two additional occupants, a news reporter from a friendly paper and a man from Scotland Yard. In this last old-fashioned campaign, Attlee led his party to another victory, but not by much. Labour still retained a respectable margin of the popular vote, outdistancing the Tories by about 2.5 percent, but due to redistricting, its majority in the Commons was sliced from 146 seats to 5. There was relief at victory, but little expectation that a government could survive long with so thin a majority.

North Korea's invasion of South Korea in 1950 brought pressure for increased defense expenditure, and this in turn exacerbated tensions within the government between those, led by Aneurin Bevan, who wanted to maintain social spending, and others, led by Chancellor of the Exchequer Hugh Gaitskell, more mindful of fiscal responsibility. Bevan was perhaps Labour's most charismatic leader and Attlee's favored successor, but his looming eclipse by the younger, colorless Gaitskell symbolized the party's loss of faith. In addition, a fault line opened between the government and the labor unions, which were chafing under wage controls and limits on strikes. Many observers expressed surprise that Attlee was able to manage as long as he did before calling another election, late in 1951.

In his speech to the party conference inaugurating that campaign, Attlee quoted from Blake's "Jerusalem":

I will not cease from mental fight,

Nor shall my sword sleep in my hand,

Till we have built Jerusalem

In England's green and pleasant land.

But the party's election manifesto made no mention of socialism nor of any new nationalizations. Labour was on the defensive. It eked out a slight plurality of the popular vote, but once again the vicissitudes of vote distribution worked to its disadvantage and the Conservatives won a majority of seats.

The Tory government of Churchill reversed the nationalization of iron and steel and of trucking while leaving intact the other elements of what Labour called its "peaceful revolution." This boast was justified not only by the reforms enacted but also by the dissolution of class barriers that occurred when the highest positions in the land were filled for the first time by men with backgrounds like Ernest Bevin's. In six years, "Labour had achieved the maximum it could, or would, do in changing the political face of Britain," writes Burridge.[66] Yet as this formula suggests, while Labour changed much it also discovered something about the limitations of change. "We have only gone a few steps towards the kind of society of which we Socialists dream," said Attlee.[67]

8

UJAMAA: NYERERE
FORGES A SYNTHESIS

THE ECONOMIC TRANSFORMATION OF BRITAIN engineered by
Clement Attlee's government failed to yield the luminous results that he
and his comrades had always envisioned. But in writing *fini* to the empire and
playing midwife to dozens of new states, they opened the door to previously
unimagined vistas for the construction of socialism. According to orthodox
Marxist doctrine, societies become ripe for socialism only after maturing industrially. But in the twentieth century the Russian and Chinese revolutions stood
this postulate on its head, and even social democrats who refused to recognize
Communist regimes as truly "socialist" nonetheless embraced the inference that
undeveloped countries need not postpone socialism. Attlee's belief that socialism and independence should go hand in hand in the former colonies met with
few demurrals in the Socialist International.

The lack of economic advancement that had once been thought an obstacle
to socialism now was seen as an exciting opportunity. A less structured society,
less encrusted with class and less burdened by history, would be easier to mold,
and socialism itself could be the antidote to backwardness. State-planned economic development seemed to offer the straightest path to modernity. This was
not only the Communist position; it became the regnant wisdom of Western
development specialists. And it was reinforced by the Cold War rivalry in the
"Third World," where socialism, not capitalism, became the West's proffered

alternative to communism as the two sides competed to help in the construction of state-centered economies. For their part, the local rulers, eager to take
help from all sides and to avoid policy or ideological straitjackets, formulated
their own fluid mixtures of "Third World socialism."

Altogether, some fifty-eight Third World states (see Appendix II) proclaimed that they were embracing socialist policies or came under the rule of
parties or movements describing themselves as socialist. Seven of these states
were in Asia, thirteen in Latin America and the Caribbean, and three in the non-
African Middle East. By far the largest number, thirty-five, was in Africa, the
most impoverished region of the world and the locus of the largest number of
newborn states. Nowhere was the challenge of development more urgent, and
nowhere was there more agreement on the solution. Much to the jubilation of
European socialists, the leaders of the African independence movements almost
all proclaimed socialism to be the key to their future. As the noted Labour Party
intellectual Fenner Brockway enthused, "Nearly every politically alert African
nationalist regards himself as a socialist. . . . Indeed, it is not too much to say that
the most dynamic socialist movement in the world to-day is in Africa. It is the
most comprehensively revolutionary continent."[1]

In celebrating the popularity of socialism among African leaders, the British
socialists were in a sense smiling at their own reflection. Where had these
Africans acquired their ideology but in European universities, where the most
promising colonial youngsters had been sent for the purpose of grooming a
native elite? Only half in jest was the London School of Economics—which the
Webbs founded and where young Attlee lectured—called the most important
institution of higher learning in Asia and Africa. This classroom transmission
of socialist ideas from North to South was dubbed the "British revolution" by
Daniel Patrick Moynihan, who said it rivaled the American and French and
Russian revolutions in its global consequences.[2]

One of the young Africans who partook of this experience was Julius
Kambarage Nyerere, who was to become his continent's outstanding theoretician of socialism. Arriving at Edinburgh in 1949 with a fellowship to pursue a
degree in biology, he was the first Tanganyikan to study in the mother country.
Julius was the son of Nyerere Burito of the village of Butiama. Burito was a
chief of the Zanaki, one of the smallest of the 120-odd tribes that made up
Tanganyika. Julius' mother, Mugaya, had been fifteen when she became the fifth
wife of Nyerere Burito, who was sixty-one at the time. He lived to a ripe age,
taking an additional seventeen or eighteen wives, in keeping with his seniority

and station.[3] Mugaya is said to have been not quite her husband's favorite, but perhaps his second favorite since she was the only one who played *bao,* the checkers-like game popular in East Africa.[4] Her second son was born in March 1922 on a rainy day, which inspired the choice of his name, Kambarage, after a rain spirit.

Kambarage's upbringing was tribal. His teeth were filed to points, and he sometimes accompanied the men on hunting trips on the Serengeti plains, dodging the British who, as he later recalled with a smile, "regarded [it] as poaching."[5] Tribal battles were also a part of his memory, and he liked to tell the story of when

> the Zanaki were attacked by the Nguruimi, who had disguised themselves as Masai by painting their bodies red with ochre and by carrying spears. The Zanaki were terrified and fled. But later the Nguruimi made the mistake of boasting too much, and the Zanaki said in disgust, "ah, it's only the Nguruimi," and beat them up.[6]

Kambarage was "a good child . . . almost too good," recalled Mugaya. "If I had to go somewhere and I told him to stay at a place, I would find him there when I came back."[7] Though they were the family of a chief, life was still poor. Kambarage would later recall how he watched his mother's constant struggle to patch their leaking mud roof or how she covered him against the cold with her cloth without having another for herself. When he was eight, he was entrusted with the chore of taking the goats to pasture and tending them for the day. He might have lived out his life in such traditional pursuits, except for a coincidence when he was twelve that gave him the opportunity for education. Two of Nyerere Burito's sons had already attended school, and two seemed like enough to him. But when the district commissioner selected the adopted son of Kambarage's older brother, Edward, to be sent some thirty miles away to a boarding school run by Catholic missionaries, Edward prevailed upon his father to send Kambarage, too, so the two boys might keep each other company.

At the Mwisenge School in Musoma on the shores of Lake Victoria, Kambarage learned Swahili, the region's lingua franca, and English. He also attended religion classes and embraced Christianity. He proved an outstanding student, and two years later was admitted to Tabora, modeled after the British "public schools" and run by the colonial administration for the most talented local youth. After six years there, he received a scholarship to study at Makerere College in Uganda.

His father had recently died, clearing the way for Kambarage to enter the Catholic Church formally. Until then he had held back for fear of hurting the older man's feelings by abandoning the tribal gods. Now, he was baptized "Julius," the name he used ever after, never straying from his Catholic faith.

When he received his degree in 1945, Julius returned to Tabora and took a job teaching biology and history at St. Mary's College, a Catholic secondary school. He became the secretary of the local branch of the Tanganyikan African Association, a national club of Africans, mostly civil servants, that was more social than political and therefore tolerated by the colonial authorities. With the once vaunted strength of the European shattered by world war, Africans in Tanganyika as elsewhere were increasingly asking why they should be ruled by foreigners. Nyerere was already beginning to be pegged as one such trouble-maker, and objections were raised on this ground to his application in 1948 to study in Britain. These were overcome, however, with the help of his friends in the Catholic hierarchy, and after securing some financial aid, which enabled him to contribute to the support of his mother and build her a house, he reached Scotland in 1949.

Disarmingly, he had applied to study biology, although he had no such inten-tion. Soon after arriving, he applied for a change of subject, his real goal being to gain the kind of knowledge that would strengthen him in the struggle ahead. He read politics, history, economics and philosophy. Scribbling in a copy book, he crystallized his ideas in a biting essay on "The Race Problem in East Africa":

> The African's capacity for bearing insult is not really limitless. . . . A day comes when the people will prefer death to insult. . . . Africa is for the Africans, and the other races cannot be more than respected minorities. . . . Should it come to a bitter choice between being perpetually dominated by a white or an Indian minority and . . . driving that minority out of East Africa, no thinking African would hesitate to make the latter choice.[8]

Edinburgh had a long reputation as a hub of left-wing thinking, and Nyerere found sympathetic interlocutors among the members of the Labour Party and the Fabian Society. As he studied their descriptions of socialism, he was struck by the resemblance to the time-honored ways of the society from which he sprang. The Zanaki, as Nyerere saw it, were natural socialists. They practiced

François-Noël "Gracchus" Babeuf, the first socialist.

Robert Owen came to the New World to organize a practical demonstration of the superiority of the "social system." (Photograph by the Indiana Historical Society of John Cranch's 1845 portrait.)

The Manchester (England) Hall of Science where Owen's followers held Sunday services, attended frequently in 1843 by the young Friedrich Engels. (Courtesy of the Central Library of Manchester.)

Friedrich Engels and Karl Marx, the high priest and oracle of the new religion of Scientific Socialism, with Marx's daughters, Laura, Eleanor and Jenny, in London in 1864. (Courtesy of the Friedrich Ebert Foundation, Trier.)

Eduard Bernstein, the leading disciple of Marx and Engels, worried that their forecasts were not coming true. (Courtesy of the Friedrich Ebert Foundation, Bonn.)

Lenin haranguing a crowd in Moscow in 1920. Trotsky, standing at his lower right, was later famously airbrushed out of the photo by Stalin. (Courtesy of the David King Collection.)

Il Duce, Benito Mussolini, exhorting Italians to win "the battle for grain." The outbreak of world war in 1914 convinced him that nation could be a more potent revolutionary principle than class. (From Rizzoli Photo Archives.)

Prime Minister Clement Attlee was a perfect British gentleman, "conservative about everything except socialism." (Courtesy of the German Historical Museum, Berlin.)

President Julius Nyerere with Chinese economic advisers laying the cornerstone of the Friendship Textile Mill, a symbol of Tanzania's socialist road to development. (From the Warder Collection.)

Alexandr Solzhenitsyn thanks George Meany "on behalf of all the prisoners" of the Soviet *gulag* for the AFL-CIO's militant defense of human rights against communism. (Courtesy of the George Meany Labor Studies Center.)

Samuel Gompers abandoned socialism for "bread-and-butter unionism." This photo was shot by a detective keeping his eye on a labor organizing campaign. (Courtesy of the George Meany Labor Studies Center.)

Below: Deng Xiaoping at a Texas rodeo during his 1979 visit to the United States, the first by a leader of the People's Republic of China. His opening to the West was a cornerstone of economic reforms that undid socialism.

Aspiring rock star Tony Blair at Oxford. By jettisoning ideology, he got the Labour Party back in tune with British voters. (Courtesy of South West News Service, Bristol.)

Moses Hess, who helped introduce Marx and Engels to communism, proclaimed that the difference between Christians and Communists was that the Communists "will have this heaven on earth." (Painting by Gustav Adolf Koettgen, 1845, by permission of the City Museum of Düsseldorf.)

THE HOTEL IN KIBBUTZ GINOSAR

Kibbutz Ginosar on the banks of the Sea of Galilee: initially some tents and huts surrounded by a stockade and watchtower, it was a verdant resort by the 1970s. (Courtesy of Ada Tsoref.)

communal ownership, collective decision making, and essential social and economic equality—leaving aside the status of women. For an angry young man
who felt that there was no worse crime of colonialism than "the attempt to
make us believe we had no indigenous culture of our own; or that what we did
have was worthless," it was profoundly gratifying to discover that his own tribal
patrimony anticipated the social ideals of Britain's most advanced thinkers.[9] He
left Edinburgh a convinced socialist.

In 1952 Nyerere completed his degree and returned to Tanganyika. Now
thirty, he married Maria, the fiancée he had left behind, and took a teaching
position at St. Francis College, a secondary school in Pugu. But neither domes-
ticity nor teaching was foremost in his mind. Colonial issues were in the air.
The electrifying Mau Mau rebellion was at full pitch in neighboring Kenya,
and stirrings could be felt even in relatively placid Tanganyika. The Tanganyikan
African Association shed its heritage as a doughty social club, changing its name
to the Tanganyikan African National Union (TANU) and adopting a statement of
purpose that was unequivocally political. Nyerere, now perhaps the most highly
educated African in the territory, assumed its presidency.

His mother did not welcome his new role. "One day I overheard them
talking about taking over the government," she recalled. "I became afraid. Later
I asked Julius if what I heard was true. When he said yes I became more frightened. I told him that what he was doing was bad. God had given him a good job
and now he wanted to spoil it."[10]

But Julius was on his way to international acclaim. In 1955, TANU cobbled
together the funds to send him to New York to address the United Nations
Trusteeship Council. While demanding "a categorical statement" that the "future
government [of Tanganyika] shall be primarily African," he offered reassurance
that to TANU "the Asian or European who has adopted Tanganyika as his home
is as much a Tanganyikan as a Tanganyika-born African."[11] This conciliatory
message confounded the image of fiery black nationalism that had been etched
by the Mau Mau, and his appearance was hailed as a triumph in the Western
media and by diplomats. Here was an authentic voice of Africa's grievance who
nonetheless could be reasoned with.

On the way home Nyerere stopped in Britain to cultivate support in the
Labour Party. The next year he was invited to address the party's annual conference, where he received an enthusiastic reception and posed for photos with
key figures including Hugh Gaitskell, who had succeeded Attlee as party leader.
After that, writes John Hatch, who was then the Labour Party's Commonwealth

officer, Labour "afford[ed] Nyerere every facility he requested, helping his fledgling party and constantly harrying Conservative governments over their policies in Tanganyika."[12] Socialism might have hit on hard times at home in Britain, but this only made it all the more heartening to see it carried forward by new disciples in new lands.

Upon his return, his once disapproving mother came to meet him at the airport and was stunned by the adoring crowd that greeted him. "That was the first time I realized that my son had become such an important person," she said.[13]

As pressure mounted on the colonial administration to take more account of Tanganyikan opinion, a plan was devised for tightly circumscribed elections to a new legislative council. The country would be divided into ten districts, each of which would elect three representatives—one seat reserved for a white, one for a black, one for an Asian. Voters could cast a ballot for all three seats in their constituency, but the electorate was sharply restricted on the basis of education, income and employment. In all, only sixty thousand voters were registered, less than 1 percent of the population.

The first reaction of the leaders of TANU was to spurn this undemocratic election as a trap designed to spread a veneer of legitimacy over minority rule. But Nyerere persuaded his colleagues that TANU could command a majority of the voters, despite the narrowness of the electorate, and that it had enough white and Asian sympathizers to field candidates even for those seats. His confidence was amply vindicated. When the first five constituencies voted in late 1958, all fifteen seats were captured by candidates backed by TANU. When the remaining five districts went to the polls in early 1959, few candidates not endorsed by TANU even bothered to run. The British government recognized that it would have to come to terms with Nyerere, and soon announced that new legislative elections would be held in 1960, with seats no longer assigned by race. Nyerere exulted: "We would like to light a candle and put it on top of Mount Kilimanjaro, which will shine beyond our borders, giving hope where there was despair, love where there was hate, and dignity where there was humiliation."

TANU approached the 1960 election with a statement of aims that committed it to building a democratic and socialist Tanganyika. It swept all seats but one, and colonial governor Richard Turnbull named Nyerere chief minister. Early the following year, London announced the decision to grant Tanganyika its independence.

• • •

December 9, 1961 was the day of *Uhuru,* the Swahili word for "freedom." A team of climbers did in fact scale Kilimanjaro and plant a torch on its summit. Then, six weeks later, Nyerere abruptly resigned as prime minister. He called in one of his close disciples, Rashidi Kawawa, and said, "Look, Rashidi, you are the prime minister from right now. Take the chair."[14] The whole nation was as stunned as Kawawa, who insisted that he was only sitting in for "the father of the nation."

Nyerere explained that he was leaving the government in order to give "full time to the work of TANU."[15] This was the first indication that he was moving away from the democratic ideas of his British teachers. In Communist regimes the top man was ordinarily the general secretary of the party, rather than the official head of state or government. Nyerere was not a Communist, nor did he want to model TANU after the Communist parties, but he wanted to reshape it from a movement of mass struggle to a governing apparatus.

And in other ways, Nyerere's decision to step back contained hints that he did not believe he could implement socialism in Tanganyika by the democratic means he had learned at Edinburgh, yet he did not want to compromise his standing as hero to Europe's social democrats, so he let someone else do the dirty work. With his encouragement, a sweeping law on preventive detention was enacted, giving the government complete discretion to throw people in jail, and this was coupled with tight restrictions on trade unions. Since Kawawa had himself been a labor leader, he was the ideal front man for such action.

Nyerere also was in a bind over racial preferences. Little would be gained, he said, by the "replacement of non-African landlords, employers and capitalists by African ones."[16] He had opposed those who would have restricted Tanganyika citizenship to blacks, likening their approach to the policies of Hitler and Verwoerd, the architect of South Africa's apartheid.[17] He was, moreover, pain-fully aware of the country's dearth of trained Africans.[18] According to a govern-ment study of the skilled professions in Tanganyika just after independence, 16 of the nation's 184 doctors were black, as were 9 of the 45 veterinarians, and 2 of the 57 lawyers. There was 1 black civil engineer, 1 surveyor, 1 zoologist—and not a single black architect, mechanical engineer or geologist. As a demonstra-tion of Nyerere's non-racialist conviction, TANU for the first time opened its doors to non-blacks. Nonetheless, he recognized that his views ran counter to an overwhelming tide of public opinion. How could Africans feel they had become masters in their own house so long as society's elite positions continued to be

filled almost entirely by whites and Asians? Better to let Kawawa, who shared
little of Nyerere's delicacy, "Africanize" the civil service.

After a year Nyerere returned to government, winning Tanzania's first
presidential election with more than 98 percent of the vote. Soon thereafter he
adopted the sobriquet "Mwalimu." It was an ostentatious gesture of humility:
Mwalimu is Swahili for "teacher," and teachers ordinarily carry this title before
their names much as professors do in the West. Nyerere told associates that he
was repelled by the grandiose honorifics that other African leaders were bestow-
ing upon themselves. For his part he would be content to be called "Mwalimu
Nyerere," just as he had been when teaching school. Usually, though, he was
called simply "Mwalimu," and, for all its modesty, there was something exalting in this, implying that he was always the teacher and his countrymen were
his perpetual pupils. For the next nearly thirty years, the nation's course was
charted by means of policy declarations that began as lectures by Nyerere. They
were rarely discussed in advance with anyone else.

Among his first acts as president was to appoint a commission to study the
transition to a one-party system. By the time of the next election, in 1965, the
constitution was amended to outlaw any party except TANU. Nyerere claimed
that he had not departed from his previous pledge "to demonstrate to the whole
of Africa that democracy is the only answer."[19] He dismissed objections to the
new setup with a bit of breezy doubletalk: "the philosophical concept of freedom
is not a matter of mechanics."[20] Yet in justifying a one-party system, he seemed
to concede that the democracy he had in mind was an attenuated version. Just as
European democracies sometimes resorted to a less competitive political system
when the nation's security was in jeopardy, he wrote, so Tanganyika needed to
maximize national unity in order to win its "war against poverty, ignorance and
disease."[21] He returned to the "war" analogy in his inaugural address in a way that
made its antidemocratic implications chillingly clear. "I look to every citizen of
our country to join in the fight," he said. "And anyone who interferes with our
war effort, I . . . shall look upon as a traitor and an enemy."[22]

Nyerere's strategy for winning the "war" was socialism. During the months
between his resignation as prime minister and his assumption of the presidency,
the TANU constitution was revised to commit the party to socialism, and
Nyerere wrote the first of his seminal pamphlets, "*Ujamaa*: The Basis of African
Socialism." His version of socialism was an original one, deviating sharply from
the Marxist tradition as well as from British-style social democracy, and betraying the earmarks of his religiosity, so rare among socialist leaders.

Nyerere rejected the materialist approach of the European Left. Socialism, he declared, "is an attitude of mind."[23] It is not contingent on economic factors. Poor people could be socialists, and so too could poor countries; it was all a question of outlook. Therefore, it was wrong to believe that Africa would have to develop capitalism before it could hope for socialism.

Despite its lack of industrial development, Africa had a great advantage in its quest for socialism, since its native tradition was implicitly socialist. This was evidenced by the absence of millionaires in Africa, which Nyerere said reflected innate egalitarianism, "for it is not . . . the amount of wealth in a country, which makes millionaires; it is the uneven distribution."[24] Nyerere said that he himself had been "brought up in tribal socialism," embodied in the term *ujamaa,* meaning "familyhood." This noble tradition had been obscured by an overlay of selfishness imported from the West. "Our first step, therefore, must be to re-educate ourselves; to regain our former attitude of mind."[25]

Toward this end, Nyerere decreed the nationalization of all land. Tanganyika is a country with a large amount of arable land relative to the size of its population, and few Tanganyikans lacked the opportunity to farm. But Nyerere argued that private ownership was "completely wrong" and "foreign."[26] Whether or not this assessment accurately represented the country's polyglot traditions, nationalization alienated many peasants from TANU and was one reason for the ban on opposition parties and other repressive measures.[27]

Nyerere encouraged members of the TANU Youth League and other idealists to form communal farms, called *"ujamaa* villages," as models of socialist development. Israel sent a team of advisers who helped with the founding of ten kibbutz-type settlements. Altogether, as many as three hundred villages were set up. Encouragement came not only from socialists abroad but even from the World Bank, which believed that denser settlement would promote agricultural efficiency.

In addition, Nyerere toyed with abolishing private commerce. That merchants bought things cheap and sold them dear without adding any value seemed to him parasitic. Here, too, his image of Tanganyika's mores may have been skewed. A study he commissioned in 1962 discouraged any major interference with existing retail and wholesale trade, but he was not completely dissuaded. "We were not satisfied that nothing could be done," he said, "and we tried to establish co-operative wholesale and retail shops by Government initiative."[28]

Building socialism at home proceeded in tandem with the fight for emancipation across Africa. When the Organization of African Unity (OAU) was founded, its most portentous decision was to create a "War and Action Council" to give political support to those fighting against colonial rule or white domination in southern Africa. Nyerere provided a headquarters for the council in Dar es Salaam, turning his capital into a main hub of activity in support of the liberation movements. Dar es Salaam was a poor city, but outsiders recall it as a wonderful place to visit in the 1960s because it teemed with heroic exiles and throbbed with the excitement of righteous struggle.

The liberation campaign hit home in Tanganyika in an unexpected way in 1963 and 1964. On the nearby islands of Zanzibar, African militants staged a coup against the Arab sultan and declared a "people's republic." Chaos reigned until Nyerere sent a force of three hundred police to help stabilize the new regime. A few months later, Nyerere and Zanzibar's ruler, a former dockworker named Abeid Karume, announced the merger of Tanganyika and Zanzibar to form Tanzania.[†] Since Karume and Zanzibar's other revolutionaries had ties to Russia, China, Cuba or East Germany, the merger pulled Nyerere's alignment toward the East.

Aside from its foreign policy consequences, the turmoil in Zanzibar had surprising and painful repercussions for Nyerere at home. Just a week after the island uprising, two battalions of troops mutinied in Tanganyika. The principal source of the mutineers' unhappiness was that the armed forces remained under British commanders. The Zanzibar revolt, with its racial impetus, served as an inspiration, and the absence of the three hundred police whom Nyerere had sent to the island to keep order there left his own government vulnerable. Although the mutineers did not molest Nyerere, they took control of the State House, the executive building, until he arranged the intervention of a team of sixty British paratroopers who subdued the rebels and restored presidential authority.

The experience of having to turn for help to the former colonial rulers was deeply humiliating, and Nyerere asked for a special session of the OAU so that he might explain his actions. He dissolved the existing forces and began to rebuild his military from scratch with a heavy emphasis on political indoctrination. In the aftermath of the crisis, hundreds of critics of his regime were arrested. Nyerere may have suspected them of encouraging the rebellion, or he may have used the occasion as a pretext for clamping down on dissent. He disbanded the labor unions, toward which he was never friendly, seeing unions as inherently selfish and thus the antithesis of a socialist "attitude of mind." They were replaced

---

† Nyerere insisted that the name of the country be pronounced with the accent on the penultimate syllable in keeping with the cadence of Swahili.

by a government union with a secretary-general chosen by himself rather than by the members. Nyerere explained his vision of its role in a subsequent essay: "Our trade union movement must shake off its British heritage, where it found its justification for existence by quarreling with the employers . . . [and] learn something from the Soviet trade unions" whose job was to raise productivity.[29]

In the aftermath of the military mutiny, Nyerere dispatched Kawawa to Moscow and Beijing in search of aid in building a new military force. The Russians characteristically demanded stiff terms, but the Chinese were far more forthcoming. China also stepped into the breach in 1965 to replace a British loan cancelled when Nyerere severed relations with London for failing to act more forcefully against the breakaway white supremacist regime in Rhodesia. Eventually, Tanzania became the leading recipient of Chinese foreign aid.

Nyerere first visited China in 1965 and believed he had found there a model more suitable for Tanzania than that of the West. "If it were possible for me to lift all the ten million Tanzanians and bring them to China to see what you have done since the liberation, I would do so," he gushed.[30] Chinese communism was quite far afield from Nyerere's oft-repeated democratic protestations. His affinity for it can best be understood, ironically, in view of the Christian rather than the Marxian roots of his thought. In Marxism, socialism is linked to the idea of abundance, whereas Nyerere's concept of socialism was ascetic; it was about selfless devotion, not self-gratification. That is what he saw, or thought he saw, in China. He explained:

> There is [a] lesson which we can learn from the Chinese revolution. It is that courage, enthusiasm, and endurance are not enough. There must also be discipline. . . . The single-mindedness with which the Chinese people are concentrating on development was the thing which most impressed me. . . . The conscious and deliberate frugality with which your people and your government efficiently and joyfully conduct their affairs was a big lesson for me.[31]

Only a year after Nyerere's first visit, the Great Proletarian Cultural Revolution was unleashed by Mao Zedong. For most Chinese, it was a time of unparalleled horrors, when frenzied adolescent gangs murdered millions and much of society's constructive activity ground to a halt. Yet Nyerere took it all in stride. Chinese premier Zhou Enlai told him that the Cultural Revolution was a popular uprising against a new elite, and Nyerere approved. He was deeply troubled by his inability to stop Tanzanian officials from looking to advance their own power and prosperity. During a visit to China in 1968 he remarked: "I must say that if you found it necessary to begin a cultural revolution, in order to make sure that the new generation would carry forward the banner of your revolution, then certainly we need one. We have seen in Tanzania how easy it is to pay lip service to the importance of socialism and the people, while in fact we behave like capitalists and petty dictators."[32] He even created a youth movement, the Green Guards, that drew on the image (although not the violent antics) of Mao's Red Guards.

By then, Nyerere had launched his own cultural revolution. It was called the "Arusha Declaration" after a speech of Nyerere's that was adopted as a resolution of the National Executive Committee in early 1967, and it aimed to accelerate radically Tanzania's transition to socialism. "We are at war," said the resolution, employing a favored metaphor. "The struggle is aimed at moving the people of Tanzania (and the people of Africa as a whole) from a state of poverty to a state of prosperity." The key to accomplishing this was socialism. And the key to socialism was government ownership:

> To build and maintain socialism it is essential that all the major means of production and exchange in the nation are controlled and owned by the peasants through the machinery of their Government and their cooperatives. . . .
>
> The major means of production and exchange are such things as: land; forests; minerals; water; oil and electricity; news media; communications; banks, insurance, import and export trade, wholesale trade; iron and steel, machine tool, arms, motor-car, cement, fertilizer, and textile industries; and any big factory on which a large section of the people depend for their living, or which provides essential components of other industries; large plantations, and especially those which provide raw materials essential to important industries.[33]

Within a week, Nyerere announced at a mass meeting the nationalization of all banks. "Cabinet ministers hugged each other in joy at this triumph over the imperialists, and soldiers shouted and waved banners," reports biographer William Edgett Smith.[34] In the following days there were more mass rallies and more announcements of nationalizations. Soon Nyerere could boast that "in the space of one week [we] have nationalized or taken control of all the large capitalist firms and institutions which could have dominated our economy."[35]

The program of nationalizations was closely tied to the Arusha Declaration's goal of self-reliance. "The policy of inviting a chain of capitalists to come and establish industries in our country might succeed in giving us all the industries we need, but it would also succeed in preventing the establishment of socialism."[36] Moreover, it would make Tanzania dependent on foreigners, when the country should instead rely on its own resources and energies.

The most controversial part of the declaration was its "leadership code," which embodied Nyerere's ascetic ethic. It forbade party or government leaders, or their spouses, from holding other jobs or owning businesses or shares or rental property. This was greeted much less warmly by Nyerere's comrades and was the one part of the declaration to which the TANU executive forced some modification.

The nationalizations were immensely popular, especially because most of the owners whose property was taken were white or Asian. Nyerere bemoaned his countrymen's lack of "understanding of socialism."[37] They did not "demand socialization; they simply demanded the replacement of white and brown faces by black ones." Worst of all, "It was not only the masses who looked upon things in this way; many leaders of the independence struggle themselves saw things in these terms. They were not against capitalism; they simply wanted its fruits." Ironically, comments Cranford Pratt, the two most prominent centers of socialist belief were a group within TANU that associated socialism with despoiling whites and Asians, and a circle of Marxist academics at Dar es Salaam University and Kivukoni College (the TANU training school), most of whom were white or Asian.

To correct this situation for the long term, Nyerere proposed to overhaul the nation's education system. He put his proposals in a pamphlet, "Education for Self-Reliance," issued a month after the Arusha Declaration. Nyerere criticized the system left over from colonial days, which was geared toward preparing students to compete for admission to secondary school and then to university. This was doubly faulty, he said. The majority of students failed to advance, leaving them discouraged and unprepared for the agricultural work at which they would have to spend their lives. The minority who succeeded took on airs of elitism. Therefore, he argued,

> we should change the things we demand of our schools. We should not determine the type of things children are taught in primary schools by the things a doctor, engineer, teacher, economist, or administrator need to know. Most of

our pupils will never be any of these things. We should determine the type of things taught in the primary schools by the things which the boy or girl ought to know—that is, the skills he ought to acquire and the values he ought to cherish if he, or she, is to live happily and well in a socialist and predominantly rural society, and contribute to the improvement of life there.[38]

Every school, he said, should have a small farm or workshop attached to it. Not only would the students learn work skills, but the planning they would have to do would help them to understand socialism. Entry to secondary school and university would no longer be based exclusively on formal criteria but instead on a combination of examinations and an "assessment of work done for the school and community."[39] The paramount function of the schools would be to "encourage the growth of . . . socialist values" so that "our students [will] be educated to be members and servants of the kind of just and egalitarian future to which this country aspires."[40]

While school reforms promised to produce an eventual solution to the dearth of ideological commitment in the country, Nyerere felt he had to take more immediate steps to gather public support for the socialist path he had chosen. At a rally on Saba Saba Day, 1967 (Saba Saba, the seventh day of the seventh month, was the anniversary of TANU's founding), "Mwalimu declared an all-out war on the remaining capitalists and exploiters."[41] Then the young members of the Green Guards were urged to undertake marches in all corners of the country in support of the Arusha Declaration. The response was trumpeted in TANU's English-language newspaper, *The Nationalist,* in reports such as this:

> Tempered and remoulded by the flames of the Spirit of Arusha, nine gallant youths from Singida have advanced their column on the longest march of all— through eight regions—in support of the Arusha Declaration, the President and the party. A long revolutionary column of one hundred and six people, of all ages, is advancing south toward the capital where the gallant marchers will make revolutionary contacts with party leaders, and pledge their support for the Arusha Declaration.[42]

A team of secondary school students scaled Mount Meru, the country's second-highest peak, where they planted copies of the Arusha Declaration and "Education for Self-Reliance," and urged Nyerere to rename it "Socialism Peak."

Then Mwalimu himself joined the marchers, leading an eight-day trek over 138 miles, addressing rallies along the way, and ending in Mwanza, where the TANU National Conference was scheduled to convene.

• • •

Nationalizations continued over the next few years, resulting in the creation of more than four hundred government corporations, called "parastatals." All commercial real estate as well as residences not occupied by their owners and worth more than £5,900 were seized by the state. But Nyerere pointed out that this was not enough. "For the foreseeable future the vast majority of our people will continue to spend their lives in the rural areas and continue to work the land," he said in the third of his seminal essays of 1967, "Socialism and Rural Development." Therefore, "if our rural life is not based on the principles of socialism our country will not be socialist."[43]

Virtually all of the communal farms created in the first years after independence had "failed miserably," as one leading official acknowledged, and the government had shut down its Village Settlement Agency.[44] Now a call went out to government, party and civic leaders across the land to spur the peasants to create new communal villages. Nyerere's intent was to rely on persuasion and exhortation, but for the most part the peasants were unresponsive, so local officials began using coercive methods. Michaela von Freyhold, a Marxist academic, headed a research team of Tanzanians and Germans that spent five months in Tanga province studying *ujamaa* villages. She describes a typical case:

> The DEO [Divisional Executive Officer] who was the son of a chief managed to mobilize a tax-collector . . . and a number of marginally established ex-migrant poor peasants from his own clan to act as enforcing agents bringing others into the village. What these enforcing agents hoped for (apart from getting free . . . uniforms), was to gain some political status in the new village and maybe in the long run also some kind of employment. . . . [T]he technique was to drive with a lorry to a person's house and tell him to shift his belongings or else.[45]

When enough such reports reached Nyerere, the TANU central committee issued a decree against coercion, and those who were known to have engaged in it undertook self-criticism. The coercion did not cease, but from then on it took nonviolent forms. Freyhold relates:

One method . . . was the collection of tax arrears after the local rate had been abolished, but only outside Ujamaa villages. Another method was the granting of extensive land rights to Ujamaa members only, turning those who lived outside into squatters. Such pressures were increasingly coupled with aid (or aid promises) of water supplies, the training of village medical helpers, the construction of dispensaries and schools. The most effective combination of compulsion and aid proved to be the distribution of famine relief in 1971 to Ujamaa villages only, forcing outsiders to work on the communal farms of villages where they were not members or to start their own. These tactics did succeed in bringing growing numbers of people into the new villages . . . although they were not helpful in generating any permanent commitment to communal farming.[46]

Faced with such heavy-handed tactics, the peasants in the villages learned to humor the waves of officials whose job it was to ensure high productivity. Freyhold reports on a typical visit by the "district planning team" to a village called Segera:

The list of different crops was read out and villagers were encouraged to mention for each crop how many hectares they would want to plant—and usually the higher figure was entered into the records. Neither the ecology nor the labour input was taken into consideration. Livestock was planned in a similar way. . . . The villagers did not take this "auction" very seriously and did not protest when they finally found that they were supposed to plant about 850 hectares in the year. After about two hours the planning team had filled all the columns of the forms and left.[47]

While TANU strained to mobilize Tanzanians behind the Arusha principles, this homespun socialist vision evoked a spontaneous outpouring of enthusiasm from the outside. Progressive-minded states and individuals hastened to offer Tanzania their support. In the "First World," socialism had proven maddeningly resistant to implementation, but its embrace by the world's youngest, most formative nations seemed to reaffirm its claim to be mankind's destiny. Socialism's past and present were riddled with disappointments, but it still had a glorious future. Western socialists looked upon the Africans like parents hoping to fulfill their dreams through their children.

Sweden's prime minister Olaf Palme was deeply impressed by Nyerere, and Stockholm made Tanzania a special focus of its foreign aid, organizing the Nordic states into a bloc of donors. Canada, under its dashing Liberal prime minister, Pierre Elliott Trudeau, became another major supporter. The American socialist writer Michael Harrington visited Tanzania and dedicated his book *The Vast Majority: A Journey to the World's Poor* to Nyerere.[48] Other Western leftists came to the country to teach at Dar es Salaam University or the party's Kivukoni College. All of this inspired the Kenyan academic Ali Mazrui to coin the neologism "Tanzaphilia." Socialist Tanzania, he said, had cast a "romantic spell" over Western intellectuals. Mazrui quoted one expatriate Marxist as having complained in the early days after independence that Tanganyika suffered not only from ignorance, poverty and disease, but also from too much "empiricism." However, Mazrui went on, since the Arusha Declaration the country had become "significantly less empirical and more ideologically committed," much to the gratification of foreign admirers.[49]

Perhaps the most surprising booster of post-Arusha Tanzania was Robert S. McNamara, who became president of the World Bank in 1968. The former corporate executive and secretary of defense seemed driven to erase the stain of having been one of the masterminds of the Vietnam War by adopting a progressive outlook and doing good deeds for the Third World. McNamara's biographer reports that he "appeared to find [a] soul mate" in Nyerere. "McNamara's drive to install packages of uplifting services in the countryside . . . fit Nyerere's plans like a glove."[50] Under McNamara, the World Bank helped to finance *ujamaa* villages as well as the government marketing boards that were formed to monopolize the purchase of crops, much to the unhappiness of the peasantry. It also financed parastatal corporations such as the Morogoro shoe factory, designed to be the largest such in the world. An in-house summary declared that the bank had "supported Tanzania's transition from a market to a socialist economy during the late 1960s and 1970s."[51]

Aid flowed from the Communist world as well, with China nudging aside Canada as the main trainer and supplier of Tanzania's military. It also built cotton, shoe and agricultural implement factories before embarking on its largest foreign aid project anywhere, the Tanzam or Tanzara railway, which ran all the way across Tanzania from Zambia's copper mining centers in the west to the port of Dar es Salaam in the east.

Nyerere and Zambian president Kenneth Kaunda wanted to free Zambia from depending on routes through the colonial or racist states of southern Africa for its overseas commerce. In addition, Nyerere believed that a line from Zambia would spur the development of Tanzania's hinterland. When the United States and other potential Western backers concluded that the project was not economically sustainable, Beijing volunteered to build it, and financed the project with an interest-free loan repayable through the purchase of Chinese imports. The results were described by the journalist J. R. A. Bailey:

> I . . . watched the Chinese coming ashore in Dar es Salaam harbour, drawn up in rows, each carrying Mao's little red book, each in an identical uniform with blank faces that look straight ahead—no laughing, no chattering, no whistling at the girls. They looked like zombies, the opposite pole of temperament compared to their Tanzanian counterparts. In return for financing and erecting the Tanzam railway—I was told it was a very old Chinese rail system and had at first been laid in China by the British—the Tanzanians had to import whatever they needed from China. A lot of it did not work too well and it came under the tradename of Fou Keng. So whenever anyone hit his thumb with a Chinese hammer—or some such—it was always "that Fou Keng hammer!"[52]

Never before had all the varieties of socialists—Swedish, Israeli, Chinese, East German, American, Cuban, British, Indian—converged so hopefully around a single national experiment. Yet such were the vicissitudes of the Cold War that the capitalist world did not turn its back on Tanzania either. Not only did the World Bank single out Tanzania for special generosity, but the flow of aid from the major Western powers—the United States, the United Kingdom, West Germany—resumed sooner or later after each rupture in relations. In all, Tanzania emerged from its declaration of self-reliance as Africa's largest per capita recipient of foreign assistance.

In terms of influence, it was the Chinese model that Tanzania seemed most often to try to emulate. As Goran Hyden has described it: " 'operations' and 'campaigns' to change the rural areas, in which all available resources have been mobilized for a single cause, have developed into the most important mode of policy-making."[53] This was redolent of Chinese practice, as was *Mwongozo,* the new party guidelines promulgated in 1971 as Nyerere grew alarmed by reports of indifference and corruption on the part of the managers of state industry. *Mwongozo* exhorted employees to form workplace party branches to oversee management. The result, as with China's Cultural Revolution, was chaos in industry which was not brought under control until a few years later, when the government reversed course and cracked down harshly on the workers.

China's influence was also evident in Tanzania's evolution toward a party-based state and society. "The responsibility of the party is to lead the masses and their various institutions," read the *Mwongozo* guidelines. "The duty of a socialist party is to guide all activities of the masses. The Government, parastatals, national organizations, etc, are instruments for implementing the Party's policies."[54]

Nyerere always insisted that his one-party system was democratic, and members of Parliament were indeed chosen in competitive elections among TANU members. But the party retained the power to veto locally chosen candidates, and after the first election no one was ever allowed to run against Nyerere for president, the only office that really mattered. The whole electoral exercise was meaningless since all of the nominal powers of the National Assembly were in practice assumed by the party National Executive Committee (NEC). In 1968, when eight Assembly members attempted to reassert the chamber's authority, they were simply expelled on orders of the NEC.

It was not only the legislature that was emasculated by the party. According to Hyden, party leaders at every level in the hierarchy received salaries at least one step above government officials of equivalent rank.[55] In addition to supplanting the institutions of government, the party did the same to the nongovernmental sector. Political scientist Joel Barkan writes that "civil society institutions in Tanzania, with the sole exception of the church, were effectively crushed.... [A]ll independent associations were either banned or brought under the control of the ruling party."[56] Ironically, the casualties of this process included not only the labor unions but also Tanzania's few other organically socialistic bodies. Tanzania had boasted Africa's most effective producer cooperatives, which marketed coffee, sisal and other cash crops. These were suppressed and replaced by government purchasing boards. Also, the Ruvuma Development Association, a group of communal farms singled out by Nyerere in "Socialism and Rural Development" as the model for *ujamaa* villages, was closed down and its expatriate leader expelled from the country for being too independent.[57]

Nor was the party itself a democratic body. Francis Nyalali, the former chief justice of the Tanzanian supreme court and engineer of much of the country's democratic reform in the 1990s, observes that while there was open debate at its conferences, the party had a "top-down" structure. "There were no established channels for input from below," he says. "The membership was not consulted."[58] Although some Tanzanian spokesmen distinguished TANU from Communist parties on the grounds that it was a mass rather than a "vanguard" organization, the Arusha Declaration vitiated this distinction. It said:

> Since the Party was founded we have put great emphasis on getting as many members as possible. This was the right policy during the independence struggle. But now the National Executive feels that the time has come when we should put more emphasis on the beliefs of our Party and its policies of socialism.... [I]f it is discovered that a man does not appear to accept the faith, the objects, and the rules and regulations of the Party, then he should not be accepted as a member.[59]

In 1977, TANU merged with Zanzibar's Afro-Shirazi party to form *Chama Cha Mapinduzi,* or Revolutionary Party. Given the Afro-Shirazis' East-bloc ties and violent history, the move further eroded the differences with a Communist Party model.

In other ways as well, the system grew increasingly undemocratic in the years after Arusha. No independent press was permitted to function. In a program of reform perversely called "decentralization," local governments were stripped of authority and replaced by centrally appointed officials. In 1970 several prominent political figures were held in preventive detention on charges of having conspired with the exiled former party chief Oscar Kambona. Eventually they were tried and convicted, although the whole story of the plot in which they were alleged to have taken part was painfully opaque, and the most prominent of the group, the TANU women's leader Bibi Titi Mohammed, was subsequently pardoned by Nyerere, equally mysteriously.

In 1971 a national militia was formed. Its purpose, writes Freyhold, was "ostensibly to guard the country's socialist achievements against outside intervention and local reaction. In practice the militia was an enforcing agent for government directives."[60] Former chief justice Nyalali summarizes the situation thus: "There was a time when a number of people felt that the country was moving toward a dictatorship. Mwalimu Nyerere himself said he had all the power of a dictator if he wanted to use it. It became apparent to some of us that what we had fought for—liberty—was in danger, that democracy was disappearing."[61]

Yet in some critical ways, Nyerere's rule was quite different from that of Communist dictators—or for that matter, from that of most African rulers. It was free of gratuitous cruelty (except by the occasional local official) and of political executions or concentration camps. It was free as well of pomposity and self-aggrandizement. Nyerere maintained a humble persona, living modestly, and there was no reason to doubt that the well-being of the country was always his paramount concern. Nor was Tanzania ever totalitarian. Not only was debate tolerated within the party, but dissentient views were often aired in the university, although not in the mass media. What led Nyerere in a dictatorial direction despite a manifest purity of intentions was his unyielding determination to bring the benefits of socialism to an unreceptive populace. As his admirer Cranford Pratt writes, "It quickly became clear that democracy, at least through...Westminster-type political institutions...was inappropriate and perhaps incompatible with the transformation which the leaders hoped Tanzania would be able to achieve."[62]

However disappointing the results, Nyerere never flagged from the march to socialism. Economic goals were organized in "five-year plans." The prices of some three thousand consumer goods were set by the state. To facilitate this, farmers were paid only a small fraction of world market prices for their crops. When the official exchange rate, which set the Tanzanian shilling at many times its market value, spurred black-market currency speculation, a force of "currency cops" emerged and dozens of Asians were placed in preventive detention.[63]

In the months after the Arusha Declaration, Nyerere had said, "How ... do we move ... to the system of *ujamaa* villages?...We must encourage and help people, not try to force them."[64] But when only a minor part of the peasantry responded to the encouragement, he grew impatient. In 1973 he decreed that the entire rural population had to be living in villages within three years. The idea of communal or *ujamaa* villages had met with almost no success. The peasants were stubbornly resistant to this approach, and the few hundred communal farms that had been created by true believers at the time of independence or in the wake of the Arusha Declaration had virtually all folded. Nyerere now was willing to make a concession: the new villages did not have to be communal. The residents could farm individual plots, although they were expected to give a certain amount of labor as well to a common plot.

Hyden recounts the angry speech on government radio in which Nyerere launched "operation planned villages":

> [He] reminded the audience about all the things that the TANU Government
> had done for the people after the Arusha Declaration: abolishing the poll tax,
> abolishing primary-school fees, building permanent, clean water supplies in
> the villages, expanding the number of health clinics and dispensaries in the

rural areas, increasing primary-school facilities, etc. He then went on to ask what the peasants had done in return for these favours. In answering that question, President Nyerere suggested that they had done virtually nothing. They had remained idle and evaded their responsibility to make a contribution to the country's socialist development. He concluded his speech by saying that he knew he could not turn people into socialists by force, but what his government could do was to ensure that everybody lived in a village. He said he wanted that to be done before the end of 1976.[65]

Although Nyerere's admirers believe that he did not intend violence to be used to enforce this edict, how else could it be achieved? As Andrew Coulson relates: "Experience in Dodoma, Kigoma, and elsewhere in previous years showed what had to be done. Occasionally the 'fire weapon' (burning of houses) was used, and with this threat hanging over them the majority of peasants decided to move first and argue later."[66] In other cases, homes were torn down by armed militia.[67] "Disaster struck soon after," says Nyalali. "People tried to leave [the new villages], and force was used to drive them back. Lives were lost."[68] Nyalali says that no one knows how many died. Nyerere, he adds, "was a humanitarian. He deplored cruelty. But he had created this monster."

To Nyerere (as earlier to the World Bank), "villagization" promised to make agriculture more efficient and productive and to make it easier for the government to provide such services as education and health care. But it wrenched people from the lives to which they were accustomed. Nyalali was a Sukuma, from Tanzania's largest tribe, which had a saying: "You build your house where you can just barely see the smoke of your neighbor's fire-place. If you could see a lot of smoke you were too close."[69] In the villages, not only were people packed together much more closely than their custom, they were also often mixed in with those of different families or tribes, which made them feel ill at ease. Because the villages were launched without sanitary facilities, the closer quarters led to the spread of disease.

To compound the problem, the same hapless officials charged with gathering the people into villages usually selected the sites, although they rarely had the skills for making such determinations. Sometimes, says Nyalali, "people were moved from places where water was accessible to places where it was difficult" or "from areas of fertile soil to areas of bad soil."[70] In still others, the villagers were left with long distances between their homes and their fields. As a result, "operation planned villages" was followed by "operation rectification" to relocate villages.[71] The overall consequences were disastrous for agriculture. A severe food shortage gripped the country, necessitating urgent imports.

By 1976, the campaign had succeeded in resettling most of the rural population. The last major piece of Tanzania's socialist transformation was initiated that year. Operation Maduka aimed to replace privately owned shops with government-sponsored "cooperatives." Nyerere had acknowledged that similar efforts in the early 1960s had had poor results. "Many of the ... co-operatives failed and the shops ... had to be closed," he said.[72] Yet he wanted to try again. According to Nyerere's executive assistant, Joan Wicken, his intention was merely to *encourage* public rather than private retail enterprise; but local officials charged with carrying out the project found it simplest just to close down private shops. It was not much more difficult to open government shops, until it came to stocking them.

In sum, says Hyden, Nyerere "did not abandon his socialist policies until almost all economic activities of any significance had been brought under political control."[73] In 1967, on the heels of Arusha, Nyerere had declared: "The transformation of our people's lives, as a deliberate government policy, is a new development in the history of man."[74] Ten years later, he delivered a long speech assessing the nation's progress since Arusha.

He began by recalling that in 1967 he had predicted that it would take thirty years to reach socialism. "I am now sure that it will take us much longer," he said, calling himself "a very poor prophet."[75] The speech was laced with acknowledgments of problems. In the course of villagization, there had been "cases of people being required to move from an area of permanent water to an area which is permanently dry" and "cases where people were rounded up without notice, and dumped on the village site, without time to prepare shelter for themselves."[76] Increases in the nation's food output had not kept pace with population growth. And there were "intermittent shortage[s]" of consumer articles. Factories and workshops were "grossly inefficient," he admitted, offering this scathing portrait of their management:

> In every parastatal we have a whole series of managers for different functions, and a General Manager on top. Each Manager has a Secretary, an office of his own, and often a car....We employ some "Sales Managers" who sit in their offices and wait for customers to search them out....We employ some "Production Managers" who do not order spare parts or the necessary raw

materials on time, or having done so just sit and complain instead of going after them if the goods are not delivered.[77]

Yet against such "difficulties" and "failures" could be counted many triumphs.[78] These included "moving virtually our entire people into villages" and preventing the nation's wealth from flowing abroad, as he said would have happened had capitalism been allowed to flourish. The country could now boast eight textile mills "capable of producing over 84 million square meters of cloth."[79] The education system had been overhauled according to plan. Now in primary schools "new emphasis [has been] given to technical and agricultural training, and the pupils no longer spend most of their time preparing for secondary school."[80] At many schools, the students produce "bricks, furniture, or clothes." And only students "who have been working in our villages or factories are eligible to go to University." Moreover, "political education has been introduced in schools, colleges, and other educational institutions" and "the English language newspaper has been nationalised so that we could rely upon it to report news accurately, and to analyze events from a Tanzanian and socialist viewpoint."[81]

"Our greatest achievement," said Nyerere, was that Tanzania was free of capitalist exploitation and "great progress" had been made in reducing income differentials. "Fortunately . . . th[e] 'creation of an African middle class,' had not gone very far." The Arusha Declaration had succeeded in nipping it in the bud.[82] In other words, equality had been fostered by keeping everyone poor.

While calling for greater discipline, efficiency and self-reliance from his countrymen, Nyerere exuded confidence that the nation was on the right course. But during the ensuing two years Tanzania was badly shaken from without. Uganda's army laid claim to northwestern Tanzania, whereupon Nyerere decided not merely to repulse the invaders but to pursue them to Kampala and put an end to the maniacal reign of Idi Amin Dada. It was a task for which much of the world and most Ugandans were grateful, but it added tens of millions of dollars to an already crushing deficit in the Tanzanian budget. Nearly simultaneously came the 1979 global oil price shock, which hit Tanzania hard since it is dependent on imported energy sources. An annual trade deficit that had run in the tens of millions of dollars in the early 1970s ballooned to half a billion. Desperate for foreign exchange, Tanzania turned to the International Monetary Fund for a major infusion of subsidized loans. The IMF, as is its custom, demanded certain shifts in Tanzanian policies, which Nyerere angrily rejected, calling the fund "paternalistic and condescending."[83] For all his confessions of difficulties, however, the country was in much worse condition than Nyerere had recognized.

Forced villagization had so disrupted agriculture that crops like maize that had once been exported now had to be imported. The situation in industry was no better. The massive Morogoro shoe factory normally operated at 4 percent of capacity, although it pushed itself to a record level of 7 percent on the occasion of a visit by its patron, Robert McNamara.[84] The Tanga fertilizer company required 140,000 tons of imports to produce 100,000 tons of fertilizer.[85] And the vast textile industry of which Nyerere had boasted was largely a Potemkin village sustained by state subsidies.

The paucity of agricultural and industrial production naturally meant that goods were scarce, and they grew catastrophically more so after the closing of private shops in Operation Maduka. Tanzanian economists T. L. Maliyamkono and M. S. D. Bagachwa describe the self-reinforcing nature of the problem: "not only do the peasants lack necessary agricultural implements like hoes and ploughs, but they have no incentives to produce more for cash when there are severe shortages of basic manufactured goods such as soap, salt, sugar, cooking oil, two-wheeled bicycles and clothes."[86]

The writer Shiva Naipaul captured the same facts rather more lyrically in his travelogue *North of South*. Arriving in the morning at Dar es Salaam's elite New Africa Hotel before his room was made up, Naipaul repaired to the restaurant. After a long wait (while "the cook forgot" his order), he reports this scene.

My breakfast arrived. I noticed there was no butter and asked for some.

"Butter you cannot have."

"Why not?"

"Because there is none."

The coffee I poured into my cup turned out to be tea. "Is anything wrong, bwana?" The waiter looked at me worriedly.

"Everything's fine. Just fine."

"Since you are satisfied with my service, you will give me nice tip?"

"Tipping is illegal in Tanzania. Do you want me to break the law?" He giggled.

"I think you are a capitalist roader. The Mwalimu will not like that."

"The Mwalimu will not know."

I handed him a hundred-shilling bill. "I want all my change back." I asked him to bring me a box of matches. Fifteen minutes later he returned, the bill intact.

"Change you cannot have."

"Is that possible?"

"The cashier has not yet been to the bank."

"What am I supposed to do about that?"

"Maybe you can ask one of these people sitting here. Maybe one of them will have change." . . .

"What about the matches?"

"Matches you cannot have."

The check (including a small tip) having been settled, I went to see if my room was ready. It was not.

"How much longer do I have to wait?"

"That is difficult to say," the clerk replied. The cleaners, he said, were attending a meeting. "They are making big protest about the racist Rhodesian fascists."[87]

The shortages, particularly when measured against the inflated production quotas to which peasants and factory managers had learned to agree willy-nilly, naturally led to suspicions and finger-pointing. In the early 1980s a crackdown on "saboteurs" was declared and the minister of home affairs announced that more than one thousand people had been arrested and the following contraband seized: 7,892 tons of salt, 9,323 corrugated iron sheets, 792 bags of rice, 17,845 hoes, 15,828 tins of kerosene, 9,956 cartons of washing soap, 192 bags of sugar and 5,519 tins of cooking oil.[88] Roadblocks were established to prevent the unauthorized shipment of food or other basic goods from one region of the country to another. Every transaction required authorization. "If you wanted a few cases of beer for a party you had to book weeks ahead," recalls Paul Sozigwa, formerly Nyerere's press spokesman.[89] The booking required a bureaucrat's stamp, and the bureaucrat often required some emolument.

Corruption thus became rampant. "In all areas of social reproduction, bribes have become the inducement to finish transactions, whether getting services in a government office, receiving goods at controlled prices, or buying a train ticket," wrote political scientist Horace Campbell after years of teaching in Tanzania.[90] With opportunity for private economic gain legally foreclosed, the easiest way that a person who did not absorb Nyerere's ascetic ethic could make a buck was by exploiting an official position. Popular cynicism, Campbell added, expressed itself through a pun on the party's initials, CCM, which were said to stand for *chukua chako mapema,* Swahili for "take yours early."[91]

Despite Nyerere's denunciations of the IMF, his government reached an agreement with it in 1980. However, Tanzania failed to meet the budget targets, largely because of ballooning subsidies to government enterprises, so the deal collapsed. In 1981 TANU announced its own National Economic Survival Program based on a major increase in Tanzania's exports. But it provided no mechanism for achieving this other than exhortation, and the economy continued to deteriorate. By 1983 foreign aid furnished 14 percent of the country's GNP.[92]

Pressure for reform mounted from a group of indigenous economists at Dar es Salaam University as well as from foreign lenders who one by one came to endorse the IMF's demands. It became irresistible when in 1984 the Nordic bloc donors, hitherto the most enthusiastic backers of Tanzanian socialism, joined in the call for change.

Even as his government continued quiet talks with the IMF, a proud Nyerere would not bow to the foreigners. If capitulation was inescapable, he himself did not have to be party to it. Instead, he reprised his 1961 maneuver of stepping back from the government, this time by announcing that he would not seek "reelection" in 1985. Just as he had once left it to Kawawa to put through the draconian law on preventive detention, so now it would fall to another of his followers to do the dirty work of signing a deal with the IMF. But for all his rhetorical defiance and defense of his record, there were moments of epiphany when he betrayed a recognition of how badly things had gone wrong. "If I called back the British to look at their estates, they would laugh at us because we've ruined them," he confessed.[93]

Nyerere continued on as party chairman and as a critic of the free-market reforms undertaken at the IMF's behest. He lamented cutbacks in social services which had been paid for in the past by foreign donors, who were now demanding tighter budgets. In 1987, the twentieth anniversary of Arusha, he showed himself unbowed. "It is not the Arusha Declaration that needs revision," he proclaimed, but its "implementation."[94] As for the criticisms of his socialist policies, the problem was not the policies but the criticisms. "Converting our people away from socialism is the objective of the capitalists and exploiters all over the world," he warned. The IMF "is not a friend of Tanzania or of any poor country," but "an institution used by the imperialist countries . . . to control the economy of a poor country and destablise the governments of countries they do not like." Although "Tanzania is not socialist yet," he said, "we have many socialist achievements" and "our first task is . . . to guard and strengthen" them. To help do this, Nyerere reversed his previously announced decision to step down as party chairman at that year's CCM congress and was elected to another three-year term.

When it expired in 1990 he did not seek another. That year he began to question the one-party system he had created. As Joel Barkan explains, "What was important to Nyerere was not the one-party state per se but a ruling party committed to socialism."[95] Since CCM had "lost its ideological compass," the rationale for its monopoly of power had evaporated. In 1992, a commission chaired by Chief Justice Nyalali recommended transition to a multiparty system, and this was approved. Nationwide multiparty elections were held in 1995.

Although relations continued to be rocky with the IMF and the World Bank—which had left behind McNamara's heritage and become a proponent of economic liberalization—Tanzania followed a path of economic reform through the 1990s. The provision in Tanzania's constitution proclaiming the country "socialist" was not rescinded, but the parastatal corporations began to be sold off or closed down. Ironically, a group of Chinese entrepreneurs bought the Friendship Textile plant, which had originally been built for Tanzania by the Chinese Communists as a model state industry. In the year 2000, Harvard University's Center for International Development declared Tanzania the most improved country in Africa in terms of economic competitiveness.

After completing his tenure as CCM chairman, Nyerere retired to his birthplace, Butiama, to a home built for him by the party on a ninety-acre farm, where he raised maize, millet and cassava. A stream of local villagers and national leaders trekked to Mwalimu's door, as did old friends from abroad like McNamara. Nyerere remained active on the international scene as an advocate for more generous wealth transfers from the advanced countries to the poor. In 1999, at age seventy-seven, he died of leukemia in a London hospital.

Tanzanians mourned the father of their country. His modest lifestyle, deep patriotism and relatively bloodless rule had helped to create a strong sense of national identity and, apart from recurrent turmoil on Zanzibar, a degree of domestic tranquility that was the envy of their neighbors. Yet economically, this incorruptible idealist left his country probably worse off than it began.

Nyerere's overriding goal had been to prevent the emergence of a middle class, since this would mean the beginnings of inequality. In his image of the country's future, all Tanzanians would prosper in unison. On the whole, Nyerere succeeded in averting the rise of a middle class, though the consequence of repressing economic activity was not shared progress, but shared stagnation. According to one World Bank study issued in 1990, the year Nyerere stepped down as party leader, Tanzania's economy had *shrunk* at an average rate of half a percent a year from 1965 to 1988.[96] Other studies produced less dire figures, although most authorities believe that the economy grew no faster than the population.[97]

The costs of Tanzania's socialism are impossible to compute. They seem benign compared to the staggering toll in human life claimed by Communist regimes in Russia, China, Cambodia and elsewhere or by bloodier "Third World socialist" regimes in Uganda, Burma, Syria and Iraq, among many others. Yet when a country is so impoverished that much of the population lives on the edges of survival, economic failure translates into hunger, disease and death. "We lost a lot of time in terms of development," said CCM's deputy secretary-general in 1995, "and are sorely trying to catch up now."[98] The best that can be said of Tanzania's record is that it was not discernibly worse than the run of the other nearly sixty states that adopted African socialism or Arab socialism or cognate creeds. Scarcely any achieved robust growth, and many suffered stagnation or even decline, although their starting points were low.

The vast majority of Third World socialist states were ruled by dictators. And some said that this, rather than their economic policies, was the nub of the problem. It was meaningless to speak of "public ownership" of the economy in a country where the citizens exercised no control over the government. Thus the failure of these states did not necessarily discredit the socialist approach to development. But the short answer to this line of argument was: India.

After winning independence in 1947, India's democratic political system flourished, its diverse and outspoken free press becoming one of the glories of the contemporary East. But its predominantly socialist economy—based on state ownership of major industry, strict control of private business, insulation from global commerce, and government planning—foundered. For decades its average annual economic growth of 3.5 percent kept just ahead of population increase, and the country remained dismally poor. Then, under Prime Minister Rajiv Gandhi in the late 1980s, India took its first faltering steps toward economic liberalization, followed in the early 1990s by more decisive measures under Narasimha Rao. The result was a near doubling of the rate of growth and substantial movement toward the ranks of middle-class countries.

One of the key influences that changed economic thinking in India as elsewhere in the Third World was the example of the so-called "little tigers" of East Asia. In some quarters, the records of the mostly socialist postcolonial states had bred despair that the poorer nations could ever lift themselves out of misery, much less catch up with the advanced. The "terms of trade," it was said, were irretrievably tilted against "late developers." Then Taiwan, South Korea, Hong Kong and Singapore made nonsense of this alibi. Though short on natural resources and living on the margins of international politics, they adopted development strategies based on private ownership and maximizing foreign trade—and accomplished astonishing rates of growth. Singapore and Hong Kong were no more than city-states, and both started from a relatively high base. Taiwan and South Korea were the more remarkable examples: they rose from poverty with a momentum that pulled them within hailing distance of the West's prosperity. The contrast between the record of the "tigers" and the scores of Third World socialist states constituted an empirical blow from which the prestige of socialism was never to recover.

Collapse

———————

9

UNION CARD: GOMPERS AND MEANY HEAR A DIFFERENT DRUMMER

IF THE CAUSE OF SOCIALISM WAS DAMAGED by its dismal performance in the Third World, its fatal weakness lay in the failure to get a foothold in America. According to Marx and Engels, the most advanced capitalist country ought to have been the most ripe for socialism; but America showed fewer socialist tendencies than almost any other country, casting a dark shadow of doubt over the claim of socialism's inevitability.[1] Not only was America recalcitrant, it became in itself a model of an alternative future. In the war of abstractions, socialism had trounced capitalism, which had precious few defenders. But in the competition between real living systems, America offered an image that was the envy and yearning of the world. America was not synonymous with capitalism; it represented more than that. But in light of its achievements, its conspicuous resistance to socialism conveyed ideological implications. What was the source of the country's unique imperviousness to socialism? It can be traced to the doorstep of America's workers and their two most influential leaders during the century of industrialism: Samuel Gompers and George Meany.

In 1979, just as the Tanzanian government was turning in despair to the IMF, Meany was bidding a last farewell to his followers in a Miami hotel ballroom. He had been an early supporter of Nyerere's, as of other independence movements, but he turned his back when Nyerere repressed Tanzanian unions and embraced Communist China. Such implacability was typical of him at home as well as abroad. After decades as the champion of the little guy and the heavy muscle behind innumerable progressive victories, he had shown nothing but contempt for the "counterculture" and the new styles of liberalism that had emerged in the 1960s. Now eighty-five and without long to live, he was often called a dinosaur.

The leadership of reform causes had passed from organized labor to more media-savvy peace and environmental activists. Meany's pugnacious devotion to the Cold War seemed to be a relic of the "inordinate fear of Communism" that President Carter had famously said Americans had gotten over. No wonder, then, that the tears of the delegates as Meany bade them farewell from his wheelchair were matched by a sense of deliverance in Communist headquarters from Moscow to New York. "The exit of George Meany" marks "the end of a very reactionary dynasty in the U.S. labor movement," exulted the American Communist newspaper, Daily World.[2]

Little did they imagine that for all the grief that the AFL-CIO had caused them during Meany's reign, worse lay ahead—as if he were haunting them from the grave. In truth, their problem was not with one man. Labor's anticommunism would not end with Meany because it had not begun with him. In Meany's own estimate, "the first American to understand and proclaim the dangers and basic evils of Communism" was none other than the founder of the AFL, Samuel Gompers, who more than anyone else had personified the American worker's unique resistance to socialist ideas of any kind, and his deathly hatred of Communism in particular.[3]

Gompers was born in East London in 1850. His parents, Solomon and Sara, were Dutch Jewish immigrants. Their London flat consisted mostly of one large room where the family slept, ate, washed and congregated. Sam shared a trundle bed with his four brothers. To escape the crowding, they spent all the time they could outdoors. In contrast to the unrelieved misery observed in this same area by Attlee a couple of generations later, Gompers recollected that despite their poverty, "life in the London streets, though precarious, was adventurous, wonderfully interesting and happy."[4]

Samuel attended the Jewish Free School from the age of six until ten, when his family needed him to go to work. He continued to study language and Talmud at an evening Hebrew school, and was apprenticed to a shoemaker. The trade did not please him, and a few months later he seized the opportunity to enter an apprenticeship in his father's trade, cigar making.

In 1863 the family decided to renew its search for a better return on

Solomon's skills by migrating to America. They packed up their possessions and boarded an old sailing vessel for a fifty-day voyage across the Atlantic. Like millions of other Jewish "greenhorns," as they called one another, they settled first on Manhattan's Lower East Side, finding a rank apartment wedged between a slaughterhouse and a brewery. For a year and a half Sam and his father worked at rolling cigars in their home before getting jobs in cigar workshops. In his spare hours, the boy took part in various social and recreational groups. He helped to organize, and became president of, the Arion Base Ball and Social Club. And along with many others too poor to matriculate, he attended free lectures and classes at Cooper Union.

The subjects included history, biography, music, mechanics, elocution, economics, electricity, geography and astronomy, but this was only a part of his education. Much of the rest came on the shop floor, where he studied politics. Cigar making was a gregarious occupation. The rolling required skill—decades after he had left the trade Gompers still liked to demonstrate his prowess—but it was quiet work, and the men would talk as they rolled. At times they would select one in the shop to read aloud to the rest, and since they were paid by the piece, each of the others would chip in a few cigars to make good the missing product of the reader's lost hours. The talk would range widely but a primary focus was the common plight of their occupation and the various ideas for bettering it.

The political debate was largely shaped by a group of immigrants who constituted the American branch of the International Workingmen's Association, then at its height. One of the members of the local IWA executive worked in the same shop as Gompers—a taciturn Swedish former seaman named Karl Malcolm Ferdinand Laurrell. Gompers said he developed a "boundless admiration" for Laurrell's "brain, heart, and character," viewing him as "the dominating mind" in their shop.[5]

Gompers felt himself "groping for something fundamental, something upon which one could base a constructive program."[6] Laurrell offered him his copy of the *Communist Manifesto,* but Gompers could not read the German, so Laurrell translated it aloud to him. The "insight into a hidden world of thought" that this afforded motivated Gompers to teach himself German so he could read the rest of the socialist canon. Yet curiously, Laurrell counseled Gompers against joining any socialist party and told him that he ought to make his "union card" his political touchstone.

Laurrell was forming the germ of an idea that Gompers was to nurture into a distinct labor philosophy. It came to be known as "bread and butter" or

"pure and simple" unionism, and it was seen as the very antithesis of revolutionary ideology. To Gompers, however, it flowed directly from the teachings
of Marx and Engels. He considered the essence of their message to be the
self-liberation of the working class. As he saw it, the trade union was the only
organization that was purely proletarian and that emerged spontaneously
from the class struggle. He called it the "natural" organization of the workers, in contrast to other movements and parties that were adulterated with
middle-class members.

It is all the more surprising that Laurrell should have pointed Gompers
in this direction at a time when unions were pathetically weak. They were
mutations of pre-industrial craft guilds as the class of independent artisans and
tradesmen began to give way to the hired hands of the assembly line. In this era,
strikes were usually defensive, precipitated by resistance to wage cuts or work
speedups rather than demands for improvements. And they usually ended in
defeat. Gompers' labor philosophy developed not only out of endless conversations with his shop mates but also from the hard-earned lessons of the struggle
to advance their position.

In 1869, they struck against the introduction of molds that made it possible for less-skilled workers to make cigars. The issue was lost, and Gompers
concluded that it was futile to resist the advance of technology. Thereafter, he
always advocated bringing unskilled workers into the union even while some of
his fellows wanted to preserve an exclusive club of the skilled. A few years later
his union tried forming a cooperative, and while their cigar outlet managed to
stay in business for many years, it did not secure enough trade to relieve them
from employment in the factories.

Perhaps the most vivid early lesson came during the bitter depression
of 1873, when many workers were idled, causing any number of destitute
families to be evicted from their homes. Members of the IWA proposed a mass
demonstration, which was organized by something called the Committee on
Public Safety—histrionically borrowing the name of the dreaded Jacobin command of the French Revolution. The planned event became a magnet for the
most radical elements and visionaries of all sorts. At the last minute, munici-
pal authorities withdrew the parade permit, but the organizers proceeded
in defiance, and the police attacked the demonstrators viciously. Gompers
barely escaped having his head cracked open in what he termed an "orgy of
brutality" on the part of the authorities. But despite his declared "outrage,"
he drew some sober conclusions:

I saw how professions of radicalism and sensationalism concentrated all the forces of organized society against a labor movement. . . . I saw that leadership in the labor movement could be safely entrusted only to those into whose hearts and minds had been woven the experiences of earning their bread by daily labor. I saw that betterment for workingmen must come primarily through workingmen. I saw the danger of entangling alliances with intellectuals who did not understand that to experiment with the labor movement was to experiment with human life.[7]

Building on these lessons, Gompers, Laurrell and Adolph Strasser, a Hungarian immigrant and veteran of the IWA, began to build a new local union of cigar makers, the hallmark of which was its inclusion of the less skilled. Gompers was chosen as its unpaid president, and by 1876 it was the largest local in the country, boasting 245 members. The next year, it initiated a string of successful strikes, demanding an increase in pay to a rate of six dollars for each thousand cigars. Soon thereafter, Strasser won election as president of the national body, the Cigarmakers International Union. At a national convention—small affairs which often drew fewer than a dozen delegates—Gompers proposed that locals be forbidden from excluding members on the basis of race or sex or degree of skill. On the last point, he was forced to compromise.

Perhaps Gompers' embrace of less-skilled workers was encouraged by one fortuitous benefit he had derived from their presence in the shops. When he was sixteen a friend had asked Sam to keep an eye on his girlfriend while he went on a trip. Sam kept both eyes on her. Sophia Julian was her name, and Gompers recalled in his autobiography that she worked as a "stripper." In the cigar world, "strippers" were those employed to separate the leaves from the stems of the tobacco. Sam thought her lovely, and on his seventeenth birthday he suggested that they and the other couple with whom they were double-dating should mark the occasion by getting married. The next day both pairs followed through on the plan, and after celebrating with dinner and a show, Sam and Sophia returned to their respective parental homes. There ensued some "hullabaloo" from the parents, but when this died down, Sophia, still sixteen, moved in with the Gomperses, and the young couple paid his parents for their food. The marriage was a close one, lasting more than fifty years and producing a dozen or more children (Sam said in the end that he could not recall the exact number), of whom six reached adulthood.

In addition to their organizing work among cigar makers, Gompers and Strasser set about pulling together a citywide body of unions, dubbing it the Amalgamated Trade and Labor Federation. Besides their own trade, it included unions of tailors, cabinet makers, wood carvers, varnishers, boot makers, fresco painters, upholsterers, cigar packers and typographical workers. It was, said Gompers, "the first federated labor body to make trade unionism a prerequisite to membership."[8] Other federations had admitted labor sympathizers or adherents of labor-oriented ideologies in addition to wage earners. It was precisely against this that Gompers and his colleagues intended to draw a line. Even though Strasser and Laurrell had been active socialists and Gompers was a devotee of Marx and Engels, their own sharp class consciousness was driving them away from the socialist movement because of its inclusion of middle-class people and the low priority it gave to meliorating the immediate conditions of the workers. Symbolizing this break, when the federation organizers decided they needed to issue a newspaper, they took over a weekly called the *Socialist* and changed its name to the *Labor Standard*.

In 1881, the Cigarmakers, the Typographical union and a few others succeeded, after several false starts, in launching an analogous federation on a national level. At its first convention, in Pittsburgh, the Federation of Organized Trade and Labor Unions adopted a long list of legislative goals including legal protections for labor unions, the eight-hour day, restrictions on child labor, a requirement that wages be paid in lawful money, and a ban against further immigration from China.[†]

The 1881 gathering was a small beginning. The federation's initial treasury of $56.10 was entirely drained by the costs of publishing the proceedings. A second convention a year later drew a grand total of nineteen delegates. Similar small gatherings were held each of the next few years, but no headquarters or structure carried on between conventions. Those who believed that a permanent umbrella organization was needed convened a gathering in 1886 in Columbus, Ohio. There, forty-two delegates representing twenty-five unions claiming a combined membership of 317,000 founded the American Federation of Labor, and what was left of the old federation was folded into it.[9] A single full-time paid position was created, that of president, and Gompers was elected to fill it

---

† Gompers, although an early and consistent advocate of equal rights for blacks and women, was nonetheless a strong advocate of Chinese exclusion. At this time, by his count, one-quarter of all of those employed in cigar making were Chinese, and because they were willing to work for less, Gompers feared that unless the influx was stopped all non-Chinese would be driven from the trade.

at an annual salary of one thousand dollars, somewhat less than he was making rolling cigars.

The new federation aimed to strengthen its affiliates not only against employers but also against a rival body, the Noble Order of Knights of Labor, which had mushroomed from around nineteen thousand members in 1881 to nearly a million by 1886. It was an omnibus organization enrolling members from every occupation, and this posed a threat to the various trade unions, each of which aimed to incorporate all of the members of its own trade. The Knights of Labor was a secretive, ritualistic fraternal organization without a clearly articulated purpose. It declared that it aimed to change society, but without specifying in what way. Its membership was not restricted to workers but was open to anyone except bankers, lawyers, liquor traffickers, gamblers and stockbrokers. Gompers said that the Knights of Labor thought of itself as something "higher and grander than a trade union."[10] Conversely, the Knights referred to the AFL as comprising "mere trade unions." Gompers denounced the presence of grocers and former police chiefs among the leaders of the Knights, which he called an "artificial" organization. In return, Knights leader Terrence Powderly referred to Gompers as a "gin guzzling, pot bellied, red nosed, scab faced, dirty shirted, unwashed, leather assed, empty headed, two faced, rattle headed, itch palmed scavenger."[11] On some occasions, alluding to Gompers' Jewish origins, he threw in "Christ slugger."[12]

Although the Knights were not socialist or otherwise well defined ideologically, the struggle with them reinforced Gompers' conviction that workers' organizations should be exclusively by and for the workers. Since virtually everywhere—from Marx, Engels and Lassalle in Germany, to Lenin and Plekhanov in Russia, to Attlee and the Webbs in England—socialism had been brought to the workers by advocates from the privileged classes, Gompers' position boded ill for socialism in America.

Initially larger than the AFL, the Knights declined almost as rapidly as they had sprung up. In part the cause may have been that Gompers was a vastly more capable leader than Powderly. But in part, too, it was that Gompers was right in calling the trade unions "natural," insofar as they arose straight from the industrial workplace, while the Knights, in contrast, harkened to the image of a happier age, either of the past or of the future, but offered little benefit in the here and now.

To grant Gompers' point that the trade unions were in some sense natural does not mean that they were self-generating. On the contrary, the movement he led was very much the product of his own vision and tireless dedication. He was not the only one considered for president at the founding meeting, but he was the only one willing to accept the job at the penurious rate of a thousand dollars a year. Even this amount was not always forthcoming since it was the president's own burden to raise the funds. Many of the affiliated unions were delinquent in their payments to the federation, and Gompers' paycheck was often delayed, causing him to despair that he would have to "giv[e] up the position . . . or starve."[13] He walked to work each day to spare carfare, wearing his single suit of clothes. His oldest son, Sam Jr., quit school and went to work as a printer to help the family make ends meet.[14]

The federation sometimes could not meet bills, and initially it had no other staff. After a year, Gompers received the board's approval to hire an errand boy at a maximum rate of $3.50 a week so as to free more of his own time for substantive work. Gompers traversed the country preaching the cause of unionization. One trip took him to Syracuse, Rochester, Buffalo, Boston, Albany, Troy, Cleveland, Columbus, Cincinnati, Indianapolis, Louisville, Evansville, Nashville, Connellsville, Peoria, St. Louis, Springfield, Kansas City, Fort Scott, Denver, Lincoln, Omaha, Sioux City, Minneapolis, South Bend, St. Paul, Milwaukee, Chicago, Grand Rapids, Saginaw, Lansing, East Saginaw, Detroit and a half-dozen other cities. At each stop, the local unions that sponsored his visit had agreed to cover the cost of that leg of his journey. He traveled by freight car and other cheap means, but still the hosts sometimes reneged, leaving him to make up the difference out of pocket and later to plead for reimbursement from a strapped AFL board.[15]

He also coaxed geographically dispersed local unions—for unions were usually formed first as local bodies—to combine into national unions of common occupations. These often called themselves "international" unions, as many included branches in Canada. (The mighty Teamsters Union was cobbled together in this manner, under the nurture and tutelage of the AFL.) To give life to these continent-wide bodies, Gompers urged each of them to hire at least one full-time paid officer, for initially most functioned merely as intermittent conventions of local organizations. And he encouraged them to carry out organizing campaigns within their trades.

After four years, the AFL's 1890 convention began to show the fruits of these efforts. In attendance were 103 delegates representing 83 unions.[16] The once fragile federation was on its way to becoming a powerful organization. Within a little more than a decade it would claim to represent 10 percent of

American wage earners.[17] As the press took increasing notice of this emergent force in American life, Gompers was dubbed the "little Napoleon of labor." Though standing barely five foot four, he earned a reputation for feistiness. Biographer Bernard Mandel recounted one of the incidents that it rested on, which took place at a fractious labor convention in Albany, New York, in 1887 at the height of the rivalry between the AFL and the Knights:

> A delegate rushed from the rear of the room, jumped over the bar and onto the platform, and pointed a gun at Gompers' breast. Gompers, without flinching, and smiling all the while, quickly stepped beside the man, threw his arms around him so as to pin his arms to his body, gradually moved his arms down to the gun, put it in his pocket, and said, "Now, beat it, while the going is good."[18]

Gompers was as opinionated as he was tough. Two issues on which his strong opinions left a distinct impact on American labor were socialism and "dual unions." He was adamantly opposed to both. Building on the ideas that he had developed on the shop floor, Gompers at first rejected socialism on the grounds that it was impractical rather than undesirable. "There is not a noble hope that a Socialist may have that I do not hold as my ideal. . . . But our methods are different," he explained.[19] In addition, he argued that there is "no other organization of labor in the entire world that is so class conscious as the trade unions."[20] The AFL preamble, no doubt largely crafted by Gompers, was faintly redolent of the *Communist Manifesto.* "A struggle is going on in all the nations of the civilized world, between the oppressors and the oppressed of all countries, a struggle between the capitalists and the laborers, which grows in intensity from year to year, and will work disastrous results to the toiling millions, if they are not combined for mutual protection and benefit," it said.[21]

As Gompers saw it, however, a clear-sighted class consciousness pointed not toward socialism, but away from it. He explained in an 1890 letter to the Second International: "Comrades, though oceans divide us, the same spirit and purpose prompts us to seek in organization the amelioration in the condition and final emancipation of the Proletariat of the world," it began. Then it added: "Of course, it is difficult to judge . . . the form that the labor organizations should assume in other countries . . . but I trust I do not trespass . . . when I suggest the thought of the importance of the organization of Trade Unions for

all wage-workers, and, at least for a time, concentrating all efforts to the economic aspect of the Movement." By the "economic aspect" he meant collective
bargaining for higher wages and better working conditions—as opposed to the
"political" goal of changing society.[22]

In this letter, Gompers suggested that the time of "political" struggle might
follow on the completion of "economic" organizing, but later his critique of
socialist impracticality grew more harsh:

> Our friends, the Socialists . . . have an excellent conception of the trouble in
> our industrial life. They say, as we say, and as every intelligent man or woman
> says, that there are miseries which surround us. We recognize the poverty,
> we know the sweatshop, we can play on every string of the harp, and touch
> the tenderest chords of human sympathy; but while we recognize the evil
> and would apply the remedy, our Socialist friends would look forward to the
> promised land, and wait for "the sweet by-and-by."[23]

At conventions of the AFL, Gompers exerted his considerable rhetorical
talents to beat back resolutions endorsing "the collective ownership by the
people of all means of production and distribution." Though the idea may have
sounded seductive, he believed that such declarations would make labor an
adjunct of the socialist movement. For like reasons, he imposed a rule against
direct representation of socialist groups within the federation. Until then, it
had been common practice in America and abroad for "labor" organizations to
encompass proclaimed sympathizers as well as workers, the former often sub-
ordinating the latter. The International Workingmen's Association, for example,
had been founded by labor leaders but was soon taken over by Marx and Engels.
Gompers would not have this. The issue came to a head in 1890 when the
New York Central Federation of Labor applied to the AFL for a charter, which
Gompers denied on the grounds that the list of its constituent bodies included
the New York chapter of the Socialist Labor Party.

"It would have been easy for me to have granted the charter automatically,"
he said. "However, I knew that course was wrong—no political organization had
a right to representation in the trade union movement. A trade union card was
the only claim to membership in the A. F. of L. which I would recognize."[24] The
New Yorkers appealed to the federation's national convention, while Gompers
sought to buttress his case by writing to Engels, whom he was sure would see
the logic in upholding the proletarian purity of the labor movement. Neither

appeal succeeded. Engels did not reply to Gompers' letter, but the AFL convention upheld his stand.

Little wonder, then, that Gompers became a main target of the socialists. Although their parties were denied direct affiliation with the federation, many trade unionists were also active socialists, and they formed a powerful bloc at AFL conventions. In 1894 they rallied behind coal miner John McBride, who succeeded in defeating Gompers for reelection, thereby causing an interregnum in his thirty-eight-year reign. He won the post back narrowly a year later, but often again faced spirited opposition backed by the socialists.

Gompers, one need hardly add, gave as good as he got. He denounced the socialists as "the men of isms and schisms" who aimed to make the labor movement a "tail to their political party kite."[25] They would subordinate the workers to someone else's goals. "The trade union movement is the only class movement," he said. "The movement often called a class movement [i.e., the socialists] is often nothing more than a party movement, and in the same degree as this party movement increases, in the same ratio does it lose its working class character."[26]

Adding fuel to the fire of battle between Gompers and the socialists was the issue of dual unions. Gompers believed that the workers of any given trade ought all to belong to a single union. Otherwise the bosses might play one union against another—as indeed happened many times. This issue lay at the heart of the AFL's early struggle against the Knights of Labor. Subsequent efforts to form national labor organizations that rivaled the AFL itself or various of its constituent unions invariably found socialists playing leading roles. The Socialist Party's perennial presidential nominee, Eugene V. Debs, was a leader of several. No less invariably these groups evoked Gompers' outrage. He dismissed the most famous of them, the Industrial Workers of the World, as "[nothing] more than a radical fungus on the labor movement."[27] And he had little more use for the American Labor Union, the Western Labor Union and the American Railway Union—all of them socialist-inspired and all threatening to fracture and weaken the movement.

Nothing, however, raised his ire more than the Socialist Trade and Labor Alliance created by the Socialist Labor Party. The SLP was led by Daniel Loeb, a university professor who changed his name to the less Jewish-sounding Daniel De Leon. A master of vitriol, he denounced the AFL leaders as "labor fakirs" and "labor lieutenants of capitalism," epithets that lived on in the lexicon of American Communists. A dual union formed by middle-class socialists epitomized everything Gompers detested—and he scarcely hid his feelings. He greeted the founding of De Leon's labor body thus:

> We note ... that the work of union wrecking is being taken up by a wing of the so-called socialist party of New York, headed by a professor without a professorship, a shyster lawyer without a brief, and a statistician who furnished figures to the republican, democratic and socialist parties. These three mountebanks, aided by a few unthinking but duped workers, recently launched, from a beer saloon a brand new national organization, with the avowed purpose of crushing every trade union in the country.[28]

When the group collapsed a few years later, Gompers was no more charitable. He chortled over "this moribund concern, conceived in iniquity and brutal concubinage with labor's double enemy, greed and ignorance, fashioned into an embryonic phthisical dwarf, born in corruption and filth; and now dying, surrounded by the vultures of its progeny ready to pounce on the emaciated carcass."[29]

After years of such warfare, Gompers ceased to minimize his differences with the socialists or to suggest they were merely about means to the same ends. At the AFL's 1903 convention he declared: "I want to tell you, Socialists ... I know ... what you have up your sleeve. ... I am entirely at variance with your philosophy. ... Economically, you are unsound; socially you are wrong; industrially you are an impossibility."[30]

It is hard to say whether Gompers' power struggles with the socialists made him more hostile to their doctrine or whether his widening disagreement exacerbated the organizational clash. But whichever was cause and whichever effect, Gompers developed a distinct labor philosophy that was quite inimical to socialist ideas. While socialists generally wanted the government to play an ever greater role in the economy, Gompers distrusted any but the most minimal government intervention. Curiously, this derived from his own version of class consciousness. In effect he accepted the view put by Marx and Engels that government was inevitably the instrument of the "ruling class." In a direct economic struggle by means of strikes or boycotts the workers might prevail, but put the issue in the hands of government, and the workers were bound to get the short end. "It has been the constant struggle of the workers through the ages to get the tentacles of government from the[ir] throats," he asserted.[31]

Gompers' distrust of government grew out of bitter experience. In 1882 he had organized a brilliant campaign to get the New York legislature to outlaw cigar rolling in tenement houses, a practice that filled homes with tobacco dust and debris, multiplying the health hazards of already squalid conditions. A pivotal role was played by a young assemblyman named Theodore Roosevelt. He believed he had been appointed to a committee on the subject because the political fixers counted him as a reliable vote for laissez faire—but they had underestimated the men they were dealing with. TR accepted an invitation from Gompers for a personally guided tour through the slums, and what he found offended his patriotism. He recalled:

> my first visits to the tenement-house districts in question made me feel that, whatever the theories might be, as a matter of practical common sense I could not conscientiously vote for the continuance of the conditions which I saw. These conditions rendered it impossible for the families of the tenement-house workers to live so that the children might grow up fitted for the exacting duties of American citizenship.[32]

With TR's active help, Gompers got his bill through, only to have it struck down by the courts. It was passed again during the next session, and thrown out again. Finally, Gompers decided on a different tack:

> we talked over the possibilities of further legislative action and decided to concentrate on organization work. . . . [W]e harassed the manufacturers by strikes and agitation until they were convinced that . . . it would be less costly for them to abandon the tenement manufacturing. . . . Thus we accomplished through economic power what we had failed to achieve through legislation.[33]

Because of such experiences, Gompers did not favor the kinds of legislative action that were to become the very hallmark of labor's political action in later decades. He opposed minimum-wage legislation as well as all manner of government social insurance except to cover physical disability. He even opposed legislation for an eight-hour work day, although few issues were closer to his heart, preferring to pursue this goal through a series of strikes.† But just

---

† In a historic irony, as part of this campaign, it was he who had chosen May 1, 1886, as an international rallying day for the eight-hour day. Thereafter "May Day" became a solemn Red holiday observed round the globe by Socialists and Communists—and despised by Gompers.

as judicial meddling had driven him from the political arena, eventually it drew him back as anti-strike injunctions impeded the kind of direct economic action that Gompers preferred. Reversing course, he concluded that only a labor-friendly legislature could clip the wings of the employer-friendly courts. The AFL formed a Labor Representation Committee, probably borrowing its name from the body formed six years before by the British Trades Union Congress that eventually became the British Labour Party, and after a shaky start it hit pay dirt with the presidential victory of Woodrow Wilson in 1912.

Upon his nomination Wilson roused little enthusiasm from labor, for he was viewed as a relatively conservative Democrat. But he turned out to be, as labor historian Henry Pelling wrote, "the first American President to pay serious attention to the advice of the leaders of organized labor ... frequently discuss[ing] matters personally with Gompers."[34] One of his earliest official acts was to create the Department of Labor, appointing as its secretary William Wilson, a former leader of the United Mine Workers. Then he signed the Clayton Act, which excluded unions from certain antitrust actions, and helped secure passage of the Seaman's Act, which liberated seamen from virtual peonage. In return, labor took a major hand in Wilson's 1916 reelection.

As American entry into World War I grew more likely, Wilson named Gompers as one of seven prominent citizens constituting an advisory commission on national defense, an appointment that symbolized labor's acceptance as a part of the American establishment. When, in the 1890s, a newly puissant America had dipped its toe in the waters of colonialism, Gompers had protested loudly. He denounced "heartless enthusiasts, grab-all monopolists, and imperialists," and he enlisted as a vice president of the Anti-Imperialist League.[35] But he was firmly convinced that America's part in World War I was just, and he responded with patriotic fervor.

Gompers convened the unions to pledge support to the government if it went to war, while asking that workers' rights be safeguarded. He met opposition from, among others, the Socialist Party, which unlike most of its kin in Europe had upheld an antimilitary posture on the theory that the working man had no real country. No idea could have been more at odds with Gompers' feelings. "It never occurred to me in all the years that I have lived in this country to question that I am an American," he said, recalling that upon settling in his new country, "the spirit of America took possession of me ... completely." Even so, he said, "I never fully plumbed the depth of my feeling for America until the World War came."[36] Thus the Socialists' neutralism aggravated his hostility.

In his eyes, it amounted to "substantial aid to Germany [making it] no longer possible for loyal Americans to continue membership."[37]

To counteract antiwar agitation within labor and radical circles, Gompers organized socialists and unionists who supported the war into the American Alliance for Labor and Democracy. "Gompers's role in fashioning a national prowar consensus was critical," writes labor historian Nick Salvatore, "for the opponents of American involvement were vocal and numerous."[38] So effective was Gompers in rallying public opinion, in fact, that late in the war he was dispatched by Washington on a tour of Europe to boost sagging morale within the allied countries. There, too, he had an enormous impact. When asked to name America's greatest contribution to the war effort, the British minister of foreign affairs, Lord Balfour, replied: "Gompers."[39]

Gompers' role in international affairs did not end with the war. He was chosen chairman of the commission that spawned the International Labor Organization, created in conjunction with the League of Nations. He also took the lead in founding the Pan-American Labor Conference. The overseas issue that aroused his most passionate response was the Bolshevik triumph in Russia. The AFL had welcomed the failed Russian Revolution of 1905, and when the tsar was overthrown in February 1917, Gompers cabled the provisional government: "We rejoice with Russia's workers in their newly achieved liberty."[40] But he saw Lenin's seizure of power as a betrayal of the hopes of the February Revolution and as a "menace to the civilization of the world."[41]

Lenin's bloodthirsty, despotic tactics were there for all to see, but they were excused by many progressives who believed that he shared their goals. The claim that Lenin's heart was in the right place, however, won no indulgence from Gompers, who had spent a lifetime battling "idealists" in and around the labor movement. His warm embrace of American principles made the Bolsheviks' undemocratic methods repugnant to him, and Lenin's claim that a revolutionary vanguard could substitute itself for the working class was a dagger pointed at his most deeply held beliefs.

Without a moment's hesitation, Gompers—who liked to say, "My legs are so short, I can never run away from a fight"—placed himself at the forefront of American anticommunism. It was a stance that the AFL was to maintain as long as communism lasted, although it sometimes set the AFL apart from liberal allies at home and fellow unionists abroad. Gompers ridiculed intellectuals who were enchanted by the Soviet experiment. Those "whose time is spent in theorizing about the salvation of society and the future welfare of Labor, [have] been made dizzy by the madness of the Bolshevist whirl . . . about as was to have been expected," he jibed, adding that "throughout the world the actual producing forces of society have not been swayed by the exotic chords of Bolshevist propaganda."[42] This was, of course, something of an exaggeration. Some labor groups were in fact attracted by the Soviets, but Gompers would not tolerate this within the AFL. When the Seattle Central Labor Council sent a delegate to the Comintern, the AFL ordered it to cease pro-Soviet activity on pain of having its charter revoked.

Nor did Gompers rest with policing the labor movement. When he got wind of sympathy being shown to Lenin's regime by members of the U.S. delegation to the Versailles peace conference, he charged that they were "committing an unspeakable crime against civilization itself."[43] Most remarkably, he took it upon himself to challenge the sympathy for Bolshevism that was widespread among American intellectuals. He wrote a series of articles in the AFL magazine that were subsequently reprinted as a pamphlet,[44] and then in 1921 he co-authored a book with William English Walling.[45] In these works, Gompers carefully dissected the pro-Soviet apologias appearing in magazines like the *Nation* and the *New Republic*. Relying almost entirely on statements and reports from Lenin and other Soviet sources, he laid bare the bloody, repressive, exploitive nature of the new Moscow regime. It made, he said, a "piteous story of cruelty and intolerance" exacted by an "autocratic . . . minority dictatorship."[46]

Gompers, it was clear, had lost none of his fight, but around seventy his health began to fail, forcing him to reduce his cigar consumption to twenty-five a day. He was heaped with honors and appreciations at his last AFL convention in 1924, after which he proceeded to Mexico, against his doctor's orders, for a meeting of the Pan-American Labor Conference, where he received an effusive reception. There he collapsed, although he hung on long enough to be carried back across the border to die on his beloved adopted soil in a San Antonio hotel room. His last words were: "God bless our American institutions. May they grow better day by day."[47]

• • •

Lenin died the same year. Communism was still in its infancy. Gompers had not lived to see it spread to rule 35 percent of the world's population, as it did by the late 1970s, fulfilling his own dire warnings. But his spirit was reincarnated in George Meany, a successor who did as much as any American to bring this juggernaut down. Meany came from a different background than Gompers, but he, too, was a self-educated proletarian with no use for middle-class theorists who appointed themselves to lead or tutor labor. He, too, was a patriot and a democrat who believed that the working man could make out all right in America thanks to the freedom to organize, to strike, to speak and to vote. And he, too, was viscerally hostile to any regime that denied those rights.

Born in 1894 in East Harlem, William George, soon known by his middle name, was the second of the ten children of Mike Meany, a plumber who rose to become an officer of his union local. Like many fathers, he wanted his son to have an easier life than was to be found plying the "hard, dirty" trade of plumbing. But like many sons, George would sooner emulate his dad than listen to him. At sixteen, after a year and a half of high school, he dropped out and secretly asked one of his father's friends for a job in plumbing. When Mike found out, he acquiesced on the condition that the boy take evening classes to learn the trade properly.

The classes lasted three years, but George still found time to play semi-pro baseball, his stocky frame making him a natural catcher. In those days, blue laws proscribed major league ball on Sundays, so the semi-pros attracted good crowds, and George was able to bring home a few dollars for each game.

Life was soon to get harder. In 1916 his father, barely past fifty, died and two years later his older brother was killed in the Great War. This left twenty-four-year-old George the sole supporter of his mother and six surviving younger siblings. It forced him to prolong his courtship of Eugenia MacMahon, a seamstress and active member of the International Ladies' Garment Workers' Union, but the two finally wed in 1919.

He also became active in his union. In a last inheritance from his father, he got elected to the local executive board, as he later said, "strictly because my name was Meany." Then in 1922, on the strength of his own rising repute, he was elected a union "business agent." This full-time position took him off the construction site for good and inaugurated his climb to the apex of American labor.

When he reached the national stage, Meany was to cut a gruffer figure than any other twentieth-century American leader. With a long stogie invariably stuck into the corner of his mouth, he exhibited utter disdain for public relations and for proper English grammar or pronunciation. (The oil workers' union would always be the "erlwoikuhs.") He never showed self-consciousness about his speech or the other mannerisms that made him seem like the plumber he was—nor about the chauffeured limousine and other perks of power that came his way. But this high school dropout read voraciously and taught himself

to paint works of art and play the piano and organ, and he learned Spanish—all
of which he kept private. He felt no need to make himself more appealing in
the eyes of higher classes or the press, but his peers saw something captivating
beneath the unpolished exterior. Paul Hall, the wizened leader of the Seafarers
Union, once explained:

> You give me one good guy on a ship who knows what he's doing and I'll
> give you a united crew with a single purpose. There is a certain . . . quality
> about . . . leadership. Meany has that quality. If Meany comes into a room and
> nobody knows who he is, he has the quality to attract the attention of other
> men. If you go aboard a ship and meet in the mess hall over a cup of coffee,
> you'll soon see who the leader is. They call that built-in-leadership quality,
> and this Meany has.[48]

In 1932 a vacancy opened on the executive board of the New York State
Federation of Labor. Meany decided to throw his hat in the ring. "Our trade
didn't have a member," he said. "Now, you weren't entitled to a member, but it
was always an argument."[49] In truth, Meany didn't need much of an argument.
He had impressed the federation's president, who engineered his elevation.
Within a mere sixteen months, that president resigned to accept an office in
the state government, and Meany decided to run for his position. The vacancy
was initially filled by the executive board, and Meany, the newest and youngest
member, lost to the most senior member by a vote of 7 to 6. But he was able
to reverse that outcome when the full convention of the state federation met
a few months later.

The same year, 1934, that Meany was chosen New York labor chief, Herbert
Lehman was elected governor and the Democrats won control of the state
senate and assembly in a landslide set off by the popularity of the New Deal. A
Jewish investment banker, Lehman was short and slight and gave off an air of
culture. He was an odd match for Meany, but the two formed a tight political
bond. Together they put through a workmen's compensation law, unemployment
insurance, social security and a raft of other labor and social welfare proposals—seventy-two bills in a single year, by one count.

New York was then the largest bastion of organized labor, home to
around one-fifth of the nation's union members, and Meany's political effectiveness caught the attention of labor's national leadership. At the AFL's 1939
convention, a delegate proposed to nominate Meany against the incumbent

president, William Green, a weak leader, who had in fact been chosen for that very reason. For nearly its first forty years the AFL had been dominated by Gompers. In structure, it was nothing but a federation of independent unions, able to wield only as much power as they chose to cede to it. But Gompers had ruled the movement by sheer force of personality. When he died in office in 1924, the heads of the individual unions wanted to reassert their prerogatives, and they picked Green because he had neither a strong base nor a strong presence.

In the fifteen years since then, the Great Depression had come, and then the New Deal. A group of unions impatient for more aggressive efforts to organize the newer, mass-production industries broke away from the AFL to form the Congress of Industrial Organizations (CIO). Some in labor believed that President Roosevelt had encouraged this split in the hope that a new body would give him less stinting support in his campaign for reelection in 1936 than he expected to receive from the AFL. The close partnership that did in fact develop between the president and the CIO was reflected in the oft-quoted Roosevelt phrase "clear it with Sydney," referring to the clothing workers' chief, Sydney Hillman, a CIO officer. Inevitably, AFL leaders began to wish that their organization cut a more effective political presence than Green was able to give it. Meany's accomplishments in New York made him a natural for that role.

Meany, however, was embarrassed by the rumor that he might stand against Green. In the structure of the federation, he had no power. He had been voted to his New York position by the convention of New York local unions. The national AFL was made up not of locals, but of the national unions. Meany did not control a single one, not even the plumbers. Moreover, at forty-five, he was considered quite a youngster in a labor hierarchy in which people rose in large degree through seniority. And while the individual unions and the federation were democratic in structure, competitive elections were relatively rare and discouraged by the movement's us-against-them mindset. Meany was not willing to go after the presidency, but he agreed to a proposal by the heads of the big unions that he become the second-ranking officer, secretary-treasurer, in the hope of invigorating the leadership without challenging Green.

At first it was not a happy move for Meany. For one thing, Eugenia refused to leave New York, hoping that George would give up his dalliance with the national body. (Eight years later she finally relented when their youngest daughter, Genevieve, completed high school, but until then he commuted by train to spend weekends at home.) In addition, the job was disappointing. Green recognized that Meany's elevation was prompted in part by dissatisfaction with himself; he had not even been consulted about it. Naturally, he felt threatened by a dynamic second-in-command twenty years his junior, so he endeavored to occupy Meany with the nuts and bolts of AFL business while keeping him at arm's length from the political work that Meany believed he was put there to do. Meany was so frustrated that he seriously considered relinquishing the post and returning to New York, but the outbreak of world war changed the picture. Meany was named a member of the National Defense Mediation Board, which became the National War Labor Board after the United States declared war. Now, he found himself bearing weighty responsibilities not only for his fellow unionists but for his country as well. He was in Washington to stay.

Before the bombing of Pearl Harbor, the AFL's position on the war, like that of the average American, was isolationist. There is no evidence that Meany's own views were much different, nor that he paid much attention to the world abroad. (Years later, he himself told the anecdote that when Green called in 1936 to ask him to go to Geneva for a meeting of the International Labor Organization, he thought at first that Green was referring to Geneva, New York.) But the war imbued him with an abiding appreciation of the importance of world politics. He discovered that this was one area in which Green was willing to give him free rein, since it was remote from union politics.

In 1944, the AFL voted to establish a Free Trade Union Committee (FTUC) as a vehicle for labor's international operations. With victory by the Allies growing more certain, Meany was among the small number who foresaw postwar conflict with the Soviet Union. Like England's Ernest Bevin, that other unvarnished proletarian who rose to lead a labor movement, Meany despised the Communists. Bevin is supposed to have said after his first meeting with Soviet leaders that they were "just like the Commies," meaning Communists he had battled in the unions. There were few if any Commies in the plumbers' union, but miners' leader John L. Lewis, who headed the breakaway CIO, employed hundreds of American Communists. Although he did not share their ideology, Lewis wanted these activists for their organizing skills, and he defended his use of them with the rhetorical question: "Who gets the bird—the hunter, or the dog?" Despite this bravado, the Communists gained influence inside many unions and in CIO headquarters itself. Meany called them "termites."

• • •

To head the FTUC and spearhead the anticipated battle against international communism, Meany turned to a flamboyant character whose chosen name was Jay Lovestone. Lovestone was working on international affairs for the International Ladies' Garment Workers' Union (ILGWU) when its president, David Dubinsky,† offered his services to Meany. Lovestone would rather have spent the war working for the OSS, but spy chief "Wild Bill" Donovan would not have him due to his years of Communist activity. Meany judged by different standards. He gave credence to Dubinsky's official pronouncement that Lovestone was kosher: "The son of a bitch is okay, he's been converted."[50]

Lovestone had been born Jacob Liebstein, the fifth and youngest child of Rabbi Barnet and Emma Liebstein. Just before his tenth birthday, Jacob, his mother and three of his siblings left their home in Poland and sailed to America to join Barnet and the oldest daughter, who had preceded them the year before. Like most Jewish immigrants, they settled in a tenement on New York's Lower East Side. Eventually they moved to the Bronx. The parents had difficulty adapting to their new land. Barnet could not find employment as a rabbi, and some years later he and Emma decided to settle in Palestine. But Jacob assimilated with a vengeance. Just as Meany earned a few extra dollars at semi-pro ball, so Jacob as a teenager took up semi-pro boxing. Makeshift rings were put up on tenement roofs, and locals paid a little to watch youngsters slug it out. Jacob was called "the Blond Jew," although he had turned fiercely against his father's faith. Years later, a friend would say that Jacob had an "anti-Semitic heart," a description justified by his many barbed remarks about Jews.[51]

In place of Judaism, Liebstein embraced socialism, joining the Socialist Party in 1915, the year he entered City College of New York. The Bolshevik triumph in Russia engendered an irreparable split among the Socialists, with the left wing breaking away in 1919 to form the Communist Party. Liebstein was among them. That same year he received his American citizenship, legally changing his name to Lovestone, its English translation, in the process.

Lovestone was the party's *wunderkind,* emerging as the number two man in a faction led by Charles E. Ruthenberg which favored a relatively pragmatic approach of working within mainstream labor and political organizations. Factional

---

† Dubinsky had become active at age fourteen in the bakers' union in his native Lodz, Poland, and in the Jewish Socialist Bund, with which it was affiliated. His efforts earned him a term in tsarist prison and then exile to Siberia. He escaped, and made his way to America at nineteen. There he took a series of odd jobs that ended in the clothing industry, where he began his ascent up the ranks of the ILGWU. He became one of the nation's most influential labor chiefs, and of all of them, he was probably Meany's closest friend.

debates were fought out in votes at party conventions, but they were also mediated by representatives from the Comintern, who exercised great authority although their powers were implicit. At the party's 1925 convention, the Ruthenberg-Lovestone group was outnumbered 2 to 1, but then the Comintern representative announced receipt of a cable from Moscow. It read in part:

> Communist International decided under no circumstances should be allowed that majority suppresses Ruthenberg Group . . . demand as ultimatum from majority that Ruthenberg retains post of [party] secretary . . . categorically insist upon Lovestone's Central Executive Committee membership . . . demand retention by Ruthenberg group of co-editorship on central organ. . . . If majority does not accept these demands then declare that, in view of circumstances of elections, unclear who has real majority.[52]

Behind this message lay the internecine intrigues afoot in Russia. Lenin had died a year before and the Bolshevik hierarchs were jockeying for position. During his travels to Russia for Comintern meetings, Lovestone had forged a bond with Nikolai Bukharin, whose star was for the moment rising, as he allied with Stalin against the left-wingers Trotsky and Zinoviev. Bukharin was now using his clout to bolster Lovestone's group. Two years later, Ruthenberg, then forty-six, died suddenly of peritonitis, and Lovestone, not yet thirty, became faction chief and party secretary.

At the next party convention, in 1929, Lovestone set out to consolidate his position. His faction controlled 95 votes out of 104. But there was a higher authority. In Moscow, Trotsky and Zinoviev had been defeated, and now Stalin turned on Bukharin, accusing him of a right-wing fallacy. Lovestone was doubly compromised: as a relative right-winger himself and as an ally of Bukharin's. He bowed to the wind and renounced Bukharin, yet he was suspect. As was often done with foreign Communists whom Stalin wanted to bring to heel, he ordered Lovestone to leave the American party and put himself at the disposal of the Comintern for "international work." Lovestone resisted and took a delegation of party leaders to Moscow to appeal the Comintern's decision.

At a formal hearing, Lovestone and several of his comrades had the temerity to argue with Stalin, even to remind him that they had the bulk of the American Communists behind them. This unwonted defiance prompted Stalin to bare his fangs:

A few words regarding the vaunting manner in which the group of Comrade Lovestone speaks and represents itself here in the name of the whole Party, in the name of 99 percent of the Communist Party of America. . . . Let me remind you that Zinoviev and Trotsky also at one time played trumps with percentages and assured everybody that they had secured or, at any rate, would secure, a 99 percent majority in the Communist Party of the Soviet Union. You know, Comrade, what a farce the vainglory of Trotsky and Zinoviev ended in. I would therefore advise you not to play trumps with percentages. You declare that you have a certain majority in the American Communist Party and that you will retain that majority under all circumstances. That is until no, comrades of the American delegation, absolutely untrue. . . . [A]t present, you still have a formal majority. But tomorrow you will have no majority and you will find yourselves completely isolated if you attempt to start a fight against the decisions of the [Comintern]. You may be certain of that, dear comrades.[53]

Stalin's forecast was accurate and Lovestone's support melted away. What Stalin understood so much better than Lovestone was that the very premise of Communist parties around the world was that Moscow was the new Jerusalem. However surprising the twists of line, to be a Communist meant to accept the Kremlin's authority. Lovestone was ordered expelled from the American party, and a campaign of "enlightenment" was launched. All those who remained faithful to Lovestone were purged, but their numbers were few: ninety-two in all, by one count.[54] The members of Lovestone's delegation headed back home, some repentant, some defiant. But Stalin ordered Lovestone to remain in Russia, and the American began to fear for his life. Fortunately, he still had a few friends in Moscow who secured him a passport (his own had been confiscated) and an airline ticket to Berlin, and he made good his escape.

Like many Communist purge victims who retained their faith in the system and its leader and blamed their fate on underlings, Lovestone was at first tempted to believe that it had all been a mistake. But over the course of the 1930s he came to see that his own treatment had been far from an aberration, and he made an irrevocable break with Stalin. The last straws for him were the 1937 suppression by Soviet agents of the POUM, the independent leftist movement that fought alongside the Communists in the Spanish Civil

War, and the trial and execution of his hero, Bukharin.[†] The former rooftop brawler now began to fight communism with the same single-minded ferocity that he had once brought to promoting it. He liked to say: "I may be wrong, but I am never in doubt."

The new Lovestone was embraced by ILGWU president Dubinsky, who had led his union into the CIO but was alarmed at the Communist influence there. He hired Lovestone and a bevy of the followers who remained devoted to him to work within the United Automobile Workers, where the Communists were on the rise. Lovestone did not in fact manage to defeat them (they lost out later to their erstwhile ally Walter Reuther), but he acquitted himself well enough for Dubinsky to recommend him to Meany, who was eager to put Lovestone's talents to work.

In later years it was often assumed that the stolid plumber must have been spoon-fed the ideology of anticommunism by the conniving ex-radical. Meany had heard such stories and said they "gripe the hell out of me.... Hell, I was fighting the Commies when Lovestone was running the Communist Party."[55] Indeed, Meany's anticommunism was so strong and his anticipation of the Cold War so acute that it led him to quietly vote for Dewey in 1944. He told interviewer Archie Robinson:

> I liked FDR, but ... I had been in and out of the White House many times. I was convinced that we were going to have real problems with the Russians after the war.... I had seen FDR [and come] to the conclusion that, physically and mentally, he had gone downhill very, very fast.... I just felt that in dealing with the Russians after the war, we would be better off with Dewey.[56]

During the war, the British Trades Union Congress had asked the American and Soviet labor unions to join in founding some kind of international labor body. Since the three countries were allied in a life-or-death struggle against a common foe, such cooperation seemed natural, and all three governments endorsed the idea. But the AFL would have none of it. To Meany and his colleagues, the Soviet state was an ally to whom it might be necessary to give military aid and cooperation—but without illusions. They had no hesitation

---

† Lovestone was not the only one for whom these events constituted an anti-Stalin epiphany. Bukharin's trial was taken as the model for the novel *Darkness at Noon* by the disillusioned Communist Arthur Koestler. And it was in the ranks of the POUM that George Orwell fought, transforming him from a sympathizer into a determined foe of communism, a story he recorded in *Homage to Catalonia*.

in supporting Lend/Lease, but to legitimate the U.S.S.R.'s state-run "unions" was unthinkable. In deference to the war effort, the AFL resisted quietly, but in April 1945, with Germany on the brink of defeat, Meany decided to take off his muzzle. In a speech that offers a nice sample of his blunt style as well as the strength of his feelings about communism, he said:

> We see no virtue in groveling in the dust of a false unity which would simply replace one form of totalitarianism with another. We do not propose to be a party to the rigging of international labor machinery to be used as a medium of infiltration or the chocolate coating of an ideology among people who would choke if they knew the consequences of what they were swallowing. . . . What could we talk about? The latest innovations being used by the secret police to ensnare those who think in opposition to the group in power? Or, perhaps, bigger and better concentration camps for political prisoners?[57]

At war's end, the AFL became the first major American organization to denounce Soviet subjugation of nations occupied by the Red Army. In 1947, Meany and Lovestone arranged publication of a map of Soviet concentration camps, offering the first glimpse of the appalling story that became household knowledge decades later through Aleksandr Solzhenitsyn's *Gulag Archipelago.* When Solzhenitsyn reached the United States, he offered the federation thanks "on behalf of all the prisoners of those times."

Like Gompers, Meany and Lovestone were thus in the "vanguard of the proletariat"—not in the mendacious sense that Lenin had used that term, but in an opposite sense. They took the lead in fighting communism because it repressed workers, and in defending their country because it gave workers the chance for a decent life even though Marxism denied that this was possible under capitalism.

Little could be done, beyond protest, about the spread of communism in Eastern Europe, but Western Europe became an active battleground between America and Russia, and the AFL threw itself into the fray. Upon the launching of the Marshall Plan, Meany accepted a seat on its advisory board. The plan amounted to the heftiest foreign aid program ever, absorbing (together with analogous aid to Japan) some 2 percent of the U.S. Gross National Product for six consecutive years. It was a time when Americans were striving to make up for the privations of war, but Meany took it upon himself to explain to workers the need for sacrifice. In a series of speeches, he told them plainly that "the program will cost us billions of dollars. . . . [I]t means postponing the day when there will be sufficient goods to satisfy all the demands of our own people . . . it means continued high taxes on our wages . . . it means further pressure on the already high cost of living." However, he went on, "if we make the tragic choice of saving some money and letting Western Europe work out its own salvation unaided by America, it is but a matter of time . . . before we will find a new neighbor on the Atlantic shore—Joseph Stalin's brutal, Fascist dictatorship."[58]

Italy, France, Germany and Austria were prostrate in the war's aftermath. Revived Communist parties hoped to exploit the social dislocation and widespread deprivation. In Italy and France, moreover, the Communists had emerged from the war with their credentials for patriotism and heroism burnished by prominence in the antifascist underground. A centerpiece of their strategy for winning power was to gain control over reborn labor movements. Meany and the AFL strained to persuade the State Department of the importance of preventing this, and Lovestone was able to get many of his own followers or allies named as labor attachés. The aim was to secure the presence of someone in local U.S. embassies who would back the efforts of the FTUC to strengthen non-Communist unions.

Lovestone's most able disciple, Irving Brown, was posted to Europe to carry out this campaign. It was financed with donations from the AFL and various unions, but labor's treasure chest was not equal to its goals (nor perhaps to the funds that the local Communists received from Moscow). U.S. government funds apparently supplied by the newly created CIA supplemented the FTUC's effort.[†] In Germany and Austria, the Communist labor bid was defeated. In France and Italy, the Communists came out on top, but smaller competing labor fronts prevented them from exercising firm control. Brown's operatives thwarted politically inspired strikes by Communist-controlled dock unions designed to impede delivery of Marshall Plan aid. There are varying estimates of how close the Communists came to taking power in one or more of the Western European states in the late 1940s; but when details of this shadowy conflict leaked out decades later, it became clear that Lovestone and Brown, under Meany's aegis, had had a large hand in ruining the Communists' game plan.

---

† Meany always denied allegations of cooperation with the CIA, but while it is probably true that the AFL-CIO itself received no funds from the CIA, it seems that the federation facilitated covert government support for anticommunist unions abroad. Lovestone's biographer, Ted Morgan, says that Meany fired Lovestone in 1974 when he discovered him flouting an order to sever his financial relationship with legendary CIA counterintelligence chief James Jesus Angleton. Other authorities, however, doubt that Meany was ever in the dark on what Lovestone was doing.

• • •

Ironically, while the AFL was fighting the Communists overseas, a backlash was building at home against the strong role of Communists inside American unions. A provision of the 1947 Taft-Hartley Act required labor officials to sign affidavits disavowing communism. At that year's AFL convention in San Francisco, Mine Workers leader John L. Lewis advocated defiance of the provision. Volatile and personally ambitious, Lewis was the nation's most colorful labor leader. Trained as an actor, his memory packed with biblical and Shakespearian quotations, he soared above every other labor leader in his oratorical skills. He used them pugnaciously to intimidate anyone who stood in his path; and when oratory would not suffice, he was always ready to supplement it with physical intimidation.

The provision was indeed humiliating, but with the Cold War aborning, the well-publicized influence of Communists in CIO unions was a public relations vulnerability for labor. When Lewis took the floor to denounce other labor leaders as cowards and traitors for their willingness to obey Taft-Hartley, he stoked resentment since he had done so much to cause the problem by deliberately hiring hundreds of Communists as CIO organizers. And his insistence on taking his miners out on strike during the war, thumbing his nose at the nation's peril, had done more than any other single action to generate a climate of opinion hostile to labor. But no one dared to cross rhetorical swords with the vindictive Lewis—until George Meany took the floor.

Meany carefully recited the history of the Communists' disruption of the labor movement and of Lewis' decision to invite them into the CIO. Then he said:

> with his right hand [Lewis] upheld the position of the United Mine Workers in uncompromising resistance to Communism; but with his left hand he made fellowship with Harry Bridges, Lewis Merrill, Michael Quill, Julius Emspak [Communist officers of various CIO unions] and all the other stinking America haters who love Moscow.
>
> So, I am prepared to sign a non-Communist affidavit. I am prepared to go a step further and sign an affidavit that I was never a comrade to the comrades.[59]

For the first time at such a conclave, Lewis was brought low. Never before had anyone risked taking him on so directly. When the issue was put to a vote, Lewis' support evaporated, and he pulled the Mine Workers out of the AFL.

Meany's courage and effectiveness sealed his status as heir apparent to the presidency, and he acceded to the post upon Green's death in 1952. The unions wanted a leader who could stand up for them the way Meany had done to Lewis.

Meany served as the labor federation's president for twenty-seven years, a year less than Green, but with far more impact. While Green had been content to reign without ruling, Meany transformed the movement. He repaired the internecine rift by bringing the CIO back to the AFL. The CIO itself had become riven with factions, and some colleagues counseled Meany to try to absorb its member unions one at a time. But Meany eschewed such an approach, believing that a more complete and durable unity would come from bringing the two federations together as equals. The spirit was symbolized by Meany's idea of calling the reunited body by the combined names of each: ergo the mouthful, AFL-CIO.

Despite the importance he attached to labor unity, Meany was ruthless in purging Communists and gangsters. The highlight of these campaigns came in 1957 when he acted to expel the corrupt Teamsters Union even though it was the largest member of the AFL-CIO, contributing 10 percent of the federation's budget. Teamsters boss Jimmy Hoffa, who was later convicted of racketeering, ducked several meetings with Meany in the course of the expulsion proceedings. A Teamsters source told Meany biographer Joseph Goulden: "Jimmy didn't want to get in the same room with Meany. Jimmy didn't scare easy, but he wasn't used to dealing with a rock like Meany."[60]

A still tougher internecine battle that Meany fought was to rid the movement of racial discrimination. This could not be won by expelling one or two unions, since the problem was widespread, stemming in part from raw prejudice and in part from the effort to monopolize jobs, a key tactic in some trades. Some unions followed the practice of admitting only the children of existing members. Meany once said he knew of plumbers' locals that would open membership only to those from certain counties in Ireland. The problem was rampant within the building trades, and there were some accusations that Meany went too easy on them, being a building tradesman himself. The tensions came to light at the AFL-CIO's 1959 convention when Meany crossed swords with A. Philip Randolph, the only black president of a national union. Meany did not like Randolph's washing labor's dirty linen in public and scolded him for not being "on the team." But neither Randolph nor most other black labor leaders doubted Meany's underlying commitment to civil rights. As *New York Times* labor correspondent A. H. Raskin wrote:

the unhappiest aspect of the bitter exchange was that it created the outward appearance of a rift over principle between the two men who had been most conspicuous in the implementation of this no-discrimination drive....Actually, their differences have never been over which way the federation should go, but over how fast its progress should be and how much pressure it should exert to make it faster.[61]

Meany created a civil rights department within the AFL-CIO, and by the late 1960s virtually the last vestiges of discrimination within the movement had been eradicated. In addition, although he was sometimes criticized for the federation's failure to endorse civil rights marches, it provided the principal lobbying muscle behind the passage of the landmark legislation of the 1960s that sounded the death knell of Jim Crow in America.

While recasting the labor movement internally, Meany also molded it into a mighty force in American life. His office at the AFL-CIO commanded a stunning view of the White House across Lafayette Park, and he joked to visitors that the American people needed someone to keep an eye on the president. Indeed, he never hesitated to criticize the commander in chief to his face or in the press. The *Washington Post* reported that Meany "went to the mat with Harry S. Truman over stabilization policy in the Korean war; challenged Dwight D. Eisenhower to demonstrate his professed concern for labor's interests and fought Lyndon B. Johnson on the minimum wage law . . . denounced Gerald R. Ford's economic policies and accused him of 'government by veto' . . . accus[ed Jimmy Carter] of insensitivity to working people."[62] The only president with whom Meany did not tangle was Kennedy, perhaps because of the avuncular regard he had for the fellow Irish Catholic a generation younger than himself, but perhaps for no other reason than the brevity of Kennedy's term. Despite the clashes, Eisenhower and Johnson each sought out private hours with the labor chief as much for sociality as for politics. It is lonely at the top, and Meany's power made him something of a peer, while his granite persona made him a trustworthy confidant.

The president with whom he got along least was Nixon. While supporting him on Vietnam, Meany went after Nixon hammer and tongs on domestic issues, organizing campaigns that defeated two successive Supreme Court nominees, Clement Haynesworth and Harrold Carswell. When Nixon's secretary of labor criticized Meany for opposing the president's wage and price controls, Meany retorted, "I don't pay much attention to the Secretary of Labor. After all when you have a problem with the landlord, you don't discuss it with the janitor."[63]

Détente made him even more sour on Nixon, and he once quipped that if Hitler were still in power "we'd have Henry [Kissinger] sitting in his lap."

Labor had mobilized as never before in 1968 behind its old friend Hubert Humphrey, who lost to Nixon by a hair's breadth, and Meany was prepared to do as much or more to oust Nixon after his first term. But when the Democrats nominated peace candidate George McGovern in 1972, Meany stopped dead in his tracks. Early in the year, he had warned with his usual straightforwardness: "There's one point . . . I will not go beyond. I will not go with a guy who advocates surrender, and this has nothing to do with the labor movement; it has nothing to do with Nixon. This is me. I will not go with a fellow running for President of the United States who advocates surrender in Southeast Asia."[64] True to his word, Meany kept the AFL-CIO neutral in the presidential race, but this signaled no reconciliation with Nixon. As the Watergate scandal unfolded early in Nixon's second term, Meany became the first major public figure to call for his impeachment.

Withholding support from McGovern despite his deep dislike for Nixon and despite pressure from the overwhelmingly Democratic unions within the federation showed the degree of Meany's anticommunism. He had once said that he was "the second most rabid anti-Communist" in America, behind only Nixon, but after Nixon launched "détente," Meany no longer gave him pride of place. He boasted that the AFL-CIO "remains the most powerful mass organization in the world in complete opposition to Communism."[65] Little wonder, then, that the Communists were happy when he finally stepped down in 1979.

• • •

If Communists believed that their torment at the hands of American labor was over, they were to be sadly disappointed. It is true that Meany's successor, Lane Kirkland, was a man of different style and background. The scion of a prominent old South Carolina family, he had been reared on tales of the "war of northern aggression." When war broke out in Europe in 1939, the seventeen-year-old Kirkland tried to enlist in the Canadian army since America was still at peace. Turned away because of his age, he soon found his way into the merchant marine, in which he served throughout the war, joining a small seafaring union called the Masters, Mates and Pilots. This intense introduction to global affairs motivated him to enroll in Georgetown University's school of foreign service when the war was over. After that he took a job with the AFL, where he became a favorite of Meany's and was groomed by "the old man" as heir. Kirkland was to change a few of Meany's policies, but one area in which there was not a shade of difference between the two was on the subject of communism.

The proof of this was not long in coming. Less than a year after Kirkland's accession, a drama began to unfold in the Baltic port city of Gdansk. A crane operator who had labored thirty years in the immense Lenin shipyard was fired for defying the authorities. A large, devout single mom in her fifties, Anna Walentynowicz was undaunted by the gigantic machinery that she handled or by the repressive state machinery that tried to handle her. She was active in a loose network of dissidents who kept alive the embers of resistance that had flamed into mass demonstrations at least once every decade. In 1970, workers protesting price increases had been fired upon by police and soldiers in a handful of cities and several had died, some directly in front of the Lenin shipyard. In the ensuing years, those workers who had dared to persist in low-key agitation had repeatedly voiced the demand for a monument to these martyrs. Now, emboldened by the recent visit of the Polish pope, a group of workers were planning a memorial meeting. Since candles, like other consumer goods, were scarce, Walentynowicz had scavenged a nearby cemetery for leftover wax from some that had already burnt. For this she had been arrested and subsequently dismissed from her job.

Other workers rallied to her defense, including the electrician Lech Walesa, who had himself been fired for disobedient activities some four years earlier. Soon the Lenin works were idled in a sit-down strike that spread to other factories throughout Gdansk and other cities. The "Independent Self-Governing Trade Union, Solidarity," was born, espousing a list of demands that added up to the end of totalitarian dictatorship.

Within days after the Gdansk sit-down began, Kirkland displayed his "class consciousness": "They are on strike and we will support it any way we can," he declared.[66] The AFL-CIO Longshoremen's union announced a boycott of all cargoes to and from Poland. Its president, Thomas Gleason, noted slyly that a hundred thousand cases of Polish ham were in transit to the United States. If the Polish strike were to be suppressed, warned Kirkland and Gleason, the AFL-CIO would organize an international labor boycott of all Polish transport.

In addition, Kirkland soon announced the creation of the Polish Workers' Aid Fund. Together with the auto workers and other unions from around the world, it rushed donations to the nascent Solidarity. Cash was less important than items difficult or impossible to buy in Poland: office machines, printing supplies, minivans, copies of Robert's Rules of Order. Here at last was the international proletarian solidarity that Marx and Engels had dreamt about but failed to achieve—except that its purpose was not to bring about communism, but to abolish it.

Labor's militancy made the U.S. administration uneasy. President Carter sent Secretary of State Edmund Muskie, himself of Polish extraction, to plead with Kirkland to avoid actions that the U.S.S.R. would find provocative. He may as well have been speaking to a stone wall. Walesa had appealed for international support, and nothing the U.S. government could say would dissuade Kirkland from providing it.

From Moscow, *Pravda* denounced U.S. labor activities, saying their aim was "to inflict damage on the socialist gains of the Polish people, to try to push Poland off the road it took."[67] Sixteen months later, the Polish regime declared martial law. Solidarity was violently suppressed, and those of its leaders whom the regime could lay hands on were imprisoned. Anna Walentynowicz was sentenced to six years.

But the movement lived on underground, nurtured by the AFL-CIO. Thousands of books and hundreds of periodicals were published illegally and circulated throughout the country. Radio *Solidarnosc,* transmitting each time from a different rooftop, broadcast messages from leaders who had slipped through the dragnet. "Flying universities" met from home to home discussing subjects banned from state classrooms. Polish civil society flourished, completely disdaining official ideology. The American labor pipeline continued to provide printing equipment, only now it was smuggled into the country, often broken down into parts stashed within packages of innocuous goods. In addition, funds were contributed for the relief of families of arrested activists and for bribing the managers of state printing houses to allow Solidarity publications to be run on their presses during the night.

This assistance, as well as labor's relentless pressure on the Reagan administration to maintain a hard line against the Warsaw regime, made the Solidarity stalwarts feel they were not alone. The endless games of cat and mouse with the authorities almost always ended in the apprehension of the activists. But according to Senator Zbigniew Romaszewski, who served a long sentence, as did his wife Zofia, for having founded Radio *Solidarnosc,* "in the prisons and detention centers we always felt the support of the AFL-CIO, knowing that we were not forgotten."[68]

Despite many arrests and massive surveillance, the Polish regime found itself incapable of stamping out the resistance or regaining any measure of legitimacy. The endurance of the illegal Polish labor union caused an irreparable fissure in the stolid edifice of the Soviet bloc. The Soviet press agency, TASS, plaintively denounced "interference in Poland's affairs," but above all it was the Poles themselves whom the Kremlin did not want to see "interfering." Since this could not be said plainly, the Soviet spokesmen concentrated their fire on "the reactionary US trade union organization AFL-CIO—the former empire of George Meany, the notorious anti-communist and reactionary, which is closely linked with the US military-industrial complex and the big monopolies."[69]

Such attacks were to no avail. By the end of the decade, Communist rule had collapsed in Poland, and then like dominoes the other regimes of the Warsaw Pact fell, too. When Kirkland died in 1999, the Polish president Aleksander Kwasniewski awarded him the nation's highest honor, the Order of White Eagle, for his patronage of Solidarity. Some cynics suggested that Kwasniewski, himself a former Communist, had the ulterior purpose of basking in the reflected glory of Kirkland's anticommunist heroism.

• • •

Not only did American labor contribute more than its share to the downfall of communism, it also proved to be one of the great obstacles to the global advance of socialism in any form. "Ideology is baloney," George Meany liked to say. Indeed, it could be said that Meany's very cast of mind was the antithesis of Marxian consciousness. In the dense theoretics of Marxism one learns that the observable universe is mere "superstructure." Meany, in contrast, believed that things should be expressed plainly and taken at face value. To him, a plumber was a plumber, not a "proletarian." A worker was a guy trying to squeeze the most he could out of his job and hoping to get a better one. And if he was something more than flesh and blood, as he assuredly was, it was not because he was an embodiment of historical processes, but rather a husband, father, worshiper, patriot, pianist, artist, baseball player.

Some socialists have believed that the distinctive absence of socialism from the American scene was because the doctrine had never been presented adequately. What else but sheer ignorance of their own true interests could have led union construction workers in the late 1960s to organize "hard-hat" brigades to violently disperse anti-Vietnam War demonstrations? Actress Jane Fonda once responded to some hecklers: "if you knew what communism was you would get down on your knees and pray for it." But labor's understanding of communism stood the test of time better than Hollywood's.

Labor leaders also understood that not all socialism was tantamount to communism. In declining to endorse either McGovern or Nixon in the 1972 election, Meany once quipped: "where is Norman Thomas now that we need him?"—a reference to the perennial Socialist Party candidate for president. Yet while they did not despise socialism in its democratic guise the way they did communism, labor leaders rejected it nonetheless as a false doctrine for the working man. Far from being born of ignorance of socialist ideas, the unique "bread-and-butter" philosophy of American labor, formulated by Gompers and carried on by Meany and Kirkland, had grown out of an intense confrontation with those ideas and with American conditions.

Such proletarian members as America's socialist parties could boast were in vast disproportion immigrants who had absorbed their ideology in the Old World. But the American experience proved to be a potent solvent in which socialist ideas were washed away. Engels was one of the first to spot this phenomenon, noting in despair what became of comrades who traversed the Atlantic for temporary employment:

> [T]he available Germans who are worth anything become easily Americanized and give up any thought of returning.... [T]he ease with which the overflow population settles on the land, the necessarily increasing tempo of the country's prosperity ... makes people consider bourgeois conditions as a *beau idéal*. Those Germans who think of returning home are for the most part only demoralized individuals.[70]

The solvent consisted not only of economic opportunity but also of self-confidence on the part of the working man. Everywhere in the world, socialism arose as an idea of middle-class thinkers who then set about selling it to the workers. Given the invidious class distinctions in Europe, workers felt they needed middle-class allies, and the socialists played this role. In gratitude, the workers were willing to accept their ideology. Nonetheless, within the socialist parties the ideologues struggled endlessly against the tendency of the labor representatives to slide back toward reformism. Unlike their European counterparts, American socialists failed to win over the unions in part because the workers felt more able to stand on their own.

America's resistance to socialism had consequences far beyond its own borders. By the late 1970s, some 60 percent of mankind was living under socialist government of the communist, social-democratic or Third World variety. Had

America, too, embraced some form of socialism, that idea's triumph would have been complete. It is not likely to have been undone merely by disappointing economic outcomes such as Tanzania and so many other countries experienced. History is replete with examples of dogged human persistence in practices not validated by their results. The use of bleeding to cure disease, of human sacrifice to appease the gods, of trial by ordeal, of mercantilism or colonialism to generate wealth—all reflected time-honored wisdom that was impervious to experience. Socialist economies yielded little growth, but economic growth has been the exception, not the rule, throughout history. People are unlikely to relinquish ineffectual practices unless they can envision a better alternative. Just as the remarkable success of East Asia's four tigers made it harder to explain away the dismal performance of Third World socialist economies, so on a grander scale, the American counter-model undermined socialism's appeal.

To be sure, America has not always been loved. It has been a target of resentment, even hatred. American leaders have been pelted with eggs and stones in foreign capitals by protestors venting their rage at the behemoth of supposed imperialism. But it is doubtful that these demonstrators have often represented more than small minorities. To millions of others America has presented a picture of freedom and abundance. It attracted the German comrades whose desertion Engels lamented, as it did Babeuf's son, Robert Owen's children and the families of Meany and Gompers. It still attracts about one million legal immigrants each year, while an even larger number gets turned away attempting to enter without authorization. Some thousands of unauthorized immigrants succeed at entering, arousing political controversy. Many millions more who do not pull up roots to try to become Americans are nonetheless drawn to the images of American life, real or fanciful, in television, cinema, sport, fashion, food and music, that dominate pop culture around the world. This great allure was deeply subversive of the socialist consensus that had been gathering elsewhere around the world for much of the twentieth century. Like Napoleon's failure to conquer Russia, socialism's failure to conquer America proved its undoing.

10

PERESTROIKA AND
MODERNIZATION: DENG
AND GORBACHEV REPEAL
COMMUNISM

O N MAY 15, 1989, SOVIET PRESIDENT Mikhail Gorbachev boarded a
jetliner for a historic visit to his Chinese counterpart, Deng Xiaoping. For
thirty years, the two principal Communist powers had been more hostile to
one another than to the United States. Scores of military divisions faced each
other along their Amur River border, where intermittent fighting had caused
thousands of casualties. Soviet diplomats had once gone so far as to sound out
Henry Kissinger about the possibility of a nuclear strike against China, while
Beijing secretly colluded with Washington in spying on the Soviets and in a tacit
alliance against "hegemony."

Now, the leaders were meeting to seal an end to the hostility that had
become pointless as a result of the reforms that each had imposed. Both had
devoted their lives to the Communist cause, climbing through the hierarchy to
its very pinnacle. Both had struggled to make the system work, only to conclude that this would require drastic renovation. Deng had concentrated on the
economy, Gorbachev on the political structure, but each had changed his country beyond recognition, abandoning the posture of revolutionary embattlement
and making it a more normal member of the community of nations. A decade

earlier Sino-Soviet rapprochement would have been momentous, but now it seemed like little more than a footnote.

As Gorbachev's jet approached Beijing, an important message came across the radio. In a last-minute change, there would be a makeshift welcoming at the airport instead of the meticulously choreographed ceremony that had been planned for Tiananmen Square. The reason was that the square was occupied by student protestors. They numbered in the tens of thousands, and their ranks were swelled by other citizens during Gorbachev's stay until the total reached one million, of which three thousand were hunger strikers. The throng so disrupted downtown traffic that the entire summit schedule was thrown off kilter. One Soviet embassy official commented wryly: "Everything has gone smoothly today. The only thing lacking was information about the time and location of our meetings and whether they would take place on time or ever."[1]

This disarray was embarrassing for the Chinese hosts, but the demonstrators' message was even more so: they were demanding the kind of political liberties that Gorbachev had instituted. Across the square they had stretched a banner in Russian and Chinese, proclaiming "Democracy—Our Common Ideal." The student leader Wang Dan held a press conference urging the Soviet president to plead the students' cause: "As a great political reformer, we urge Mikhail Gorbachev to talk to the government on our behalf for humanitarian reasons." Other signs and banners directly needled Deng: "Welcome to a real reformer—Gorbachev," said one. "The Soviet Union has Gorbachev. Who does China have?" said another. "You're 58 and I'm 85," said a third, referring to the two leaders' ages.[2]

Gorbachev tried to ease the tension with humor. "I came to Beijing, and you have a revolution," he kidded. But Deng's fury was not easily assuaged. He had led China out of the dark night of the Cultural Revolution. He had opened the country to the outside, making possible the presence of the international press corps to which the students so cannily tailored their actions. He had instituted the changes that had more than doubled the average annual income, putting China on the brink of being a modern nation. Now, in his waning years, was his reward to be ridicule rather than honor?

． ． ．

Like Mao Zedong and many of the other top Communists, Deng had been a child of privilege. He was born on August 22, 1904, in the village of Paifang in Sichuan province. Deng Xiansheng, as he was originally called, was raised largely by nannies in a twelve-room brick house with his own bedroom. His father, Deng Wenming, was a prosperous landowner who leased most of his holding to tenant farmers while hiring laborers to work the rest. He spent his own time supervising and serving in various civic offices, including village head. Xiansheng was born to his father's second wife or concubine. Two more wives or concubines followed. By some accounts, Wenming took them in succession upon the deaths of their predecessors, while in other tellings they formed part of the household simultaneously, as would not have been untoward given his station.[3]

An observant Buddhist, Wenming wished for his son to become a man of learning. The name Xiansheng means "sage," and when the boy was five, his first teacher convinced the father that it was not an appropriate name for a child, so it was changed to Xixian, which means one aspiring to be a sage. At the age of eleven, he completed primary school, which was as much education as Paifang could offer. To continue he had to go to Guang'an, the county seat, where there was a boarding school.

In 1918, at age fourteen, Deng took off with a seventeen-year-old uncle for the big city, Chongqing, some three hundred kilometers away. There they enrolled in high school for a few months before learning of a program combining work and study for Chinese students in France.[4] This was a period of recrimination and searching that came to be called the May 4th Movement for the student demonstrations in Beijing on that date in 1919. Young Chinese were anguished by their country's inferior position in comparison to Japan and the West. Many were eager to travel abroad in the hope of acquiring the knowledge necessary to change this. Deng spent a year and a half at a special preparatory school and then set sail from Shanghai just after his sixteenth birthday. "China was weak and we wanted to make her stronger, and China was poor and we wanted to make her richer," he said. "We went to the West in order to...find a way to save China."[5]

However well intended, the program in which Deng had enrolled was a fiasco. Apart from furnishing the students with steerage-class transport, it had little to offer. Schooling was available only on a pay-as-you-go basis, and even those who could afford it mostly lacked the language skills to study in French. Nor was employment provided. To earn tuition, the participants needed to work, but jobs were hard to come by in the postwar economic downturn. Some students briefly received public assistance from the French government, and the Chinese embassy provided a meager food allowance. None of this was enough to make ends meet, and many of the students camped out in a tent on the grounds of the program's headquarters. To make matters worse, the Chinese students were socially isolated. Deng, for example, acquired bits of French culture—a lifelong love of soccer and croissants—but after five years, he came away still not fluent in French.

These frustrating conditions constituted a hothouse for radical politics. Nationalism and communism competed for the students' allegiance. Of the 1,500 Chinese students, at least 200 enrolled in one of these causes.[6] More than twenty went on to become famous figures in the Communist movement alone. In addition to Deng, their ranks included future premier Zhou Enlai and three who became vice premiers of the People's Republic: Chen Yi, Nie Rongzhen and Li Fuchun.[7]

While supporting himself with jobs in a rubber plant, a steel works and the Renault auto factory, Deng became active in the Communist Youth League, which was founded in 1922. By 1924, when he was nineteen or twenty, Zhou recruited him to the staff of the league's publication, *Red Lights.* The two were close, and Deng later said that he regarded Zhou "as my elder brother."[8] At first Deng's job seems to have been largely technical; apparently he was in charge of the duplicating process. But he came to play more of a substantive role, and according to his daughter, Deng Maomao, he soon became a member of the secretariat of the league's European branch.

His revolutionary activities caused the French police to take an increasingly active interest in him, to the point of raiding his apartment, where they found a bunch of duplicating equipment. In January 1926, fearing arrest, Deng and several comrades fled France for the U.S.S.R.[9]

In Moscow, Deng was admitted first to Eastern University where, by chance, one of his fellow students was Chiang Chingkuo, son of Nationalist leader Chiang Kaishek, who at this time still looked to the Soviet Union for aid and leadership. A half-century later, these two classmates would joust as the respective heads of the two Chinas. After a few months at Eastern, Deng switched to the newly opened Sun Yat-sen University, where the curriculum was devoted entirely to Marxism, Leninism and other subjects designed to mold effective cadres.

Classroom indoctrination was reinforced by the living experience in Russia. Not many people would trade the joys of Paris for those of Moscow. But the Chinese students had faced poor conditions and a sense of rejection in France, whereas in Moscow they were furnished with adequate food, quarters, even recreation and were made to feel welcome as fellow crusaders. In a party document he wrote there, Deng declared: "When I came to Moscow, I had already made up my mind to give my whole life to our Party."[10] He left with redoubled commitment.

As a first assignment, Deng was sent back to China by truck through Mongolia to bring munitions as well as his own services to a northern warlord who had momentarily allied with the Communists in the Hobbesian all-against-all war of regions and factions into which China had devolved. Over the next several years, Deng was assigned alternately to the underground apparatus in Shanghai and to party outposts or other friendly warlords in the provinces.

Even as they worked together to subdue the country, the various ranking Communists jockeyed for position within the movement. Purges and internecine fights were waged with scarcely less brutality than was shown toward the party's enemies. *New York Times* correspondent Harrison Salisbury described an episode in Ruijin county where Deng was named party secretary. "Several thousand Party members had been arrested, and many had been executed," charged with being members of an antiparty conspiracy, a label borrowed from Stalin's purges. "Supposed conspirators were persecuted with devilish cruelty," continues Salisbury. "One group of local Party leaders was paraded through a village street, each man led by a rusty wire that penetrated his testicles. At the village square all were shot."[11] Salisbury says that Deng brought this particular reign of terror to an end, but according to biographer Benjamin Yang, several documents suggest that, at least in its early stages, Deng "sided with the security agency" that carried out the purge rather than with its victims.[12]

In 1932, it was Deng's turn to find himself on the wrong end of a factional battle even though he was on the same side as Mao Zedong, who was not often a loser. Deng was not executed nor even expelled from membership. Rather he was "struggled against." An official directive spelled out what this bit of party terminology entailed: "an attack without mercy and a struggle with brutality." Deng was imprisoned, denied food, probably tortured, and subjected to public "criticism" sessions to which he himself was obliged to contribute.

After three years in purgatory, Deng achieved rehabilitation during the Long March. So romanticized has this chapter of the Chinese Revolution been by Western writers that Americans often use the expression in other contexts to signify a prolonged advance (as in the phrase "the long march through the institutions"). In reality, it was a low ebb in Communist fortunes, a relentless retreat in which most of the participants perished. The winnowing ordeal reshuffled the party's factional balance, with Mao assuming an increasingly prominent role. Although regular party congresses could not be convened under such circumstances, a 1935 leadership meeting at Zunyi confirmed Mao's ascendancy and also reinstated Deng as secretary of the Central Committee, a title he had held briefly in the Shanghai underground.

Relegated to the hinterlands, the Communists found salvation in the outbreak of war with Japan in 1937. The Japanese had occupied Manchuria five years earlier, and Japan's militarist faction had made no secret that it had larger designs on China. Because they were weak, the Communists had appealed for national unity; because he was strong, Chiang had spurned them. He hoped to finish with the Communists before gathering his forces against the foreign threat. Now that China proper was under attack, Chiang reversed himself and endorsed the united front.

When the Japanese surrendered, the civil war between the Communists and the Nationalists recommenced almost at once. By some accounts, Deng's forces were the ones that initiated the resumption of hostilities.[13] He had served since 1938 as political commissar of the 129th division, which made him, says Yang, "de facto guardian of one-third of [all Chinese Communist] military forces."[14] His troops, renamed the Second Field Army, were instrumental in the Communists' eventual triumph, among other feats capturing Chongqing, the Nationalists' last major redoubt on the mainland. He had returned as conqueror to the city from which he had departed for France as an ill-prepared sixteen-year-old.

He briefly journeyed to Beijing to join Mao and the seven other principal Communist leaders in proclaiming the birth of the People's Republic. Standing side by side, they reviewed their victorious forces in Tiananmen Square from atop the Gate of Heavenly Peace, at the entranceway to the Forbidden City, the seat of the Chinese Empire. Mao's dominance within the party had grown decisive during the war, culminating in the seventh party congress of 1945 where his authority was codified in the party constitution, which declared "Mao Zedong thought" to be one of its ideological pillars.

Simultaneously, the nexus between Deng and Mao had grown stronger. Deng was named governor of Chongqing and ruler of all of southwestern China, one of the six administrative regions into which the Communists initially divided the country. In addition to pacifying remaining pockets of resistance, overseeing the 1951 conquest of Tibet and setting in place the machinery of a new government, Deng was entrusted with what turned out to be the first of several grandiose and slightly mad projects conceived by Mao: to relocate a great part of the country's industry deep inland in preparation for an American invasion.

These early years of the People's Republic also witnessed the regime's first agricultural reform program. Land was redistributed, and landlords and rich peasants were hauled before mass meetings for verbal and physical abuse by former tenants or poorer neighbors egged on by party cadres. According to some estimates, as many as a million may have been killed in the process. As ruler of Sichuan, Deng was able to protect his own family from such treatment, although his father had already been brutally murdered ten years earlier under mysterious circumstances.

Having acquitted himself well as regional chief, Deng was summoned in 1952 to the capital, where he was named deputy premier of the state administrative council. In rapid succession between 1954 and 1956, he was promoted to a series of high offices. The first was secretary-general of the Central Committee, a post he had held before but which was more important now that the party was in power. Next he was named a member of the Politburo, and then general secretary of the party. This made him, by most reckonings, the fourth-highest official in the regime, but his real power may have exceeded even that, for Deng had worked himself deeply into Mao's good graces.

Throughout this period, Mao subjected one Politburo member after another to public criticism, ostensibly for errors of policy or theory but actually in order to exert his supremacy. As had been the case with a "rectification" campaign a decade earlier, Deng was exempted from this rough treatment. "Deng was regarded as 'Mao's man,'" writes David Goodman, "his loyal, most trusted and able follower."[15] He was also a ready hatchet. As Lucian Pye remarks, "Mao discovered early [that] Deng could be called upon to slander and vilify any current 'enemy' of the Party."[16] But it was not only for such duties that he valued Deng. Mao seems to have had genuine respect for his abilities. Khrushchev recalled that Mao expressed disdain for his other comrades, but spoke of Deng differently: "See that little man there? He's highly intelligent and has a great future ahead of him."[17] Deng had become, says Harrison Salisbury, "Mao's golden boy."[18]

Mao derived policies from some inner vision, and Deng stood ready to devote his considerable administrative talents to executing them. In the spring of 1957, Mao took many of his colleagues by surprise in suddenly calling for a new freedom of expression. "Let a hundred flowers bloom, a hundred schools of thought contend," was the slogan. Writers, intellectuals and students were exhorted to speak their minds even to the detriment of the authorities. The outpouring of criticism of leaders, policy and doctrine that ensued may have surprised Mao, or perhaps his intent was to lure doubters into the open. Whatever the original motive, after little more than a month, he had had enough. The "flowers" were abruptly cropped in an "anti-rightist campaign" orchestrated by Deng that destroyed hundreds of thousands of lives.[19]

Great numbers of intellectuals were sent to labor camps or to the countryside to be reeducated at the foot of the peasantry. The latter refinement would be employed more widely a decade later in the Cultural Revolution, in which Deng was to suffer. Ironically, it was he who thought up the method, with Mao's enthusiastic approval.[20]

Later that year, with Deng's assistance, Mao began to concoct one of the zanier campaigns of his rule. The purpose of the "Great Leap Forward" was to gather all of China's hundreds of millions of peasants into vast "people's communes," which could combine industry with farming. Mao convinced himself that this system would yield great increases in productivity, thus accelerating China's development and enabling it to overtake the West in the foreseeable future. Some of the comrades had their doubts, but not Deng. "Among the top party leaders, Deng was the most conspicuous in siding with Mao," says Yang.[21]

The whole scheme was symbolized by "backyard steel mills," since the communes were encouraged to produce this ultimate symbol of industrial prowess. Salisbury describes the result:

> By the autumn of 1958, ninety million Chinese peasants had abandoned farm work for dawn-to-dusk (or late-night) labor at ramshackle smelters set up in each commune. The peasants had no ore or pig iron to feed into the smelters. Into the smelting pots instead went every piece of iron or steel they could lay hands on—picks, shovels, hoes, rakes, axes, hammers, pitchforks, crowbars, soup pots, wagon hubs, water buckets, pipes, all the iron on the farm. Galvanized iron roofs, nails, bolts, hinges, barbed wire, locks, angle irons, even small tractors were thrown in. The country looked as though it had been picked clean by iron-eating ants.[22]

Needless to say, the steel produced in this manner was virtually useless, while the loss of tools and the diversion of labor caused a famine that came to be known as the "three bitter years." Western Sinologists estimate variously that

20, 25 or 30 million people perished.[†] The only member of the leadership who dared to criticize Mao over the debacle was purged. Nonetheless, Mao gave up his government title, retaining his positions as chairman of the party and of the military commission. Steering the country to recovery was entrusted to Liu Shaoqi and Deng.

Until then, Deng had been a fervent yes-man to Mao, but his new responsibility marked the beginning of an ominous change in their relationship. He and Liu soon recognized that one key to restoring agricultural output would be the so-called "responsibility system." This was code for a partial undoing of communization. It entailed giving small work teams or individual households plots of land to farm on their own with the freedom to dispose of the produce after delivering a share or a tax to the state. It was in justifying this approach in a 1962 speech that Deng first gave voice to the metaphor that later became his trademark. He said:

> New conditions have appeared in the villages. I believe that altogether the various types of household contracts now make up more than twenty percent of the villages in agriculture. In deciding on the best production system we might have to embrace the attitude of adopting whichever method develops agricultural production most easily and rapidly and whichever method the masses desire most. We must make the illegal legal. To quote an old saying from Sichuan province..."It doesn't matter if the cat is yellow or black as long as it catches the mouse."[23]

Although Mao had yielded formal authority, he resented deviations from his policies. He had already begun criticizing "household responsibility," and the very same day that Deng made this speech, Mao announced that his own research had convinced him that the peasants preferred communal farming. A worried Deng tried to get the record of his remarks revised to eliminate the conflict with Mao. But the idea had now been planted that the faithful golden boy might be capable of straying. This germ was to bear bitter fruit a few years later during the Cultural Revolution.

•   •   •

---

† Chen Yizi, the former director of the official Institute for the Reform of the Economic Structure, who fled China after the 1989 Tiananmen Square massacre, told me in 1991 that he had been commissioned by party officials to conduct a secret study which concluded that the death toll of this man-made tragedy had reached fifty million.

The Cultural Revolution had no formal beginning or end. Its purpose was to restore revolutionary spirit and discredit the pragmatic approach that had led the government to pull back from some of Mao's pet policies. Mao's authority was reasserted by mass displays of veneration and by the destruction of much of the established party leadership which had come to distrust his judgment.

Students were exhorted to scrutinize teachers, neighbors and other adults for any sign of "bourgeois deviationism"—an indiscreet remark, a faulty background or an inappropriate possession, perhaps a book or a drawing. Those who fell afoul were "struggled against," hauled before jeering crowds to be denounced, humiliated, beaten and tortured. After a while the schools were closed, and the youngsters organized into companies of "Red Guards" who were given free rail transport to roam the country ferreting out any derogation from Maoist purity. No one knows how many millions were killed or driven to suicide by them, but years later when interviewer Oriana Fallaci commented to Deng that Stalin had taken more lives than the Cultural Revolution, he replied: "I am not sure about that. Not sure at all."[24]

Although it appeared spontaneous, much of the mayhem was orchestrated by a group close to Mao. The mobs generally acted with implicit official sanction, and many of their victims were arrested. Mao observed slyly in a letter to Jiang Qing, his third wife: "great disorder across the land leads to great order."[25] Jiang was a shrill, vindictive woman who took control over cultural affairs, insisting that all forms of art must serve as revolutionary propaganda. She was one of those whose influence rose as the old cadres were knocked down. Another was Defense Minister Lin Biao. He had been promoted to the Politburo in 1955 along with Deng Xiaoping, and he may have set his sights on supplanting Deng as Mao's favorite. Around the same time that Deng ruffled the chairman by endorsing the "household responsibility" system, Lin ingratiatingly compiled various Mao quotes into the *Little Red Book*, which he ordered distributed to all members of the armed forces. It became the bible of the Red Guards.

One after another, the men who had fought side by side with Mao to bring communism to China were denounced. None had the courage or decency to speak up in defense of any other. Each joined in the denunciations, hoping to spare his own skin. Only Zhou Enlai managed to succeed at this strategy.

The head of state, Liu Shaoqi, whose book *How to Be a Communist* was the best seller in the history of Communist China before the *Little Red Book* appeared, was declared to be China's leading advocate of the "capitalist road." He was subjected to repeated beatings and tortures, which culminated in his death. Anticipating the outcome, Liu asked his wife and children to "spread my ashes in the sea as was done for Engels," but the authorities refused to turn over his remains.[26]

Deng was denounced as the number two "capitalist roader" but was spared the worst. He was not even expelled from the party, perhaps because Mao anticipated that he might someday use Deng again. He was arrested late in 1966 and kept in prison, apparently most of the time in solitary confinement, until October 1969. At times he was dragged before mobs for abuse and ridicule, driven through the streets in a dunce cap, but he was not seriously injured. Other members of his family suffered worse on his behalf. His youngest brother, Deng Shuping, was driven to suicide — a common fate of those "struggled against." Deng's oldest son, Deng Pufang, hurtled from a fourth-story window at the conclusion of a long beating on the campus of Beijing University. He could not recall whether he had jumped or been thrown, but he was permanently paralyzed.

Released from prison, Deng Xiaoping was banished to a remote village in Jiangxi province. For the next three years he and his wife worked in a tractor factory while living under a form of house arrest. As the Cultural Revolution lost steam, Deng wrote two letters to Mao abasing himself, renouncing his black cat/yellow cat metaphor, and begging to be allowed to return to official work. On Mao's decision, a Central Committee resolution in March 1973 restored Deng to the leadership, almost as if nothing had happened. In the blink of an eye the notorious "capitalist roader" was named first vice premier, vice chairman of the party, and chief of staff of the armed forces.

Mao's motives in this remain somewhat obscure. The fall of Defense Minister Lin Biao, who died in a mysterious plane crash in Mongolia in 1971, may have aroused anxieties about the allegiance of the army. As Red Guards had rampaged out of control, troops had been called upon in many locales to restore order. The result was a marked shift in power toward the People's Liberation Army, which had been shielded from the brunt of the Cultural Revolution. "Regional military commanders had displayed an alarming tendency to defy Beijing's political authority," writes Sinologist Richard Baum. "Visibly concerned, Mao, [Defense Minister] Ye [Jianying], and Zhou agreed that Deng Xiaoping's prestige and influence among senior army leaders could prove useful in counteracting regional PLA defiance."[27]

Deng's rehabilitation did not assure him smooth sailing. Mao liked to keep his underlings at odds with one another. Toward that end, he maintained a balance between the remnant of the old cadres led by Zhou and Marshal Ye, now joined by Deng, and the radicals led by his wife Jiang Qing and three others, dubbed the Gang of Four. The two camps battled over power and policy.

The conflict came to a head in 1976, following Zhou's death. Deng's wings had been clipped by Mao for advocating that the "verdicts" of the Cultural Revolution against many old cadres be reversed. Then on Qing Ming, a holiday of homage to the dead, Tiananmen Square witnessed a great display of mourning for Zhou, culminating the next day in a riot. It was apparent that this was in a sense a demonstration against the Cultural Revolution. "As much as for Zhou Enlai, the people seemed to be grieving for themselves and their country," observes Baum.[28] Deng was accused of having orchestrated the outpouring, and once again he was denounced and purged. Marshal Ye, however, knowing that Mao was near death, conspired with other senior commanders to shelter Deng from the radicals.

When Mao died of Lou Gehrig's disease later that year, the leaders made plans to encase his body in clear crystal for permanent veneration. Mao had led the Communists to power. Thanks to him, China's long ordeal of national humiliation had been brought to an end. The PRC was strong enough to frighten even the superpowers, and it was admired as an example by developing countries like Nyerere's Tanzania. Indeed, all around the world, radicals who viewed the Soviet model as having gone stale turned their eyes to the "red sun in the East" where revolutionary zeal still glowed hot.

But Ye and others in the inner circle knew things about Mao that had been hidden from the eyes of foreign admirers. While the citizenry was required to live in abstemious devotion to the socialist future, denied even such indulgence as colored clothing or the free choice of a mate, Mao had enjoyed a life of exemplary hedonism. He had taken up residence in a magnificent palace which had been named by the Qing emperor who built it the Hall of Respect for Elegance.[29] It was located in the central Beijing compound of Zhongnanhai, "a hidden fairyland of lakes and parks and palaces where Marco Polo strolled and Kublai Khan built his pleasure domes," in Harrison Salisbury's description.[30]

As a voluptuary, Mao outdid the former denizens. He supped on delicacies like bear paw and enjoyed the ministrations of a harem of young women, often in their teens, who serviced him singly and in groups. Special guesthouses were reserved for him in other major cities on the chance that he might visit, each furnished with a swimming pool and a harem, so that he might enjoy his two principal recreations. Girls (and occasional boys) in whatever numbers apparently did not suffice, so he had his aides assemble a private library of erotica, surpassing that of any emperor.[31]

Many of his top comrades were scandalized by these goings-on, but none dared utter a reproach. Most of the hierarchy had suffered punishments and demotions at his hands for offenses far smaller than questioning his lifestyle. Now that he was gone, the Communist hierarchs wanted a leader who would preserve Mao's political legacy, which was the basis of their legitimacy, without the megalomania. No one fit the bill better than Deng. He had been through all the struggles: a large share of the republic's military commanders had served under him during the wars against the Japanese and the Nationalists. And yet he had adopted the moniker Xiaoping, which means "plain and small." What a welcome contrast to the overbearing former chairman!

Deng, however, languished in political purgatory, and Mao had designated Hua Guofeng, an obscure regional leader identified neither with the old cadres nor with the Gang of Four, as his successor. Hua evidently recognized that he lacked the weight to perpetuate Mao's balancing act, so he made the only sensible decision, which was to throw in with the old guard against the far more dangerous radicals. The night of October 6, 1976, exactly four weeks after Mao's passing, Hua convened a meeting of the top leaders in Zhongnanhai. Its announced purpose was to discuss the release of a posthumous edition of Mao's works; but the meeting was a trap. As each member of the Gang of Four arrived, carefully screened soldiers emerged from an adjacent room and took him into custody. When the most fearsome of the four, Mao's widow Jiang Qing, failed to appear, a squadron was sent to her home to complete the roundup.

These events were not announced, but as the news leaked out, the response was like when Oz had learned that the wicked witch was dead. The university quarter sold out of alcoholic beverages in the rejoicing.[32] The arrests signified the end of the Cultural Revolution's reign of terror.

In a series of meetings throughout the late 1970s, a widening circle of victims of the Cultural Revolution and other purges were rehabilitated. The action against Liu Shaoqi was officially proclaimed to have been the "biggest frame-up our party has ever known."[33] This was cold comfort since he was already dead. But others, like Deng, who was recalled to office, were very much alive. With the Gang of Four defeated and reviled, the tide of "reversing the verdicts" ran strong. Hua could not oppose it, but each reversal swelled the ranks of the so-called rehabilitated cadres faction, of which Deng was the recognized leader. Gradually Deng's position grew so strong as to allow him an effortless check-mate, and Hua yielded power peacefully.

• • •

The party's 1978 plenum endorsed Deng's program of "four modernizations"— of industry, agriculture, the military and science. Why such a "second revolu-tion," as it was called, would be necessary was inexplicable in Marxist theory; but the stark fact was that nearly thirty years after communism had "liberated" the common man, the average Chinese survived on about one dollar a day. The twin pillars of Deng's program were economic liberalization and openness to the outside. The most consequential agricultural reform was the promotion of the "household responsibility" system. Years before, when he attempted to engineer a recovery from the Great Leap Forward, Deng had become persuaded of its superiority over communal farming. Mao had forced him to abandon it, but Deng had not changed his opinion.

Although he set a direction, Deng had no master plan. Instead, with his approval, the initiative fell to some local leaders. In Anhui province, peasants had nicknamed the private plots they were allowed to farm after the Great Leap "life-saving land."[34] The memory had remained, and with cover from a reform-minded provincial chief, Wan Li, various little groups decided to try it again. In view of previous crackdowns, this experiment took courage. Sinologist Joseph Fewsmith reports that "When peasants and cadres in the extremely poor Xiaogang Production Brigade . . . decided to put the household responsibility system into effect in the spring of 1978, they first convened and swore an oath of loyalty in which the eighteen households in the community vowed to take care of the dependents of any production team cadres who were arrested for allowing the household responsibility system to go into effect."[35]

This time no one was arrested, and within about a year Anhui began to report impressive improvements in output. So did Sichuan, which undertook similar policies under the aegis of Zhao Ziyang, then the province's party secretary. In 1979, researchers in a government-sponsored study reported that peasants told them, "If you want rapid [development], mass action will not work. If the household responsibility system is adopted, 80 percent will become wealthy."[36] Soon, central government policy shifted from tolerating to encouraging household responsibility. In 1980, Zhao Ziyang and Wan Li, its two local patrons, were both named vice premiers of the State Council. In addition,

Wan Li, who derided the communes as "labor camps," was appointed head of the State Agriculture Commission.[37]

In January 1982, the party officially proclaimed the household responsibility system to be a legitimate form of "socialist" enterprise.[38] By then, an estimated 45 percent of production brigades had adopted it, and following this declaration the number jumped to 72 percent. Communal farming—which Mao, like Stalin, had killed millions to impose—melted away almost overnight.

The new openness toward the capitalist world was heralded on December 19, 1978, when Boeing announced Beijing's purchase of three 747 jetliners and Coca-Cola unveiled a deal to build a bottling plant in Shanghai. The next month Deng paid the first visit by a ruler of the People's Republic to the United States. He toured assembly lines, laid a wreath on Martin Luther King's grave, and took the controls of a space ship on a simulated mission. In Seattle he got a taste of American free speech: he was greeted with protests not only by supporters of Taiwan but also by a group of thirty American Maoists who staged a "Little Red Book March" through the university district, chanting "death to Deng" and "Long Live Mao Tsetung."[39] In Houston he was feted with a barbecue and a rodeo, where he posed in a ten-gallon hat, and aides confided that he was a fan of western movies. He told a luncheon audience that he had come "to learn from the American people, creators of an advanced civilization."[40]

Deng had been impressed by the remarkable performance of the so-called "little tigers" of East Asia. Their export-led growth was changing international thinking about economic development, undercutting the popularity of Third World socialism. Since three of the four tigers were populated by Chinese, he found their example especially compelling. In 1979, Deng decided to launch a similar experiment, designating four coastal areas as "special zones for export." The name was soon changed to "special economic zones," and the number of them was substantially increased in ensuing years. Tax and other incentives were offered to encourage international capital to develop these areas. Deng said he hoped they would catch up with the four tigers.

By the mid-1980s, the focus of economic reforms turned from agriculture to industry. As peasants prospered farming their own plots, many of them saved enough capital to launch little businesses. In addition to myriad household trades, a number bought surplus trucks from the military and offered shipping services. With government encouragement, the tally of officially registered household enterprises reached 11.7 million by 1985.[41] Larger industry remained state-owned, but the government began to devolve authority to enterprise managers. State companies were allowed to keep half of their after-tax profits, which could be used for bonuses. They also were given permission to fire unproductive employees, and they were increasingly exposed to market pressures.

These operational reforms were accompanied by a major shift in the message that the regime conveyed to the public. "To get rich is glorious" became an official slogan. A Shanghai newspaper published the inspirational story of a group of poor spinsters who prospered through the household responsibility system, with the result that they found themselves awash in suitors.[42]

Deng's goal in fostering these changes remained what it had been when he left for France as a sixteen-year-old: to make China rich and strong. He did not wish to abandon socialism but rather to build "socialism with Chinese characteristics." As he explained, "after years of practice it turned out that the old stuff didn't work."[43] He told the party Central Committee, "we can hardly convince the masses of the advantages of socialism if its productivity is always lower than that of capitalism."[44]

All his life, Deng had been a doer, not a theoretician. He boasted of never having read *Das Kapital*. Now he directed China's "theoretical workers," that is, its academicians, to validate the Marxian pedigree of his policies.[45] But obliquely, he confessed the hopelessness of the task. "Marx sits up in heaven," said the hard-of-hearing Deng. "He sees what we are doing, and he doesn't like it. So he has punished me by making me deaf."[46]

During the Cultural Revolution, when Mao had accused such lifelong Communists as Deng and Liu Shaoqi of being "capitalist roaders," the charge had all the antic absurdity of Stalin's claim that his Bolshevik rivals were "Trotskyite-Hitlerite wreckers." And yet in his own mad way, Mao was on to something. It turned out that the household responsibility system—the proximate spur of Mao's wrath—did indeed put China on the road to capitalism.

The results were astounding. China's annual economic growth rate rocketed to a level of 12 or 13 percent and remained there for more than a decade. Nothing in world history could compare—except the four tigers. In the wake of the bitter upheavals of the Cultural Revolution, the Communist Party's legitimacy came to rest, ironically, on its success in bringing the Chinese people the fruits of capitalism.

Implicitly this raised the question of whether China needed Communist rule at all. The party's monopoly of power had been justified on the grounds that it constituted the "dictatorship of the proletariat." The "bourgeoisie" had to be repressed lest it prevent the people from reaping the benefits of socialism. But now the public was being encouraged to pursue riches, and the regime was exerting itself to lure foreign capitalists to China. Who, then, was to be repressed, and why?

The dizzying transformation of the economy inevitably generated pressure for political liberalization. Under Mao, the entire nation had been compelled to live like members of a cult. The most personal acts required official sanction. Everyone wore Mao suits and joined in tireless displays of veneration. Suddenly all this was out the window. Chinese were free to dress themselves, to find their own jobs, to open shops, to pursue hobbies and cultural interests (although not to procreate). These freedoms of expression only whetted the appetite for more. A further impetus was given by the leadership's own description of the Cultural Revolution as "an appalling catastrophe" and a "decade of suppression, tyranny, and bloodshed."[47] If suppression was bad, then implicitly its opposite—freedom—must be good.

Early in the reform period, Deng seemed alive to such considerations. Freer airing of public opinion served his interest as he struggled to subdue more conservative forces. In 1978 the constitution was amended to protect the people's right to put up "big character posters," which attracted large crowds of readers along what came to be called "Democracy Wall" in central Beijing. And they inspired other forms of expression. Independent journals begin to spring up. Tiananmen Square became a gathering place for spontaneous debate like London's Hyde Park. The topics included long-forbidden ideas and diverse individual grievances. In renouncing the Cultural Revolution, the authorities had promised to redress injuries. But so many had suffered that there was no possibility of making good on this. Some of the disappointed grew so bold as to stage protest demonstrations.

By March 1979, Deng had had enough. Like Mao and his "hundred flowers," Deng wanted to give the people the freedom to say things he wanted to hear. Instead, he found he had opened the floodgates to a torrent of criticism that spared neither Mao nor himself. He responded by affirming "four cardinal principles": socialism, the dictatorship of the proletariat, leadership by the party, and Marxism-Leninism-Mao Zedong thought. A decree threatened punishment for any opposition to these orthodox tenets. The police had already begun arresting Democracy Wall activists. Deng's most caustic critic, Wei Jingsheng, was sentenced to fifteen years.

In 1980 the constitution was amended to delete the "four bigs" of 1978, which had legalized big character posters and enshrined other aspects of free speech. The restrictive mood of the leadership in 1980 was reinforced by the terrifying example of the rise of Solidarity in Poland. Party officials unfurled the slogan "oppose bourgeois liberalization." When some anti-regime candidates won experimental contested elections for low-level office, the results were disallowed.

Repression proceeded in tandem with continuing economic liberalization. This dichotomy was the hallmark of Deng's rule. He managed to create an increasingly free economy within an unfree political system, although the two were in constant tension. Economic modernization required computers, fax machines, cell phones and the like, which made it hard for the government to control the flow of information and ideas. It also required interaction with free countries, especially America, which set an example of democracy and criticized violations of human rights. Foreign investors wanted assurances that Chinese courts would enforce the laws fairly and that information relevant to their businesses would be available. In response to the tension, the regime oscillated. After an episode of repression, it would loosen its grip in order to keep the economy rolling. The relaxation would bring forth new expressions of independent thought from elements of the public, and this would touch off another round of repression.

For example, the emergence of an innovative school of "Marxist humanism" in 1983 was followed by a crackdown against "spiritual pollution." In 1986, student demonstrations in Shanghai and Beijing led to the dismissal of the party's secretary general, Hu Yaobang, an advocate of political liberalization who was accused of sympathizing with the protesters.

Hu was replaced by Zhao Ziyang, Deng's other principal disciple. Zhao, the innovator from Sichuan, was more of an economic than a political reformer. But perhaps influenced by the younger intellectuals with whom he surrounded himself, Zhao perpetuated the liberal tone that Hu had set. One visible indicator was the removal of the outsize portraits of Marx, Engels, Lenin and Stalin from Tiananmen Square. Emboldened, various intellectuals began to issue open appeals for human rights.

Once again a period of leniency gave rise to popular demands for greater freedom. The sudden death of Hu, who collapsed at a party meeting in April 1989, touched off demonstrations that spilled out from the campuses to Tiananmen Square and then to cities outside Beijing. The students mourned Hu as a champion of their freedoms, much as demonstrators in Tiananmen had mourned Zhou Enlai in 1976. Then, Deng had been blamed for instigating the protests; now it was he who ordered a harsh response to them.

The students were not easy to deal with, and their banners were sometimes cruel. "Those who should die haven't; those who shouldn't, have," read one. Sometimes they were mocking, calling on the people, tongue in cheek, to support the party's correct leadership. They had no clear lines of organization nor consistent demands. What they did have was an immense reservoir of support among an urban populace that yearned for greater freedom and a more responsive government.

The ranks of the protestors swelled over the course of a month to include not only an apparent majority of college students but also large numbers of workers and professionals. When martial law was declared, the citizenry of Beijing seemed to rally as one to protect the students and prevent the soldiers from reaching them. The sympathizers included party cadres all the way up the ranks to General Secretary Zhao, who sacrificed his position and even his freedom in opposing the use of force against the demonstrators. But Deng was unyielding. "Concessions in Poland led to further concessions," he said.[48] In a speech to the Politburo he exhorted his comrades not to be afraid of three things: foreign pressure, domestic opinion and the shedding of blood.[49]

Once the throng of foreign reporters that had covered his summit with Gorbachev had dissipated and military units of undoubted reliability were in place, Deng gave the word for the troops to clear the square. Many hundreds, more likely thousands, were mowed down; but since the killing took place off the square and in surrounding neighborhoods, no solid estimates exist.

Zhao was placed under house arrest, and some of his liberal advisers, as well as some of the student activists, were imprisoned or fled abroad. Leaders of worker groups that had joined the protests did not get off so lightly. They were mostly shot, although again no one knows how many. Zhao was replaced by Jiang Zemin, the Shanghai party chief who mirrored Deng's combination of economic liberalism and political conservatism. Together with Premier Li Peng, they struck an unapologetic pose. In the ensuing months, as Communist regimes crumbled across Eastern Europe, they claimed vindication. Jiang blamed Gorbachev, likening him to the traitor Trotsky.[50]

So deep ran the abhorrence of the bloodshed among the party's rank and file, not to mention among the general citizenry of Beijing, that a "rectification campaign" designed to root out protest sympathizers proved an embarrassing flop. Within the party hierarchy, however, it was a different story. In purging the party's liberals, Hu and Zhao and their supporters, Deng mortgaged himself to conservatives. As a result, he was forced to retreat on economic policy during the years following the massacre.

It was not until 1992 that he could get economic liberalization back on track, and it took his last strength. At eighty-eight, sometimes requiring assistance in walking and in communicating as his speech had grown slurred, Deng took off on a tour of the Special Economic Zones. He praised their progress and urged that reform move forward boldly, not like "women with bound feet." In a notable change of line, he called the Left (those opposed to reform) a greater threat than the Right (those who wanted reform in the political realm, too).

Party conservatives† resisted, and at first the controlled press did not even report his tour. But Deng fought back hard, bluntly warning his comrades that the party's grip on power depended on economic performance. "Had it not been for the fruits of reform . . . we would not have been able to pass the test of June 4 [the Tiananmen massacre]," he told them.[51] He bludgeoned Jiang into line and rallied other supporters to the fight. In a contentious debate, one of them, Vice Premier Tian Jiyun, ridiculed reform opponents. In contrast to Deng's Special Economic Zones, he proposed the creation of Special Leftist Zones:

> Let us carve out a piece of land where policies favored by the Leftists will be practiced. For example, no foreign investment will be allowed there, and all foreigners will be kept out. Inhabitants of the zone can neither go abroad nor send their children overseas. There will be total state planning. Essential supplies will be rationed and citizens of the zone will have to queue up for food and other consumer products.[52]

In the end, the conservatives were routed. The next year, the National People's Congress enshrined the phrase "socialist market economy" in the constitution. Overall direction of the economy was taken from the relatively conservative Li Peng and placed in the hands of Zhu Rongji, the former mayor of Shanghai who had a reputation as a strong supporter of reform.

It is said that Deng's daughter, Deng Maomao, and others close to him had encouraged the 1992 tour of the Special Economic Zones out of concern for his legacy. Just as Deng himself had campaigned for reversing the verdicts of

---

† The terminology can be confusing to Americans, but since the status quo of the PRC was very far to the Left, the terms "Leftist" and "conservative" are usually treated as synonyms, and the same is true for "Rightist" and "liberal."

the Cultural Revolution and the 1976 Tiananmen Square demonstrations, they were haunted by the prospect of a future reversal of the official assessment of the 1989 demonstrations. Would Deng be remembered as the author of China's prosperity or as the "butcher of Beijing"?

Deng himself showed no such cares. "Properly draw the lesson from the former Soviet Union," he exhorted his comrades in his last message before going to his grave at age ninety-two. "The [Chinese Communist Party's] status as the ruling party must never be challenged."[53] By then, the anticommunist workers' leader, Lech Walesa, was ruling Poland, and the members of the for-mer Politburo were scrambling to avoid being put on trial. The story was much the same in Czechoslovakia, Hungary, Bulgaria and the rest. The Soviet Union itself, where Deng had spent that inspiring year when he was twenty-two, was no more. The worst story was in Romania, where President Nicolae Ceauşescu, together with his wife, had been gunned down like a dog by a kangaroo court. Deng gathered some top colleagues to watch tapes of the executions culled from Western news broadcasts.[54]

It was the independent-minded Ceauşescu who had brokered Deng's historic 1989 summit with Gorbachev, which turned into such a fiasco. Deng surely wished to warn Gorbachev off the dangerous course he was on, but with the streets outside their meeting aswarm with students lionizing Gorbachev, he must have been too embarrassed to do so. Gorbachev, naturally, was impressed by the demonstrators. He later noted that the "tens if not hundreds of thou-sands of Beijing's residents [who] came out to see us off . . . were by no means stooges."[55] His two hours with Deng were correct but cool. It was with the soon-to-be-purged Zhao Ziyang that he really hit it off. "The whole conversa-tion proceeded in a spirit of goodwill and mutual understanding," he said, for the two of them were wrestling with similar concerns:

> Zhao Ziyang posed a seemingly rhetorical question, stressing that we all had to answer it together: "Can a one-party system ensure the development of democracy? Can it implement effective control over negative phenomena and fight the corruption in Party and government institutions?" In this question I read all my own doubts.[56]

Gorbachev had more reason than Deng to be appalled by the breakup of the U.S.S.R., for it had cost him his power. But however much he rued the outcome, he did not regret having embarked on the course that had led to it, for he had no second thoughts about his judgment that the system he had inherited was deeply rotten. It does not appear that he harbored such a view at the time of his selection as general secretary in 1985. Certainly none of the men who chose him suspected it, nor was there anything in his background to foreshadow it.

• • •

Mikhail Gorbachev was born in the tiny village of Privolnoye, in the district of Stavropol in the northern Caucasus, the relatively warm, fertile land bridge bordered on the east by the Caspian Sea and on the west by the Black Sea and the Asov Sea. "Privolnoye would be twenty-four hours by train from Moscow," observes Gail Sheehy, one of Gorbachev's many biographers, "but . . . there is no train."[57]

Gorbachev's father, Sergei, had grown up in Privolnoye and married the girl next door, Maria Panteleyevna Gopkalo. Both had descended at least in part from Ukrainian ancestors who were part of the eastward Cossack migration a century before. They were simple farmers, and Maria was illiterate. On March 2, 1931, she bore a son whom they named Viktor, and for sixteen years they had no other children. Such infertility was unusual among peasant families, but these were unusual times.

The following years, 1932 and 1933, were the height of what Robert Conquest calls the "terror-famine" visited upon rural Russia, Ukraine and Kazakhstan by Stalin. With the New Economic Policy (NEP) of 1920, Lenin had ordered a tactical retreat in the Bolsheviks' war against the peasantry, but now his successor had renewed the offensive, determined to carry it through no matter what the cost. Mass starvation—effectuated by depriving the growers of seed and fertilizer and by confiscating at gunpoint whatever they grew—was used to eradicate the last traces of resistance. The survivors were reduced to automatons, part of the machinery of the collective farms. Gorbachev recounts that "a third, if not half, of the population of Privolnoye died of hunger. Entire families were dying, and the half-ruined ownerless huts would remain deserted for years."[58] Three of his father's five siblings were among those who perished.

Sergei's parents did not take readily to Bolshevization. Having worked their way up from the category of "poor peasants" to "middle peasants," they continued to farm their own plot for as long as they could, rather than join a collective. They took their infant grandson to the local church for baptism, and in this rite the birth name, Viktor, was superceded by the Christian name, Mikhail. The child's maternal grandmother, Vasilisa, was also devout and reportedly a party to the baptism. Her husband, Pantelei Gopkalo, was a nonbeliever, but the couple was tolerant of one another, and her icons shared space on their mantel with his portraits of Lenin and Stalin.

In contrast to Mikhail's paternal grandparents, Gopkalo embraced the new regime wholeheartedly and hastened to become a founder of the local collective. Ironically, the dutiful grandfather fared no better than the recalcitrant grandfather when Stalin unleashed his vast purges, and both men were arrested. Andrei Gorbachev, Sergei's father, was charged in 1933 with having failed to "fulfill the plan," that is, to deliver sufficient grain to the state, notwithstanding that he had been given no seed and three of his children had starved to death. Pantelei Gopkalo was charged in 1937 with being a member of a "counter revolutionary right-wing Trotskyist organization." Gorbachev, who was then six and lived most of the time with the Gopkalos, recalled: "They took him away in the middle of the night. . . . [N]eighbors began shunning our house as if it were plague-stricken. Only at night would some close relative venture to drop by. Even the boys from the neighborhood avoided me."[59]

Mercifully, both grandfathers survived and, under circumstances that remain murky, were permitted to return to their homes within a year or two. Mikhail remembered his grandfather Gopkalo's first night back. With a few close relatives gathered around his table, he described his ordeal, and then never spoke of it again. This is what the seven-year-old boy recalled:

> Trying to get him to confess, the investigator blinded him with a glaring lamp, beat him unmercifully, broke his arms by squeezing them in the door. When these "standard" tortures proved futile, they invented a new one: they put a wet sheepskin coat on him and sat him on a hot stove. [He] endured this, too, as well as much else.[60]

There is an old Russian saying, "if only the tsar knew," used to explain away the abuses by local officials that the subjects were sure their benevolent sovereign would not tolerate. It was in just this spirit that Gopkalo responded to his own suffering. "He was convinced that Stalin did not know about the misdeeds of the NKVD and he never blamed the Soviet regime for his misfortunes."[61] Soon he was reelected chairman of the collective. Even the once independent paternal grandfather fell in with the system after his return from the gulag. He "joined the kolkhoz [collective] immediately" and "soon he was managing the kolkhoz pig farm."[62]

Mikhail's reaction seems to have been little different. At age fourteen, almost as soon as he was eligible, he joined the Komsomol, the party youth organization, and began his long ascent into the establishment. Far from exhibiting any dissident sentiments, young Gorbachev comes across as suffocatingly earnest. No doubt this had much to do with the war. Mikhail had been ten when Hitler betrayed his partnership with Stalin and invaded the U.S.S.R. Mikhail's father, Sergei, was called to the front almost at once. In 1942, an emergency decree lowered the working age for rural children from sixteen to twelve. "I had to take care of a multitude of household chores," recalled Gorbachev. "Our way of life had changed completely. And we, the wartime children, skipped from childhood directly into adulthood."[63]

At war's end, Sergei returned home and Mikhail was able to resume his education with a new dedication. The final examination was an essay on the theme "Stalin: our combat glory; Stalin: the elation of our youth." Mikhail's essay received the highest grade and was held up as an example to subsequent classes.

Nor was this his only distinction. When school was not in session, Mikhail worked with his father on the kolkhoz. In 1948 the Gorbachevs paired with another father-and-son team to accomplish a prodigy of socialist labor. Working up to twenty hours a day, they managed to produce a grain harvest five to six times the average. For their achievement the fathers each received the Order of Lenin while the two youngsters got the Order of the Red Banner of Labor.

Gorbachev later said that he was prouder of this medal than any of the others he received in his illustrious career. It also brought practical benefits, for it became his ticket out of Privolnoye. Combined with his top grades, his status as a "worker or peasant," and the fact that he was already a candidate member of the party, the Red Banner of Labor won him a place in the prestigious Moscow State University.

Despite the university's eminence, living conditions were spartan. Four to six students shared a room, while a single bathroom served a whole corridor. But Gorbachev thrilled to his intellectual surroundings. The lectures of famous scientists and academicians, he said, "revealed a new world, entire strata of human knowledge hitherto unknown to me."[64] Compared with his fellows, most of whom came from Moscow or Leningrad, he appeared something of the country bumpkin, an image reinforced by the frequency with which his chest sported the Red Banner of Labor medal. But he strove to remedy his cultural deficiencies by taking in plays, exhibitions, concerts and recitals. More than one female student was willing to assist in his instruction. He was then thin, mustachioed and handsome.

One in particular stood out, a beauty named Raisa Titorenko. She, too, was of Ukrainian extraction, although also apparently one-quarter Jewish.[65] She, too, had had a grandfather taken in the purges, although unlike Mikhail's, hers never returned.[†] And she, too, was of humble origins, the daughter of a railway engineer from Siberia. Her drive to transcend that modest background was even stronger than his. Where he had won a silver medal for high school studies, she had taken a gold. She majored in philosophy, in which she later earned a doctorate, and she learned to read English in order to expand her literary horizons. After a courtship consisting of many long walks, they wed in the unsentimental, atheist ceremony considered proper for Communists. His roommates cleared out so the newlyweds could spend a night together before resuming their lives in separate dorms until a room for married students became available.

Gorbachev chose law as his major, an unusual choice in a country ruled mainly by dictate. More important to his political prospects was activity in the university branch of the Komsomol, and in his fourth year (out of a standard five) he was appointed its chief. Along the way he also became a full member of the party. Yet his conformism does not seem to have been tainted with cynicism. Classmates have recounted several incidents that show the young man to have had both spine and principle. When one professor devoted class after class to reading aloud from a recent book of Stalin's, Gorbachev and a fellow student slipped a note onto his lectern pointing out that *"this is a university, and they admit . . . people who can read by themselves."*[66] When confronted, Gorbachev owned up to being the author. In another story, he rushed to the defense of a Jewish friend who was being subjected to anti-Semitic taunts at the time when Stalin's discovery of a fictitious "doctor's plot" had sounded the clarion for a campaign against Jews. And during a summer internship in a prosecutor's office near his home, he wrote to Raisa of his "disgust" with the behavior of local officials, including "their acceptance of convention" and "subordination." When you look at one of them, he said, "you see nothing outstanding apart from his belly."[67]

These anecdotes speak well of Gorbachev's character, but scarcely portray him as a freethinker. When Stalin died in 1953, Gorbachev recalls, he interrupted his studies and, on his own initiative, walked "for a day and a night" in an "endless, slow-moving line" to pay last respects to the tyrant.

---

† When he became president of the country, Gorbachev ordered up the secret police files on his and Raisa's grandfathers. Hers, he learned, had been "shot dead—for no reason other than that he was a kulak." Gorbachev, "The Legacy of a Monster That Refuses to Die," *Guardian* (London), 27 February 1993, p. 21.

Upon graduation in 1955, Gorbachev applied for a position in the office of the federal prosecutor, but he discovered that a recent secret decree closed such positions to new law graduates. With no other prospects in Moscow, he decided to return to Stavropol, the capital of the district by the same name. He and Raisa rented a tiny room without heating or interior plumbing. After ten unhappy days in the local prosecutor's office, he seized the offer of a position as deputy chief of agitation and propaganda for the regional Komsomol.

That year, 1956, the twentieth party congress was convened, at which Khrushchev delivered his epochal denunciation of Stalin's crimes and "cult of personality." After a copy was smuggled abroad, reportedly by Israeli intelligence, the text was published in the West. Within the U.S.S.R. it remained secret, circulated briefly within the party before being withdrawn. Because he was a party functionary, albeit of low rank, Gorbachev says he "managed to get my hands on it." It left him "shocked, bewildered and lost."[68] He knew of the persecutions from the experience of his own family, but he could no longer comfort himself with the belief that these were the fault of local officials who had gone astray. In his memoirs, Gorbachev comments that "those 'at the top' realized immediately . . . that to criticize Stalin was tantamount to criticizing the system as a whole."[69] But he makes no claim to having realized this himself. On the contrary, it seems that like most Communists he quickly absorbed the new catechism which said that the system was grand but unfortunately a maniac had seized the helm.

Over the next twenty years, Gorbachev ascended through the ranks of the Stavropol party. In 1958 he was named second secretary of the regional Komsomol. Three years later he rose to first secretary. That year, too, he was chosen for the first time as a delegate to a national party congress, the twenty-second, which was the high point of Khrushchev's rule. This time an array of party leaders joined in a fervent exposé of Stalin's crimes, and the former leader's corpse was removed from its pickle alongside Lenin's in the mausoleum and buried in the Kremlin wall. In addition, the congress adopted an economic plan designed to vindicate Khrushchev's famous "we will bury you" remark by surpassing the United States in per capita production within ten years.

The next year, 1962, Gorbachev got his first job in the adult party, as agriculture chief in the Stavropol region. With characteristic earnestness he enrolled in a correspondence course, and within a few years added a degree in agricultural science to the practical knowledge from his background on the kolkhoz. He won more promotions until in 1970 he became regional first secretary, a post that made him master of the fief at the unusually tender age of thirty-nine. He was marked as a comer, and the following year he took his first step up the national party ladder by being named a member of the Central Committee.

Stavropol was not an especially important outpost except in one respect: it is the site of many natural mineral springs. Russians believe strongly in the curative powers of these waters, and the party elite, whose lifestyle was none too healthy, came frequently for therapy. It was customary for the region's first secretary to greet the highest-ranking visitors, and not uncommon for him to ply them with gifts intended as quid pro quo. There is no hint of corruption in Gorbachev's record, but he exerted himself to assure the comfort of high-level guests. They all seem to have been impressed by his attentiveness as well as his élan. Fortuitously, two key figures in the hierarchy, Yuri Andropov, the KGB head who became ruler of the country in 1982, and Mikhail Suslov, the party's chief ideologist, both had roots in Stavropol. Although they were reportedly bitter rivals, each took a shine to Gorbachev.

His rising stature gave Gorbachev the opportunity to go abroad for the first time. In 1969, only months after the liberal "Prague Spring" had been snuffed out by Warsaw Pact military forces, he traveled to Czechoslovakia as a member of a Soviet delegation. Gorbachev's inclusion in the mission at this sensitive time shows that his superiors harbored no doubts about his ideological reliability. In the 1970s he got to visit France, Italy and the Low Countries, taking Raisa with him. What they saw made a mockery of the twenty-second party congress' plan to overtake the West by 1971. Although his political faith remained strong, a deeply subversive seed had been planted that was to blossom fatefully. "The question haunted me," he said, "why was the standard of living in our country lower than in other developed countries?"[70]

Aside from playing host to vacationing bigwigs, Gorbachev's responsibilities as regional boss focused largely on agriculture. Ever since Stalin won his war against the peasantry and forced the survivors onto collective farms, the country had been unable to feed itself. Gorbachev experimented with the use of incentives for individual production teams and with expanding the freedom for people to grow produce for sale on tiny private plots. But he did not make himself a champion of such liberal measures, and when the prevailing winds blew in a different direction, he bent with them. Thus, in 1977 his Stavropol predecessor, Fedor Kulakov, who had moved up to become Central Committee secretary for agriculture, sponsored a new harvesting scheme. It entailed the mobilization of vast amounts of equipment and manpower, much in the tradition of the grandiose methods that Stalin had favored. Gorbachev was chosen to implement it, and far from demurring, he embraced the assignment with enthusiasm. As with many such projects, the first results were encouraging because ideal conditions were selected and extraordinary resources were put at the project's disposal. But the method was counterproductive in regions where soil or climate conditions were less suitable, and while assets were concentrated in one area, crops rotted in others.

However, before the theory could prove its bankruptcy, Kulakov suddenly died, and Gorbachev was chosen to succeed him. After twenty-three years he was out of Stavropol and back in Moscow. Now he was truly a part of the national leadership. There were hundreds of members of the Central Committee but only nine secretaries, who together with the members of the Politburo constituted the ruling oligarchy. At age forty-seven Gorbachev was younger than any other member of this inner core. And having spent five years at university, not to mention his correspondence degree in agriculture, he was among the best educated.

Gorbachev was informed of his promotion a day in advance by General Secretary Leonid Brezhnev's trusty factotum, Konstantin Chernenko. "Leonid Ilyich assumes that you are on his side, that you are loyal to him," explained Chernenko.[71] Gorbachev says he was puzzled by the remark. "Did this imply that there was another side, and if so where was it, what was it like, and who was on [it]?" he wondered.[72]

The young leader from Stavropol may have been innocent of Kremlin intrigues, but Brezhnev had cause to assume that Gorbachev was a faithful follower. Earlier that year the first volume of Brezhnev's ghostwritten memoirs had appeared. They were as stolid as the man himself, offering up such profundities as: "we tend to underrate the importance of humor, yet a good joke often helps matters." Gorbachev not only ordered the mind-numbing work serialized in two regional newspapers in order "to meet the innumerable requests of the workers of Stavropol," as he put it; he added his own fawning gloss:

> In number of pages the book . . . is not very large, but in the depth of its ideological content, in the breadth of the author's generalizations and opinions it has become a great event in public life. . . . Communists and all the workers of Stavropol are boundlessly grateful to Leonid Il'ich Brezhnev for this truly party-spirited, literary work in which the sources of the great feat of our heroic nation, its spiritual and moral strength, its steadfastness and courage are depicted with deep philosophical penetration.[73]

Gorbachev may have been laying it on rather thick, but there is no reason to doubt that he admired Brezhnev.

This attitude was to change once Gorbachev got to work with the party chief up close. On his first day as secretary for agriculture, the eager beaver secured an appointment with Brezhnev to outline his ideas about agricultural policy. He was taken aback by the reception he received. "Not only did [Brezhnev] not take up the conversation, but he showed no response at all, neither to my words nor to myself. I had the impression that he was, at this moment, completely indifferent to my presence. The only sentence he uttered was: 'It's a pity about Kulakov, he was a good man.'"[74]

Brezhnev and the other aging oligarchs were content to enjoy their high offices, taking little interest in policy, and a go-getter like Gorbachev chafed under this regime. He found something of a kindred spirit, and a benefactor, in Yuri Andropov. The KGB chief was certainly no liberal, despite stories planted by his agents when he became general secretary, but with the wealth of information at his disposal he was more aware than others of the country's true condition. He also apparently was truly appalled by the corruption that suffused Brezhnev's inner circle. When a teary-eyed Soviet television anchorman announced Brezhnev's demise in 1982, Andropov had already elbowed aside the lackluster Chernenko as the successor.

While Andropov was prepared to face problems that Brezhnev preferred to ignore, he offered little in the way of solutions. He hoped to get the stagnant Soviet economy growing again by restoring labor discipline and cracking down on corruption. He did not seem to grasp that these were only symptoms, nor did he have much success at ameliorating them. Although he deplored the high national rate of alcoholism, he oversaw the introduction of a cheaper brand of vodka, which a grateful nation affectionately dubbed "Andropovka." A few months after taking power his kidneys failed, and he was reduced to the role of absentee ruler from his hospital room. Gorbachev acted as his liaison with the rest of the government and as unofficial deputy.

In early 1984, after barely fifteen months in office, Andropov breathed his last. Although Gorbachev was his preferred successor, the Kremlin's old guard, discomfited by Andropov's anticorruption measures, was wary of letting power pass to the relative newcomer. The same dynamism that appealed to Andropov struck them as a force to be distrusted. Rather than face such a risk, they closed ranks behind Chernenko.

But Chernenko, they all knew, had always been a nonentity, and he, too, was now on his last legs. By tradition, the changing of the guard was signaled by the funeral arrangements. A bevy of Politburo comrades would serve as pall-bearers, and the places in which they stood as well as the order in which they spoke revealed the new ranking. At Andropov's funeral, however, Chernenko could not summon the strength even to go through the motions of carrying the casket, however many the helpers, so the ritual was dispensed with. He could not so much as hold his hand up long enough to salute the passing military guard.[75] With his physical powers waning, Chernenko proposed that the energetic Gorbachev head the Central Committee secretariat and chair Politburo meetings in his absence. After only a year, Chernenko, too, was in his grave.

Having thus capped off the passing of three geriatric general secretaries in little more than two years, the regime was becoming a laughing-stock both at home and abroad, and the pressure to turn to a more vigorous leader mounted. Gorbachev had demonstrated his verve during a well-publicized recent visit to England, where he parried with the Iron Lady, Margaret Thatcher, eliciting her respectful assessment: "I like him. We can do business together." Viktor Grishin, the long-serving party boss of Moscow, had attempted to paint himself as the heir apparent by getting Soviet television to broadcast scenes of himself and Chernenko casting ballots together shortly before Chernenko's death. But since the putative polling place was recognizable as a hospital suite, the ploy came off badly. When the Politburo deliberated on the succession, Grishin's name was put in nomination, but the oldest of the old guard, Foreign Minister Andrei Gromyko, gave Gorbachev a ringing endorsement. The two had not been allies, but Gromyko must have recognized a collective interest in ending the vacuum at the top, and the others soon concurred in making their youngest member the new general secretary.

The outside world noticed the surface change immediately. "He walks, he talks, and his suit fits," noted *Washington Post* reporter Dusko Doder.[76] Even more remarkable was the pretty and stylish Raisa, who resigned her position teaching philosophy to serve as an unpaid assistant to her husband, a relationship similar to the later partnership between Bill and Hillary Clinton, except without the appearance of mutual exploitation.[77]

•   •   •

Gorbachev's first move as general secretary was to consolidate power. Within six weeks, he had three of his own men added to the Politburo to assure his control. The next month, he traveled to Leningrad to give a speech undercutting the local party boss, Grigory Romanov, who happened to have been the one who had nominated Grishin against Gorbachev. In fact, Romanov himself, who was younger than Grishin, was seen as a more formidable potential rival. Gorbachev soon had him removed from the Politburo. Gromyko, despite the key part he played in Gorbachev's victory, was kicked upstairs to the ceremonial role of president. He was replaced as foreign minister by Gorbachev's Georgian friend Eduard Shevardnadze, who also was added to the Politburo. Late in 1985 Grishin was replaced as secretary of the Moscow party by Boris Yeltsin. Within a year, says Jack Matlock, then the U.S. ambassador, Gorbachev's "position was as firm as that of any of his predecessors, save only Stalin's at the height of his power."[78]

Gorbachev's initial program was not reform but "acceleration." "The very system was dying away," he lamented. "The sluggish senile blood no longer contained any vital juices."[79] From top to bottom, corruption, absenteeism and featherbedding were rampant. Everything produced was shabby, broken or unavailable. Having seen the West, Gorbachev was anguished by the comparison. The Soviet Union produced its own trucks, but they were of such poor quality that four times as many people were employed in repairing them as in their manufacture. Soviet televisions were often made with cardboard components that sometimes combusted spontaneously in viewers' homes. And each year the country scoured world grain markets in order to feed itself. To paraphrase an American president, Gorbachev wanted to get the Soviet Union moving again.

His first remedy was a new agency to monitor the quality of goods. Faulty items would be junked as they came off the assembly line. But discarding the most defective units out of a universe of shoddy merchandise had little impact on the overall level. And since the whole bureaucratic system of production was lubricated by the exchange of favors, the inspectors soon became just another part to be oiled. The second major initiative was a campaign to reduce the country's intake of alcohol—the only civilian product for which it could boast the world's highest rate of consumption. There were five million officially registered alcoholics; each year fifteen million arrests were made for drunkenness and fifty thousand people died of acute alcohol poisoning.[80] One-fifth of all deaths were deemed alcohol-related.[81] As a result, male life expectancy was plummeting, making the U.S.S.R. the only industrialized country where this was happening.

Gorbachev had the price of vodka doubled and redoubled. The hours for its sale were drastically curtailed in shops and restaurants. Soviet embassies were ordered to serve soft drinks at diplomatic receptions. The militia confiscated nine hundred thousand stills.[82] And Georgia's famous vineyards were plowed under. A shortage of sugar ensued because it was bought up for use in home

brew. More seriously, desperate drinkers resorted to consuming lethal intoxi-
cants. So many imbibed aftershave or cologne that limits were placed on the
quantities of these allowed for sale. And the secret but large state budget deficit
mushroomed because the sale of booze had accounted for almost 15 percent
of government revenues.

Gorbachev did bring a new tone to his office, barnstorming the country for
meetings with common people, speaking without prepared texts and dispensing
with some of the pompous rituals of his predecessors, such as the presentation
of armfuls of bouquets to the party secretary by bevies of maidens at every place
he visited. In agriculture, the realm with which he felt most comfortable, he
inaugurated some minor reforms to encourage private initiative. He also put
through a measure allowing private purchase of certain building materials, but in
an early indicator of how hard it was going to be to reform the Soviet economy,
this innovation proved idle since the permitted items were nowhere to be found.

In his memoirs Gorbachev describes his first year in office as a time of
discovery rather than of launching any preconceived plan:

> Gradually we freed ourselves of conventional ideological stereotypes and
> made our first attempts to understand the kind of society we had created, to
> what extent it matched Lenin's ideas, and the place it occupied in the world.
> We tried to see what our own history would look like in an undistorted
> mirror. We began a plan to renew society within the framework of socialist
> choice.[83]

In 1986, he says, he "reflected more and more often that the problem lay not
only in the people . . . there would have to be some reform of the system itself."[84]

Two developments in the course of that year spurred him along the path of
reform. One was the disaster that struck the country's largest nuclear generating
plant at Chernobyl, one of the prides of Soviet industry. The accident, which
revealed errors in design, construction, operation and maintenance, drove home
in one devastating moment how far the U.S.S.R. was from being able to keep
pace with the West. And the pathologies of the system were on display as well,
with officials withholding information in order to minimize embarrassment
even though this compounded the jeopardy to the health of millions of citizens.

The second impetus was Gorbachev's disappointment with the response to
perestroika, the term for economic reform that he had highlighted at that year's
party congress. He emphasized that to energize the system, local initiative

would have to be encouraged, but he had no idea how difficult it would be to reverse seventy years of enforced servility. A cartoon captured what Gorbachev was up against: it showed a local factory official sending to headquarters a telegram saying, "We have successfully completed perestroika. Await further instructions." Gorbachev summarized his frustration: "It was as if no one was against perestroika, everyone was 'for it,' but nothing was changing."[85]

Thus in mid-1986 Gorbachev began to emphasize the second of his principal watchwords: *glasnost,* or openness. He recognized that he could not bring about economic change without political change, for it was the political officialdom that was thwarting economic reform. *Glasnost* was not tantamount to free speech, much less democracy, but it invited freer speech, aiming to mobilize public criticism as a spur against the immobile bureaucracy.

Print and broadcast journalists were encouraged to report more freely, even about the failures and wrongdoing of officials. Censorship was sharply reduced, and banned novels like Pasternak's *Doctor Zhivago* and Rybakov's *Children of the Arbat* were published for the first time in their home country. Several further economic innovations were announced by Gorbachev, who invoked Lenin's NEP as his model. Collective farms would henceforth be allowed to sell 30 percent of their produce directly to retailers. Factories were allowed to deal directly with foreign buyers or sellers, and various forms of private work were legalized. The latter measure, said the dissident writer Zhores Medvedev, was "the most important economic decree of . . . 30 years."[86]

Capping off the year, in December the leading dissident, physicist Andrei Sakharov, was released from internal exile in the closed city of Gorky. After years of isolation and physical abuse by the KGB, Sakharov suddenly found workmen in his apartment to install a telephone. Soon after it was hooked up it rang, and none other than Gorbachev was on the line to inform Sakharov personally that he was free to return to Moscow and continue his "patriotic work." Since Sakharov, the "father" of the Soviet atom bomb, had long since been barred from military research, Gorbachev's phrase apparently referred to Sakharov's advocacy of human rights. In short, Gorbachev was encouraging him to further his role as scourge of the system.

Within the country and without, many found Gorbachev's behavior incomprehensible. The key was to be found in the boy who had won the Red Banner of Labor and the young man who had disdained time-serving apparatchiks. Gorbachev was the last true believer in the revolution's ideals. He felt they had gotten buried beneath a thick accretion of bureaucracy and that his job was to recover the strength and purity of unsullied socialism. Domestic and foreign criticism was suddenly welcome because it could provide some of the solvent to wash away the undesirable encrustation.

In January 1987, in anticipation of a state visit by Prime Minister Thatcher, the Soviets stopped jamming the radio broadcasts of the BBC. It did not resume when the visit was over, and soon the jamming of Voice of America and Germany's Deutsche Welle ceased, as well. That same month saw the release in Moscow of the groundbreaking film *Repentance*, a bitter allegory on the crimes of Stalin and the complicity of his heirs. Gorbachev was reported to have encouraged it to be screened widely enough for the whole country to see it.

Also that month, at a Central Committee plenum, he delivered a withering account of the reign of his predecessor, Brezhnev, as an era of corruption and stagnation. To move forward, he said, "we need democracy like air."[87] He pushed through a proposal to allow multiple candidates in local party elections and another to open some top government positions to nonmembers of the party. Additional reforms aiming to readjust the balance of power between the citizenry and the party were turned back by the committee. But Gorbachev would not accept a partial victory. To outmaneuver the Central Committee he announced the intention to convene a special party conference, where he could trump the Central Committee without waiting for the next scheduled party congress, still four years away.

Matlock comments: "The policies of 1985 and 1986 were much like the earlier . . . attempts to apply superficial correctives to a system whose defects were inherent. . . . But Gorbachev's proposals in 1987 were directed at the system itself."[88] In February, Gorbachev renounced the longstanding practice, immortalized in George Orwell's *1984,* of redefining reality to fit the party line. "There should be no forgotten names or blanks, either in history or in literature," he said. The next autumn, the existing history textbooks, which had been tailored to official dogma, were withdrawn and schoolteachers were told to fend for themselves until more honest editions could be issued. In April, during a visit to Czechoslovakia, Gorbachev's spokesman was asked to explain the difference between his policies and those of liberalizer Alexander Dubček that were crushed by Warsaw Pact tanks in 1968. "Nineteen years," he replied.

In the months that followed, Gorbachev's pace quickened. He began to speak favorably of "pluralism," a Western concept entirely at odds with Marxist thinking. He told a foreign newspaper that his government had decided to withdraw its troops from Afghanistan. And he pushed through the Central Committee a "law on socialist enterprises" which aimed to decentralize the economy. During the summer he retreated from public view to write the book *Perestroika,* which was published before the end of the year.

Perestroika contained an unsparing indictment of the system over which Gorbachev presided. He said that Soviet society had suffered "a gradual erosion of . . . ideological and moral values," elaborating:

> Propaganda of success—real or imagined—was gaining the upper hand. Eulogizing and servility were encouraged; the needs and opinions of ordinary working people, of the public at large, were ignored. In the social sciences scholastic theorization was encouraged and developed, but creative thinking was driven out. . . . Similar negative tendencies also affected culture, the arts and journalism, as well as the teaching process and medicine. . . . At some administrative levels there emerged a disrespect for the law and encouragement of eyewash and bribery, servility and glorification.

Like Hamlet asserting that "something is rotten in the state of Denmark," Gorbachev insisted that the problem of the Soviet Union went deeper than poor economic performance. The quest for change did not arise from mere "pragmatic . . . considerations," but from "our troubled conscience." The ruler himself was calling for a "revolution."[89]

Over the next three years Gorbachev's revolution had three high points. The first was the election of the Congress of People's Deputies. Gorbachev had forced this proposal through the June 1988 party conference during its confused closing moments after the delegates had turned aside some of his democratizing reforms. The election was to be the first exercise in genuine democracy in the country since Lenin's strong-arm men had closed down the Constituent Assembly in 1918. When the vote was held, entrenched party officials all across the country were repudiated by the newly empowered voters in favor of insurgents of various stripe. In Moscow, Yeltsin—who had been stripped of his authority and ostracized for criticizing the slow pace of change—chose to run for a citywide seat against the official party candidate and amassed more than 90 percent of the vote. One-third of the seats in the new body had been reserved for representatives of various official organizations rather than the electorate at large. This provision had been designed to help assure party dominance, but it backfired, and many of the reserved seats were captured by dissidents. The most prominent of them, Sakharov, was chosen to represent the Soviet Academy of Sciences.

The congress convened in May 1989, just after Gorbachev's return from his fateful visit to Beijing. At the outset, Gorbachev announced that Communist Party deputies would not be expected to vote as a bloc. A caucus of democrats led by Sakharov pulled in one direction and a bloc of conservatives pulled in the other, while nationalists from each of the republics pursued their various agendas. In a strange mix of authoritarianism and democracy, Gorbachev held the chair, controlled the microphones, and bantered back and forth as if in perpetual dialogue with the newly pluralistic country. And the whole unprecedented exercise was broadcast live on television to a rapt populace that had never before had a voice in its own government nor the right to view its deliberations.

The next climacteric in the revolution was the retreat from empire. In the latter half of 1989, Moscow looked on impassively as Communist regimes toppled one after another throughout the Soviet bloc. The first domino was Poland, where the government of General Wojciech Jaruzelski negotiated a form of power-sharing. Contested elections were to be held for the first time, but the balloting would be rigged to assure Communist control of the more powerful lower house of Parliament, the Sejm. The illegal labor union, Solidarity, captured 99 out of 100 freely contested seats for the upper house, the Senate. And even the intended Communist dominance in the Sejm was undermined when a majority of voters managed to defeat the unopposed Communist leaders by crossing out their names. Such was the humiliation that Communist ranks crumbled, and the government fell into Solidarity's hands.

Within a week, the regime in Hungary, the most liberal in the bloc, began talks with its opposition. In this case, just the agreement to hold elections in a few months was enough to shatter the Communist Party, as its brighter and more ambitious leaders read the handwriting on the wall and began to reposition themselves. In Bulgaria, a rebellion within the Politburo, probably encouraged by Moscow, replaced party boss Todor Zhivkov with reformers pledged to democratization. In Czechoslovakia and East Germany, conservative Communist regimes struggled to hang onto power even in the face of popular demonstrations, but public statements by Gorbachev and other Soviet spokesmen about the imperative of reform sapped their determination. Finally, in Romania, Nicolae Ceauşescu, the one Communist despot who was determined to shed blood rather than relinquish power, was toppled and killed in the brief, violent upheaval so traumatic to Deng Xiaoping. When the smoke had cleared around the region, Andrei Grachev, an official of the Soviet Communist Party's international department, declared: "Gorbachev had his eyes wide open when he started this, calculating the inevitable effects it would have in Eastern Europe."[90]

Finally, in February 1990, the Central Committee, as Sovietologist Charles Fairbanks summed it up, "voted for Gorbachev's proposal to end its monopoly of power, agreeing in principle to a multi-party system, and to end its opposition to private property, thus abolishing the core of Leninism and the core of Marxism in one three-day meeting."[91] The Achilles' heel of the totalitarian system turned out to be the principle of obedience to the leader. When Gorbachev in effect ordered the party to commit suicide in the name of saving "socialism," the hierarchs could not bring themselves to resist.

· · ·

While Gorbachev succeeded at democratizing the Soviet Union, his economic reforms fell flat. Although he decentralized and liberalized, he remained, as he repeatedly insisted, a "convinced socialist," and he balked at wholesale privatization. Citizens gained the right to open small restaurants or shops, but the bulk of the economy remained under centralized control. The old methods, depending on administrative reward and coercion more than economic incentive, had worked poorly. Now, the instruments of command had been weakened more than market mechanisms had been strengthened. Economic performance, woeful as it had been, deteriorated further.

As the economy stalled, strikes spread across the country, spearheaded by miners in the Donets and Kuznets basins. The first walkouts were triggered by something so simple as the absence of soap with which the men could wash when they emerged from the pits. This was scarcely the only complaint. Conditions were so dreadful that the life expectancy of miners was calculated at forty-eight years. One work stoppage followed another over a span of a few years, adding further to the economic downturn.

Without the balm of material progress, Gorbachev could not hold the center against the centrifugal forces of conservatism, liberalism and especially nationalism. In late 1990, he veered toward the conservatives, replacing many of his top aides with men who had been lukewarm to his reforms. The most prominent liberal in the inner circle, Foreign Minister Shevardnadze, resigned, warning of the danger of a new dictatorship. In March 1991, Gorbachev sponsored a countrywide referendum aiming to rally a constituency for holding the Soviet Union together. So far had the process of disintegration advanced that six of the U.S.S.R.'s fifteen republics refused outright to take part. But what proved the most consequential response came in Russia itself. The Russian Republic had by now created its own skeletal political institutions, differentiated from those of the U.S.S.R. They were headed by Yeltsin, who, as the leading spokesman for the radical democrats, had become Gorbachev's nemesis. Russian authorities agreed to hold the referendum but added a second question to the ballot, asking whether to establish a Russian presidency. Both questions won approval.

Accordingly, three months later the first-ever election was held for a president of Russia, and Yeltsin won with a substantial majority. Although his legal powers were obscure, he now was robed with a greater degree of legitimacy than Gorbachev, who filled the newly created position of president of the U.S.S.R., a post to which he had been elected by the Congress of People's Deputies, not by the public.

For Gorbachev, time was running out. Much as he had come to hate the goad, Yeltsin, he was desperately eager to reach agreement with him and leaders of the other republics on a new treaty of union that would hold together at least most of the U.S.S.R. In August 1991 a draft treaty was in hand. This was the final straw for the conservatives, including those with whom Gorbachev had surrounded himself in his political retrenchment of late 1990. A group of top aides burst in on him in his vacation retreat in the Crimea and placed him under house arrest.

They asked him to declare a state of emergency, insisting that they intended to turn power back to him as soon as they had restored order in the country. When he refused to cooperate, the decree was issued in the name of the State Committee for the State of Emergency. The announcement also explained that Gorbachev was ill and unable to perform his duties and had been supplanted by Vice President Gennady Yanaev. Military units were ordered to take up positions around Moscow. But hundreds of thousands of citizens poured into the streets to defend the White House, seat of the Russian government, where Yeltsin clambered atop a tank and denounced the "right-wing, reactionary, anti-constitutional coup d'état." His display of courage and determination contrasted dramatically with the image projected by Yanaev, whose hands shook uncontrollably at a televised press conference. Some soldiers joined the demonstrators, and military commanders were uncertain what the response of the others would be to an order to storm the White House. Plans for such an action were drawn up, but the coup leaders could not find the courage to launch it. Within three days their effort collapsed.

Gorbachev rushed back to the Kremlin, but the foiled coup had left him a spent force. These were his own deputies who had betrayed him and tried to turn back the clock. The hero of the hour was Yeltsin, whose authority now came—in an ironic reprise of Lenin—from the street, as well as from the electorate. Gorbachev had no mandate from either. Yeltsin issued a decree that in effect outlawed the Communist Party. The next day, August 24, Gorbachev resigned as general secretary and dissolved the Central Committee. Four months later, the Soviet Union itself officially ceased to exist.

• • •

Gorbachev and Deng were the *yin* and *yang* of communism's demise. Each was honest enough to confront the fact that the system he had come to rule was not working, and each was patriotic enough to find this intolerable. Their predecessors, in contrast, had been more concerned with personal power and privilege, content to command listing ships so long as they could enjoy the perquisites of captaincy.

The failures that alarmed Deng and Gorbachev were in the first place economic, but their courses of action quickly diverged. Although Gorbachev tirelessly invoked Lenin, it was Deng who was the real Leninist. For him, the dictatorship of party was the essence of socialism; all else was negotiable. The system he left behind he called socialism with Chinese characteristics, but it might better be called capitalism under the rule of the Communists. His gamble, and that of his successors, was that capitalism could bring the populace enough material rewards to keep them from challenging too vigorously the party's monopoly of power.

On the other hand, it was Gorbachev who was the real socialist. "I am a . . . convinced Communist," he replied to those who complained that he was dismantling the system. Early on he decided that what was wrong with the economy was the lack of democracy. Although he did not renounce Lenin, he attempted to undo the division in the socialist movement that Lenin had inaugurated in 1903 when he founded Bolshevism. Gorbachev, like other Communists in Eastern Europe, strove to return the movement to its roots in social democracy. He started to call himself a social democrat, looking back wistfully to an ideal that had appeared so promising at the dawn of the twentieth century. Alas, he had returned too late. Not only was there the matter of millions of lives that had been snuffed out by the Bolsheviks and their offspring, but now in the West, as the century waned, real existing social democracy was in the throes of its own crisis.

11

THE PARTY OF BUSINESS: BLAIR REDEFINES SOCIAL DEMOCRACY

SURVEYING THE SOVIET COLLAPSE, the eminent pro-socialist economist Robert Heilbroner wrote: "Less than seventy-five years after it officially began, the contest between capitalism and socialism is over: capitalism has won."[1] But others on the Left demurred. Communism, they insisted, was not socialism, but only a perverted form of it. Therefore, sweeping inferences should not be drawn from its defeat. As the *New York Times* reported, "To some thinkers, the collapse of Communism, far from presaging the downfall of Socialism, could be the source of its renewal."[2]

When the Socialist International gathered in Berlin for its nineteenth congress in 1992, British Labour Party leader John Smith denounced the "myth" that the "agenda of democratic socialism" was exhausted. "It is the ideas of the Right that have run out of steam," he said.[3] Socialist ranks were fortified by erstwhile Communists who hastened to realign themselves as social democrats, following Gorbachev's lead in repealing Lenin's decision eighty years earlier to form the Bolsheviks into a separate movement. From Bulgaria to Italy to Nicaragua, these parties queued up for admission to the International, and Gorbachev himself was a highlight speaker at the congress.

On the surface, these hopes for a renaissance of social democracy were vindicated: by the decade's end the parties of the Socialist International were governing twelve of the fifteen states of the European Union. Yet electoral victory masked ideological surrender. As early as 1985, the American socialist writer Irving Howe observed that "socialism . . . as a living idea . . . is something different from the mere survival of European social-democratic parties as established institutions."[4] His worry was well founded, for the socialists' success at the polls in the latter half of the 1990s was accomplished exactly by assuring the voters there was no danger that they would implement socialism.

The most successful of all the new socialist politicians, and the model for many of the others, was Britain's Tony Blair. In 1997, after the Labour Party had languished in opposition for eighteen years, he led it to a landslide victory that surpassed even Attlee's triumph in 1945.

Like Attlee, Blair had come from a comfortable background. He, too, was the son of a lawyer. He, too, had studied the law himself but found little interest in it. And he, too, came to politics and to socialism only in full adulthood. But while Attlee had struggled against innate shyness, Blair was at home in the limelight. Perhaps it was in his genes; his paternal grandparents had both been actors. While co-starring in a production, they had an adulterous affair which resulted in pregnancy. The baby was given up for adoption to Glasgow shipyard rigger James Blair and his wife, who named him Leo.

Leo was politically precocious, serving at age fifteen as the secretary of the Scottish Young Communist League.[5] After earning a law degree and a Ph.D. at Edinburgh University, he secured appointment as a lecturer at Durham University, moving there with his wife, Hazel, in 1953, the year their second son was born. Although Leo never spoke of his own complicated origins, they named the boy Anthony Charles Lynton Blair, the middle names taken from Leo's natural father. They enrolled him and his older brother, Bill, in the Choristers School, which has supplied choirboys to the Durham Cathedral for hundreds of years.

As Leo's legal career blossomed, his political aspirations flourished. But his views had changed considerably. He became chairman of the Durham Conservative Association and began to scout out constituencies where he might stand for Parliament. Then, at age forty, he was felled by a massive stroke. He survived, but regained his power of speech only over the course of three years, which ended his political dreams—until they were reborn through his son.

At thirteen, Tony was sent to Fettes College, a British "public school." With the loss of Leo's earning power the family would not have been able to afford this had Tony not won a scholarship. At first he hated Fettes because new boys were obliged to "fag" for upperclassmen, in effect acting as their servants with few constraints against abuse and humiliation. But once he survived his first unhappy year, Tony settled in and flourished. He earned good grades, distinguished himself on the cricket and rugby teams, and became the school's outstanding dramatic performer.

From Fettes, Blair went on to St. John's College at Oxford to study law. In contrast to his father, who had been so politically earnest so young, Tony had shown no interest in politics throughout high school, and this did not change at St. John's. "There is precisely nothing from what Blair joined or did at Oxford to suggest that he had even the faintest glimmer of a political ambition in him," says biographer Jon Sopel.[6] His only political activity was to participate in a discussion group organized by an older Australian student, Peter Thomson, which batted around various Marxist and Christian Left ideas. It was the Christian thread, more than the Marxist, that drew Tony. He had renewed his religious devotions, which had flagged in high school, and was confirmed during his second year at St. John's. Blair credits the discussion group, and Thomson in particular, with having influenced his thinking, yet neither he nor his biographers have succeeded in specifying the ideas that he came away with. At bottom, he still was not very deeply engaged. Peter Mandelson, an Oxford contemporary who was to become something of a Svengali to Blair during his parliamentary career, was once asked whether he had known Blair at college. "No, why should I have done?" he replied sardonically. "I was interested in politics!"[7]

What held a much firmer grip on Blair's attention was rock 'n' roll. His training at the Choristers School paid off when he auditioned successfully for lead singer in a rock band called "The Ugly Rumors." It had a short, unmemorable career. Tony, who kept up his acting during college, was a good performer even though his voice did not rise above the mediocre level of the band's other musical elements. "He would strut onto the stage, à la [Mick] Jagger, punching the air and wagging his finger at the audience," says Sopel.[8] He wore his hair long in what a band mate called a "Three Musketeers" look, and sported purple pants, cowboy boots and a cut-off T-shirt to flaunt his abs. Leo later recalled going to visit his son at Oxford and encountering this bizarre-looking fellow: "I wondered who the hell it was. Then he said, 'Hi, Dad.'"[9]

As befits the lead of a rock band, Tony had lots of girls, some of them great beauties. But unlike so many other performers, he was not known for exploiting women. One of them recalled: "I always thought of Tony as the only 'nice' person that I ever went out with at Oxford. He was very good looking, in a kind of sweet way, and wasn't at all predatory."[10]

It was not until he had left college that he fell in love. Cherie Booth was not as beautiful as some of his girls, but she won him with her brains and force of personality. Law graduates in the British system serve a term of unpaid apprenticeship as "pupils" in a firm. Tony discovered that a young woman had applied for the same position he was after. Since she came out top in the bar exam, while he was far down the list, she got the spot. But Tony made such an impression in the interview that he was taken on as well. Thereafter, he and Cherie competed for a permanent position with the firm and courted as they dueled.

Cherie was more political than Tony, or at least more ideological. She may have been influenced by her father, who was something of an activist on the Labour Left. By the time Blair joined the party in 1975 at age twenty-two, she had already been a member for three years. They, too, gravitated to the Left, although without attaching themselves too firmly to any one of the party's several Left tendencies.

They had not been active long when, in 1976, the party was convulsed by a crisis that confronted Britain's Labour government. A run on the pound impelled Prime Minister James Callaghan to turn to the International Monetary Fund for support. Third World countries like Tanzania found the IMF's terms humiliating; how much more so Great Britain? Yet the government felt it had no choice but to submit to the fund's demands for austerity. "We used to think that you could spend your way out of a recession," Callaghan told a Labour conference. "I tell you in all candour that that option no longer exists."[11] With inflation running around 25 percent, the government imposed an "incomes policy" to restrain prices and wages, but the unions ultimately rebelled. Years of frustration culminated in a wave of strikes during the 1978-79 "winter of discontent," symbolized by uncollected garbage and unburied coffins. A public backlash swept Labour from office in May 1979.

The Conservatives were led by Margaret Thatcher, the first female prime minister in European history. Whereas Tory leaders mostly came from society's upper crust, she had grown up in a cold-water flat above her parents' grocery store. And whereas her predecessors had been paragons of compromise—giving rise to the neologism "Butskellism" to designate the indistinguishable policies of Labour leader Hugh Gaitskell and Tory Chancellor R. A. Butler—she was an ideologue.

• • •

Thatcher laid Britain's doldrums at the door of socialism. "No theory of government was ever given a fairer test or a more prolonged experiment in a democratic country than democratic socialism received in Britain," she said. "Far from reversing the . . . decline of Britain . . . it accelerated it."[12] Unlike previous Conservative administrations that had "merely pitched camp in the long march to the left," Thatcher set out to "kill" socialism.

She got off to an inauspicious start. Her anti-inflation policy drove unemployment into double digits, igniting a wave of urban riots. Her approval rating dropped to 28 percent, the lowest in the history of British polling.[13] Many businessmen and Tories joined the ranks of her detractors. Among the Conservatives, only a minority of party members said they wanted her to continue as their leader.

Political rescue came from an unexpected direction. In faraway Argentina, the military regime of President Leopoldo Galtieri sent forces to seize the nearby Falkland Islands, a British possession which the Argentines regard as rightly their own. Galtieri apparently hoped to boost his deteriorating popularity, but instead he gave Thatcher the opportunity to show her mettle. Despite rumblings by the Soviets, denunciations by the Organization of American States, and peace appeals from the pope and the secretary general of the United Nations, Thatcher ordered British forces to fight on until Argentina surrendered. It made dramatic contrast with the fecklessness of Labour governments, which had been paralyzed by the milder challenge of runaway labor unions. The outcome was a military victory for Her Majesty's forces and a reversal in political momentum in Britain.

It was while the Falklands war was raging that Tony Blair ran his first race for office, securing the Labour Party's nomination for a vacant seat from Beaconsfield, a reliably Tory constituency some twenty miles northwest of London, in a 1982 by-election.

Blair ran a dismal third behind both the Conservatives and the Social Democrats, the centrist party formed by the defection of part of the right wing of the Labour Party. He drew only 10 percent, half what Labour had won the previous election without the Social Democrats in the field, but party leaders did not fault him for the poor showing in what they knew was a hopeless district. On the contrary, he was widely credited with having conducted himself well, and he received a warm consolation note from Michael Foot, the left-winger who had replaced Callaghan as party leader following Thatcher's 1979 victory.

Foot had upset the more conservative Dennis Healey as the Left had seized the initiative within the party, arguing that Callaghan's defeat demonstrated how pointless it was to try to move rightward with the Tories. A group called the Labour Coordinating Committee, with which Tony and Cherie identified, promoted a more radical Alternative Economic Strategy, calling for the immediate nationalization of twenty-five major firms. Led by the radical aristocrat Anthony ("Tony") Wedgewood Benn, the Left had gained the upper hand in the party's National Executive Committee and secured the adoption of its program, titled *Peace, Jobs, Freedom,* at a special policy conference in May 1980. This plus the election of Foot had prompted four leading figures from Labour's Right— Shirley Williams, Roy Jenkins, David Owen and William Rodgers—to bolt in 1981 and found the Social Democratic Party.

Blair got another chance within a year when Thatcher called general elections, and the Beaconsfield party invited him to carry their standard again. But he had no wish to fall on his sword a second time, so he scoured the country for a winnable seat. By luck, redistricting had created an open constituency in Sedgefield, adjacent to his home county of Durham. In the British system, there are no primaries; candidates are chosen in a series of meetings. Blair examined the list of township party committees within Sedgefield and found one, Trimdon, that had not yet nominated anyone. He got an appointment with the township leaders, whom he found watching a soccer game. Blair watched along, joining in the male-bonding badinage to show that he was a regular guy. When the final whistle blew, he made his pitch.

The men agreed to back him, and they put him forward at the nominating meeting of the constituency as a whole. One of them brandished the consolation note that Michael Foot had sent after the Beaconsfield campaign, which said he hoped that Blair would soon find his place in Parliament, and misrepresented it as an endorsement of Blair in the current contest. Aided by their lobbying and shenanigans, Blair won the nomination on the fifth ballot.

Labour's 1983 campaign reflected its new leftward tilt. Its manifesto called for nationalizing an additional batch of industries, imposing barriers to foreign trade and currency transactions, withdrawing from the Common Market, and doing away with Britain's nuclear weapons unilaterally. All of this and more was spelled out in earnest, tedious detail in what Gerald Kaufman, a disaffected Labour MP, called "the longest suicide note in history." Foot, gray-haired and carrying a cane, came across as good-hearted but ineffectual—the ideal foil for the Iron Lady. Columnist Peter Jenkins called him "a walking obituary for the Labor Party."[14] The Conservatives garnered the largest margin in a British election since Attlee's 1945 triumph, polling 42 percent of the vote to 28 for Labour and 25 for the Social Democrats. This translated into an advantage of 144 seats in Parliament. Thatcher exulted that it was "the single most devastating defeat ever inflicted upon democratic socialism in Britain."[15]

Fortunately for Blair, Sedgefield was a safe Labour seat. Just thirty, he took his place in Parliament as the youngest representative of a party badly in need of new directions. However, he was not yet a significant innovator, and his maiden speech was laced with familiar socialist themes. "I am a socialist," he said, "...because I believe that, at its best, socialism corresponds most closely to an existence that is both rational and moral. . . . It stands for equality, not because it wants people to be the same but because only through equality in our economic circumstances can our individuality develop properly."[16]

Foot resigned days after the 1983 polling. In the contest to succeed him, Blair backed Neil Kinnock, who represented the "soft Left," which Blair favored. Later, he joined its official faction, the Tribune Group. Kinnock, in turn, saw in Blair the kind of freshness that he wanted the party to project, so just seven months after Blair entered Parliament, he was moved to the front bench. Only once before had an MP won this promotion so fast.

Also in the interest of refurbishing the party's image, Kinnock created a "Campaigns and Communications Directorate" to do public relations and polling. Innocuous though it sounds, this was looked upon askance by the hard Left. As two of its leading intellectuals put it, such an operation "represented . . . a decisive shift away from the concept of the party as a shaper and leader of opinion towards the idea of the party as marketing products—products which could themselves be more or less indefinitely modified in the light of 'market testing.'"[17] The left was all the more grieved by the man chosen to head the directorate, Peter Mandelson, whom it viewed as an unprincipled master of "spin." Punning on Gorbachev's reforms, the critics called Mandelson the inventor of "glitznost."

Blair, in contrast, became Mandelson's strongest admirer and turned to him increasingly for support and counsel. When some journalists likened Blair to the dashing young John F. Kennedy, Blair's staff began calling Mandelson "Bobby," jocularly analogizing the close bond between Blair and Mandelson to that between the Kennedy brothers.

Despite the Left's unease, the changes Labour undertook in the mid-1980s remained in the realm of technique and image. When Thatcher called new elections for 1987, the party's advertising concentrated on Kinnock's persona. He cut a far more attractive figure than Foot had done in 1983, and opinion polls reflected his appeal. But if the approach was new, the Labour platform was not. It still advocated additional nationalizations, and Gordon Brown, another bright young star in Labour's firmament, joked that its theme was "TSB"—tax, spend and borrow.[18] The Labour vote edged from 28 to 31 percent, while the Tories held steady at 42. The parliamentary margin slipped from 144 to a still insurmountable 101 seats.

This third consecutive thorough beating convinced many Labour leaders that the party required more than cosmetic change. In an article in the *Times,* Blair assessed Thatcher's success in running against the legacy of Attlee's admin-istration. She had "been able to challenge the post-war consensus because it was weak and people were tired of it. Labour has failed to recognise this and shift its ground," he said.[19]

His was not an isolated voice. The Labour National Executive Committee, at Kinnock's prompting, launched a "policy review" process to reexamine the party's program. As a result, the party began to make its peace with some elements of Thatcherism, just as the Tories had once acquiesced in many of Attlee's reforms. It repealed its pledge to renationalize the industries that the Conservatives had privatized; dropped its promise to rescind legislation restricting labor union activities; and abandoned its call for unilateral nuclear disarmament.

Labour's search for new ground was prompted not only by electoral duress. All across Europe, socialist parties were absorbing the economic lessons of their movement's boldest experiment of recent memory. It had been conducted in France under the leadership of the charismatic socialist convert François Mitterrand, who dominated French politics like no other twentieth-century figure except Charles DeGaulle.

In 1981, Mitterrand had defeated incumbent Valéry Giscard-d'Estaing to claim the presidency. He immediately dissolved the National Assembly and called parliamentary elections, in which the Socialists captured nearly 70 percent of the seats. Socialists had served in French governments before, even led them; but those were coalition arrangements typical of the Third and Fourth Republics, with limited freedom of action and limited aspirations for social change. This time, under the rules of the Fifth Republic with its strong executive, they won a degree of power beyond what they had ever held before. And with an ambitious program of socialist transformation spelled out in their campaign platform, they were prepared to make the most of it. *"La rupture"* was their watchword, signifying a clean break with the capitalist past.

Mitterrand's platform, "Socialist Project for France in the Eighties," was 371 pages burning with the millenarian rhetoric of an earlier era. Its aim was to "free the workers from age-old oppression and to provide all those who are exploited . . . with the instruments for their own self-emancipation."[20] In his inaugural address Mitterrand promised to "forge a new alliance between socialism and freedom." At once he and his party began to implement measures creating new public-sector jobs, nationalizing industries and mandating increases in wages, pensions and welfare.

Within a year, the French economy was in such a tailspin—output stagnant, trade balance collapsing, inflation soaring—that Mitterrand ordered an abrupt about-face. "The aim is to bring about a real reconciliation between the left and the economy," explained Socialist Party general secretary Lionel Jospin tellingly.[21] Even the leader of the party's Marxist Left, cabinet minister Jean-Pierre Chevenement, acknowledged: "France has understood, thanks to the crisis, the reality of economic struggle. . . .The private sector is recognized as the creator of social wealth."[22]

Eventually, the economy responded to the austerity program implemented by the chastened Socialists, but nonetheless the party lost its parliamentary majority in 1986. As Mitterrand prepared to run for reelection in 1988, he cut a very different figure than in his 1981 campaign. "References to socialism disappeared from socialist documents," writes socialist historian Donald Sassoon, "except to stress how far the [Mitterrand] government had strayed from it."[23]

• • •

Left-wingers in the other European socialist parties, including in Britain, had long argued that their party would prosper if it had the courage of its convictions instead of settling for pallid compromises. But Mitterrand's turnaround sapped their resolve. That and a string of electoral defeats pushed the Labour Party to the right and brought about a shift in factional alignments. The division between Left and Right gave way to a debate between "traditionalists" unmoved by the decade's events and "modernizers," an alliance of rightists and soft leftists like Tony Blair and Gordon Brown who wanted to redefine the party.

In 1988 Blair, in the role of shadow employment secretary, made his mark as an apostle of change by engineering a reversal of Labour's traditional opposition to the open shop. He argued that the closed shop—a workplace open only to union members—violated the Social Charter of the European Commission, which asserted the right to belong, or not to belong, to a union. But beneath this argument lay the conviction that the Labour Party needed to move away from its original purpose of representing the unions in the political arena. Blair put it plainly: "The trade union movement is a tremendously important, integral part of British society *but* it's important that Labour speaks for the whole community."[24]

The unions remained the party's backbone, so it was not easy to effect a policy change that cut against their interests. Blair approached the union leaders directly and won grudging praise for his straightforward dealing. His success in securing their acquiescence marked him as a comer in the eyes of Kinnock even though his public reputation was still modest. As the party geared up for the 1992 election, Blair was named to a five-member leadership team designated to speak for the economic program that Labour hoped would be the key to victory.

With the country in the throes of an eighteen-month recession (the longest in fifty years), unemployment nearing 10 percent, and the national health service beginning to split at the seams, the Conservatives were vulnerable. They would be seeking a fourth consecutive mandate, something no British party had achieved in the better part of two centuries. And they showed the hallmarks of having governed too long. Internal feuding forced Thatcher to step aside. Worse, the man who had opposed her, Michael Heseltine, had also fallen short, necessitating a compromise in the person of the lackluster John Major. Rather than run on their record, the Tories were relying on a scare campaign about the opposition.

But they had lost their most potent bugaboo. Voters had distrusted Labour's approach to national security ever since it abandoned the muscular anticommunist policies of Attlee and Bevin and moved toward accommodation and unilateral nuclear disarmament. The Soviet collapse now made that issue moot. In addition, Labour had spruced up its image and streamlined its campaign operations. The red flag had been replaced as the party's symbol by a red rose, and Oscar-winning actress Glenda Jackson added some Hollywood sparkle to its list of parliamentary candidates. Pundits called Labour's new approach "designer socialism," and polls showed that the voters were impressed. When asked which party had "campaigned most impressively," they placed Labour well ahead. Asked whom they were going to vote for, they gave Labour a lead throughout the campaign.

Election Day, however, brought a rude surprise. It turned out to be "the worst ever performance for the pollsters," confessed a spokesman for Marketing Opinion Research International.[25] The Tories had won again. "Our whole country deserves better," moaned Kinnock, who had led the party to defeat for the second time. "I simply don't know how the British mind works to produce this result," chimed in deputy leader, Roy Hattersley. But the explanation was clear enough.[26]

While Hattersley and Kinnock seemed to be faulting the voters for making the wrong choice, Blair responded differently. He was inclined to accept the truth of columnist Peter Jenkins' bleak observation that "Labor lost because it was Labor."[27] It was the sixth consecutive election in which the party had failed to achieve so much as 40 percent of the vote. Blair had been a key supporter of Kinnock's effort to modernize the party, but he knew it had not gone far enough. "He was angry," commented one colleague. "Angry with the small c conservatism of the Labour Party. Angry at its resistance to change. It was as though he wanted to pick the Party up and shake it by the scruff of the neck."[28]

There were some who thought Blair should replace Kinnock. Polls showed that he had come across on television better than any other member of Labour's leadership team. But he was still only thirty-eight, not yet ready. The overwhelming choice was John Smith, the well-liked Scotsman from the party's Right. Blair toyed with running for deputy, but when Smith announced that he wanted a woman in that spot, Blair dropped the idea. Instead, he accepted the position of home secretary in the shadow cabinet and made himself a spokesman for those seeking to transform the party. "The reason Labour lost in 1992, as for the previous three elections, is not complex," he wrote, "it is simple: society had changed and we did not change sufficiently with it."[29]

As for the substance of change, Blair took inspiration from Australia's Labour prime minister Robert Hawke, who had put through a package of tax reductions, privatization and deregulation that cut against the socialist grain. But a still more powerful model was on offer from the United States. While British Conservatives were riding high, their American counterparts had been brought low. Their conqueror, Bill Clinton, had studied at Oxford during the 1960s, and it was reported that in 1992 Conservative officials had complied with a request from the Republicans to scour Home Office files for any records from those years that might be used against him. After his election, Clinton owed the Tories a bad turn, and his political team offered to share the lessons of victory with Labour.

One way that Clinton had established his identity as a "new Democrat" was to return to Arkansas during the campaign in order to assure the execution of Ricky Ray Rector, a murderer who had sustained brain damage from a police bullet during his capture. Within days of returning from a series of private briefings by Democratic operatives in Washington, Blair began sketching the outlines of "New Labour" by unveiling the slogan "we must be tough on crime and tough on the causes of crime." Whatever the second phrase may have meant, it was the first phrase that was seen as a newsworthy departure for Labour.

Crime fell within Blair's portfolio as shadow home secretary, and the subject was much on the nation's mind in the wake of a horrifying story that had chilled Britain's soul. Two-year-old Jamie Bulger had been found beaten to death, and a security video camera captured footage of the killers leading the toddler by the hand from a shopping mall. They were two ten-year-old boys. However important the issue of crime, this incomprehensible event pointed to deeper questions, and Blair attempted to confront them:

> A solution to this disintegration doesn't simply lie in legislation. It must come
> from the rediscovery of a sense of direction as a country and most of all from
> being unafraid to start talking again about the values and principles we believe
> in and what they mean for us, not just as individuals but as a community. We
> cannot exist in a moral vacuum. If we do not learn and then teach the value
> of what is right and what is wrong, then the result is simply moral chaos
> which engulfs us all.[30]

Mandelson says that the advance text of this speech made some of Blair's advisers nervous for fear it was "redolent of the religious right in America."[31] At a minimum its stress on the limits of government departed from socialist tradition. Yet Mandelson adds that "more than any other speech this one defined the man and imprinted his character on the public's mind."[32]

One other "new Democrat" feature that Blair reprised in 1993 was the demonstration of independence from interest groups. In the 1992 campaign Clinton had profited from ostentatiously dressing down the black "rap" singer Sista Souljah for some anti-white remarks. In Britain, the interest group whose hold on Labour compromised its electoral prospects was the unions. Already having bearded them on the closed shop, Blair took a lead in engineering party reforms that watered down their block vote in party councils.

In May 1994, John Smith died suddenly of a heart attack. Blair at once decided to run for leader. The sticky part was that his closest colleague, Gordon Brown, also intended to run. Until only a year before, Brown, who was more senior than Blair, had been widely regarded as Smith's natural successor. Since then, Blair had come on strong in the fight to reduce the union block vote and in realigning the party on social issues. Both knew that if they ran against each other they would divide the modernizers and run the risk of allowing a traditionalist to prevail. Blair, however, told Brown that he was determined to run regardless, and Brown yielded to his steelier determination.

Blair ran on a platform of "change" that was not sharply defined; the essential change contemplated would be to stop losing elections. Many old party hands were uneasy about the degree to which Blair was willing to jettison time-honored Labour positions, but most felt he offered the best hope of leading them out of the wilderness of perpetual opposition, and he won by a commanding majority.

The next day, in an interview on BBC radio, he heralded a new era by rhetorically severing the umbilical cord (as one headline phrased it) between the party and the unions. "The trade unions will have no special and privileged place within the Labour Party," he said. "They will have the same access as the other side of industry. . . . We are not running the next Labour government for anyone other than the people of this country."[33]

Many other dramatic changes soon followed as Blair set about filling out the image of "New Labour." "I want to rebuild this party from its foundations," he declared.[34] In his first nine months as leader the party's positions changed on taxes, inflation, minimum wage, private schooling, and a variety of constitutional and international issues. He decried "penal rates of taxation" of individuals and called for reviewing corporate taxes, too, since "companies will not invest without decent profits."[35] He urged reduction in the welfare rolls, saying: "a nation at work, not on benefit—that is our pledge."[36] He proclaimed, "the Labour Party is now the party of law and order."[37] And he underlined his social conservatism with the statement: "governments don't raise children—families do."[38]

While jettisoning unpopular Labour policies and embracing the main tenets of the Thatcher revolution, New Labour still needed to distinguish itself. Blair identified a series of small differences with Tory positions and highlighted them with strong oratory. He endorsed a minimum wage, opposed certain privatization measures within the health service, and supported lowering the age of legal consent to sixteen for homosexual acts to bring it into line with the law for heterosexual intimacy. Columnist Anne Applebaum wrote that New Labour's program amounted to "an elaborate rhetoric that describes a modest set of proposed solutions."[39] Blair also announced some catchy goals, such as making Britain a "young country again," but was vague about how he would do it. For this, some critics labeled him "Tony Blur."

In addition to distancing the party from unions and changing its policies on issues, Blair took its fundamental ideology in his sights. That had been defined since 1918 by "Clause IV" of the party's constitution, written by Sidney Webb. The party's purpose, it said, was "to secure for the workers . . . the full fruits of their industry and the most equitable distribution thereof that may be possible upon the basis of the common ownership of the means of production, distribution and exchange." This summary of socialist philosophy was reprinted on the back of every party membership card.

The few party leaders who had in the past suggested tampering with this holy writ had been made to regret that they had ever broached the subject. Former Labour prime minister Harold Wilson had said that to amend Clause IV would be like removing Genesis from the Bible. And John Smith, although of the party's Right, reportedly "blew his top" when a member of the shadow cabinet suggested changing the clause.[40] Despite this forbidding history, just three months after winning the leadership Blair called for a special party conference to review Clause IV. Then "he ordered a high-profile crusade for change to be mounted in every part of the country," write Peter Mandelson and Roger Liddle. "What's more, he decided to lead it himself, and his [calendar] for the next three months was cleared for the purpose."[41]

The miners' hard Left leader Arthur Scargill said that Blair's action was like a bishop tearing up the Ten Commandments. But when the delegates gathered at Methodist Central Hall in Westminster, where Clause IV had first been adopted seventy-seven years before, 65 percent voted to approve the new language. It called for:

> A dynamic economy, serving the public interest, in which the enterprise of the market and the rigour of competition are joined with the forces of partnership and co-operation to produce the wealth the nation needs and the opportunity for all to work and prosper, with a thriving private sector and high quality public services, where those undertakings essential to the common good are either owned by the public or accountable to them.

If this was a little murky, it was nonetheless a far cry from Webb's version as well as from Attlee's diatribes against "wasteful competition." It opened the way for a closer embrace of capitalism during the two years leading up to the next general election. "The battle between market and public sector is over," declared Blair.[42] Labour's goal was "not to abolish the market, but to make it dynamic and work in the public interest."[43]

Taking aim squarely at the socialist tradition, he said: "The days of the all-embracing theories of politics—religious in nature, whose adoption would solve all human problems—are over."[44] Labour could not win if it remained shackled to an "outdated ideology."[45] Blair spoke of the need to "cross the old boundaries between left and right, progressive and conservative." And he took to describing his political camp as "left-of-centre" rather than "the Left."[46]

Blair proposed replacing the term "socialism" with "social-ism," meant to suggest a general spirit of human empathy rather than a rigid economic doctrine. He explained:

> Socialism to me was never about nationalisation or the power of the state; not just about economics or politics even. It is a moral purpose to life; a set of values; a belief in society, in cooperation, in achieving together what we are unable to achieve alone. It is how I try to live my life.
>
> The simple truths: I am worth no more than anyone else. I am my brother's keeper. I will not walk by on the other side. We aren't simply people set in isolation from each other, face to face with eternity, but members of the same family, the same community, the same human race. This is my socialism.[47]

In view of such statements and Blair's religious devotion, several analysts called his beliefs a form of Christian socialism, but it was hard to see how these ideas might be differentiated from "Christian capitalism" or just plain Christianity.

Blair often implied that he was merely summoning the party back from the leftist excesses of the Tony Benn era in the early 1980s. But much of his revision went too far even for veterans of the party's Right. One such figure, former deputy leader Roy Hattersley, wrote an article in 1995 lamenting the abandonment of the "bedrock ... principle" of "redistribution of power and wealth."[48] As the leftist writers Leo Panitch and Colin Leys noted, Blair's "big idea was ... that socialism, if it still meant anything at all, was a set of values that should guide public policy *under* capitalism, nothing more."[49]

As the 1997 election campaign took form, Blair moved further rightward. Speaking to the City of London (that is, the British stock exchange) he "formally tore up his party's longstanding opposition to the sale of public assets," reported the *Times*.[50] Until two years before, the party was still on record in favor of "social ownership" of the whole economy. Now, Blair embraced Thatcherite privatization. He said he wanted to create "a nation of entrepreneurs."[51]

Blair turned away not only from socialism but even from some policies of nonsocialist progressives. The "era of tax and spend is dead and buried," he said.[52] And while endorsing the implementation of a minimum wage, he boasted that nonetheless his policies "would amount to less labour market regulation than in the US."[53] Competing with the Conservatives for their core constituency, one campaign slogan proclaimed: "Labour is the party of business." Blair issued a special "Manifesto for Business," calling himself "the entrepreneur's champion" and promising "stable prices with an inflation target of 2.5 per cent or less, coupled with tough rules on borrowing and spending, and no rises in income tax."[54]

Martin Jacques, the former editor of *Marxism Today,* the journal of the Labour Left, bemoaned Blair's tactics:

> For anyone on the Left, or anyone who believes the Left has something distinctive to offer, the [campaign has] been deeply depressing. Labour's lead in the polls remains colossal and yet, with the Tories divided, exhausted and demoralised, it is still their arguments, their philosophy, their priorities, that are defining the agenda on which New Labour thinks and speaks.... [Blair's] principal concern is to reassure everybody that practically nothing will change under New Labour.[55]

However much it dismayed the Left, Blair's strategy worked to perfection. Labour rolled to its largest win ever, surpassing even Attlee's record triumph of 1945. The voting, coincidentally, was held on May 1, a date that was marked in bygone days by red banners and fiery speeches. But there was not the least rosy tint to this victorious May Day. David Marquand summed up the race as an exercise in jujitsu. "Thatcherism was, above all, an anti-socialist crusade," he said, and as a result of Blair's stands, "the Thatcherites found themselves in the undignified position of a contestant in a tug-of-war whose rival suddenly lets go of the rope."[56]

• • •

In office, Blair showed that he had learned from Clinton's mistakes as well as his successes. In 1994 the Gingrich-led Republicans profited from a backlash by voters who felt that Clinton had turned left after having campaigned to the right. Blair, in contrast, hewed closely to the stance struck during the election. In his first major speech as prime minister, he offered a program for moving a quarter-million people from "welfare to work." In rapid sequence he also proposed to cut the child allowance to single mothers and reform the disability system to make it less costly to the government. All this was laced with some bracing rhetoric: "A decent society is not based on rights. It is based on duty."[57]

Under the lead of Gordon Brown as chancellor of the Exchequer, the government reaffirmed its campaign pledge to hold inflation below 2.5 percent. It transferred authority for setting interest rates to the Bank of England, thus shielding the process from political pressures much as is done in the United States or Germany. Blair also made good his promise that the unions would be treated with "fairness not favours." Union leaders were given access to the government, but no more than businessmen. Into the third year of Blair's administration, the *Economist* observed that "big business and New Labour are closely entwined in a clammy embrace."[58] The government privatized the Commonwealth Development Corporation and mooted proposals for doing the same with the London Underground.

This is not to say that Blair governed exactly as the Tories would have done. He moved Britain closer politically to the Continent, including signing the Social Chapter of the Maastricht Treaty, which contains some rights and regulations to which the Conservatives objected.[†] He won enactment of a minimum wage and put forward what the *Economist* called "a bewildering array of worthy small initiatives on health and education," causing some businesses to complain about increased regulation.[59] He declared the goal of ending child poverty in Britain, although he did not accompany this with a program to achieve it. He advanced some offbeat ideas, notably to "rebrand" Britain, that is, to change its image abroad so as to make its exports more alluring.

The area in which he brought the most dramatic change was constitutional reform. He put through measures to devolve power to regional governing bodies in Scotland and Wales, to establish an elected mayor of London, to remove most of the hereditary members of the House of Lords. He also secured adoption of human rights and freedom of information acts.

---

† Confusingly, the Social Chapter supplanted the Social Charter.

Blair attempted to provide a theoretical framework for his policies by christening his ideology the "Third Way." Its essence was to "unit[e] the two great streams of left-of-centre thought—democratic socialism and liberalism—whose divorce this century did so much to weaken progressive politics across the West."[60] What he was alluding to specifically was the splintering of the pro-labor wing of the Liberal Party at the beginning of the twentieth century, which eventuated in the formation of the Labour Party. The leading American scholar of British politics, Samuel Beer, remarked: "the leader of the Labour Party is telling us that the founding of the Labour Party was a great mistake and that he looks forward to reversing that fatal deviation."[61] Ironically, just as Gorbachev was trying to return Bolshevism to its roots in social democracy, Blair was proposing to return social democracy to its roots in liberalism.

Willy Brandt, the former German chancellor and chairman of the Socialist International, liked to say that social democracy offered a "third way" between capitalism and communism. But the coordinates of Blair's "Third Way" lay further to the right, designating a mean between the mixed economy (itself a kind of midpoint) and laissez-faire. On the political spectrum this is hard to distinguish from pre-Thatcher Toryism. The goal, said Blair, was to advance four core values: "equal worth" (meaning civil equality or equal rights), opportunity for all, responsibility and community. There is little in this that could not be endorsed by conservatives except perhaps the last point, and even this would not be objectionable to religious or traditionalist conservatives. Blair said that "community" implies "strong government," but in his lexicon this was not the same as "big government," which he repudiated. Blair's approach undoubtedly ascribed a larger role to government than the Thatcherites would do, but not too large a role, and its exact dimensions remain murky. "The Third Way recognises the limits of government in the social sphere, but also the need for government within those limits," he explained none too helpfully.[62]

Looking beyond the frontiers of Britain, Blair explored creating an organization that would include "other center-left parties which might not be socialist"—in other words, a kind of international movement of the Third Way to supplant the Socialist International.[63] A fourteen-nation summit of this kind was hosted by German chancellor Gerhard Schroeder in Berlin in June 2000. It issued a communiqué that echoed almost to the word the four "values" enunciated in Blair's Third Way declaration. The participants included social democrats from industrialized countries, as well as President Bill Clinton, President Thabo Mbeki of South Africa and several heads of state from Latin America.

Schroeder had been as much a student of Blair's as Blair had been of Clinton's. In his 1998 campaign, Schroeder had declared his intention to be "tough on crime and its causes," and his pro-business effusions led some disillusioned leftists to brand him "comrade of the bosses." A *New Statesman* essayist who visited Germany during that campaign wrote that when he switched on the television, he thought he was watching "new Labour . . . dubbed in German."[64]

In September 2000, Blair and Schroeder joined with the social-democratic prime ministers of Holland and Sweden in a declaration that "progressive politics has been liberated from old attitudes." It called for "active government," "strengthen[ing] civil society" and more help for poor countries—but all within a context of "sound macroeconomic policy," "free trade" and an appreciation of "responsibilities as well as rights."[65]

As this suggests, Blair was at the vanguard of a strong current. Schroeder, declaring that his party was "breaking with . . . statist social democratic attitudes," put through an overhaul of the tax system that substantially reduced personal and corporate rates and eliminated entirely a major category of capital gains tax.[66] And he proposed reforms to the national pension system designed to stimulate greater reliance on individual investment. Spain's Socialist prime minister, Felipé Gonzalez, explained a like transition on the part of his party by saying that "capitalism is the least-bad economic system in existence."[67] And even Sweden's Social Democrats moved to lower tax rates, reduce government spending and privatize some state assets.

The only important holdout among socialist governments was Jospin's in France. He mocked the Third Way as "an excuse to abandon our socialist principles."[68] There was, however, some distance between Jospin's rhetoric and his practice, which continued to reflect the lessons of Mitterrand's *rupture*. The *Christian Science Monitor* reported: "[Jospin] has privatized more state-owned companies than his two conservative predecessors combined [and] has stood aside as a wave of mergers and aggressive takeovers have reshaped French capitalism along US lines."[69] For his part, Jospin confessed: "On some subjects I have surprised even myself."[70] And, softening his criticism, he said: "I believe that in fact the 'third way' is the national form that the effort to reshape theory and policy has taken in the UK, the same project as that which has been embarked upon by all the socialist and social democratic parties in Europe."[71] Thus it seemed that the French dissent to the Third Way was less a matter of policies than of provenance. "There is a certain originality in French socialism that must be preserved," Jospin insisted.[72]

So the French socialists would not have the Third Way; they would have something of their own. But Jospin's policies would no more have satisfied Babeuf or the Mitterrand of 1981 than Blair's policies would have satisfied Owen or Attlee. Parties with the name "Socialist," "Labor" or "Social Democrat" continued to win elections, but they shed all but a few remnants of the philosophies on which they were founded. What they came to stand for in the 1990s was more accepting of markets, private enterprise and economic inequality than were the parties of the Right in Europe in the 1950s and 1960s.

But to say that is also to acknowledge that the Right in the democratic world long ago yielded to certain positions of the Left, and at its core this was not under challenge. Every democratic capitalist economy includes a large public sector the bounds of which far exceed the narrow police and military functions of the "night watchman state" of laissez-faire theory. Everywhere, government functions include education, health care, social insurance for the old, the disabled and the indigent, and more. Some of the strands in these social safety nets were woven by socialists and some by conservatives out to steal the socialists' thunder. No major parties propose to tear them out wholesale.

This has occasionally led leftists to boast, and rightists to lament, that "we are all socialists, now." But the opposite is nearer to the truth. From the birth of socialism until late in the twentieth century, social democrats believed that the piecemeal reforms they championed—though gradual and democratic—would eventually add up to a socialized economy. By the century's end, however, even the French and Swedish socialists, not to mention the British and the German, came to deny any such intent. They recognized the limits of the welfare state, which are in part political: while voters have hefty appetites for government benefits, they rebel when taxes grow too high.

Still more profound are the economic limits. Socialists used to believe that state ownership or planning would prove more efficient than private competition, making socialism not only more just but also more productive than capitalism. That turned out to be a pipe dream. Today, it is all but universally acknowledged that the wealth that sustains the public sector is created in the private sector. This means that any attempt to expand the public sector beyond a certain point will backfire: if the private sector is squeezed too hard, government revenues will dry up. Thus, it is within the context of predominantly capitalist economies that democratic societies continue to debate about and experiment with relatively minor variations in taxes and social services. The parties of the mainstream Left may pour the cream that lightens the coffee of capitalism, but they are not offering any other beverage. And they have long ago ceased to dream of an elixir that would transport us to an earthly paradise.

12

—

THE KIBBUTZ
GOES TO MARKET

FROM NEW HARMONY TO MOSCOW, from Dar es Salaam to London, the story of socialism was the story of a dream unrealized, a word that would not be made flesh. The little utopias erected by the likes of Owen disintegrated soon after they began. Lenin found a way to seize power and to abolish capitalism by expropriating property and suppressing the former owners. But the societies the Communists created were a miserable caricature of the socialist vision. Social democrats like Attlee recognized that the use of coercion was a fatal error, but they discovered that the democratic path never led to anything more than a modified capitalism. And Third World socialism made a sorry tale.

There was, however, one exception to this unbroken record of disappointment. In the biblical promised land, the promise of socialism was at last fulfilled. It took the form of communities called *kibbutzim* (the plural of the Hebrew noun *kibbutz*) where, on average, four to five hundred people lived a life of sharing, cooperation and mutual support. Small as those settlements were, socialists of many stripes took heart from them. When Gorbachev visited Israel some six months after the dissolution of the Soviet Union, he toured kibbutz Ein Gedi and exclaimed: "this is what we meant by socialism."[1] The stalwart American socialist writer Irving Howe once said it was the kibbutz that proved that socialism was indeed possible despite all the disappointments.[2] And the philosopher Martin

Buber observed that, as distinct from all other efforts to construct socialism, the kibbutz stood out as "an experiment that did not fail."[3]

Unlike the denizens of the communes inspired by the nineteenth-century utopians, the kibbutzniks were not escaping from the larger society; rather, they were the spearhead of Jewish resettlement in Palestine. They were not fanciful types like Owen and Fourier, beguiled by images of taming lions and whales and other beasts in a universe of perfect harmony. They were all too aware of being up against a forbidding environment that demanded the full measure of their energy and practicality.

The first kibbutz, Deganya, was founded in 1910. Over the next seventy years there came to be some 270 kibbutzim. At their height, they were home to some 130,000 people, not enough to constitute a nation but far too many to dismiss as a negligible social experiment.

The kibbutzim practiced socialism of a very pure kind. The members rotated jobs, took their meals in a common dining hall, lived in identical little dwellings and deposited their offspring while still in swaddling clothes in children's homes. The youngsters lived and studied with their peers, save for a few hours' visit with parents each evening.

The movement officially adopted Marx's formula "from each according to his ability, to each according to his needs." Kibbutzniks rarely saw money, for goods were distributed according to exquisite standards of fairness. The goal was to go beyond mathematical equality to "human equality," taking into account discrepancies in biological, familial and other circumstances. Committees were formed to weigh special requests, and were in turn answerable to a general assembly, usually held weekly, in which every member was eligible to participate. Everything was thoroughly democratic.

It was not only in creating true socialism that the kibbutzim were successful. Their many remarkable accomplishments were instrumental to the birth and flourishing of the state of Israel. During the years that the Jewish settlement in Palestine struggled to lay physical claim to lands to which title had been purchased, it was the kibbutzim that staked out the furthest, most isolated and perilous outposts. They furnished many of the young men and women of the pre-statehood Jewish defense forces and later the Israeli army. Although the kibbutzim rarely comprised more than 3 percent of the population, they provided an estimated 20 percent of Israel's top military officers. They also produced a great part of the nation's agricultural goods and a disproportionate share of its industrial output.

Typical was kibbutz Ginosar, founded in 1937 in a narrow valley on the northwestern banks of the Sea of Galilee, in reality a lake called the "Kinneret" in Hebrew. It is a venue memorable to Christians for the miracle of loaves and fishes and other highlights of Jesus' ministry, and to Jews for resistance to Roman rule. The kibbutz lies in the shadow of Mount Arbel, on whose apex, a flat rocky cliff, the Jews built a fortress that for a time confounded Roman military engineers, much like the more famous fortress at Massada. Below, on the "sea" itself, Josephus tells us that the desperate Jews took to fishing boats in a hopeless confrontation with Roman warships.

I have known Ginosar since 1960, the year I turned thirteen. Bar mitzvahs were unheard of in my socialist family, but my mother's mother, a Zionist, took me to Israel instead. For part of the visit we stayed with distant cousins—a woman named Judith and her family—who lived at Ginosar. In 1972 I returned to Israel as the leader of a delegation of young American socialists invited by our Israeli counterparts. By chance, the model kibbutz to which they took us was Ginosar. I have returned to it periodically, including in 2001, when I found it in the throes of wrenching changes about which I interviewed a number of the older members.

Judith (pronounced *yoodeet* in Hebrew) was one of the original group of settlers at Ginosar. They had met as teenagers at Tel Aviv's A. D. Gordon School, named after the Zionist prophet of the "religion of labor." There were numerous strands of Zionist philosophy, but the exaltation of manual labor was common to most of them. It embodied the belief that the Jews could reclaim their ancestral home not merely by purchasing land but by mixing their labor with it. It drew on the feeling, too, that the Jewish nation had been deformed by exclusion from many manly vocations. And the influence of Marxism, which was strong among the secularized Jews who made up the larger part of the Zionist movement, added an ironic fillip. In this view, it was not the Jews who were the "chosen people," but the proletariat, and the Jews stood in unique danger of missing out on membership in this elect group because they numbered too many intellectuals and too few workers.

Upon graduation, some dozen or two of the Gordon School adolescents pledged to stick together to redeem by their own sweat another patch of the Palestinian wilderness for the Jewish nation. The Jewish Agency, the main Zionist organization, was buying as much land as it could in Palestine, which was governed by Britain as a "trust" territory, for distribution to Jewish pioneers. After some further study at an agricultural school and a period of apprenticeship at kibbutz Kinneret and kibbutz Deganya, this particular group settled in 1934 in the village of Migdal, overlooking the Ginosar valley, to await assignment to a piece of land.

In the interim, its ranks were augmented with occasional recruits. One was Avshalom, who became Judith's husband. He had made his way to Palestine at age fourteen after being expelled from his yeshiva in Lithuania because he preferred the soccer field to the synagogue. Through such accretions and the birth of five babies, the group's numbers passed thirty. To support themselves, they hired out as farm hands, while filling their evenings with intense discussions of their dreams and philosophies.

But they were marking time, and being young and eager, they found the delay excruciating. They would have gone wherever the Zionist authorities sent them, but in their limbo they cast a covetous eye on the Ginosar valley below. It had been purchased by Baron Rothschild, who had created his own Zionist corporation, the Palestine Colonization Association (PICA). PICA intended the land to be used for individual Jewish home-sites, not for a commune, but external events worked to the purposes of the would-be kibbutzniks.

A bloody Arab uprising in opposition to Jewish settlement broke out across Palestine in 1936. Aside from Migdal, there was no Jewish presence along the vulnerable road that connected Tiberius at the southern end of the Sea of Galilee with Sefat twenty kilometers north. Both ancient cities contained sizable Jewish populations, and it was perilous for them to be cut off from one another. So the Haganah, the Jewish defense force, helped the young Gordon School graduates to move down into the valley to help protect the Tiberius-Sefat road which ran through it. The settlement was to be temporary, in response to military necessity.

In the manner characteristic of the time, the colonists at once threw up a stockade and watchtower, the components of which they had constructed at Migdal. They lived in tents, and, apart from the tasks of self-defense, devoted themselves to clearing the land. It would yield nothing until they carted off myriad heavy stones and hacked their way through the dense spiny branches of hundreds of *sheizaf* trees to dig up their deep, interwoven roots. Their only immediate source of livelihood within the settlement was from fishing the lake, the return from which was not nearly enough to support them. So a large share of the men took jobs outside to bring income to the fledgling kibbutz.

Some toiled as stevedores in the port of Haifa, others in road construction, and the largest group at the potash works on the Dead Sea. One of these was

Ovadia—a swarthy man, tall and wiry but now in his eighties somewhat bent—who had come at age sixteen from Baghdad's once flourishing Jewish community to Tel Aviv, where he was swept off his feet by a socialist lecturer. He recalled to me how he used to commute back to Ginosar in part by boat after each three-week shift and would find the valley's temperatures, which often reach one hundred degrees, a respite from the ungodly heat of the Dead Sea basin.

Once they put down roots at Ginosar, the youngsters had no intention of leaving, no matter what the understanding between the Haganah and PICA. The Arab uprising ended in 1939, but they stayed put. PICA's overseer, they knew, did not work on the Sabbath, so one Saturday they mobilized all their manpower to build a permanent structure that would strengthen their claim to the land. Ottoman law, taken over by the British mandatory authorities, forbade the destruction of a roofed building even if it were erected by squatters. The more the settlers worked the land and built upon it, the stronger their legal rights became.

However, the dispute between the Ginosar settlement and PICA deterred the Zionist authorities from giving the new kibbutz such material assistance as was given to others. Compounding the problem, Ginosar's workforce was depleted in 1940 when ten of the men were arrested by the British authorities for the slaying of the *mukhtar,* or chief, of an Arab village with which the kibbutz quarreled over the use of one of the streams that fed the lake, and they were sentenced to long terms in prison in the ancient city of Akko. While those who worked outside turned over every penny to Ginosar, survival was a struggle. The kibbutzniks continued to live in tents, and their meager diet featured the daily ration of half an egg.

The world war brought additional burdens. As throughout Palestine, some of the men enlisted in the British army to fight against Hitler. Other men and women joined the Haganah or its elite commando force, the Palmach, which was founded in a eucalyptus forest on Ginosar in 1941. The forest continued to serve as the base for its first company, led by Yigal Allon, a young agriculture school graduate who had joined Ginosar the year of its founding. The Palmach cut its teeth assisting the Allies in the invasion of Syria and Lebanon, where its guerrillas served as scouts, guides, intelligence collectors and saboteurs.

The war's end meant demobilization for the Allies, but for the Jewish forces it only opened the way to new battles. To preserve itself with few financial resources, the Palmach became a kibbutz-based force. Each platoon was stationed on a kibbutz where its members did enough agricultural labor to support themselves while leaving time for their military duty. The platoons of closely located kibbutzim formed companies which were linked with neighboring areas into battalions. Yigal Allon became the commander of the entire Palmach and was regarded by many as the most important military leader in Israel's 1948 War of Independence.

Ginosar lost three men in the war, but with the achievement of statehood and relative security, the kibbutz grew and began to prosper. New manpower arrived in the form of refugees from the Holocaust. The painstakingly cleared land proved highly fertile, and there was more of it as the kibbutz absorbed some lands from which Arabs had fled. Moved by Allon's stature as a national hero, PICA relented to the squatters. Legitimized, Ginosar at last began to appear on maps, and it became eligible for loans and other benefits which the new state's Labor[†] government bestowed on the kibbutzim. The members were able to quit their outside jobs and to secure a livelihood within the settlement. Food in the dining hall became plentiful and the tents gave way to cottages. In 1952, running water was installed in the dwellings, but only in bathrooms, for introducing it into the kitchen area would have detracted from the practice of communal dining.

This is not to say that life was luxurious. After a morning in the fields or banana groves, the kibbutzniks would pour water over the concrete floors of their cottages before going for their midday dinner. The evaporation provided a kind of makeshift air conditioning as they passed the hottest hours of the day in siesta before going out again for their afternoon shifts.

The kibbutz cultivated bananas, cotton, grapes, citrus, olives, palms, mangoes, avocados, corn, alfalfa, soybeans and vegetables. It raised chickens, fish, dairy cattle and honeybees. It cooperated in fishing with kibbutz Ein Gev, located on the eastern banks of the lake at the foot of the Golan Heights, from which Syrian gunmen shelled its fields. They fished by night because the cotton nets they used were visible to the fish in daylight, yet their operation was productive. Each night they gathered tons of St. Peter's fish and a small fish called *lavnun* or Tiberias sardines that were canned in a plant operated jointly by the two kibbutzim. In addition to its economic rewards, the fishing served to assert Israel's claim to the lake against that of Syria.

---

† Most of the Zionist movements and parties included "labor" in their names or philosophies. There were many of them, and over the years they had many splits and fusions. After statehood, the system of proportional representation used to elect Israel's parliament further encouraged this tendency. For simplicity, I refer here to the governments of Israel's first thirty years as "Labor," eliding the changing party names and alliances.

The early 1950s witnessed a split in the main kibbutz federation. It was not about any practical matter, but over socialist theory and how to assess the Soviet Union. The split tore Ein Gev down the middle, and the impassioned disagreement proved intolerable within the intimate community of the kibbutz. Some 140 of the more pro-Soviet members of Ein Gev left and joined Ginosar.

In the 1960s and 1970s, the children of the original settlers reached maturity. Some received advanced agricultural training, and the innovations they introduced further advanced Ginosar's prosperity. The cottages were improved, as were the houses where the children lived. Each member began to receive modest cash allocations for clothing, furniture and travel. Cultural and recreational facilities were added. A Holocaust memorial was erected in the kibbutz's cemetery.[†]

This period also saw the kibbutz diversify its economy beyond farming and fishing. The reason was not strictly economic, for Ginosar's agricultural sector was booming; but the kibbutzniks discovered that an agricultural worker's productivity in the valley's harsh heat diminishes notably after the age of forty. In view of the strong ethos of productive labor, it was important to find employment for aging members. And, too, increases in productivity meant that fewer hands were required to work the kibbutz's land. A small plastics factory was opened. Later this was transformed to produce electrical switches, then medical appliances.

Ginosar's picturesque location on the shores of the lake, prized by Israeli vacationers for its water sports and by Christian pilgrims for its association with Jesus, made it a natural spot for tourism. So the kibbutz opened *Nof Ginosar,* or Ginosar View, a guesthouse and restaurant. When a wooden boat that two of Ginosar's fishermen found preserved in the mud of the lakeshore turned out to be two thousand years old, it was made the centerpiece of a little museum. Kibbutz publicists advertised that it might have been used by Jesus himself.

---

† This remarkable sculpture of Joseph Cafri's is one of the most moving Holocaust monuments in the world, although it is probably the least known. It consists of a black stone pedestal perhaps a foot high and some twenty meters long on which a set of railway tracks is mounted representing the transports that carried the victims to the camps. Crosswise between the tracks are white marble slabs, each engraved with the names of murdered parents or siblings of Ginosar's members. No relatives other than immediate family are included, but still the toll is 250. Avshalom, the soccer-loving yeshiva delinquent, for example, listed both parents and five siblings who had remained in Lithuania. The tracks terminate at a large, black, slightly broken Star of David, which leads the eye directly across the lake to a particular spot on the opposite overlook. It is Gamla, another fortified mountaintop settlement, like Arbel and Massada, where the Jews resisted the Romans until only two women remained alive, according to Josephus.

. . .

The golden age for Ginosar and the other kibbutzim lasted into the 1980s, but there was turbulence beneath a placid surface. The election of conservative Menachem Begin as Israel's prime minister in 1977 ended a stretch of Labor rule that extended back beyond the birth of the state. With it went a policy of generosity to the kibbutzim that included subsidies, tax breaks and government contracts. The change was psychological as well as financial. Part of the reward of being a kibbutznik was the feeling of belonging to what political scientist Shlomo Avineri calls a "serving elite," like Plato's "Guardians." The kibbutzniks, as author Tom Segev puts it, "were the nobility and priesthood of the national ideology."[4] Prime Ministers David Ben-Gurion, Levi Eshkol, Golda Meir, Shimon Peres and Ehud Barak were all at one time kibbutz members.

Because the kibbutz movement constituted such an important part of the Labor establishment, Begin was bound to view it with antipathy. His constituency was largely made up of Sephardis, Jews who had immigrated from the Arab countries. They were poorer and less inclined toward socialism than the European-born Ashkenazis who dominated Israel in its early years. Most Sephardis shunned the kibbutzim, so for Begin it was good politics to direct barbed comments their way. "Millionaires with swimming pools," he called the kibbutzniks. The characterization might easily have been laughed off, but it came as a shock to people who saw themselves as a selfless vanguard.

Ruder shocks were in store. The following years saw inflation in Israel reach 400 or 500 percent. Interest rates did not keep pace, so the inducement to borrow was overwhelming. To take a loan at even 100 or 200 percent interest was like receiving free money, a temptation that most kibbutzim, and many other Israeli citizens and companies, could not resist. When the government finally took drastic measures to halt the inflationary spiral, the kibbutzim faced payments they could not meet. The principal amounted to $30,000 for each kibbutznik, a burden thirty times the size of Mexico's per capita debt. To make matters worse, the kibbutz movement had invested its cash reserves in the markets to prevent their erosion during the time of high inflation, but the kibbutz leaders had little experience at this. They were easy marks for shady operators, and they placed their faith in some speculative ventures that turned out badly.

"What destroyed the kibbutz movement were the mistakes of its financial elite," laments Aharon Yadlin, a former cabinet minister and secretary of the United Kibbutz Movement.[5] In truth, the financial crisis did not destroy the kibbutzim. The government engineered a series of bailout agreements in 1989, 1996 and 1999. The banks wrote off hundreds of millions of dollars of debt, the government covered some and the rest was rescheduled. The debt crisis was not fatal to the kibbutzim but it was a symptom of something deeper. What was so devastating about all the borrowing, Yadlin points out, was that little of the money had been used as capital to boost the kibbutzim's earnings. Instead, it had been spent to raise the standard of living. The impulse to do this did not grow out of hedonism, but in the hopes of stemming the loss of members. By some point in the 1970s the majority of kibbutz-raised children were leaving.

This high rate of desertion reflected what Yaacov Oved calls "the problem of the third generation." Oved, a kibbutznik and a scholar at Yad Tabenkin, the research and documentation center of the United Kibbutz Movement, studies the history of communes around the world. Typically, he says, the founders are individuals burning with enthusiasm. Their children live to some degree "in the shade of their fathers and tend to maintain some of their spirit."[6] But the next generation "is always the problematic one." It is "prone to promote changes or even to disavow all the ideals of their fathers," says Oved.

An American example of this phenomenon, he points out, was Amana, the German Protestant sect that settled in Iowa in the 1800s to live a communal life. Their seven colonies prospered by producing household appliances. But in the 1930s, when the grandchildren came to dominate the community, they rebelled against the system. The church's commercial assets were broken into shares and divided among the members. Amana was integrated into the capitalist economy, and its appliances continue to grace American kitchens.

The idea that a similar process would unfold in the kibbutzim was unthinkable to the founders. They expected just the opposite. They themselves had to struggle to surmount their bourgeois upbringings; but they believed that "our children who are being raised in the ethos of the kibbutz would be the best kibbutzniks," recalls Yoel Darom, a founder of kibbutz Kfar Menachem and editor of one of the movement's journals.[7] An original leader of Deganya had explained: "For people to feel and think as they should in a life of complete equality and complete partnership, they have to be born into it."[8]

Thus did the kibbutzim become the sites of history's most serious effort to achieve socialism's perennial goal of a new man. Stalin, Mao and Hitler had proclaimed a similar purpose, but no reasonable person could believe that terror and mass murder were the methods that would produce a better human being. Here, in contrast, in a brotherly and nurturing environment, children were raised to socialism from infancy. It was largely in order to bring them up to be good socialists that they lived together in children's homes rather than sleeping in their parents' cottages.[†] "The child-parent link was deliberately downgraded," says Israeli author Daniel Gavron in his highly sympathetic study.[9] The community's strict rules of equality were engines of socialization, and the lessons were reinforced by classroom instruction in the values of the kibbutz.

Yet the results disappointed. As Gavron explains,

> For seventy years, the kibbutz as an institution exerted unprecedented influence over its members. No totalitarian regime ever exercised such absolute control over its citizens as the free, voluntary, democratic kibbutz exercised over its members. . . . [I]t organized every facet of their lives: their accommodations, their work, their health, their leisure, their culture, their food, their clothing, their vacations, their hobbies, and—above all—the education and upbringing of their children. Despite these optimal conditions . . . [those] who grew up in the new environment . . . were not imbued with communal and egalitarian values.[10]

In the end, rebellion against communal childrearing constituted the first major breakdown in the kibbutz system. Increasingly, the demand was heard for children to sleep in their parents' homes. Those who voiced it were primarily young mothers. At Ginosar, it was women who had married into the kibbutz who took the lead, but they alone would not have been enough to force such a big change, and on most kibbutzim it was the "natives" who championed home-sleeping. Most kibbutz-raised children spoke warmly of their upbringing, and yet these same individuals upon reaching adulthood did not want their children raised as they had been. Was it that their parental instincts overwhelmed their memories? Or was there a darker side to the communal rearing that was unacknowledged or unrecalled?

Certainly, not all had been happy in that system. One of my cousins, a daughter of Judith and Avshalom, recalled that from the age of kindergarten she begged her parents to move the family to the city so they could live together and she could follow her own interests rather than having to conform to her peers.

---

† Ironically, Deganya was a rare exception to this practice insofar as the children's sleeping arrangements were concerned. As the oldest kibbutz, it settled into its own ways before communal sleeping for children was established as a kibbutz norm.

That such feelings were not rare is attested in two books published in Israel in 1991. One is a collection of searing reminiscences of the children's houses gathered by Nurit Leshem, a kibbutz-raised psychologist.[11] The other is a novel, *Murder on a Kibbutz,* by Israel's popular mystery writer Batya Gur.

Though she writes fiction, Gur is prized for her portraits of Israeli life. In this work, the central character, Moishe, a middle-aged leader of the kibbutz and son of two of its founders, explodes at a community meeting:

> I remember vividly how [my father] used to take me back to the children's house when I ran away to their room at night.... I'm not saying there wasn't anything good about the way we grew up, but what about the misery, the nights when we woke up to a non-mother instead of a mother and a non-father instead of a father.... I want to tuck in my children at night myself... and when they have a nightmare I want them to come to my bed, not to some intercom, and not to make them go out at night in the dark looking for our room, stumbling over stones, thinking that every shadow is a monster, and in the end standing in front of a closed door or being dragged back to the children's house.[12]

A number of kibbutzim made the shift to family sleeping in the 1970s. Ginosar did it only in the late 1980s. As late as 1994, one kibbutz, Baram on the border with Lebanon, defeated a motion in its general assembly to end the system of collective sleeping. At the time, Baram was the last holdout. A few years later, it, too, gave in. One of the Baram idealists who fought against the change explained, "The abolition of the old system in all the other kibbutzim... is eventually leading to the disintegration of the kibbutz."[13]

Such fears seemed overstated. Could something as tangential to the economic system of the kibbutz as the children's living arrangements have such a powerful impact? In fact, it did. As a practical matter, the change required the enlargement of each residential unit to add more bedrooms. This massive construction project was a major reason for the heavy borrowing that wreaked havoc with the kibbutzim's ledger books. But there was also a more subtle consequence that was ultimately more profound.

In his imaginary republic, Plato had his "Guardians" raise their children in common, for he believed that family ties were the opening wedge to selfish individualism, which he wanted to eradicate. As he explained, parents who look upon all of the community's children as their own will not rend the community asunder by each applying that word "mine" to different things and dragging off whatever he can get for himself into a private home, where he will have his separate family, forming a centre of exclusive joys and sorrows. Rather they will all, so far as may be, feel together and aim at the same ends, because they are convinced that all their interests are identical.... [T]hey will be free of those quarrels that arise from ownership of property and from having family ties.[14]

In comparison with the kibbutz, Plato's republic—where a Guardian did not even know which of the shared offspring were biologically his own and where wives, too, were held in common—appears a grotesque parody. And yet the relationship between family feeling and selfish materialism played out on the kibbutz much as it had in Plato's imagination. Moving the children in with their parents "led to privatizing of many things," said Shlomo Avineri, Israel's foremost socialist thinker. "It was an across-the-board reorganization of public and private space."[15] Menachem Rosner, the senior scholar at Haifa University's Institute for Research on the Kibbutz and the Cooperative Idea and a kibbutznik himself, explains that the kibbutz was transformed from "an afamilistic to a highly familistic society," a change that amounted to a "revolution" in its sociology.[16]

One sign of this transformation was a new mode of dining. The dining hall, which had pulled the community together three times a day, had been the backbone of the traditional kibbutz. Now with increasing frequency meals were prepared at home. The cooking facilities in the dwellings were enhanced, and, like most other kibbutzim, Ginosar opened its own small supermarket called Hyper Ginosar.

The new sleeping and eating arrangements fed an efflorescence of individualism that ate away at the ethos and structure of the kibbutz. Yet they were not the underlying source of this process. Indeed, from the earliest days, the history of the kibbutz was an endless chain of compromises between the stringent communal ideals of the founders and the germ of egoism which they could never fully conquer. At Ginosar as elsewhere, the early kibbutzniks had decided to foreswear possessing even their own clothing. Garments were handed in to the central laundry each week, and clean ones of the appropriate size (more or less) were received in exchange. After a couple of years, the women could stand this no longer, and the kibbutz made its first bow to private property. Typically, the second bow, says Darom, occurred when the men who had volunteered for the British army in World War II returned with electric teakettles or some other small furnishing. The kibbutz could not force members to relinquish such prizes, but they introduced an intolerable element of inequality. The solution? Buy a kettle for each household. However, with a teakettle in each dwelling the first step had been taken in undermining communal dining. In subsequent similar cycles, each member was furnished with a refrigerator and then a television.

Even when clothes were individually owned, they were at first usually purchased in bulk by the kibbutzim; but in time the members asserted the desire to select their own, so the system of cash allowance was instituted. Eventually, the same was done for furnishings, toiletries and travel. A further transition came in the 1980s when Ginosar's membership, and that of the majority of kibbutzim, voted to combine these separate allocations into "inclusive budgets" which members could use for whatever they wished. This was called "privatization."

The growth of private budgets was encouraged not only by the demand for greater consumer choice, but also by the desire to hold down costs in the face of the debt crisis and the recognition that providing things free encouraged wastefulness. "The electricity used to burn by day and by night," Moshe told me. He was one of Ginosar's original fishermen, a bear of a man with weather-beaten skin capped by sparse, crew-cut white hair. "And food was free so people would bring friends and even new acquaintances to meals. Sometimes strangers would just wander in and eat." Finally, Ginosar and other kibbutzim began to charge for electricity in the cottages and for meals in the dining hall, enlarging the members' private budgets accordingly and causing a sharp drop in food and energy use.

• • •

The shoots of individual identity and self-interest had always managed to force their way through the crevices in the kibbutz's edifice of selfless collectivism, but the financial crisis of the 1980s exacerbated this erosion to the crumbling point by undermining the sense of security. The kibbutzim were facing insolvency, and although the government did arrange bailouts, the kibbutzniks knew that the nation no longer relied on them to settle the land and guard the borders. How long would it continue to underwrite them? The question haunted those at the end of their working years. Because they had never imagined reaching such a pass, no pensions had been put aside. It was assumed that the kibbutz would be there always and that it would provide.

"The older people are frightened," said Isaac, a short man in his seventies with a thick crop of white hair, the spokesman for Ginosar's seniors. What would become of them if the kibbutz went bankrupt, and how could they provide for themselves if it were put entirely on a market basis, as Ginosar's leaders were now planning? We spoke in 2001 as he showed me around the little private orchard of perfectly cultivated citrus, palm and other tropical trees surrounding his cottage. He had reached Israel after enduring Auschwitz and surviving a Nazi firing squad, and was sent to Ginosar where he became an agricultural expert. The kibbutz's leaders during its time of transition, mostly the age of Isaac's children, had agreed to measures that would safeguard the elders, but they would not retreat from the process of converting the kibbutz to a new economic system. "We will take care of you; but who will take care of us?" they asked.

Although the elderly were the most vulnerable, the sense of insecurity was felt by all. It became common for people with private income—pensions from outside jobs, gifts from family members off the kibbutz, or reparations to Holocaust survivors from the German government—to deposit it in personal bank accounts rather than contribute it to the collective as the rules required. There was a visible weakening of the communal ethic. "It used to be that no one would walk on the lawns or litter, but that has changed," rued one lifelong kibbutznik.[17]

Selfish behavior was not entirely new: every kibbutz had slackers. It was "paradise for parasites," quipped one Ginosar veteran. Yuval Dror, a specialist on kibbutz education at Tel Aviv University and a member of kibbutz Hamadya, told me: "People like me who started as socialists concluded that you can work hard and get nothing while others don't work hard. It is so unfair."[18] Such problems "were there all along," explains one of my cousins, who left Ginosar in his forties, "but the pride people took in being kibbutzniks enabled them to tolerate these things." With the days of pioneering long past and the kibbutzim "looked upon as miserable beggars," as Aharon Yadlin remarked bitterly, that feeling became a thing of the past.[19]

The ill-judged borrowing and speculation were but symptoms of an underlying issue. Agriculture could not furnish the kind of standard of living that Israelis, including kibbutzniks, came to desire. "We wanted to make a modest life," Moshe the old fisherman told me wistfully. "The children today don't even want to hear the word 'modest.'" Diversifying from agriculture to production and service industries, as Ginosar did with its factories and guesthouse, boosted revenues, but much about the economy of the traditional kibbutz was uneconomic.

At Ginosar, several successful enterprises—reflecting the talent and ingenuity of many of the members—arose alongside reminders of less well-conceived ventures—reflecting a lack of seasoned management. Ginosar's fields are remarkably fruitful: its banana groves have long been the most productive in the country. The plastics and electronics factories were succeeded by a biotech operation cloning plant tissue and marketing banana seedlings to growers in Central America. When ostrich farming seemed like a coming thing in America, Ginosar raised ostriches and shipped fertilized eggs to Texas. The former children's houses were converted into cabins for vacationers seeking a longer stay at cheaper rates than at the guesthouse.

On the other side of the score sheet, the kibbutz became home to a flock of feral peacocks, the last vestige of a long-forgotten petting zoo. Along the Tiberias-Sefat road, which the founders guarded against the Arabs, stands a restaurant where the feature once was "chicken and gloves." The gloves were of the medical kind because some kibbutznik had the notion that diners would enjoy ripping and eating their roasted birds with their hands without getting messy. After that venture failed, which did not take long, the facility was leased to an entrepreneur who opened a successful establishment featuring Lebanese cuisine.

Even where kibbutzim abandoned job rotation in order to keep talented managers in place, they discovered that their closely knit social structure militated against efficient administration. How do you fire or demote your neighbor? A couple of Ginosar's ablest administrators, including one of Avshalom and Judith's sons, took jobs managing other kibbutzim while continuing to live at Ginosar. Meanwhile, Ginosar hired a nonmember as its manager. "We bring in outside experts and professionals," Isaac told me pointedly, "because they have relations with no one."

A kibbutz's prospects for survival depended not only on effective management but also on its ability to stanch the loss of membership. Often, the most economically productive members were the ones most tempted to leave. It was said that the kibbutz was a great place for children and the elderly but not for those of working age: people who can make a good living on the outside were the ones most likely to chafe under the traditional egalitarianism. Dror told me that the outflow of professionals and managers from Hamadya included a majority of those who served as kibbutz secretary (CEO) during the preceding decades.

The kibbutzim long ago departed from the founders' emphasis on the sanctity of Jewish labor. The question of "who will collect the trash" was an old bone of socialist theoretics. The kibbutz discovered that the answer was no one—at least no one from within the community. Eventually, Thais were hired to work in Ginosar's fields and Arabs to clean the hotel guestrooms and serve the meals. While hired labor could be imported to perform the least desirable jobs, a further departure from socialist ideals proved necessary to stem the outflow of the kibbutz's most skilled workers, namely the introduction of pay differentials.

At first, a proposal merely to pay extra for overtime was controversial because it violated the principle "to each according to his needs." But in 1997 the more radical step of assigning wages according to skill level was adopted at Ginosar. The first kibbutz to do this, Ein Zivan in the Golan, was threatened with expulsion from the kibbutz movement in 1993, but before long many others followed its example. Pay grades were assigned according to what it would cost to hire an outsider; however, differentials were limited to a ratio of five to one if the community was to retain the tax status of a kibbutz. In addition, kibbutzniks are free to find jobs outside the kibbutz, as about a fourth of Ginosar's working members did as of 2001. They keep whatever wages they are able to make on the open market—after a substantial part is taken in taxes. These include a steep national income tax and an additional tax imposed by the kibbutz that goes to furnishing a safety net for the elderly and for other community overhead.

As the numbers of the pensionless older generation thin, the taxes are likely to be reduced. There is concern that the high rates discourage earning. A young divorced mother of two who worked outside Ginosar as an accountant told me she had turned down the offer of a promotion. "If I make more I'll end up with less," she joked. Her true motive, I suspected, was to avoid losing time with her children, but the small amount of the raise that would have remained in her pocketbook clearly entered into her decision.

Ginosar shifted entirely to a cash economy. With their after-tax earnings, the members pay not only for food and electricity but for all the goods and services they receive, even education. Only some property maintenance, basic medical coverage and landscaping of the common areas comes free. And at Ginosar, as at other kibbutzim, members took ownership of their dwellings. Many kibbutzim have built or have made plans to build adjacent housing for sale to the public. With their well-tended lawns and gardens, they are often idyllic environments. The idea is to attract suburbanites to whom the kibbutz sells various services, like education and dependent care

In addition to establishing ownership of dwellings, some kibbutzim have privatized their productive assets by distributing shares to the members. Henry

Near, author of the standard history of the kibbutzim, explains the motives this way:

> During most of the history of the kibbutz movement social change was justi-
> fied (or resisted) on grounds which stemmed from, or were compatible with,
> a socialist world-view. From about 1980 onwards, however, the ideologi-
> cal background changed....The improvisations were still ideologized, but
> the ideology was no longer that of socialism, but of late twentieth-century
> capitalism.[20]

A former head of the kibbutz movement and an opponent of the new trends, Muki Tsur, said mockingly in 2001: "Some of the most romantic images of capitalism in the world can be found today on the kibbutzim."[21]

Led by men like Tsur and Yadlin, some 40 out of the 270 kibbutzim formed a group called the "Collective Trend" to resist the abandonment of socialism. But this was little more than a rearguard action, for these forty differed from the majority only in the pace, not the direction, of change. "It is not an exaggeration to describe the condition of the kibbutz as terminal," wrote Daniel Gavron in 2000.[22] As he foresaw, the communities built by the pioneers have not disappeared; rather, they evolved into "communities, with certain enterprises commonly owned, with a measure of cooperation and mutual assistance, with some Jewish festivals celebrated together, and with an egalitarian tradition that will diminish year by year."[23]

In April 2001, the *Jerusalem Post* reported that Mishmar David in central Israel became "a pioneer among kibbutzim . . . the first one [to] dismantl[e] itself in order to become an ordinary Israeli community."[24] Its members voted 50 to 1 in favor of a transformation that gave each of them title to his own dwelling and a share in the kibbutz's factory while selling off some land to liquidate the community's collective debt. This, however, proved atypical. Mostly kibbutzim cohered as they transformed into communities of private ownership. In this new guise they experienced a resurgence of sorts, as younger couples found them to be affordable and attractive environments in which to live and raise families away from urban bustle.

The story of the kibbutzim bears resemblance to the history of New Harmony and other communes founded in America in the nineteenth century. Those created for the explicit purpose of practicing socialism collapsed quickly. But many religious communes, in which socialism was ancillary to a binding faith, succeeded for long periods. Only a small fraction of the kibbutzim were religiously based, and those held up better than most. For others, the burning commitment to Zionism was the functional equivalent of a religious faith, and the old veterans look back with satisfaction on what they accomplished. "I am not sorry about how I spent my life," reflects Isaac. "I feel proud; I feel like I did something."

With the passing of the heroic pioneering phase of Israel's development, however, the communal way of life proved difficult to sustain. Ovadia, who sweated to support the kibbutz by mining potash from the Dead Sea, told me: "Now I think the system is a mistake because not all people will give their best if they can get things free." And Isaac admits: "We were abnormal." Driven by the most powerful motivations—rebuilding a country, rescuing a people—they accomplished great feats. But one goal defied them utterly. As an old member of Kibbutz Kinneret put it, they had "tried to change human nature and create a new man. To my regret, the kibbutz did not succeed at this task."[25]

•   •   •

Kibbutz Kinneret lies just a few kilometers from Ginosar traveling south along the edge of the Sea of Galilee. It is here that the founders of Ginosar apprenticed and that Ovadia joined up with the group. When statehood was achieved, a special section of its cemetery was established to provide a final repose for the earthly remains of the most important founders of Zionism that were gathered back from the Diaspora. Notable among them is Moses Hess, whose extraordinary personal story points to answers to the central mysteries of socialism.

Those mysteries are two: How could an idea that so consistently showed itself to be incongruent with human nature have spread faster and further than any other belief system ever devised? And how did an idea calling upon so many humane sentiments lend its name to the cruelest regimes in human history?

Before Hess' bones were carried to Kinneret to lie with those of the other Zionist heroes, they had found a different honor at their original resting place. His grave in Cologne had been marked with a headstone commissioned by the Social Democratic Party and engraved with the words: "Father of German Social Democracy." An apposite tribute it was, for long before he became a Zionist, Hess had been, as a young Engels wrote in an article in Owen's *New Moral World,* "the first Communist in the party." It was Hess who had played the major part in winning Marx and Engels to communism.

A "tall, scrawny man with benevolent eyes and a cock-like curve to his neck," as Marx described him,[26] Hess was renowned for his "purity of character" and "saintly" ways.[27] After fleeing the cudgels of a benighted rabbinic teacher who tried to beat the Talmud into him, Hess had turned away from religion and immersed himself in the ideas of the Enlightenment. But his spirit was uneasy. He confided in his diary: "I worked without rest to rediscover my God, whom I had lost. . . . Nor could I remain a skeptic for the rest of my life. I had to have a God—and I did find him, after a long search, after a terrible fight—in my own heart."[28]

The God he found was communism. In a catechism composed in 1846, Hess contrasted his new faith with the one that prevailed in the society around him. Whereas Christians invest their hopes "in the image of . . . heavenly joy . . . We, on the other hand, want this heaven on earth."[29] He credited Babeuf with having "laid the groundwork for . . . the new ethics."[30] And he took it upon himself to translate Buonarroti's memoir of the Conspiracy of Equals into German.

Although Hess was several years Marx's senior and led him in the embrace of communism, he soon deferred to the younger man's superior polemical and theoretical gifts, calling Marx his "idol" who "will give the final blow to all medieval religion and politics."[31] Despite the deference, however, many of the ideas associated with Marx's name—about alienation, class struggle, the withering away of the state and other subjects—were foreshadowed in the writings of Hess. So were some famous passages of Marxian rhetoric, including the *Communist Manifesto*'s reference to "the specter of Communism" and what became the kibbutz movement's guiding slogan: "From each according to his ability; to each according to his needs."[32]

Marx's intellectual debt to Hess "was not always publicly—or privately—acknowledged," observes Shlomo Avineri gently.[33] Neither was the debt of loyalty. Hess continued for many years to offer Marx assistance—even at times representing him at meetings of the First International—although he disagreed on some matters of doctrine and he objected to Marx's rough handling of dissident comrades. For his part, Marx would not forgive Hess his deviations, especially his persistence in trying to ground socialism on an ethical basis rather than on historical inevitability. Hess, Marx wrote to Engels, was one of "those pieces of party excrement" that Lassalle "keeps on collecting for his manure factory."[34] And Engels wrote Marx gleefully about having seduced Hess' wife.[35]

The ethical element in his thought, which Marx and Engels found so contemptible, combined with anguish over the persistence of anti-Semitism to lead

Hess to the idea of Zionism. In 1862, with little to foreshadow it, he published *Rome and Jerusalem,* which reasserted a profound sense of Jewish identity. He declaimed:

> Here I stand again in the midst of my people, after being estranged from it for twenty years, and actively participate in its feasts and fasts, in its memories and hopes, in its inner spiritual struggles....A mental picture again vividly arises before me: a picture of my people inseparably united with my ancestral heritage, the Holy Land, the Eternal City, the place where the belief in the divine unity of life and the future brotherhood of man was born.[36]

Hess did not abandon socialism, nor did he return to strict Jewish observance. His focus was on regathering the Jewish people in their ancestral home. But as the foregoing passage makes clear, his newfound nationalism was rooted in religious sensibility and ethical concerns. The point of rebuilding Zion was not simply national fulfillment but, as Jewish tradition held, the inauguration of the messianic age. This was different from the "heaven on earth" of his youthful catechism. In Jewish belief the focus of messianism is not on eternal reward but on progress toward moral perfection.

Although Hess was a pioneer, it was only in this last phase that he diverged from the temper of the times. His early writings formed part of the swell of what Isaiah Berlin calls the "historico-theological systems" that came flooding out of German universities in the early 1800s, aiming "to find in art or science the path to individual or national salvation which the orthodox Christian churches seemed no longer capable of providing for critical minds."[37] A similar quest was pursued in England, Italy and, of course, France, which had done the most to create the vacuum that the new systems were designed to fill.

France was the capital of the Enlightenment, an eighteenth-century intellectual movement spearheaded by writers who called themselves *philosophes.* They had waged a campaign of relentless criticism of the church and revealed religion, which their leader Voltaire called "the infamous thing." The crusade was so effective that by 1778, when an eighty-three-year-old Voltaire returned to Paris after decades away, he was received like a "victorious general," as Peter Gay describes it.[38] The Jesuit order had been suppressed, and various indicators showed a decline in devotion among the public. The effects were most profound in the ranks of the articulate and highborn. "Frank atheism was still comparatively rare, but among the enlightened scholars, writers, and gentlemen who set the intellectual fashions of the later eighteenth century, frank Christianity was even rarer," writes historian E. J. Hobsbawm.[39]

The decline of faith was fueled by a rise of science, but not all who lost faith became scientific. "Fashionable women kept books of science on their dressing tables, and, like Mme. de Pompadour, had their portraits painted with squares and telescopes at their feet," say the Durants.[40] Nonetheless, "a thousand superstitions survived side by side with the rising enlightenment."[41] The same Madame de Pompadour, Louis XV's mistress, frequented a fortune-teller who read the future in coffee grounds. Other leading figures of his court did the same.

Like Voltaire, those who were neither Christians nor atheists usually were deists. Deism affirmed the existence of God, or better, of some "supreme being" or "eternal cause," but denied the legitimacy of the church and the authority of Scripture. What separated deists from atheists was a need to explain creation or a fear of the moral consequences of a godless world.

Deism enjoyed its apotheosis in the French Revolution with the replacement of the Christian calendar by one in which the days, months and seasons were renamed for plants and animals and types of weather. But this transformation, like other innovations such as changing the name of the Cathedral of Notre Dame to the Temple of Reason, did not last long; for it served only to illustrate the depth of the human impulse to religion. Diderot, whose *Encyclopédie* was the flagship of the Enlightenment, confessed that he could not watch religious processions "without tears coming to my eyes."[42]

Most anthropologists agree that religion is a universal; they have yet to discover a civilization of logical positivists. As the eminent scholar Edward O. Wilson said in his acceptance speech upon receiving the 1999 Humanist of the Year Award:

> There is no doubt that spirituality and religious behavior of some kind are extremely powerful and, it appears, necessary parts of the human condition. . . . The inability of secular humanist thinkers to satisfy this instinct, even when evidence and reason are on their side, is surely part of the reason that there are only 5,300 members of the American Humanist Association and sixteen million members of the Southern Baptist Convention.[43]

Accordingly, the Enlightenment's discrediting of Christianity left Europe in the early nineteenth century hungering for a new faith. Robert Owen's movement with its church-like "halls of science" aimed to fill the need, but he was unable to fashion a coherent doctrine. Had socialism remained the work of such fanciful souls as he, it would have been as marginal as humanism, pacifism, ethical culturism, vegetarianism, prohibitionism and so many other goodhearted but feckless theories.

Engels and Marx, however, succeeded in recasting socialism into a compelling religious faith, and their socialism absorbed or eclipsed all others. Attlee, for example, claimed in *The Labour Party in Perspective* that his thinking was rooted in Christianity and Owen rather than in Marx, but like Molière's *bourgeois gentilhomme* who had been "speaking prose without knowing it," Attlee's idiom reverberated with Marxist concepts. He spoke of class struggle, historical materialism, the supersession of socioeconomic systems in response to technological change and the like. Nothing akin can be found in Owen or the Gospels.

Marxism made socialism a religion by reducing all of history and all problems to a single main drama. "Communism is the riddle of history solved," said Marx. Solving the riddle meant not only comprehending the past but foreseeing the future. It "transferred the centre of gravity of the argument for socialism from its rationality or desirability to its historic inevitability," said Hobsbawm, giving it "its most formidable intellectual weapon."[44] In truth, the claim of inevitability was not an intellectual weapon but a religious one. It had no logical weight but great psychological power, paralleling Engels' boyhood faith of Pietism, which embodied a doctrine of predestination.

Nor was this the only way that socialism echoed revelation. It linked mankind's salvation to a downtrodden class, combining the Old Testament's notion of a chosen people with the New Testament's prophecy that the meek shall inherit the earth. Like the Bible, its historical narrative was a tale of redemption that divided time into three epochs: a distant past of primitive contentment, a present of suffering and struggle, and a future of harmony and bliss. By investing history with a purpose, socialism evoked passions that other political philosophies could not stir. As the American socialist intellectual Irving Howe put it,

> Not many people became socialists because they were persuaded of the correctness of Marxist economics or supposed the movement served their "class interests." They became socialists because they were moved to fervor by the call to brotherhood and sisterhood; because the world seemed aglow with the vision of a time in which humanity might live in justice and peace.[45]

Most socialists would deny that their creed is religious in character. Did not Marx say that religion is an opiate? But many have given evidence of the religious quality of their belief. Michael Harrington, a fallen-away product of Jesuit education who became the preeminent American socialist of his generation, once wrote: "I consider myself to be—in Max Weber's phrase—'religiously musical' even though I do not believe in God. . . . I am . . . a 'religious nature without religion,' a pious man of deep faith, but not in the supernatural."[46] A Harrington disciple, sociologist Norman Birnbaum, has been more blunt. "Socialism in all its forms," he writes, "was itself a religion of redemption."[47]

Harrington may not have made as clean a break with the supernatural as he liked to believe. To be sure, Marxism contained no gods or angels, yet it had its own mystical elements. It claimed that human behavior was determined by abstract, exterior forces: people do what they do not for the reasons they think, but because of the mode and means of production and the class structure. To compound the mystery, Marx and Engels did not believe that the forces they described governed their own actions, but they did not explain why they were exempt.

Nonetheless, Marxism's departure from empiricism was less glaring than that of revealed religions and did not prove fatal to its claim to be scientific. Marx and Engels were pioneers in applying the terminology of science to human behavior. The term "science" had only come fully into vogue in the early nineteenth century, replacing the older "natural philosophy," and it carried a powerful cachet. Every day science was finding explanations for things that had long seemed inexplicable, so Marxism's claim to having broken the code to history did not seem implausible.

Before Marx, Robert Owen always characterized his activities as scientific (as did Saint Simon, Fourier and the other utopian socialists), and the claim was valid. Owen hit upon the idea of socialism and then set about to test it by creating experimental communities. Such experimentation is the very essence of the scientific method. Owen strayed from science only at the point that he chose to ignore his results rather than reconsider his hypothesis. Engels and Marx replaced experimental socialism with prophetic socialism, and claimed thereby to have progressed from utopia to science.

Thus, part of the power of Marxism was its ability to feed religious hunger while flattering the sense of being wiser than those who gave themselves over to unearthly faiths. In addition, the structure of rewards proffered by socialism was so much more appealing than in the biblical religions. For one thing, you did not have to die to enjoy them. Ernest Belfort Bax, the most voluble of the founders of British Marxism, wrote a book titled *The Religion of Socialism* that reprised the young Hess:

> Socialism . . . brings back religion from heaven to earth. . . . It looks beyond the present moment . . . not . . . to another world, but to another and a higher social life in this world. It is in . . . this higher social life . . . whose ultimate possibilities are beyond the power of language to express or thought to conceive, that the socialist finds his ideal, his religion.[48]

The same ecstatic tone reverberated in Trotsky's forecast that under socialism the average person would exhibit the talents of a Beethoven or a Goethe, and in Harrington's vision of "an utterly new society in which some of the fundamental limitations of human existence have been transcended. . . . [W]ork will no longer be necessary. . . . The sentence decreed in the Garden of Eden will have been served."[49]

The biblical account of Adam and Eve's fall explained the hardships of life. It also portrayed mankind's capacity for evil as well as good, suggesting that we might ameliorate the hardship by cultivating our better natures. As Harrington's bold promise suggests, socialism made things easier. Not only did it vow to deliver the goods in this world rather than the next, but it asked little in return. At the most, you had to support the revolution. At the least, you had to do nothing, since ineluctable historical forces would bring about socialism anyway. In either case you did not have to worship or obey. You did not have to make sacrifices or give charity. You did not have to confess or repent or encounter that tragic sense of life that is the lot of those who embrace a non-secular religion. No doubt, many or most of those drawn to socialism felt some sense of humane idealism, but its demands were deflected outward onto society as a whole.

If this is what made the religion of socialism so attractive, it also explains what made it so destructive. Religion is ubiquitous, reaching far back into the human dawn: prehistoric cave drawings depict what appear to be mythical images. But early ideas about the cosmos reflected little that we would recognize as moral content, as the bawdy shenanigans of the Greek deities illustrate. The Bible changed this. And the advent of the Bible was only a part of a global transformation that historian Herbert J. Muller places around the sixth century B.C., with the rise of Zoroastrianism, Hinduism, Buddhism, Confucianism and Taoism, as well as the culmination of the prophetic movement in Judaism. These faiths, he says,

> all moved away from the immemorial tribal gods and nature gods, toward more universal, spiritual conceptions of deity or the cosmic order. Their primary concern was no longer the material success of the nation or the assurance of good crops, but the spiritual welfare of man. They offered visions of some Good beyond the flux of earthly life, rescuing man from his long obsession with food and phallus. They proposed different ways of treating the powers above, but ways alike more amenable to his ideal purposes. Their service of deity was far from mere servility.[50]

From then on, each of the world's major faiths connected some theory of the nature of the world with a moral code. Two and a half millennia later, the religion of socialism sundered that connection. What was different about it was not the absence of God, since Buddhism and Confucianism also have no God, but rather the absence of good and evil or right and wrong. This opened the doors to the terrible deeds that were done in the name of socialism.

To be sure, terrible deeds have also been done in the name of the traditional religions. One can cite the Crusades, the Inquisition, the World Trade Center and more. The idea of ultimate salvation—religious or secular—can be used to justify many things. Religious zealots have rationalized their depredations by selective interpretation of holy texts, finding authority for attacks against outsiders or coreligionists whom they deem wayward. But in so doing they also ignore or suppress core elements of their creeds that address moral commands to the believer himself, constraining his actions. Socialism, in contrast, lacks any internal code of conduct to limit what believers may do. The socialist narrative turned history into a morality play without the morality. No wonder, then, that its balance sheet looks so much worse. Over about three centuries the Crusades claimed two million lives; Pol Pot snuffed out roughly the same number in a mere three years. Regimes calling themselves socialist have murdered more than one hundred million people since 1917. The toll of the crimes by observant Christians, Muslims, Jews, Buddhists or Hindus pales in comparison.

By no means were all socialists killers or amoral. Many were sincere humanitarians; mostly these were the adherents of democratic socialism. But democratic socialism turned out to be a contradiction in terms, for where socialists proceeded democratically, they found themselves on a trajectory that took them further and further from socialism. Long before Lenin, socialist thinkers had anticipated the problem. The imaginary utopias of Plato, More, Campanella and Edward Bellamy, whose 1887 novel, *Looking Backward*, was the most popular socialist book in American history, all relied on coercion, as did the plans of the Conspiracy of Equals. Only once did democratic socialists manage to create socialism. That was the kibbutz. And after they had experienced it, they chose democratically to abolish it.

Afterlife

13

EPILOGUE:
RISING FROM THE ASHES

BY THE END OF THE TWENTIETH CENTURY the idea of socialism had withered and died. It had germinated in the French Revolution, gradually grown up over the nineteenth century, then borne fruit, mostly bitter, over the sixty-odd years following World War I. Its denouement had appeared most vividly in the collapse of its mightiest branch, the Soviet Communist empire that fell with the Berlin Wall in 1989. Less dramatically but no less definitively, socialism's various other manifestations had gone the same way. Chinese Communists had discovered that "to get rich is glorious." European social democracy had begun to bill itself "the party of business." The Third World had forsaken state planning, striving instead to replicate the commercial wizardry of the "four tigers." Even the kibbutzim—working socialist utopias in snow globes—had opted to go private. History, said Francis Fukuyama, had ended.

But then a new generation began to come of age without direct memory of "history." And like the phoenix, socialism seemed to rise from the ashes and weave its spell once again. The image of equality, harmony and easy abundance still tantalized; it gained new cachet as a panacea for the pains of globalization, migration and industrial obsolescence.

And even as the glitter of socialism was enticing innocents in some corners, the dead hand of history was making its weight felt to lamentable effect in others. The socialist behemoths, Russia and China, did not follow the paths to free market democracy that had seemed to be laid out before them. Instead, they veered off in menacing new directions, shaped almost invisibly by their socialist past, but now driven not by illusory ideals, rather just by the grim satisfactions of power.

Could the world, once terrified by Soviet or Chinese Communism, now be haunted by their ghosts? Or, could nations be beguiled, or beguile themselves, down the barren blind alleys or fatal trapdoors of the previous hundred years? This had been unthinkable in the immediate aftermath of socialism's fall, but in one place and then another voices were raised proposing exactly that, and they found attentive listeners.

• • •

The siren song of socialism was first heard again in 1998 when Venezuelans, chafing under austerity imposed in response to plummeting revenues from oil exports, elected Hugo Chávez Frías their president. This vote was a sad omen of a crisis of democracy that was to beset the world a decade later.

In 1992 as a young colonel, Chávez had attempted to assassinate the elected president and seize power in a coup, so no one could have illusions about his fidelity to democracy. Admirably, Venezuela had preserved democracy through-out the 1960s and 1970s when almost every other Latin American country had succumbed to military dictatorship. Now, desperate Venezuelans gambled their freedom on a charismatic soldier who presented himself as savior.

He called his philosophy "Bolívarian," whatever that might mean. Simón Bolívar had been the hero of South American independence, but his own politi-cal philosophy was obscure enough that he was later claimed as a hero by both right and left.[1] Perhaps the most distinctive feature of Chávez's philosophy was his vituperation toward America and his indiscriminate embrace of its enemies, especially Fidel Castro but also Saddam Hussein and Mahmoud Ahmadinejad. The day after 9/11 Chávez jeered: "The United States brought the attacks upon itself, for their arrogant imperialist foreign policy."[2] The *Atlantic*'s Franklin Foer wrote that "this anti-American bent has helped make Hugo Chávez a hero of the international Left—a title that he has aggressively courted. . . . , [and] has turned Caracas into a refugee camp for socialists displaced since the tumultu-ous events of 1989."[3]

Chávez practiced a back-to-the-future mix of statist economics and pater-nalistic rule that bore fewer earmarks of Bolívar than of Perón, Mussolini, Mao and Fidel. He required the nation's television networks to keep him on the air for long stretches most days, including four to eight hours every Sunday, creating the image of an omnipresent father, stern but benevolent. And he treated his Twitter followers to such megalomaniac messages as: "Chávez is the People!! We are all Chávez! Chávez is the nation!"[4]

On economics, Chávez at first equivocated, favoring "an effective state that regulates, promotes, pushes economic development" alongside a "market, where the laws of supply and demand are able to exist."[5] By 2005, however, he declared his approach unambiguously socialist, proclaiming that Venezuela and Cuba were pursuing "one and the same revolution."[6] He coined the slogan "Fatherland, socialism, or death."[7]

Chávez could ignore socialism's failures elsewhere because Venezuela possesses the world's largest known oil reserves, larger even than Saudi Arabia's. And he enjoyed the good fortune of an unprecedented run of oil prices. In 1998, the year of Chávez's first election, oil sold at twelve dollars a barrel; in 2012, his last full year in office, the price was nearly ten times higher, filling government coffers.

This windfall underwrote a raft of social programs, including food and housing subsidies, new clinics largely staffed by Cuban medical personnel and adult literacy programs. While Chávez deployed these for political impact, they undoubtedly succored recipients. According to official figures the proportion of households living in poverty fell from over 49 percent in 1998 to 29 percent in 2009.[8]

But that year the price of oil began a long decline, the poverty rate climbed back up and the toll of statist economics rose. Shortages of basic goods like milk, sugar, coffee and toilet paper had appeared even as early as 2007 when oil was still high.[9] Venezuela by then had fallen to 164th place out of 175 countries on the World Bank's "ease of doing business" scale.[10] Inevitably, those inefficiencies dragged down the state oil company, too. Production began to crater around the time that Chávez died of cancer in 2013.

He left crumbling infrastructure and a deteriorating economy, and the collapse accelerated under his handpicked successor, Nicolás Maduro. Starting in 2015, Bloomberg ranked Venezuela annually "the world's most miserable economy."[11] It dropped to 188th place out of 190 countries on the "ease of doing business" scale, ahead of only Eritrea and Sudan. In July 2018, the IMF forecasted that inflation would reach 1,000,000 percent that year. The bolívar officially between three and ten to the dollar, traded at two hundred and fifty thousand to the dollar. In the three years 2016-2018, Venezuela's economy contracted by about one-half, considerably more than the U.S. drop in the Great Depression.

The reduction of poverty had once been the revolution's proudest boast, but now 80 percent sank below the poverty line. Hunger became endemic with three-quarters of Venezuelans reportedly losing nearly twenty pounds on what was sardonically called "the Maduro diet."[12] More than 11 percent of young children suffered from life-threatening acute malnutrition. Health care broke down, leading to, among other things, the return of malaria.[13] From 2016 to 2018, around 10 percent of the population emigrated, creating a refugee crisis in neighboring states.

Increasingly unpopular, Maduro intensified repression. Independent newspapers were censored and starved of newsprint, forcing many to close.[14] In 2014 student protests were met with violence, leaving dozens dead and hundreds injured. When, in 2015, the opposition won a majority in the National Assembly, Maduro responded by transferring authority to a new body, the Constituent Assembly, a simulacrum of a legislature made up entirely of regime supporters, generally voting by unanimity.[15] In 2018, he had himself reelected in a vote widely seen as rigged.[16]

The transformation of Venezuela was now complete. Chávez had turned it from a democracy into a "hybrid" of democracy and autocracy. Maduro erased what had remained of democracy, leaving it, as the *New York Times* put it, a country "rule[d] with an authoritarian fist."[17] It had been the second most prosperous country on the continent, after Argentina; now it was among the poorest.

Twenty years after Chávez reached power, his "Bolívarian socialism" had reenacted the whole sordid saga of European Communism or Third World Socialism as if its destiny was to exemplify Marx's dictum that history repeats itself first as tragedy, then as farce. The failure of numerous other socialist experiments in developing countries often had been explained away by reference to impoverished beginnings and the lack of capital. But Venezuela was not poor when Chávez took office, only when he left. And its oil reserves constituted an immense source of capital. Its sad destiny was to demonstrate that not even a most favorable endowment could make such a system work.

•   •   •

While most of the world looked on aghast as the romance with socialism turned the once-middle-income democracy of Venezuela into an impoverished dictatorship, one important Westerner saw only beauty in the project, like the Fairy Queen in *A Midsummer Night's Dream* gazing in rapture on the ass-headed Bottom. British Labour Party MP Jeremy Corbyn took to Twitter upon news of Chávez's death in 2013 to say: "Thanks Hugo Chavez for showing that the poor matter and wealth can be shared. He made massive contributions to Venezuela and a very wide world."[18] The next year Corbyn demonstrated his support for Maduro by calling in live as a guest on Maduro's radio broadcast.[19] Pressed in 2017 to condemn Maduro's regime for killing scores of protestors, Corbyn refused, saying: "What I condemn is the violence that's been done by any side and all sides."[20]

The reason Corbyn was grilled about Venezuela in 2017 was that he was by then no longer just an MP but the leader of the British Labour Party, a likely future Prime Minister. His position was being scrutinized less because of concern for Venezuela than for what it might reveal about him and where he wished to take his own country.

Corbyn, as the *Economist* put it, was a "left-wing firebrand," standing well outside the political mainstream.[21] He disdained the compromise that had brought so much electoral success to social democrats across Europe in the twentieth century. They had found their calling in reforming the system rather than replacing it. In contrast, Corbyn said he was out "to challenge global capitalism."[22]

An earlier Labour leader, Tony Blair, had seemed to seal Labour's break with its socialist past by engineering the repeal of the famous Clause 4 of its constitution calling for "common ownership of the means of production, distribution, and exchange." Corbyn now asserted the wish to reenact it. To say that Corbyn wanted to lead his party back to where it stood before Blair would be an understatement. Never had the party been led by someone so far to the left. In the approving eyes of Richard Seymour, "this is the first time in Labour's history that it has a radical socialist for a leader."[23]

As Seymour recounted, Corbyn "appealed for a new type of society where, 'we each care for all, everybody caring for everybody else: I think it's called socialism.'"[24] Was he a Marxist, BBC talk show host Andrew Marr asked Corbyn. "That is a very interesting question actually," came the uneasy reply. The evasion went on:

> I haven't thought about that for a long time. I haven't really read as much of
> Marx as we should have done. I have read quite a bit but not that much. I think

Marx's transition of history and the analysis of how you go from feudalism to
capitalism and move on to a different stage is fascinating.[25]

In sum, Marx "was a fascinating figure...from whom we can learn a great
deal."[26]

The reason for such obfuscation was apparently that Corbyn doubted that
his countrymen were ready to swallow his true beliefs. He had become party
leader not through a profound shift in public opinion, but through a perfect
storm of chance decisions and miscalculations by other politicians. Many U.K.
journalists reported that Corbyn himself was surprised by the position he had
reached.

If he had not read as much Marx as he should have, it was not for want of
opportunity. Born in 1949, the youngest of four sons, Corbyn had been raised
in bucolic Shropshire. His biographer notes that his home was "so posh that it
doesn't have a number, just a name,"[27] and it was awash in left-wing politics. His
mother subscribed to the pro-Communist Left Book Club, and his father "built
up a large collection of books about the Soviet Union and Communism."[28] They
had met in 1936, campaigning for solidarity with republican Spain, and he once
described them as "committed socialists."[29]

Coming of age in the late sixties and early seventies, Corbyn bore the
earmarks of his generation, sporting a beard and scruffy clothes, and practicing vegetarianism and bicycling. For him, these affectations were a fillip to his
parents' leftism, not a substitute for it.

The true mark of Corbyn's worldview was to be found neither in his lifestyle nor his tergiversations about Marx but in the causes he championed and the
political associations he forged. Upon entering Parliament in 1983 he enrolled
in the Socialist Campaign Group, generally recognized as the caucus of the
"hard left." He became a tireless advocate for the Irish Republican Army during
its terror campaign against Britain, speaking each year at London's Connolly/
Sands commemoration, honoring fallen IRA militants and "prisoners of war."
The program for the 1988 event minced no words about the honorees: "in the
war to rid Ireland of the scourge of British imperialism...force of arms is the
only method capable of bringing this about."[30] He also hosted a meeting in
Parliament for IRA members who had been convicted of terrorism.[31]

In 1984, when an IRA bomb exploded at the Conservative Party conference, killing five and wounding thirty-one others, the leftist newsletter, *Labour
Briefing*, of which Corbyn was a mainstay and reportedly general secretary of

the editorial board,[†] ran an implicitly approving editorial saying, "the British will only sit up and take notice when they are bombed into it."[32] Farther from home, he took a keen interest in Latin America. Active in the Cuban Solidarity Campaign, he lionized Fidel Castro as "a huge figure of modern history, national independence and 20th century socialism [whose] achievements were many."[33] Corbyn also described himself as a supporter of the Sandinista government of Nicaragua, complaining bitterly that their "social advancements" and "social gains" had been destroyed when in 1990, after eleven years of one-party rule, the Sandinistas were forced to hold free elections and were voted from power.[34] He described himself as "supporting" the "people of El Salvador," by which he meant the Communist guerrilla group FMLN.[35] In addition, he said he was "very involved in supporting the Grenadan revolution," under the Marxist-Leninist New Jewel Movement.[36]

The other turbulent region on which Corbyn focused was the Middle East, despite the absence of Marxist regimes of the type that commanded his esteem elsewhere. There, instead, Corbyn devoted himself to the Palestinian cause. He sponsored an event in Parliament for a delegation from Hizbullah, saying it was his "pleasure and honor" to host these "friends." He complained bitterly that Israel had thwarted his wish also to host "friends" from Hamas, which the European Union officially designated a terrorist organization. He described the two groups as "dedicated towards the good of the Palestinian people and bringing about long-term peace and social justice and political justice in the whole region."[37] Consistent with this, he has repeatedly affirmed the Palestinians' "right to return to their homes"[38] or "right to return home"[39]—phrases that point to the abolition of Israel, which is what Hamas and Hizbullah say is their aim.

So fierce was Corbyn's opposition to Israel that he was accused of anti-Semitism, a charge he strongly denied. But in 2018, one revelation after another cast these denials in doubt. He had hosted an event on Holocaust Memorial Day at which Israel was likened to the Nazis. He had taken to Iranian state television to celebrate the release of Hamas terrorists whom he called "brothers." He had shared a platform with Holocaust deniers. He had laid a wreath on

---

† Confronted with this thirty years later, Corbyn denied he had even belonged to the editorial board, much less been its general secretary, and he made out that he was merely a contributor to the publication. However, Internet sleuths reproduced several items from that era listing Corbyn as the host of *Labour Briefing* gatherings and as the person to contact to join its mailing list. ("The Question of Labour Briefing and Jeremy Corbyn's Affiliation," *Cult Exploits*, June 4, 2017. https://cultexploits.wordpress.com/2017/06/04/the-question-of-labour-briefing-and-jeremy-corbyns-affiliation/.)

the graves of the terrorists who perpetrated the Munich Olympics massacre. All of this prompted Britain's three main Jewish newspapers to publish an unprecedented joint front-page editorial in July 2018, voicing their fear that "a Jeremy Corbyn-led government" would pose "an existential threat to Jewish life in this country."[40]

Nonetheless, his defenders continued to insist that he was being pilloried for mere opposition to Israeli policies. Then, however, a video surfaced in which he said of "Zionists": "Having lived in this country for a very long time, probably all their lives, they don't understand English irony."[41] He was not speaking about Israel, but about Jews. "This was classic anti-Semitism," wrote the New York correspondent for the *Sunday Times*, a Labour supporter, speaking for many Jews and non-Jews.[42]

Some analysts parsing Corbyn's dalliance with anti-Semitism recalled the ferocious "anti-Zionism" of the U.S.S.R. This inference was hard to assess. His open embrace of Communist movements around the globe did not extend to the Soviet Union as it apparently had for his parents, although he was not strongly critical of it, either. "There were many things wrong with what happened in the Soviet Union," he conceded in a debate on socialism before the Oxford Union in 2013, adding, "I am not here to defend Stalin and his strange views."[43] This sounded more like a grudging disclaimer than a denunciation and seemed curiously mealy coming from a mouth that often breathed fire about the faults of the United States, Israel or the U.K. For example, Corbyn called for Tony Blair to be tried as a "war criminal" for Britain's participation in the Iraq war. Corbyn's discomfort with Stalin's "strange views" also paled in comparison to the denunciation of Stalin by his own successor, Khrushchev, in his famous secret speech to the twentieth Congress of the Communist Party of the U.S.S.R. in 1956.

Since that speech, precious few in the West have harbored illusions about the Soviet tyrant. But Corbyn seemed to surround himself with some of this rare breed. In 2015, he brought on Seumas Milne as his director of strategy and communications, and in early 2017 added Steve Howell as Milne's deputy. After Prime Minister Theresa May called a snap election in 2017, Corbyn hired Andrew Murray to help run his campaign. These three men had all been associated with *Straight Left*, the mouthpiece of a subgroup within the Communist Party of Great Britain that favored strict loyalty to the Soviet Union and were branded "tankies" by other, more liberal Communists, a sardonic allusion to their support for Moscow's armored invasion of Hungary in 1956 and Czechoslovakia in 1968.

In 1999, Murray, who served a tour as a U.K. correspondent for *Novosti*, the Soviet press agency (most of whose correspondents abroad worked for Soviet intelligence[44]), wrote a column to commemorate the 120th birthday of Joseph Stalin, saying:

> if you believe that the worst crimes visited on humanity this century, from colonialism to Hiroshima and from concentration camps to mass poverty and unemployment have been caused by imperialism, then [Stalin's birthday] might at least be a moment to ponder why the authors of those crimes and their hack propagandists abominate the name of Stalin beyond all others.[45]

In a similar vein, Milne wrote in 2006:

> For all its brutalities and failures, communism in the Soviet Union, eastern Europe and elsewhere delivered rapid industrialisation, mass education, job security and huge advances in social and gender equality. It encompassed genuine idealism and commitment . . . and provided a powerful counterweight to western global domination.[46]

Why did Corbyn bring men with such outré views as these into the heart of his political circle? Because his career has been entwined with theirs, and his outlook differs little if at all from theirs. When Milne was named chief strategist and publicist, Corbyn's campaign tweeted: "Seumas shares Jeremy's worldview almost to the letter . . . they sing from the same hymn sheet."[47] Murray's paean to Stalin had appeared in the *Morning Star*, a newspaper for which Corbyn, too, was a columnist and which was formerly the *Daily Worker*, official organ of the Communist Party.

Corbyn and Murray alternated as chairman of the ultra-left Stop the War Coalition. This group did not merely oppose the war in Iraq, it went so far as to endorse the jihadists and Baathists who were fighting American and British forces, affirming "the legitimacy of the struggle of Iraqis, by whatever means necessary." Later, when Stop the War felt pressure to criticize the Syrian government's use of chemical weapons, it added the caveat that this outrage was not as harmful as the Western bombing of ISIS.

Given these positions and associations, and that he had voted against his own party more than any other Labour MP,[48] Corbyn's 2015 election as party

leader defied odds that the *Guardian* pegged at 100 to 1. How did he pull off one
of the more surprising upsets in modern British political history?

The choice is made by rank-and-file members from nominees put forward
by the party's MPs. Corbyn's parliamentary faction, the Socialist Campaign
Group, was so small that in previous leadership contests it had been unable
even to get one of its own on the ballot. This time, however, the faction
appealed for help outside its ranks, arguing that to include Corbyn in the
field would "widen the debate." Thus, a dozen MPs who supported other
candidates nonetheless lent their names to Corbyn's nomination, qualifying
him for the race just barely.[49]

Then he took advantage of a new rule allowing nonmembers to vote simply
by registering online for a nominal fee as a Labour "supporter." Alone among the
Labour competitors his campaign's website bore a link to the utility for signing
up as a party "supporter."[50] Many who did were activists from the anti-war and
pro-Palestinian movements and other cause groups that Corbyn had championed. As Hilary Wainwright, editor of *Red Pepper* magazine, wrote, "[running]
on his own radical terms [he] stepped outside the party, mobilizing social forces
that previously found Labour repellent."[51] Nonmember "supporters" accounted
for one-fourth of the total vote cast, and they almost all went for Corbyn.

Younger voters, whether "supporters" or full party members, were attracted to Corbyn, much as their American counterparts were to Bernie Sanders,
by his unconventional and rebellious image; by his promises of free university
tuition and other apparently new government benefits (one disgusted Labour
MP likened Corbyn's platform to "a ten-year-old's letter to Santa Claus"[52]);
and by his skillful use of social media (his Twitter account reportedly had 1.3
million followers).[53]

Corbyn also scored strongly with the union vote, reflecting a change in
labor's role within the party. Traditionally British unions had provided ballast
for moderation, but in recent decades they had grown more radical as industries shrank and so, too, had union membership. Powered by unionists, youth
and radical activists, Corbyn left his opponents in his dust, amassing nearly 60
percent of the vote in a field of four.

In all, however, only a tiny fraction of Labour voters participated in this
process, and most Labour parliamentarians remained unreconciled to Corbyn's
leadership. Their discontent crystallized in 2016 under the shock of the U.K.'s
referendum vote to leave the European Union. Critics charged that Corbyn
had failed to campaign effectively against it, hampered by his own history and

ideology. While the campaign to withdraw from the EU had been led by the UK Independence Party, and most of the energy behind it came from the right, the far left also endorsed leaving, viewing the EU as a tool of the capitalists. This had long been Corbyn's position. As party leader, with most Labour voters and parliamentarians favoring the EU, he switched and advocated a vote to "remain," but his opposition seemed half-hearted and ineffective.

A motion of no confidence in his leadership among Labour MPs carried by the crushing margin of 172 to 40, and most of his shadow cabinet resigned. MPs, however, were powerless to replace him; they could only force a rerun of the previous year's leadership vote. Once again, a small percentage of party members took part, and once again he carried the day, even slightly upping his margin.

Nonetheless, Corbyn's position remained precarious in light of polls showing Labour trailing the Conservatives by fifteen to twenty points. Prime Minister May read these polls, too, and saw an opportunity to widen her majority in Parliament and thereby afford herself a cushion as she undertook the fraught task of negotiating Britain's extrication from the European Union. In the spring of 2018, she called a "snap election" although no balloting was required for another three years.

To her shock and dismay, when the votes were counted a mere seven weeks later, Labour had come roaring back. Far from widening her majority, May had lost it entirely. Clinging to a narrow plurality, she managed to hang on to office only by forming a coalition with the small Democratic Unionist Party of Northern Ireland. The outcome was seen widely as a defeat for her and a triumph of sorts for Labour. It hadn't won, but it had "pulled off the most stunning surge in British political history," as one partisan chronicler exulted. "There was simply no precedent for a party coming from so far back in such a short time."[54]

Corbyn expressed confidence a new election would have to be called soon due to the fragility of May's coalition and that he would win it. Neutral observers agreed. "Bookmakers have him as favourite to be Britain's next prime minister," reported the *Economist*.[55]

Labour's improbable comeback to the brink of victory in 2017 finally cemented Corbyn's hold on his party two years after he became its leader, although it still struck many as something of a freak occurrence. "Rarely in Britain has such a marginal, ideological group become so dominant in a party, so influential in how other parties and the country discuss fundamental issues, and so electorally powerful," observed the *Guardian*.[56]

What would happen if Corbyn's Labour Party ever won a national election? Its 2017 platform called for nationalizing railways, energy delivery, mail and water and for endowing a National Transformation Fund and a National Investment Bank. The platform also offered free university tuition, free childcare for preschoolers, free lunches for all primary school students, a slew of other benefits as well as government construction of one million housing units. In addition it proposed large tax increases on high earners, increases in the minimum wage and legal limits on the differentials between high and low salaries.

Corbyn appointed John McDonnell, a self-described Marxist, as his shadow Chancellor, the post most responsible for economic policy.[57] McDonnell had long been Corbyn's closest ally in Parliament, focusing on domestic issues while Corbyn worked foreign policy. McDonnell advocated "root and branch radical change right across our economy."[58] He favored creating an "entrepreneurial state," a euphemism for government-owned industries, as well as various other socialist instruments, such as cooperatives and worker-controlled enterprises. Speaking in 2018, he decried "leaving the economy in the hands of the market."[59]

Corbyn and McDonnell seemed to have the wind at their backs. Popular impressions of socialism had shifted since the end of the Cold War and the fall of the Soviet empire. In 2016, the British polling agency YouGov asked respondents their views on capitalism and socialism. Thirty-three percent of Britons counted themselves "favorable" to capitalism, while 39 percent were "unfavorable." Toward socialism, the plurality reversed, with 36 percent favorable as against 32 percent unfavorable.[60]

The meaning of such polls is not self-evident without knowing how respondents interpret these terms, but Britain seems in a very different mood from the 1980s when Margaret Thatcher set out to "kill socialism" or even from the turn of the century when Tony Blair promised he would not undo Thatcher's legacy. Buffeted by globalization and immigration and perhaps other less obvious dislocations, British politics seem sharply polarized, with the nationalist UK Independence Party at one end and Corbynistas, as they are called, at the other,[†] much as in the United States where supporters of Donald Trump are arrayed opposite progressive Democrats.

In 2018, the *Financial Times* speculated that Britain might be on a path spelled out in a 1951 Communist Party text, *The British road to Socialism*: "Step one is a leftwing takeover of the Labour party (check), followed by electoral

---

† The extremes came together, as polar opposites sometimes do in politics, in favor of leaving the EU but not much else.

triumph (incomplete), taking control of the state (incomplete) and building a Socialist society as a transition to Communism (incomplete)."[61]

Whether a hope or a fear, this scenario may be overdrawn. Labour under Corbyn could win an election and form a government, but the final box on this checklist would require much more than a tick of the pen. Attlee led Britain the furthest down the road to socialism that it has ever gone and soon was forced to turn back. Corbyn undoubtedly dreams of restoring Attlee's policies and going much further, but the obstacles will prove formidable.

Corbyn's impact, should he come to power, would likely be felt more in the realm of foreign policy. He had always deemed American "expansionism" to be the main global problem. As he explained in a parliamentary newsletter in 1991, "The aim of the war machine of the United States is to maintain a world order dominated by the banks and multinational companies of Europe and North America."[62]

That was the year Washington led a UN-sponsored coalition to rescue Kuwait from forcible absorption by Iraq. In truth, wrote Corbyn, America had been seeking a "pretext [for] war with Iraq."[63] In a similar vein, he charged that North Korea's nuclear program was only an excuse for U.S. sanctions, the true aim of which was "to weaken, if not destroy, the North Korean economy in order to ultimately force . . . the spread of free market capitalism into North Korea."[64]

Conversely, he has always exhibited understanding, if not outright sympathy, toward any adversary of America's, not only Cuba and Vietnam and other Communist regimes, but even regimes and forces that laid no claim to leftist ideals, for example, Putin's Russia. In addition to justifying its invasion of Ukraine, he initially defended it against the accusation, doubted by almost no one else at the time or since, that Russia was responsible for the nerve-agent poisoning of a former Russian intelligence officer in Salisbury, England.[65]

He has also often leapt to the defense of Jihadis, even groups more extreme than Hamas and Hizbullah. In the wake of 9/11, he pronounced, "we have to look to the causes of this act. A quarter of the world's population is in poverty."[66] When American forces killed Osama Bin Laden, Corbyn called it "tragic."[67] When ISIS conquered much of Iraq, he called for "an acceptance and understanding of why so many people have apparently been prepared to accept the ISIS forces" whose brutality, he claimed, was no greater than that of "the Americans."[68] As the heterodox leftist blogger James Bloodworth explained Corbyn's logic, "Because the US is the beating heart of capitalism . . . any movement that points a gun in its direction must invariably have something going for it."[69]

Certainly, a Corbyn government would spell the end of the "special relationship" between the U.K. and the U.S. Even were he to muffle his hostility, it is hard to see how U.S. military planners or intelligence services could continue sharing strategies and secrets with a government he led.

NATO would also, in all likelihood, be done for, having already been weakened by Donald Trump's peevish animus and Turkey's virtual defection from the Western camp. Campaigning in 2017, Corbyn mouthed support for the alliance, but his opposition to it had been longstanding and vociferous. He had denounced it in 2014 as "a very, very dangerous Frankenstein of an organization."[70] He also penned a column that year in the *Morning Star* (the former *Daily Worker*), titled "NATO Belligerence Endangers Us All" (a headline that must have seemed numbingly familiar to longtime subscribers). His wrath was stirred by the conflict in Ukraine, which, parroting Vladimir Putin, he blamed not on the Russian invasion but on Ukrainian "Nazi groups" and the "expansionism of the post-1990 United States."[71]

Whatever he might do in office, Corbyn symbolizes the socialist dream's enduring capacity to envenom the idealism of compassionate individuals who eat no meat and constrain their carbon footprint. Frustrated in their efforts to erect utopia in their own countries, they are childishly credulous toward any claimed sighting of it abroad, squeezing their eyes shut and embracing the most bloodthirsty tyrants so long as they claim to be enemies of capitalism.

•   •   •

If the United States was its beating heart, as Corbyn and his fellow anti-Americans believed, then capitalism was suffering from angina that grew more intense in 2016 when Bernie Sanders nearly upset Hillary Clinton for the Democratic nomination for U.S. president, an outcome still more stunning than Corbyn's near-upset of May. Sanders did not even belong to the party whose candidate he proposed to become but had spent his career as an official "independent," a curiosity among politicians.

He had moved from his native Brooklyn to Vermont in the 1960s, part of a migration of "flower children" drawn to the pastoral settings of the Green Mountain State and its culture of toleration, bred perhaps by long harsh winters that force neighbors to rely on one another. Unlike most of these newcomers who were content to enjoy their nonconformist lifestyles in a nonjudgmental environment, Sanders never ceased trying to change the world through politics. He ran for various offices on miscellaneous third-party tickets before winning the mayoralty of Burlington as an independent, which proved a springboard to seats in the U.S. House and the Senate. In Congress, he caucused with the Democrats, since parties assign committee seats, but he doggedly refused to join the party.

Surprising as it was for a non-Democrat to enter the Democratic race, more surprising still was Sanders' decision to advocate "political revolution" and to declare himself a "democratic socialist." This is a term long favored by members of the Socialist Party and others to emphasize their difference with Communism. They sought extreme transformation of the economy but by parliamentary methods. Unlike the Communist Party, which never polled many votes, the Socialist Party had garnered 6 percent of the presidential vote in 1912 and won some seats in Congress and some mayoralties. But its support ebbed away after that, and the label "socialist" has been anathema in U.S. elections since, all the more so because many Americans took "socialist" to mean Communist.

Yet, despite his socialist rhetoric and his party, or rather non-party, status, Sanders gave frontrunner Hillary Clinton a strong challenge although she was backed by the country's most formidable political machine and could boast the near unanimous support of Democratic officials. All told, as against Clinton's 16.8 million votes, Sanders pulled down 13.2 million, carrying 23 states or territories. "No candidate since 1972 started that far down to a front-runner and came so close to winning," reported the numbers-crunching website FiveThirtyEight of Sanders' achievement.

Much like Donald Trump in the Republican primaries, Sanders seemed to have sensed a feeling among voters that conventional politicians had missed. For Trump it was about, or was symbolized by, illegal immigration. For Sanders, it was about economic inequality. Unease over it had been building for some years.

The American Dream that each rising generation would enjoy a higher standard of living than its parents seemed to have evaporated. Statistically, real wages had scarcely risen over the preceding half-century, roughly since the 1960s. And what increase could be detected in cumulative data was attributable mostly to the rising incomes of those at the top of the pay scale. Even above them on the economic ladder stood other tiers of those who did not receive wages of any kind, rather whose compensation or earnings were based on corporate profits, which multiplied over these years, a period when the billionaire replaced the millionaire as the image of a rich person in popular culture.

The Sanders movement had been previewed in 2011 when several hundred protestors "occupied" Wall Street. They took aim at "corporate greed" and at what they called "the 1%" who they said dominated the economy, while they themselves claimed to speak for the balance, the "99%."

They did not actually occupy Wall Street but rather Zuccotti Park, three blocks away. Ironically, this three-quarter-acre treed plaza, a postage stamp of spatial relief amidst the towering glass and steel of the financial district, was a monument to corporate generosity, not greed. Worth countless tens of millions of dollars, this space was owned and maintained by a private business, which consecrated it to the free enjoyment of chess players, picnickers and the public in general—until, that is, the "occupiers" took it over, camping out there, using it as an arena for nightly assemblies and a base from which to launch periodic protest marches into the surrounding streets.

Although the sociological math of the "1%" and the "99%" was debatable, it pointed to the genuine issue of stagnant wages and the increasingly skewed distribution of income. The collapse of the housing bubble in 2008 and the "great recession" it triggered, which were still reverberating through the lives of Americans, gave this issue an edge. Many resented that banks and other giant companies were bailed out while private citizens lost their equity and were left to face the economic damage on their own. This put wind beneath the wings of the protest. An early poll by *National Journal* found that Americans "overwhelmingly support" the Occupy movement.[72]

For a moment, then, "Occupy" captured the public imagination, even overseas. The Wall Street action was imitated in scores of cities around the country. A month after it began, similar protests took place in London, Frankfurt, Madrid, Rome, Sydney, Hong Kong, Berlin, Stockholm, Sarajevo, the Philippines and perhaps elsewhere.[73]

But a Pew survey in late October recorded less public support, with 39 percent favorable and 35 percent unfavorable,[74] and by mid-November, Public Policy Polling found "public opinion souring pretty quickly" on the Occupy movement.[75]

Part of the public's change of heart stemmed from the demonstrators' style and trappings—lots of drums and guitars and drugs and various young and not-so-young women going topless, sometimes wearing only panties or body paint for the shock value. It seemed to reflect, said *New York Times* columnist Ginia

Bellafante, a "wish to burrow through the space-time continuum and hunker down in 1968."[76]

The deeper problem was the movement's inability to explain what, exactly, it stood for. It was clearly anti-capitalist, thus implicitly socialist, but only implicitly. The third night of the occupation the group issued a list of twenty-three broad and deep grievances, encompassing economics but also race, gender, the environment, foreign policy, civil liberties and more, capped with the caveat, "These grievances are not all-inclusive." However, when it came to setting down proposed remedies, the Occupiers foundered.

In time, the media value of the protests dissipated, the occupiers drifted away, the police cleared out the remnant, and Zuccotti Park was returned to the public. But the issue that Occupy had momentarily captured remained salient, and in 2014, it returned to the fore in a format that could scarcely have been more different.

Astonishingly, a 700-page academic tome on economics rocketed to the top of bestseller lists, leaving Harvard University Press scrambling to print enough copies to catch up with back orders. *Capital in the Twenty-First Century* by French economist Thomas Piketty had been published first in his home country to no great notice, but the release of its English translation made Piketty an instant "rock star" in the U.S. The *New York Times*'s Paul Krugman said Piketty deserved the Nobel Prize.

Rich in data, Piketty's book claimed he had discovered an economic law of capitalism—"$r>g$"—that would lead to such extreme concentration of wealth as to be unsustainable. $R>g$ means that return on investment exceeds economic growth, causing an imbalance that Piketty said would "undermine the meritocratic values on which democratic societies are based" and might culminate with the owners of wealth "accumulat[ing] claims on the rest of the population so extensive that they would easily come to own everything that can be owned."[77]

Piketty argued that this process had been underway throughout the nineteenth century, cresting in the *Belle Époque*. The trend had then been interrupted by the two world wars, which burned through great quantities of accumulated capital. It had resumed, however, in the second half of the twentieth century and was continuing its destructive course into the twenty-first.

Although the book's chosen title was an unmistakable bow to Karl Marx and his masterwork, Piketty insisted that he had been "vaccinated for life" by the fall of the Soviet Union, "against the conventional but lazy rhetoric of anticapitalism. I have no interest in denouncing inequality or capitalism per se—especially since social inequalities are not in themselves a problem as long as they are justified."[78]

Rather than challenge private ownership, Piketty proposed only to level the mountainous inequality of wealth, first by raising high-end tax rates on income to what he called approvingly the "confiscatory" levels that the U.S. and European countries had mostly abandoned. He proposed to add a global tax on wealth—global because wealth is movable—although he acknowledged that it would be difficult to enact such a thing. He also mused about enlarging the size of the public sector in European countries from its current level of about one-half the economy to two-thirds or three-quarters. (He would naturally also hike it in the U.S., where the current level was less.) It did not seem to matter much to Piketty how the additional tax receipts would be spent. Rather their purpose would be to level the distribution of wealth.

If this did not add up to socialism, as such, it embodied some of the same impulses without the gloss of hope and optimism that gave socialism easy entrée into the human heart. Whereas Marx and other socialist thinkers invoked a heavenly future, Piketty proffered his solution mostly as a map for avoiding hell.

Inevitably, discussion of Piketty's book faded,[†] as had the Occupy movement. But the issue of inequality remained, echoed by such personages as President Barack Obama who called it the "defining challenge of our time"[79] and Pope Francis who tweeted in 2014 that it "is the root of social evil."[80]

Then, in the 2016 election season, the issue found its fullest expression in Sanders' novel presidential candidacy. Many veterans of the Occupy movement were among the first to enroll in the campaign, joined by thousands of others. Voters and volunteers young enough to be his grandchildren professed to "feel the Bern" or to be "Bernie brothers."

Excitement even reached beyond U.S. borders. In England, the labor union UNITE, which had powered Corbyn's campaign for party leadership, gave free facilities for the Sanders effort to round up votes from "Democrats abroad." In Venezuela, President Nicolás Maduro said he supported "our revolutionary friend" Sanders, and, ironically in light of his own massive vote rigging,

---

† The eclipse of Piketty's book was perhaps hastened when, the next year, he published a scholarly paper recanting his main argument. "I do not view r>g as the only or even the primary tool for forecasting changes in the path of inequality in the twenty-first century. . . ." he wrote. "[R]>g is certainly not a problem in itself." (Thomas Piketty, "About *Capital in the Twenty-First Century*," *American Economic Review*, Papers and Proceedings 2015, 105(5), pp. 48-49.)

claimed Sanders would win "if the elections were free."[81] In France, Thomas Piketty himself took to the columns of *Le Monde* and the *Guardian* to exult that Sanders' strong showing proved that "another Sanders—possibly younger and less white—could one day soon win the US presidential elections and change the face of the country."[82]

Perhaps the reason Sanders did as well as he did was that the country—or at least the electorate—was already changing. According to a Pew survey, 42 percent of Democratic (or Democratic leaning) voters considered themselves "liberal" in 2015, a large increase over the 27 percent who so identified in 2000.[83] Polls also showed that this liberal swing entailed a new openness to "socialism," making it impossible for opponents within the Democratic Party to dismiss him with a scare word. Hillary, pressed on MSNBC by Chris Matthews to explain "the difference between a socialist and a Democrat," refused to answer.[84] Sanders' unexpectedly strong showing in Iowa launched him toward a crushing victory in the New Hampshire primary where, according to exit polling, 32 percent of Democratic voters called income inequality the most important issue, and 70 percent of these chose Sanders.[85]

In short, although Sanders' ideology made him seem initially an unlikely contender, instead it helped him tap a current that was welling inside the Democratic Party. And his other curious attributes—lack of party affiliation, fusty appearance, advanced age, peculiar diction—may also have redounded to his benefit in a year when voters in both parties seemed eager to embrace outsiders. So, too, may have his white hot rhetoric of indignation, which is peppered with words like "grotesque," "horrific" and "abysmal" to "signal moral ferocity," as the *New Yorker*'s Margaret Talbot explained it.[86]

Sanders' accent bears the stamp of Brooklyn where his parents settled. He often refers to them as "Polish immigrants," but in Poland they would have been seen as Jews sooner than Poles, and most likely would have seen themselves that way as well. He may have been slightly embarrassed to say "Jewish immigrants," although he does not seem much given to embarrassment. Perhaps he thought that "Polish" sounded more proletarian, a mark of honor among socialists. He sometimes likes to say his father was "a worker," but acknowledges he was a paint salesman. And he suggests he knew poverty in childhood by recounting a scolding from his mother for buying groceries at the corner store rather than the supermarket, which was less expensive—as if household frugality was a distinction of the downtrodden. Had he known genuine poverty he surely would have more poignant anecdotes.

At the University of Chicago he joined the Young People's Socialist League, the youth wing of the Socialist Party, as well as the Student Peace Union and the Congress on Racial Equality, two organizations favored by Socialists and also by Communists and miscellaneous radicals.[†] His own trajectory from there remains murky. His sympathetic biographer, Harry Jaffe, conveys frustration on this score: "For Sanders, allowing a journalist to delve into his past to understand his motivation, his character, the genesis of his political positions is a waste of time. He has no interest in revealing himself."[87]

Although Sanders seems to have had a lifelong attachment to Eugene V. Debs, the four-time Socialist presidential nominee, about whom he made a biopic and whose portrait hangs in his office, Sanders' tenure in the Socialist Party was apparently brief. In 1964, a year or two after he joined, the Young People's Socialist League (YPSL) broke apart in an internecine brawl won by a faction too radical for the adult party to abide. Many of its members, apparently including Sanders, made their way instead into the burgeoning New Left.

Two broad currents fed the counterculture of the 1960s: political radicalism, and lifestyle bohemianism. Sanders immersed in both. His move to Vermont was part of a larger migration of longhaired, pot-smoking, sexually liberated youth escaping the urban jungles of New York. He fathered a child with a casual girlfriend and wrote freelance articles on the harm of office work, the use of television for social control and the psychosomatic causes of cancer, especially breast cancer, which he attributed to sexual repression.[88]

But old-fashioned radical politics attracted Sanders more than quirky lifestyle issues did. His leftism seems to have been eclectic in the extreme. Jaffe reports that "the Russian Revolution captivated young Sanders. He fell for the Bolsheviks."[89] This was presumably before he joined YPSL, but Jaffe offers no details. Sanders also, says Jaffe, worked briefly for the "United Meatpackers," by which he presumably means the United Packinghouse Workers, a union known in Chicago for Communist domination. In addition, he spent six months on a kibbutz affiliated with Israel's pro-Soviet party, Mapam—the latter factoid unearthed by an Israeli journalist after Sanders made a mystery of it.[90] Most oddly, he chose to honeymoon in the Soviet city, Yaroslavl, which he had made a sister city of Burlington's when he became mayor.

---

† I speak from direct experience, having by chance joined these three organizations at the same time as Sanders although I was in high school in New York while he was in college in Chicago, and to the best of my recollection we never met.

These connections with the Communist world and its advocates were quite strange for a member of YPSL, as the Socialist Party was strongly anti-Communist. Thickening the stew further, Jaffe reports that Sanders was an "elector" to the Socialist Workers Party convention of 1980 and even reportedly sought that party's nomination for vice president. The Socialist Workers Party (as distinct from the Socialist Party) was Trotskyist. No one outside the radical left could be expected to keep straight these different groupings, but Socialists, Communists and Trotskyists despised one another. For an activist to dally with all three was unheard of.

What, then, defined Sanders' socialism of 2016? In the campaign he advocated Medicare for everyone, free college tuition, full employment by means of public works projects, family leave for parents, as well as some non-economic causes like combating climate change.

However, he also said, "I don't believe the government should own the means of production."[91] And although he had earlier boasted of his radicalism, he seemed to play it down in his presidential campaign to the point of incoherence. He pointed out mockingly that "almost everything [Franklin Roosevelt] proposed was called 'socialist'" and that much the same was true for President Lyndon Johnson.[92] Opponents of those presidents' programs had indeed tried to discredit them by flinging the "S word" at them baselessly. But in Sanders' case it was he himself who brandished the label. Did he intend to suggest that when he called himself a socialist he was smearing himself?

Such obfuscation prompted the author of a *New York Times* profile to call him "frustratingly non-responsive" to efforts to pin him down on how far he would go in changing the American system[93] and to cause his friendly biographer to use the phrase: "whatever Sanders means in his slippery identification with socialism."[94]

Perhaps from disdain or perhaps to make him seem less threatening, Noam Chomsky volunteered that Sanders was "a decent, honest New Dealer," rather than a socialist.[95] Other radical leftists have typed Sanders as a liberal or a social democrat rather than a democratic socialist. But his older brother, Larry, who first introduced him to such ideas when Bernie was still in his teens and who remains close to him personally and ideologically, insists to the contrary:

> Bernard is a genuine socialist in his sense of class warfare—that he thinks there is not a national interest so much as there is an interest [on the part of]

sectors of the population. In that sense, his passion and the sense of conflict between the major owners and the rest of the population is very socialist—as socialist as Corbyn.[96]

Sanders set forth his interpretation of contemporary American dynamics in his book *Our Revolution*:

[S]adly, today, there are people of incredible wealth and power who, instead of moving forward, want to undo the progress we have made and roll back the clock of history. These oligarchs are threatened by what ordinary people can accomplish through the democratic process. In order to protect their vast financial holdings, they utilize their incredible resources to make us a less democratic society. They want more power for themselves, and less power for ordinary Americans. . . . They want to move our country toward an oligarchic form of society in which almost all economic and political power rests with a handful of multibillionaire families. . . . They want to make it virtually impossible for ordinary Americans to make the changes necessary to improve their lives. Tragically, they are succeeding.[97]

These words were not written during Donald Trump's presidency but rather Barack Obama's. And they described a reality that in Sanders' eyes appeared eternally true. *Tablet* magazine's Jas Chana interviewed a correspondent for the *Burlington Free Press* who covered Sanders' first run for mayor in 1980 and said that Sanders' pitch in the presidential race was "word for word" identical to what he had said running for mayor back then. "The only difference is he's changed the word millionaire to billionaire."[98]

In addition to "class warfare," Sanders' main issue, he always took an interest in foreign policy, even as mayor. His consistent theme has been alarm at the possible over-aggressiveness of America or its allies more than at the actions of its adversaries. When Saddam Hussein's regime annexed Kuwait, which President George H. W. Bush declared would "not stand," Sanders said, "the real challenge of our time is to see how we can stop aggression in a nonviolent way."[99] In response to Middle Eastern terrorism, he argued it was "important to address the root causes underlying these brutal acts."[100] When Hamas led Gazans in 2018 in an attempted "march of return" into Israel, leading to the deaths of dozens of the invaders by Israeli fire, Sanders posted a series of videos on social media blaming only Israel.[101]

Most distinctive about Sanders' foreign policy was his approach to Communist governments. As mayor of Burlington, he forged sister city arrangements not only with the Soviet Union but also with Nicaragua, where he traveled in 1985 for the celebration of the sixth anniversary of the seizure of power by the Sandinista Liberation Front. "No one denies they are making great progress giving power to the poor people, to the working people,"[102] declared Sanders upon his return. But by this time, the non-Communists who had allied with the Sandinistas in overthrowing the dictatorship of Anastasio Somoza had all gone into opposition, some of them even taking up arms, and the "progress" Sanders claimed to have seen (and claimed that "no one" denied) was indeed denied vociferously by the leading independent newspaper, the main human rights organization, the religious leadership, the labor unions and the political spokesmen of the Miskito Indians, the principal indigenous group.

Having apparently spoken only to Sandinista government representatives, Sanders parroted their party line that "illiteracy has been reduced from 50 percent to 13 percent" and that "the government has substantially more support among the Nicaraguan people than Ronald Reagan has among the American people."[103] While this was back in the 1980s, he never recanted even when plentiful evidence to the contrary emerged, and thirty years later he extolled the Cuban Communist government in a similar way, saying it had done "a lot of positive things." He said he had visited there two or three times and his wife had gone there for "some educational work."[104]

To many "democratic socialists," democracy came first. Where democratic socialism did not exist, they preferred democratic capitalism to dictatorial socialism. But the reverse seemed true for Sanders: he spoke more favorably about undemocratic socialist regimes than democratic capitalist ones.

This, however, scarcely mattered in the 2016 election. Most Democratic primary voters may not have known what to make of "democratic socialism," but it went over far better than seasoned political observers would have expected. A survey of likely participants in Iowa's Democratic caucuses, where Sanders first established himself as a serious challenger to Clinton, found that 43 percent called themselves "socialists."[105]

National polls showed that, when asked their reaction to various terms, Democrats were as favorable to socialism as to capitalism.[106] Among the public as a whole, capitalism still evoked more positive responses by a wide margin, although for those under thirty, the balance was virtually even.[107] Two years later, in 2018, Gallup registered a continuing trend to socialism among Democratic voters, who now favored "socialism" over "capitalism" by a ten-point margin.[108]

These results suggested that self-identified "socialists" could fare well in future Democratic nominating contests. And indeed some did. In 2018, Alexandria Ocasio-Cortez, an outspoken socialist, scored a stunning primary upset of a high-ranking Congressman in a secure Democratic district representing parts of the Bronx and Queens, New York, while a second woman of like views, Palestinian-American Rashida Tlaib, won a multi-candidate Democratic primary for an open seat in Detroit that Republicans did not contest. Other proclaimed socialists won state and local contests that year.

Ocasio-Cortez, a charismatic twenty-eight-year-old of Puerto Rican background, became the youngest woman ever elected to the House and her surprise victory generated something of a media frenzy, with non-stop appearances on late-night television and a fawning profile in the *New Yorker*, among numerous stories and features in other publications. Sympathetic journalists attempted to shield her from conservative critics by suggesting that her views amounted to nothing more radical than Roosevelt's New Deal or the Scandinavian welfare state.

But the group to which Ocasio-Cortez and Tlaib professed allegiance, Democratic Socialists of America, propounded a far-reaching economic transformation, proclaiming that "the workers and consumers who are affected by economic institutions should own and control them"[109] and that "working people should run both the economy and society."[110] Ocasio-Cortez's own patter slid effortlessly into Marxist jargon, with phrases such as, "we are in a crisis of late-stage capitalism."[111] (To Marxists, capitalism is always in "crisis.")

Like Ocasio-Cortez and Tlaib, most "democratic socialist" candidates were women or members of ethnic minorities or both. They symbolized a transformation of Marxism away from "economism." The most distinctive feature of Marx and Engels's thought was its emphasis on conflict. In contrast to millennia of preceding philosophers who focused on identifying the ideal society, they focused on how an ideal society would come about. This would happen through "class struggle," when the proletariat would defeat the bourgeoisie. While Marx and Engels had dwelled exclusively on conflict between economic strata, latter-day Marxists saw the struggles of women, ethnic minorities and gays as being equally important, much as Mao and Mussolini had given Marxism a nationalist twist. Ergo, these "democratic socialists" were as bent on racial and gender causes as on economic ones, for example demanding "reparations" to the descendants of slaves.

Whether such a candidate could win a general election in a contested district, or even the presidency, would depend on whether the attitudes of the under-thirty cohort would change with age or would endure and be matched by those coming up behind them. Historically socialism always appealed most to the young, giving rise to an aphorism sometimes misattributed to Churchill but in fact coined by conservative French politician Clemenceau, who had begun as a leftist journalist: "any man who is not a socialist at twenty has no heart, and any who is still a socialist at forty has no brain." Whatever this dictum implies about the prospect of Sanders or Ocasio-Cortez or Tlaib ever winning the presidency, they managed to make socialism more respectable in America, the great citadel of capitalism, than it had been since the heyday of the Socialist Party a century before.

• • •

While Corbyn and Sanders demonstrated that the socialist idea lived on even after a century of failure and even as one more country, Venezuela, fell to ruin under its allure, still socialism's larger impact in the twenty-first century could be found not in new iterations but in the afterlife of old ones. Russia and China, which had once been the world's most consequential socialist experiments, had each now turned in a new direction. And yet their socialist pasts were still in some ways shaping them—and haunting the rest of the world.

In the heady moment after the Berlin Wall came down it was widely supposed that they were destined to transition to free market democracy. And briefly Russia did indeed move in that direction. In 1991, the first full year it stood alone (not as part of the U.S.S.R.), Russia was rated "partly free" on the annual survey of Freedom House. China registered no similar advance, its progress aborted by the bloody suppression of the 1989 Tiananmen Square protests. Still, most observers believed that this was only a temporary setback in a trajectory of liberalization driven irreversibly by privatization and rapid economic growth. President Clinton had acted on this hope in extending China's "most favored nation" trade status in 1993, even though as a candidate he had decried "coddling" China.

But then history started up again. Russia's score on the Freedom House scale, rather than progressing into the "free" category, declined a tick in 1992 and then another the next year and the next. A few years into the new century, it receded to an unambiguous "not free" status, and Russia's scores only continued to worsen from there. China did loosen up a little. People could now choose a spouse without official approval; bear a second child if they wished; wear clothes with bright colors. But this new minuscule degree of personal autonomy only illuminated the astounding severity of the totalitarian past rather than a path to a free future.

For all the verbiage about the proletariat, Communism had rested on two institutions, the party and the secret police—and these had not gone away. In Russia, when Communism toppled, the secret police only retreated to the shadows for a moment before reemerging with a new name, FSB instead of KGB. Then, one of their own, Vladimir Putin, reached power. He had termed the demise of the U.S.S.R. the "greatest geopolitical catastrophe of the twentieth century," but he made no effort to re-create Communism. Instead, he used state power to concentrate the economy in the "private" hands of a small number of favored "oligarchs" beholden to him. And he set about systematically to restore dictatorship and to reassemble such pieces of Soviet Russia's empire as he could lay hands on at acceptable risk.

In China meanwhile, even while socialism was largely supplanted by private enterprise, the Communist Party continued to rule, dominating the society in the manner distinctive to Communism. The party was not akin to political parties in democracies, which exist to contest elections. Under Communism, "elections" are not contested. Rather, the party serves as a ruling elite, internally hierarchical, disciplined and subservient, and outwardly repressive. This did not change.

Thus, Russia and China each settled into a form of post-socialist authoritarianism that seemed relatively settled rather than transitional. The Russian regime rested on the secret police; the Chinese on the party. Each of these organizations was an instrument of pure power, forged originally by men obsessed with bringing about socialism. But they proved to be robust and durable, outliving their original rationale, now adapted for use in a post-socialist society.

Consequential as this had been for Moscow's and Beijing's own subjects who had momentarily tasted the forbidden fruit of freedom, or at least inhaled the aroma, before finding themselves once again under the pitiless boot, these regimes also had an impact on others. Russia invaded Georgia and Ukraine and intervened in Syria's civil war, inviting speculation about the extent of its neo-imperial ambitions. It meddled aggressively in Western elections and conducted intimidating military maneuvers. Driven by the FSB, post-Communist Russia yearned to recapture superpower status, a quest bound to be disruptive to international relations. But it did not appear capable of doing much worse than disrupt, short of the suicidal option of resorting to its still-formidable nuclear arsenal. The danger of Cold War days that Russia could conquer the rest of Europe no longer loomed.

China was another story. By 2018 its economy had reached second place among nations, eclipsing Japan's and Germany's and trailing only that of the U.S. Given its faster rate of growth, many prognosticators saw it overtaking the U.S. sometime in mid-century or before. In its day, the U.S. had moved into first place, surpassing the United Kingdom around year 1900, and this stature helped to make the following hundred years the "American century." Would the twenty-first become the "Chinese century"?

And what might that mean? For now, China was less belligerent than Russia, but only out of prudence, not principle. Nonetheless, it insisted on its "right" to absorb Taiwan, a flourishing country of 24 million that had been independent for 70 years. In violation of a solemn commitment to "one country, two systems," it systematically eliminated Hong Kong's freedom. It worked to erase the distinct identity of Tibet, a once independent country that it had swallowed. And it asserted outsized claims in the South and East China Seas in conflict with those of many neighbors. At least close to home, China was not reluctant to throw its weight around. And its weight was growing. Would it eventually throw it farther? With ten times the population of Russia and an economy eight times as large, its ambitions or potential ambitions seemed more important than Russia's and more ominous.

The anxiety was heightened by the words and policies of Xi Jinping, who ascended to paramount office in 2012. Over the two preceding decades Western observers had been able to find evidence that China was evolving in the direction, if not at the pace, they wished. In addition to the abatement of its intrusion into the most intimate details of the personal lives of its citizens, there was a general loosening of the state's grip. NGOs, albeit not with overtly political purposes, were allowed to spring up. Indeed, they were sometimes encouraged to fill vacuums of social services as the economy privatized. A new emphasis on "rule according to law" opened the way for lawyers to pursue human rights issues, and some made a specialty of this. The press was not free but journalists found some leeway, even sometimes reporting official misdeeds if they did not directly blame the regime. And the Internet was freer still, enabling Chinese to absorb ideas from the outside and to share ideas with one another. Slow though it was, China seemed to have resumed the step-by-step march to freedom interrupted in Tiananmen Square in 1989.

Then came Xi. His rise was meteoric, spurred by his management of the 2008 Olympics in Beijing. The games came off smoothly, a logistic and diplomatic triumph that boosted China's prestige. The selection of this dynamic leader to succeed the immobile Hu Jintao inspired hopes of accelerated reform. *New York Times* columnist Nicholas Kristof wrote from Beijing:

> Here is my prediction about China: The new paramount leader, Xi Jinpeng, will spearhead a resurgence of economic reform, and probably some political easing as well. Mao's body will be hauled out of Tiananmen Square on his watch, and Liu Xiaobo, the Nobel Peace Prize-winning writer, will be released from prison.[112]

As it turned out, Xi drove China in exactly the opposite direction. The only one of Kristof's predictions borne out was the release of Liu, who was sent home with advanced liver cancer but not allowed to travel abroad for treatment. He died three weeks later, suggesting he was freed neither for justice nor mercy but only so the state could avoid the embarrassment of having him die in prison. As for Mao, far from being given a burial like an ordinary mortal, he was celebrated more enthusiastically by Xi than by any of his other successors.

In an era of populism around the globe, Xi cast himself as the exemplar of a Chinese version. Although largely unknown to the public before taking power, he cultivated grassroots enthusiasm by launching a fierce campaign against corruption. This always played well with the Chinese because corruption is endemic to a system like China's, in which ordinary citizens have little recourse against officials, and it is always deeply resented.

Mao used campaigns against corruption to renew his own power at the expense of state and party structures. Adopting Mao's lingo, Xi targeted "tigers," meaning high officials, and "flies," lower ones. By mid-2018, according to a database assembled by the website *Chinafile*, 232 "tigers" and 2,125 "flies" had been brought down.[113] This amounted to "the largest purge of the upper echelon of the Chinese Communist Party since the fall of the Gang of Four in 1976," according to China scholar Victor Shih.[114] That the accused received scant due process seemed not to dampen public approval.

Corruption, however, was not the sole target of Xi's populist offensive. Speaking to a 2013 party conference on "propaganda and ideology" he decried the indifference to Marxism and socialism among party members.[115] Even more alarming, apparently, was the presence of party members whose views deviated from Xi's or were disloyal to him. "We found that the damage done by political indiscipline is far greater than that caused by corruption," explained a high official of the party's Discipline Commission.[116] Thus, as American China-watcher Orville Schell put it, the campaign "morphed from an anticorruption drive into a broader neo-Maoist-style mass purge aimed at political rivals and others with differing ideological or political views."[117]

While purging the party of corruption and political deviation, Xi also worked to strengthen its hand over society. Control over news media was tightened, including Xi's demand that outlets owned by the party or the state function as "publicity fronts" for the authorities.[118] A 2017 Cybersecurity law constrained Internet streaming and chat, as well as commentary. A 2018 decree gave the party's Department of Propaganda control over films, books and newspapers.[119] Xi also demanded subservience from the nation's universities. China should "build universities into strongholds that adhere to Party leadership," he said, adding, "Adherence to the Party's leadership is essential to the development of higher education."[120]

The 19th party congress in 2017, which officially conferred on Xi a second five-year term as general secretary, adopted a new party constitution. A team of China specialists at University of California, San Diego noted:

> the 2017 document emphasizes that the Party leads everything, not just over the "political, ideological and organizational areas" as it was phrased in 2012; maintains "absolute" (newly added word) control over the military; and aims to build a modern "powerful country," not just a modern [one].[121]

Xi also moved to elevate his own role as party leader. Elizabeth Economy, director of Asia studies at the Council on Foreign Relations, put it:

> Pushing aside decades of institutionalized collective decision-making that acknowledged the general secretary of the CCP and president of the country as first among equals, Xi Jinping, like Mao before him, has established himself as simply first.[122]

The press and the party's propaganda machinery fostered a cult of personality around Xi unmatched since the days of Mao. His words and photograph appeared on the front pages many times a day, more than was true for any of his recent predecessors. Art students were sometimes tested for college admission by having to draw his likeness. And "Xi Jinping thought" was added to the constitution, along with the thought of Marx, Lenin and Mao, as touchstones of the national belief system.

The hallmarks of Xi thought were the power of the party over society ("the government, the military, the people, the academia and all circles, the party leads all") and conformity within the party ("strengthen inner party supervision, comprehensively purify the political ecology within the party, resolutely correct all kinds of unhealthy tendencies").[123]

In addition to strengthening his hand, Xi paved the way to lengthening his tenure. Traumatized by Mao's tyranny that culminated in the chaos of the Cultural Revolution, the party's leadership had adopted term limits. However, at the 2017 party congress, Xi declined to appoint a deputy to be groomed to succeed him as general secretary, a departure from the practice of his immediate predecessors, which suggested he intended to hold on to that office longer than they had done. Then, the next year, the National People's Congress voted 2,958 to 2 to amend the constitution to eliminate term limits for one of his other posts, the presidency.

With the elevation of Xi to a position of concentrated power unmatched since Mao, as well as his drives to bring the party to heel and to tighten its authority, China was "entering a new era—the counter-reform era," in the words of China scholar Carl Minzner.[124] The very gradual expansion of freedoms over the prior two decades was reversed. Some two hundred lawyers specializing in rights were arrested; churches were closed, as were various NGOs; Internet access was severely curtailed and professors were warned about expressing unorthodox views in their classrooms. They were admonished to avoid seven "unmentionable" topics: universal values; press freedom; the civil society; citizens' rights; the party's historical aberrations; the "privileged capitalistic class" and independence of the judiciary.[125]

Why this heightened repression and concentration of power? In his report to the 19th party congress, Xi used the term "socialist" or "socialism" 146 times.[†] Yet it was often in the phrase "socialism with Chinese characteristics," coined by Deng Xiaoping as a euphemism for encouraging private enterprise. Clearly, socialism and Marxism remained integral to the regime's claim of legitimacy, but practice was at variance with the economic theory they connoted. True, state-owned enterprises represented a significant share of the economy and

---

† By my count in the official English version.

enjoyed favored treatment. But the essence of socialism is equality, and in its pursuit of economic dominance China was moving in the opposite direction.

Were there such a thing in China as an election campaign, a Chinese Bernie Sanders could have a field day denouncing the country's billionaires. China expert Carl Minzner argued that economic stratification had "risen dramatically," and pointed out that "official statistics now place China in the ranks of the top 25 percent most unequal nations in the world," as measured by "Gini coefficients," the metric commonly used by economists.[126] Moreover, the party had officially redefined itself to welcome entrepreneurs as well as workers, with ironic consequences. A *Wall Street Journal* study in 2012 found that of the country's 1,024 wealthiest individuals, 160, with an average net worth well above a billion dollars apiece, held seats that year in high party or government bodies.[127]

Given such brazen contradictions of traditional socialist thinking, the party looked for additional bases of legitimacy and found them in nationalism. Maoist Communism had long included this element. When Mao reviewed his victorious forces upon their seizure of Beijing in 1949, he is said to have declared, "China has stood up." Alluding to these words, the Xi administration propounded the slogan "Under Mao the Chinese people stood up; under Deng the Chinese people got rich; and under Xi the Chinese people are becoming stronger."[128] Upon taking office, Xi had asserted, "the greatest dream is the rejuvenation of the Chinese nation." He was speaking less about internal renewal than about the country's power in the world.

Toward that end, he provided substantial increases year after year in military spending, aiming to assure a force that in his words could "fight and win." He inaugurated a "made in China" technology policy aiming for global leadership in key emergent industries like robotics and artificial intelligence. He oversaw establishment abroad of four hundred Confucius Institutes to spread Chinese language and culture and spoke of the Chinese model as an alternative to Western democracy for developing countries to emulate. His signature initiative was the giant octopus-like "Belt and Road Initiative" to build roads, railways, ports, utilities, industrial and educational facilities, altogether an infrastructure to link China more closely in commerce and communications with Asia, Europe, Eurasia and Africa and to undergird an enhanced global role.

The essence of Xi's "rejuvenation" plan, said Elizabeth Economy, was to put China at the center of the world stage where it could compete with the United States.[129] The *New Yorker*'s Jiayang Fan thought Xi's ambitions went even further: "He seems to believe that the more power he amasses, the easier it will be for him to enact the kind of monumental changes necessary to transform China into the world's leading superpower."[130]

Although it has been a cautious power, it is hard to imagine that China would exercise such a position benignly or that it could get there without overcoming ferocious resistance. Neither picture—of the climb or the reign—affords comfort. Could it be that following a century so horribly blighted by the mad pursuit of the will-o'-the-wisp of socialism will come another century turned bloody by its afterlife?

APPENDIX I

SOCIALISM AT HIGH TIDE: 1985[†]

Communism
Afghanistan
Albania
Bulgaria
Cambodia
China
Cuba
Czechoslovakia
East Germany
Hungary
Laos
Mongolia
Nicaragua
North Korea
Poland
Romania
U.S.S.R.
Vietnam
Yugoslavia

Social Democracy
Australia
Austria
Finland
France
Greece
Israel
Italy
New Zealand
Portugal
Spain
Sweden

Third World Socialism
Algeria
Angola

---

† Year during which the largest number of countries was governed by socialists. For some
Third World countries with dictatorial governments, state-run economies and close ties to the
Soviet bloc, it becomes a fine judgment whether to count them as "Communist" or "Third World
Socialist"—and for my immediate purpose it is not very important. I have chosen to include
Nicaragua in the former category and Ethiopia and South Yemen in the latter. Other students of the
subject might differ.

Barbados

Benin

Burkina Faso

Burma (Myanmar)

Burundi

Cape Verde

Congo

Costa Rica

Curaçao

Democratic Republic of Congo
 (Zaire)

Dominican Republic

El Salvador

Ethiopia

Guinea-Bissau

Guyana

India

Iraq

Kenya

Madagascar

Mali

Mauritius

Mozambique

PDR Yemen

Peru

Rwanda

São Tomé and Príncipe

Senegal

Seychelles

Sierra Leone

Somalia

Sudan

Suriname

Syria

Tanzania

Togo

Tunisia

Venezuela

Zambia

Zimbabwe

APPENDIX II

THIRD WORLD SOCIALIST COUNTRIES†

Africa

Angola, 1975–1990/91
Benin, 1972–1989
Burkina Faso, 1983–1987
Burundi, 1966–1993
Cape Verde, 1975–1991
Congo, 1963–1991
Democratic Republic of Congo
   (Zaire), 1970–1991
Equatorial Guinea, 1968–1979
Eritrea, 1993–present
Ethiopia, 1974–1991
Ghana, 1957–1966
Guinea, 1958–1984
Guinea-Bissau, 1974–1991
Kenya, 1965–1991
Madagascar, 1975–1992
Mali, 1960–1968, 1974–1992
Mauritius, 1982–1993
Mozambique, 1975–1990
Namibia, 1989–present

Rwanda, 1975–1991
São Tomé and Príncipe, 1975–1990
Senegal, 1952–present
Seychelles, 1977–1993
Sierra Leone, 1967–1991
Somalia, 1969–1991
South Africa, 1994–present
Tanzania, 1962–1992
Togo, 1967–1992
Tunisia, 1957–1987
Uganda, 1966–1971
Zambia, 1965–1991
Zimbabwe, 1980–1991

Middle East

Algeria, 1962–1991
Iraq, 1968–present
Egypt, 1954–1980
Sudan, 1969–1985
Syria, 1963–present
PDR Yemen, 1967–1990

---

† By self-description of the government or the ruling party.

Asia

Bangladesh, 1970–1975

Burma (Myanmar), 1962–1988

Cambodia, 1955–1970

India, 1947–present

Indonesia, 1949–1967

Nepal, 1959–1960, 1994–1995

Pakistan, 1971–1977

Sri Lanka, 1956–1977, 1994–present

Latin America & Caribbean

Argentina, 1946–1955, 1973–1976

Aruba, 1989–1994

Barbados, 1976–1986, 1994–present

Bolivia, 1952–1964

Chile, 1932, 1970–1973

Costa Rica, 1942–1948, various
  from 1949–present

Curaçao, 1979–1984, 1985–1988

Dominican Republic, 1962,
  1978–1986

El Salvador, 1979–1992

Grenada, 1979–1983

Guatemala, 1944–1954

Guyana, 1953, 1957–present

Jamaica, 1972–1980, 1989–present

Peru, 1968–1975, 1985–1990

Suriname, 1980–1987

Venezuela, 1969–1989

ACKNOWLEDGMENTS

I am profoundly grateful to the Lynde and Harry Bradley Foundation, which generously supported my work over many years including the years I spent working on the original edition of this book. I am also grateful to the president and trustees of the American Enterprise Institute, my institutional home at that time and for many years.

Amanda Schnetzer's brilliant labors as my research assistant laid a great part of the foundation of this book. While the book was still in progress, she moved to another state, but continued to give me occasional help, simply out of kindness. For a time I despaired of replacing her, but eventually I found another gifted researcher, Krista Shaffer, who ably saw me through to the completion of the project and contributed numerous important insights. In writing the additional material included in the second edition of the book, I received superb freelance assistance from Jared Sorhaindo, which the Charles Koch Institute kindly helped pay for.

AEI's librarian, Gene Hosey, helped me in countless ways, and I had a terrific staff assistant, Gwen Wilbur, during the early phases of the project. I benefited as well from the help of others at AEI, including Karlyn Bowman, Leigh Tripoli, Catherine Keane, Kelly O'Neal and Elizabeth Tencza.

I am indebted to Leon Aron and Charles Fairbanks for their helpful suggestions about sources on Russia, to Arthur Waldron, Merle Goldman, Andrew Nathan, Sarah Cook and Chong Pin Lin about China, and to James Q. Wilson about anthropology. Mark Kahan and Rabbi Reuben Landman helped me to understand some theological questions, and I learned many valuable things from my conversations with John Earl Haynes, Arch Puddington, Michael Novak, Seymour Martin Lipset, Ronald Radosh, Roy Godson, Herb Romerstein, Michael Allen and Chris DeMuth.

A number of people went to pains to facilitate my research in Israel, including Hillel Halkin, Dan Polisar, Allen Roth, Amnon Tsoref, Ada Tsoref, Bracha Buberman, Michael Makavsky, Laurie Verson and Hillel Fradkin. Similarly, my research in Tanzania owed much to the help of Joel Barkan, Goran Hyden,

Prosper Youm, Terry Townsend and Dave Peterson. I received information or materials that otherwise would have been difficult or impossible to track down about Babeuf from Ian Birchall, about Owen from John Hatton Davidson of the Robert Owen Memorial Museum and Kate Underman of Historic New Harmony, about Meany from Peter Hafer and Robert Reynolds of the George Meany Memorial Archives, about Nyerere from George Shepperson of Edinburgh University, about Tanzania from Rene Vandendries of the World Bank, and about several subjects from Henry Palka.

I am grateful to many people who granted me interviews, but I shall not list them save for Joan Wicken, Julius Nyerere's executive assistant throughout his presidency, who, although facing challenges to her health, showed me kind hospitality throughout a day-long interview knowing well that my perspective on the subject would not please her.

Paul Johnson; Ben Wattenberg; my wife Sally; our daughter, Stephanie and her husband, Jon Shields, read the manuscript of the original edition and gave me valuable suggestions and corrections, as did Amanda Schnetzer and Krista Shaffer. I owe a special debt to my cherished friend Peter Collier, who did much to design the project, who provided counsel, guidance, encouragement and edits. I am thankful, too, to Carol Staswick, who copy edited the original edition, and to Katherine Wong of Encounter Books, who shepherded the second edition.

I benefited from the help of a number of interns, many of whom performed work that belied their young ages. Among them were Zainub Ashraf, Yitzchak Meirovich, Demetrios Datch, Sonny Lee, Julie Hernandez, Jonathan Lippman, Duncan Long, Kenneth MacPhail, Theodore Obenchain, Monika Tjia, Wouter Kolk, Matthew Ketchum, Rachel Rosenberg, Ondrej Matejka, Leanne Powner, David McCormack, Simonetta Capobianco, Melissa Habel and Jamie Fly. Interns Maria Anderson, Wilson Alexander and Ross Babineau assisted me greatly with the second edition.

My beloved wife, Sally, and the other members of my family put up with a lot during the years I labored on the original edition—and then with a bit more while I prepared the additional material for the second edition. I am most grateful for their indulgence.

Finally, I thank those lifelong socialists, my parents, Emanuel and Miriam, of blessed memory.

NOTES

PROLOGUE: CHANGING FAITHS

1 Michael Harrington, *Socialism* (New York: Bantam, 1973), p. 131.

CHAPTER ONE: CONSPIRACY OF EQUALS

1 James Billington, *Fire in the Minds of Men: Origins of the Revolutionary Faith* (New York. Basic Books, 1980), p. 25.

2 Gracchus Babeuf, *The Defense of Gracchus Babeuf before the High Court of Vendome*, ed. and trans. John Anthony Scott (Amherst, Massachusetts: University of Massachusetts Press, 1967), pp. 60, 48.

3 David Thomson, *The Babeuf Plot: The Making of a Republican Legend* (London: Kegan, Paul, Trench, Trubner, & Col, Ltd , 1947; reprint, Westport, Connecticut: Greenwood Press, 1975), p. 1 (page citations are to the reprint edition).

4 Quoted in R. B. Rose, *Gracchus Babeuf: The First Revolutionary Communist* (Stanford, California: Stanford University Press, 1978), p. 22.

5 Ibid., p. 54.

6 "Lives of the French Revolutionists," *Quarterly Review* (London), vol. 7 (March & June 1812), p. 436.

7 Ernest Belfort Bax, *The Last Episode of the French Revolution: Being a History of Gracchus Babeuf and the Conspiracy of Equals* (London: Grant Richards Ltd., 1911), p. 62.

8 Rose, *First Revolutionary Communist*, p. 118.

9 Ibid., p. 124.

10 Ian H. Birchall, *The Spectre of Babeuf* (New York: St. Martin's, 1997), p. 39.

11 Ibid., p. 134; Philippe Buonarroti, *Babeuf's Conspiracy for Equality*, trans. Bronterre O'Brien (London: H. Hetherington, 1836), p. 30.

12 Rose, *First Revolutionary Communist*, p. 220.

13 Reprinted in Albert Mathiez, *The Fall of Robespierre and Other Essays* (New York: Augustus M. Kelley, 1968; reprint of 1927 translation by Williams & Norgate Ltd. of London), p. 243.

14 Ibid., pp. 246–47.

15 Quoted in "French Revolution: Conspiration de Babeuf," *Quarterly Review* (London), vol. 45 (April & July 1831), p. 179. The quote is in French; the translation is mine.

16 Ibid., p. 180.

17 Billington, *Fire in the Minds of Men*, p. 76.

18 Ibid., p. 66.

19 Birchall, *Spectre*, p. 40.

20 Buonarroti, *Babeuf's Conspiracy*, p. 90.

21 Sylvain Maréchal, "Manifesto of the Equals," in Birchall, *Spectre*, p. 167.

22 Buonarroti, *Babeuf's Conspiracy*, p. 159.

23 Birchall, *Spectre*, p. 169.

24 "Manifesto of the Plebeians," in Birchall, *Spectre*, p. 172.

25 Ibid., p. 171.

26 "Babeuf's Reply to a Letter Signed M.V.," reprinted in Buonarroti, *Babeuf's Conspiracy*, p. 370.

27 Letter to Dubois de Fosseux, 8 July 1787, in *Socialist Thought: A Documentary History*, ed. Albert Fried and Ronald Sanders (Garden City, New York: Anchor Books, 1964), p. 49.

28 Babeuf, *Defense*, p. 57.

29 "Draft Economic Decree," in Birchall, *Spectre*, p. 174.

30 Buonarroti, *Babeuf's Conspiracy*, p. 164.

31 "Draft Economic Decree," in Birchall, *Spectre*, pp. 175, 174.

32 From *Le Tribun du Peuple*, reprinted in Buonarroti, *Babeuf's Conspiracy*, p. 371.

33 Babeuf, *Defense*, p. 57.

34 Buonarroti, *Babeuf's Conspiracy*, p. 204.

35 Ibid., p. 207.

36 Ibid., p. 159.

37 Ibid., p. 172.

38 Ibid., p. 230.

39 Ibid., p. 30.

40 Patrice L.-R. Higonnet, "Babeuf: Communist or Proto-Communist?" *Journal of Modern History*, vol. 51, no. 4 (December 1979), p. 778.

41 Simon Schama, *Citizens: A Chronicle of the French Revolution* (New York: Alfred A. Knopf, 1989), p. 730.

42 Quoted in "French Revolution," *Quarterly Review*, pp. 205–6.

43 Quoted in R. B. Rose, "Gracchus Babeuf: The First Modern Revolutionary," *Encounter*, vol. 47, no. 1 (July 1976), p. 31.

44 Buonarroti, *Babeuf's Conspiracy*, p. 115.

45 Rose, *First Revolutionary Communist*, pp. 239–40.

46 Buonarroti, *Babeuf's Conspiracy*, p. 143.

47 Bax, *Last Episode*, p. 150.

48 Buonarroti, *Babeuf's Conspiracy*, p. 147.

49 R. B. Rose, "Babeuf, Dictatorship and Democracy," *Historical Studies*, vol. 15, no. 58 (April 1972), p. 233.

50 Rose, "Dictatorship and Democracy," p. 234.

51 Buonarroti, *Babeuf's Conspiracy*, p. 230.

52 Rose, *First Revolutionary Communist*, p. 214.

53 Buonarroti, *Babeuf's Conspiracy*, p. 210.

54 Birchall, *Spectre*, p. 69.

55 William Doyle, *The Oxford History of the French Revolution* (New York and Oxford: Oxford University Press, 1989), p. 246.

56 Buonarroti, *Babeuf's Conspiracy*, p. 73.

57 Rose, *First Revolutionary Communist*, p. 294.

58 Bax, *Last Episode*, p. 193.

59 Ibid., p. 221.

60 Ibid., p. 204.

61 Babeuf, *Defense*, p. 36.

62 Ibid., p. 86.

63 Thomson, *The Babeuf Plot*, p. 59.

64 Bax, *Last Episode*, p. 238.

65 Babeuf, *Defense*, p. 24.

66 Elizabeth L. Eisenstein, *The First Professional Revolutionist: Filippo Michele Buonarroti (1761–1837)* (Cambridge: Harvard University Press, 1959), p. 67.

67 "Robiquet, Buonarroti et la Secte des Égaux," p. 187, quoted in ibid., p. 98.

68 G. D. H. Cole, *A History of Socialist Thought*, vol. 1, *The Forerunners, 1789–1850* (London: Macmillan, 1967), p. 19.

69 Julius Braunthal, *History of the International*, vol. 1, *1864–1914*, trans. Henry Collins and Kenneth Mitchell (New York: Praeger, 1967), pp. 35–36. Eventually it did appear in German, and also Italian and Russian.

70 Babeuf, *Defense*, p. 45.

CHAPTER TWO: NEW HARMONY

1 "First Discourse on a New System of Society," *Selected Works of Robert Owen*, vol. 2, *The Development of Socialism*, ed. Gregory Claeys (London: William Pickering, 1993), p. 3.

2 "Second Discourse on a New System of Society," *Selected Works*, vol. 2, p. 26.

3 Philippe Buonarroti, *Babeuf's Conspiracy for Equality*, trans. Bronterre O'Brien (London: H. Hetherington, 1836), p. 213f.

4 Friedrich Engels, *Herr Eugen Dühring's Revolution in Science (Anti-Dühring)*, ed. C. P. Dutt (New York: International Publishers, 1966, c1939).

5 Robert Owen, *Selected Works*, vol. 4, *The Life of Robert Owen, Written by Himself*, ed. Gregory Claeys (London: William Pickering, 1993), pp. 83, 82.

6 Ibid., p. 112.

7 Ibid., pp. 109, 110.

8 Frank Podmore, *Robert Owen: A Biography* (New York: Haskell House, 1971; orig. pub. 1906 by London: Hutchinson & Co.; London: Allen & Unwin; and New York: Augustus M. Kelley), vol. 1, p. 82n.

9 Ibid., vol. 1, p. 165.

10 Robert Dale Owen, *Threading My Way* (New York: Robert M. Kelley, 1967; orig. pub. 1874), p. 95.

11 Owen autobiography in *Selected Works*, vol. 4, pp. 132–33.

12 Ibid., p. 191.

13 R. D. Owen, *Threading*, p. 93.

14 Quoted in Podmore, *Robert Owen*, vol. 1, p. 89.

15 Owen autobiography in *Selected Works*, vol. 4, p. 201.

16 Ibid., p. 215.

17 R. D. Owen, *Threading*, p. 90.

18 Harriet Martineau, *Harriet Martineau's Autobiography* (London: Virago Press, 1983; orig. pub. 1877), vol. 1, p. 233.

19 Robert Owen, *Selected Works*, vol. 3, *The Book of the New Moral World*, ed. Gregory Claeys (London: William Pickering, 1993), pp. 33, 20.

20 Ibid., p. 26.

21 Owen autobiography in *Selected Works*, vol. 4, p. 155.

22 Ibid., p. 67.

23 Quoted in Podmore, *Robert Owen*, vol. 1, p. 247.

24 "Report to the Committee of the Association for the Relief of the Manufacturing and Labouring Poor," *A Supplementary Appendix to the First Volume of the Life of Robert Owen* (London: Effingham Wilson, Royal Exchange, 1858; London: Frank Cass & Co Ltd, 1967), 58–59. Also quoted in Podmore, *Robert Owen*, vol. 1, p. 219.

25 Quoted in Rowland Hill Harvey, *Robert Owen, Social Idealist*, ed. John Walton Caughey (Berkeley: University of California Press, 1949), p. 87.

26 G. D. H. Cole, *The Life of Robert Owen*, 3rd ed. (Hamden, Connecticut: Archon, 1966), p. 185.

27 Owen, *New Moral World*, part 5, p. 290.

28 Ibid.

29 Ibid., p. 291.

30 Ibid., p. 292.

31 Ibid., part 4, p. 208.

32 *The Black Dwarf*, vol. 12, p. 447 (1 June 1824), quoted in Harvey, *Robert Owen, Social Idealist*, pp. 50–51.

33 Owen autobiography in *Selected Works*, vol. 4, p. 37.

34 See Harvey, *Robert Owen, Social Idealist*, pp. 97–98; Podmore, *Robert Owen*, vol. 1, p. 287; "Why New Harmony" (unpublished) from the New Harmony press kit distributed by Historic New Harmony (New Harmony, Indiana; received October 2001), p. 1; and R. D. Owen, *Threading*, p. 239.

35 R. D. Owen, *Threading*, p. 244.

36 Ibid., p. 240.

37 *Diary of William Owen*, ed. Joel W. Hiatt (Clifton, New Jersey: Augustus M. Kelley, 1973), pp. 14–15.

38 Ibid., p. 44.

39 Owen to William Allen, 21 April 1825, reprinted in Arthur Bestor, *Backwoods Utopias: The Sectarian Origins and the Owenite Phase of Communitarian Socialism in America: 1663–1829*, 2nd ed. (Philadelphia: University of Pennsylvania Press, 1970; orig. pub. 1950), pp. 113–14; and in Karl J. R. Arndt, ed., *Harmony on the Wabash in Transition, 1824–1826* (Worcester: Harmony Society Press, 1982), pp. 533–34.

40 "Address Delivered by Robert Owen, of New Lanark," *Selected Works*, vol. 2, pp. 38, 41. Also in George B. Lockwood, *The New Harmony Movement* (New York: AMS Press, 1971; orig. pub. New York: D. Appleton & Co., 1905), pp. 83–84.

41 *Diary of William Owen*, pp. 129–30.

42 Arndt, *Harmony on the Wabash*, p. 656.

43 Bestor, *Backwoods Utopias*, p. 164.

44 William Owen to Robert Dale Owen, 14 October 1825, in Arndt, *Harmony on the Wabash*, p. 655.

45 Paul Brown, *Twelve Months in New-Harmony* (Philadelphia: Porcupine Press, 1972), p. 36.

46 *New Harmony: An Adventure in Happiness*, Papers of Thomas and Sarah Pears, ed. Thomas Clinton Pears Jr. (Clifton, New Jersey: Augustus M. Kelley, 1973), p. 26.

47 William Owen to Robert Dale Owen, 14 October 1825, in Arndt, *Harmony on the Wabash*, p. 655.

48 R. L. Baker to Frederick Rapp, 20 November 1825, in Arndt, *Harmony on the Wabash*, p. 718.

49 Pears to Benjamin Bakewell, 2 September 1825, in Pears, *New Harmony*, p. 24.

50 Pears, *New Harmony*, p. 24.

51 Ibid., p. 26.

52 Ibid.

53 Brown, *Twelve Months*, p. 26.

54 Wm. H. Shephard to R. H. Baker, 12 November 1825, in Arndt, *Harmony on the Wabash*, p. 706.

55 Brown, *Twelve Months*, p. 25.

56 Indiana Historical Commission, *New Harmony as Seen by Participants and Travelers* (Philadelphia: Porcupine Press, 1975), p. 44.

57 Brown, *Twelve Months*, p. 36. Brown was a voluble malcontent, but his account on this issue is echoed in the correspondence of Owen's partner in New Harmony, William Maclure. See *Education and Reform at New Harmony*, Correspondence of William Maclure and Marie Duclos Fretageot, 1820–1833, ed. Arthur E. Bestor Jr. (Clifton, New Jersey: Augustus M. Kelley, 1973), p. 378.

58 Pears, *New Harmony*, p. 28.

59 Indiana Historical Commission, *Participants and Travelers*, pp. 32, 29, 31.

60 Pears, *New Harmony*, p. 41.

61 R. D. Owen, *Threading*, p. 260.

62 Lockwood, *New Harmony Movement*, p. 104.

63 Quoted in ibid., p. 111.

64 Ibid., p. 105.

65 Ibid., p. 114–15.

66 Ibid., p. 117.

67 The interview was conducted by A. J. MacDonald in the 1850s and is contained in his manuscripts at the Yale University library. I am quoting it from John Humphrey Noyes, *History of American Socialisms* (New York: Dover, 1966), p. 56. A slightly different version appears in Lockwood, *New Harmony Movement*, p. 179.

68 Quoted in Lockwood, *New Harmony Movement*, p. 246.

69 Robert Owen, "Oration, Containing, a Declaration of Mental Independence," reprinted in Arndt, *Harmony on the Wabash*, p. xx.

70 Quoted in Harvey, *Robert Owen, Social Idealist*, p. 158.

71 Podmore, *Robert Owen*, vol. 2, pp. 490–91.

72 Harvey, *Robert Owen, Social Idealist*, p. 158.

73 Bestor, *Education*, p. 355.

74 Brown, *Twelve Months*, p. 86.

75 Lockwood, *New Harmony Movement*, p. 157.

76 Ibid., pp. 169, 172.

77 Ibid., p. 175.

78 Quoted in Brown, *Twelve Months*, pp. 111–12.

79 Owen autobiography in *Selected Works*, vol. 4, p. 333.

80 Quoted in Podmore, *Robert Owen*, vol. 2, p. 360.

81 Lockwood, *New Harmony Movement*, p. 185.

82 Arndt, *Harmony on the Wabash*, p. 435.

83 See, for example, Yaacov Oved's *Two Hundred Years of American Communes* (New Brunswick, New Jersey: Transaction Books, 1988) and Julia Elizabeth Williams' "An Analytical Tabulation of the North American Utopian Communities by Type, Longevity and Location" (Master's Thesis, University of South Dakota, 1939).

84 Owen autobiography in *Selected Works*, vol. 4, p. 303.

85 Quoted in Harvey, *Robert Owen, Social Idealist*, p. 147.

86 Cole, *The Life*, p. 236.

87 Ibid., p. 237.

88 Podmore, *Robert Owen*, vol. 2, p. 471.

89 Reprinted in ibid., p. 473.

90 Ibid., p. 533.

91 Isaac Ironside, quoted in ibid., p. 571.

92 Ibid., p. 594.

93 Owen autobiography in *Selected Works*, vol. 4, p. 253.

94 Ibid., p. 285.

95 George Jacob Holyoake, *Life and Last Days of Robert Owen*, 2nd ed. (London: John Watts, 1859), p. 7.

96 Podmore, *Robert Owen*, vol. 2, p. 629.

97 Cole, *The Life*, pp. 33–34.

98 Robert Dale Owen, "To Amos Gilbert. Letter 11," *Free Enquirer*, vol. 4, no. 18 (25 February 1932), p. 140.

99 Robert Dale Owen, "To Amos Gilbert. Letter 18," *Free Enquirer*, vol. 4, no. 28 (5 May 1832), p. 223.

100 Quoted in Noyes, *History of American Socialisms*, p. 42.

101 Victor Lincoln Albjerg, *Richard Owen* (Lafayette, Indiana: The Archives of Purdue, 1946), p. 22.

102 R. D. Owen, "To Amos Gilbert. Letter 18," p. 223.

CHAPTER THREE: SCIENTIFIC SOCIALISM

1 From the *Schweizerischer Republikaner*, no. 51 (27 June 1843), in Karl Marx and Frederick Engels, *Collected Works*, vol. 3, *Marx and Engels, 1843–44* (New York: International Publishers, 1975), pp. 387–88.

2 Marx and Engels, *Collected Works*, vol. 3, *Marx and Engels, 1843–44*, p. 385.

3 Quoted in Gustav Mayer, *Friedrich Engels: A Biography* (New York: Alfred A. Knopf, 1936), p. 5.

4 Quoted in Terrell Carver, *Friedrich Engels: His Life and Thought* (New York: St. Martin's, 1990), p. 34.

5 Quoted in W. O. Henderson, *The Life of Friedrich Engels* (London: Frank Cass, 1976), vol. 1, p. 14.

6 Karl Marx, "Toward the Critique of Hegel's Philosophy of Law," quoted in Saul K. Padover, *Karl Marx: An Intimate Biography* (New York: McGraw-Hill, 1978), p. 164.

7 Henderson, *The Life*, vol. 1, p. 5; Terrell Carver, *Marx and Engels: The Intellectual Relationship* (Bloomington: Indiana University Press, 1983), p. 9.

8 Quoted in Henderson, *The Life*, vol. 1, p. 14.

9 Carver, *Friedrich Engels*, pp. 69, 76ff.

10 David McLellan, *Friedrich Engels* (New York: Viking, 1978), p. 21.

11 Hal Draper, *The Marx-Engels Chronicle* (New York: Schocken, 1985), p. 13.

12 This originally appeared in *Deutsches Bürgerbuch für 1845* and was then published in English in the *New Moral World*. Reprinted in Karl Marx and Frederick Engels, *Collected Works*, vol. 4, *Marx and Engels, 1844–45* (New York: International Publishers, 1975), pp. 214–28.

13 Marx and Engels, *Collected Works*, vol. 4, *Marx and Engels, 1844–45*, pp. 222, 223, 227.

14 Mayer, *Engels*, p. 56.

15 Carver, *Marx and Engels*, p. 36.

16 David McLellan, *Karl Marx: His Life and Thought* (New York: Harper Colophon, 1977), p. 6.

17 Quoted in Henderson, *The Life*, vol. 1, p. 27.

18 Quoted in Padover, *Intimate Biography*, pp. 212–13.

19 Quoted in Lewis S. Feuer, *Marx and the Intellectuals* (Garden City, New York: Anchor Books, 1969), p. 43.

20 Henderson, *The Life*, vol. 1, p. 61.

21 Gareth Stedman Jones, "Engels and the History of Marxism," in *The History of Marxism*, vol. 1, *Marxism in Marx's Day*, ed. Eric J. Hobsbawm (Bloomington: Indiana University Press, 1982), pp. 296–97, 321.

22 Heinrich to Karl, 2 March 1837, in *The Letters of Karl Marx*, comp. and trans. Saul K. Padover (Englewood Cliffs: Prentice Hall, 1979), pp. 500–1.

23 Padover, *Letters*, pp. 163–64.

24 Heinrich and Henriette to Karl, 18 November 1835, in Padover, *Letters*, p. 493. Padover gives the letters as written, which means, in the case of Mrs. Marx, without punctuation, for apparently she had never learned it. I have added punctuation.

25 *New Moral World*, no. 21 (18 November 1843), reprinted in *Collected Works*, vol. 3, *Marx and Engels, 1843–44*, p. 407.

26 Feuer, *Marx and the Intellectuals*, pp. 41–42.

27 Paul Annenkov in *Reminiscences of Marx and Engels* (Moscow: Foreign Languages Publication House, 1961), quoted in McLellan, *Karl Marx*, p. 157.

28 Quoted in Padover, *Intimate Biography*, p. 233.

29 Engels to Marx, [25]–26 October 1847, in *Collected Works*, vol. 38, *Marx and Engels, 1844–51* (New York: International Publishers, 1982), pp. 138–39.

30 Engels to Marx, 23–24 November 1847, in *Collected Works*, vol. 38, *Marx and Engels, 1844–51*, p. 149.

31 Frederick Engels, *Karl Marx*, in *Collected Works*, vol. 21, *Marx and Engels, 1867–70* (New York: International Publishers, 1985), p. 61.

32 Carver, *Marx and Engels*, p. 78.

33 Quoted in Carver, *Engels: Life and Thought*, p. 197.

34 Quoted in Carver, *Engels: Life and Thought*, p. 219.

35 Mayer, *Engels*, p. 77.

36 Padover, *Letters*, p. 199.

37 Quoted in Carver, *Engels: Life and Thought*, pp. 144–45. Padover gives a more awkward translation of the same letter and points out that the words "lose caste" were written by Marx in English. *Letters*, p. 235.

38 Reprinted in Robert C. Tucker, ed., The Marx-Engels Reader, 2nd ed. (New York: W. W. Norton, 1978), pp. 506–7.

39 Feuer, *Marx and the Intellectuals*, p. 16.

40 Quoted in Max Nomad, *Apostles of Revolution* (New York: Collier, 1961), p. 102.

41 Quoted in Henderson, *The Life*, vol. 1, p. 154.

42 Quoted in Nomad, *Apostles*, p. 102.

43 Quoted in Henderson, *The Life*, vol. 1, p. 44.

44 Feuer, *Marx and the Intellectuals*, p. 32.

45 Quoted in Mayer, *Engels*, p. 196.

46 Edmund Wilson, *To the Finland Station* (New York: Farrar, Straus & Giroux, 1972), p. 245.

47 Padover, *Intimate Biography*, p. 331.

48 Henderson, *The Life*, vol. 2, p. 395.

49 Quoted in ibid., p. 563.

50 Henderson, *The Life*, vol. 1, p. 205.

51 Peter Flora, Franz Kraus, and Winfried Pfenning, eds., *State, Economy, and Society in Western Europe, 1815–1975*, vol. 2, *The Growth of Industrial Societies and Capitalist Economies* (Frankfurt: Campus Verlag, 1987), p. 368.

52 Padover, *Intimate Biography*, p. 341.

53 McLellan, *Karl Marx*, p. 310.

54 Carver, *Marx and Engels*, p. 46.

55 Wilson, *Finland Station*, pp. 338–89.

56 McLellan, *Karl Marx*, p. 353.

57 Padover, *Intimate Biography*, p. 359.

58 Henderson, *The Life*, vol. 2, p. 404; Mayer, *Engels*, p. 197; Padover, *Intimate Biography*, p. 368. Padover puts the number of these reviews at seven, Henderson at ten. Other biographies of Marx or Engels have a number in between.

59 Padover, *Intimate Biography*, p. 394.

60 Quoted in McLellan, *Karl Marx*, p. 402.

61 Quoted by Marx in "After the Revolution: Marx Debates Bakunin," in Tucker, *Marx-Engels Reader*, p. 546.

62 Padover, *Intimate Biography*, p. 423.

63 Wilson, *Finland Station*, p. 361; Henderson, *The Life*, vol. 2, p. 400.

64 Padover, *Intimate Biography*, p. 489.

65 Quoted in ibid., p. 464.

66 Quoted in McLellan, *Karl Marx*, p. 438.

67 Quoted in Henderson, *The Life*, vol. 2, p. 716.

68 Eduard Bernstein, *My Years of Exile: Reminiscences of a Socialist*, trans. Bernard Miall (Westport, Connecticut: Greenwood, 1986), p. 197.

69 Bertram D. Wolfe, *Marxism: One Hundred Years in the Life of a Doctrine* (New York: Dial Press, 1965; reprint, Dell, 1967), p. xiii.

70 Padover, *Intimate Biography*, p. 370.

71 Ibid., p. 360.

72 Mayer, *Engels*, p. 235.

73 Eric J. Hobsbawm, "The Fortunes of Marx's and Engels's Writing," in Eric J. Hobsbawm, *History of Marxism*, vol. 1, p. 34.

74 Quoted in Carver, *Engels: Life and Thought*, p. 250.

75 Gary P. Steenson, *Karl Kautsky, 1854–1938: Marxism in the Classical Years* (Pittsburgh: University of Pittsburgh Press, 1978), p. 46.

76 Karl Kautsky, *Frederick Engels: His Life, His Work and His Writings*, trans. May Wood Simons (Chicago: Charles H. Kerr & Co., 1899), p. 17.

77 George Lichtheim, *Marxism: An Historical and Critical Study* (New York: Praeger, 1961), p. 241.

78 Stedman Jones, "Engels and the History of Marxism," p. 293.

79 Quoted in Mayer, *Engels*, p. 331.

80 Quoted in Henderson, *The Life*, vol. 2, p. 725.

81 Quoted in McLellan, *Karl Marx*, p. 131.

CHAPTER FOUR: WHAT IS TO BE DONE?

1 Quoted in David McLellan, *Karl Marx: His Life and Thought* (New York: Harper Colophon, 1977), p. 435.

2 Quoted in Peter Gay, *The Dilemma of Democratic Socialism: Eduard Bernstein's Challenge to Marx* (New York: Collier, 1962), p. 46.

3 Eduard Bernstein, *My Years of Exile: Reminiscences of a Socialist*, trans. Bernard Miall (Westport, Connecticut: Greenwood, 1986), pp. 152–53.

4 Ibid., p. 153.

5 Manfred B. Steger, *The Quest for Evolutionary Socialism: Eduard Bernstein and Social Democracy* (Cambridge, England: Cambridge University Press, 1997), p. 25. For these several paragraphs about Bernstein's childhood and youth, I have relied to a great extent on Steger's account.

6 Gay, *The Dilemma*, p. 25.

7 Bernstein, *Years of Exile*, p. 107.

8 Gary P. Steenson, *Karl Kautsky, 1854–1938: Marxism in the Classical Years* (Pittsburgh: University of Pittsburgh Press, 1978), pp. 45–46.

9 Quoted in Bernstein, *Years of Exile*, p. 108.

10 Steger, *The Quest*, p. 49.

11 Quoted in Gay, *The Dilemma*, p. 50.

12 Quoted in ibid., p. 1.

13 Steenson, *Kautsky*, p. 13.

14 Ibid., p. 48.

15 Steger, *The Quest*, p. 50.

16 Ibid., p. 58.

17 Quoted in Gay, *The Dilemma*, p. 73.

18 Eduard Bernstein, "General Observations on Utopianism and Eclecticism," *Die Neue Zeit*, 28 October 1896, trans. in *Marxism and Social Democracy: The Revisionist Debate, 1896–1898*, ed. H. Tudor and J. M. Tudor (Cambridge, England: Cambridge University Press, 1988), p. 74.

19 Quoted in Gay, *The Dilemma*, p. 74.

20 Quoted in Steenson, *Kautsky*, p. 80.

21 Quoted in ibid., p. 122.

22 Parvus, "Bernstein's Statement," *Sächsische Arbeiter-Zeitung*, 9 February 1898, trans. in *Marxism and Social Democracy*, ed. Tudor and Tudor, p. 194.

23 Peter Nettl, *Rosa Luxemburg*, abridged ed. (London: Oxford University Press, 1969), p. 32.

24 Rosa Luxemburg, "Practical Consequences and General Character of the Theory," *Leipziger Volkszeitung*, 28 September 1898, trans. in *Marxism and Social Democracy*, ed. Tudor and Tudor, pp. 270–71.

25 Luxemburg, "Practical Consequences," p. 272.

26 Rosa Luxemburg, "The Method," *Leipziger Volkszeitung*, 21 September 1898, trans. in *Marxism and Social Democracy*, ed. Tudor and Tudor, p. 252.

27 Gay, *The Dilemma*, p. 80; Steenson, *Karl Kautsky*, pp. 122–23.

28 "The Party Conference at Stuttgart: The Debate on the Press," trans. in *Marxism and Social Democracy*, ed. Tudor and Tudor, pp. 297, 294, 298.

29 Ibid., p. 302.

30 Peter Flora et al., *State, Economy, and Society in Western Europe, 1815–1975*, vol. 2, *The Growth of Industrial Societies and Capitalist Economies* (Chicago: St. James, 1983), pp. 381–82, 398–89. Also, Angus Maddison, *Monitoring the World Economy, 1820–1992* (Paris: OECD Development Centre, 1995), table D-1a, pp. 194, 196.

31 Gay, *The Dilemma*, p. 128.

32 Eduard Bernstein, *Evolutionary Socialism* (New York: Schocken, 1961), pp. 209–10.

33 Steenson, *Kautsky*, p. 118.

34 Robert Payne, *The Life and Death of Lenin* (New York: Simon & Schuster, 1964), p. 133.

35 V. I. Lenin, *Collected Works*, vol. 37, *Letters to Relatives, 1893–1922* (Moscow: Progress Publishers, 1977, 3rd printing), p. 281.

36 Quoted in Edmund Wilson, *To the Finland Station* (New York: Farrar, Straus & Giroux, 1972), p. 447.

37 Nikolay Valentinov, *Encounters with Lenin*, trans. Paul Rosta and Brian Pierce (London: Oxford University Press, 1968), p. 184.

38 Nikolai Valentinov, *The Early Years of Lenin*, trans. and ed. Rolf H. W. Theen (Ann Arbor: University of Michigan Press, 1969), pp. 16–17.

39 *Pravda*, 16 April 1927, quoted in Louis Fischer, *The Life of Lenin* (New York: Harper & Row, 1964), p. 17.

40 Tibor Szamuely, *The Russian Tradition* (New York: McGraw-Hill, 1974), p. 213.

41 Valentinov, *Encounters with Lenin*, p. 64.

42 Karl Marx, Letter to Friedrich Adolph Sorge, 5 November 1880, in *The Letters of Karl Marx*, comp. and trans. Saul K. Padover (Englewood Cliffs: Prentice Hall, 1979), p. 330.

43 Jerzy Gliksman, *Tell the West* (New York: Gresham Press, 1948), p. 350.

44 Quoted in Bertram D. Wolfe, *Three Who Made a Revolution: A Biographical History* (New York: Dial Press, 1964; reprint, Dell, 1978), p. 120.

45 Pravda, 30 May 1923, quoted in Fischer, *Life of Lenin*, p. 655.

46 Quoted in Bertram D. Wolfe, *An Ideology in Power: Reflections on the Russian Revolution* (New York: Stein & Day, 1969), p. 13.

47 Jacques Barzun, *Darwin, Marx, Wagner* (Garden City, New York: Doubleday, 1958), p. 219.

48 Steenson, *Kautsky*, p. 91.

49 Adam Ulam, *The Bolsheviks: The Intellectual and Political History of the Triumph of Communism in Russia* (New York: Collier, 1968), p. 138.

50 V. I. Lenin, "The Immediate Tasks of the Soviet Government," in *Collected Works*, vol. 27, *February–July 1918* (Moscow: Progress Publishers, 1977, 3rd printing), p. 267.

51 V. I. Lenin, "Materialism and Empirico-Criticism," in *Collected Works*, vol. 14, *1908* (Moscow: Progress Publishers, 1977, 3rd printing), p. 326.

52 V. I. Lenin, "The Three Sources and Three Component Parts of Marxism," in *Collected Works*, vol. 19, *March–December 1913* (Moscow: Progress Publishers, 1977, 4th printing), p. 23.

53 Leon Trotzky [sic], *Lenin* (Garden City, New York: Garden City Books, 1959), p. 61.

54 Wolfe, *Three Who Made*, p. 229.

55 Quoted in ibid., p. 611.

CHAPTER FIVE: REAL EXISTING SOCIALISM

1 Quoted in Lavender Cassels, *The Archduke and the Assassin* (London: Frederick Muller, 1984), pp. 176–77.

2 Leszek Kolakowski, *Main Currents of Marxism*, vol. 2, *The Golden Age*, trans. P. S. Falla (Oxford: Clarendon, 1978), p. 1.

3 All of these figures are taken from Donald Sassoon, *One Hundred Years of Socialism: The Western European Left in the Twentieth Century* (New York: The New Press, 1996), p. 10. I have borrowed them from Sassoon's table 1.1. However, I have rounded them off to whole numbers.

4 Carl E. Schorske, *German Social Democracy, 1905–1917* (Cambridge: Harvard University Press, 1955), p. 83.

5 Quoted in Bertram D. Wolfe, *Three Who Made a Revolution: A Biographical History* (New York: Dial Press, 1964; reprint, Dell, 1978), p. 522.

6 Quoted in Leonard Schapiro, *The Communist Party of the Soviet Union* (New York: Vintage, 1964), pp. 89–90.

7 V. I. Lenin, "Speech for the Defence (or for the Prosecution of the Menshevik Section of the Central Committee) Delivered at the Party Tribunal," in *Collected Works*, vol. 12, *January–June 1907* (Moscow: Progress Publishers, 1977, 4th printing), pp. 424–26. Emphases in original.

8 Maria Essen, quoted in Louis Fischer, *The Life of Lenin* (New York: Harper & Row, 1964), p. 43.

9 See Adam B. Ulam, *The Bolsheviks: The Intellectual and Political History of the Triumph of Communism in Russia* (New York: Collier, 1968, c1965), p. 283.

10 V. I. Lenin, *Collected Works*, vol. 43, *December 1893–October 1917* (Moscow: Progress Publishers, 1977, 3rd printing), p. 406.

11 Quoted in Wolfe, *Three Who Made*, p. 610.

12 Julius Braunthal, *History of the International*, vol. 1, *1864–1914*, trans. Henry Collins and Kenneth Mitchell (New York: Praeger, 1967), p. 355.

13 Donald Sassoon, *One Hundred Years*, p. 27.

14 Quoted in Julius Braunthal, *History of the International*, vol. 2, *1914–1943*, trans. John Clark (New York: Praeger, 1967), pp. 13–14.

15 Quoted in Carl Landauer, *European Socialism: A History of Ideas and Movements* (Berkeley: University of California Press, 1959), vol. 1, p. 510.

16 Quoted in Ulam, *The Bolsheviks*, p. 303.

17 Wolfe, *Three Who Made*, p. 577.

18 Maxim Gorky, *Days with Lenin* (New York: International Publishers, 1932), p. 23.

19 Quoted in David Shub, *Lenin* (Baltimore: Penguin, 1966), p. 158.

20 Quoted in Ulam, *The Bolsheviks*, p. 306.

21 Isaiah Berlin, *The Sense of Reality* (New York: Farrar, Straus & Giroux, 1997), p. 139.

22 Bertram D. Wolfe, *An Ideology in Power: Reflections on the Russian Revolution* (New York: Stein & Day, 1969), p. 28.

23 According to economist Paul Bairoch, Germany's GNP per capita in 1850 amounted to the equivalent of $308, measured in 1960 U.S. dollars, whereas Russia's in 1913 was $326. See "Europe's Gross National Product: 1800–1975," *Journal of European Economic History*, vol. 5, no. 2 (Fall 1976), p. 286, table 6.

24 Quoted in Fischer, *Life of Lenin*, p. 480.

25 Milovan Djilas, *The Unperfect Society*, trans. Dorian Cooke (New York: Harcourt, Brace & World, 1969), p. 131.

26 Richard Pipes, *The Russian Revolution* (New York: Alfred A. Knopf, 1990), p. 731.

27 Quoted in Richard Pipes, *Russia under the Bolshevik Regime* (New York: Alfred A. Knopf, 1993), p. 374.

28 Shub, *Lenin*, p. 324.

29 Leon Trotzky [*sic*], *Lenin* (Garden City, New York: Garden City Books, 1959), p. 123.

30 Trotzky, *Lenin*, pp. 147–48.

31 Fischer, *Life of Lenin*, p. 344.

32 Bertrand Russell, *Bolshevism: Practice and Theory* (New York: Harcourt, Brace & Howe, 1920), p. 35, quoted in Fischer, *Life of Lenin*, p. 407.

33 Angelica Balabanoff, *Impressions of Lenin*, trans. Isotta Cesari (Ann Arbor: University of Michigan Press, 1964), p. 5.

34 Quoted in Wolfe, *Three Who Made*, p. 494.

35 "Comrade Workers, Forward to the Last Decisive Fight!" in V. I. Lenin, *Collected Works*, vol. 28, *July 1918–March 1919* (Moscow: Progress Publishers, 1981, 3rd printing), p. 57.

36 Quoted in Ulam, *The Bolsheviks*, p. 384.

37 Quoted in Trotzky, *Lenin*, p. 137.

38 Ibid., pp. 137–38.

39 Quoted in Fischer, *Life of Lenin*, p. 278. Also Shub, *Lenin*, p. 360.

40 Quoted in Shub, *Lenin*, p. 360.

41 Ibid., p. 345.

42 Gorky, *Days with Lenin*, p. 44.

43 Ibid., p. 39.

44 Quoted in Shub, *Lenin*, p. 274.

45 Quoted in ibid., p. 429.

46 Pipes, *Russian Revolution*, p. 638.

47 Quoted in ibid., p. 807.

48 Pipes, *Bolshevik Regime*, p. 456.

49 Fischer, *Life of Lenin*, p. 260.

50 Adam B. Ulam, *Expansion and Coexistence: Soviet Foreign Policy, 1917–73*, 2nd ed. (New York: Holt, Rhinehart, 1974), p. 110.

51 Quoted in Shub, *Lenin*, p. 388.

52 "Political Report of the Central Committee RKP(b) to the Ninth All-Russian Conference of the Communist Party," trans. in *The Unknown Lenin: From the Secret Archive*, ed. Richard Pipes (New Haven: Yale University Press, 1996), p. 96.

53 Ibid., p. 107.

54 In Pipes, *Unknown Lenin*, p. 114.

CHAPTER SIX: FASCISM

1 Jonathan D. Spence, *The Search for Modern China* (New York: W. W. Norton, 1990), p. 338.

2 Margherita G. Sarfatti, *The Life of Benito Mussolini*, trans. Frederic Whyte (New York: Frederick A. Stokes, 1925), p. 261.

3 Angelica Balabanoff, *My Life as a Rebel* (New York: Harper, 1938), p. 45.

4 Benito Mussolini, *My Rise and Fall* (New York: Da Capo Press, 1998), vol. 1, p. 3.

5 Denis Mack Smith, *Mussolini* (New York: Alfred A. Knopf, 1982), p. 1.

6 *Opera Omnia di Benito Mussolini*, a cura di Edoardo e Duilio Susmel, vol. 1, *Dagli inizi all'ultima sosta in Romagna (1 Dicembre 1901–5 Febbraio 1908)* (Firenze: La Fenice, 1951), p. 27. Translated by Simonetta Capobianco.

7 Balabanoff, *My Life*, p. 50.

8 Paolo Monelli, *Mussolini: The Intimate Life of a Demagogue*, trans. Brigid Maxwell (New York: Vanguard, 1954), p. 46.

9 A. James Gregor, *Young Mussolini and the Intellectual Origins of Fascism* (Berkeley: University of California Press, 1979), pp. 42–43.

10 V. I. Lenin, *Collected Works*, vol. 18, *April 1912–March 1913* (Moscow: Progress Publishers, 1978, 5th printing), p. 172.

11 Gregor, *Young Mussolini*, p. 135.

12 Ibid., p. 133.

13 Mack Smith, *Mussolini*, p. 23; Gregor, *Young Mussolini*, p. 161.

14 Quoted in Sarfatti, *The Life*, p. 263.

15 Mussolini, *My Rise*, vol. 1, p. 36.

16 Quoted in Gregor, *Young Mussolini*, p. 179.

17 Jasper Ridley, *Mussolini* (New York: St. Martin's, 1997), p. 71.

18 Mussolini, *My Rise*, vol. 1, p. 25.

19 Zeev Sternhell with Mario Sznajder and Maia Asheri, *The Birth of Fascist Ideology*, trans. David Maisel (Princeton: Princeton University Press, 1994), p. 30.

20 Mack Smith, *Mussolini*, p. 36.

21 Robert O. Paxton, "The Five Stages of Fascism," *Journal of Modern History*, vol. 70, no. 1 (March 1998), p. 15.

22 Sternhell, *The Birth*, p. 224.

23 Gregor, *Young Mussolini*, p. 227.

24 Sarfatti, *The Life*, p. 264. Also see A. James Gregor, *The Faces of Janus: Marxism and Fascism in the Twentieth Century* (New Haven: Yale University Press, 2000), pp. 137, 141.

25 Mussolini, *My Rise*, vol. 1, p. 96.

26 Monelli, *Intimate Life*, p. 95.

27 Ridley, *Mussolini*, p. 162.

28 Mussolini, *My Rise*, vol. 1, p. 231.

29 Joseph E. Davies, *Mission to Moscow* (Garden City, New York: Garden City Books, 1943), p. 244.

30 Richard Washburn Child, Foreword to Mussolini, *My Rise*, vol. 1, p. vii.

31 Mack Smith, *Mussolini*, p. 135.

32 Herman Finer, *Mussolini's Italy* (New York: Grosset & Dunlap), pp. 503–4.

33 Mussolini, *My Rise*, vol. 1, p. 277.

34 Quoted in Finer, *Mussolini's Italy*, pp. 501–2.

35 Mussolini, *My Rise*, vol. 1, p. 129.

36 George Slocombe, *The Tumult and the Shouting* (New York: Macmillan, 1936), p. 150.

37 Pipes, *Russian under the Bolshevik Regime* (New York: Alfred A. Knopf, 1993), p. 253.

38 Mack Smith, *Mussolini*, p. 242; Gregor, *Faces of Janus*, p. 147.

39 Gregor, *Faces of Janus*, p. 147.

40 Mack Smith, *Mussolini*, pp. 154, 187.

41 Charles Maurras, *Dictionnaire Politique et Critique*, vol. 5 (Paris: Fayard, 1931–33), p. 213, quoted in Sternhell, *The Birth*, p. 82.

42 Marcel Déat, *Révolution Française et Révolution Allemande, 1793–1943* (Paris: Editions du R.N.P., 1943), p. 29.

43 Sternhell, *The Birth*, p. 246.

44 Quoted in ibid., p. 311.

45 Quoted in John Weiss, *The Fascist Tradition: Radical Right Wing Extremism in Modern Europe* (New York: Harper & Row, 1967), p. 89.

46 Max H. Kele, *Nazis and Workers: National Socialist Appeals to German Labor, 1919–1933* (Chapel Hill: University of North Carolina Press, 1972), pp. 34–35.

47 Adolph Hitler, *Mein Kampf*, trans. Ralph Manheim (Boston: Houghton Mifflin, 1943), pp. 496–97.

48 Quoted in Max Nomad, *Apostles of Revolution* (New York: Collier, 1961), p. 102.

49 Karl Marx, "On the Jewish Question," originally appeared in the *Deutsch-Französische Jahrbücher*, February 1844. Reprinted in Karl Marx and Frederick Engels, *Collected Works*, vol. 3, Marx and Engels, 1843–44 (New York: International Publishers, 1975), pp. 170–74.

50 Hitler, *Mein Kampf*, p. 483.

51 Quoted in David Schoenbaum, *Hitler's Social Revolution: Class and Status in Nazi Germany, 1933–1939* (Garden City, New York: Anchor Books, 1967), p. 57.

52 Hermann Rauschning, *Hitler Speaks: A Series of Political Conversations with Adolf Hitler on His Real Aims* (London: T. Butterworth Ltd., 1939), p. 185.

53 Reginald H. Phelps, ed., "Hitler's 'Grundlegende' Rede ueber der Antisemitismus," *Vierteljahreshefte für Zeitgeschichte*, vol. 16, no. 4 (1968), p. 415. Translated by Krista Shaffer.

54 Joseph Goebbels, *Die zweite Revolution. Briefe an Zeitgenossen* (Zwickau, Sa.: Streiter-Verlag, 1926), p. 47.

55 Schoenbaum, *Hitler's Social Revolution*, p. 58.

56 Hitler, *Mein Kampf*, p. 681.

57 *Völkischer Beobachter*, 15 May 1923; quoted in Kele, *Nazis and Workers*, pp. 63–64.

58 Quoted in Monelli, *Intimate Life*, pp. 129, 130.

59 Mack Smith, *Mussolini*, p. 152.

60 Quoted in Ridley, *Mussolini*, p. 261.

61 Quoted in Monelli, *Intimate Life*, p. 187.

62 Mussolini, *My Rise*, vol. 2, pp. 56, 62.

63 Max Ascoli, "Preface" to Mussolini, *My Rise*, vol. 2, p. 48.

64 Mack Smith, *Mussolini*, p. 311.

65 Quoted in Monelli, *Intimate Life*, p. 248.

66 Mack Smith, *Mussolini*, pp. 282–283.

67 Quoted in Monelli, *Intimate Life*, p. 253.

68 Quoted in Ridley, *Mussolini*, p. 365.

CHAPTER SEVEN: SOCIAL DEMOCRACY

1 Socialist International, *Aims and Tasks of Democratic Socialism, Frankfurt Declaration*, 1951, point 8.

2 "The Man Who Built the Welfare State," *Economist*, 11 November 1989, p. 23.

3 Alan Bullock, *Ernest Bevin, Foreign Secretary, 1945–1951* (Oxford: Oxford University Press, 1985), p. 25.

4 Quoted in Charles L. Mee Jr., *Meeting at Potsdam* (New York: Dell, 1967), p. 212.

5 Clement R. Attlee, *As It Happened* (London: William Heinemann, 1954), p. 5.

6 Ibid., pp. 15–16.

7 Francis Beckett, *Clem Attlee* (London: Richard Cohen Books, 1997), p. 19.

8 Attlee, *As It Happened*, pp. 20–21.

9 Quoted in Roy Jenkins, *Mr. Attlee: An Interim Biography* (London: William Heinemann, 1948), p. 30.

10 Anne Fremantle, *This Little Band of Prophets: The British Fabians* (New York: New American Library, 1960), p. 16. The quote within the quote is attributed to Malcolm Muggeridge.

11 Kenneth Harris, *Attlee*, rev. ed. (London: Weidenfeld and Nicolson, 1995), p. 28.

12 Beckett, *Clem Attlee*, pp. 41–42.

13 Attlee, *As It Happened*, p. 12.

14 Quoted in Jenkins, *Mr. Attlee*, p. 67; Beckett, *Clem Attlee*, p. 44.

15 Trevor Burridge, *Clement Attlee: A Political Biography* (London: Jonathan Cape, 1985), p. 42.

16 Beckett, *Clem Attlee*, p. 44.

17 Attlee, *As It Happened*, p. 40.

18 Harris, *Attlee*, pp. 36–37.

19 Attlee, *As It Happened*, p. 40.

20 In Beckett, *Clem Attlee*, p. 51.

21 Quoted in Burridge, *Clement Attlee*, p. 46.

22 George Bernard Shaw, *The Fabian Society: Its Early History*, Fabian Tract no. 4 (London: Fabian Society, 1892), p. 4.

23 Harris, *Attlee*, p. 43.

24 Beckett, *Clem Attlee*, p. 59.

25 Attlee, *As It Happened*, p. 51.

26 Harris, *Attlee*, p. 52.

27 Ibid., p. 54.

28 Quoted in ibid., p. 55.

29 Reprinted in Beckett, *Clem Attlee*, p. 73.

30 Quoted in Attlee, *As It Happened*, pp. 58–59.

31 Ibid., p. 74.

32 "Italian Challenge to Mr Attlee," *Times* (London), 9 July 1935, p. 14.

33 Harris, *Attlee*, p. 56.

34 Beckett, *Clem Attlee*, p. 201.

35 Quoted in Harris, *Attlee*, p. 77.

36 Clement R. Attlee, *The Labour Party in Perspective* (London: Victor Gollancz Ltd., 1937), p. 10.

37 Ibid., p. 132.

38 Ibid., p. 147.

39 Ibid., pp. 152, 153, 198.

40 Ibid., p. 153.

41 Ibid., p. 279.

42 Ibid., pp. 83, 132.

43 Ibid., p. 10.

44 Ibid., p. 18.

45 For example: Anthony Dell, "Sweden's Secret," *Contemporary Review*, vol. 139, no. 784 (April 1931), pp. 477–83; Marquis Childs, "Sweden: Where Capitalism Is Controlled," *Harper's Monthly*, November 1933, pp. 749–58; Roger L. Simons, "The Garden of Sweden," *North American Review*, vol. 238, no. 5 (November 1934), pp. 414–20; "Swedish Democracy Bids Farewell to Depression," *Christian Century*, 6 February 1935; Isaac F. Marcosson, "The Swedish Recovery," *Saturday Evening Post*, vol. 298 (22 February 1936), p. 23; Hubert Henning, "The Incredible Sweden," *Harper's*, November 1936, pp. 632–43.

46 Attlee, *Labour Party in Perspective*, p. 224.

47 Ibid., p. 270.

48 Harris, *Attlee*, p. 169.

49 Winston S. Churchill, *The Second World War*, vol. 2, *Their Finest Hour* (Boston: Houghton Mifflin, 1949), p. 12.

50 "A London Diary," *New Statesman and Nation*, 4 August 1945.

51 Quoted in Harris, *Attlee*, p. 244.

52 Ibid., p. 187.

53 Quoted in Kenneth O. Morgan, *Labour in Power, 1945–1951* (Oxford: Oxford University Press, 1985), p. 37.

54 Burridge, *Clement Attlee*, p. 182.

55 Attlee, *As It Happened*, pp. 162–63.

56 Quoted in Harris, *Attlee*, p. 424.

57 Burridge, *Clement Attlee*, p. 191.

58 Attlee, *As It Happened*, p. 163.

59 Morgan, *Labour in Power*, pp. 105–6.

60 Ibid., p. 331n; also see Harris, *Attlee*, p. 335.

61 Quoted in Morgan, *Labour in Power*, p. 160.

62 Quoted in ibid., pp. 412–13.

63 Sidney and Beatrice Webb, *Soviet Communism: A New Civilization?* (New York: C. Scribner's Sons, 1936), p. 1072.

64 Attlee, *As It Happened*, pp. 146–47.

65 Ibid., p. 169.

66 Burridge, *Clement Attlee*, p. 312.

67 Quoted in Harris, *Attlee*, p. 549.

CHAPTER EIGHT: UJAMAA

1 Fenner Brockway, *African Socialism* (Chester Springs, Pennsylvania: Dufour Editions, 1963), pp. 14, 17.

2 Daniel Patrick Moynihan, "The United States in Opposition," *Commentary*, vol. 59, no. 3 (March 1975), pp. 31–32.

3 William Edgett Smith, *Nyerere of Tanzania* (London: Victor Gollancz Ltd., 1973), p. 40, and John Hatch, *Two African Statesmen: Kaunda of Zambia and Nyerere of Tanzania* (Chicago: Henry Regnery, 1976), p. 1, as well as various news stories which may have relied on these sources, give the number of Nyerere Burito's wives as twenty-two. However, Joan

Wicken, who served more than thirty years as Nyerere's executive assistant, says that he always spoke of his father's having had twenty-three.

4 Smith, *Nyerere*, p. 43.

5 Ibid, p. 42.

6 Ibid.

7 Annie Smyth and Adam Seftel, *Tanzania: The Story of Julius Nyerere through the Pages of DRUM, Bailey's African History Archives* (Kampala: Fountain, 1998), p. 28.

8 Quoted in Smith, *Nyerere*, pp. 49–50. The version of this essay printed in Julius K. Nyerere, *Freedom and Unity* (London: Oxford University Press, 1967), pp. 23–29 omits the passages about Africa for the Africans and driving out the others.

9 Nyerere, "President's Inaugural Address" in *Freedom and Unity*, p. 186.

10 Smyth and Seftel, *Tanzania*, p. 31.

11 "Oral Hearing at the Trusteeship Council," in Nyerere, *Freedom and Unity*, p. 37.

12 Hatch, *Two African Statesmen*, p. 202.

13 Smyth and Seftel, *Tanzania*, p. 31.

14 Ibid., p. 68.

15 "Resignation as Prime Minister," press statement issued 22 January 1962 in Nyerere, *Freedom and Unity*, p. 158.

16 Julius K. Nyerere, *Ujamaa: Essays on Socialism* (Dar es Salaam: Oxford University Press, 1968), p. viii.

17 Cranford Pratt, *The Critical Phase in Tanzania, 1945–1968* (New York: Cambridge University Press, 1976), p. 65.

18 George Tobias, *High-Level Manpower Requirements and Resources in Tanganyika, 1962–67*, Government Paper no. 2 of 1963 (Dar es Salaam: Government Printer, 1963), table 10, pp. 33–36, reprinted in Pratt, *The Critical Phase*, table 1, p. 93.

19 Smyth and Seftel, *Tanzania*, p. 47.

20 Ibid., p. 105.

21 Pratt, *The Critical Phase*, p. 68.

22 "President's Inaugural Address," in Nyerere, *Freedom and Unity*, p. 177.

23 Reprinted in Nyerere, *Ujamaa*, p. 1.

24 Reprinted in ibid., p. 2.

25 Reprinted in ibid., p. 6.

26 "Ujamaa: The Basis of African Socialism," in ibid., p. 7.

27 Goran Hyden, *Beyond Ujamaa in Tanzania: Underdevelopment and an Uncaptured Peasantry* (Berkeley: University of California Press, 1980), p. 70.

28 "After the Arusha Declaration," in Nyerere, *Ujamaa*, p. 154.

29 Ibid., p. 170.

30 Smith, *Nyerere*, p. 160.

31 Quoted in Hatch, *Two African Statesmen*, p. 204.

32 Quoted in Pratt, *The Critical Phase*, p. 163.

33 "The Arusha Declaration," Nyerere, *Ujamaa*, p. 16.

34 Smith, *Nyerere*, p. 171.

35 "Socialism Is Not Racialism," in Nyerere, *Ujamaa*, p. 42.

36 "The Arusha Declaration," Nyerere, *Ujamaa*, p. 26.

37 All quotes in the paragraph are from "Introduction," Julius K. Nyerere, *Freedom and Socialism* (Dar es Salaam: Oxford University Press, 1968), pp. 26–27.

38 "Education for Self-Reliance," Nyerere, *Ujamaa*, p. 63.

39 Ibid., p. 71.

40 Ibid., pp. 74–75.

41 Smyth and Seftel, *Tanzania*, p. 137.
42 Quoted in Smith, *Nyerere*, p. 176.
43 "Socialism and Rural Development," Nyerere, *Ujamaa*, p. 118.
44 Juma Volter Mwapachu, "Operation Planned Villages in Rural Tanzania: A Revolutionary Strategy for Development," in *African Socialism in Practice: The Tanzanian Experience*, ed. Andrew Coulson (Nottingham: Spokesman, 1979), p. 115. Mwapachu was District Development Director of Shinyanga.
45 Michaela von Freyhold, *Ujamaa Villages in Tanzania: Analysis of a Social Experiment* (New York: Monthly Review Press, 1979), p. 46.
46 Ibid., p. 47.
47 Ibid., pp. 138–39.
48 Michael Harrington: *The Vast Majority: A Journey to the World's Poor* (New York: Simon & Schuster, 1977).
49 "Tanzaphilia," *Transition*, no. 31 (June–July 1967), pp. 20, 25.
50 Deborah Shapley, *Promise and Power* (Boston: Little, Brown, 1993), pp. 531, 531.
51 "Tanzania Country Assistance Evaluation," The World Bank, Operations Evaluation Department, Report 20902-TA, 13 September 2000, p. i.
52 J. R. A. Bailey, "Preface" to Smyth and Seftel, *Tanzania: The Story of Julius Nyerere*, p. iv.
53 Hyden, *Beyond Ujamaa*, p. 135.
54 "TANU Guidelines on Guarding, Consolidating and Advancing the Revolution of Tanzania, and of Africa (Mwongozo)," reprinted in Coulson, *African Socialism in Practice*, pp. 37–38.
55 Hyden, *Beyond Ujamaa*, p. 177.
56 Joel D. Barkan, "Divergence and Convergence in Kenya and Tanzania: Pressures for Reform," in *Beyond Capitalism vs. Socialism in Kenya and Tanzania*, ed. Barkan (Boulder: Lynne Rienner, 1994), p. 20.
57 "Socialism and Rural Development" and "Progress in the Rural Areas," Nyerere, *Ujamaa*, pp. 143, 181.
58 Interview with Francis Nyalali, Dar es Salaam, 21 September 2000.
59 "The Arusha Declaration," Nyerere, *Ujamaa*, p. 35.
60 Freyhold, *Ujamaa Villages*, p. 56.
61 Nyalali interview.
62 Pratt, *The Critical Phase*, p. 2.
63 Smyth and Seftel, *Tanzania*, p. 167.
64 "After the Arusha Declaration," Nyerere, *Ujamaa*, pp. 174–75.
65 Hyden, *Beyond Ujamaa*, p. 130.
66 Coulson, *African Socialism in Practice*, p. 8.
67 Hyden, *Beyond Ujamaa*, p. 144.
68 Nyalali interview.
69 Ibid.
70 Ibid.
71 Hyden, *Beyond Ujamaa*, p. 145.
72 "After the Arusha Declaration," in Nyerere, *Ujamaa*, p. 154.
73 Goran Hyden, "Party, State, and Civil Society: Control Versus Openness," in *Beyond Capitalism vs. Socialism*, ed. Barkan, p. 88.
74 "The Varied Paths to Socialism," Nyerere, *Ujamaa*, p. 87.
75 Julius K. Nyerere, *The Arusha Declaration Ten Years After* (Dar es Salaam: Government Printer, 1977), p. 1.
76 Ibid., p. 42.

77 Ibid., pp. 34–35.

78 Ibid., pp. 3, 7.

79 Ibid., p. 9.

80 Ibid., pp. 12–13.

81 Ibid., p. 22.

82 Ibid., pp. 5, 7, 16.

83 Quoted in James M. Boughton, *Silent Revolution: The International Monetary Fund, 1979–1989* (Washington: IMF, 2001), ch. 13.

84 Horace Campbell, "The Politics of Demobilization in Tanzania: Beyond Nationalism," in *Tanzania and the IMF: The Dynamics of Liberalization*, ed. Campbell and Howard Stein (Boulder: Westview, 1992), p. 96.

85 Coulson, *African Socialism in Practice*, p. 6.

86 T. L. Maliyamkono and M. S. D. Bagachwa, *The Second Economy in Tanzania* (London: James Curry, 1990), p. 8.

87 Shiva Naipaul, *North of South: An African Journey* (London: Penguin, 1978), pp. 245–46.

88 Maliyamkono and Bagachwa, *The Second Economy*, p. xiii.

89 Interview with Paul Sozigwa and Philip Mangula, Dar es Salaam, 23 September 2000.

90 Campbell, "The Politics of Demobilization," p. 87.

91 Ibid., p. 101.

92 "On the Road to Somewhere; Tanzania: The Failed Experiment," *Economist*, 20 June 1987, p. 14.

93 Mary Anne Fitzgerald, "Tanzania: Drifting Back to Capitalism?" *Christian Science Monitor*, 30 July 1985, p. 7.

94 "Speech by Mwalimu Julius K. Nyerere, Chairman of Chama Cha Mapinduzi, on the 20th Anniversary of Arusha Declaration and 10th Anniversary of Chama Cha Mapinduzi," 5 February 1987 at Dodoma, pp. 6, 12, 17, 21–22. (I have a photocopy of a published text, given to me by the Mwalimu Nyerere Foundation of Dar es Salaam. It does not say by whom or when it was published.)

95 Barkan, "Divergence and Convergence," p. 31.

96 Michael T. Kaufman, "Julius Nyerere of Tanzania Dies; Preached African Socialism to the World," *New York Times*, 15 October 1999, p. B10.

97 See the World Bank's "Country Assistance Evaluation" for Tanzania, Report No. 20902-TA, 13 September 2000, p. i.

98 Judith Matloff, "Where Marx Left His Harshest Marks," *Christian Science Monitor*, 5 September 1995, p. 7.

CHAPTER NINE: UNION CARD

1 For a discussion of this, see Seymour Martin Lipset and Gary Marks, *It Didn't Happen Here: Why Socialism Failed in the United States* (New York: W. W. Norton, 2000), pp. 16–20.

2 George Morris, "Three Presidents in 97 Years," *Daily World*, 28 November 1979.

3 Quoted in Philip Taft and John A. Sessions, "Introduction" to Samuel Gompers, *Seventy Years of Life and Labor* (New York: E. P. Dutton, 1957), p. 6. (Note: This is a different edition of the Gompers autobiography than cited elsewhere in this chapter.)

4 Samuel Gompers, *Seventy Years of Life and Labor*, ed. Nick Salvatore (Ithaca, New York: ILR Press, 1984), p. 8.

5 Ibid., p. 25.

6 Ibid., p. 26.

7 Ibid., pp. 34–35.

8 Ibid., p. 43.

9 Philip Taft, *The AF of L in the Time of Gompers* (New York: Harper & Bros., 1957), p. 37.

10 Gompers, *Seventy Years*, p. 76.

11 Quoted in Bernard Mandel, *Samuel Gompers* (Yellow Springs, Ohio: Antioch Press, 1963), p. 108.

12 Gerald Emanuel Stearn, "Introduction," in *Gompers*, ed. Gerald E. Stearn (Englewood Cliffs: Prentice Hall, 1971), p. 9.

13 Quoted in Taft, *The AF of L*, p. 44.

14 Mandel, *Samuel Gompers*, p. 89.

15 Taft, *The AF of L*, p. 45.

16 Ibid., p. 58.

17 Nick Salvatore, "Introduction," in Gompers, *Seventy Years*, p. xxvi.

18 Mandel, *Samuel Gompers*, p. 76.

19 Quoted in ibid., p. 115.

20 Quoted in William M. Dick, *Labor and Socialism in America: The Gompers Era* (Port Washington, New York: Kennikat Press, 1972), p. 114.

21 Quoted in Mandel, *Samuel Gompers*, p. 75.

22 Quoted in ibid., p. 116.

23 "Against Socialism," in *Gompers*, ed. Stearn, p. 50.

24 Gompers, *Seventy Years*, p. 114.

25 *Gompers*, ed. Stearns, pp. 48–49.

26 Quoted in Taft, *The AF of L*, p. 73.

27 Gompers, *Seventy Years*, p. 126.

28 Quoted in Daniel Bell, "The Great Totem," in *Gompers*, ed. Stearn, p. 156.

29 Quoted in ibid., p. 156.

30 Gompers, *Seventy Years*, p. 117.

31 Quoted in Dick, *Labor and Socialism*, p. 115.

32 Theodore Roosevelt, *The Autobiography of Theodore Roosevelt* (New York: Scribner's, 1958), pp. 79–80.

33 Gompers, *Seventy Years*, p. 62.

34 Henry Pelling, *American Labor* (Chicago: University of Chicago Press, 1960), p. 118.

35 Mandel, *Samuel Gompers*, pp. 204–5.

36 Gompers, *Seventy Years*, p. 135.

37 Ibid., p. 201.

38 "Introduction" to ibid., p. xxxvi.

39 Mandel, *Samuel Gompers*, pp. 415–16.

40 Quoted in Taft, *The AF of L*, p. 444.

41 Samuel Gompers, *The Truth about Soviet Russia and Bolshevism* (pamphlet of articles republished from the *American Federationist*) (Washington, D.C.: American Federation of Labor, 1920), p. 13.

42 Ibid., p. 15.

43 Taft and Sessions, "Introduction" to Gompers, *Seventy Years*, p. 42.

44 Gompers, *The Truth*.

45 Monroe Smith, *Out of Their Own Mouths: A Revelation and an Indictment of Sovietism* (New York: E. P. Dutton, 1921).

46 Gompers, *The Truth*, p. 12.

47 Quoted in Mandel, *Samuel Gompers*, p. 529.

48 Archie Robinson, *George Meany and His Times* (New York: Simon & Schuster, 1981), p. 23.

49 Joseph C. Goulden, *Meany: The Unchallenged Strong Man of American Labor* (New York: Atheneum, 1972), p. 28.

50 Ted Morgan, *A Covert Life: Jay Lovestone—Communist, Anti-Communist and Spymaster* (New York: Random House, 1999), p. 141.

51 Ibid., p. 107.

52 Quoted in Theodore Draper, *American Communism and Soviet Russia* (New York: Viking, 1960), p. 144.

53 "Speech to the American Commission of the Presidium of the Executive Committee of the Communist International," *Stalin's Speeches on the Communist Party U.S.A.* (New York: Central Committee, Communist Party, USA, 1931), pp. 30–31.

54 Morgan, *Covert Life*, p. 103.

55 Goulden, *Meany*, p. 122.

56 Robinson, *George Meany*, p. 121.

57 Goulden, *Meany*, pp. 125–26.

58 Quoted in ibid., p. 135.

59 Ibid., p. 152.

60 Quoted in ibid., p. 250.

61 Quoted in Jervis Anderson, *A. Philip Randolph: A Biographical Portrait* (New York: Harcourt Brace Jovanovich, 1972), p. 304.

62 J.Y. Smith and Kenneth Crawford, "George Meany, 85, Giant of U.S. Labor Movement," *Washington Post*, 11 January 1980, p. B5.

63 *Associated Press*, "Washington Date-line," 10–11 January 1980.

64 Quoted in Robinson, *George Meany*, p. 321.

65 "Introduction" to Gompers, *Seventy Years* (New York: E. P. Dutton, 1957), p. 6.

66 "Longshoremen Boycott of Polish Goods Set," *Associated Press*, 20 August 1980, A.M. cycle.

67 Quoted in Dudley Clendinen, "U.S. Unions Slip Money into Poland," *New York Times*, 1 September 1980, p. A4.

68 Correspondence (by e-mail), 19 February 2001; copy in author's file.

69 "Solidarity's 'Center of Provocations' in New York," text of commentary by Yury Kornilov, *Telegraph Agency of the Soviet Union*, 25 September 1981, translated by the *British Broadcasting Corporation*, BBC Summary of World Broadcasts, 28 September 1981.

70 Quoted in Lewis S. Feuer, *Marx and the Intellectuals: A Set of Post-Ideological Essays* (Garden City, New York: Doubleday, 1969), p. 214.

CHAPTER TEN: PERESTROIKA AND MODERNIZATION

1 Quoted in Daniel Benjamin, "State of Siege: With Tiananmen Square the Epicenter, a Political Quake Convulses China," *Time*, 29 May 1989.

2 John Pomfret, "Students Ask Gorbachev to Take Their Case to China's Leaders," *Associated Press*, 15 May 1989, A.M. cycle.

3 According to Harrison E. Salisbury in *The New Emperors: China in the Era of Mao and Deng* (Boston: Little, Brown, 1992), p. 28, only the first two mates were simultaneous. Benjamin Yang, *Deng: A Political Biography* (Armonk, New York: M. E. Sharpe, 1998), pp. 17–18 suggests they were simultaneous.

4 This is Yang's account in *Deng*, pp. 22–24. Deng Maomao, in *Deng Xiaoping: My Father* (New York: Basic Books, 1995), p. 41, has it that Deng's father was already in Chongqing and brought him there expressly to prepare to go to France. Although she was close to her father, Deng Maomao acknowledges that he was tightlipped about his childhood, and she was forced to rely on indirect sources. There is no reason, therefore, to treat her version as more authoritative, and Yang's contains more compelling detail.

5 Quoted in Yang, *Deng*, p. 32.

6 Yang, *Deng*, p. 32, gives the number of 200 as a combined total for the two movements, while Nora Wang, "Deng Xiaoping: The Years in France," *China Quarterly*, no. 92 (December 1982), p. 704, says that there were 200 Communists alone.

7 Deng, *My Father*, p. 100.

8 Oriana Fallaci, "Deng: Cleaning Up Mao's 'Feudal Mistakes,'" *Washington Post*, 31 August 1980, p. D4.

9 Deng Maomao, *My Father*, p. 97, says flatly that "the French police were going to arrest them." Yang, *Deng*, p. 45, finds it "doubtful" that the situation was that clear-cut.

10 Deng, *My Father*, p. 108.

11 Salisbury, *Emperors*, pp. 40–41.

12 Yang, *Deng*, p. 69.

13 Ibid., pp. 98–99.

14 Ibid., p. 87.

15 David S. G. Goodman, *Deng Xiaoping and the Chinese Revolution* (London: Routledge, 1994), p. 19.

16 Lucian W. Pye, "An Introductory Profile: Deng Xiaoping and China's Political Culture," *China Quarterly*, no. 135 (September 1993), p. 432.

17 Nikita Sergeevich Khrushchev, *Khrushchev Remembers*, trans. and ed. Strobe Talbott (Boston: Little, Brown, 1973), p. 253.

18 Salisbury, *Emperors*, p. 130.

19 Jonathan Spence, *Mao Zedong* (New York: Viking, 1999), p. 131.

20 Pye, "Profile," p. 438.

21 Yang, *Deng*, p. 143.

22 Salisbury, *Emperors*, p. 149.

23 "New conditions": Quoted in Ruan Ming, *Deng Xiaoping: Chronicle of an Empire*, trans. and ed. Nancy Liu, Peter Rand, and Lawrence R. Sullivan (Boulder: Westview, 1994), pp. 4–5.

24 "Deng: A Third World War Is Inevitable," *Washington Post*, 1 September 1980, p. A10.

25 Quoted in Salisbury, *Emperors*, p. 247.

26 Quoted in ibid., p. 269.

27 Richard Baum, *Burying Mao: Chinese Politics in the Age of Deng Xiaoping* (Princeton: Princeton University Press, 1994), p. 29.

28 Ibid., p. 33.

29 Salisbury, *Emperors*, p. 49.

30 Ibid., p. 3.

31 Regarding the guesthouses and the erotica, see Salisbury, *Emperors*, pp. 74, 218. Regarding the taste for the occasional boy, see Li, *The Private Life*, pp. 358–59.

32 Baum, *Burying Mao*, p. 42.

33 Ibid., p. 91.

34 Joseph Fewsmith, *Dilemmas of Reform in China: Political Conflict and Economic Debate* (Armonk: M. E. Sharpe, 1994), p. 25.

35 Ibid., p. 28.

36 Quoted in ibid., p. 29.

37 Ibid., pp. 20, 41.

38 Ibid., p. 48.

39 Robert B. Cullen, *Associated Press*, 3 February 1979, A.M. cycle.

40 "China's Teng Ends U.S. Visit; Tours 3 Cities before Leaving," *Facts on File World News Digest*, 9 February 1979, p. 83 C2.

41 Baum, *Burying Mao*, p. 173.

42 Ibid., pp. 169–70.

43 Quoted in Barry Naughton, "Deng Xiaoping: The Economist," *China Quarterly*, no. 135 (September 1993), p. 512.

44 Quoted in Cheng Xiaonong, "Dilemmas of Economic Reform in China," *World Affairs*, vol. 154, no. 4 (Spring 1992), p. 155.

45 Robert C. Hsu, "Economics and Economists in Post-Mao China," *Asian Survey*, vol. 28, no. 12 (December 1988), p. 1218.

46 Quoted in George J. Church, "China: Deng Xiaoping Leads a Far-Reaching, Audacious but Risky Second Revolution," reported by David Aikman/Washington, Richard Hornik/Peking, and James O. Jackson/Moscow, *Time*, 6 January 1986, p. 24.

47 Marshal Ye Jianying's speech to the fourth plenum, 29 September 1979, quoted in Baum, *Burying Mao*, p. 87.

48 Quoted in Goodman, *Deng Xiaoping*, p. 109.

49 Pye, "Profile," p. 424.

50 Baum, *Burying Mao*, p. 304.

51 Quoted in Willy Wo-Lap Lam, *China after Deng Xiaoping: The Power Struggles in Beijing since Tiananmen* (New York: John Wiley & Sons, 1995), pp. 18–19.

52 Quoted in Baum, *Burying Mao*, p. 353.

53 Quoted in ibid., p. 394.

54 Yang, *Deng*, pp. 256–57.

55 Mikhail Gorbachev, *Memoirs* (London: Bantam, 1997), p. 634.

56 Gorbachev, *Memoirs*, pp. 632–33.

57 Gail Sheehy, *The Man Who Changed the World: The Lives of Mikhail Gorbachev* (New York: HarperCollins, 1990), p. 30.

58 Gorbachev, *Memoirs*, p. 34.

59 Ibid., pp. 29–30.

60 Ibid., p. 33.

61 Ibid., p. 33.

62 Ibid., p. 34.

63 Ibid., p. 36.

64 Ibid., p. 54.

65 Dusko Doder and Louise Branson, *Gorbachev: Heretic in the Kremlin* (New York: Viking, 1990), p. 21.

66 Sheehy, *The Man*, p. 71.

67 Archie Brown, *The Gorbachev Factor* (New York: Oxford, 1997), p. 36.

68 Mikhail Gorbachev, "The Legacy of a Monster That Refuses to Die," *Guardian* (London), 27 February 1993, p. 21.

69 Gorbachev, *Memoirs*, p. 78.

70 Ibid., p. 130.

71 Ibid., p. 5.

72 Ibid., p. 11.

73 Quoted in Zhores Medvedev, *Gorbachev* (New York: Norton, 1987), p. 216.

74 Gorbachev, *Memoirs*, p. 18.

75 Medvedev, *Gorbachev*, p. 139.

76 Quoted in Jack F. Matlock, *Autopsy on an Empire* (New York: Random House, 1995), p. 50.

77 Doder and Branson, *Gorbachev*, p. 20.

78 Matlock, *Autopsy*, p. 53.

79 Gorbachev, *Memoirs*, p. 216.

80 Ibid., p. 283.

81 Leon Aron, *Yeltsin: A Revolutionary Life* (New York: Saint Martin's, 2000), p. 179.

82 David Pryce-Jones, *The Strange Death of the Soviet Empire* (New York: Metropolitan, 1995), p. 79.

83 Gorbachev, *Memoirs*, p. 453.

84 Ibid., p. 251.

85 Ibid.

86 Medvedev, *Gorbachev*, p. 276.

87 Doder and Branson, *Gorbachev*, p. 192.

88 Matlock, *Autopsy*, pp. 65–66.

89 Mikhail Gorbachev, *Perestroika: New Thinking for Our Country and the World* (New York: Harper & Row, 1987), pp. 10, 22–24, 25, 49.

90 Michael Dobbs, "E. Europe Owes Peaceful Change to Gorbachev," *Washington Post*, 31 December 1989, p. A1.

91 Charles H. Fairbanks Jr., "The Nature of the Beast," *National Interest*, no. 31 (Spring 1993), p. 54.

CHAPTER ELEVEN: THE PARTY OF BUSINESS

1 Robert Heilbroner, "Reflections: The Triumph of Capitalism," *New Yorker*, 23 January 1989, p. 98.

2 Frank J. Prial, "Ideas and Trends: The Socialists' New Class Struggle: How to Survive Communism's Fall," *New York Times*, 14 October 1990, p. D4.

3 Philip Sherwell, "Socialism Looks to a New World," *Daily Telegraph*, 18 September 1992, p. 12.

4 Irving Howe, "Thinking about Socialism, 1985," in Irving Howe, *Selected Writings, 1950–1990* (New York: Harcourt Brace Jovanovich, 1990), p. 488.

5 John Rentoul, *Tony Blair* (London: Little, Brown, 1995), p. 15.

6 Jon Sopel, *Tony Blair: The Moderniser* (London: Michael Joseph, 1995), p. 22.

7 Ibid., p. 88.

8 Ibid., p. 27.

9 Ibid., p. 25.

10 Ibid., p. 24.

11 Quoted in Donald Sassoon, *One Hundred Years of Socialism: The West European Left in the Twentieth Century* (New York: The New Press, 1996), p. 500.

12 Margaret Thatcher, *The Downing Street Years* (New York: HarperCollins, 1993), p. 7.

13 Chris Ogden, *Maggie: An Intimate Portrait of a Woman in Power* (New York: Simon & Schuster, 1990), p. 177.

14 Quoted in ibid., pp. 197–98.

15 Thatcher, *Downing Street Years*, p. 339.

16 Quoted in Sopel, *Tony Blair*, p. 78, and Rentoul, *Tony Blair*, p. 143.

17 Leo Panitch and Colin Leys, *The End of Parliamentary Socialism* (London: Verso, 1997), p. 221.

18 Rentoul, *Tony Blair*, p. 167.

19 Quoted in ibid., p. 180.

20 Quoted in Sassoon, *One Hundred Years*, p. 545.

21 *Le Monde*, 9 October 1982, p. 14. Translated in *FBIS*, October 1982, VII, p. K6.

22 Quoted in Sassoon, *One Hundred Years*, p. 559.

23 Ibid., p. 570.

24 Quoted in Rentoul, *Tony Blair*, p. 232.

25 Glenn Frankel, "Conservatives Win 21-Seat Majority; Vote Called a Rejection of Labor Party," *Washington Post*, 11 April 1992, p. A13.

26 Craig R. Whitney, "Tories Remain in Power in Britain; Major Sees 'Magnificent Victory,'" *New York Times*, 10 April 1992, p. A1.

27 Quoted in Glenn Frankel, "What's Left of Europe's Once-Mighty Left Today?" *Washington Post*, 12 April 1992, p. A1.

28 John Monks, quoted in Jon Sopel, *Tony Blair*, p. 129.

29 Quoted in ibid., p. 138.

30 Quoted in ibid., p. 157.

31 Peter Mandelson and Roger Liddle, *The Blair Revolution: Can New Labour Deliver?* (London: Faber & Faber, 1996), pp. 47–48.

32 Ibid., p. 48.

33 Jon Hibbs, "POLITICS: Blair Will Not Offer Downing Street Favours to Unions," *Daily Telegraph*, 23 July 1994, p. 7.

34 Tony Blair, *New Britain* (Boulder: Westview, 1997), p. 8.

35 Ibid., p. 112.

36 Ibid., p. 46.

37 Ibid., p. 313.

38 Ibid., p. 249.

39 Anne Applebaum, "Tony Blair and the New Left," *Foreign Affairs*, vol. 67, no. 2 (March–April 1997), p. 49.

40 Richard Heffernan, *New Labour and Thatcherism: Political Change in Britain* (New York: St. Martin's, 2000), p. 82.

41 Mandelson and Liddle, *Blair Revolution*, pp. 53–54.

42 Blair, *New Britain*, p. 213.

43 Ibid., p. 32.

44 Ibid., p. 55.

45 Ray Moseley, "New Leader Subdued Labour's Socialist Bent," *Chicago Tribune*, 2 May 1997, sect. 1, p. 8.

46 Quoted in Panitch and Leys, *End of Parliamentary Socialism*, p. 250.

47 Blair, *New Britain*, p. 62.

48 Quoted in Panitch and Leys, *End of Parliamentary Socialism*, p. 232.

49 Ibid., p. 14.

50 Phillip Webster, "Blair Drops Opposition to Privatisation," *Times* (London), 8 April 1997, p. 1.

51 Stephen Timewell, "UK: Blair's Britain," *Banker*, vol. 147, no. 856 (1 June 1997).

52 Quoted in Michael White, "The Election: Blair Opts for 'Third Way,'" *Guardian*, 8 April 1997, p. 11.

53 Quoted in Heffernan, *New Labour*, p. 23.

54 Quoted in ibid., p. 74.

55 Martin Jacques and Stuart Hall, "The Election: Blair: Is He the Greatest Tory since Thatcher?" *Observer*, 13 April 1997, p. 31.

56 David Marquand, "Can Labour Kick the Winning Habit?" *New Statesman*, vol. 127, no. 4408 (23 October 1998), p. 25.

57 Quoted in Irwin M. Stelzer, "Tony Blair's Coronation," *Weekly Standard*, vol. 3, no. 5 (13 October 1997), p. 24.

58 "A New Corporatism," *Economist*, 14 August 1999.

59 "Things Will Have to Get Better," *Economist*, 31 July 1999.

60 Tony Blair, *The Third Way: New Politics for the New Century*, Fabian pamphlet 588 (London: The Fabian Society, 1998), p. 1.

61 Samuel Beer, "Liberalism Rediscovered," *Economist*, 7 February 1998, p. 23.

62 Blair, *ThirdWay*, p. 14.

63 Thomas B. Edsall, "Clinton and Blair Envision a 'Third Way' International Movement," *Washington Post*, 28 June 1998, p. A24.

64 Mark Leonard, "New Labour, but Not Quite in Synch?" *New Statesman*, vol. 127, no. 4404 (25 September 1998), p. 54.

65 Tony Blair, Wim Kok, Goran Persson, and Gerhard Schroeder, "The New Left Takes on the World," *Washington Post*, 6 September 2000, p. A19.

66 Quoted in Seymour Martin Lipset, "The Americanization of the European Left," *Journal of Democracy*, vol. 12, no. 2 (April 2001), p. 81. I am indebted to Lipset for several of the examples cited in this section.

67 Quoted in Lipset, "Americanization," p. 81.

68 Quoted in Martin Walker, "Europe's Third Way Labs," *New Democrat*, May–June 1999, p. 8.

69 Peter Ford, "Europe Struggles to Follow a 'Third Way' Path," *Christian Science Monitor*, 7 October 1999, p. 7.

70 Quoted in Robert Philpot, "Blair's 'Little Local Difficulty,'" *New Democrat*, July–August 1999, p. 22.

71 Lionel Jospin, "Only on Our Terms; Global Capitalism Is a Fact but Europe Must Act in Concert to Regulate It," *Guardian* (London), 16 November 1999, p. 17.

72 Quoted in Philpot, "'Local Difficulty,'" p. 22.

CHAPTER TWELVE: THE KIBBUTZ GOES TO MARKET

1 Quoted by Muki Tsur, former secretary of the United Kibbutz Movement, interview, Yad Tabenkin Institute, Kfar Efal, Israel, 14 March 2001.

2 Quoted by Shlomo Avineri, interview, Jerusalem, 18 March 2001.

3 Martin Buber, *Paths in Utopia* (New York: Collier, 1988), p. 139.

4 Tom Segev, *One Palestine, Complete*, trans. Haim Watzman (New York: Henry Holt, 2000), p. 260.

5 Interview, Kibbutz Hatserim, 12 March 2001.

6 Interview, Yad Tabenkin, Kfar Efal, 14 March 2001.

7 Interview, Yoel Darom, Kibbutz Kfar Menachem, 13 March 2001.

8 Quoted in Daniel Gavron, *The Kibbutz: Awakening from Utopia* (Lanham, Maryland: Rowman & Littlefield, 2000), p. 31.

9 Ibid., p. 163.

10 Ibid., p. 158.

11 See ibid., pp. 167–70.

12 Batya Gur, *Murder on a Kibbutz*, trans. Dalya Bilu (New York: HarperCollins, 1994), pp. 322–24.

13 Quoted in Yossi Melman, "Is the Dream Dead?" *Moment*, February 1995, p. 49.

14 *The Republic of Plato*, trans. and ed. Francis MacDonald Cornford (New York: Oxford University Press, 1945), p. 166.

15 Interview with Shlomo Aveneri, Hebrew University, 18 March 2001.

16 Interview with Menachem Rosner, Kibbutz Reshafim, 20 March 2001.

17 Interview with Amnon Lahav, Kibbutz Gal'ed, 19 March 2001.

18 Interview with Yuval Dror, Tel Aviv, 15 March 2001.

19 Interview with Aharon Yadlin, Kibbutz Hatserim, 12 March 2001.

20 Henry Near, *The Kibbutz Movement: A History*, vol. 2, Crisis and Achievement, 1939–1995 (London: Littman Library of Jewish Civilization, 1997), pp. 357–58.

21 Interview with Muki Tsur, Yad Tabenkin Institute, Kfar Efal, 14 March 2001.

22 Daniel Gavron, "Communal Change," *Jerusalem Post*, 10 November 2000, p. 12.

23 Gavron, *Awakening*, p. 281.

24 Leora Eren Frucht, "Every Man for Himself," *Jerusalem Post*, 27 April 2001, p. 4B.

25 Quoted in Melman, "Is the Dream Dead?" p. 46.

26 Howard M. Sachar, *A History of Israel: From the Rise of Zionism to Our Time*, 2nd ed. (New York: Alfred A. Knopf, 1996), p. 10.

27 Isaiah Berlin in *The Life and Opinions of Moses Hess* (Cambridge, England: W. Heffer & Sons, 1959), p. 10, and Sidney Hook in *From Hegel to Marx* (Ann Arbor: University of Michigan Press, 1962), p. 187; both use both terms in characterizing Hess.

28 Quoted in Shlomo Avineri, *Moses Hess: Prophet of Communism and Zionism* (New York: New York University Press, 1985), p. 11.

29 Quoted in Svante Lundgren, *Moses Hess on Religion, Judaism and the Bible* (Abo, Finland: Abo Academy Press, 1992), p. 62.

30 Quoted in Avineri, *Moses Hess*, p. 98.

31 Quoted in ibid., p. 15.

32 Lundgren, *Moses Hess*, p. 44.

33 Avineri, *Moses Hess*, p. 133.

34 London, 15 August 1863, in *The Letters of Karl Marx*, comp. and trans. Saul K. Padover (Englewood Cliffs: Prentice Hall, 1979), p. 478.

35 Engels to Marx, Paris, 14 January 1848, Karl Marx and Friedrich Engels, *Briefwechsel*, Marx/Engels Gesamtausgabe, Dritte Arbeitung, Band 1 (Berlin: Marx-Engels-Verlag G.M.B.H.: 1929), pp. 91–92.

36 Moses Hess, *Rome and Jerusalem*, trans. Rabbi Maurice J. Bloom (New York: Philosophical Library, 1958), not paginated.

37 Isaiah Berlin, *Life and Opinions*, p. 8.

38 Peter Gay, *Voltaire's Politics: The Poet as Realist* (New York: Vintage, 1965), p. 334.

39 E. J. Hobsbawm, *The Age of Revolution, 1789–1848* (New York: New American Library, 1964), p. 259.

40 Will and Ariel Durant, *The Age of Voltaire* (New York: Simon & Schuster, 1965), p. 508.

41 Ibid., p. 493.

42 Quoted in Franklin L. Baumer, *Religion and the Rise of Scepticism* (New York: Harcourt, Brace, 1960), p. 60.

43 Edward O. Wilson, "The Two Hypotheses of Human Meaning: Transcendentalism and Empiricism," *Humanist*, vol. 59, no. 5 (1 September 1999), p. 30.

44 Hobsbawm, *Age of Revolution*, p. 289.

45 Irving Howe, "Thinking about Socialism, 1985," in Irving Howe, *Selected Writings, 1950–1990* (New York: Harcourt Brace Jovanovich, 1990), p. 488.

46 Michael Harrington, *The Politics at God's Funeral* (New York: Holt, Rinehart, 1983), p. 10.

47 Norman Birnbaum, *After Progress: American Social Reform and European Socialism in the Twentieth Century* (New York: Oxford University Press, 2001), p. 1.

48 Ernest Belfort Bax, *The Religion of Socialism* (Freeport, New York: Books for Libraries Press, 1972), pp. 52–53.

49 Michael Harrington, *Socialism* (New York: Bantam, 1973), pp. 421, 452.

50 Herbert J. Muller, *Freedom in the Ancient World* (New York: Bantam, 1961), pp. 107–8.

EPILOGUE: RISING FROM THE ASHES

1 Enrique Krauze, "The Shah of Venezuela," *New Republic*, 1 April 2009.

2 Javier Corrales and Michael Penfold, *Dragon in the Tropics: Venezuela and the Legacy of Hugo Chavez* (Washington, D.C.: Brookings Institution, 2015), second edition, Kindle edition, loc. 2,159.

3 Franklin Foer, "The Talented Mr. Chavez," *Atlantic*, May 2006.

4 "Ten Memorable Hugo Chavez Moments," *New York Times*. (This online article is not dated. The tweet is dated 12 July 2012.) https://archive.nytimes.com/www .nytimes.com/interactive/2013/03/05/world/americas/chavez-anecdotes .html?_r=0&hp#/#time229_6918.

5 Quoted in Corrales and Penfold, *Dragon*, loc. 1,095.

6 "Mission Accomplished: 15 Years of Cuba-Venezuela Pact," *Telesur*, 30 October 2015.

7 Rory Carroll, "'Socialism—or Death! I Swear It,'" *Guardian*, 10 January 2007.

8 Corrales and Penfold, *Dragon*, loc. 1,687.

9 Rory Carroll, *Comandante: Myth and Reality in Hugo Chavez's Venezuela* (New York: Penguin, 2013), Kindle edition, loc. 1,874.

10 World Bank, *Doing Business 2007: How to Reform*, Washington, D.C., 2006, p. 6.

11 Michelle Jamrisko and Caterina Saraiva, "These Are the World's Most Miserable Economies," *Bloomberg*, 14 February 2018.

12 Editorial Board, "Venezuela's Sham Election," *New York Times*, 21 May 2018.

13 Ibid.

14 Corrales and Penfold, *Dragon*, loc. 3,483.

15 Kirk Semple, "Venezuela's Two Legislatures Duel, but Only One Has Ammunition," *New York Times*, 3 November 2017.

16 Flora Charner, Paula Newton and Natalie Gallón, "Opponents Slam Venezuelan President Nicolas Maduro's Election Victory as a Sham," *CNN*, 21 May 2018.

17 Nicholas Cascy and Vanessa Herrero, "Critics Say He Can't Beat a Dictator. This Venezuelan Thinks He Can," *New York Times*, 17 May 2018.

18 https://twitter.com/jeremycorbyn/status/309065744954580992?lang=en.

19 "Jeremy Corbyn MP and President Nicolas Maduro Discuss Legacy of Tony Benn," Youtube.com, 7 April 2014. https://www.youtube.com/watch?v=7eL8_wtS-0I.

20 "British Opposition Leader Corbyn Declines to Condemn Venezuela's Maduro," *Reuters*, 7 August 2017.

21 "Jeremy Corbyn: Britain's Most Likely Next Prime Minister," *Economist*, 23 September 2017.

22 Sam Knight, "Enter Left: Will a Fervent Socialist Reshape British Politics or Lead His Party to Irrelevance?" *New Yorker*, 23 May 2016.

23 Richard Seymour, *Corbyn: The Strange Rebirth of Radical Politics*, second edition (London and New York: Verso, 2017), Kindle edition, loc. 512.

24 Ibid., loc. 729.

25 Corey Charlton, "So Is He a Marxist? Jeremy Corbyn Dodges the Question but Says 'I Haven't Really Read as Much of Marx as We Should Have Done,'" *Dailymail.com*, 26 July 2015. http://www.dailymail.co.uk/news/article-3174996/So-Marxist-Jeremy-Corbyn -dodges-question-says-haven-t-really-read-Marx-done.html.

26 Brian Wheeler, "The Jeremy Corbyn Story: Profile of Labour Leader," *BBC*, 24 September 2016. http://www.bbc.com/news/uk-politics-34184265.

27 Rosa Prince, *Comrade Corbyn: A Very Unlikely Coup: How Jeremy Corbyn Stormed to the Labour Leadership* (London: Biteback, 2016), Kindle edition, loc. 128.

28 Ibid., loc. 596.

29 Prince, *Comrade Corbyn*, loc. 588.

30 Andrew Gilligan, "Revealed: Jeremy Corbyn and John McDonnell's Close IRA Links," *Sunday Telegraph*, 11 October 2015.

31 Prince, *Comrade Corbyn*, loc. 1,710.

32 See endnote 30 above.

33 "Fidel Castro: Jeremy Corbyn Praises 'Huge Figure,'" *BBC*, 26 November 2016.

34 Jeremy Corbyn, "Rogue States" in Farah Reza, ed., *Anti-Imperialism: A Guide for the Movement* (London: Bookmarks, 2003), p. 36.

35 Ibid., p. 37.

36 Ibid., p. 36.

37 https://www.youtube.com/watch?v=pGj1PheWiFQ.

38 "Amid Gaza Unrest, Jeremy Corbyn Calls for UK to Review Arms Sales to Israel," *Times of Israel*, April 9, 2018. https://www.timesofisrael.com/amid-gaza-violence-jeremy-corbyn-calls-for-uk-to-review-arms-sales-to-israel/.

39 Asa Winstanley, "Listen: Palestinians Deserve Right to Return, Says British MP Jeremy Corbyn," *Electronic Intifada*, 9 August 2015. https://electronicintifada.net/blogs/asa-winstanley/listen-palestinians-deserve-right-return-says-british-mp-jeremy-corbyn.

40 "United We Stand," *Jewish Chronicle*, 25 July 2018.

41 https://www.youtube.com/watch?v=nEB9PwKYmmA.

42 Josh Glancy, "Getting Off the Fence about Jeremy Corbyn's Anti-Semitism," *New York Times*, 27 August 2018.

43 https://www.youtube.com/watch?v=pZvAvNJL-gE.

44 *Soviet Active Measures*, Hearings before the Permanent Select Committee on Intelligence, House of Representatives, Ninety-seventh Congress, second session, 13–14 July 1982, testimony of Stanlislav Levchenko (Washington, D.C., U.S. Government Printing Office, 1982), p. 162.

45 Andrew Murray, "Eyes Left," *Morning Star*, 17 December 1999, reprinted in Michael Mosbacher, "British Anti-Americanism," *Social Affairs Unit*, 2004, p. 6. http://socialaffairsunit.org.uk/digipub/index2.php?option=content&do_pdf=1&id=12.

46 Seumas Milne, "Communism May Be Dead, but Clearly Not Dead Enough," *Guardian*, 16 February 2006.

47 Michael Mosbacher, "The Stalinist Past of Corbyn's Strategist," *Standpoint*, December 2015. David Patrikarakos, "Corbyn's New Stalinist Voice," *Politico*, 27 October 2015.

48 "Jeremy Corbyn and the Labour Whip," *Revolts: Philip Cowley and Mark Stuart's Research on Parliament*. http://revolts.co.uk/?p=932.

49 Prince, *Comrade Corbyn*, loc. 3,743.

50 Patrick Wintour and Nicholas Watt, "The Corbyn Earthquake—How Labour was Shaken to Its Foundations," *Guardian*, 25 September 2015.

51 Hilary Wainwright, "The Making of Jeremy Corbyn," *Jacobin*, 9 March 2016. https://www.jacobinmag.com/2016/03/tony-benn-corbyn-thatcher-labour-leadership.

52 Alex Nunns, *The Candidate: Jeremy Corbyn's Improbable Path to Power* (New York and London: OR Books, 2018), p. 376.

53 Prince, *Comrade Corbyn*, loc. 5,829.

54 See note 52.

55 Jeremy Corbin: Britain's "Most Likely Next Prime Minister," *Economist*, September 23, 2017.

56 Andy Beckett, "The Wilderness Years: How Labour's Left Survived to Conquer," *Guardian*, 3 November 2017.

57 Gordon Rayner and Laura Hughes, "John McDonnell Faces Labour Revolt as He Suggests There Is a 'Lot to Learn' from Karl Marx's *Das Kapital*," *Telegraph*, 7 May 2017.

58 John McDonnell and Hilary Wainwright, "The New Economics of Labour," *Open Democracy UK*, 25 February 2018. https://www.opendemocracy.net/uk/hilary-wainwright/new-economics-of-labour.

59 McDonnell and Wainwright, "The New Economics."

60 Will Dahlgren, "British People Keener on Socialism than Capitalism," https://yougov. co.uk/news/2016/02/23/british-people-view-socialism-more-favourably-capi/.

61 Joshua Chaffin, "Communist Party of Britain Embraces Comrade Corbyn," *Financial Times*, 10 May 2018.

62 Prince, *Comrade Corbyn*, loc. 2,382.

63 Corbyn, "Rogue States," p. 40.

64 Ibid., p. 35.

65 Isabel Hardman, "Jeremy Corbyn Backs His Spokesman on Russia," *Spectator*, 15 March 2018.

66 Knight, "Enter Left."

67 "Jeremy Corbyn Calls Death of Osama bin Laden a 'Tragedy,'" *Telegraph*, 31 August 2015.

68 Prince, *Comrade Corbyn*, loc. 2,566.

69 James Bloodworth, "James Bloodworth: A Left-Wing Case against Comrade Corbyn," *International Business Times*, 4 August 2015.

70 https://www.youtube.com/watch?v=k1T6s4mx1CA.

71 Jeremy Corbyn, "NATO Belligerence Endangers Us All," *Morning Star*, 16 April 2014.

72 Matthew Cooper, "Poll: Most Americans Support Occupy Wall Street," *Atlantic*, 19 October 2011. https://www.theatlantic.com/politics/archive/2011/10/poll-most -americans-support-occupy-wall-street/246963/.

73 Adam Gabbatt, Mark Townsend and Lisa O'Carroll, "'Occupy' Anti-Capitalism Protests Spread around the World," *Guardian*, 15 October 2011.

74 "Public Divided over Occupy Wall Street Movement," Pew Research Center, 24 October 2011. http://www.people-press.org/2011/10/24/public-divided-over-occupy -wall-street-movement/.

75 Eric Kleefeld, "Poll: Public Turning against Occupy Wall Street," *TPM*, 16 November 2011. https://talkingpointsmemo.com/dc/poll-public-opinion-turning-against-occupy -wall-street.

76 Ginia Bellafante, "Gunning for Wall Street, with Faulty Aim," *New York Times*, 23 September 2011.

77 Thomas Piketty, *Capital in the Twenty-First Century* (Cambridge, MA: Belknap, 2014), pp. 1, 6.

78 Ibid., p. 31.

79 "Remarks by the President on Economic Mobility," The White House, Office of the Press Secretary, Washington, D.C., 4 December 2013.

80 https://twitter.com/Pontifex/status/460697074585980928.

81 Girish Gupta, "Venezuela's Maduro Rooting for 'Revolutionary Friend' Sanders in U.S. Campaign," *Reuters*, 31 May 2016.

82 Thomas Piketty, "Thomas Piketty on the Rise of Bernie Sanders: The US Enters a New Political Era," *Guardian*, 16 February 2016.

83 Rob Suls and Jocelyn Kiley, "Democratic Voters Increasingly Embrace the 'Liberal' Label—Especially Whites, Millennials and Postgrads," Pew Research Center, 9 February 2016.

84 Derek Hunter, "Hillary Can't Explain the Difference between a Democrat and a Socialist," *Daily Caller*, 6 January 2016.

85 Randy Yelp and Cecilia Reyes, "Who Voted in New Hampshire and How," *Wall Street Journal*, 9 February 2016.

86 Margaret Talbot, "The Populist Prophet," *New Yorker*, 12 October 2015; and Jaffe, *Why Bernie Sanders Matters*, p. 61.

87 Harry Jaffe, *Why Bernie Sanders Matters* (New York: Regan Arts, 2015), Kindle edition,

loc. 52. (Note: In the Kindle edition of this book, the Introduction gives only location numbers, while in the balance of the book, page numbers are provided.)

88 See note 86.

89 Jaffe, *Why Bernie Sanders Matters*, p. 176.

90 Steven Erlanger, "Bernie Sanders's Kibbutz Found. Surprise: It's Socialist," *New York Times*, 5 February 2016.

91 "Senator Bernie Sanders on Democratic Socialism in the United States," prepared remarks, Georgetown University, 19 November 2015. https://berniesanders.com/democratic-socialism-in-the-united-states/.

92 "Sanders on Democratic Socialism."

93 Mark Leibovich, "The Socialist Senator," *New York Times Magazine*, 21 January 2007.

94 Jaffe, *Why Bernie Sanders Matters*, p. 182.

95 Okla Elliott, "What Does Sanders Mean by Democratic Socialism?" *The Hill*, 4 March 2016.

96 Nico Hines, "Bernie Sanders's Brother: He Backs 'Class Warfare,' Bill Clinton Was Worse than Bush," *Daily Beast*, 19 February 2016.

97 Bernie Sanders, *Our Revolution: A Future to Believe In* (New York: St. Martin's, 2016), Kindle edition, p. 188.

98 Jas Chana, "Straight Outta Brooklyn, by Way of Vermont: The Bernie Sanders Story," *Tablet*, 20 August 2015.

99 Jaffe, *Why Bernie Sanders Matters*, p. 123.

100 "Sanders on Democratic Socialism."

101 Ron Kampeas, "Bernie Sanders, Focusing on Foreign Policy, Blasts Israel on Gaza," *Jewish Telegraphic Agency*, 7 June 2018.

102 "Bernie Sanders: Nicaragua Interview (8/8/1985)," https://www.youtube.com/watch?v=_6liJbu9ZCY.

103 Ibid.

104 "Bernie Sanders on the Life and Legacy of Late Cuban Revolutionary Fidel Castro," *Democracy Now!*, 29 November 2016. https://www.youtube.com/watch?v=Mkat7UYPJWA.

105 Aaron Blake, "This Number Proves Bernie Sanders Can Win Iowa," *Washington Post*, 17 January 2016.

106 Frank Newport, "Americans' Views of Socialism, Capitalism Are Little Changed," Gallup, 6 May 2016. "Little Change in Public's Response to 'Capitalism,' 'Socialism,'" Pew Research Center, December 28, 2011. YouGov, 25–27 January 2016. https://d25d2506sfb94s.cloudfront.net/cumulus_uploads/document/467z1ta5ys/tabs_OP_Socialism_20160127.pdf.

107 In addition to the Gallup, Pew, and YouGov polls cited above, see Max Ehrenfreund, "A Majority of Millennials Now Reject Capitalism, Poll Shows," *Washington Post*, 26 April 2016.

108 Frank Newport, "Democrats More Positive about Socialism than Capitalism," Gallup, 13 August 2018.

109 https://www.dsausa.org/about-us/what-is-democratic-socialism/.

110 https://www.dsausa.org/.

111 David Remnick, "Alexandria Ocasio-Cortez's Historic Win and the Future of the Democratic Party," *New Yorker*, 23 July 2018.

112 Nicholas Kristof, "Looking for a Jump-Start in China," *New York Times*, 5 January 2013.

113 "Catching Tigers and Flies," https://anticorruption.gistapp.com/catching_tigers_and_flies.

114 Victor Shih, "The Pros and Cons of Centralizing Power in China," *Xi Takes Charge: Implications of the 19th Party Congress for China's Future*, Twenty-First Century China Center, UC San Diego, 2017, p. 18.

115 Elizabeth C. Economy, *The Third Revolution: Xi Jinpeng and the New Chinese State* (Oxford: Oxford U., 2018), Kindle edition, loc. 903.

116 Chun Han Wong, "China's Xi Jinping Puts Loyalty to the Test at Congress," *Wall Street Journal*, 1 March 2016.

117 Orville Schell, "Crackdown in China: Worse and Worse," *New York Review of Books*, 21 April 2016.

118 "China's Xi Underscores CPC's Authority in News Reporting," *Xinhua*, 19 February 2016.

119 Chris Buckley, "China Gives Communist Party More Control over Policy and Media," *New York Times*, 21 March 2018.

120 "China: Xi Calls for Stricter Ideological Control of Universities," *BBC*, 9 December 2016.

121 Susan Shirk, Lei Guang, Barry Naughton, Victor Shih, and Tai Ming Cheung, "The 19th Party Congress: A Retrospective Analysis," in *Xi Takes Charge*, p. 39.

122 Economy, *Third Revolution*, loc. 495.

123 "His Own Words: The 14 Principles of 'Xi Jinping Thought,'" *BBC Monitoring*, 18 October 2017.

124 Carl Minzner, *End of an Era: How China's Authoritarian Revival Is Undermining Its Rise* (Oxford, Oxford U., 2018), Kindle editions, loc. 733.

125 Willy Wo Lap Lam, "China's Reform Summed Up: Politics, No; Economics, Yes (Sort of)," *China Brief*, vol. XIII, issue 11, Jamestown Foundation, 3 May 2013.

126 Minzner, *End of an Era*, loc. 1,033, 1,040.

127 James T. Areddy and James V. Grimaldi, "Defying Mao, Rich Chinese Crash the Communist Party," *Wall Street Journal*, 29 December 2012.

128 Susan L. Shirk. "The Return of Paternalistic Rule," *Journal of Democracy*, vol. 20, no. 2 (April 2018), p. 27.

129 "'The Third Revolution: Xi Jin Ping and the New Chinese State,' by Elizabeth C. Economy," Council on Foreign Relations, Past Event, 17 May 2018. https://www.cfr.org/event/third-revolution-xi-jinping-and-new-chinese-state-elizabeth-c-economy.

130 Jiayang Fan, "At the Communist Party Congress, Xi Jinping Plays the Emperor," *New Yorker*, 18 October 2017.

INDEX

Page numbers with italic "*n*" indicate footnote